D1538360

THE COMPLETE GUIDE TO

WALKS & TRAILS

IN SOUTHERN AFRICA

Trails are not dust and pebbles on a hill,
Nor even grass and wild buds by a lake;
Trails are adventure and a hand to still
The restless pulse of life when men would
    break
Their minds with weight of thinking. Trails
    are peace,
The call to dreams, the challenge to ascent;
Trails are the brisk unfolding of release
From bitterness and from discouragement.
Trails are the random writing on the wall
That tells how every man, grown tired at
    heart
Of things correct and ordered, comes to
    scrawl
His happy hour down – then goes to start
Life over with new eagerness and zest
Who builds a trail finds labor that is rest!

Trails
Helen Frazee-Bower

JAYNEE LEVY

THE COMPLETE GUIDE TO

WALKS & TRAILS

IN SOUTHERN AFRICA

STRUIK

Struik Publishers (Pty) Ltd (a member
of The Struik Group (Pty) Ltd)
Struik House, Oswald Pirow Street,
Foreshore, Cape Town 8001.

Reg. No: 63/00203/07

First published as *Everyone's Guide to Trailing &
Mountaineering in Southern Africa* in 1982
First published as *The Complete Guide to Walks
and Trails in Southern Africa* in 1987
Second edition 1989
Second impression 1991

Text © Jaynee Levy
Photographs © Jaynee Levy, except for the
following: Norman Larson, p. 52 (centre) and
p. 316; Zelda Wahl, p. 66; Port Elizabeth
Publicity Association, p. 93 (top); Gunther
Komnick, p. 106 (centre); Greater East London
Publicity Association, p. 108 (top); Qwa-Qwa
Government Service, p. 132 (left) and p. 144
(bottom right); Barry Cleveland, p. 199 and
p. 200; Alan Job, p. 201 (above); David Steele,
p. 187, p. 188, p. 189, p. 191, p. 203, p. 205
(right), p. 206, p. 208, p. 211 (top), p. 212,
p. 215, p. 216; Pilgrim's Rest Museum, p. 239.

Maps by Anne Westoby. (Many of the maps were
adapted from those drawn by Peter Slingsby for
Jaynee Levy's *Everyone's Guide to Trailing and
Mountaineering in Southern Africa*, C. Struik,
1982.)

Edited by Tracey Hawthorne, Cape Town.
Designed by Valerie Phipps-Smith, Cape Town.
Photoset by McManus Bros (Pty) Ltd, Cape
Town.
Reproduction by Unifoto (Pty) Ltd, Cape Town.
Printed and bound by Tien Wah Press Pte Ltd.
Singapore

Poem on title page by Helen Frazee-Bower. It
first appeared in *Good Housekeeping*, a magazine
published by the Hearst Corporation, in March
1939. Quote on p. 12 by John Cleare, from
Collin's Guide to Mountains and Mountaineering,
published by Collins, London, 1979.

All rights reserved. No part of this publication
may be reproduced, stored in a retrieval system or
transmitted, in any form or by any means,
electronic, mechanical, photocopying, recording
or otherwise, without the written permission of
the copyright owners.

ISBN 1 86825 056 3

PUBLISHER'S NOTE

Trails: Living in a multilingual country such
as South Africa, confusion often arises as to
the correct form of proper names. Every
attempt has been made to use the standard,
accepted version of place, mountain and
river names; where doubt existed, we used
the English form.

In the trail descriptions, the available
literature is obtainable from the relevant
authority-in-charge, unless otherwise stated.
Maps: It should be noted that the maps in
this book have been designed as simple
visual guides to the area concerned, and are
not intended for use in the field.

Although every effort has been made to
ensure the accuracy of the maps, a personal
field-study was not possible in every
instance. Use had therefore to be made of
the best source material available. This
varied considerably in quality from area to
area, and this variation will inevitably be
reflected in the maps presented in these
pages.

KEY TO MAP SYMBOLS

 Overnight hut   Lighthouse

 Forest station   Camp-site

 Forestry land   Hotel

Cave   Entry points and parking

Picnic place

ABOUT THE AUTHOR

Jaynee Levy has been intricately involved in
outdoor recreation and environmental education development in southern Africa
since 1975, when she joined the South African Forestry Branch of the Department of
Environment Affairs. During the past 12
years, she has assisted in the development of
the National Hiking Way System, and has
served as Environmental Education Officer
for the Cape Province, Tourist Development Consultant for the Ciskei Tourist
and Holiday Trust and Chief Recreational
Development Officer for the Ciskei Tourist
Board.

Born in America and educated at Cornell
(B.Sc.) and Yale (M.F.S.) universities, Jaynee served both in the Environmental Conservation Department of her native New
York State and in Israel, before arriving in
Africa. A highly experienced backpacker,
having hiked in more than 36 countries in
Africa, North and South America, Europe
and Asia, Ms Levy finds this the ideal way
of pursuing her other interests of nature
photography and bird-watching. She is also
a keen canoeist, cyclist, skin-diver and
skier.

CAPTIONS

Captions to photographs appearing on the
opening pages of each chapter can be found
on page 352.

COVER PHOTOGRAPHS

Front: Gerald Cubitt
Back: (top left) David Bristow
       (top right) Walter Knirr
       (bottom left) John Yeld
       (bottom right) John Yeld

CONTENTS

PREFACE

I came to South Africa in 1975 to assist in planning the National Hiking Way System – an exciting position within a burgeoning recreational activity. The potential for expansion and development in the field of outdoor recreational and environmental education was wide open. My work was multifaceted – I was either bushwacking up a slope with a team of foresters, lecturing to 'Veld and Vlei', constructing a trail through thick indigenous forest with a group of youngsters, being an interpretive naturalist on the Wild Coast, or selecting backpacking gear for the mountain catchment team. I developed a deep respect for the mountains and their animals and plants. Weekends and public holidays found me exploring new ranges, peaks or gorges and, during my annual leave, I flew to neighbouring countries to investigate their mountains and trails. My professional life and private hours fused – and I loved it.

This book was written out of sheer self-defence for, invariably, whenever I went hiking, one of the members of the party would trigger a barrage of questions. How long is the Outeniqua Trail? Is it more difficult than the Boland Hiking Trail? How many nights do you sleep out? Where can I make bookings? What about the Wild Coast? I heard you organized an expedition up Mulanje – how was it? Have you hiked the Fish River Canyon? Would my children be able to manage it? What footwear do you recommend? The questions were endless and I encountered them every time I hit the trail. Willingly providing advice and information to each hiker, it struck me as ironic that I, an American who had lived in southern Africa for only a few years, was the target of all these queries. It also emphasized the very real need for a practical and comprehensive book which would answer this sort of question.

Although I knew that all the information existed somewhere, it became obvious that nowhere did it exist in a single reference work. So I reluctantly traded mountaineering time to combine the facts and experience that appear here. Compiling up-to-date information on trails in southern Africa is like trying to write the latest on world politics – both are constantly developing and changing. Although the directory of trails and mountaineering areas is as comprehensive and accurate as possible (as of April 1987), alterations to routes and other changes are inevitable. Some mountaineering and kloofing regions were purposely excluded at the request of their landowners. As a whole, the selections, descriptions and opinions expressed are entirely personal, based on my experience in southern Africa from 1975 to 1987.

This edition differs in several ways from its predecessor, *Everyone's Guide to Trailing & Mountaineering in Southern Africa*. More than one hundred new trails are described, all of which have been developed since 1982. The trails concept has been broadened to include canoeing, kayaking, white-water rafting and horse-riding adventures. In addition, emphasis is placed on the many new trails mushrooming in southern Africa's new national states and homelands. All information on equipment, resources and references has also been brought up to date.

By popular demand, the structure of the book has been changed so that the trails are arranged geographically (by province or country), replacing the ecological zone concept. This was done to facilitate practical needs when planning a trailing holiday. The information on the ecological zones has been retained, however, in order to assist understanding a trail's natural environment.

I hope that the second edition proves to be not only as popular as the first, but also a practical and inspirational guide for everyone's exploration of southern Africa's rich natural and historical heritage. Trailists and mountaineers should unite as an active voice, encouraging wise use and preservation of the land on which they tread.

This book is my tribute to the magnificent mountains and other natural areas I have been introduced to and the wonderful people I have met while in southern Africa.

ACKNOWLEDGEMENTS

FIRST EDITION
(Everyone's Guide to Trailing & Mountaineering in Southern Africa)
I arrived in southern Africa with little practical knowledge of its wild areas. This book is therefore a compilation of the work of many people – not only those who assisted me in producing the manuscript but also those hikers who were familiar with exciting mountaineering terrain and who enthusiastically shared these areas with me.

In my graduating year Professor Francois Mergen, former Dean of the Yale School of Forestry and Environmental Studies, suggested that I work in South Africa. Once I had arrived here Danny Ackerman, Secretary of the then-Department of Forestry, gave me tremendous encouragement by supporting my rather unconventional requests and ideas. Paul van Zyl, a former officer of the Department of Forestry, introduced me to the National Hiking Way System. Don Bands and the western Cape forestry mountain catchment team deserve thanks for letting me be 'one of the guys' on our exploratory missions. Mrs Ethelwyn de Vos, who heads the Noord-Transvaalse Avontuur-Vereniging, presented me with marvellous opportunities by requesting my presence as an interpretive naturalist on the dramatic Wild Coast and Drakensberg expeditions.

Instrumental in my mountaineering education was the MCSA (Mountain Club of South Africa). Although it is unfair to single out individuals, Hans Billman, former Chairman of the Northern Transvaal Section, has my thanks for encouraging me to join the club, as do Jan de Groot, Arnie Ruch and many other MCSA member friends who took me into the lesser-known areas.

In Malawi, Gordon Beldon, Chairman of the Mountain Club of Malawi, introduced me to many of that country's mountains and John Hough, of the Department of Parks and Wildlife, supplied data about these regions.

I am indebted to the many individuals who gave their time and expertise to supply basic information. Theuns van Rensburg of the National Hiking Way Board and the then-Directorate of Forestry and Environmental Conservation, was invaluable in supplying details of South Africa's foremost trails. Chris van der Merwe, of the Department of Nature and Environmental Conservation of the Cape Provincial Administration, together with many other government officials and private landowners in southern Africa, summarized their latest trail developments. Helen Robertson and Sandra Fowkes helped me with information on the trails operated by the Wildlife Society of Southern Africa. Other individuals such as Kevin Wall, Dr Richard Melville, Elana Katz and Anne Mayne shared with me their experiences in areas with which I was not so familiar.

When the time came to add the final touches, Rheina Epstein taught me how to write South African English, the staff of Struik contributed their editing expertise, and Lorna Kingon and Valerie Smollan assisted with typing at the critical moment.

I am particularly indebted to Dr Peter Penny who generously permitted me to use, after hours, the office facilities of Herbert Penny (Pty) Ltd.

Finally my sincere appreciation goes to the Provincial Secretary of the Cape of Good Hope Provincial Administration, the Director of the Department of Nature and Environmental Conservation of the Cape, and the Director of the then-Directorate of Forestry and Environmental Conservation for their kind permission to use the knowledge I accumulated while serving as an officer in their respective departments.

SECOND EDITION
(The Complete Guide to Walks and Trails in Southern Africa)
The second edition was made possible with the assistance of both old and new colleagues. Peter Millian's store of knowledge about Lesotho opened up a vast new hiking terrain. Horst Windisch, National Chairman of the Hiking Federation of South Africa, was forever discovering obscure but tantalizing trails. Jimmy Baker, with superhuman energy and fitness, reported on all trails that I did not have the opportunity to walk myself, and generously offered to review the draft. Peter Penny sent me notes on trails he walked, correcting imperfections in the first edition. My late friend David Hanaburgh gave me tremendous encouragement from overseas to continue when the going got tough.

Many thanks again to the authorities-in-charge of trails and private individuals who co-operated in answering my endless questions and who were extremely generous in their hospitality during my research visits. I would like especially to note John Burchmore and Klaas Boonzaaier of Lebowa; Liz and Ted Reilly, James Culverwell, and Norah and Murray Meikle of Swaziland; Alta and Joseph Mostert and Jap van Eeden of Fouriesburg; J.H. van Jaarsveld and Frans Viljoen of Ficksburg; and Margo and Don MacKay of Knysna. In addition, John Bridgman of the Ciskei Tourist and Holiday Trust and the Ciskei Tourist Board understood the importance of this work and granted me liberal leave allowance.

Much appreciation is also extended to my friends and little dog, Wiggles, who either braved new horizons in the name of research or patiently tolerated my long periods of hibernation with my typewriter. And lastly, thanks to my Mom and Dad who waited another five years until we met again, and began to understand.

WALKS AND TRAILS IN SOUTHERN AFRICA

Are trails necessary?

The myriad trails in southern Africa today, most of them established less than 15 years ago, is stirring up the question: 'Are trails a positive influence in the ecology, or are they merely another human means of manipulating nature for selfish goals?'

Some people are of the opinion that hiking trails should not be built because wild lands are shrinking, and that those remaining should be closed to the public and saved for future generations. Another argument is that by having your ability to explore and move where whim takes you limited, you develop 'tunnel vision' and your interest in the outdoors is destroyed. Others are concerned that trails create an artificial need and avenue for people to explore our natural areas, and by doing so, overpopulate them. Arguments are heard that inexperienced people, unsupervised by clubs or guides, destroy the environment and so the experience for the 'real' mountaineer.

Some arguments point to the ills of hiking in the USA, where millions of hikers utilize hundreds of thousands of kilometres of hiking trails annually, and solitary experiences are shattered by the popularity of the pastime; *Giardia*, a water-borne disease, is spread by backpackers to remote high altitude streams; the 'carrying capacity' of a camp-site is inversely proportional to the distance campers must walk to collect dead firewood; and prime camp-sites and trails are littered and show other ugly scars of overuse.

Strangely, I, who have dedicated the past 12 years of my life to planning and constructing trails, and publicizing and using them for environmental education, sympathize with these arguments. I recall how excited I was when I arrived here in 1975: southern Africa seemed, in comparison to my American homeland, a big wilderness area, where I seldom met another hiking party on a peak climb or traverse, where I could drink from every mountain stream,

and where the animals were not yet food raiders and tent invaders. So I am asked, 'Why do you do it? Why do you plan more trails and write trail guides? Why are you updating this book?'

The answer is simple. The world's population is increasing, and while people are acquiring more leisure time and dispensable income, development and technology are creating more stress and moving humans further from their natural roots. People are looking to our untouched areas for relief, relaxation, education, exercise, spiritual, mental and physical refreshment, and as pleasant places to reunite with their families, friends and lovers. If we do not create proper facilities for these people, they will invade and destroy the wilderness. By creating a hierarchy of trail types – physically easy to strenuous, one hour to one week, on the beach to the high escarpment, self-guided to group involvement, walking to kayaking, primitive camping to luxurious overnight lodges – we cater for the diverse levels of interest, degrees of involvement and physical capabilities of the public. Hiking, riding and canoeing trails are relatively low-impact developments with high-impact benefits.

We compromise some natural regions for purity of others: by creating financially vi-

able recreational zones, we prevent these areas from meeting worse fates – industrial and agricultural developments, overgrazing or resettlement. By awakening and exposing more people to the beauties and challenges of their natural heritage, we develop a population of alert individuals, a pressure group who will join the 'elite mountaineer' in influencing public decision-making.

Trails also create an informal, relaxed zone for meeting people with whom you would not interact in the urban setting. And sometimes, trails are the incentive to restore damaged ecosystems.

I view trails as part of the strategy to preserve the natural environment. More importantly, I view them as a tool for educating people to work together to preserve the foundation of our very existence.

I believe that you cannot keep a good thing a secret for long. Therefore, if trails are to be publicized, let this be in an informative and comprehensive manner which conveys responsibility to the user for his conduct, for others' enjoyment and safety, and for the environment itself.

Trail types

The trails directory, which begins on page 34, concentrates on trails and areas for mountaineering under the jurisdiction of South Africa's Department of Environment Affairs, National Botanic Gardens, the National Parks Board, the four provincial nature conservation departments, local authorities (divisional councils and municipalities), the Wildlife Society of Southern Africa, and other independent organizations. In Namibia, the Directorate of Nature Conservation

Opposite page: Hikers ascending the Slanghoek Needle in the Western Cape.

Left: Demands on public facilities have brought about restrictions and conditions for use, and all of our recreational areas are burdened with necessary 'don'ts'.

and Recreation Resorts is the controlling body, as are parallel government departments in Botswana, Swaziland, Lesotho, Ciskei, Bophuthatswana, Venda, Lebowa, Zimbabwe and Malawi.

Trails can be grouped into types, based on characteristics such as length and difficulty, experience and type of equipment needed, and educational value.

NATURE TRAILS

These are self-guided interpretive trails laid out with a specific educational objective. Trailists are provided with education aids, usually a written brochure, describing ecological or historical features *en route*. Nature trails run by the National Hiking Way Board, trails through botanical gardens and bird sanctuaries, and nature rambles (similar to interpretive trails, but in which educational material is not provided), also fall into this category.

Nature trails can be completed in less than a day.

URBAN TRAILS

These are trails which are laid out through towns and cities, and which emphasize features of historical and architectural interest.

CANOEING OR KAYAKING TRAILS

Often guided, canoeing or kayaking trails can extend over a few hours or a few days. They include white-water rafting trails.

CYCLING TRAILS

These are trails completed by bicycle, either thin-tyre (racing) or fat-tyre (all-terrain) cycles being used. Those featured in this book are all guided.

HORSE-RIDING TRAILS

Trails on which participants ride horseback. Some trails offer horses for hire, while others operate on a 'bring-your-own' basis.

HANDICAPPED TRAILS

These trails are designed specifically for those confined to wheelchairs, or having some other physical disability, such as blindness.

SNORKELLING TRAILS

These include trails where interpretation is provided underwater and the participant, wearing a snorkel and mask, 'swims' the trail.

DOG TRAILS

Dogs are welcomed, and encouraged, on these trails.

AUTO TRAILS

These trails, set out in game reserves, allow the motorist to spot game and study the ecology of an area from his vehicle.

GUIDED (WILDERNESS) TRAILS

The term 'wilderness trail' is special to Africa, for here it has grown to imply a walk guided by a game ranger or conservation officer – usually carrying a rifle – through an area rich in big-game animals, some potentially 'dangerous'. *En route* the guide explains the ecology and management of the area, emphasizing conservation principles and ethics. These trails are physically less demanding than hiking trails, but their value in terms of environmental education is unsurpassable. They usually extend over several days, although some are shorter.

Those guided trails that do not go through big game country, but are led by a reserve officer, knowledgeable ecologist, game scout, caver, boatsman or river rafter, are also labelled guided trails.

BACKPACKING OR HIKING TRAILS

These are continuous footpaths through natural environments. As these trails are two or more days long, the hiker must carry essential overnight equipment and food in a backpack or rucksack. Overnight camping sites or huts, remote from built-up areas, are provided. Such trails are essentially 'do-it-

yourself' adventures, and do not have trails officers. Detailed brochures and maps are available, however. The National Hiking Way System's overnight trails fall into this category. Trails vary widely in their levels of difficulty, and many have stages that are demanding. For example, the hiker can expect to ascend and descend ravines, ford rivers and hike for long stretches over rugged terrain. As discussed on page 11, the aspirant trailist must be prepared, mentally and physically, to meet these challenges.

WILDERNESS TREKKING AND MOUNTAINEERING

'Trailing' is defined as following or walking on a footpath, nature walk or hiking trail, or participating on a guided trail. Thus a 'trailist' is a walker, rambler or hiker who follows a trail or a trails officer. The wilderness trekker differs from the trailist in that he or she sets off into a mountainous area such as a water catchment zone or wild coastal region where no designated footpaths exist. Wilderness trekking varies from the strenuous but fairly straightforward traverses and climbs where enthusiasm and energy are more prerequisite than sophisticated equipment, to very difficult rock or ice ascents where ropes, pitons and other aids are essential. Irrespective of the grade, however, trekking and mountaineering are highly demanding recreations, and climbers often have to cope with fast-changing and extremely rigorous weather conditions. Those participating in these activities should be experienced in outdoor survival and first-aid, and have a basic knowledge of map-reading. Descriptions of rock and ice climbing routes are beyond the scope of this guide.

The National Hiking Way System

'NHWS' stands for the National Hiking Way System, a complex of hiking trails and nature walks in South Africa and its independent states, each accompanied by a comprehensive information brochure and map.

Before 1975, most mountain catchment areas, plantations and private farms were inaccessible to the public, as authorities and landowners were reluctant to allow general access to their land. A change came in the mid 'seventies, however, when the Forestry Branch initiated a trial project – a system of hiking and nature trails which, at first, was modelled on the popular Appalachian Trail in the eastern United States, and the European hiking trails. The South African trails evolved a distinctive character and today explode with unpredicted popularity.

The National Hiking Way System was established on 30 April 1975 when it was granted statutory recognition in the Forest Amendment Act of 1975. It is co-ordinated and managed by the National Hiking Way Board, an autonomous body representing State Departments, Provincial Administrations, Parks Boards, mountain and other outdoor clubs, as well as influential private citizens.

At one time it was envisaged that a continuous footpath would stretch for thousands of kilometres from the Soutpansberg in the north, along the whole length of the Escarpment, to the Cedarberg in the western Cape. However, experience taught the National Hiking Way Board two important lessons: circular trails (those which begin and end at the same point, thereby easing the hiker's transport problems) are most popular; and trails in prime country, with attractive scenery, wildlife and other natural or historical assets, are used more frequently than those developed solely to link up the prime trails. For this reason, the NHWB today concentrates on developing trails with the trailist

and natural attributes of a region in mind. The continuous footpath is no longer a priority goal.

The Fanie Botha Hiking Trail, the first hiking way, was opened in 1973. Since then over a thousand kilometres of the system have been developed. These completed sections are attracting more and more enthusiasts and obviously, with such heavy usage, a trails environment can be threatened by erosion and pollution. To prevent this, every hiker must abide by certain rules if he is to be a guest on the NHWS.

Along the entire length of each trail, white footprints painted on tree trunks and rocks mark the NHWS route to be followed. Nature trails are marked with theme pictograms, for example, the elephant on the Elephant Walk near Knysna (see page 80). Hikers must remain on the trail and hike in the stated direction only. They must stay overnight at hiking huts or camps – located about 3-8 walking hours (or 10-22 kilometres) apart, depending on the terrain. Every hut is different in structure and provision, ranging from simple shelters to converted farmhouses and foresters' houses. Most have fireplaces, firewood, water, toilet facilities and sleeping bunks. The trail brochure is essential, however, to learn exactly what is provided at each site; the length of

each trail stretch; beginning, end and parking places; climatic data; specific rules and regulations; precautions; closures; fees, etc.

The NHWS brochures also contain information on natural and cultural history as well as maps of excellent environmental educational value. Despite its comprehensiveness, this guide is by no means a substitute for any of the NHWS brochures and/or maps.

Fees for trails

A fee is charged on every NHWS trail, and on most other hiking trails. At the time of writing, this was R6,00 per night for adults on NHWS trails. Trailists on nature walks require permits, but access is usually free or at a nominal tariff.

I do not indicate fees for any facilities or amenities, huts, accompanied trails, entry into wilderness areas, trail booklets, or en-

trance to reserves, because these change frequently. However, the trailist can assume that a charge will be levied on most trails and that this charge will be much higher for privately run trails than for those organized by government authorities or run by societies and clubs.

Before setting out

THE PRACTICAL ASPECTS OF PREPARATION

Wouldn't it be idyllic to venture on to the trail clad in nothing more than a T-shirt and shorts, with no paraphernalia on our backs or hanging from our necks or shoulders? Idyllic – but impractical – and virtually impossible, for this would imply 'living off the land' to survive. Not only are we ill-equipped for such adventuring, but also destroying wild plants and animals for both food and shelter are 'luxuries' that man can no longer afford. Whether we like it or not we are products of twentieth century society – seeking recreation on a shrinking planet.

Today, our natural areas are under so many pressures from over-population by the ever-increasing human species, that more

and more space is needed for food production, industry, housing, dams . . . and recreation. Great demands on public facilities have brought about stringent restrictions and conditions for use, and even our playgrounds are burdened with necessary 'don'ts'. The Cape Town City Council's sign in the Table Mountain Nature Reserve underlines the seriousness of the situation:
'Camping, erecting structures, lighting fires, using gas or paraffin cookers, gathering flowers and plants, hunting, fishing and interfering with any animal, fish, bird or insect, selling or displaying for sale any articles or distributing any pamphlets or playing a radio, allowing dogs unleashed *without authority are prohibited*.
'Riding motorcycles, bathing, polluting water, littering, feeding baboons, rolling and throwing stones or missiles, damaging or defacing any rock or indigenous flora, removing any rocks or soil, causing a nuisance, obstruction or disturbance *are prohibited in terms of the parks by-law*.'

When we leave the security of our homes to go trailing, whether on foot, horseback, in a canoe or on skis, we must cater constantly for our needs – hunger, thirst, protection from heat or cold, sleep, cleanliness and safety – and, of course, our curiosity. Since we can no longer live off the land, or interfere with it, we must prepare ourselves like an astronaut does for a journey in a spaceship. We must venture into the wilds carrying all our creature comforts in a backpack, taking care to leave as little trace of our passage as possible. This is the new wilderness ethic. Fortunately, the technology of our space-probing era has produced an array of foods, equipment, clothing and first-aid items that are astonishingly compact, lightweight, efficient and simple to use.

The following, together with the detailed trail checklist on page 336, will help you sort out what is needed for each trail type, starting with the most essential prerequisites – physical and mental fitness, knowledge and experience.

PHYSICAL AND MENTAL FITNESS

A basic fact is that the fitter you are, the more you will enjoy trailing. Physical fitness is twofold: fitness of the heart, and muscle fitness (especially important for backpacking, in the legs and knees, lower back and arms, and upper body). Fitness of the heart, or cardiovascular fitness, is simply how efficiently your heart-lung machine can use oxygen to supply energy to working muscles. You inherit 90 per cent of your fitness potential, while the remainder can be devel-

Opposite page: Choose your degree of difficulty: from interpretive nature trails (bottom) to hiking and mountaineering (top).
Above: Read the trail brochure (left) carefully to discover what amenities (right) are available.

oped by endurance exercises such as jogging, bicycling and swimming. However, the best sport to get your heart tuned for hiking *is* hiking. The best way to strengthen muscles used to carry packs *is* backpacking. Books recommended on page 338 show how to get fit and stay fit.

Another type of fitness develops from trail use – mental fitness. A hike must be both a mental and physical challenge – you must feel a sense of achievement on reaching your destination, a 'Wow, I made it!' To many hikers the feeling of complete independence and solitude is as exhilarating as the breath-taking scenic beauty experienced on most trails. To those who have never hiked, the trail can be many things – wonderful, pleasant, unpleasant, harrowing or disastrous. Some hikers emerge from the mountains with the scent of bushes and ferns on their clothing and dust on their boots – enriched physically and mentally. Others stumble out exhausted, footsore, sunburnt, dehydrated or soaked to the skin – sadder but wiser for their ordeal. Others are even less fortunate, but basically the outcome of these ventures depends largely on the hiker: his preparation, his clothing and equipment, his physical condition and his good sense.

The question often asked is, 'How far can I walk?' Here are some guidelines:
33 kilometres a day if you are in top shape and don't want to see anything more than a blur.
25 kilometres a day if you are in good shape and don't dawdle.
20 kilometres a day if you are in poor shape and want to suffer.
10 kilometres a day if you are in fair shape and want to enjoy yourself.
five kilometres a day if your companion is an attractive person and you both enjoy wildflowers!

Remember that the trail is not a suitable place for anyone who considers it a loss of face should he decide to turn back when conditions require it; and it is no place for backbiting or sensitivity over small slights. Most of the fun you have from backpacking depends on mental attitude. I quote the American Harold Allen:

'A trail is
remote for detachment
narrow for chosen company
winding for leisure
lonely for contemplation.
The trail leads not merely North or
   South,
but upward to the body, mind and soul
   of man.'
This is the beauty of the trail and what backpacking is all about.

EXPERIENCE AND KNOWLEDGE

Don't do what I did on my first mountaineering trip. I flew into a remote section of Alaska, shoddily equipped with a pack, no experience and little knowledge of the area.

The pilot was three days late in returning, during which time I ran out of food and spent miserably sleepless nights uncomfortably clad in all my clothes as my sleeping bag was of poor quality and I didn't have a foam pad. I wandered aimlessly without a map and narrowly escaped grizzly bears because I was ignorant of their habits. Good weather, an abundance of non-poisonous berries and fat-filled migrating fish – caught in my hat as they jumped rapids – helped me to survive. Others aren't so lucky – and have only themselves to blame.

Each type of trail demands different degrees of fitness, experience and knowledge. Realize your limitations, choose dependable and experienced trail leaders and gain your experience trailing with them.

Nature trails: Nature trails (and here I emphasize trails for which trail guide booklets and educational brochures are available or which have visitor centres with interpretive displays) lead to an awareness of skills we have lost because we have become dependent beings in some huge machine, spinning around and around, too dizzy to see what we look at and too preoccupied to care. These skills are knowing how to use your senses, your eyes, your nose, your hands, your ears, your tongue.

Accomplished outdoorsmen aren't born experts; they have simply given their senses a chance to develop. Just as your heart and lungs need to be exercised to reach maximum efficiency, so do your nerve endings. The nature trail is where you can start as, unburdened by sleeping bags and tents, you can walk slowly and explore, observe and record, using binoculars and field guides to aid your senses and expand their potential. For many people, rambling, bird-watching, photographing nature or just reaching a point and taking in sounds, scents and movements is an incomparable 'high'. Try it, but beware . . . nature trails are addictive and lead you towards the longer and more challenging hiking trails.

Guided (wilderness) trails: The fortunate novice will begin trailing on a guided or wilderness trail, such as those run by the Wilderness Leadership School or Educational Wildlife Expeditions. The degree of fitness required is that of any healthy, keen individual and distances covered each day are relatively short. Because the trail is led by an experienced ranger, he will modify its length, route and strenuousness, taking into consideration the weather and his party. You carry a minimum of items, as most of your essentials are transported by porters, mules or jeep. Having an experienced trails officer with you, you will be warned of sudden dangers (such as puff adders in the path or lightning storms), and first-aid will be readily available.

Much time is taken up with discussions and observations in the veld – a most impor-

tant aspect, where the trails officer will help you achieve the right orientation towards trailing – to become aware of what you are 'looking at', by imparting his knowledge of the region, its plants and animals as well as the archaeology and bush lore.

Hiking trails: The main difference between rambling or walking and hiking or backpacking is one of degree – hikers go farther, stay out for one or more nights and carry more need-satisfying items. The hiker must be familiar with various skills such as basic first-aid; recognizing the symptoms of hypothermia, hyperthermia and mountain altitude sickness; using a compass and map-reading; using equipment and knowing its limitations; and – most important – being environmentally 'literate'. When hiking you should be able to use all your senses to 'read' nature – wind direction, vegetation, bird species, wildlife habits, insects flying about, sounds and smells all provide clues for understanding your surroundings. Environ-

mental literacy and hiking skills develop slowly and with experience; by starting to hike with qualified members of mountain clubs or organized expeditions, you will be pointed in the right direction.

Wilderness trekking and mountaineering: Unlike the hiker, the wilderness trekker and mountaineer must carry everything he needs (including his shelter) into a pathless environment in which he must be able to navigate and survive. Mountaineering is physically very demanding, requiring peak fitness for full enjoyment. It is often the natural culmination of experience and knowledge gained from nature walks and hiking trails. John Cleare in his *Guide to Mountains and Mountaineering* puts it succinctly:

'Mountaineering is a selfish and anarchistic sport and long may it remain so! The competent all-round mountaineer must master a wide range of skills. Besides being a proficient performer on steep rock, ice and

Above: The feeling of independence and solitude can be as exhilarating as the breath-taking scenery.
Opposite page: A knowledge of map-reading is essential in a wilderness area.

mixed ground, he must be a useful off-piste skier, an expert back-packer and something of a navigator and survival specialist.'

INSOMNIA ON THE TRAIL

We are led to believe that the great outdoors is a natural tranquillizer which relaxes our minds and bodies, and that when darkness envelops us, we blissfully fall into a deep sleep. The fact that many people suffer sleepless nights in the outdoors may come as a surprise to you, as your fellow hikers are often too embarrassed to admit it.

There are several factors that may contribute to a poor night's sleep on the trail. You may be uncomfortable because your mattress is too thin, too narrow or too short, or you may have forgotten to bring one. (I neglected to take a mattress when I went to Alaska, and discovered that sleeping on permafrost was akin to retiring on an ice skating rink.) You are probably accustomed at home to one or two pillows and have sacrificed these to lighten your load; your lumpy pile of clothes does not substitute well. You may be conscious of a throbbing injury and not have any pain killers. You may be too hot, especially in the summer when tents block out breezes and good down sleeping bags turn into sauna baths. More likely, you are too cold. Perhaps you feel constricted, short of leg room or claustrophobic in your new mummy bag.

You may be sensitive to unfamiliar surroundings and strange noises; everything from the monotonous chirp of crickets or the flapping of fly sheets to the buzz of a mosquito or the snorer in the next tent has been blamed for disturbing the peace. Too much coffee, tea or alcohol before retiring is certainly a physiological cause of insomnia. If you are worried about the next day's route, having to ford a river in the rain, or poor weather conditions, you may ponder all night. If you worry about not being able to fall asleep, you won't. High altitude (usually above 3 700 metres, which excludes trails in this book), is a definite cause of sleeplessness; it is associated with headache, rapid heartbeat and heavy breathing.

There are remedies for sleeplessness on the trail. Worries about unfamiliar surroundings and the following day should disappear once you gain confidence and physical fitness. Always hike with a leader whom you trust and respect. Uncomfortable sleeping conditions can be alleviated with the correct equipment. Air mattresses may suit you better than closed-cell foam; a small down pillow may be a worthwhile investment (or wrap your down jacket around your ears). Try a dome tent to eliminate fly sheets flapping in the wind. Your first-aid kit should always carry pain killers of differing intensities. Cold and heat packs (see page 22) can help to adjust your 'in-bag' temperature.

I find that irregular noises keep me awake so I try to sleep far away from known snorers and 'bed tossers', and near a stream. Running water always soothes the nerves. Avoid sipping coffee, tea or alcohol late at night over the deep, warm coals of your fire. Rather substitute decaffeinated and non-alcoholic drinks such as hot chocolate, which will provide liquid, warmth and kilojoules. If you are sleeping in the open, stargaze, with your eyes fixed to the heavens. My astronomer hiking friend says this always makes him dozy. Carry along a lightweight book and read with a head torch, but without disturbing others with your light or shuffling pages.

Ear plugs, eye covers and sleeping pills are last resorts. Ear plugs and eye covers can be a nuisance and a cause of irritation rather than a remedy. Pills are crutches and do not psychologically solve the problem; sleeping pills are especially dangerous to use because they are addictive, and some leave you feeling groggy in the morning. Consult your doctor for the correct prescription, letting him know that you are planning to use the

pills while camping. Remember, sleeping pills should not be taken at high altitudes.

If you try these suggestions and still have problems getting a good night's sleep on the trail, do not get upset: even with less sleep than is usual for you, the following morning you will still function better on your hike than you would at your office or school desk!

IS HIKING A FAMILY ACTIVITY?

To share with your children a walk in the woods, the flight of a loerie, or the crimson sunset over the high peaks is a wonderful experience, but is it practical, possible and realistic to hike with the whole family? How many times has the old story been repeated: the keen varsity hiker graduates to a job, joins a hiking club, finds a spouse, then has a family. Suddenly he feels trapped – the woods and mountains are no longer his domain, and his fitness and spirit fade. And all that backpacking gear just gathers dust . . .

This doesn't have to happen. In fact, the thrill of hiking and camping can be enhanced by sharing it with your children. However, there are changes, compromises and new methods to adapt for successful family outings. These are largely dependent on the ages of your children.

Parents who take children hiking who are less than three years old must be prepared to carry not only their own loads but also those of their children, *and* the toddlers as well! Infants take to front and back carriers very well. Front carriers allow the parent to attend to a baby's needs while hiking. Toddlers enjoy negotiating the trail on their own, with an occasional free ride in the backpack from Mom or Dad. School-going children (five to six years old) can begin to help carry some of the load, even if this is only a book, snack, water bottle or a whistle to blow if they get lost.

Child carriers are now being manufactured overseas in greater varieties and quantities, although this area is still an experimental field. Many of these models should percolate to the camping stores in South Africa. Women should not carry children high up, but rather centre the weight lower down on the body to take advantage of their own weight distribution and musculature.

To reduce weight, parents must trim some of theirs for the children – food, sleeping bag, nappies, clothes, and also those special little extras such as a story book and stuffed animal, which make camp more like home and add to the child's feeling of security. It is also a wise idea to camp in one large dome-type tent (rent it if necessary) with a lantern – children younger than eight or 10 years can become frightened in a tent by themselves or alone with other children. Before the hike, let the kids camp in the tent in the back yard. If you pack smaller, two-person tents, have a parent sleep in each tent.

If your child is likely to urinate in the sleeping bag, I suggest using only synthetic fill bags which wash easily and remain warm when wet.

To feed babies and small children on the trail, take along bagged bottles, which can be prefilled with powdered formulas and reconstituted along the way. Children often don't perceive dehydration, so it is sometimes a problem to get your child to drink enough water. Try filling water bottles with lemonade or orange juice and freezing the bottle before you set out. Alternatively, buy small cartons of juice available in cafés and supermarkets. To make the trip pleasant, carry foods children enjoy.

Dress your child properly in bright colours (so he can be seen if he gets lost), and in wools and tough fabric blends which are able to withstand the vigours of outdoor wear. Layering for warmth, although time-consuming, is necessary. Boots in children's sizes are scarce, so sturdy running shoes, preferably with high tops for ankle support, are the best alternative. Children's daypacks are easily purchased whereas sleeping bags are not.

Children are born nature enthusiasts. Small children love large animals and older children favour small animals. Most children hate 'slimy and dirty' snakes and 'hairy and creepy' spiders. All children exhibit an exploratory behaviour and display intense curiosity about their surroundings. Parents must be prepared to stop frequently on a walk, giving their children lots of time to explore, and to explore with them. You will be astonished how your children will open up new worlds for you through their eyes. Try to take with you some simple identification picture books and magnifying glasses to make the hike a learning experience.

On the trail, young girls (eight to 12 years) are most interested in hiking and learning, while boys of the same age are in-

terested in animals, things to eat and chase, adventure and climbing. Girls from 12 to 16 are more interested in socializing with boys, while boys are interested not only in girls, but also in physical challenges and wildlife. In contrast, senior citizens are interested in traditions, how their ancestors used to live and eat, and natural foods, medicines and poisons.

Children must be kept busy on a hike. Give them responsibilities such as reading a map, taking the lead, determining the route or finding the next trail marker. Let the fittest and fastest carry a heavier weight as you must always walk at the pace of the slowest child. After the hike your children will talk about the special moments, so plan something unusual – a braai, flying kites, exploring a cave, etc. And when you get home, sew a patch on their daypack for a small memento of the experience.

First hikes should start small to avoid boredom. A day hike should be no more than four hours, with a long rest stop, while an overnight hike for three nights is sufficient. For the first overnight hike, go to a place from which you can retreat fast if nec-

essary. Setting up camp in a pleasant area and doing day walks should be considered.

Camping with more than one family has its advantages. Although planning logistics are more difficult, the children will enjoy the company of others their age, and parents will also have a diversion. It will also lessen your children's demands for constant parental attention and coaching.

To hike with your family is to bridge the generation gap. It is one of the few activities which is fairly inexpensive to do *en masse*, where all members can share in the fun and chores, each having a function and responsibility. Hiking with your children will undoubtedly bring the family closer together.

Equipment

Look through the checklist provided on page 336 – but don't despair. Believe it or not, a well-equipped mountaineer can carry everything he needs in a backpack with a mass of between one quarter to one third of that of his body. The secret is the 'light-style'. The lighter your gear, the longer and farther you can walk. Buy only quality equipment to prevent frustration and unnecessary replacements.

BOOTS

Boots are the foundation of a comfortable hike. Buy carefully! Trail boots are always recommended, although on short nature walks a pair of well-cushioned velskoens, or tennis or jogging shoes may be sufficient if your ankles are strong. In boots, look for full-grain leather uppers that are foam-padded at the ankles with a padded 'scree guard' around the top for comfort. The toe and heel should be hard. The tongue should be sewn to the uppers to keep out dirt, water and snow.

The midsole (layers of leather or rubber between the boot upper and the bottom sole) determines the stiffness of the boot. Climbers need very rigid boots for support, whereas those for walkers and hikers need not be so heavy. Remember, a kilogram of boot when worn is the equivalent of four kilograms carried on your back. The most popular sole is the black, knobby lugged sole, its high carbon content ensuring long life. Its major drawback is that the rugged, deep-patterned sole forms a reverse imprint in the soil. A constant stream of deep footprints breaks up the soil, thus making it susceptible to erosion. Tyre-sole boots are sufficient for nature trails and summer hiking.

The fit of the boot is critical. A poorly made or badly fitting pair not only leads to painful blisters but also causes the feet to tire much more quickly than a well-fitting boot with good support. Take your own socks with you when trying on boots. A heavy wool ragg outer sock should be fitted

over a lighter cotton or light wool sock. Push your foot forward in the unlaced boot until your toes touch the front. There should be room to insert your index finger between the back of the boot and your heel. Tap your heel back into place and tightly lace the boot; your toes should never touch the end of the boot, even when hiking at full stretch. There should be lots of room to wiggle them about.

In recent years, a new kind of hiking boot has been developed. Improving on all the features of the classic European mountaineer's boot, the hiking boot weighs little more than a pair of running shoes. Although they seldom last as long as the classic boots and cost the same, I highly recommend them for any trail in this book. They are painless to break in, thus eliminating the discouraging 'blister' period. Other features include their abrasive resistant and waterproof uppers, insoles offering superb cushioning and arch support, moulded heel counters and other supporting devices, and engineered soles that claim not only to eliminate slipping (and mud clogging, which also decreases gripping power), but also to reduce damage to ground cover, the first stage of erosion.

Before using boots on the trail, treat the leather parts with boot polish, Neatsfoot oil or a similar product. Wear them at home, in town and on short walks to break them in, so that the leather moulds to your feet. A good pair of climbing boots needs at least 75 kilometres of walking to wear them in properly. If you participate in a variety of different trails, you will find it worthwhile to own more than one pair of boots, each of different mass and quality, saving the best boots for the rugged expeditions.

A final point: even though hiking boots often get very wet, never dry them next to a fire or in direct heat. It cooks the life out of the leather. Rather allow them to air dry, stuffed with newspaper to retain their shape.

BACKPACKS

Today a multitude of backpacks of different designs is available: some have rigid metal frames, others flex as your back flexes; some are mounted on external frames, while others conceal an internal frame. Each has advantages and disadvantages.

External frame packs are stable, able to carry heavy weights or odd-shaped loads, and cool – the backpacks allow some air between the back and the pack. Internal frame packs are firm, flex to allow freedom of movement and are favourites when climbing, skiing, canoeing and bushwacking. The newest models are adjustable to fit your body shape perfectly. Their suspension systems, which adjust and draw the load tight in all directions, combined with close body contact, enable a well-designed internal frame pack to approach or equal the load-carrying capacity of a framepack.

Soft packs flex to allow excellent freedom of movement and they hug the body. They are often the choice of the climber, skier or canoeist (for portaging) to whom stability is the prime concern. Some soft packs hug the body so closely that they are too hot for use in warm weather. I own both an external-frame bag for hiking trails, and an internal-frame, soft pack for mountaineering and kloofing trips. I prefer to travel with the latter as it is more acceptable to airlines and can be squeezed more easily into the boot of a car.

Whether you choose a soft pack or an external frame model, buy one which has a firm, foam-padded hip belt and shoulder straps. The hip belt takes much of the load from your shoulders and the padding is essential to prevent sore, bruised muscles and bones.

To keep the top of the pack from falling over backwards, look for the new suspension system which uses the shoulder harness. Better packs have 'load-lifter' straps that can be adjusted to lift the top of the shoulder straps right off your shoulders. The only contact is against the front of your upper chest.

As with boots, fit your backpack in the store before buying it. Make sure that the hip belt wraps around your hips and not your waist or torso. Do not buy a pack that rides more than five centimetres above your head. Women, be aware that most packs are designed for longer-bodied men, although very recently 'women-only' packs have been manufactured. These take into consideration a woman's lower centre of gravity, wider hips, narrower shoulders and shorter torso.

You can purchase top-loading or front-loading bags, or a combination. The bag itself comprises one, two or three compartments, often with two to four pockets. Be sure these zipped or buckled pockets are large enough for items you want handy – water bottle, bird guide, first-aid kit, camera, etc. A top-loading bag is best for oversized and protruding loads – make certain the storm flap that covers the top is large enough to cover the largest load you will carry. Front-loading bags with large, zipped flaps are most accessible and easiest to keep your gear organized.

Nylon-coil and plastic-toothed zip fasteners are preferable to the older metal zips. Check for clean stitching, reinforced at stress points. Also, look for the new, fast-releasing plastic buckles which are not only more convenient, but safer in some situations, such as when crossing streams or falling in snow. Lift tabs are also useful as they make tightening or loosening your shoulder straps easier, which in turn makes it easier to get a proper adjustment. This lessens back strain, prevents blisters and gives the legs more freedom.

When loading your bag, pack the densest items closest to your centre of gravity. In other words, place the heaviest items on top and to the back of your pack, with the

smaller equipment in the lower side pockets; the water bottle should be placed in an upper side pocket.

Women should realize that they often suffer from weight packed too high because they do not have the upper body strength of men. This weight can interfere with arm movement and breathing. Therefore, a good suspension system and hip belt are essential.

Although colour choice is personal, remember that bright colours aid identification in dense bush, heavy mist or snow and low light intensities.

DAYPACKS

On nature and/or guided wilderness trails, you will need only a daypack (providing 9 000 to 16 000 cubic centimetres of space). Some daypacks have padded backs, which come in handy as you don't have to concern yourself with packing the bag too comfortably. To be inconspicuous near large game, wilderness trail participants must avoid brightly coloured (orange, red or yellow) packs. Daypacks should have one or two easily accessible side pockets and should be large enough to contain all your cold-weather needs and interpretive equipment (guide books, camera, binoculars, etc).

Another consideration when buying a daypack is that it should fit comfortably into your larger backpack. Many hiking trails allow you to reach the hut by lunch-time, leaving the afternoon free to ramble or climb to a nearby peak. Many people on mountaineering trips camp in an area and then make day trips from their base. Daypacks are also useful as hand baggage on airlines. Some backpacks are now made with a removable, zippered compartment that, when detached, can be worn as a small daypack.

Kloofing trips require fully waterproof packs. Such a pack can be dropped in a river or pool and float freely downstream over and under rapids, without any of its contents getting wet. The best way to waterproof a pack is to place all critical items (items that must be kept dry) in a heavy-duty, double-seamed plastic bag, twisting the opening and tying it securely with a bootlace. A second bag over the first provides extra protection. Garbage bags, shopping bags and even some sports bags are not strong enough for waterproofing packs. The most reliable bags can be purchased at camping stores. Place the bag inside the major compartment of your backpack. Non-critical items (water bottle, plates, tinned food, etc.) are carried in side pockets.

For any regular outing, place a waterproofing bag inside your pack and simply fold over the opening. This will ensure dry gear at the end of a rainy trek. I use a brand new, heavy-duty bag for each kloofing expedition to ensure that there are no small holes and then place the 'used' bag in my pack for the more usual mountaineering or hiking trips.

Bearing all this in mind, if you should ask for a porter to assist your climb on Malawi's Mount Mulanje, in the Drakensberg, or elsewhere in Africa, do not be too surprised if he empties the contents of your smartly styled pack into a duffel-bag and then proceeds up the mountain carrying it on his head!

SLEEPING GEAR

The major consideration involved when buying a sleeping bag is warmth. If you plan to hike during winter or in regions with sharp nocturnal drops in temperature, waterfowl down filling is highly recommended. Down is not only warm but also soft, easily compressible and capable of complete recovery after being stuffed into a carrying sack for long periods. Duck (as opposed to goose) down is slightly less efficient, but cheaper. Some manufacturers combine the two to produce a more economical bag. The biggest drawback of any down is that it will not keep you warm if it gets soaked. It is also allergenic and is becoming increasingly expensive.

The highest quality man-made fibre fills, however, have none of these drawbacks and, most importantly, they will keep you warm even when wet. They dry quickly and are easily washed at home and, being less compressible, insulate you better from the ground. On the minus side, they are not as light or compact as down. However, new fillings and constructions have narrowed the gap between synthetics and down considerably in recent years. Some of the fillings you are apt to see in the near future are Thinsulate, Polar Guard, Hollofil 808, Hollofil II

Invest in the right equipment, such as boots and a good backpack (opposite page and above).

15

and Quallofil, this last being the most compressible and warmest for its weight.

Whichever you choose, make sure your zip fastener is nylon, backed by a 'draft tube' filled with down or fibre to keep out the cold. Unless your sleeping bag is used only in warm temperatures, you should avoid sewn-through constructions, which cause cold spots along stitch lines. If you buy a bag for cold weather but also plan to use it in warm weather, make sure that it has a double zipper so that you can vent the lower end to keep cool.

Never buy a sleeping bag made of waterproof material. When you sleep, you perspire and the resultant condensation will soak you and your bag if it cannot evaporate. I find the ideal combination to be a cotton inner lining with a water repellent but breathable nylon material used for the outside.

The shape of the bag is also important. Mummy bags (form-fitting and with a hood) give maximum warmth, and are more compact than rectangular bags.

Mattresses are only really necessary for wilderness trekkers and mountaineers or hikers using camp-sites. Most huts in southern Africa supply them and they are usually provided on wilderness trails. Some people carry air mattresses that can double as a lilo, but these puncture easily and can burst if over-heated by the sun. If a mattress is required, a closed-cell foam mattress is ideal, being both waterproof and very light.

A reasonably comfortable pillow can be made by stuffing clothes into the bag used to carry your sleeping bag during the day.

TENTS

When selecting a tent, look for one with a waterproof floor and roof and a 'breathing' ceiling. Until recently, all quality tents were double-skinned, with a ceiling of breathable nylon, having a few centimetres or more below a waterproof fly. Body moisture passes through the ceiling, condenses on the impermeable fly and drips off harmlessly outside.

There are new waterproof materials available which let out body miosture yet repel rain. These materials are patented as Goretex, Bion, Entrant and Helly-Tech. Although single-layer tents are constructed from these fabrics, the smaller, one-person tents have proven most successful.

Today's lightweight tents come in a multitude of shapes – tepee, A-frame, dome, 'half-dome', tunnel or hoop and star. Any is satisfactory if it has the specifications I have mentioned. However, dome or half-dome designs will stand without pegs or guyropes, which makes them particularly useful where staking is difficult – on beaches or river banks, on frozen ground or in snow. Dome designs have flexible poles which tense inside fabric sleeves, pushing outwards on the walls to support the tent.

Other features to look for when buying a tent are tight, preferably double- and triple-row stitching; reinforced stress points; mosquito netting for doors, windows and vent openings; and nylon-coil or Delrin-toothed zips. A two-person backpacker's tent should weigh less than three kilograms. Good tents are expensive but can last a lifetime, so don't compromise on quality.

STOVES

It is virtually impossible to go trailing today without a camp-stove if you want to cook food or have hot fluids. The camp-stove is the symbol of the environmentally conscious trailist. In most areas under government control, fires are prohibited – either because of depletion of natural wood supplies, fire danger or simply to prevent unsightly campfire remains from spoiling the environment. Hence, with the exception of organized (guided) trail safaris, camp-stoves are necessary for all trail users and mountaineers.

Like tents, there is a myriad stoves from which to choose and although selection is largely a matter of personal preference, it is important to know what to look for. Among the aspects to be considered are type of fuel needed, its availability and price; the stove's mass; accessories included, such as pots; ease of packing; safety, stability and reliability; boiling speed; cold-weather performance; starting and running ease; cleaning; noise; and environmental concerns such as disposing of fuel cartridges.

Fuel, especially its availability, is a very important consideration. Camp-stoves operate on either white gas (benzine), butane and propane, paraffin, solid fuel or alcohol. There is one stove on the market, designed by Mountain Safety Research in Seattle, Washington, that operates on all fuel types. White gas or benzine stoves (such as the classic Swedish Optimus 123R, 8R and 111B models) work well in low temperatures. Disadvantages are the delicate task of refuelling and in preheating, which involves creating a dangerous flare. In Africa generally, benzine is not readily available except in the larger towns.

Butane and propane fuels come in pressurized steel cylinders. These fuels are popular with beginners because they are convenient, refuelling is simple (either push or screw in a new cylinder) and they start easily. The problems are possible leakage of gas between the stove and the canister, the sheer bulk and mass of the cylinders, and what to do with the 'empties'. Butane is a poor coldweather fuel because it will not vaporize below 0 °C; in addition, the heat output decreases as the amount of fuel in the cartridge decreases. Propane is a better fuel for cold weather and at high altitudes but, because it must be stored under greater pressure, the canisters are stronger and therefore heavier.

Paraffin stoves such as Optimus 45 and 111 are safer and burn hotter than those that run on benzine. Another 'pro' of paraffin is that it is relatively cheap and readily available, making it an excellent choice for groups and expeditions. The 'cons' include its smokiness, smell and starting difficulty.

Solid fuel stoves are best kept for emergencies – they have low heating power and less delicate simmering control, but they are safe and relatively impervious to cold.

Alcohol (methylated spirits) stoves include my favourite, the Optimus stormstove. It weighs only 0,68 kilograms and includes two large saucepans, a frying pan, a wind-shield and a pot grip. The main disadvantage of an alcohol stove is that more fuel is needed to produce as much heat as gasoline or paraffin stoves. However, unlike most other stove fuels, it is not a petroleum product. The storm-stove is quiet, stable, reliable and poses no problems in starting or refuelling. Alcohol spirit is available throughout Africa.

Compatibility is critical. Observe your friends' stoves, know the conditions you will be trailing in and then decide what to buy.

Warning: Never use a camp-stove inside your tent. They have been known to cause

Above: Lilos, sometimes used when kloofing, double as air mattresses.

Opposite page: Choose your tent and stove according to your needs.

carbon monoxide poisoning, and they can flare up and turn all your petroleum-based synthetic equipment into a blazing inferno.

CLOTHES

High, exposed windy summits; warm, sun-heated valleys; hot midday sun; and cold nights – these may all be experienced in a 24-hour hiking day. Always be prepared for a wide range of temperatures, humidity or precipitation. Two important principles to keep in mind are that several light layers are more adaptable than a single, heavy garment, and that wool is the only fabric that retains its warmth even when wet. Wearing wet cotton clothing actually makes you feel colder than walking naked.

Use the 'layered look' and be as warm or as cool as you like. Here are suggestions, starting with extremities: light wool, silk or polypropylene socks under heavy woollen ones (avoid cotton socks inside boots as cotton holds moisture next to the skin, promoting soft skin and blisters); thin leather glove liners and wool or fibrefill insulated mittens; a brimmed cotton hat for daytime and a woollen hat or balaclava for cold or night; cotton shorts or long pants for daytime; long fishnet underwear, long wool pants for winter or high altitudes; water repellent, breathable nylon wind pants; a thin, cotton, long-sleeved shirt for summer, a woollen one for cold or altitude; a wool jersey or a down or fibrefill vest; a down or fibrefill hooded parka; and a waterproof/breathable hooded shell parka and long pants for rain.

Choose versatile clothes. For example, a long-sleeved cotton shirt can be worn buttoned or unbuttoned, sleeves rolled up or down, and collar up or down, and it has pockets for handkerchief, glucose sweets or tissues. A T-shirt has none of these. A small but useful hint for day hikers – leave a change of warm clothes at your base camp. It is most encouraging to look forward to if you become cold and wet after a strenuous outing.

The biggest clothing dilemma hikers face is choosing between waterproof and water-repellent outerwear. If, when trailing, you walk wearing a waterproof jacket and pants, you keep out the rain but keep in body moisture. Water-repellent clothes allow body moisture to escape but, as the repellent wears off, will eventually prove useless in keeping out rain. If you do not have a Goretex rain suit, it is inevitable that in prolonged rain you will get wet. Waterproof rain gear has the advantage, however, of keeping out wind associated with rain and thereby allowing your body to warm its trapped moisture. In this way, the waterproof jacket and/or pants work like a diving wetsuit.

An alternative to Goretex rain suits is the waterproof gear with new design features such as fuller cut or zipped underarm vents, a hood with a rain visor to keep water out of your face, and few seams, with none over the top of the shoulders.

Some people have expressed dissatisfaction with Goretex, Entrant and similar fabrics that claim to be windproof and waterproof while allowing condensation to evaporate. This is because these fabrics work well only if the rate of perspiration is low, there are significant temperature and relative humidity differences between the outside and the inside of the material, and the outer surface is not coated with a layer of water, such as during a torrential downpour. These are also the reasons why the large dome Goretex tents have failed while the tiny, one-person Goretex tents work well.

In pouring rain you will get damp no matter what you wear. How wet you get will depend on how ingeniously you arrange your clothing layers.

Underwear and pyjamas: Select your underwear by taking into consideration the weather conditions you are likely to encounter. The coolest types of underwear are those made from pure cotton or cotton-and-nylon wash-and-wear combinations. I prefer the quicker-drying (synthetic) fabrics on

long trips when washing must be done. Cold weather underclothing requires more thought. Long johns made of cotton in a conventional weave or net construction are warm, but woven wool and silk combinations are even warmer. Net underwear traps the layer of air next to the skin, adding warmth in winter. In really cold conditions wear two- or three-ply thermals – which usually consist of a wool outer layer, with silk or cotton next to the skin.

For winter nightwear, I use long wool underwear – either for lounging in a tent or as pyjamas. In the summer, a cotton track suit or clean, light underwear is all that is necessary.

Never wear your walking clothes in your sleeping bag. Apart from reasons of hygiene, the fibres of your walking clothes compress and fill with dirt and moisture so that they are no longer able to trap and hold warm air.

A new 'underwear' synthetic is gaining widespread popularity. This product, called polypropylene, works well for active, perspiring people. Instead of absorbing moisture, as do natural fibres like cotton, polypropylene repels water. In order for perspiration to escape from the material, your polypropylene underwear (or undersocks) must be thin and in close contact with your skin. A top layer, of another fabric, will enhance the effectiveness of polypropylene by absorbing expelled moisture.

SMALL ITEMS

Included here are some hard-learned hints about some small items I suggest in the checklist.

Space blanket (sportsman's blanket): This is a true space-age product and has rapidly become indispensable. Incredibly light (340 grams), it consists of a centre fibre net with an aluminium film laminated in a different colour on either side of the fibre. The silver side reflects heat while the red serves as an emergency signal. I have used my space blanket as a groundsheet, blanket, rain poncho, tent, heat reflector, signal to a lost companion, waterproofer in my pack and even as a 'tablecloth'.

Mug or cup: Metal ones burn your lips when you are drinking hot fluids and can freeze to your lips when the mercury drops, so the heat-resistant, strong plastic type is preferable.

Wristwatch: I never concerned myself with time until I started leading hikes and realized how important a watch is. Days are not endless – darkness does fall and most of us are not particularly good judges of sun-time. Watches are essential in emergencies – to arrange meeting or search times. Some reserves close their gates at certain times, especially in day-use areas. At low altitudes (below about 3 000 metres), the average hiker can climb 300 metres in an hour or hike between 2,5 and 3,5 kilometres an hour on a trail. Watches, in conjunction with maps, can give you an idea of how to pace yourself and how long your meal and swim breaks can be.

Torch (flashlight): Headlamps, such as those worn by miners or dentists, are most convenient and leave your hands (and mouth) free for other things. However, small, bright hand-torches weigh less. Always use long-life, alkaline batteries and carry spares, plus an extra bulb. To prevent accidental switch-on and draining, invert the batteries and place a piece of paper between them and the contact.

Binoculars: When hikers think of binoculars they immediately think of watching birds. However, binoculars on the trail have much broader uses – identifying wildlife, picking out landmarks for a compass bearing, searching for lost souls, sighting distant beacons and structures, studying a cliff face or rough terrain, or just generally taking in the 'big picture'. In the past their bulky size and heavy weight made binoculars an item sure to be left behind. However, the new generation of binoculars allows for more magnifying power and brightness, and can weigh as little as 200 grams. The 'roof prism' models, in which the prisms are inside the straight barrel of the instrument, are among the lightest and trimmest of all.

FOOD

Everyone's favourite subject and the hardest to agree on. I find it enormously amusing to hike with a group of people and watch the various foods produced from their packs – everything from tins of smoked oysters to hard, fishmeal squares, commonly referred to as 'dog biscuits'. Many factors govern what foods to take – length of trip, number of people, distance to be travelled, time of year and overnight facilities.

In general, hiking food should be nutritious, lightweight, low in bulk, and prepared with a minimum of fuss and fuel. I divide food into five categories: fresh, tinned, dried, dehydrated and freeze-dried.

Fresh foods such as oranges, apples, cold meats, tomatoes, bread and eggs, spoil easily when exposed to the sun, and are heavy and bulky. They are great for one-day nature walks, but for mountaineering and hiking only the strongest members of the party will feast on them. I find, however, that the enjoyment of one fresh fruit a day on any type of hike is worth the extra muscle strain!

Tinned foods are totally unsuitable. The tins and the opener add extra mass, and once the contents have been eaten you must put the smelly tin with its rough edges back in your pack and carry dead weight. No, you cannot bury the tin. Exceptions to carrying tins can be made on canoeing or kloofing

trips when waterproofing is essential and space for waterproofed items is dear.

Dried foods (figs, raisins, crispbreads, sweets, nuts, health bars and energy bars) will form your diet's bulk, make great trail snacks and are usually packed with energy-giving kilojoules. Some retain a moisture content of as much as 25-30 per cent, however, and must therefore not be stored for too long.

Dehydrated foods such as dried soup mixes, isotonic drinks, non-fat milk powders, instant potatoes, some breakfast cereals, and certain brand meats or soya, are important hiking foods. They need little storage space, have a long storage life and a higher long-term nutritive value than any other type of food. Their only disadvantage is that preparation takes a little longer. Dehydrating removes 98 per cent of moisture, making the food shrink in size. The shrivelled outer covering contracts and tends to protect nutritive values for long periods. Dehydrated foods are usually less costly than dried or off-season fresh foods, and are certainly less expensive than those which are freeze-dried. (Note: in some African countries dehydrated foods are not cheap, but can easily be airfreighted for expeditions, or carried in your baggage.)

Freeze-dried foods ('Mountain House' and other specialized brands) are sliced or processed, immersed or sprayed with a preserving agent, and frozen. The moisture content in the food turns to ice. The food is then placed in a vacuum chamber and subjected to microwaves. As a result of this, the ice is evaporated, leaving the cellular structure of the food essentially the same. The food is lightweight and porous and, when immersed in water, rapidly soaks it up to become reconstituted and ready to use. The convenient and extremely lightweight nature of freeze-dried foods makes them indispensable for strenuous mountaineering trips. However, they are hard to find in Africa, very expensive and within six months their nutritional value is lower and deteriorates faster than dehydrated products. Two of the more unusual freeze-dried foods that are my favourites are freeze-dried pizza and ice-cream!

When planning meals remember the following guidelines:
1. Energy: Kilojoules required by the average hiker walking with a moderate load during a cool summer's day vary between 14 700 and 16 800 a day. Hard, mountain walking in winter, such as in the Drakensberg, can increase needs to 25 200-33 600 kilojoules a day.
2. Properly planned meals, including snacks, need not exceed one kilogram per person per day.
3. Seasonings are important and give a necessary sparkle to the trail traveller's meal.
4. Always carry extra, high-energy and quickly digestible food, some of which can be eaten cold, in a separate re-sealable plas-

tic bag. Suggestions include glucose tablets, nuts, dried fruit, chocolate, instant soup and 'health' bars (for example, Noogy Bars, PVM bars and Muesli Bars). Always carry more tea than you think you will need; *not* coffee or alcohol, both of which if drunk in excess can cause hypothermia.

If this section was too much to digest, stick to guided wilderness trails where all your meals are chosen and prepared for you.

Emergencies on the trail

I hesitate to write this section and hope you never need it. I hesitate because it is not a substitute for a proper first-aid course or mountain survival training. Statistically, besides common blisters, burns, insect bites, scratches and sprains, most of you will never be affected by mountain altitude sickness (the trails included in this guide book are all under 3 700 metres), hypo- or hyperthermia, malaria or bilharzia. However, you will not be affected only if you are aware of how to avoid the dangers.

Analysis of survival cases has proved that mental stress associated with emergencies – especially with being lost and alone – produces fear and anxiety. In turn, these psychological stresses detrimentally affect judgement and attitudes. The prepared hiker can certainly curb, if not eliminate, such stresses. Before embarking on a hike or trail:
1. Obtain adequate information about your route by reading this guide and the relevant hiking pamphlet thoroughly.
2. Be physically fit to follow your planned route and have the proper equipment, clothes and emergency items.
3. Know how to use your equipment. Be familiar with the use of a compass, reading a map, lighting a camp-stove, navigating by the stars, setting up a tent, fixing a broken pack frame, preparing powdered foods, using a first-aid kit, administering snake-bite serum and using water purification tablets. It is beyond the scope of this guide to provide instruction on all these aspects; however, it is the responsibility of the hiker to prepare himself with such knowledge before setting off.
4. Allow ample time between overnight points. Taking into consideration stops *en route* for rest, nature study, food and water, the hiker should average at least two to three kilometres an hour. Remember, however, that more time may be needed for steep climbs.
5. Before your hiking tour, discuss with members of your party plans of action for all foreseeable emergencies. Make sure that each member carries his own water, trail snack, emergency rations and first-aid. Never hike alone.

In an emergency, stop immediately. Review your situation thoroughly, consider possible solutions by analysing the weather, terrain, available resources and time of day, and only then plan a course of action which best suits your available energy, health and resources.

Above all, stay calm (remember that, nowadays, a crisis is generally short-term, lasting less than 72 hours).

The following are suggestions which will help you to cope with common emergencies.

GETTING LOST

If you lose your way on a constructed hiking trail, retrace your route, returning to some clear indication of the trail. Make certain that you have not overlooked a change in trail direction. If you find yourself completely lost, stay put. Usually if the hiker does not wander aimlessly, he will not be far from the trail. Signal for help audibly and visibly – blow three times on your whistle, flash a mirror three times to the sun.

Dense smoke, produced by placing green leaves or grass in a fire, will generally be seen from look-out towers. Don't start a veld fire! Repeat your distress signal regularly. If you have not wandered far from the trail, there is a good chance of other hikers or officials responding to your signals. Air searches can be assisted by placing a large, bright object, such as your space blanket, in a conspicuous place.

AIR, WATER, SHELTER AND FOOD

Air, water, shelter and food are essentials for survival. You can live for three weeks or more without food, three days without water, three hours without protection in hostile weather and three to five minutes without air (see Artificial Respiration, page 20). It is, therefore, imperative that the hiker be familiar with techniques to provide these essentials for life if confronted with a survival situation.

Water: If lost without sufficient water, conserve body fluids by moving only in the cool of the day, talking as little as possible and keeping your mouth closed.

Study the immediate terrain, searching for clues to water sources, such as dense reeds or thickly marked, converging game trails. Large movements of animals (including doves and game birds) during sunset and sunrise usually indicate the directions in which water will be found. Dig beneath the surface of dry riverbeds, especially near the base of big rocks and cliffs where an abnormal amount of vegetation is growing, or at the base of large sand dunes on the shady or steep sides. Ore dumps and tailings indicate that water might be nearby in an old mine shaft or pit.

Many of the water-securing techniques of the Bushmen can teach modern man how to survive. For example, if you find water by digging, preserve the hole with bark lining and bury a grass bundle with two reeds projecting. The bundle acts as a sieve, and the reeds (once thoroughly perforated) act as a straw. Dew or moisture from rocks and plants can be gathered, using a cloth to gently mop up the moisture and wring it into a container. During the rainy season, collect water by digging a hole and lining it with a groundsheet or poncho.

The probability of having to resort to the extremes described above in order to find water while trailing is very slight. However, the possibility that water on the trail is contaminated with diarrhoea-causing bacteria or disease-causing viruses (for example, hepatitis) or protozoa (for example, amoeba) is growing. In November 1981 a woman contracted typhoid on the Otter Trail on the Tsitsikamma coast, and in Natal cholera has become a real problem. All water not originating from high mountain areas should be sterilized by boiling or by adding the appropriate chemicals.

The use of an aqueous solution of iodine is one of the simplest, safest, easiest-to-carry, most rapid and effective methods of water sterilization. Add 15 millilitres of a saturated solution of iodine to one litre of water (strained or filtered if necessary) and leave to stand for 30 minutes. The water will be sterilized of entero-viruses, bacteria and their spores, algae, and protozoas and their cysts. The aqueous iodine technique is superior to other common chemicals used to sterilize water, such as commercial tincture (alcohol solution) or iodine or chlorine tablets.

Water contaminated with bilharzia (see page 20) must be boiled, as cercariae (the snail parasites) can pass through a simple sand filter or strainer. As an alternative, water can be strained free of snails and then allowed to stand for 48 hours, so that all the cercariae die. However, this latter treatment will not prevent other infections such as typhoid and cholera.

Shelter: When building a shelter, avoid expending excess energy. A cave or natural depression is far superior to a complicated wooden structure. Your shelter must minimize body heat loss and maximize body protection. Choose an area protected from the wind. Avoid valleys, stream beds or areas close to rivers. Avoid camping near anthills as snakes are often prevalent here. Also avoid fig trees, as they are infested with flies and insects teem around them. Urine on paths leading into your camp-site helps to discourage wildlife visitors.

The simplest shelter in timbered country, the lean-to, can be constructed from wood and vegetation. Basically, lean-tos are windbreaks and are only temporary structures. They should be three-sided to provide protection from the prevailing night winds. Use trees and sticks as supports and cover them with leaves or grass; start thatching from the bottom, using bark or rope to secure the covering. Matting and grass used for a floor covering should be removed from the shelter and then re-spread for protection against snakes. Heat should radiate into a shelter. You can construct heat reflectors at the back of a fire from logs, rocks, boulders, green boughs or a space blanket.

Food: In an emergency, food is your least important worry and excess energy should not be expended searching for edible plants and animals.
Remember:
1. No grasses are poisonous and the soft stem, swollen roots and seeds are edible.
2. Anything monkeys and baboons eat can be eaten by humans. Avoid fruits with smooth yellow or green skins and thorns on leaves or stems; avoid dark purple fruits from plants with milky juice but no thorns (except wild figs); and avoid fruits of carpet-like, low-growing plants. If the first taste of the central pulp is bitter, do not eat the fruit. Spit out seeds. Do not eat any mushrooms unless you are absolutely sure of their identification and edibility.
3. Insects such as locusts, flying ants, dragonflies, hairless caterpillars, beetles and grubs can be eaten if cooked.
4. Honey can be obtained by smoking a wild beehive.
5. Most fish are edible.
6. All birds' eggs, when fresh, are edible.

FLOODED RIVERS

In 1978 I was caught with forty children on the Transkei's Wild Coast in a flood reputed to be the worst in that country's history. In 1981 I was on the Springbok Hiking Trail during the infamous Laingsburg Floods which took many lives and virtually destroyed several Karoo towns. I have experienced numerous occasions where a flooded river presented a major obstacle between myself and the hiking hut or another destination. Because of these dramatic experiences I have learned to respect the tremendous force of rushing water and its potential hazards.

If you are confronted by a flooded watercourse *do not attempt to cross it*. If mountaineering, set up camp on high ground well away from the river. A swollen river usually returns to normal flow almost as quickly as it rises. Wait until the waters subside. If hiking on a trail, return to the last accessible shelter or examine the route map for emergency exits. In either case, do not feel you are 'losing face' or failing by turning back. Rather sleep safe and dry than be mentioned in Monday's newspaper headlines.

AILMENTS, INJURY AND ILLNESS

The wise trailist has a thorough knowledge of basic first-aid. Common sense dictates that all outdoors people should be prepared for emergencies – by taking a course run by the Red Cross, St. John or an equivalent first-aid society and by carrying a comprehensive first-aid kit including a first-aid manual, such as the small, lightweight, concise booklet issued by the Red Cross Society.

Most trailists will experience at least one of the following problems (listed here alphabetically). I have encountered most, either personally or as a mishap to a companion.

Artificial respiration: Hikers may need to administer artificial respiration if a victim is struck by lightning, drowns, is crushed by ice, snow or rock, chokes, falls or suffers a head blow, or is suffering from inadequate ventilation in his tent. If an individual has difficulty in breathing, artificial respiration must be applied within minutes or death will occur.

Lie the victim on his back. Remove all foreign matter from his mouth and open the air passage by pulling the chin upwards until the head is fully tipped back. Form a tight seal by placing your mouth over the victim's mouth (with a small child, place your mouth over both nose and mouth) while exhaling. With adults, exhale one vigorous breath every five seconds. For small children, exhale shallow breaths every three seconds. If at all possible, don't give up until a doctor arrives.

Bilharzia: Also known as schistosomiasis, bilharzia is a dangerous disease contracted by contact with contaminated water (see page 19). When in a bilharzia area, avoid drinking, swimming or washing in water along the edges of quiet pools, dams, streams or irrigation canals, especially those near human habitation. Unless you are trailing for a very long time, bilharzia will not be noticed until you return home. Signs of blood in your urine or faeces should be reported immediately to a doctor. A word of caution: bilharzia is on the increase in southern Africa.

Bites and stings: *Bees, wasps and spiders:* If a person is not allergic, then bee and wasp stings and spider bites produce only local irritation and swelling which can be treated by cold compresses and aspirin. Remove the sting, being careful not to irritate the affected area in doing so. Allergic reactions to bees and wasps include shortness of breath, shock and unconsciousness, and all allergic persons should carry a special anti-allergy kit at all times. Poisonous spider bites will produce similar reactions to the bites of scorpions.

Scorpions: Scorpion stings cause local burning pain, a prickling sensation, agitation, increased muscle tone, salivation and perspiration, impaired visual acuity, sneezing and vomiting. Scorpion stings should be treated as snake bites, sometimes requiring injections of appropriate serums.

Snake bite: A little advice is dangerous, as the bite of each species must be treated differently. Consult the reference in the appendix (see page 339) for thorough coverage.

Ticks: Tick bites are characterized by local redness and itching. Pull off all ticks that have not burrowed into the skin. If the tick has burrowed into the skin, cover it with oil or margarine to close its breathing pores. If the entire tick does not back out within a few minutes and gentle pulling does not succeed, the area must be cleansed and covered, and medical assistance must be sought.

Blisters: Blisters will probably be your most common emergency and are caused mainly by friction from ill-fitting boots or pack straps. As soon as you feel discomfort, cover the tender area with moleskin or an adhesive tape such as 'Elastoplast'. If a blister has already formed, cut a hole in the moleskin which is equal to the size of the blister and place the moleskin around the blister – the purpose being to reduce rubbing on the tender area. Contrary to popular belief, placing plaster strips on blisters serves only to increase friction, not reduce it. Broken blisters should be kept clean to prevent infection.

Burns: Prevent sunburn by wearing a hat and long-sleeved shirt and by using protective creams. Never apply a lotion to a second degree burn (a deep burn with blistering). Instead, immerse the burn in cold water, blot dry and cover with a dry, sterile dressing. Third degree burns (those causing underlying tissue damage, charring and cell destruction) should be treated with sterile dressings and then wrapped in plastic to exclude air and possible infection. Ice packs can be applied over the plastic for pain relief. Treat the victim for shock.

Choking: In the event of a companion choking, remove any objects from the mouth but do not attempt to prise out anything lodged in the throat.

If this does not dislodge the object, do the 'Heimlich hug'. Stand behind the victim with his back against you, and encircle his waist with your arms. Make a fist with one hand and clasp it with your other. Then push your fist sharply upwards into the diaphragm (in the middle of the body below the ribs). The object should be expelled with the air in the windpipe. Repeat the manoeuvre if necessary. If the victim is not breathing, begin artificial respiration immediately.

Dehydration: Dehydration in extreme heat can lead to hyperthermia (heat exhaustion or sunstroke). Symptoms are a headache, dizziness, rapid heart rate, nausea, vomiting, muscle and abdominal cramps, unconsciousness or loss of reasoning. Death can occur if timely action is not taken. At the first signs of dehydration or heat exhaustion, seek shade if possible. If no shade is available, the space blanket can be used as a sun guard. Remember to place the silver side facing the sun. Strip the victim, sprinkle him with cool water and fan him to create an artificial sweat.

Dislocations: Injuries in which the normal relationship of a joint is disrupted, are indicated by pain aggravated by motion, tenderness, swelling, discoloration, limitation of motion and deformity of the joint. Correction of dislocation is dangerous if attempted by amateurs. Therefore, treat dislocations as fractures – immobilize by splinting. Dislocation of a finger, however, can be corrected by gently pulling on the injured digit and then splinting by taping it to an adjacent, uninjured finger.

Eyes: Tree sap in the eye can cause inflammation. Bathe the eye with milk or water. If foreign particles get into the eye, natural lavage should dislodge them and wash them away. If not, gently lift particles with a moist corner of a sterile gauze pad. If an object becomes lodged in the eye, prevent further harm by placing a doughnut bandage over the eye (encircle the orbit), and bandage both eyes. To prevent further harm the victim must be carried so there is absolutely no temptation to use the injured eye.

Fainting: Simple fainting occurs as a result of a reduced blood supply to the brain. The symptoms of fainting can be alleviated by making the victim sit with his head between his knees, or, if he has fainted, by lying him down and elevating his feet. Should the victim not regain consciousness within minutes, fainting may be a symptom of a more serious problem (such as heat exhaustion or a stroke).

Food poisoning: Meat or other foodstuffs that have been contaminated by bacteria, can make a person ill. Symptoms such as vomiting, diarrhoea and stomach cramps are the most common signs of food poisoning. Give frequent sips of electrolyte solution, but if this is impossible, give Coca-Cola or plain water; although these are not ideal, they may prevent dehydration in an emergency if the vomiting and diarrhoea are severe.

Fractures and related injuries: The first-aid treatment for fractures is immobilization – splints above and below the fracture, and keeping adjacent joints as still as possible. Signs of a fracture include severe pain and tenderness, swelling and discoloration, deformity and/or shortness of the limb, abnormal mobility, shock and the inability or disinclination of the patient to move the broken limb.

Not all fractures are easily detected. I hiked on a stress fracture for five weeks before the pain and discomfort drove me to an orthopaedic surgeon who put me in a cast for three months. A stress fracture is not a sharp break and you do not feel sudden pain. Rather, it is many micro-fractures caused by continual strain, such as carrying too heavy a backpack, running on the wrong surfaces or ballet dancing. If you feel localized pain and cannot understand why, see your doctor. X-rays are the only means of identifying a stress fracture, but such a fracture may appear on film only three to four weeks after the onset of symptoms.

Frostbite: Southern Africa is not always warm and sunny, and many mountain regions, especially in the Drakensberg and western Cape, are regularly snow-capped in winter. In such conditions frostbite is a real danger. It occurs when water in the cells and between the skin and capillaries freezes, thus injuring tissues both physically and chemically.

There are two types of frostbite, and each is treated differently. Superficial frostbite occurs when the skin is a pale, greyish-white colour, and is cold or numb. This occurs because the skin and adjacent subcutaneous tissues are frozen. Treatment includes covering the area with a dry, insulating windproof material, placing a warm body next to it, and applying firm, steady pressure. In no case should the affected area be rubbed! Immerse the limb in water with a temperature of 42-44 °C and administer warm food and non-alcoholic drinks to the patient.

In contrast, deep frostbite occurs when tissue muscle, bone and tendons are frozen and the patient does not feel pain but the tissues are hard. Deep frostbite cases should never be thawed if in danger of refreezing. When properly sheltered, immerse the affected area in a large waterbath at 42-44 °C under sterile conditions for no longer than 20 minutes at a time. After re-warming, clean the affected area gently with disinfectants and apply antibiotic creams to the broken skin. Elevate the affected area to reduce swelling and seek medical assistance as soon as possible.

Hypothermia: Southern African hiking trails have been the stage of avoidable and unnecessary deaths from hypothermia. This can easily be avoided with the correct equipment, the right attitude and some rudimentary knowledge.
What is hypothermia? Hypothermia is a 'cold injury' where the body's heating system breaks down and cannot produce as much heat as it loses. When cold reaches the brain, the body's core temperature plummets and if not halted, death occurs in two hours.
What causes hypothermia? Hypothermia occurs when heat is lost from the body because of cold weather injuries; dampness from sweating, rain, mist, snow or wind; fatigue from over-extending yourself; and excessive drinking of alcohol or coffee.
How to avoid hypothermia: Wear woollen clothes which insulate when wet; do not hike in jeans or corduroys. Dress in layers and adjust heat by taking off or putting on as desired. Carry top-quality rainwear. Protect

What are the symptoms and treatment of hypothermia?

Symptoms	Treatment
Shivering Difficulty in manual movements Unusual responses Loss of clothing goes unnoticed Stumbling Intense shivering Difficulty in speech Sluggish thinking Loss of memory	Stop immediately Drink hot, sweet liquids Eat high-energy foods Protect against the elements Rewarm with dry clothes

Increased shivering
Muscle rigidity and jerky
  movements
Frequent stumbling
Sluggish responses
Skin blue and puffy
Loss of memory
Irrational behaviour
Drowsiness
Pulse and respiration slows
	Drink fluids as hot as possible
	Eat only quickly digested foods such as
	  soup, sweet liquids and candy bars
	Get out of wind and wet into
	  a sheltered location
	Get into sleeping bag after stripping
	  off wet clothes
	Continue drinking hot liquids
	Build fire to warm the camp
	Do not fall asleep!

Unconscious
No response to the spoken word
No reflexes
	All of the above plus:
	Apply skin to skin reheat with two
	  naked, warm donors, in the same
	  sleeping bag

Erratic heartbeat	Keep victim awake; sleep means death
Respiratory and cardiac failure Oedema and haemorrhage in lungs Death	All of the above plus: Seek professional medical treatment

Remember: If you are tired, wet and cold, hypothermia can still strike – even at 10 °C!

your head and neck with a balaclava, hat or scarf. Carry warm mittens with a waterproof outer covering. Eat regularly when hiking, including energy-rich foods like nuts, chocolate, sweets, raisins and dried fruit. Drink sweet, hot fluids like soup, tea with honey, or hot chocolate; avoid coffee and alcohol. Do not be headstrong or goal-orientated if difficulty upsets your trailing schedule. If one of your group develops symptoms react intelligently – act to restore warmth.
What can I do if my body loses heat faster than it produces it? Stay dry by getting out of the elements. Find protection from the wind. Put on dry clothes and a woollen hat. Eat high-energy foods. Drink hot, energy-rich fluids. Rest, set up camp, give up your goal – tomorrow is another day!

Malaria: Malaria occurs in Zimbabwe, Malawi, northern Botswana, the northern and eastern Transvaal, the north-eastern Cape and coastal Natal. You can contract the disease if bitten by an infected *Anopheles* mosquito. Before entering a malaria zone, take prophylactic tablets according to instructions. Consult the health authorities for the best type of malaria pill, as these change as new strains of the disease develop. (See also page 29.)

To avoid bites, spray the inside of your tent or hut with an insecticide, cover as much bare skin as possible with long sleeves, long trousers and thick socks, use mosquito repellents on bare or thinly covered skin and sleep under a mosquito net. As with bilharzia, you will not know you have contracted malaria until you get home. Fever and high temperature alternating with chills are symptoms which demand immediate medical attention.

Mountain altitude sickness: It is generally (and incorrectly) believed that altitude sickness occurs only above 4 250 metres. It can affect any mountain traveller who attains altitude too quickly – even at 2 500 metres. Therefore it is a potential problem for two areas described in this guide: the Mulanje Massif in Malawi, and the Drakensberg in Natal and Lesotho.

People affected by altitude sickness display some of these symptoms: Loss of appetite, sleeping difficulty, severe headaches and nausea. More serious cases are characterized by vomiting, irrational behaviour, loss of energy or unconsciousness. Although the most severe forms of mountain altitude sickness (pulmonary and cerebral oedema) are possible at altitudes as low as 2 500-3 500 metres, they are usually associated with climbers at higher elevations.

When mountaineering at high altitudes, allow your body time to acclimatize. In other words, by climbing slowly (at a rate at which you feel comfortable) and resting between climbs, your body will gradually adapt. If symptoms persist, stay put or descend until you feel better. If you have a cold, influenza, a cough, asthma or are feeling unwell, do not proceed to high altitudes as these conditions will become exaggerated above 2 500 metres.

An individual's bodily reponse to altitude change is difficult to predict and although pre-trip physical conditioning will make your trip easier, it does not guarantee prevention of altitude sickness. I have witnessed the fittest and keenest member of a climbing party become afflicted with severe altitude sickness because of over-exertion and refusal to walk slowly and rest frequently.

Nosebleeds: Minor nosebleeds can be stopped by applying direct pressure against the nostril or by clamping the tip of the nose. The patient should sit with the head tilted slightly forward, so that blood does not drain back into the throat. Cold applications to the nose should also aid coagulation.

Shock: Shock – circulatory failure that leaves bodily functions in a depressed condition – can be caused by fractures, loss of fluids (either blood, plasma or perspiration) or any significant injury combined with cold and/or pain. When a person is suffering from shock he feels cold and clammy to the touch. His pulse is slow, but later turns rapid. He feels faint. If shock is suspected:
1. The person should lie down with his feet raised (except in cases of head injury, breathing difficulty, an unsplinted fractured lower extremity, or pain). In the case of deep cuts or wounds, control bleeding if possible.
2. Maintain body heat but *do not overheat!* Insulate the patient from the ground and keep him dry and covered (especially head and neck); protect him from the weather, and provide external warmth. Placing him in a warmed sleeping bag with another person is a fast and effective method of providing external warmth.
3. Give no food or fluid by mouth.

Sprains: Sprains (torn or stretched soft tissue surrounding joints) result in local haemorrhaging and painful swelling. Elevate the injury and apply cold compresses locally to the affected joints. Sprained ankles should be supported by a figure-of-eight bandage put on over the hiking boot.

If you forget these tips, remember 'PRICE'. This stands for the Principles of Rest, Ice (if possible), Compression and Elevation for this type of injury.

Strains: Strains (stretched muscles) are accompanied by minor haemorrhaging and should be treated with warm compresses to aid circulation.

More common injuries, bursitis, tendonitis and shin splits are caused by inflammation of the tendons or the fluid lubricating them. Hikers unaccustomed to the use of certain muscles for an extended length of time may initially feel stiff. Apply moist heat and take aspirin for relief. If it is necessary to continue using the affected area, the application of an ice bandage may relieve pain.

Unconsciousness: Unconsciousness may be caused by a number of factors, for example, shock, a blow on the head, or heat. The most important immediate action is to keep the air passages open. If the neck is not broken, lie the victim on his side (so his tongue falls forward instead of backwards) and pull his jaw forward, tilting his head back. If the victim vomits, keep his head lower than his chest and turned to the side. Never administer food, fluids or medication by mouth to an unconscious person. If the victim has false teeth or contact lenses, remove them.

Wounds: A wound is a break in the skin's surface. A major wound, accompanied by severe bleeding (usually arterial), is best treated by applying direct pressure on brachial or femoral arteries, or elevating the wound and applying a cold compress. The use of a tourniquet is dangerous and should be applied only as a last resort. If used, a tourniquet should be wide so that it does not cause further injury.

If internal organs are exposed, *do not* attempt to push them back into the body cavity. Moisten with a saline solution (5 millilitres salt to a litre of clean, sterile – boiled – water); cover with sterile dressings; bandage lightly without applying pressure (unless to control bleeding).

Minor wounds (abrasions and punctures) should be cleaned and dressed under sterile conditions. If further injury or bleeding could result from removal of foreign objects embedded in the wound, leave them. Lacerations or incisions must be washed with a sterile compress and antibacterial soap; rinse with clear running water, if possible. Open wounds should be closed with butterfly bandages. Tincture of benzoin applied to the area around the wound acts as an adhesive and helps to keep the butterfly bandages closed. Cover with a sterile dressing and bandage (preferably roller gauze covered with a triangular bandage). Elastic bandages can impede circulation.

FIRST-AID 'AIDS'

The chart on page 336 lists small items to carry in your personal first-aid kit. Here I describe other aids which are suggested for more comprehensive or group kits.

Disposable plastic chemical cold pack: The cold pack consists of chemicals in a double-walled plastic bag. When the inner pouch is squeezed the chemicals mix, and in three seconds the temperature of the pack drops to approximately 0 °C, at which it stays for about/30 minutes. Cold packs can be applied to injuries in order to slow bleeding, and lessen pain and muscle spasm; reduce temperature; lessen swelling resulting from burns, insect bites and other causes; and help in the management of heat exhaustion and heatstroke.

Disposable plastic instant heat pack: The heat pack works on the same principle as the cold pack, producing a source of immediate heat for therapy where needed, such as for hypothermia or superficial frostbite, or as a 'hot water bottle' in your sleeping bag.

Braces and sleeves: Many hikers, especially those who also jog or run, are afflicted with knee or ankle pains which can unexpectedly flare up in the 'middle of nowhere'. There are several lightweight knee and ankle braces and sleeves available, including pneumatic braces which can be carried (or worn) to give the trailist greater security or aid his retreat to base camp or home. All braces, sleeves and aircasts should be used only after a thorough examination and prescription by your physician. There are variations in the models and it is essential that the correct type is worn. In South Africa, these devices are distributed by Medac in Cape Town.

'THE CARRY'

Evacuation of a victim should only be attempted if the accident takes place near the trail, if the injuries are not major, if the party is strong and sufficiently large, if the distance to help is no longer than 8-12 kilometres and if the victim is strong enough.

The following carries are used if rope is unavailable: when two men are present, a two-man carry chair can be made by grasping one of your own wrists and one of the other carrier's. Over rough terrain, 'backpack' the victim out. A one-man carry involves tying the patient's wrists to his ankles with strips of cloth, then carrying him like a pack. An unconscious person can be packed out in this fashion.

A stretcher can be made from two poles and a blanket (or sleeping bag, if necessary). The patient's weight keeps the top layers from slipping.

BACKGROUND AND BASICS

TRAILING AND THE ENVIRONMENT

Perhaps it is ironic that an American should write a book on how to see southern Africa on foot. My Capetonian hiking companions often joke, 'Meet an American, see the Cape'. In 1975 when I was 'imported' by the then-Department of Forestry, there existed only a handful of trails for the public and an overriding reluctance among many government authorities to permit the public access to natural areas under their control.

As I write, the entire scene has changed – the trails era has hit southern Africa. Suddenly it appears as if everyone has taken up trailing in one or more of its many forms: hiking, rambling, backpacking, snorkelling, jogging, canoeing, caving, horse-riding . . . and with government authorities planning and constructing trails and private entrepreneurs organizing expeditions, would-be trailists are inundated with fascinating, yet sometimes confusing, new opportunities. This guide has been compiled to put these trails into perspective, and to provide background and a detailed directory of what exists and 'what's coming'. So whether you are a resident wanting to explore your surroundings as the trailblazers of earlier times did (well, almost), a teacher/youth leader wanting to capture the attention and interest of your students, a traveller seeking the adventure approach to touring, or an amateur naturalist, this book will serve as your companion while discovering the wonderful diversity of southern Africa's natural environment.

In *Everyone's Guide to Trailing & Mountaineering in Southern Africa*, I grouped the trails into broad ecologically based regions. My reasoning was that when you decide to go trailing or mountaineering, you are, consciously or otherwise, making a decision to travel to a specific environment because it promises the climate, scenery, wildlife, terrain and type of atmosphere or mood you wish to experience. Hence, an ecological directory seemed better able to allow you to choose your travels and prepare yourself for the natural elements you were likely to encounter.

However, feedback from many users of the first edition indicated that grouping trails in traditional geo-political boundaries better facilitated their trip planning. Ecological groupings are educationally expedient, but regional groupings are more practical. Therefore, although I still emphasize 'eco-trail zones' throughout the text, readers of this edition will find that all trails are grouped in close proximity to each other; that is, either in one of South Africa's four

provinces or its independent states, or in other countries of southern Africa.

'Ecology', 'ecosystems' and many other 'conservation orientated' terms are much bandied about, and in the process, very often misused. Each has its specific meaning. Ecology is the study of relationships between animals and plants and the environment in which they live, while an ecosystem is the whole community of organisms interacting within a particular environment, for example, a pond or a forest. Major ecological regions with distinct groups of plants and animals extending over large natural areas such as the savannah, coastal forest or desert, incorporate a number of ecosystems and are known as biomes. In compiling this guide I have adopted the following ten major biomes: fynbos; semi-desert and Karoo; acacia savannah (Kalahari); coastal desert; eastern evergreen temperate forests; coastal bush and subtropical forests; eastern grasslands; Drakensberg; highveld; and dry woodlands. Malawi, the only region dominated by the Rift Valley system, is considered separately as the eleventh major eco-region.

The limits of these regions lack the rigidity of man-devised boundaries. Nevertheless, each biome is, by virtue of its living and non-living components, distinct. These include physical factors such as soil type; climatic factors such as temperature, rainfall, wind, light intensity, air pressure and humidity; physiographic factors such as the general topography, altitude, slope of the land, drainage and presence of water; and finally, biotic factors, which are the plant and animal communities interacting in the region.

When the biomes meet, the transition from one to the next is seldom abrupt. More typically, the changeover is gradual, providing an 'in-between' region referred to by ecologists as an edge or ecotone. Ecotones are often richer in species diversity than either of the adjacent biomes because they harbour species from both. An intertidal rocky coast is such an edge, the meeting of the sea and the land creating a unique habitat for a profusion of plants and animals: birds, fish, invertebrates, seaweeds – the myriad forms of intertidal life.

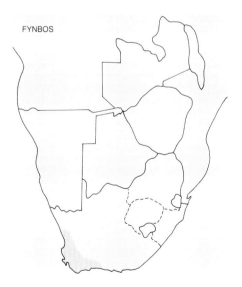

FYNBOS

FYNBOS

From the Olifants River in the west and tailing out beyond the Cedarberg to the north, the fynbos extends southwards to the sea and then eastwards to Port Elizabeth along two mountain chains, the inland ranges of Swartberg-Baviaanskloof and the coastal

Langeberg-Outeniqua-Tsitsikamma ranges. Traversed by numerous nature and hiking trails, and offering endless opportunities for mountaineering, this irregular, L-shaped region is one of southern Africa's most popular trailing zones. It is a region of striking contrasts. Sweeps of unspoilt beach, interrupted by rocky promontories where mountains slide into the sea, encourage countless hours of rambling. But it is inland that real adventure and challenge await the addicted outdoorsman, for the narrow coastal plain rapidly gives way to a rugged mass of high peaks that tower over fertile, river-veined valleys.

Hiking through these magnificent folded mountains inevitably leads to questions concerning their origins. During the Upper Silurian to Lower Carboniferous times (the Paleozoic pre-Karoo Era), the Cape formations – known technically as Table Mountain quartzitic sandstones and shales, Bokkeveld shales and Witteberg shales, sandstones and quartzites – were deposited under water. In Karoo times (Permo-Triassic), geological forces of unimaginable power heaved and buckled these sediments into the tortured convolutions and folds of the Cape mountains. Today, the Witteberg rocks are scarce, brutally weathered and eroded through time, and the Bokkeveld shales form the economically important basin and valley soils. It is, therefore, the more resilient Table Mountain sandstone outcrops with their intricate mass of knobs and pinnacles, which are responsible for the spectacular mountaineering challenges.

The 'variegated' cliff faces always attract the hiker's attention – worn to an overall whitish-grey, but gashed with reddish-brown or broken surfaces where deposits of iron oxides have formed. The rough surface of the weather-beaten sandstones is frequently hollowed out into shallow depressions which hold water for some time after rains – a welcome refreshment for tired, parched hikers when no other source of water is available.

This rugged terrain is tough on hikers' boots: durable soles are essential. I recommend investing in a pair of boots with the closely spaced, lugged soles which pick up less debris and therefore cause less damage to the environment.

As breathtaking and spectacular as the contorted landscape undoubtedly is, however, the true wonder of the region surely lies in its dense and shrubby vegetation. The mountain complex yields a nutrient-deficient sandy soil which, ironically, supports the most diverse and puzzling plant kingdom in the world. Known as fynbos – an Afrikaans term meaning 'fine bush', alluding to the fine-leaved form of many of the shrubs and their bushy habit – this remarkable vegetation type occupies less than one thousandth of the total area covered by the earth's six floral kingdoms. Yet it contains more species per square metre than any-

where else in the world. Furthermore, a great number of these plants have a very limited distribution range; for example, the snow protea, *Protea cryophila*, is seen in nature only on the high peaks of the Cedarberg, where winter snowfalls are common.

The fynbos, therefore, is a zone to be enjoyed by trailists with a sensitive botanical eye; although at first the sheer numbers of different plants is bewildering, once aware of the three main 'elements', you will have a framework for identifying individual plants. The dominant element – the restioids – comprises the 'Cape reeds', which many people confuse with grasses. On closer inspection, however, these are distinguished by their tufted, near-leafless, tubular or wiry stems. The ericoids – sometimes referred to as heaths, which so often paint mountain slopes in bright colours – are small shrubs with narrow, rolled leaves. It is the proteoid element, however, which although not always present, is so characteristic of the Cape. The most easily recognized of the Proteaceae family is the genus *Protea*, as many produce large, showy flowerheads.

The fynbos is threatened on many fronts. Already 60 per cent has been destroyed by indiscriminate use of fire and other human actions, agriculture, careless urban sprawl and alien plant species. These 'exotic' invaders were introduced, deliberately or inadvertently, from overseas and now seriously threaten indigenous flora. Hakea, rooikrans and wattle are some of the more than 50 alien plants that are rapidly changing the veld and, in the process, endangering the many animals reliant on the fynbos for their survival. Endemic birds such as the Cape sugarbird, the protea seedeater and the orangebreasted sunbird, are vulnerable to diminution of the fynbos, but it is the mammals which are particularly at risk. Many have been ruthlessly exterminated or have had their habitats destroyed. Species such as the klipspringer, grey rhebok, baboon and dassie are still readily seen by hikers, but others such as the bontebok exist only in reserves or on farms.

When trailing in the fynbos, always keep a wary eye on the sky as, of all eleven trailing zones, the weather patterns in this region are the most unpredictable. This is very largely because of the Cape's diverse topography, and is further complicated by the marine temperature differences between the cold west coast and warmer southern waters. Long-term forecasting for mountaineers is particularly difficult as temperature, visibility and precipitation often vary, not only from range to range but also with altitude.

I love the fynbos for its unbelievable diversity – in winter when softly hued light reflects off rain-laden clouds, in spring (September and October) when the veld explodes with floral colour unequalled elsewhere on earth, and during the long, hot, lazy days of summer which invite boulder-hopping and swimming in the clear, refresh-

ing waters of kloofs. Whenever you choose to hike, however, respect the mountains and their latent power. Be prepared – always carry warm clothes, emergency rations and waterproof bags – and you will be able to appreciate fully the Cape's many-faceted character.

SEMI-DESERT AND KAROO

I once drove a boy from Johannesburg to Cape Town who insisted that 'nothing' existed between these two cities. Obviously he had never hiked in the Karoo for if he had, he would have come to know and appreciate the great natural wealth of these seemingly endless scrubby plains, punctuated occasionally by rocky outcrops and rondavel-shaped koppies.

Perhaps, though, my companion had a point, for certainly the region is very different from what it must have been like in early times. The great herds that once roamed the plains have been hunted almost out of existence and replaced with flocks of merino sheep, regimented into camps whose barbed wire perimeters line kilometre after kilometre of the national highway. Such farming has also placed great pressure on the natural vegetation and, despite advanced farming practices, erosion is extensive in places.

There are parts, although often remote, where the trailist can enjoy glimpses of the Karoo's past. Also, a renewed interest in preserving the Great Karoo's natural heritage has motivated the creation of many new reserves, such as the Karoo National Park in Beaufort West and the Karoo Nature Reserve in Graaff-Reinet, where the aim is to recreate a balanced Karoo ecosystem. Hiking trails designed to encourage people to discover the Karoo are an integral part of these programmes.

The semi-desert and Karoo, one of the larger trailing and mountaineering regions discussed in this book, is a vast tract of land that sweeps down diagonally from the northwest to the barrier of mountains along the

Cape coast. It encompasses the Kaokoveld in northern Namibia; the Damaraland Plain, between the Otavi and Khomas highlands; Great Namaqualand and Bushmanland, a very dry area which extends southwards from Damaraland and the Kalahari to the Orange River; Little Namaqualand, from the Atlantic coast to the hilly escarpment edge; the Little Karoo, the dry plains lying to the north of the southern Cape folded mountains; and the Great Karoo, the large basin, 600-900 metres above sea level between the highveld escarpment and the Little Karoo.

Geologically, the region is very young. It comprises mostly the Karoo System which was laid down only some 280-180 million years ago. Despite its comparatively short history, the region has passed through many developmental stages.

The story of the Karoo begins in the humid heat of 'Dwyka times', about 250 million years ago, when most of southern Africa was a low-lying basin, a natural sump in which sediments – accumulated from riverborne sand, mud and silt – settled to form shales. Vleis and swamps with primitive vegetation evolved. But then the earth froze and huge rivers of ice deposited rocks and mud into the basin. This material hardened into what is termed Dwyka tillite.

As the earth again grew warmer, the glaciers retreated and mud and coarse sand were carried into the swampy Karoo basin to form the Ecca Series. A temperate climate prevailed and diversified plant life evolved. Early conifers, club-mosses, horsetails, ferns and large trees flourished in the conge-

nial conditions, and these were eventually to fossilize into the great coal deposits that underlie the Karoo veld. Then temperatures and rainfall rose, and animals dependent on the verdant vegetation, evolved. Reptiles populated the swamps in great abundance.

The next series laid down, the Stormberg, comprises sediments deposited in desert conditions and capped by lava which poured through fissures. Less susceptible to weathering than the shales and sandstones into which they intruded, these Stormberg lavas formed the dolerite ridges, koppies and cliffs so characteristic of the Karoo landscape of today.

The parts of Namibia falling within the semi-desert and Karoo ecological zone have an older geological history. Namibia is composed of pre-Cambrian rocks (more than 500

million years old), which originated when life on earth barely existed. Predominant are the Damara System of the Late pre-Cambrian era, and the even older Nosib System. These series contain limestones, shales and sands which were deposited in a deep sea and then metamorphosed into marble, schist, gneiss, granite and sandstone. The Damara and Nosib systems have produced copper, lead, zinc, iron and vanadium deposits – all of which are important to the country's economy.

The popular mountaineering area of the Waterberg is formed from the Karoo System, while the Brandberg, Spitzkoppe and Erongo mountains are the granitic cores remaining from intense volcanic activity that metamorphosed triassic sandstones of the Stormberg Series. The canyons of the Kuiseb, Swakop, Kunene and Fish rivers, also of particular interest to the mountaineer, were formed by vigorous erosion in a humid climate that coincided with the Pleistocene ice-age in the northern hemisphere.

In the north-west the Karoo's contact with the highveld, grassveld and savannah is abrupt, but in the south, transition with the fynbos is gradual and suggests that Karoo vegetation is an environmental modification of fynbos. Plants of the Karoo are basically of two types – succulents and woody shrubs.

Succulents, except for some outlying populations in the Little Karoo, occupy the driest, western parts of the Karoo area, and the drier the region, the shorter the bushes. Low succulent bushes, those less than 20 centimetres tall, include ericoid shrublets and fleshy-leaved mesembryanthemums. Kraalbos and yellow milkbush are common. In the western winter rainfall area, geophytes – plants which survive the harsh winters by storing food in subterranean buds – provide the rich spring flower displays for which Namaqualand is so justly famed. Tall succulent bushes, those over a metre high, include euphorbias, cotyledons, aloes, crassulas and portulacas.

Along river courses, even though many are dry for much of the year, trees grow abundantly; common species include sweet thorn, white karoo (a willow-like bush), and kunibush.

Woody shrubs thrive in the more easterly parts of the Karoo where conditions are less harsh. They comprise the taller mountain plants growing along ridges and on koppies, and the smaller Karoo bushes, covering the flat plateau area. These smaller shrubs are well adapted to conserving moisture – they are spaced apart to reduce competition, their leaves are small to reduce transpiration and they have spreading root systems with the main roots penetrating very deep. Common Karoo bushes include pentzias, daisies, the sweet resin bush and bitter Karoo bush, the 'gannas' and the saltbushes.

Karoo animals, too, are well attuned to their dry habitats. Once the plains thronged with large herds of antelope such as spring-

bok, eland, gemsbok and hartebeest. Although their numbers were huge, reports by early travellers indicate that the game was never uniformly scattered, but was concentrated in massive, migrating herds. These animals were subsequently decimated by indiscriminate hunting during the 1700s and 1800s but even today, animals abound in the more remote areas. For example, the Namibian plateau still supports kudu, duiker, steenbok, zebra, warthog and leopard, as well as smaller mammals such as the wildcat, meercat, field-mouse, skunk, hare, dassie, bats and the scaly anteater. The *Agama planiceps* is a commonly seen, brightly coloured rock lizard, while mountain tortoises and leguans are also present.

The central plateau of Namibia, studded with prominent termite mounds, hosts land snails, unusual for such a dry region, long stick insects and many centipedes, giant millipedes, solifuges and spiders, including the large baboon, or trap-door, spider. The totally red sand lizard, *Eremias undata rubens*, well camouflaged in its red sandstone habitat, is also occasionally spotted by the alert hiker.

Trailists with an interest in bird-watching will not be disappointed as, considering the overall aridity of South Africa's semi-desert and Karoo, birdlife is surprisingly plentiful. My favourite is the rosyfaced lovebird. Some of the region's 'specials' are, in Damaraland, the Monteiro's and Bradfield's hornbills, Rüppell's parrot and the whitetailed shrike; in Great Namaqualand and Bushmanland, the Scaler's and red lark and the sociable weaver; and in the Karoo, the rufouseared warbler, Layard's titbabbler, the Karoo green warbler and the Namaqua prinia.

Climatic variations in the semi-desert and Karoo zone are extreme. In the Karoo, the main rainy season is March and April, while for the rest of the region, the rain (250 millimetres annually) is distributed fairly evenly throughout the year. Thunderstorms are common. Temperature fluctuations, both diurnal and seasonal, are extreme, so much so that even after the hottest of summer days – the average for January is 32 °C – the temperature can drop sharply when the sun sets and reduce trailists to a huddle around a camp-fire. Such fluctuations are even more drastic during winter, and although daytime temperatures may be pleasantly cool to warm – the average for July is 18 °C – temperatures regularly plummet well below freezing under the crystal-clear night skies. From June to August, frosts are common, as are snowfalls on the mountain peaks. Backpackers in the semi-desert and Karoo region must be well equipped, therefore, to ensure daytime comfort and warmth at night.

In Namibia, although rainfall is low and droughts can be prolonged, flash floods are not uncommon. Such spates can be extremely hazardous for the unwary hiker and camp-sites must be chosen with care. Never pitch your tent in a dry water course – this is asking for trouble. Sudden floods are not restricted to Namibia, and, as evidenced by the devastating 1981 floods of Laingsburg, are possible throughout the region.

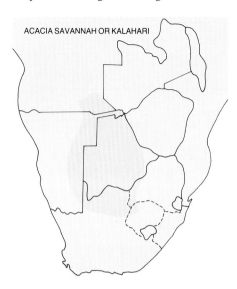

ACACIA SAVANNAH OR KALAHARI

ACACIA SAVANNAH OR KALAHARI

Sprawling across the centre of southern Africa, embracing much of Botswana and encroaching into Namibia, Zimbabwe and the northern Cape, is a vast sea of undeveloped sand and swampland ideal for rambling and wilderness exploration. Ecologically, this huge basin, lying 915-1 067 metres above sea level, is known as acacia savannah, but more commonly it is referred to as the Kalahari, thornveld or simply 'bush'.

Basically, the Kalahari is two contiguous regions. In the north-east, the predominantly summer rainfall exceeds 500 millimetres a year and feeds the swamplands formed by the Okavango, Linyanti and Zambezi rivers. Apart from these 'oases', however, the northern parts are characterized by sand, scrub, a few trees and grassland. By contrast, the drier south-western Kalahari, which reaches southwards from Ovamboland to the Orange River where it merges with the semi-desert and Karoo ecological zone (see page 24), is a region of sparsely vegetated red sandveld, dissected by corridors of 'dry forest' along waterless riverbeds.

But for the occasional rocky projection providing some relief, the entire Kalahari basin is mantled with sand. In places it is fluvial in origin, but mostly it derives from the Stormberg Series of the Karoo System. Whatever its origins, however, its distribution results from wind action under desert conditions. It is this sand, not the meagre annual rainfall, which contributes largely to the region's 'dehydrated' appearance, as the loosely packed particles allow water to drain away too rapidly to benefit plant life.

Synonymous with the stark Kalahari landscape is the camelthorn, *Acacia erioloba*.

This tall tree, with its spreading branches, sparsely leaved and wickedly armed with long, needle-like thorns, is welcomed by animals and hikers alike, for it provides all-too-scarce shade from the relentless sun. Other trees include the deciduous commiphoras, burkeas and terminalias, which vary in density from fairly close cover, through scattered parkland to almost pure grassland. Even where the savannah is thickest, however, the covering of short and tall Bushman grasses is interrupted by bald patches of all-pervading dry red sands.

Surface water is very seldom available and trailists must always carry sufficient liquid for their needs. In a few localities, calcification has sealed the porous sand and here, in pans and depressions, water collects during infrequent downpours. The few Bushmen who still subsist in the Kalahari make their homes near these pans which are criss-crossed with tracks of cattle and wildlife in search of water.

Animals of the acacia savannah, especially the beetles, are closely allied to those of the Namib (see Coastal Desert ecological zone). Gemsbok, hartebeest, springbok, lion and ostrich are as much part of the Kalahari as the thornveld and sand, but perhaps the most evocative image is that of huge sociable weaver nests which often envelop the crowns of tall trees. These unmistakable 'condominiums' represent highly integrated communities comprising many individual nest chambers. They are used continuously for many, many years and extend beyond the housing needs of the weaver birds themselves: rosyfaced lovebirds, pygmy falcons, and scalyfeathered and redheaded finches are some of the 'uninvited guests', while giant eagle owls often nest atop the communes. These intruders cause little direct harm to the weavers, unlike the Cape cobra which raids the nest for eggs and the honey badger which will claw it to shreds in search of chicks.

Other birds commonly seen in the Kalahari are the chat flycatcher, sandgrouse, pied babbler and many lark species. The dry riverine forests throng with Cape and Burchells' glossy starlings and yellowbilled hornbills. Trailists camping near water are likely to be woken by turtle and Namaqua doves which fly in for their daily drink, and on cloudy or dewy mornings, harvester termites emerge from their sandy retreats, unwittingly providing a handsome feast for a variety of birds from warblers to vultures.

Throughout the Kalahari, beware of puff adders and scorpions. Solifuges, or sun-spiders, should also be treated with respect, for although their bite is not poisonous, they can deliver nasty wounds. They are extremely savage hunters and will devour any arthropod they can conquer.

Hiking in this region is most comfortable in winter. Mosquito netting during the night is recommended for those sensitive to biting insects; and although uncomfortable in the

heat of the day, thick clothing helps guard against the bite of the tsetse fly that infests the northern swamps.

If you are a novice to the Kalahari, including its northernmost wilderness, the Okavango swamps, I strongly recommend experiencing this area under the guidance of a reputable organization. The Wilderness Leadership School and Educational Wildlife Expeditions, for example, run fantastic adventures into the remotest areas. Although more expensive than a do-it-yourself safari, these organizations not only transport you by light aircraft and canoe into the heart of the primeval setting, but also have as their objective interpreting its ecological intricacies for their trailists. In comparison, self-generated treks require thorough and judicious planning. A rugged vehicle – a four-wheel drive is recommended – fully equipped with spare parts, extra petrol and water tanks, and a mechanically minded trailist, are minimum prerequisites for exploration off the 'tourist track'.

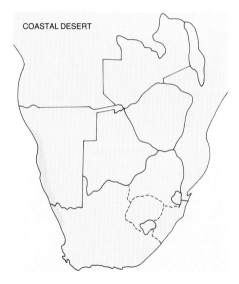

COASTAL DESERT

COASTAL DESERT

Steep, shifting sand dunes, rocks laid bare by wind and the ceaseless pounding of the sea, great time-worn canyons, sliced through the earth's crust . . . all are part of the beautiful but forbidding landscape of the Namib, a 50-80 kilometre-wide coastal belt which stretches northwards from the Orange River to southern Angola – a distance of some 1 600 kilometres.

There is irony in the Hottentot name, as although *namib* means 'large plain' or 'desert', it can also be interpreted as 'place where there is nothing'. Admittedly, vegetation is sparse or non-existent and wildlife often less than obvious, but within the gravels of raised beaches from Conception Bay southwards to the Groen River mouth, lies the unimaginable wealth of one of the world's greatest deposits of diamonds. The region is a gem collector's paradise, with beryl, agate and amethyst being just a few of the semi-precious stones which occur in great abundance.

For the trailist, the Namib is a fascinating region, a fascination enhanced by the inherent dangers of hiking in an environment of such extreme aridity. Unfortunately, however, much of it is out of bounds. The southern parts form the *Sperrgebiet*, the restricted diamond fields, while the northern reaches fall within the military 'operational area' or war zone. A further impediment to hiking is the almost total lack of amenities for hundreds of kilometres on end – enough to deter all but the most stout-hearted adventurer. Trailing and mountaineering experiences, therefore, are virtually confined to a few areas, of which the Fish River Canyon is the most accessible and popular.

From the Kunene River, the boundary between Namibia and Angola, to just north of Lüderitz, the coast is geologically fairly homogeneous, low-lying and sandy. Occasionally, low rock platforms protrude; these were formed by the same Stormberg lavas responsible for the Drakensberg escarpment. Some of the rivers along this coastal stretch (the Swakop, Ugab, Omaruru and Hoarusib) are susceptible to flash-flooding in summer – a very important factor for campers to bear in mind.

The southern Namib from Lüderitz to Chamais Bay is rugged, a precipitous and rocky coastline formed from ancient eroded crystalline rocks, Nama quartzites, and dolomites with softer intervening shales.

Although the Karoo and Kalahari are also often referred to as deserts, only the Namib, with a rainfall of less than 150 millimetres a year, is truly so. Plant life is most prolific in the south, where two of the more unusual plants are the 'half-mens' or 'elephant's trunk' and the kokerboom, which forms fascinating, forest-like stands. To the north, the cover of low succulents gradually thins until, on the Namib sand dunes, there is little or no plant growth, and only scanty desert grass and acacia trees in the valleys.

Northwards from the Kuiseb River near Walvis Bay, grows the unique *Welwitschia mirabilis*. This prehistoric plant has adapted well to its hostile habitat; it even helps support desert life, as many plant-eating animals are partial to its long, sprawling evergreen leaves. Also in this area, river courses support a good growth of trees such as camelthorn, ana, African ebony, tamarisk and the leadwood.

For the greater extent of the Namib, the Great Escarpment limits its sprawl into the interior and forms a distinct border between the coastal desert and the semi-desert and Karoo. North of the Swakop River and north of the dune area, however, the escarpment is ill-defined and the desert gives way more gradually to a landscape softened by sparse grass and thornveld.

Within this harsh yet beautiful Namib landscape of ancient bare rock, high dunes and cliffs, and weird plants, a fascinating

animal life thrives. A large number of the smaller desert dwellers are nocturnal and escape the heat of the day in deep burrows. The Namib gerbil, when it does emerge, is seen scurrying across the parched sand on wide, furry feet. Gemsbok, springbok and ostrich are among the larger animals adapted to the scarcity of water. Birds special to the area include pallid larks, Layard's chat and Rüppell's korhaan, all ground birds whose pale plumage blends well with the desert sands. Birds of prey include the lappetfaced vulture, pygmy falcon and martial eagle.

As with other coastal deserts of the world (for example, the Atacama in South America), the Namib, despite its extreme aridity, is relatively cool. These low temperatures are attributed to the Benguela current which originates in the Antarctic and sweeps up the west coast of Africa. Thick fog frequently gathers above these icy waters and, propelled by onshore winds, rolls in over the land. This misty blanket not only shields the desert from the fierce sun but also supplies life-giving moisture to a number of superbly adapted smaller desert animals, particularly the dune beetles such as *Lepidochora* species which dig trenches in the sand to trap condensing fog. The story of *Onymacris unguicularis*, however, is without parallel. This tenebrionid beetle senses the fog rolling in and climbs to a ridge where it points its abdomen upright to the wind. Moisture condenses on its raised body and runs down to its mouth. These and many other small desert creatures obtain nourishment from wind-blown organic debris which settles on the dunes.

The desert is also snake territory and some of these animals have developed unusual ways and means of coping with their environment. For instance, Peringuey's desert or side-winding adder, a small reptile confined to the sandy Namib, has evolved a sideways-on mode of locomotion which facilitates maximum traction over the loosely compacted sands while keeping to a minimum contact with the often hot surface. The grooves of its 'spoor' are most distinctive.

Many of the most venomous scorpions are found in the desert and one species, *Parabuthus villosus*, can squirt its venom – as toxic as that of a cobra – with such force that it can reach a person's eyes.

Hiking in the drought-wracked Namib holds obvious dangers and common sense at all times is paramount. Never venture far from your base without carrying plenty of water; protect yourself from the sun; and avoid camping in dry riverbeds during summer, especially between January and March, when sudden floods are more likely. As in many arid regions, differences between day and night temperatures can be dramatic, so be prepared. Contracting rocks 'exploding' in the cool night air can be disquieting for the uninitiated. May through August are the preferred hiking months, as though the winter nights can be bitter, any discomfort is compensated for by the pleasant, warm days.

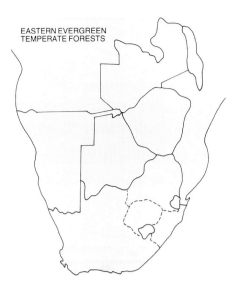

EASTERN EVERGREEN
TEMPERATE FORESTS

EASTERN EVERGREEN TEMPERATE FORESTS

When I arrived in southern Africa I was frequently asked: 'Why would a foreigner educated in forestry come here to work?' This was a valid question in many respects, as natural forest covers only about 0,25 per cent of South Africa and, except for Malawi, the proportion is even less for the rest of the sub-continent. What people do not always realize is that forestry embraces a number of related disciplines and its students naturally develop a very broad interest in the ecology of the land. However, this ecological region does concentrate on trees.

Perhaps my formal forestry training prejudiced me towards favouring forest trails as the idyllic hiking environment. They offer a soothing escape into a microcosm of peace and tranquillity. On closer inspection, however, a struggle is constantly being waged for life's necessities – space, light and water – among the earth's largest and longest-living giants. The outcome of this struggle determines the character of the forest – a character which is everchanging through the seasons and decades of time. To familiarize yourself with a forest trail is to know and understand its scents, sounds and textures, individual trees, fungi, flowering herbs and rotting logs. Forests provide man with many products (oxygen, food, drugs, shelter, building material) and services (weather modification, pollution filtration, erosion control and soil fertilization). Yet to the trailist they offer shade and refreshing water and, most importantly, rejuvenation and inspiration.

Forests have several basic requirements, a constant supply of adequate soil nutrients, as well as year-round moisture and sunlight being the most important. Forests also flourish best where diurnal and seasonal temperature variations are small. These conditions are fulfilled in only a few localities in South Africa: the eastern parts of the southern continuous rainfall area; the narrow eastern coastal zone; parts of the Great Escarpment in the eastern midlands and farther north; and parts of the high central plateau facing the rain-bearing winds blowing in from the low Mozambique plain.

In southern Africa, the three principal forest types are temperate, subtropical and montane. The largest and best known temperate forest blankets the landscape from Mossel Bay westwards to the Wit Els River. Within this area the broad mountain belt of the Outeniqua range supports the famous 'Knysna Forest'. Known as the Cape Fold, these mountains and their sub-parallel chains form an impenetrable barrier to humid air moving in off the sea. Rain-heavy clouds gather and eventually discharge themselves over the south-facing slopes which form a sharp divide between the moist coastal belt and the dry Karoo plains to the north.

In the eastern Cape interior, conditions are similar and the sea-facing escarpment, formed by the Winterberg and Hogsback-Amatola ranges, is heavily forested.

Coastal forests with their milkwoods, white stinkwoods, erythrinas and wild figs are slightly different in character from those inland which comprise mostly yellowwoods, assegais, black stinkwoods and Cape chestnuts. Other valuable inland forest species include black ironwood, Cape beech, sneezewood and white ironwood. Where rainfall is heaviest, trees grow 18-30 metres tall, the dense foliage of their upper limbs forming a closed canopy. Trailists with an interest in photography will need fast film and probably a flash as well, if they are to enjoy any success in these dark woods.

Many trees along the trail are labelled with their national tree list numbers. A list of trees corresponding to these numbers is usually provided in the trail's brochure. If not, purchase the *National List of Trees*, a tiny, inexpensive and very useful publication by Winter and Vahrmeijer. Forests are more than just trees, however, and other plant life abounds, especially climbers, mosses, ferns, fungi, lichens, grasses and many herbs.

Unfortunately, as with so many of South Africa's indigenous plant communities, exotic invader plants pose a threat to the survival of natural forests that is even more serious than previously uncontrolled exploitation for valuable timber. Southern forests are invaded by Australian myrtle, black wattle, blackwood and other aliens, while the main enemies of eastern Cape forests are black and golden wattle, jointed cactus and the Port Jackson willow.

The two other principal forest types occurring in South Africa are Coastal Bush and Subtropical Forest, which is discussed separately, and montane forests – located on the high east- and south-facing aspects of the Great Escarpment in the Transvaal, Zimbabwe and Malawi – which are found in isolated patches only, and are therefore described as part of the broader ecological zones within which they fall.

Forest birdlife is plentiful, but trailists intent on bird-watching must be prepared for frustrations, as individual birds are difficult to pick out in the thick tangle of branches and leaves. Crashing through the forest and chatting loudly to your fellow hikers is no way to see forest birds. If, however, you take the trouble to wait quietly in a clearing or shady glade, you will soon be rewarded by the arrival of a surprising variety of birds. Choose a fruiting tree as your post and you may even witness a 'mixed flock', a loose gathering of many species working their way through the forest in search of food. Some of the larger colourful birds characteristic of temperate forests are the Knysna loerie, Narina trogon, Rameron pigeon, gymnogene, redbilled hoopoe, blackheaded oriole and Knysna woodpecker.

Mammals of the forest are also shy; footprints and droppings are often the only evidence of their presence. Spoor you are most likely to come across are those of bushbuck, grysbok, blue duiker, bushpig and leopard. Baboons and vervet monkeys, like the birds, are more often heard than seen.

Be alert for the well-camouflaged boomslang (usually bright green, but many varieties occur). Its venom can prove fatal, but these back-fanged reptiles seldom strike at humans and are only aggressive when cornered. Many other snakes, frogs and lizards, woodlice, millipedes, centipedes, spiders, flatworms and scorpions live in the trees or litter-strewn floor, all interacting within the intricate web of forest life. Most common among these forest dwellers is the peripatus. This biological curiosity – restricted to high humid environments – has characteristics of both worms and insects and is thought to be the evolutionary link between the two. It looks like a squat velvet worm with fifteen pairs of stumpy legs and its eyes are situated at the base of soft, filamentous antennae.

The weather in temperate forests is usually mild, with rain and mist possible year-round. Snow can fall in June, July and August. Because trails in these forests (such as the Outeniqua and Tsitsikamma hiking trails) usually traverse other ecosystems (such as fynbos or grassland) as well, trailists are advised to study the climatic patterns of the entire region in which they intend walking.

All trailing environments hold dangers of one kind or another and forests are no exception, for within these often dark surroundings it is easy to lose your bearings. If for any reason you do lose your companions or stray far from the trail, do not bash through thick undergrowth. Stay in one spot, signal and wait for help. Never walk through dense forest after dark; with the meagre, dappled light of day gone you are liable to miss your footing on the excessively slippery forest floor and the chances of losing your sense of direction are even greater.

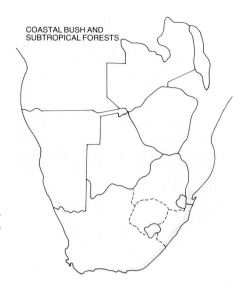

COASTAL BUSH AND SUBTROPICAL FORESTS

COASTAL BUSH AND SUBTROPICAL FORESTS

Tangled bush and dense evergreen forests mantling river-dissected, steeply rolling ridges, coastal plains, swamps, dunes, estuaries, beaches and mudflats . . . these are the challenging environments awaiting trailists within a narrow belt extending along southern Africa's eastern seaboard from the Gamtoos River, near Port Elizabeth, northwards through Transkei and Natal to northern Mozambique.

In the past, most of the region, from sea level to an altitude of some 300-400 metres, was forested, but here, as with southern Africa's all-too-few other natural forests, over-exploitation has taken its toll. Today valuable timber trees such as Cape box, Cape mahogany and Cape ebony, and their lianes, have been largely replaced by plantations of sugar-cane and other agricultural crops.

The natural areas remaining embrace several forest types; the following summary is abstracted from *Veld Types of South Africa* by Acocks (1975).

Typical Coast-belt Forest occurs in small patches on steeply rolling terrain where the soil is stable. Today, these forests, in which umzimbeet, red beech and Natal strelitzia are common, are being invaded by scrubby thornveld.

Zululand Palm-veld – a short, jungle-like tangle of lianes, palms and wild bananas within patches of scrubby thornveld – characterizes the poorly drained, sandy soil of the coastal plains north of the Tugela River.

Transitional Coastal Forest blankets the region between the Kei and Keiskamma rivers, respectively north and south of East London. It is similar to the drier parts of the 'typical forest', but its species composition is slightly different.

Mangrove Forests thrive on the eastern coast in salty, shallow waters, an environment hostile to all other trees. Mangrove trees actually help to create land, as they send out underwater roots which trap sediments and debris, thereby building up the soil. A rare animal community depends on the perpetuation of mangrove swamps. This unique ecosystem is described in greater detail in The Transkei Hiking Trail – Wild Coast (see page 160).

Alexandria Forest occurs south and west of Port Elizabeth to the Gamtoos River and northwards from Alexandria to just east of Port Alfred. The plants of these parts, such as the principal trees – Cape plane, white pear and kooboo-berry (the latter bearing edible fruit) – and the numerous scrambling shrubs such as cat-thorn, are more drought-resistant than those of the coastal forests to the north. Walking through the relatively short Alexandria forest is difficult, as it grows very thickly. However, in a number of the recognized trailing and rambling areas, paths have been cleared.

One of the most fascinating features of the vegetation within the coastal area between the Gamtoos and Fish rivers is that it comprises four main floral types. Topography, which plays a significant role in determining local climatic conditions in this transitional area, is responsible for the varied vegetation. Hence, it is not unusual for the trailist to hike through subtropical flora in sheltered kloofs, fynbos on coastal plains, succulent thorny scrub in wide river valleys, and then ascend grassy hills or mountain peaks.

Where protected, coastal forest and bush generally support diverse plant and animal communities. Some of the birds endemic to this ecological zone are the pinkthroated longclaw which inhabits the grasses of marshy areas, the blackbellied glossy starling, the grey waxbill and the olive sunbird.

If you intend hiking in this region in summer you must be prepared to endure hot, humid and rainy weather. As you move inland, however, the climate becomes refreshingly cooler and in the dry winters, frost is possible.

Warning: Malaria is endemic – meaning present and contractable year-round – in northern Zululand (or north of latitude 28°S, Richard's Bay). September to April are times of greatest risk, while May and August are the months of lowest transmission. Trailists should protect themselves against the bite of the 8-10 millimetre-long disease-carrying female *Anopheles* mosquito by taking these precautions: at sunset, dress in long-sleeved, light-coloured shirts and trousers; leave perfumes, colognes and after-shave lotions at home, instead applying a mosquito repellent with the active ingredient N-diethyl-meta-toluamide to all exposed skin surfaces (all repellents evaporate within two to three hours and should be re-applied at regular intervals); if possible sleep in a tent or hut in which mesh mosquito netting is provided; if you are in a hut, spray the interior thoroughly with a Pyrethrin insecticide; lastly, and most importantly, take an antimalarial drug at prescribed intervals

throughout your trip, beginning before departure and continuing for four weeks after leaving a malarial region – even if you spend only *one* night in an infected area. The South African Department of Health recommends that adults use tablets containing pyrimethamine (15 mg) and chloroquin (150 mg) in combination. Children are particularly vulnerable to malaria and prescriptions should be carefully followed in accordance with their age.

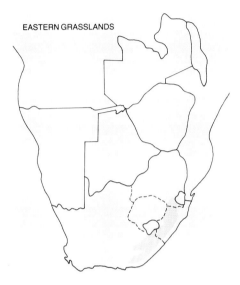

EASTERN GRASSLANDS

EASTERN GRASSLANDS

Transcending the boundaries of many eco-regions, grasslands occur over great areas of southern Africa and together form what is regarded as one of the most vital of all ecosystems. A renowned botanist once assessed the value of grasses in no uncertain terms: 'Whether civilization in South Africa survives or not will be determined by the way we manage our grasslands'. Although the statement may sound a little melodramatic, it has the ring of truth, for wildlife and domesticated stock and, indirectly, humans as well, depend on grass for food, and seldom does an ecological discussion not elaborate on grassland management for our survival.

Although improved agricultural know-how and conservation practices have benefited the state of grasslands, the ravages of mismanagement are still evident. Under particular stress are the eastern grasslands blanketing the broad undulating plateau which sweeps up between the Great Escarpment foothills and the coastal bush, from the eastern Cape through to northern Natal.

However, despite the poor state of ecology in many parts, there are pockets – the Ntendeka Wilderness Area, Umgeni Valley and Bosberg nature reserves, and the Umfolozi Game Reserve to name a few – where the trailist can experience to the full the beauty of unspoilt grasslands.

This zone is not a challenge to the physically orientated mountaineer (the close prox-

imity to the Drakensberg fills that niche) but rather, an excellent area for naturalists and scholars to experience and observe the intricacies of a life-supporting environment. Therefore, many of the trails in this region have education as their principal objective. To participate in a guided wilderness trail is to become involved, physically and spiritually, in the primeval drama of life and to understand that man's future is dependent on the continued existence of these wild areas.

The eastern grasslands of today, as with much of inland southern Africa, were once a huge shallow sea which, hundreds of millions of years ago, thronged with reptilian life. Fossils of these prehistoric lizards lie locked in the sediments – mainly the Beaufort Series of the Karoo beds – deposited through time, while the plants of the steamy swamplands formed the vast coalfields of the Natal Midlands.

Rivers have carved broad valleys through the easily eroded sandstones of the Beaufort Series: the remaining spurs or interfluvial ridges, as well as the 'table mountain' and koppie structures which characterize the landscape of the western parts, are monuments to the harder dolerite intrusions which capped the softer sedimentary sandstones. Jointed cliffs in northern Natal, such as those of Ntendeka, were formed from these doleritic dykes and sills.

Grasslands divide naturally into 'sweet' and 'sour' types. Sweet veld grasses remain nutritious throughout the year, even in winter when they are dry, while sourveld species are nutritious only in the early stages of growth; after about three months their protein and mineral content decreases rapidly and they become unpalatable and indigestible to animals.

Examples of the two grassveld types occur in the northern and eastern grassland of the Cape Province. Here the sweet veld grows in dry areas south of the Kalahari thornveld and is characterized by genera such as *Eragrostis* and *Stigagrostis*. The sourveld occurs in higher rainfall, more mountainous areas where *Eylyonurus argentus* and *Harpochloa falx* are dominant.

Within the eco-region, grassland is more or less 'pure' to an altitude of about 1 220 metres. Below, and ranging down to the coastal evergreen bush, short and tall grasses carpet the uplands while mixed grass and bush thrive on the deeper valley floors. In the moister regions, temperate forests have developed but the majority have fallen to agricultural expansion and have regressed to poor, unproductive veld. In the lower-lying part of the region, where Table Mountain sandstone and granite formations occur, soils are sandy and infertile. This veld, a mixture of acacia thornbush and *Aristida* grass, makes poor pasture.

Irwin's *Field Guide to the Natal Drakensberg* is a useful handbook for the naturalist wishing to identify the many grass species.

The great migrating herds of animals which once roamed the African grasslands have been severely reduced and today exist only in protected areas. According to Roberts' *Birds of Southern Africa*, the eastern grasslands do not have any birds endemic to its area. The birds are allied to both the highveld and eastern lowveld species. To blend in with their habitat, most grassland bird species are well camouflaged and fly less than those found in an arboreal environment. Some of the birds common to open veld include the secretarybird, blue crane, blackheaded heron, cattle egret, bustards and korhaans.

Hikers in this region can expect warmer and drier weather than in the Drakensberg, with snow in winter occurring only on mountain tops. Rainfall in summer is frequently accompanied by violent thunderstorms.

In the Usutu-Pongola floodplain and other northern parts, malaria is a constant threat, especially in hotter months. The precautions against infection set out on page 29 should be followed. Also in these more tropical areas, rivers are the domain of the crocodile, so take care when hiking along river banks. Swimming or wading in any of these bilharzia-infested waters should, in any case, be avoided.

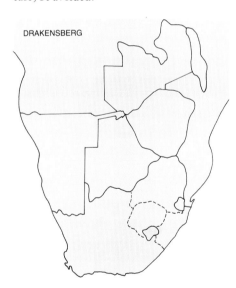

DRAKENSBERG

DRAKENSBERG

Quathlamba, a barrier of upward-pointing spears, is the Zulu name for the craggy pinnacles that form the most spectacular section of the Great Escarpment, southern Africa's watershed; and no less apt is the Dutch-derived epithet meaning 'mountain of the dragon', for the forbidding, jagged peaks seem a natural domain for these fabled creatures. In its fullest extent, the Drakensberg range describes a great arc from the northern Transvaal through Natal and Transkei, eventually petering out in the eastern Cape. For the purposes of this book, however, I have limited the discussion of this range to the 200-kilometre stretch from Mont-aux-Sources in the Royal Natal National Park, southwards to Bushman's Nek in Lesotho's Sehlabathebe National Park. The region spans an altitude of some 1 500 metres from Thaba Ntlenyana (3 482 m) in Lesotho, its highest point – also the highest point south of Kilimanjaro – to the Little 'Berg, its eastern foothills.

The Drakensberg is an invigorating experience for the rambler, hiker or mountaineer: the scenery is superb, the air crystal-clear and the plant and animal life fascinating. But it is, perhaps, the all-pervading sense of great age, the awesome primordial forces that moulded these mountains, that leaves the most indelible impressions. I well recall my own response: a sudden realization that, after several days of hard climbing, I was standing on the original surface of the earth, Gondwanaland, the super-continent that existed 180-120 million years ago.

Three hundred million years ago, a shallow sea existed where the Drakensberg is today, and in these waters sedimentary layers of the Karoo System were deposited. Then Gondwanaland, the vast land mass that gave birth to present-day southern Africa, India, Australia, South America and Antarctica, began to break apart. Unimaginable stresses opened great fissures in the earth's crust, and through them poured lavas which reached from present-day Lesotho to the coastline of present-day Natal. During the following 140 million years, at an average of one centimetre every six to seven years, wind and water eroded the hardened lavas, the Stormberg basalts, which receded 200 kilometres to form the steep descent to the Natal Midlands of today.

The Little 'Berg's underlying sedimentary rocks, moulded into large, rounded foothills and at places protectively capped by Stormberg basalts, were rapidly eroded, giving rise to the many caves, deep valleys and gorges. Appropriately named the 'cave sandstones', these less durable rocks are now known as the Clarens formation, which spans an altitude of approximately 1 700-2 000 metres.

Crystals of great beauty await discovery in the Drakensberg. Amygdales, originally veins in basalt, are most common, while others include amethyst, a semi-precious purple or blue-violet quartz; clear quartz; chalcedony, a quartz and opal mixture; and chert, a white to grey, opaque stone. With luck, you may find agate, which is chert in variegated concentric layers. In fact, chert may have been responsible for the original settlement of the 'Berg by Bushmen, as it is the only rock in this area suitable for making arrowheads and spear tips.

'Berg vegetation grows in characteristic belts, each influenced by the parent rock, sharp altitude differences and aspect – north-facing slopes are warm and gradients more gentle, those that are south-facing are cold and steep. The 'montane belt' is the lowest and, ranging from 1 280-1 829 metres, occurs in the river valleys of the Little 'Berg up to the cave sandstone. The 'sub-alpine belt', 1 829-2 865 metres, extends from the base of the cave sandstone to the foot of the basalt cliffs on the main escarpment, and the highest, the 'alpine belt', ranges from the basalt cliffs up to and including the summit plateau.

Grasses dominate the three belts and are largely responsible for the carpet of summer green and the yellow-russet brown hues of winter. The principal species, 'red grass', makes excellent pasture, but mismanagement and overburning have unfortunately led to its replacement by hardier, more xerophytic, deeper-rooted members of the genus *Eragrostis* and *Aristida*, the 'needle grass'. In places *Protea roupelliae* or *P. caffra* invade the grasslands to form protea savannah. Indigenous tree growth above the cave sandstone cliffs is absent, probably because of the severely cold, dry, windy winters, and only kloofs and sheltered ridge slopes are forest-clad.

Fynbos is one of the typical plant communities occurring around 2 000 metres but, unlike the Cape fynbos, that of the Drakensberg is dominated by small, hard-leaved plants, and not restios and proteas. Two unusual species found in this fynbos (which I will never forget after being sunburnt and trapped in a tangle on a steep slope) are the berg cypress and berg cycad. The berg cypress, closely related to the Clanwilliam cedar, has scratchy, dry branches while the berg cycad, a living fossil of Mesozoic times, has narrow-leaved, prickly fronds.

Alpine vegetation characterizes the harsh plateau environment, with evergreen dwarf woody shrubs – predominantly ericas and everlastings – scattered among temperate grasses.

In total, some 1 200 species clothe the Drakensberg and form the basis of a food web which embraces more than 43 large and small mammal species, over 250 bird species, 17 frog species, 24 snake species, 4-6 lizard families, and a myriad other creatures. Irwin's *Field Guide to the Natal Drakensberg* gives excellent coverage of these animals as well as aids to their identification.

Throughout the Drakensberg, weather patterns are fairly cyclic. Winter (April or May to September) is favoured for mountaineering. During these months, days are usually sunny and temperatures can climb as high as 22 °C, but at night they can rapidly drop to below freezing. Heavy frosts are the norm and although snow can be expected at any time of the year, it is obviously most common during the winter months. As a result of temperature inversions, the river valleys are colder than the mountain slopes. For this reason, camping under the shelter of a tent or in a cave to prevent radiant heat loss is recommended. Temperatures on the summit plateau are much lower than on the slopes and range from 10 °C during the day to -8 °C at night. Dry, warm 'Berg winds, at their fiercest in late July or August, often indicate an approaching cold front.

In view of the extreme weather in the Drakensberg, hikers must be wise and remember to take basic precautions against exposure (cold exhaustion) and hypothermia (severe, accidental lowering of the body's temperature). Most important, be aware that even a healthy and physically fit adult can succumb to exposure or hypothermia if over-fatigued by exercise and anxiety – conditions not uncommon to mountaineers who lose their way in wind and snow or rain. Watch your party carefully for any of these symptoms: slow physical or mental responses, stumbling, cramps and shivering, slurred speech, vision impairment, irritability or other unusual behaviour. React immediately by seeking shelter or erecting a tent within which the victim can rest and sip warm drinks. If at all possible, the victim should change into dry clothing or lie in a warm sleeping bag.

To treat frostbite, which usually occurs on the ears, nose, chin, fingers and/or toes, the victim must again be sheltered, given warm drinks and all constrictive clothing should be removed. Never rub or apply direct heat to frostbite; rather thaw the affected part gradually – but never do this if there is a possibility that it will refreeze. A frostbitten victim complains that the affected part is cold, painful or numb and stiff, with no power of movement. Severe cases of frostbite require prompt medical attention; therefore, the victim should be helped down the mountain and treated as soon as possible.

Summer (October to March) is the least popular hiking season because of the prevalence of violent, late afternoon thunderstorms which produce a deluge of water and cold, swollen rivers which should not be forded. Summers can also bring many hot sunny days – but, just as readily, fog that envelops the mountains, reducing visibility to no more than a few paces. Air temperatures range from 15 °C to 33 °C and nights are cool to warm. Summer hiking has one compensation, though – the 'Berg flowers are at their best.

A special note on maps: Peter Slingsby, in conjunction with the Forestry Branch of the Department of Environment Affairs, has produced a comprehensive, updated series of 1:50 000 maps for the entire Drakensberg mountaineering area. This set of Mapcape maps comprises: map number 1, Drakensberg North (Mt. Aux Sources to Cathedral Peak); map number 2, Drakensberg North (Cathedral Peak to Injasuti); map number 3, Drakensberg Central (Injasuti, Giant's Castle, Highmoor); map number 4, Drakensberg Central (Highmoor, Mkhomazi, Loteni); map number 5, Drakensberg South (Vergelegen, Cobham, Garden Castle); and map number 6, Drakensberg South (Garden Castle, Boesmansnek, Sehlabathebe).

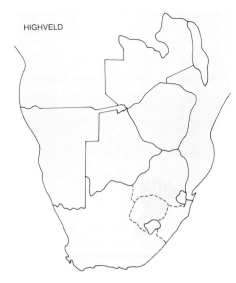

HIGHVELD

HIGHVELD

To be honest, the Highveld (with the notable exceptions of the Magaliesberg and the Witwatersrand) is not a mountaineer's delight. Although bird-watchers and nature ramblers have endless opportunities to study natural history, the recreation potential of this area is not faring well against competition from farming, mining, industry and urban development.

However, due to the recent commendable efforts of the local municipal authorities, a system of urban walks, available not only to ramblers but also to joggers, horse-riders and canoeists, leads trailists along scenic spruits within and on the outskirts of the Highveld's bustling metropolitan centres. This 'linear park system' links valleys, ridges, gardens, zoos and bird sanctuaries, and historical and archaeological features in a complex of long and short circular walks. In an age where petrol is dear, and distances to the wilder, pristine areas of the Transvaal and bushveld are far, the urban park system is a welcome alternative to the fully fledged wilderness experience.

Very simply, the Highveld is an elevated grassland region. The large part of the Highveld lies between 1 200 and 1 829 metres above sea level. From the Great Escarpment it extends inland, terminating in the north at the popular Magaliesberg range, beyond which sprawls the bushveld. In the northwest, the Langeberg and Korannaberg ranges of the Waterberg separate the Highveld from the Kalahari, while in the south and east, the boundaries coincide roughly with the plateau's edge. The character of Lesotho's landscape differs so drastically from the true Highveld, however, that I have included it with the Drakensberg ecological zone (see opposite page).

Some 280 to 180 million years ago (mid-Carboniferous to Triassic periods), in Karoo times, the Highveld lay buried under thick, horizontally arranged layers of shales and sandstones. These were later intruded by

dolerite dykes and sills and capped by basaltic lava. By early Cretaceous times, however, erosion had done its work and the high central plateau must have looked very much as it does today, a flat plain, occasionally relieved by koppies capped with resistant sandstone or dolerite. In the northern Orange Free State and southern Transvaal – an area of tremendous mineral wealth – the geomorphology is far more complex, for here the Karoo cover has been uplifted and so severely eroded that ancient ridges of the Transvaal and Witwatersrand quartzites are exposed.

Plant life varies from locality to locality. The vegetation of the Magaliesberg and Witwatersrand, the prime hiking areas, is discussed in the relevant entries (see pages 270 and 276 respectively). South of the Magaliesberg, the vegetation is generally referred to as 'Bankenveld', open tree savannah giving way to dense scrub on koppies and stony areas. Important tree species include many of those common to the bushveld: highveld protea, common hook-thorn and white stinkwood. The rolling hills are covered with grass, marking the transition to true highveld grassveld. In the grassveld, woody species are confined to the protected mountain slopes and river banks. Dominant grasses are represented by the genera *Themeda* and *Cymbopogon*, with many other species intermingled.

This exposed, often windswept region is subject to considerable temperature extremes and, as with the plant life, the Highveld animal inhabitants have adapted accordingly. Because soil is cooler in summer and warmer in winter, it presents a far more stable habitat than the surface, and burrowing mammals such as the spring hare, bateared fox and mole-rat are therefore common. Large mammals indigenous to the Highveld include black wildebeest, red hartebeest, blesbok, eland, duiker, steenbok, gemsbok, zebra and cheetah.

Grassveld birds are usually inconspicuous in colouring and habit and the majority are ground-living species such as larks, pipits, ostriches, secretarybirds, blue cranes, herons, cattle egrets, bustards, coursers, plovers, dikkops, guineafowls, quails, grass owls and marsh owls, not to mention 'LBJ's' (little brown jobs) such as the cisticolas and grass warblers. Many Highveld birds are, in fact, migrants and during their summer sojourns in southern Africa's grasslands, they lack the colourful nuptial plumage reserved for their breeding habitats in the northern hemisphere. Seed-eaters such as waxbills, weavers and parasitic whydahs feed on grass seeds in late summer, but otherwise prefer to feed in bush, vlei or reedbeds.

The intricately woven grass and reed oval nests of the spottedbacked, Cape and masked weavers, as well as those of the smaller and unmistakably coloured red bishop, golden bishop and Cape widow birds, provide a distinctive feature to hanging branches, upright reeds and exotic gum trees which line marshes, rivers and vleis. To observe a weaver bird build these fascinating structures (each species possessing its characteristic technique and design) is one of the highlights of rambling along the various spruits incorporated in the urban Highveld walks. In addition, waterbirds are abundant in artificial dams and vleis – spoonbills, glossy ibises, dabchicks, purple gallinules and geese, to name a few.

Generally, the Highveld is characterized by low rainfall, cloudless skies, and considerable day/night and seasonal changes in temperature. Summers are warm and rainy with hot winds blowing from the northwest, common also in spring. Summer days in the western Highveld are markedly warmer. Winters, on the other hand, are dry and cloudless, usually with cool to warm days and colder, sometimes bitterly cold, nights. Daytime temperatures during mid to late winter can also be unpleasantly cold, especially when the bone-chilling south winds roar across the plateau from the snow-clad Drakensberg and Malutis. Heavy frosts are not uncommon.

Although frequently dramatic and visually stimulating, the often violent thunderstorms, common from November to March, can be hazardous for those caught in the open. The sudden deluges can turn shallow streams and spruits into raging torrents literally within minutes, while vicious bolts of lightning stab randomly at the veld. Keep an eye on the weather, therefore, and if you see that a storm is imminent, keep away from any potential river race, and avoid high, exposed ground where the chances of a lightning strike are always greater. January and February are the hottest months.

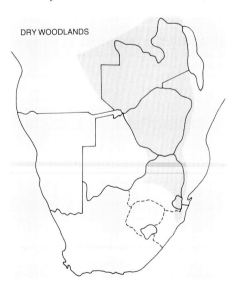

DRY WOODLANDS

DRY WOODLANDS

'The African bush', bushveld, lowveld, savannah, tree veld, dry woodlands – all refer to the vast tract of land stretching both westwards and northwards from Mozambique

through Zimbabwe and Zambia into Malawi; southwards through the northern and western Transvaal, including most of Swaziland, Lebowa and Zululand; and westwards to the accacia savannah or Kalahari.

The bushveld is largely the 'classical' African ecosystem, the one vividly portrayed in so many epics about Africa and the one where wilderness-type trails gained their popularity. The areas near Lake Kariba and the Tuli Block have always held a special appeal for all big-game lovers, as do the more recently established foot tours in the Kruger National Park and the contiguous private reserves.

But wilderness trails are only a part of the plethora of trailing opportunities in this vast area: the eastern and northern Transvaal, particularly, with its numerous lengthy and dramatic hiking stretches, is a backpacker's paradise. It is also a region of hiking 'firsts': the first NHWS trail (the Fanie Botha Hiking Trail, see page 234), the first hiking trail to incorporate a train-ride *en route* (the Elandskrans Hiking Trail, see page 231) and the first trails through areas of the prospecting boom of last century.

Some private hotels in the eastern Transvaal and Swaziland have grounds which present rambling opportunities, while many Zimbabwean towns offer peaceful walks through pleasant urban green areas. Zimbabwe also boasts the world's most sensational nature trail alongside the Victoria Falls. The ancient mountains of Chimanimani in eastern Zimbabwe and the Wolkberg in the northern Transvaal beckon the fittest outdoorsmen to the African bush.

From the air, the bushveld appears endlessly brown, with occasional muddy, greenmargined rivers where the thornbushes, acacias, baobabs and yellow-barked fever trees, so evocative of Africa, grow more thickly. These – as well as patches of montane forest and high plateau and floodplain grassland – although providing some of the finest trailing environments on the sub-continent, are no more than local interruptions in an otherwise continuous woodland association.

The aerial impression is misleading, however, as the uniform rusty-grey vista belies a diversity in altitude (the region varies between 150 and 1 375 metres), climate, geomorphology and soil conditions which give rise to a number of woodland types, each supporting a wealth of animal life.

Very ancient rocks underlie most of southern Africa and, known broadly as the Basement Complex, they comprise highly metamorphosed sediments as well as igneous rocks – schists, slates, quartzites, granites and gneisses. Further sediments and the sands of time have largely hidden the sub-continent's foundation, but here and there throughout the bushveld, outcrops occur, adding interest to the landscape and providing fine challenges for the mountaineer and serious backpacker. Examples of these primitive outcrops include the Mur-

chison range and Barberton Mountain land in the eastern Transvaal and Swaziland, the Gold Belt in Zimbabwe and the Basement schists, quartzites and volcanic rocks of the Malawi plateaux.

Towards the close of the pre-Cambrian Era, a great intrusion of igneous rock, the Bushveld igneous complex, occurred in the eastern Transvaal. This is the base of the lowveld plateau which abuts the Highveld, and here the Waterberg plateau, Pietersburg plateau and the Soutpansberg, all in the north of the basin, also present their weathered krantzes and kloofs to test the climber's skills. Farther north, old granites underlie much of the woodlands plain, with dolerites and quartzites giving rise to the eastern highlands of Zimbabwe.

Dry woodlands divide naturally into three basic vegetation types – mixed savannah, *Brachystegia-Julbernardia* veld, and mopane veld.

In mixed savannah the balance of trees to grass varies; either a forest-type association, or an open parkland in which grasses dominate, is formed. Both evergreen and deciduous trees occur and most have adapted to long periods without water, their small leaves, deep roots, water-storing organs, and thorns replacing leaves all helping to conserve liquid. In South Africa, mixed savannah occurs principally in the northern and eastern Transvaal and Zululand, and to the south it is transitional with the eastern grasslands, Karoo or fynbos. Acacias and boabads are common in the eastern Transvaal and Zululand, while in the drier areas aloes and euphorbias dot the landscape. Most regions host deciduous broad-leaved trees such as the marula, a highly valued fruiting tree, species of *Sterculia* (chestnuts), and pod mahogany. *Hyphaene* and *Borassus* palms occur in river valleys. Mahogany logs are used by local tribesmen for their dug-out canoes, while the palms are also popular, as a potent liquor is made from their sap.

Brachystegia-Julbernardia woodland is basically parkland but can vary from open grassland to almost closed forest. Dominant among the intermingling trees are *Brachystegia spiciformis* and *Julbernardia globiflora*. Often referred to as miombo woodland, this deciduous association sprawls across a large part of Zimbabwe. The red hues of young brachystegia foliage mantle the woodlands in spring and, together with the soft pinks and fawns of *J. globiflora* leaves, make a colourful display.

Frost-free situations – the warm valleys around the Limpopo and Zambezi rivers and the continental basin of the interior – are the domain of the mopane tree. Its butterfly-shaped leaves turn their edges to the sun during the heat of the day to reduce dehydration. Even in full leaf, therefore, a mopane forest provides little shade. The leaves and pods are a popular food source for both wild and domesticated animals, while the leaf-eating mopane worms, the caterpillars of a large brownish-grey moth species, are roasted and eaten by locals for their protein content. Stands of baobab are often found within the mopane woodland, and other associated trees include members of *Sterculia*, *Acacia*, *Combretum*, *Euphorbia* and *Terminalia*, all well-known bushveld genera.

When summer rains come late to the bushveld and grass is scarce, many animals feed on the foliage of trees and shrubs, all of which leave before the first downpours. Because of the great numbers of trees, dry woodlands are home to many browsers and some of the mammals that live off savannah trees, either partially or entirely, are elephants, black rhino, giraffe, steenbok, suni and forest dwellers such as the blue and common duiker. Many – impala, sable antelope and hartebeest, for example – are both browsers and grazers, while white rhino, zebra, warthog, hippo and oribi are chiefly grazers. Among the predators of the region are lion, leopard, jackal, hyaena, caracal and serval cat.

Birdlife is always fascinating in these woodlands. According to K. Newman in *Bird Life in Southern Africa*, of the 833 species recorded for southern Africa (excluding Malawi), 711 are recorded within bushveld and thornveld (Kalahari). The reasons for this disproportionately large number of species are, firstly, the great diversity of habitats available in wooded areas, which provide a myriad niches to be filled, and secondly, that the whole northern limit of southern Africa is woodland and so the many tropical birds penetrating just south into this region are also included. Species typical of all vegetation associations and easily identified are the beautifully coloured lilacbreasted roller, yellowbilled hornbill, redbilled hoopoe, longtailed shrike, brownheaded parrot and purplecrested loerie.

Smaller vertebrates and invertebrates, especially insects and spiders, thrive in the trees, shrubs, creepers and grass. Snakes and lizards also abound, while the Nile crocodile, living only in the dry woodland areas, is confined to rivers, lakes and swamps. Because of its man-eating proclivities, hikers must be careful when travelling in these areas, especially while crossing rivers. Another large reptile found mainly in savannah and open bush is the rock or tree leguan.

Woodland seasons are well defined: wet and dry. The wet season occurs from October to the end of March, with October often being referred to as 'suicide month' because it is the hottest period before the rains break. To the trailist, the advantage of wet-season hiking is the sight of the veld when the trees are fruiting and in leaf, the herbs blooming and the birds breeding. The disadvantages are that insects such as mosquitoes (which carry malaria) and tsetse flies (carriers of sleeping-sickness) are more plen-

tiful too, the game is dispersed because water is readily available, and transport is hindered by wet, muddy road conditions. During the dry season, wildlife concentrates at waterholes, so the chances of spotting game through the dry, dead grass are much improved.

MALAWI

MALAWI

Geologically, Malawi is part of the East African Rift Valley system – a 6 500 kilometre-long graben created by land subsiding between two roughly parallel fault lines, and the uplifting of the valley's shoulders. The central feature of the valley is the lake which forms the greater part of Malawi's eastern boundary. In the north, the basin of this long, narrow stretch of water is strongly faulted, evidenced by the impressive escarpment. The southern part of the basin and the Shire River Valley, however, are folded and therefore relatively shallow.

Rising from the valley floor of softer schists and gneisses, metamorphosed intrusive rocks form inselbergs and extensive highlands such as the Michiru, Ndirande, Soche and Thyolo in the south and, in the central and northern area, the Dedza and Chongoni peaks. These formations also underlie the Nyika plateau. In the post-Karoo (or late Jurassic) period, a large portion of present-day Malawi lay beneath Karoo sediments and, intruding into these, a grey crystalline igneous rock, syenite, formed the spectacular massifs of Mulanje and Zomba, as well as other mountains of the south.

Technically, Malawi – spanning altitudes from 220 metres below sea level (the lake floor) to 3 300 metres on Mount Mulanje – embraces a number of ecological zones. The three major regions are the Shire Valley and Lake Malawi – including cataracts, bird-rich marshes and lake-shore plains; the medium plateau of the Shire highland, Central and Northern provinces – between 762 and

1 372 metres; and the highlands of Mulanje, Zomba, Kirk, Dedza, Dowa, Mafingi, Misuku, Viphya and Nyika – averaging 1 372 to 2 934 metres, but with higher peaks.

Plant life reflects this topography and geology. Most widespread are montane forests and grasslands and *Brachystegia-Julbernardia* woodlands, but also covering large tracts are *Combretum-Acacia-Piliostigma* woodlands and mixed savannah woodlands.

On the Viphya, Nyika and Zomba plateaux as well as on the isolated Mulanje massif, Mangochi and Thyolo mountains, heavy rains and frequent mists carried by easterly winds combine with the deep soils of gentle slopes to produce conditions well suited to forest growth. Evergreen trees dominate, their trunks clad in a profusion of mosses and ferns and other epiphytes, which find in these more elevated situations the essential moisture and light, unavailable on the ground because of the dense forest canopy. The montane forests of Mulanje are unique and harbour such valuable endemics as the Mulanje cedar, found either in pure stands or as isolated individuals, and the yellowwood, *Podocarpus milanjiana*. The mighty cedars grow as tall as 42,5 metres and are exploited for building timber (the huts on Mulanje are constructed from their timber).

Blanketing the peaks and highlands above the tree line are grasslands interspersed with a variety of flowering plants such as buttercups, orchids and everlastings, and proteas. These grasslands probably owe their origin to destruction of the original forests by fire.

Other major vegetation types include *Brachystegia-Julbernardia* woodland which covers the greater part of Malawi (see opposite page for its description). The lower slopes of Nyika provide a fine example of such woodland, while on the plateau montane grassland predominates. Also characteristic of highlands are the dambos, broad shallow depressions that soak up the rains in much the same way as the bogs of the northern hemisphere. These sponge-like reservoirs are the lifeblood of plateau streams, often providing them with water throughout the year. Short grassland covers the dambos, and geophytes as well as other herbs abound.

Because of Malawi's large rural population, larger mammals are scarce and mostly restricted to reserves. But birds are everywhere, and to aid identification of the more than 600 species – an impressive diversity for such a small country – keen birders should purchase the detailed checklist, *Birds of Malawi*, by Benson and Benson. Snakes, lizards, frogs, butterflies and other invertebrates are also well represented, but the most special aspect of Malawi's animal life is probably the strikingly beautiful fishes waiting to delight the snorkeller in Lake Malawi. Over 220 species – most of which are endemic – thrive in these waters.

TRAILS DIRECTORY

Western Cape
1. Ramskop Nature Reserve
2. Cedarberg Wilderness Area
3. Groot Winterhoek Wilderness
4. Rocher Pan Nature Reserve
5. Columbine Nature Reserve
6. Langebaan National Park
7. Sandveld Trails
8. Tinie Versveld Flora Reserve
9. Kalkbaskraal Nature Reserve
10. Ceres Mt. Fynbos Reserve
11. Hex River Mountains
12. Karoo Botanic Gardens
13. Boland Hiking Trail
14. Canoeing
15. Bobbejaan River Waterfall
16. Elandspad River Kloofing Trip
17. Hawequas State Forest
18. Paarl Mountain Nature Reserve
19. Durbanville Nature Reserve
20. Tygerberg Nature Reserve
21. Kirstenbosch Botanic Gardens
22. 'City on Foot'
23. Table Mountain
24. Tokai Nature Trail Complex

25. The Karbonkelberg Traverse
26. Cape of Good Hope Reserve
27. World of Birds
28. Silvermine Nature Reserve
29. Rondevlei Bird Sanctuary
30. The Vineyard Trail
31. Stellenbosch, various trails
32. Jan Marais Wildflower Garden
33. Assegaaibosch Trail
34. Jonkershoek State Forest
35. Helderberg Nature Reserve
36. The Dog Trail
37. Boland Hiking Trail
38. Steenbras Dam
39. Harold Porter Botanic Gardens
40. Houwtama Educational Trails
41. Kleinmond Nature Reserve
42. Perdeberg and Three Sisters
43. Lebanon State Forest
44. Riviersonderend Canyon Trip
45. Villiersdorp Nature Reserve
46. Bundu Farm
47. Caledon Nature Reserve
48. Vogelgat Private Reserve
49. Fernkloof Nature Reserve

50. Hermanus Cliffs and Lagoon
51. Salmonsdam Nature Reserve
52. Greyton Nature Reserve
53. Boesmanskloof Traverse
54. Bredasdorp Mountain Reserve
55. De Hoop Nature Reserve
56. De Mond Nature Reserve
57. Swellendam Hiking Trail
58. Boosmansbos Wilderness Area
59. Heidelberg Wildflower Garden
60. Garcia State Forest
61. Pauline Bohnen Nature Reserve

Southern Cape
62. Ruitersbos Forest Walks
63. Outeniqua Hiking Trail
64. Woodville Walk
65. Groeneweide Forest Walk
66. Wilderness Lake Area
67. Bushbuck Trail
68. Terblans Nature Walk
69. Kranshoek Coastal Walk
70. Goukamma Nature Reserve
71. Goudveld State Forest
72. Garden of Eden

73. Diepwalle State Forest
74. The Elephant Walk
75. Robberg Nature Reserve
76. Keurbooms River Reserve
77. De Vasselot Nature Reserve
78. Tsitsikamma Hiking Trail
79. Tsitsikamma Forest N.P.
80. Grootkloof Nature Walk
81. Otter Trail
82. Nature Trail Complex
83. Garden Route Cycle Trail
84. Cockscomb State Forest
85. Cape St. Francis Reserve
86. Loerie Dam Nature Reserve
87. Groendal Wilderness Area
88. Uitenhage Nature Reserve
89. Van Stadens Reserve
90. Maitland Mines Nature Reserve
91. Sardinia Bay/Sylvic Reserves
92. Cape Recife Nature Reserve
93. Bushbuck Nature Trail
94. Swartkops Aloe Reserve
95. Suurberg National Park
96. Settler's Park
97. Riverside Walk
98. Donkin Heritage Trail
99. Fishwater Flats
100. Bluewater Bay to Coega Mouth

Eastern Cape
101. The Alexandria Trail
102. Dias Cross
103. Kowie Canoe Trail
104. Thomas Baines Nature Reserve
105. 1820 Settlers Garden
106. Valley Bushveld Trail
107. Ecca Pass Nature Reserve
108. Bosberg Nature Reserve
109. Mountain Zebra Trail
110. Commando Drift Reserve
111. Blanco Private Nature Reserve
112. Hogsback State Forest
113. Kologha State Forest
114. Kologha Hiking Trail
115. King William's Town Reserve
116. Cove Rock
117. Fort Pato Nature Reserve
118. Bridledrift Nature Reserve
119. Umtiza Nature Reserve
120. Amalinda Nature Reserve
121. Potter's Pass Reserve
122. The Urban Trail
123. Nahoon River Estuary
124. Gonubie Nature Reserve
125. Gulu/Cape Henderson Reserves
126. Bosbokstrand Nature Reserve
127. The Strandloper Trail
128. Ocean View Guest Farm
129. Black Eagle Wilderness Trail
130. Madeira Guided Trails
131. Koos Ras Nature Trail
132. The Ecowa Hiking Trail
133. Maclear Trails
134. Mountain Shadows Walks
135. Rhodes Hiking Trail
136. Die Berg
137. Oviston Nature Reserve
138. Doornkloof Nature Reserve

Karoo and Northern Cape
139. Little Karoo Cycle Trail
140. Karoo Nature Reserve
141. Springbok Trail
142. Swartberg Hiking Trail
143. De Hoek Nature Walk
144. Cango Caves

145. Greystone Cheetah Wild Park
146. Gamka Mountain Reserve
147. Montagu Mountain Reserve
148. Dassieshoek Nature Reserve
149. Vrolijkheid Nature Reserve
150. Nieuwoudtville Nature Reserve
151. Namaqualand Coast Trail
152. Namaqualand Daisy Cycle Trail
153. Ian Myers Nature Walk
154. Richtersveld Canoeing Trail
155. Klipspringer Hiking Trail
156. Orange Gorge Kayak Trail
157. Kokerboom Trail
158. Doringberg Hiking Trail
159. Rolfontein Nature Reserve
160. Orange River Game Trail
161. Vryburg Hiking Trail

Orange Free State and Qwa-Qwa
162. Drakensberg Botanic Garden
163. Rhebok Hiking Trail
164. Houtkop Hiking Trail
165. Brandwater Hiking Trail
166. Wynford Holiday Farm
167. Imperani Hiking Trail
168. The Korannaberg Hiking Trail
169. Steve Visser Nature Walk
170. Orange Free State Gardens
171. Mayaputi Gorge Canoeing Trail
172. Tussen-die-Riviere Game Farm
173. Qwa-Qwa Conservation Area

Ciskei
174. Tsolwana Game Park
175. Katberg/Readsdale Complex
176. Mpofu Game Park
177. The Amatola Hiking Trail
178. Pirie and Sandile Nature Walks
179. Sandile Dam Walk
180. Ntaba Ka Ndoda
181. The Double Drift Hiking Trail
182. The Shipwreck Hiking Trail

Transkei
183. Transkei Hiking Trail

Lesotho
184. Lesotho
185. Sehlabathebe National Park
186. Lesotho Horse Trails

Natal Drakensberg
187. Holkrans Hiking Trail
188. Royal Natal National Park
189. Upper Tugela Location
190. Mlambonja Wilderness Area
191. Mdedelelo Wilderness Area
192. Spioenkop Nature Reserve
193. Giant's Castle Game Reserve
194. Kamberg/Vergelegen Reserves
195. Burnera Trail
196. Loteni Hiking Trail
197. Mzimkulwana Nature Reserve
198. Drakensberg Hiking Trail
199. Coleford Nature Reserve
200. Mount Currie Nature Reserve

Natal and KwaZulu
201. Tugela Drift Nature Reserve
202. Weenen Nature Reserve
203. Old Furrow Trail
204. Mhlopeni Nature Reserve
205. Dargle River Trail
206. Umgeni Valley Nature Reserve
207. Howick Town Trail
208. Midmar Nature Reserve

209. Natal National Botanic Garden
210. Queen Elizabeth Park Reserve
211. Ferncliffe Forest Walks
212. Green Belt Trail
213. Pietermaritzburg Town Trails
214. Doreen Clark Nature Reserve
215. Cedara Forest Trail
216. Ngele Hiking Trail
217. Lorna Doone Forest Trails
218. Umtamvuna Nature Reserve
219. Uvongo River Reserve
220. Oribi Gorge Nature Reserve
221. Vernon Crookes Reserve
222. Ilanda Wilds Nature Reserve
223. Kenneth Stainbank Reserve
224. North Park Nature Reserve
225. Durban's Self-guided Trails
226. Beachwood Mangroves Reserve
227. Paradise Valley Nature Reserve
228. Palmiet Nature Reserve
229. New Germany Nature Reserve
230. Ingweni Hiking Trail
231. Krantzkloof Nature Reserve
232. The Hawaan Bush
233. Umhlanga Lagoon Reserve
234. Remedies and Rituals Trails
235. Amatikulu Nature Reserve
236. Umlalazi Nature Reserve
237. Ocean View Game Park
238. Dlinza Forest Nature Reserve
239. Nyala Game Ranch
240. Swamp Trail
241. Mihobi Nature Reserve
242. Launch Tours
243. Game Park Trails
244. St. Lucia Wilderness Trails
245. Mvube Trail
246. Mapelane Nature Reserve
247. Dugandlovu Trail
248. Mziki Trail
249. Isikhova/Umkhiwane Trails
250. Nyalazi State Forest
251. Umfolozi Wilderness Trails
252. White Rhino Trail
253. Mbhombe Forest and Auto Trails
254. Ubizane Game Ranch
255. Sodwana Bay National Park
256. Kosi Bay Nature Reserve
257. Ndumu Game Reserve
258. Mkuzi Bushveld Trail
259. Ntendeka Wilderness Area
260. Vryheid Hiking Trail
261. Itala Nature Reserve

Swaziland
262. Meikles Mount
263. Mlilwane Wildlife Sanctuary
264. Malolotja Nature Reserve
265. Mlawula Nature Reserve

Northern and Eastern Transvaal, KaNgwane and Lebowa
266. Gold Nugget Hiking Trail
267. Fortuna Mine Nature Trail
268. Middelburg Hiking Trail
269. Baboon/Suikerbos Trails
270. Klein Aasvoëlkrans Walks
271. Loskop Dam Nature Trail
272. Elandskrans Hiking Trail
273. Kaapsehoop Hiking Trail
274. Sudwala Caves and Walks
275. McManus Nature Walk
276. Lowveld Botanic Garden
277. Trails in KaNgwane
278. Gustav Klingbiel Reserve

279. Fanie Botha Hiking Trail
280. Loerie and Forest Falls Walks
281. Blyderivierspoort Hiking Trail
282. Morgenzon Hiking Trail
283. Mount Sheba Nature Reserve
284. Rambler's and Bridle Trails
285. Prospector's Hiking Trail
286. Echo Caves
287. Eerste Liefde Hiking Trail
288. Kadishi Valley Trail System
289. Swadini Nature Trails
290. Kruger Park Wilderness Trails
291. Sabi Sabi Game Reserve
292. Londolozi Game Reserve
293. Timbavati Wilderness Trail
294. Klaserie Lowveld Trail
295. Jock of the Bushveld Trail
296. Selati Ox-wagon Trails
297. Hans Merensky Nature Reserve
298. Rooikat Nature Trail
299. Lekgalameetse Nature Reserve
300. Wolkberg Wilderness Area
301. Magoebaskloof Hiking Trail
302. Ben Lavin Nature Reserve
303. Soutpansberg Hiking Trail
304. Soutpansberg Hiking Trail
305. Baobab Hiking Trail
306. Greater Kuduland Safaris
307. Messina Nature Reserve
308. Limpopo Wilderness Trail
309. Langjan Nature Reserve
310. Pietersburg Municipal Reserve
311. Percy Fyfe Nature Reserve
312. National Zoological Gardens
313. Doorndraai Dam Reserve
314. Mosdene Private Nature Reserve
315. Nylsvley Trail
316. Lapalala Wilderness Weekend Trails
317. Gold River Game Resort
318. Hans Strijdom Dam Reserve
319. Haakdoorndraai Reserve
320. Moletsi Nature Reserve
321. Potlake Nature Reserve
322. Strydom Tunnel Hiking Trail
323. Mapulaneng Nature Trails
324. Thabina Nature Reserve
325. Modjadji Nature Reserve

The Highveld
326. Magaliesberg
327. Rustenburg/Peglerae Trails
328. Moreleta Spruit Nature Trail
329. Union Buildings
330. Pretoria Botanical Garden
331. Wonderboom Nature Reserve
332. Austin Roberts Bird Sanctuary
333. Verwoerdburg Trail
334. Sterkfontein Caves
335. Krugersdorp Game Reserve
336. Witwatersrand Botanic Garden
337. Kloofendal Nature Reserve
338. Witwatersrand Trails System
339. The Wilds
340. Rondebult Bird Sanctuary
341. Suikerbosrand Trails Complex
342. Abe Bailey Nature Reserve
343. Barberspan Nature Reserve

Bophuthatswana
344. Maria Moroka National Park
345. Botsalano Game Reserve
346. Montshiwa Nature Reserve
347. Pilanesberg National Park
348. Borakalalo National Park

Venda
349. Mabuda-Shango Hiking Trail

Zimbabwe
350. Matobo National Park
351. Mushandike Sanctuary
352. Great Zimbabwe Park
353. Lake Kyle Recreation Area
354. Gonarezhou National Park
355. Chirinda Forest Reserve
356. Chimanimani National Park
357. Bunga Forest Botanical Reserve
358. Vumba Botanical Gardens
359. Cecil Kop Nature Reserve
360. M'Tarazi Falls National Park
361. Nyanga National Park
362. Ngezi Recreation Park
363. Sabakwe Recreation Park
364. Lake McIlwaine Recreation Park
365. Ewanrigg Botanical Gardens
366. Chinhoyi Caves National Park
367. Canoeing and Rafting Trails
368. Mana Pools National Park
369. Ruckomechi Camp Safaris
370. Charara Safari Area
371. Mutasadona National Park
372. Chizarira National Park
373. Hwange National Park
374. Matetsi Safari Area
375. Kazuma Pan National Park
376. Victoria Falls/Zambezi N.P.

Botswana
377. Mashatu Game Reserve
378. Mashatu Ivory Trail
379. Fish Eagle Trail
380. Okavango Discovery Trail

Namibia
381. Waterberg Plateau Park
382. The Brandberg
383. Spitzkoppe
384. The Ugab River Hiking Trail
385. Gross-Barmen Hot Springs
386. Tsaobis-Leopard Reserve
387. Daan Viljoen Game Park
388. Namib-Naukluft Desert Park
389. Hardap Dam and Resort
390. Fish River Canyon

Malawi
391. Lengwe National Park
392. Elephant Marsh
393. Thyolo Mountain
394. Mulanje Mountain
395. Majete Game Reserve
396. Shire River Cataracts
397. Chiradzulu Mountain
398. Soche Mountain
399. Zomba Plateau
400. Ndirande Mountain
401. Michiru Mountain Area
402. Liwonde National Park
403. Lake Malawi National Park
404. Dedza Mountain
405. Chongoni Mountain
406. Lilongwe Nature Sanctuary
407. Malawi Cycle Trail
408. Dzalanyama Range
409. Nkhotakota National Park
410. Kasungu National Park
411. Viphya Plateau
412. Vwaza Marsh Game Reserve
413. Nyika National Park
414. Manchewe Falls/Livingstonia

WESTERN CAPE

The diverse terrain commonly referred to as the Western Cape stretches from the Atlantic Ocean in the west, north to Lambert's Bay, and eastwards along the Indian Ocean to the Gouritz River mouth. It includes the great inland ranges of the Cedarberg, Groot-Winterhoek, Hex River Mountains, Franschhoek, Slanghoekberg, Groot Drakenstein Mountains, Du Toit's Berg, Wemmershoekberg, Riviersonderend and the Langeberg.

Rugged sandstone peaks and extensive fynbos-covered ranges cut by deep kloofs harbouring crystal rushing streams, form the interior of this area. The mountains are edged by a narrow coastal belt where cliffs drop into the sea. This coastal berg interface is considered to be one of the most dramatic in the world. Hikers, ramblers and mountaineers need no encouragement to explore the Western Cape's plentiful wilderness areas, hiking trails, nature and forest reserves, and botanical gardens. The main population centre, Cape Town, boasts Table Mountain, the most-climbed massif in the world.

The Western Cape has a Mediterranean climate which means cold, wet winters and dry, windy summers. Beware of the summer south-easter, which often reaches gale force, and can envelop mountains in heavy moist clouds; the 'table cloth' which sometimes covers Table Mountain is a well-known example.

ECOLOGICAL ZONE: FYNBOS

Mountaineering in the fynbos
To describe mountaineering opportunities within a 200-kilometre radius of Cape Town is like counting stars on a crisp, moonless night. Folded and jumbled sandstones and

shales, blanketed with a variety of flowering delights endemic to this tiny region of the earth's surface, make the Western Cape a mountaineer's mecca. There exists a myriad peaks which can be ascended and descended within a day by walking and scrambling, and an endless maze of traverses across ridges, through valleys and over grassy domes – as endless as the explorer with a topographical map and a strong pair of legs can devise.

Today's 'weekend mountaineers' can be a lazy bunch. They prefer to drive right to the foot of their climb or traverse, avoiding all superfluous walking. This is possible in the western Cape's montane fynbos, and undoubtedly contributes to its mountaineering popularity. Bain's Kloof Pass, running 30 kilometres along the Wit River; the Du Toit's Kloof Pass, its more southerly sister pass; Franschhoek Pass, overlooking the Groot Drakenstein Mountains; and Sir Lowry's Pass, continuing eastwards of the N2 and running south of the Cape folded mountains, are the four major access routes to virtually all the best mountaineering areas. For example, the Wit River Valley is a popular access route to the scenic peaks of Groot-Wellington Sneeukop (1 685 m), Slanghoek Peak (1 696 m), Kromrivier Peak (1 457 m), Kromrivier Dome (1 388 m), New Year Peak (1 327 m) and the Witteberg (1 633 m), all of which can be ascended without ropes if you know the easy route. One of the peaks most easily accessible from Cape Town, the Witteberg, is a rock climber's paradise. The south face is a real challenge; however, scramble, jump and worm your way through the west-facing slope's gigantic boulders and your ascent is much eas-

WESTERN CAPE

0 15 30 45 60 75 km

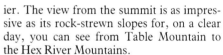

ier. The view from the summit is as impressive as its rock-strewn slopes for, on a clear day, you can see from Table Mountain to the Hex River Mountains.

I have included only the more popular mountaineering areas, not the 'sacred domains' of unusual and less frequented regions. Some areas are best left unpublicized to avoid contributing to the increasing dilemma of man 'loving his mountains to death'. Keen mountaineers will eventually discover new delights for themselves – which is half the challenge of the sport.

Remember that all land is owned by either a private individual, organization or government authority. There are no 'free zones'. Therefore, before you take your first step up the slope, it is your responsibility to obtain the necessary permits from the authority-in-charge or to gain permission from the relevant landowner. Forest guards, honorary nature conservation and forestry officers, and local landowners have the authority to question your right to be on private or government land. Trespassers not only are prosecuted, but make future access for other mountaineers even more difficult.

Mountaineering is a privilege. It is not a right. Treat all areas with the same care and respect you would if they were yours.

Top: Stettynskloof Dam, in the Wemmershoek Mountains.

Above: Camp-site at first light.

Left: Wemmershoek Dam, a major water source for the Cape Peninsula.

1. Ramskop Nature Reserve

CLANWILLIAM

AUTHORITY-IN-CHARGE: Municipality of Clanwilliam, P.O. Box 5, Clanwilliam 8135.
SIZE: 120 hectares; 7,5-hectare wildflower garden.
MAIN ATTRACTIONS: Displays of characteristic plant species, for example the orange Namaqualand daisy; great diversity of plants in this area, which is located on the edge of the coastal fynbos and the succulent Karoo; views of Clanwilliam, Cedarberg peaks, Olifants River and the Pakhuis Pass.
FACILITIES/AMENITIES: Footpaths; seeds and bulbs for sale; adjoins caravan park; roof-top tearoom, open only in spring.
PERTINENT INFORMATION: Flowers are best from June to October; the mass display of thistles and daisies for which the area is renowned is at its best from mid-July to early September.
AVAILABLE LITERATURE: Included in publicity brochures for the town.
CLIMATE: Winter rainfall area.

2. Cedarberg Wilderness Area

CITRUSDAL/CLANWILLIAM

AUTHORITY-IN-CHARGE: Western Cape Forest Region, Forestry Branch, Department of Environment Affairs★.
SIZE: 71 000 hectares.
MAIN ATTRACTIONS: Impressive rock formations; wilderness atmosphere; endemic flora.
FACILITIES/AMENITIES: Algeria camping and caravanning area with modern ablution blocks, located near the forest station; Waenhuis, accommodating 8 people, with shower, toilet and bunkbeds; Uitkyk forest refuge, accommodating 16 people in four rooms, with kitchen, bath, toilet and bunkbeds (youth groups and students receive priority for bookings); patrol shelters within the wilderness area at Sleeppad, Sneeukop, Crystal Pool, Middelberg, Sneeuberg and Boontjieskloof; Ribboksvlei picnic site on the Pakhuis Pass road; Sanddrif camp-site, enquiries to the Nieuwoudt Brothers, Dwarsrivier, P.O. Cedarberg 7341 (also for permits to the Wolfberg Cracks); camping at Driehoek Farm, enquiries to Mr P.L. du Toit, Driehoek, P.O. Citrusdal 7340; Cedarberg Tourist Park with furnished bungalows, enquiries to A.P.C. Nieuwoudt and Son, Kromrivier, P.O. Citrusdal 7340 (brochure

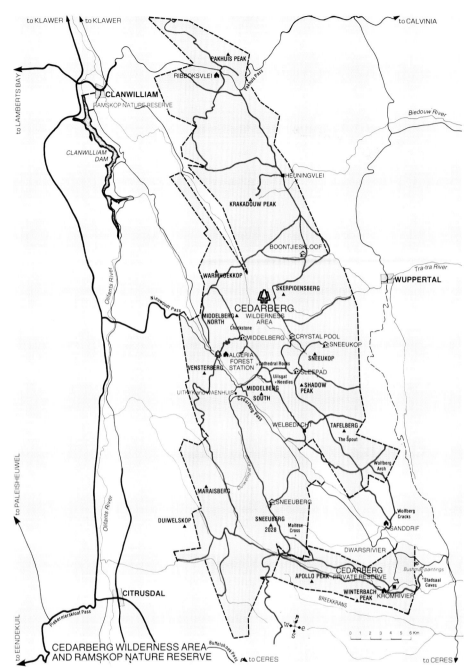

available, shop on premises); extensive network (254 km) of unmarked, well-maintained footpaths; excellent rock climbing.
PERTINENT INFORMATION: Permits necessary, obtainable from The Forester, Cedarberg State Forest, P.O. Citrusdal 7340; tel. (02682) 3440. Book camp-site three months in advance for Easter, September and December school holidays. Entry on foot only. No fires allowed. Officers of the Forestry Branch, on duty, have precedence at patrol shelters. The Mountain Club of South Africa owns a 4 200-hectare reserve named Breekkrans in the southern Cedarberg; access is available to MCSA members and two accompanied guests per member; contact the Cape Town office of the MCSA for further details.

AVAILABLE LITERATURE: *Sederberg Wilderness Area*, comprehensive colour booklet (no maps included), available from the Forestry Branch; *Northern Cedarberg and Southern Cedarberg*, topocadastral maps issued by the Forestry Branch; *Clanwilliam Flowerland and the Cedarberg*, map by Mapcape; *Kromrivier Cedarberg Tourist Park*, map by Mapcape.
CLIMATE: Average annual rainfall: 800-1 000 millimetres, falling mostly in winter. Snow is possible from May to the end of September. September to April is the best hiking season.

My introduction to the Cedarberg Wilderness Area was a punishing seven-day backpacking trip through virtually impenetrable riverine bush in the relatively unexplored

Duiwelsgat Kloof. Spattered with blood from scratched legs and arms, soaking with sweat and from unplanned slips into rock pools, I finally emerged, with tears in my eyes, on to one of the constructed footpaths. But tired as I was, the tears were those of elation from the loveliness and wildness of the 'never-to-be-dared-again' adventure into this challenging kloof.

Not everyone need experience this type of adventure to fall in love with the Cedarberg. It is so diverse in form and structure, so valuable for its plants and animals and so unique in its landscape, that any nature lover, trailist or mountaineer will find its opportunities and challenges difficult to exhaust.

Only 250 kilometres from Cape Town, this mountain complex is managed principally for pure, silt-free water, conservation and extensive recreation. Geological formations can generally be clearly seen in Western Cape mountains, but erosional processes

in the Cedarberg appear to proceed one step further, fashioning a bizarre landscape highlighted by such famous natural rock sculptures as the Maltese Cross, a 20-metre rock pillar graded as an F3 climb; the Wolfberg Cracks, a vertical cleft some 30 metres or more high; the Wolfberg Arch; the Tafelberg and its Spout. Note that the Wolfberg Cracks, Stadsaal Caves and Bushman paintings are on private property and the permission of the owners should be obtained before visiting these places.

The highest peak, Sneeuberg (2 028 m), is one of the few homes of one of the world's rarest plants, *Protea cryophila*, the snow protea. Another unusual species found in the Cedarberg is the Clanwilliam cedar, after which the mountain range is named. This tree was once threatened with extinction from over-exploitation and uncontrolled burning, but today the Clanwilliam cedar is protected in this wilderness area. It is hoped that fewer fires and strict management will foster its growth. Two plants of considerable economic importance – rooibos tea (*Aspalathus linearis*) and round-leaved buchu (*Agathosma betulina*) – are also present.

Animal life is diverse in species but not high in numbers, as a result of their low breeding rate, the reasons for which are not yet clear. Mammals commonly seen include baboon, dassie, grey rhebok and klipspringer. Bird diversity is not great (81 species) but the fynbos specials – sugarbirds, orangebreasted sunbirds, Cape rockjumpers, and others – are present, in addition to the frequently sighted black eagles, rock kestrels and jackal buzzards. Geckos, lizards and agamas are commonly seen on the rocks. Watch out for the berg adder and puff adder, two of the fifteen resident snake species.

The forestry maps are essential: all paths and huts are marked on these and are easy to find. Ideally, wilderness areas are supposed to be devoid of modern human artefacts; however, the simple, rustic huts, providing nothing more than shelter, were left stand-

ing when this area was proclaimed. On those blizzardy, snowy winter nights, you will appreciate why. The only hiking amenity lacking in the Cedarberg is large swimming holes; however, drinking water and 'cooling off' pools are adequate.

Located *in* the winter rainfall area, the mountains receive their precipitation and possible snowfalls mainly between May and September, with north-west winds, but be prepared for rain even in summer. The summers are hot, but cooled by the prevailing south-east to east winds.

Mountaineers and environmentalists almost lost the Cedarberg to the National Parks Board in 1984, when that organization planned to carve a recreational complex out of the wilderness. However, the sincere and dedicated efforts of an outraged public, who preferred to see the Cedarberg and its surrounding private land continue to be one of South Africa's few examples of a pristine, balanced environment, won a tense political battle. The Cedarberg's silence has been left undisturbed . . . at least for the near future.

3. Groot Winterhoek Wilderness Area

PORTERVILLE

AUTHORITY-IN-CHARGE: Western Cape Forest Region, Forestry Branch, Department of Environment Affairs★.
SIZE: 19 468 hectares.
MAIN ATTRACTIONS: Groot Winterhoek Peak (2 078 m); rugged, dramatic mountain terrain; large swimming pools; fynbos vegetation.
FACILITIES/AMENITIES: 90 km of footpaths.
PERTINENT INFORMATION: Permits necessary, obtainable from The Forester, Groot Winterhoek State Forest, P.O. Box 26, Porterville 6810; tel. (02623) 2900. Maximum of 12 people per group; 40 people admitted per day, but only 15 per day to Die Hel.
AVAILABLE LITERATURE: *Groot Winterhoek Wilderness Area*, guide; 'Groot Winterhoek Wilderness Area', in *Forestry News*, March 1986.
CLIMATE: Winter: cold and wet (80 per cent of annual rainfall occurs between April and September); snow possible; nights are cold (0-3 °C) and frost occurs April to November. Summer: dry and cool, but be prepared for rain, mist, cold weather and snow throughout the year.

As a forestry officer in the Western Cape, I spent many weeks exploring the Groot Winterhoek Wilderness Area: the Vier-en-Twintig Riviere; Die Hel; Klein Kliphuisrivier; the grounds surrounding the old farms of Groot Kliphuis, Groot Winterhoek, De

GROOT WINTERHOEK WILDERNESS AREA

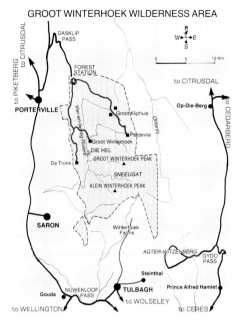

ROCHER PAN NATURE RESERVE

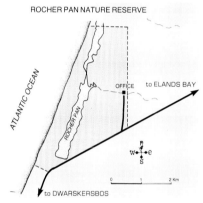

Opposite page, top: Hikers in the Cedarberg Wilderness Area ascending Sneeukop.

Opposite page, bottom: The Middelberg Falls in the Cedarberg.

Below: The rugged beauty of the Groot Winterhoek Wilderness Area.

Below right: Kayaking on Rocher Pan at Velddrif.

Tronk and Perdevlei; the Sneeugat terrain near the Tulbagh Valley; and the Klein and Groot Winterhoek peaks.

Many kilometres of bushwacking through dense kloofs and along old buchu-pickers' paths, scrambling up hills to explore high mountain caves, boulder-hopping through shallow rivers, traversing plateaux of weather-beaten rocks and climbing steep slopes to the summit of the Groot Winterhoek (2 078 m), have left me with deep-seated impressions. This is an extremely rugged region, very hot in summer and cold in winter, lush with montane fynbos flowers, lacking in readily observable wildlife except baboons, klipspringers, snakes, sunbirds and predatory birds, and still satisfyingly wild. I admire the men and women who inhabited the isolated farm complexes still standing today and who managed to eke a living from the infertile sandstone soils.

Many of these old farmhouses are in a state of disrepair and all but De Tronk will be demolished. At present, hikers can use any building for shelter but must not depend on their 'waterproofness' or even their existence. De Tronk, however, has a watchman living on the premises and can be used by small organized groups as a base camp. From De Tronk, you can hike to Die Hel, an amazing place where the Vier-en-Twintig Riviere suddenly enters a gorge and drops as a sheer waterfall into a mysterious, cold, dark basin, surrounded by cliffs.

Access to the Groot Winterhoek Wilderness Area is limited – a factor undoubtedly contributing to its unsullied, wild character. The southern approach, from the head of the Tulbagh Valley by way of a footpath into the 'Sneeugat', necessitates crossing valuable private farmland. This access point is closed to the general public. The other entrance point is through Dasklip Pass (an approximately 45-minute drive from Porterville), where a new forest station has been constructed.

4. Rocher Pan Nature Reserve

VELDDRIF

AUTHORITY-IN-CHARGE: Department of Nature and Environmental Conservation, Cape Provincial Administration.

SIZE: 390 hectares.

MAIN ATTRACTIONS: 150 species of birds, especially waterfowl (Cape shoveler, Cape teal, African shelduck, dabchick); West Coast strandveld vegetation; long, shallow seasonal pan (important breeding and feeding area).

FACILITIES/AMENITIES: Observation towers and bird hides; picnic spots.

PERTINENT INFORMATION: Spring is the best time to visit (birds numbers are high and flowers are in full bloom). Permits are necessary, obtainable from The Reserve Manager, Private Bag, Velddrif 7365.

AVAILABLE LITERATURE: Included in annual reports of the Department of Nature and Environmental Conservation.

CLIMATE: Winter rainfall area.

5. Columbine Nature Reserve

NEAR VREDENBURG

AUTHORITY-IN-CHARGE: Municipality of Vredenburg-Saldanha, Private Bag X12, Vredenburg 7380.

SIZE: 263 hectares.

MAIN ATTRACTIONS: Strandveld vegetation on sandy coastal plains and rocky outcrops.

FACILITIES/AMENITIES: Rock angling; crayfish diving.

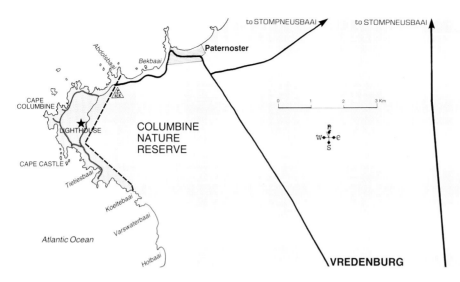

PERTINENT INFORMATION: Located north-west of Vredenburg and north of Saldanha.
AVAILABLE LITERATURE: *The West Coast*, poster-map available from the Municipality of Vredenburg-Saldanha.
CLIMATE: Winter rainfall area.

6. *Langebaan National Park*

SALDANHA

AUTHORITY-IN-CHARGE: National Parks Board.
SIZE: Approximately 6 000 hectares, including the islands and lagoon.
MAIN ATTRACTIONS: Langebaan Lagoon (46 hectares); the islands of Malgas

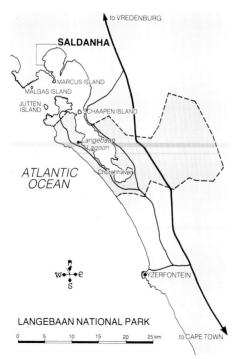

LANGEBAAN NATIONAL PARK

(18 hectares), Jutten (43 hectares), Marcus (17 hectares) and Schaapen (29 hectares); spring wildflowers; world-renowned for its birdlife, especially migrant waders; Pliocene fossils; diversity of coastal habitats; strandveld vegetation.
FACILITIES/AMENITIES: To be developed; motorboating, sailing, waterskiing, rowing, swimming and angling are permitted in specified zones.
PERTINENT INFORMATION: Nature and hiking trails in the area, including a beach walk, are planned. Mediterranean-type climate.
AVAILABLE LITERATURE: *Langebaan National Park*, brochure and map; *South Africa's National Parks*, booklet; *Custos*, October 1985, available from the National Parks Board.
CLIMATE: Average annual rainfall: 250 millimetres, falling mostly in winter. Warm, sunny summers.

7. *Sandveld Trails*

YZERFONTEIN

AUTHORITY-IN-CHARGE: For short trails and bungalows/hut: Blombos Farm, c/o Mrs Wrightman, 14 Higgo Crescent, Higgovale 8001, Cape Town. For longer trail: Western Cape Forest Region, Forestry Branch, Department of Environment Affairs.
LENGTH/DURATION: Trail 1: 16,5 km/ 4-5 hours. Trail 2: 8 km/2-3 hours. Trail 3: 3,5 km/1-2 hours.
MAIN ATTRACTIONS: Nature trails over easy terrain; rich birdlife, buck, small mammals and tortoises; wildflowers in season; coastal scenery and salt pans.
FACILITIES/AMENITIES: Two informal self-contained bungalows for hire near start of the trail, fully equipped, with 6 beds each, kitchen (gas stove, geyser and chest fridge), bathroom and outdoor shower, no cutlery, bedding or electricity; 'Witpan se hut' with

6 beds, braai area, bush shower and water, no accessories; well-marked footpaths.
PERTINENT INFORMATION: Payment for trails includes the use of the trail hut. Permit necessary for Trail 1, obtainable from either the forester at Darling or the Regional Office in Cape Town.
AVAILABLE LITERATURE: *Sandveld Trails (Wandelpaaie): Blombos Bungalows*, pamphlet with map, available from Mrs Wrightman, tel. (021) 24-2755 or Blombos Farm, tel. (02245) 589.
CLIMATE: Winter rainfall area. September and October are best times to walk.

If you are looking for a day's outing that is not as strenuous as most Western Cape trails but every bit as interesting, then explore the Sandveld Trails near Langebaan Lagoon. Definitely the main attractions of these three nature walks are the plethora of wildflowers which bloom in the spring, and the birdlife.

The sandveld, with its associated rich indigenous stunted dune bush (fortunately, few aliens are seen *en route*), large salt pans and coastal environment, ranks as one of the richest bird habitats in the Cape Province. In addition to hundreds of species of birds, duiker, steenbok, grysbok and tortoise (the latter laboriously plodding through the sandy terrain) are commonly spotted.

Many of the footpaths are actually four-wheel drive tracks or fence lines. However, on forestry ground, walkers bushwack up and down short vegetated dunes, following poles in the sand. These dunes are much smaller, and their pole markers much shorter than those on the Alexandria Trail in the Eastern Cape (see page 96). There is also the delightful four-kilometre stretch of 16 mile beach (between Yzerfontein and Rocky Point, Postberg Nature Reserve) where lucky trailists may spot dolphins playing in the Atlantic Ocean. Kelp gulls and oystercatchers are plentiful, as is marine life, although there are no tidal pools.

Because of the soft nature of the terrain, it is best to wear running shoes instead of

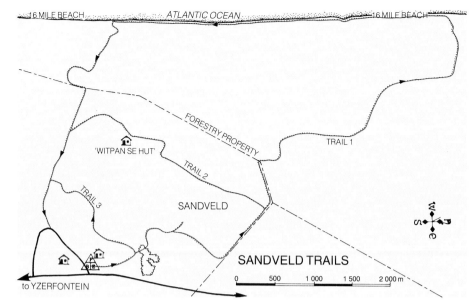

'WITPAN SE HUT'

FORESTRY PROPERTY

TRAIL 1

TRAIL 2

TRAIL 3

SANDVELD

to YZERFONTEIN

16 MILE BEACH — ATLANTIC OCEAN — 16 MILE BEACH

SANDVELD TRAILS

0   500   1 000   1 500   2 000 m

hiking boots. For people who wish to sleep near the bird-rich salt pan, a rustic hut for six, 'Witpan se hut', is available. Water is supplied at the hut and the bungalows, but trailists are advised to carry a water bottle while walking.

Although pleasant all year round, and a good venue when the Cape mountains are covered in mist, the Sandveld Trails excel in spring when the annual wildflowers bloom and the migrant birds return to the west coast to avoid northern winters.

8. *Tinie Versfeld Flora Reserve*

DARLING, see Regional Map page 38

AUTHORITY-IN-CHARGE: National Botanic Gardens.
SIZE: 22 hectares.
MAIN ATTRACTIONS: Sandveld flora such as *Babiana*, *Spiloxene*, *Geissorrhiza* and *Lachenalia*.
FACILITIES/AMENITIES: Network of footpaths only.
PERTINENT INFORMATION: Although this reserve is accessible to the pedestrian public year-round, it is only worth visiting during the spring flower season, when a spectacular display of colour can be seen.
CLIMATE: Winter rainfall area.

Opposite page: Asteraceae.
Right: Oskloof in the Witzenberg, the north-east wall of the Breede River Valley, overlooking Tulbagh. Views of the Witzenberg range are an attraction in the Ceres Mountain Fynbos Reserve.

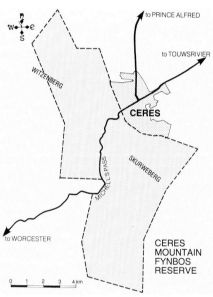

to PRINCE ALFRED

to TOUWSRIVIER

WITZENBERG

CERES

SKURWEBERG

MICHELL'S PASS

to WORCESTER

CERES MOUNTAIN FYNBOS RESERVE

0   1   2   3   4 km

9. *Kalkbaskraal Nature Reserve*

MALMESBURY, See Regional Map page 38

AUTHORITY-IN-CHARGE: Divisional Council of Swartland, Malmesbury.
SIZE: 35 hectares.
MAIN ATTRACTIONS: Swartland flowers.
FACILITIES/AMENITIES: None.
PERTINENT INFORMATION: Visitors can walk anywhere in the reserve.
AVAILABLE LITERATURE: Included in annual reports of the Department of Nature and Environmental Conservation.
CLIMATE: Winter rainfall area.

10. *Ceres Mountain Fynbos Reserve*

CERES

AUTHORITY-IN-CHARGE: Municipality of Ceres, Ceres 6835.
SIZE: 6 800 hectares.
MAIN ATTRACTIONS: Witzenberg and Skurweberg mountain scenery; montane fynbos and marshland; Bushman paintings; 'aridarium' (greenhouse for succulents).
FACILITIES/AMENITIES: Information centre with nature displays; accommodation available at Pine Forest and The Island public resorts (rondavels, bungalows, caravanning, camping and resort facilities).
PERTINENT INFORMATION: For bookings (accommodation): The Manager, Public

Resorts, P.O. Box 44, Ceres 6835. Hiking trails are planned.

AVAILABLE LITERATURE: Included in publicity brochures for the town, available from the Information Bureau, P.O. Box 44, Ceres 6835.

CLIMATE: Average annual rainfall: 1 000 millimetres, falling mostly in winter.

11. Hex River Mountains

NEAR WORCESTER

AUTHORITIES-IN-CHARGE: Private farmers; Western Cape Forest Region, Forestry Branch, Department of Environment Affairs.

MAIN ATTRACTIONS: Most rugged and dramatic of all Western Cape mountains.

FACILITIES/AMENITIES: Shelters for members of the Mountain Club of South Africa only; otherwise none.

PERTINENT INFORMATION: Large parts of this area are privately owned; farmers must be contacted for permission to cross their land. This area is for expert hikers and climbers only; it is best to hike with someone who knows the mountains well. The Hex River Mountains are known as 'waterless' mountains – very little water is available on traverses and peak climbs.

CLIMATE: Winter rainfall area.

Cradled between the road running from Michell's Pass to Worcester and the Hex River lies a complex of the highest and most rugged mountains in the Western Cape. Excluding the Drakensberg, no other South African mountains have been so well described in the journals of the Mountain Club of South Africa.

Only the fittest will fully appreciate the Hex's mass of awe-inspiring peaks and pinnacles, sheer exposures, interlaced ridges, gorges and kloofs, dense bush and high waterfalls. Opportunities for long, strenuous traverses, in addition to 'peak-bagging', are endless. Mountains such as Fonteintjiesberg (1 992 m), Sentinel (1 839 m), the Twins (2 034 m), Buffelshoek Peak (2 063 m), Milner Peak (1 996 m) and Matroosberg (2 250 m), and kloofs such as Groothoek, Waaihoek, Boskloof, Dome Kloof, Moraine Kloof and Kleurkloof, conjure up vivid memories for all serious Cape mountaineers.

Jan du Toit's Kloof, not to be confused with the more southerly Du Toit's Kloof, is one of the Hex's easiest and most popular day kloofing trips. Its entrance lies between Chavonnesberg and Waaihoek Ridge. The huge sandstone structures of Mt. Superior on the left and Fonteintjiesberg on the right provide the runoff which feeds the numerous waterfalls, rock pools and riverine bush of this breathtaking gorge. The variety of scenery while boulder-hopping up the kloof is impressive in both its diversity and massiveness. You need half a day to reach the 'ladder', originally placed in the bed of the kloof by buchu gatherers during World War I to facilitate climbing past an 18-metre waterfall. It has since been replaced by a fixed rope. Any further exploration of Jan du Toit's Kloof should be attempted by expert rock climbers only.

There is very little water for hikers on this range, as most rain runs off the steep ridges, slopes, peaks, rock faces and traverses into kloofs and the valley below. The Hex River Mountains are most popular during the cooler winter months when skiing is possible on the slopes of the Matroosberg.

Bear in mind that although the Hex River Mountains are an important catchment area, much of the land is in private ownership and access permission must be obtained from the farmer whose land you wish to cross. For example, Jan du Toit's Kloof is situated on forestry land, necessitating permits, but access is by way of private land. In the interests of conservation, numbers are restricted. Permits are available from the Kluitjieskraal Forest Station at Wolseley, tel. (023232) 7; in addition, Mr van Zyl of 'Somarso', tel. (0231) 93746, must be phoned for permission to park on and traverse his farm.

12. Karoo National Botanic Garden

WORCESTER

AUTHORITY-IN-CHARGE: National Botanic Gardens.

SIZE: 119 hectares.

MAIN ATTRACTIONS: Special collections of plants from the Karoo and arid areas of South Africa and Namibia; rugged Hex River Mountain scenery.

FACILITIES/AMENITIES: Footpaths; toilet block; carpark.

PERTINENT INFORMATION: Open 08h00-17h00. Entrance is free.

AVAILABLE LITERATURE: *Karoo Botanic*

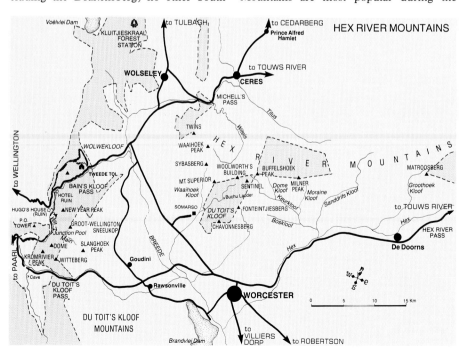

Garden, Worcester, comprehensive brochure and sketch map; trail guide and map; bird list.

CLIMATE: Average annual rainfall: 130-200 milimetres. Great daily and seasonal changes in temperature (4-42 °C).

Unusual in shape and structure, brilliant in colour and full of predator-evading devices, xerophytic (drought-resistant) plants such as aloes, vygies, spekbome, succulents or 'vet-plantjies', spring flowers, buttertrees, lithops and euphorbias attract the attention of even the least botanically minded rambler. The plants are labelled and described in the comprehensive trail guide, and the well-

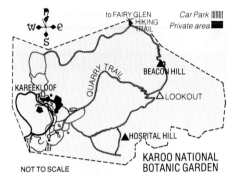

constructed footpaths offer 10-60 minute, easy rambles in the shadow of the formidable Hex River Mountains.

The Breede River Valley Centre of the Wildlife Society is presently involved in a project to extend the Quarry Nature Trail from the Karoo National Botanic Garden into a five-hour walk, crossing private farmland and terminating in the catchment area of the Hartebeest River in the Fairy Glen Kloof. The walk (and its supporting trail brochure) is due for completion in 1987.

13. Boland Hiking Trail (Limietberg Section)

DU TOIT'S KLOOF AND BAIN'S KLOOF

AUTHORITY-IN-CHARGE: Western Cape Forest Region, Forestry Branch, Department of Environment Affairs*.
LENGTH/DURATION: 37 km/2 days, 1 night.
MAIN ATTRACTIONS: Spectacular mountain scenery; floral wealth; red disas; natural swimming pools.
FACILITIES/AMENITIES: One hut with 24 beds in four rooms, situated next to a rock pool.
PERTINENT INFORMATION: Transport requires shuttling of cars (parking provided at both ends). No fires allowed, including at hut; stoves are essential. No lanterns or cooking utensils are provided.
AVAILABLE LITERATURE: *Boland Hiking Trail: Limietberg Guide*, with map, available from the Forestry Branch.
CLIMATE: Winter rainfall area.

The opening of the Limietberg Section of the Boland Hiking Trail links up well-known day walks such as the Bain's Kloof to Du Toit's Kloof Traverse, and passes camping spots such as Junction Pool. Hikers start at Hawequas Forest Station, near the foot of Du Toit's Kloof Pass. They wind their way along the Witteberg range between New Year Peak (1 327 m) and Kromrivier Peak (1 457 m), and descend to Happy Valley, where Wit River Hut is situated (19,5 kilo-

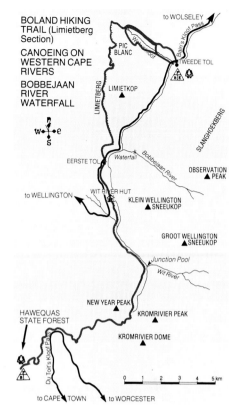

metres). The second day (17,5 kilometres) crosses Bain's Kloof Pass (a national monument, built in 1853), ascends the slopes of the Limietberg (1 174 m), and terminates with the descent into Wolwekloof. The trail ends at the popular Tweede Tol camping and picnic site on Bain's Kloof.

As with most hiking trails in the Western Cape Floral kingdom, stupendous views, proteas and swimming pools rival for attention. Wildlife is difficult to spot; consider yourself fortunate to see klipspringer, grysbok, grey duiker or leopard. Dassies, baboons and red hares are more common, as are rock kestrels, Cape francolins, sunbirds and black eagles.

Although the trail has its ups and downs, it is easily within the capabilities of the average hiker. Transport presents the major problem as cars must be shuttled between Tweede Tol and Hawequas Forest Station.

If you have friends or family picking you up at Tweede Tol, they can arrive early and ramble on its 30 kilometres of circular mountain footpaths, well-endowed with wildflowers, large natural pools and lovely patches of indigenous evergreen forest. The Wolwekloof Circle takes approximately three hours to complete.

Opposite page: On the way to Dome Kloof in the dramatic Hex River Mountains.

Left: Du Toit's Peak (1 995 m), which overlooks Du Toit's Kloof. The Limietberg Section of the Boland Hiking Trail begins near the foot of Du Toit's Kloof Pass.

14. Canoeing

ON WESTERN CAPE RIVERS, see map
page 45

AUTHORITY-IN-CHARGE: Western Cape
Forest Region, Forestry Branch,
Department of Environment Affairs★.
MAIN ATTRACTIONS: Spectacular kloofs,
valleys, gorges and rapids; wildflowers;
mountain scenery and clear waters.
FACILITIES/AMENITIES: None.
PERTINENT INFORMATION: Canoeing rivers:
Hawequas and Kluitjieskraal river systems,
Wit River from Eerste Tol to Tweede Tol
(June, July and August only),
Molenaarsrivier from below Protea Park
Hotel to Leeuklipkop. For experienced
canoeists only. Permits necessary,
obtainable from the Regional Office in Cape
Town.

15. Bobbejaan River
Waterfall

BAIN'S KLOOF, see map page 45

AUTHORITY-IN-CHARGE: Western Cape
Forest Region, Forestry Branch,
Department of Environment Affairs★.
MAIN ATTRACTIONS: Waterfall; spectacular
mountain scenery.
FACILITIES/AMENITIES: None.
PERTINENT INFORMATION: To get to the
waterfall, walk from Eerste Tol village,

cross the Wit River, and go up the west
bank of the Bobbejaan River. Permits
necessary, obtainable from The Foreman-
in-Charge, Tweede Tol, tel. (02324) 607.
Maximum of 24 people (maximum of 12 per
group) admitted per day.
CLIMATE: Winter rainfall area.

16. Elandspad River
Kloofing Trip

DU TOIT'S KLOOF MOUNTAINS

AUTHORITY-IN-CHARGE: Western Cape
Forest Region, Forestry Branch,
Department of Environment Affairs★.
LENGTH/DURATION: 28 km/an ascent takes
8 hours.
MAIN ATTRACTIONS: Spectacular gorge
scenery; steep rock walls; riverine
vegetation; large, deep rock pools.
FACILITIES/AMENITIES: None.
PERTINENT INFORMATION: This trip is for
agile mountaineers, adept at rock
scrambling, boulder-hopping and
swimming in cold water, as there are
compulsory swims of up to 30 metres.
Maximum of 12 people admitted per
weekend. Packs must be waterproofed.
Permits necessary, obtainable from The
Forester, Hawequas State Forest, P.O. Box
74, Huguenot 7645; permission to enter
necessary, obtainable from the owner of
Elandspad, Mr Visser, tel. (0231) 91287.
AVAILABLE LITERATURE: Sections of the
kloof can be researched in *Trout in the
Kloofs*, Cape Piscatorial Society, 1962;

located on Government Printer's
topographic maps '3319 CC Franschhoek'
and '3319 CA Bain's Kloof'.
CLIMATE: Winter rainfall area.

Once your body is in tune for hopping,
splashing, climbing, walking, wading,
swimming, reaching, scrambling, jump-
ing . . . and you let the magnificent gorge
scenery of steep sandstone walls, deep red,
rock-scoured pools, riverine scrub vegetation, rounded boulders, sun-bleached sand
banks and the flittering of small birds pen-
etrate your mind, then you are appreciating
what kloofing is all about. Like the Riviersonderend, the Elandspad River Gorge expedition is difficult to describe to people
who have never kloofed before, and unnecessary to describe to those who have.

There are two ways to explore this gorge.
The general public, after obtaining a permit
from the Forestry Branch, can follow the
river course upstream from under the new
bridge on Du Toit's Kloof Pass or follow the
footpath to Fisherman's Cave, on the eastern bank of the river. The beginning of this
path has been obscured by the tunnel works.
However, you will know when you reach
Fisherman's Cave because it is usually very
polluted by human debris. The second way
to gain access is through private property,
but you must first obtain permission from
the farmer, Mr Visser.

In the lower reaches of the Elandspad, between Fisherman's Cave and 'Gog and Ma-
gog' (outstanding twin rock pinnacles),
there is a tributary on the river's western
bank. The climb up the 'side kloof' is not
easy as it involves complicated scrambling
and slippery rocks. However, within an
hour (or less) you reach a lovely waterfall

and a large, cold, dark pool – well worth the effort.

The same precautions for all kloofing trips with compulsory swims are relevant to Elandspad – don't proceed in cloudy, rainy or threatening weather. The gorge can become a death-trap if the river comes down in flood. Wear jogging shoes or similar footwear and, if sensitive to cold water, a wetsuit jacket or thin woollen jersey. Waterproof your backpack carefully. Frameless packs are recommended. Carry warm clothing and a camp-stove: hot fluids are very welcome when the shivers set in. Lilos and waterproof cameras are optional but popular kloofing gear.

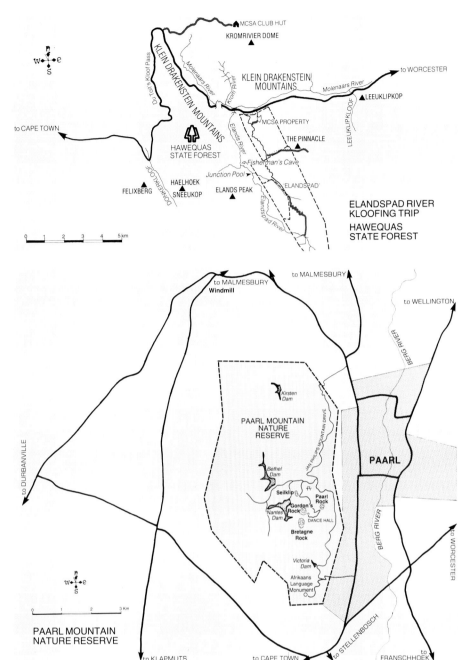

ELANDSPAD RIVER
KLOOFING TRIP
HAWEQUAS
STATE FOREST

17. Hawequas State Forest

DU TOIT'S KLOOF PASS

AUTHORITY-IN-CHARGE: Western Cape Forest Region, Forestry Branch, Department of Environment Affairs.
LENGTH: Krom River Waterfall Walk: 2,5 km each way. Eland River Cave Walk: 3 km each way. Donkerkloof Walk: 3 km each way.
MAIN ATTRACTIONS: Waterfalls; swimming; spectacular mountain scenery; fynbos.
FACILITIES/AMENITIES: None.
PERTINENT INFORMATION: Krom River Waterfall Walk: parking 100 m east of the road tunnel. Eland River Cave Walk: start at the road bridge and walk up the east bank of the river. Donkerkloof Walk: from the freeway, up the kloof to the plateau – *lock your car*. Maximum of 24 people (maximum of 12 per group) admitted per day. Permits necessary, obtainable from The Forester, tel. (02211) 27562.
CLIMATE: Winter rainfall area.

18. Paarl Mountain Nature Reserve

PAARL

AUTHORITY-IN-CHARGE: Municipality of Paarl, P.O. Box 12, Paarl 7622; tel. (02211) 22141.
SIZE: 2 895 hectares.
MAIN ATTRACTIONS: Unique geological formations; three gigantic granite peaks; diversity of flora and birdlife; stone implements from earliest times.
FACILITIES/AMENITIES: Picnic/braai site adjoins the Paarl Wildflower Garden; fishing, with permit.
PERTINENT INFORMATION: Paarl Mountain was declared a national monument in 1963.

PAARL MOUNTAIN
NATURE RESERVE

AVAILABLE LITERATURE: *Paarl Mountain Nature Reserve*, brochure and map.
CLIMATE: Winter rainfall area; precipitation differs substantially in different parts of the reserve.

The Paarl Mountain Nature Reserve includes the famous granite massif whose domed summits are visible from the national highway and from many distant, higher vantage points. These summits, with the exception of Gordon's Rock, are easily reached, and for modest exertion the rambler is rewarded with an incredible 360° panorama of the Cape's popular climbing peaks and mountain ranges, famous vineyards, valleys and towns.

The town of Paarl is named after the Rock (529 m), which glistens like a pearl after

rain. On the summit stands a cannon, one of the many between Signal Hill and Saldanha Bay which were used in the early days of the Cape Colony to notify the Table Bay Fort of ships passing Saldanha. The ascent of Bretagne Rock (649 m) is assisted by chains, but these serve merely as a hand support to prevent your slipping on the granite's smooth surface. Gordon's Rock (653 m) is located just north of Bretagne Rock and here the ascent is very dangerous and should not

Opposite page, top: A refreshing shower under a waterfall in Arch Kloof, off Bain's Kloof.

Opposite page, bottom: Ericas carpet Du Toit's Peak.

be attempted by inexperienced climbers. Large cave-like shelters occur on the lower slopes.

The granite domes also form their own landscape, with kloofs and cracks where indigenous trees and shrubs such as wild olive, bastard saffron, wild currant, proteas, aloes and wildflowers grow in profusion. The birdlife is therefore extremely good. Black eagles and rock pigeons are commonly seen gliding on the thermals, while sunbirds and sugarbirds are found feeding in the Proteaceae. The Cape bunting, Cape widow, Cape robin and redwinged starling, guineafowl, francolin and goose, are just a few of the common species of the region.

Many footpaths and narrow dirt drives (some no longer open to vehicles) criss-cross the reserve, providing hours of rambling. Note, though, that the paths are not marked and some are overgrown with vegetation.

The Paarl Mountain Nature Reserve also offers the approximately 15-hectare Paarl Wildflower Garden and a picnic and braai area. The gardens, open from 09h00 to

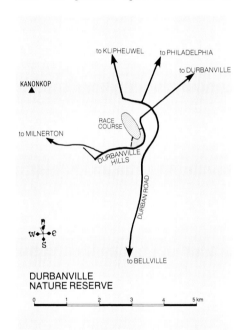

DURBANVILLE
NATURE RESERVE

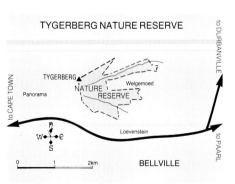

TYGERBERG NATURE RESERVE

BELLVILLE

Opposite page, top: Kirstenbosch's Braille Trail caters for the elderly and the blind.

Opposite page, centre: Dietes grandiflora.

Opposite page, bottom: Protea eximia.

18h00 daily, are well-endowed with contour paths but their trees and shrubs are poorly labelled. Fishing for black bass in the municipal reservoirs, Bethel Dam and Nantes Dam, is allowed with a permit, obtainable at the municipal offices on Bergrivier Boulevard in the town.

To reach Paarl Mountain Nature Reserve, follow the Jan Philips Mountain Road from Paarl's Main Street.

19. Durbanville Nature Reserve

DURBANVILLE

AUTHORITY-IN-CHARGE: Municipality of Durbanville, P.O. Box 100, Durbanville 7550.
SIZE: 6 hectares.
MAIN ATTRACTIONS: Indigenous wildflowers and a large variety of proteas; Cape sugarbirds and malachite sunbirds.
FACILITIES/AMENITIES: Toilets; parking; table and benches; information centre and herbarium; nursery.
PERTINENT INFORMATION: Open daily 08h00-16h30. Entrance is free. Best time to visit is between September and the end of February. No picnicking or camping allowed.
AVAILABLE LITERATURE: *Durbanville Nature Reserve*, brochure, and *Bird Notes*, available from the Municipality of Durbanville.
CLIMATE: Winter rainfall area.

20. Tygerberg Nature Reserve

BELLVILLE

AUTHORITY-IN-CHARGE: Municipality of Bellville, Parks Department, P.O. Box 2, Bellville 7530.
SIZE: 68 hectares.
MAIN ATTRACTIONS: Renosterveld vegetation and its birdlife; views of Table Mountain and surrounding cities and towns.
FACILITIES/AMENITIES: Network of footpaths; picnic sites.
PERTINENT INFORMATION: Entry by permit only (issued free at the gate). Open weekdays 08h30-16h30; Saturdays, Sundays and public holidays 09h00-18h00.
AVAILABLE LITERATURE: *Tygerberg Nature Reserve*, information sheet with map.
CLIMATE: Winter rainfall area.

Tygerberg Nature Reserve protects a portion of the renosterveld on the slopes of the Tygerberg. This veld type, much abused in

the past by farming and urban development, contains trees such as wild peach and wild olive in the kloofs. Their fruits attract a wide variety of birds, including Cape francolins, Cape bulbuls, speckled mousebirds and Cape white-eyes. Larger mammals, except for grysbok, are absent, but the reserve has a wealth of reptiles as well as the Cape grey mongoose, porcupine, mole-rat and gerbil. The name of the reserve stems from the spotted pattern of fallow grass when viewed from afar, and not from the existence of *tygers* (leopards), as is commonly assumed.

The well-constructed foothpaths offer a network of rambles, ranging from five minutes to an hour. To experience the peak flowering season, visit the reserve in spring.

21. Kirstenbosch National Botanic Gardens

CAPE PENINSULA, see map page 50

AUTHORITY-IN-CHARGE: National Botanic Gardens.
SIZE: 528 hectares
MAIN ATTRACTIONS: Attractively laid-out gardens featuring selected plants from all over South Africa in the magnificent Table Mountain setting; forest walks; mountain streams and plentiful birdlife.
FACILITIES/AMENITIES: Conducted and self-guided walks; nature study school run by the Cape Provincial Administration; information kiosk and office; facilities for disabled visitors, including the Braille Trail; labelled display of plants; lecture hall used for exhibits and shows; herbarium and nursery (closed to the general public); restaurant, open every day except Christmas Day; toilets.
PERTINENT INFORMATION: Open 08h00-18h00 April to August, 08h00-19h00 September to March. Tuesdays free from 15h00, admission charged on other days; Botanical Society members are admitted free of charge. Dogs allowed, on leash. No picnicking allowed. Public transport available to and from Mowbray and Claremont bus stations.
AVAILABLE LITERATURE: *Kirstenbosch Botanic Garden*, illustrated booklet; *Kirstenbosch*, comprehensive brochure and map; *Two Easy Routes*, trail guide; bird and tree lists; notes on cultivation of various plant groups; *Teacher's Field Guide to Kirstenbosch*, by Northern Suburbs Primary School Science Teachers' Study Group; *Braille Trail*, brochure.
CLIMATE: Winter rainfall area.

Kirstenbosch, 11 kilometres from Cape Town on the eastern slopes of Table Mountain, is one of the world's great botanic gardens. Apart from its natural assets, it has a centre fully equipped with environmental education materials and teaching aids. This makes Kirstenbosch the ideal place to initiate a study of Cape fynbos. Both the guided tours and self-guided walks with route maps and directional signs are physically easy. The approximately 45-minute Weaver Bird Walk in the central garden and the Silver Tree Stroll are suitably gentle, allowing for wheelchairs, prams and the less agile.

A specially laid-out, half-kilometre trail through the lovely forested slopes on the upper reaches of Kirstenbosch Gardens below Castle Rock, caters for the young, the elderly and the blind. A guide rope provides direction and support, while notices, a brochure and tape describe the flora. The Braille Trail ends at the fragrance garden where aromatic plants such as perlargoniums, mint and buchu growing in raised beds stimulate trailists to use their senses of touch and smell. The smooth, interlocking brick tread, metal guide rails and wooden bridge make the fragrance garden easily accessible to blind and wheelchair trailists. More challenging walks up the slopes of Table Mountain, for example to Skeleton Gorge and Nursery Ravine, also start from Kirstenbosch Gardens.

22. 'City on Foot'

CAPE TOWN, see map page 50

AUTHORITY-IN-CHARGE: Visitors' Information Bureau, Cape Town.
DURATION: 2-hour guided urban trail.
MAIN ATTRACTIONS: Interesting stories and anecdotes; one of the world's most scenic cities.
FACILITIES/AMENITIES: Those present in the city.
PERTINENT INFORMATION: Trail departs from Government Avenue, at the top of Adderley Street, on Saturdays.
CLIMATE: Winter rainfall area.

23. Table Mountain

CAPE TOWN

AUTHORITIES-IN-CHARGE: Western Cape Forest Region, Forestry Branch, Department of Environment Affairs; Public Works Department; Department of Defence; National Botanic Gardens; Municipality of Cape Town; Divisional Council of the Cape; Table Mountain Aerial Cableway Company; other private landowners.
SIZE: 6 500 hectares.
MAIN ATTRACTIONS: Spectacular setting of a mountain amidst a city; easily accessible wild areas; rich flora and indigenous forested kloofs.
FACILITIES/AMENITIES: Some well-constructed footpaths; picnic sites; cableway; three mountain huts: MCSA hut

(members only), Boy Scout hut (members only) and Coloured People's Mountain Club hut (members only).
PERTINENT INFORMATION: The Table Mountain range has been sorely abused. Walkers have contributed to its gradual degradation (soil erosion, flower picking, vandalism such as mutilation of trees, defacing rocks, arson and littering). Restrictions – such as a prohibition on all fires and overnight camping – are strictly enforced. All users of the mountain must obey these rules (see page 11), but, despite the efforts of forestry officials, the destruction continues. Proof of this was the fires that swept across the range in March 1982, devastating 300 hectares, and again in December 1986, destroying 500 hectares.

Table Mountain claims, on average, two lives each year. It is very easy to lose your way and become disorientated in mist. Weather changes rapidly on the mountain and can be very different to that in the city below. No matter how settled the weather appears to be, never venture on to the mountain without a warm jersey, waterproof anorak, map, compass, torch and spare food. Stick to well-defined routes and, until you feel confident about knowing your way, hike with an experienced leader or organized club. New trails are being constructed on the western table, and hikers are expected to use only these marked trails.
AVAILABLE LITERATURE: *Table Mountain Guide: Walks and Easy Climbs on Table Mountain, Devil's Peak and Lion's head*, MCSA; *The Cape Peninsula*, Cape Peninsula Fire Protection Committee; *A Map of the Table Mountain*, Mapcape; *Report on the Future Control and Management of Table Mountain and the Southern Peninsula Mountain Chain*, Dr D. Hey; *A Path and Recreation Report of Table Mountain*, D. McLachlan and E. Moll (see also appendix).

CLIMATE: Winter rainfall area. October to March, gale-force south-east winds can blow and cover the mountain in thick mist. January to February, hottest months. May to August, north-west winds often bring rain. June and July, rains are heaviest. **Note:** the only predictable aspect of Table Mountain's weather is its unpredictability and rapid changes – be prepared!

Table Mountain could well be the world's most-climbed mountain. It includes the Table (the large 1 000-metre plateau at the northern end of the Cape Peninsula), Lion's Head (669 m), Signal Hill (350 m) and Devil's Peak (1 001 m). The highest point is Maclear's Beacon (1 087 m). Southwards, the mountain drops from the upper table to the lower table (800 m). Five reservoirs are located on the lower table, as is Orange Kloof, a large open valley bounded by the Twelve Apostles extending south-west along the Atlantic Coast to Hout Bay Corner. To the east lies Constantia Nek which the Peninsula mountain chain extends to Cape Point (see Cape of Good Hope Nature Reserve, page 53).

One never tires of the contrast between the dramatic beauty of the mountain and the sea and city below. However, this impressive complex of peaks, tables and ridges is, from an ecological point of view, in a sorry state. Table Mountain is home to more than 1 400 plant species (the entire British Isles has 1 750 species); but it is disturbing that ten species on the mountain have become extinct in recent decades and others are endangered. Alien vegetation is posing a serious problem. Soil erosion and rock slides have taken their toll, partially caused by the ever-increasing use by tourists, walkers, hikers, rock climbers and joggers – incredibly, this mountain complex can boast of over 550 walks and climbs. Large mammal life is rare today and one seldom sees buck, but dassies and grey mongoose are common. Baboons have reached the 'cheeky' stage in parts of the mountain and can present a threat to hikers. Birdlife is reasonable – red-winged starlings, rock pigeons, bokmakieries, sunbirds and sugarbirds are usually seen and black eagles occasionally soar overhead.

Only the Drakensberg Mountains can equal the amount of literature available in the form of printed guides and maps. Not wishing to duplicate too much information, therefore, the following sets out only some of the more popular nature rambles and includes a few of my favourites.

The Pipe Track and its radiating ascents

The Pipe Track, originally a service path for maintaining pipes leading from the high reservoirs, is a beautiful stroll in itself, and also serves as an access to the paths leading up to the Twelve Apostles ridge. Leaving Kloof Nek, opposite the toilet facilities, the track passes the red brick water filtration plant, crosses Diepsloot where an alien vegetation removal programme is in progress, and winds around several bends and through thick bush for about seven kilometres before reaching the Woodhead Tunnel (Slangolie Ravine). From here it continues as a contour path.

Metal signs mark the steep Blinkwater and Kasteel's Poort ascents. Diagonal's path is situated between the two – it is a particularly interesting route because it crosses three buttresses (Porcupine, Jubilee and Barrier) and two ravines, ending in an ascent of Barrier Ravine to the Valley of the Red Gods. These footpaths are subjected to tremendous erosional pressures from hikers; the authorities have reconstructed the treads

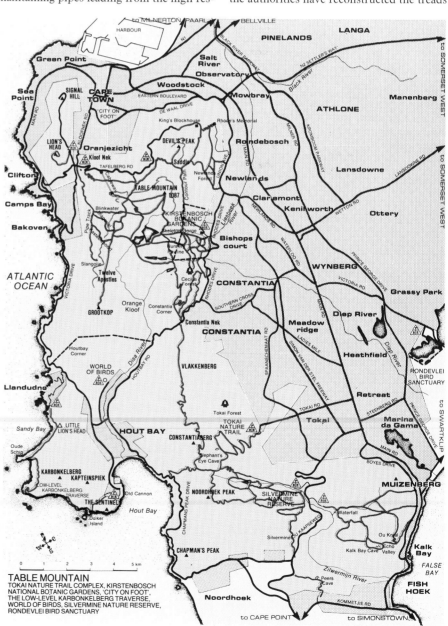

TABLE MOUNTAIN
TOKAI NATURE TRAIL COMPLEX, KIRSTENBOSCH NATIONAL BOTANIC GARDENS, 'CITY ON FOOT', THE LOW-LEVEL KARBONKELBERG TRAVERSE, WORLD OF BIRDS, SILVERMINE NATURE RESERVE, RONDEVLEI BIRD SANCTUARY

with stone steps and zigzags. Please do not take short-cuts and always carry off the mountain all bottles, bags and other litter that you carry up. Other ascents off the Pipe Track exist but are less popular.

Grootkop

The excursion to Grootkop is my favourite – probably because so few people go there and the view from the summit is one of the best on the whole range. Once you reach the lower table, take the well-worn southern path along the ridge of the Twelve Apostles. It leads you to Grootkop. The ascent is more tricky than difficult; although marked with beacons, the path is indistinct and the description on the MCSA's *Table Mountain Guide* is most helpful. Beware of snakes on Grootkop – I've seen my share!

Lion's Head

The 35-60 minute climb to the summit of Lion's Head (669 m) provides the best scenery for the least amount of effort in the whole fynbos region. At dusk, dawn and full moon, the city, sea and Table Mountain are mantled with soft light, a particularly beautiful sight from Lion's Head. The path begins at the dirt road (which has a chain across it) opposite the parking area, off the tarred road running from Kloof Nek to the summit of Signal Hill.

In recent years the rock has worn smooth and the trail is becoming increasingly indistinct because of braiding (many parallel paths developing) and short-cutting. Proceed slowly and cautiously. If you lose the path, remember that it spirals around the peak and then follows, in general, the line of pine trees. Fixed chains make the short vertical stretches easier to scale.

Skeleton Gorge and Nursery Ravine

One of my first tasks when I arrived as a forestry officer in the Western Cape was to help re-route and mark the extremely eroded and loose paths up Skeleton and Nursery gorges. I also added tree identification tags (small yellow squares); sadly, few remain, as most of them have either vanished or been badly damaged.

Skeleton Gorge (Smuts Track) ascends from the 310-metre contour path above Kirstenbosch Gardens (see page 48). There

are only a few short sections which necessitate scrambling. Once on top, near the Hely-Hutchinson Dam, I suggest you follow the southern leg of the intersection to the top of Nursery Ravine. The descent of Nursery brings you back to the 310-metre contour path which can be followed back to Kirstenbosch Gardens.

Both walks are in shady, indigenous forested gorges.

Devil's Peak and Newlands Forest and Ravine

There are many routes up Devil's Peak. I have included only one – the most direct route to the top which is really a long, steep slog. Once you have conquered this route, surveyed the topography, read maps and guide book information, you can explore the other ascents.

About two kilometres beyond the lower cableway station on Tafelberg Road (400 m)

you come to some well-constructed zigzags called the Saddle Path. Follow these – without being tempted to short-cut – and they will eventually level out at 650 metres. Continue on the main track northwards to the Saddle and then ascend the (eroded) firebreak from 700 to 1 000 metres.

On my first ascent of Devil's Peak, I was confronted by a herd of Himalayan tahrs. These alien, agile wild goats grew rapidly in numbers after a pair escaped from the zoo in 1937. Culling was necessary to control the tahrs, which were causing great damage to mountain vegetation, and although now scarce, their numerous paths remain as evidence of their past abundance.

If you do not mind ending up on the other side of the mountain from your car, descend to the Saddle. Then follow the south-easterly path across the Saddle which gradually winds up to the top of Newlands Ravine, an easy, pleasant descent (or ascent). Upon reaching the 360-metre contour path, you can descend into the very popular and beautiful Newlands Forest. If you have time, however, follow the contour path all around the northern side of the mountain, past the

King's Blockhouse, back to the original zigzag path. This round trip requires approximately five hours.

Constantia Corner Path

I like the Constantia Corner Path because of its distant views, its winding and undulating pattern and the rock formations near the top. Starting at Constantia Nek, walk up the east side of the picnic area opposite the restaurant and into Cecilia State Forest. About 30 metres beyond the gate, the path leads off to the left from the dirt road. Although it is obscure in places, you can follow the path up the crest of Constantia Ridge to the service road linking Constantia Nek to Cecilia Plantation and the Woodhead Reservoir.

Cape Peninsula Hiking Trail

A hiking trail from Table Mountain to Cape Point is planned. Details were not available at the time of writing. Contact the Department of Environment Affairs for the latest information.

24. Tokai Nature Trail Complex

TOKAI STATE FOREST

🚶

AUTHORITY-IN-CHARGE: Western Cape Forest Region, Forestry Branch, Department of Environment Affairs.
LENGTH/DURATION: Six routes, approximately 37 km of trails. Interpretive trail: approximately one hour, one way.
MAIN ATTRACTIONS: Tokai arboretum; Elephant's Eye Cave and lookout; montane fynbos and American redwoods; mountain scenery.
FACILITIES/AMENITIES: Interpretive centre; nature trail and paths to Silvermine, Elephant's Eye Cave, Hout Bay, Constantia Peak and Noordhoek Peak; picnic site in pine plantation; horse-riding allowed.
PERTINENT INFORMATION: The nature trail zigzags up the mountain and is steep.
AVAILABLE LITERATURE: *The Tokai Nature Trail*, trail guide, and *Teacher's Guide to Tokai*, booklet, both issued by the Forestry Branch.
CLIMATE: Summer: south-east winds bring cloud. Winter: north-west winds bring rain.

The Tokai Nature Trail starts at the gates of the Tokai arboretum, an interesting collection of early 1900 trial plantings, and then continues into a shady *Pinus radiata* planta-

Opposite page: A rugged piece of natural 'sculpture' guards the route up Pimple Gorge on the 'back table' of Table Mountain.

Above: Relaxing on Lion's Head.

Left: Meerkats, small carnivores of the family Viverridae.

tion with patches of indigenous forest in moist ravines. Emerging from the plantation, on the upper slopes of the Constantiaberg, the trail enters the world of Cape montane fynbos. After visiting Elephant's Eye Cave, reputed to have been the stronghold of a woman-led tribe of Hottentots, you can descend the trail or take any of a number of alternative walks. Allow an hour to reach the top of the trail as the ascent is steep.

The available literature about the trail and the State Forest is particularly valuable, especially the *Teacher's Guide*. Concepts, facts, activities and references concerning forest and fynbos ecology and conservation, as well as forest management, are presented in such a way that teachers, youth leaders and adult educationalists can use Tokai's facilities and amenities as an effective outdoor 'living' classroom. A building furnished with interpretive, forestry-orientated educational displays, has been provided at the trail base. The trail guide leaflet also adds educational value to this popular nature walk in South Africa's oldest forest reserve.

25. The Low-level Karbonkelberg Traverse

(OR HOUT BAY TO SANDY BAY)
CAPE PENINSULA, see map page 50

AUTHORITY-IN-CHARGE: Several landowners; however, public land between high and low water mark.
LENGTH/DURATION: Approximately 12 km/6 hours.
MAIN ATTRACTIONS: Spectacular coastal scenery; seals on Duiker Island; the Sentinel and the Karbonkelberg; bathing beach (Sandy Bay).
PERTINENT INFORMATION: This is not an easy hike. It requires boulder-hopping and, depending on the tides, traversing steep, exposed, rocky slopes. Plan this hike for low spring tides. Water must be carried.
AVAILABLE LITERATURE: See Table Mountain, page 49.
CLIMATE: Winter rainfall area. Prone to sea mists.

Cape Town mountaineers tend to head for the heights of the Cape Peninsula mountain chain; however, there is a challenging hike near sea level, and one which is often below the north-west or south-east clouds and mist. Basically, this 270° hike is a combination of several shorter walks. It is not a hike for beginners; depending on the tides, it can be treacherous and an entire day should be set aside for its leisurely completion.

Start at the Old Cannon, near the café at Hout Bay. The path begins at the rubbish

dump (most unpleasant) and rises as the mountain slope steepens. Follow the edge of vegetation and boulders around the curve of the bay. The track skirts the base of the Sentinel's impressive frontal cliffs, leads the trailist across the tumbled scree, above granite boulders, across a rocky beach, on to a headland, into another scree inlet, down to a stony beach and then passes by a small, rocky promontory and Duiker Island. On this small islet seals are usually seen in the late morning; binoculars are very useful. If you then want to return to Hout Bay, take

the path rising on to the nek between Kapteinspiek and the Sentinel.

To continue on the longer route, follow the path and shoreline around the Karbonkelberg, but take care on the rock faces and watch out for breaking waves. I recommend that someone who knows the route leads at this point. Once you emerge from the coastal bush near Oude Schip, a little peninsula, the track becomes much easier. At irregular intervals, rocks painted with blue stripes mark the path through the bush and across the open slope. The route descends on to the rocks and, following a short boulder-hopping stretch, emerges at Sandy Bay, one of the most beautiful and controversial beaches in the Cape Peninsula. Famed as a nudist haunt, it is now under threat of development and in danger of losing its secluded atmosphere. At Sandy Bay, you can pause for a dip in the sea (be wary of the strong undertow) and then proceed to Llandudno on a braided and well-used path through alien acacia bush.

Once at Llandudno, if you have no transport to return to Hout Bay, consider walking the return route over the sand dunes behind Sandy Bay and between the Karbonkelberg and Little Lion's Head.

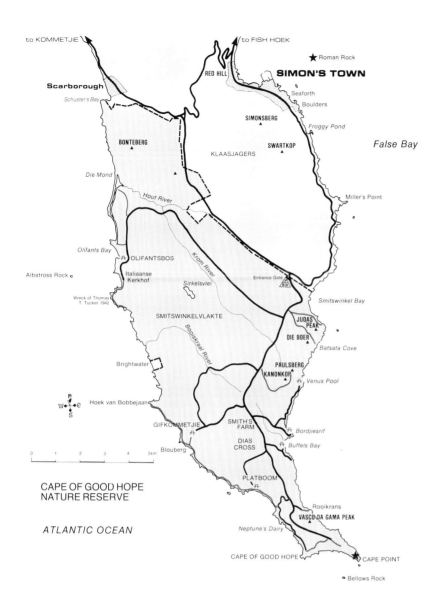

to KOMMETJIE
to FISH HOEK
★ Roman Rock
SIMON'S TOWN
RED HILL
Scarborough
Schuster's Bay
Seaforth
Boulders
SIMONSBERG
Froggy Pond
BONTEBERG
KLAASJAGERS
SWARTKOP
False Bay
Die Mond
Hout River
Miller's Point
Olifants Bay
OLIFANTSBOS
Krom River
Albatross Rock
Italiaanse
Kerkhof
Sirkelsvlei
Entrance Gate
Wreck of Thomas
T. Tucker 1942
Smitswinkel Bay
SMITSWINKELVLAKTE
JUDAS
PEAK
DIE BOER
Booiskraal River
Batsata Cove
Brightwater
PAULSBERG
KANONKOP
Venus Pool
w•e
Hoek van Bobbejaan
GIFKOMMETJIE
SMITH'S
FARM
Bordjiesrif
0 1 2 3 4 5km
Blouberg
DIAS
CROSS
Buffels Bay
PLATBOOM

**CAPE OF GOOD HOPE
NATURE RESERVE**

Rooikrans
VASCO DA GAMA PEAK
ATLANTIC OCEAN
Neptune's Dairy
CAPE OF GOOD HOPE
★ CAPE POINT
Bellows Rock

26. *Cape of Good Hope Nature Reserve*

CAPE PENINSULA

AUTHORITY-IN-CHARGE: Divisional Council of the Cape.
SIZE: 7 765 hectares.
MAIN ATTRACTIONS: Cape Point and Cape of Good Hope; coastal scenery; rare fynbos vegetation; game-viewing; tidal pools.
FACILITIES/AMENITIES: Walking, fishing, skin-diving and snorkelling are allowed in most sections of the reserve; braai sites; boat-launching ramp; refreshment kiosk and curio shop; restaurant; bus service from the carpark to the look-out point; maps, firewood and dog kennels available at entrance gate.
PERTINENT INFORMATION: The west coast of the reserve is a marine reserve; the catching of any fish or marine animals

between Schuster's Bay, Scarborough and Cape Point is prohibited, with the exception of the daily quota of five crayfish per person between Hoek van Bobbejaan and Cape Point; the eastern coastline of the reserve is open for rock angling. An entrance fee to the reserve is charged.
AVAILABLE LITERATURE: *Cape of Good Hope Nature Reserve*, brochure with sketch map, available at the entrance gate; *Cape Peninsula*, detailed map by Mapcape; *Cape Point*, Odden and Lee.
CLIMATE: Winter rainfall area. Strong winds and summer mists.

Although few specific trails have been constructed in the Cape of Good Hope Nature Reserve, an unlimited potential for day walks exists. I recommend obtaining the *Cape Peninsula* map by Mapcape or the 1:50 000 Government Printer's topographic map, '3318 CD Cape Town', and using your initiative to explore.

Suggested routes include a stiff climb up Paulsberg (366 m) via Kanonkop, for a mag-

nificent panoramic view of the Cape Peninsula, and a half-day, round-trip, game-viewing walk across the veld to Sirkelsvlei, a freshwater, spring-fed lake. A surprising number of animals such as baboon, bontebok, zebra, springbok, grey rhebok, eland, Cape grysbok, steenbok and grey mongoose, and over 150 species of birds, including the black oystercatcher, black eagle and ostrich, are seen by ramblers, but seldom by motorists.

When the Cape Peninsula Hiking Trail is built, from Table Mountain to Cape Point, the final stage of the trail will traverse this reserve.

Opposite page, top: Elephant's Eye Cave in the Tokai State Forest.
Opposite page, centre: African Black Oystercatcher.
Opposite page, bottom: The Cape Peninsula from Paulsberg.
Above: The blister-bush, Peucedanum galbanum.
Left: Aristea sp.

through indigenous forest is to the Kalk Bay Mountains via a detour to Ou Kraal and Echo Valley.

The reserve can be reached on foot by ascending Elephant's Eye Nature Trail (Tokai Nature Trail) in Tokai State Forest (see page 51), or by car via Ou Kaapseweg.

27. *World of Birds*

HOUT BAY, see map page 50

AUTHORITY-IN-CHARGE: Walter Mangold, Valley Road, Hout Bay 7800.
SIZE: 3,2 hectares.
MAIN ATTRACTIONS: Walk-through aviaries in a pleasant setting.
FACILITIES/AMENITIES: Labelled bird displays; kiosk, toilets and benches; tearoom and educational programmes planned.
PERTINENT INFORMATION: Open daily 09h00-18h00. An entrance fee is charged.
AVAILABLE LITERATURE: *World of Birds Newsletter and Guide.*
CLIMATE: Winter rainfall area.

Although the inclusion of the 'World of Birds' does stretch the trails concept somewhat, this privately owned and run wild bird sanctuary has attracted so much attention in the Cape that it is well worth mentioning. Located in the fynbos-blanketed Hout Bay Valley in the Cape Peninsula, the World of Birds is a haven for injured, sick or young deserted birds, as well as small mammals such as dassies, bushbabies, meerkats and monkeys. Tortoises are also present. The variety of birds to be observed while walking within and among the large aviaries includes ducks and geese, ostriches, blue cranes,

Top: Rondevlei attracts more than 200 species of resident and migrant birds, including flamingos, herons, swallows, martins and pelicans (pictured here).

Opposite page, top: The Simonsberg, near Stellenbosch, a well-known and beautiful landmark range which stands isolated from the cluster of south-western Cape folded mountains.

Opposite page, bottom: The view from a nek in the Simonsberg.

lovebirds, owls, egrets, parrots, vultures and a number of raptors.

Besides serving the important function of caring for and feeding disabled animals, this sanctuary has developed into a valuable education centre. It is an area where any person, regardless of fitness level, can observe, photograph and learn about common southern African species. Money collected from entrance fees and newsletters is used for maintenance and to buy animal food.

28. *Silvermine Nature Reserve*

CAPE PENINSULA, see map page 50

AUTHORITY-IN-CHARGE: City of Cape Town.
SIZE: 2 151 hectares.
MAIN ATTRACTIONS: Cape Peninsula mountain scenery; caves; indigenous forest and montane fynbos.
FACILITIES/AMENITIES: Nature walks; picnic sites, water and litter bins.
AVAILABLE LITERATURE: *Silvermine Nature Reserve*, comprehensive brochure and map.
CLIMATE: Winter rainfall area. Strong winds.

The Silvermine Nature Reserve forms part of the Cape Peninsula mountain chain and offers numerous easy to moderate walks which take from half an hour to half a day. In addition, there are twelve caves in the reserve, but these should be visited only if you are equipped with a strong torch and, preferably, accompanied by a member of the Spelaeological Association.

Seven walking routes are described in detail in the brochure. The most popular, however, is a seven-kilometre circular route from the reservoir near the parking area to Noordhoek Peak and back. Another interesting walk with excellent views and

29. *Rondevlei Bird Sanctuary*

CAPE PENINSULA, see map page 50

AUTHORITY-IN-CHARGE: Divisional Council of the Cape.
SIZE: 137 hectares.
MAIN ATTRACTIONS: One of the finest bird habitats in the Western Cape.
FACILITIES/AMENITIES: Nature walks; bird hides and observation towers; landscaped artificial pond with tame waterfowl; Leonard Gill Memorial nature museum featuring birdlife, mammals, amphibians and reptiles of Rondevlei.
PERTINENT INFORMATION: Open daily 08h00-17h00. An entrance fee is charged. To get to the sanctuary, take the M5 motorway to Plumstead, turn off, and follow the signs to Zeekoeivlei and Rondevlei.
AVAILABLE LITERATURE: *Rondevlei Bird Sanctuary*, information booklet and brochure, and *Rondevlei Bird Sanctuary*, annual report including species list, both issued by the Divisional Council of the Cape.
CLIMATE: Average annual rainfall: 670 millimetres, falling mostly in winter. Often very windy.

Rondevlei Bird Sanctuary is one of the best bird habitats in the Western Cape. With level walks along the banks of the vlei, this reserve offers a serene atmosphere in which to appreciate the more than 200 species of resident and migrant birds such as pelicans, flamingos, herons, ducks, geese, swallows, martins and swifts. Many of these birds also move to and from the nearby sewage ponds, another popular bird-watching site in the Cape Peninsula. Blackheaded and grey herons, darters and reed cormorants, and even little bitterns, rare in this area, are just a few of the approximately 50 nesting species. The clearance of alien vegetation is greatly increasing the likelihood of also seeing the many bush-dwelling species.

Used as a study area by students at nearby universities, Rondevlei's natural wealth has contributed to many scientific publications on ornithology. The resident mammals (grysbok, steenbok, genet cat, mongoose and porcupine) are seldom sighted. Over the years the vlei has become overgrown with vlei grass and bulrush and, in an attempt to keep this vegetation at bay, hippopotamus were introduced to the area. These huge

herbivores were last known in the Peninsula in 1772 and their return has undoubtedly provided an added attraction at Rondevlei.

Unfortunately the reserve is beset with various problems, such as the pressure of the high-density Cape Flats housing development which surrounds the area, making further expansion difficult, and the inaccessibility of the sanctuary by means of public transport. But despite these problems, a bird walk at Rondevlei is certainly a rewarding experience; your bird identification field guide such as *Roberts'* and binoculars are a must! Although the length of the walk is only about two kilometres, a keen 'birder' could easily spend a very enjoyable and rewarding 3-4 hours here.

30. The Vineyard Trail

STELLENBOSCH

🚶

AUTHORITY-IN-CHARGE: Stellenbosch Divisional Council.
LENGTH: 24 km (shorter variations of 15 km or 17 km possible).
MAIN ATTRACTIONS: Vineyards; rolling hills; coastal renosterveld; old tin mine; views of the Cape.
FACILITIES/AMENITIES: Parking only.
PERTINENT INFORMATION: Trains can be used to return from Kuils River to Stellenbosch; check the train schedule

before you begin the trail so you can return easily to Stellenbosch. The trail is open on Wednesdays and Saturdays only, and is closed during the grape harvesting season. Permits necessary, obtainable from the Stellenbosch Publicity Association, 30 Plein Street, Stellenbosch 7600. Carry drinking water.
AVAILABLE LITERATURE: *The Vineyard Trail*, brochure and map issued by the Stellenbosch Publicity Association.
CLIMATE: Winter rainfall area.

The Vineyard Trail, a full day's ramble, is unusual in that it follows a route almost entirely through privately owned wine estates. It starts at the Oude Libertas Centre near

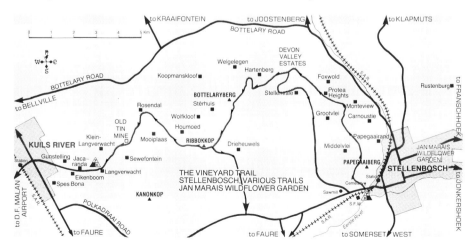

55

the cemetery in which historical figures, such as Dr D.F. Malan, a former Prime Minister of South Africa, have been laid to rest. The trail meanders through farm vineyards, cultivated land, plantations, along gravel tracks and over large hills, until it reaches a minor tarred road leading into Kuils River, from where you can catch a train back to Stellenbosch.

One of the indigenous floral features of the trail is the coastal renosterveld on Ribbokkop, near the 14-kilometre mark. Only four per cent of the original area of this veld type remains, due to urbanization, grazing, exotic plant invasion, and the cultivation of red grapes which favour the same soil type. Bottelaryberg (476 metres) is worth climbing as it is the highest point on the trail and the 360° view of the Cape Peninsula and the inland mountains is superb.

31. Stellenbosch, various trails

STELLENBOSCH, see map page 55

AUTHORITY-IN-CHARGE: Municipality of Stellenbosch, P.O. Box 17, Stellenbosch 7600.
LENGTH/DURATION: Jan Marais Wildflower Garden: variable. Eerste River Trail: 4 km. Stellenbosch Mountain Trail: 6 km/1,5 hours.
MAIN ATTRACTIONS: Historic city set in attractive mountain scenery.

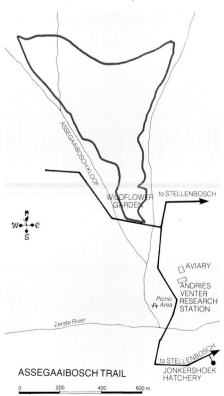

ASSEGAAIBOSCH TRAIL

FACILITIES/AMENITIES: Those present in the city.
PERTINENT INFORMATION: Jan Marais Wildflower Garden: strolls on level ground. Stellenbosch Mountain Trail: northern slopes. Eerste River Trail: starts near Volkskombuis Restaurant at the bridge. Publicity Association's Walking Tour: emphasis on historical buildings.
AVAILABLE LITERATURE: Contact the Stellenbosch Publicity Association, 30 Plein Street, Stellenbosch 7600.
CLIMATE: Winter rainfall area.

32. Jan Marais Wildflower Garden

STELLENBOSCH, see map page 55

AUTHORITY-IN-CHARGE: Municipality of Stellenbosch, P.O. Box 17, Stellenbosch 7600.
SIZE: 23 hectares.
MAIN ATTRACTIONS: Over 1 000 fynbos species.
FACILITIES/AMENITIES: Footpaths; benches; toilets.
PERTINENT INFORMATION: Permits necessary, valid for one year. Open daily 07h30-18h00 (April to September), 07h30-19h30 (October to March).
AVAILABLE LITERATURE: Contact the Stellenbosch Publicity Association, 30 Plein Street, Stellenbosch 7600.
CLIMATE: Winter rainfall area.

33. Assegaaibosch Trail

ASSEGAAIBOSCH NATURE RESERVE, JONKERSHOEK

AUTHORITY-IN-CHARGE: Department of Nature and Environmental Conservation, Cape Provincial Administration.
SIZE: 160 hectares.
LENGTH: 2-km nature trail.
MAIN ATTRACTIONS: Wildflower garden; spectacular mountain scenery.
FACILITIES/AMENITIES: Footpaths on northern slopes of Stellenboschberg; day

Top: The view on the ascent of the Jonkershoek Twins. Many of the footpaths running through the Jonkershoek State Forest provide mountaineers with access to this and other peaks.
Opposite page: On the Helderberg, with the Hottentots Holland range in the background.

picnic facilities; aquarium displays.
PERTINENT INFORMATION: The reserve breeds indigenous waterfowl, and cultivates rare and endangered proteas, heaths and other fynbos species. Permits to enter the reserve and walk the trail necessary, obtainable during office hours at the Jonkershoek Hatchery.
AVAILABLE LITERATURE: *Cape Conservation Series No. 4: Some Plants of the Assegaaibosch Nature Reserve*, booklet; included in annual reports of the Department of Nature and Environmental Conservation.
CLIMATE: Winter rainfall area.

34. Jonkershoek State Forest

NEAR STELLENBOSCH

AUTHORITY-IN-CHARGE: Western Cape Forest Region, Forestry Branch, Department of Environment Affairs.
SIZE: 10 930 hectares, of which 730 hectares are under pine.
MAIN ATTRACTIONS: Mountain scenery and wooded ravines; indigenous montane fynbos.
FACILITIES/AMENITIES: Numerous footpaths; horse-riding is allowed; mountaineering; picnic sites; angling, with permit (obtainable from the Forestry Branch); circular drive.
PERTINENT INFORMATION: Day use only. Permits necessary, obtainable at the gate. Open 07h30-17h00 weekends and public holidays, other opening times available from the Regional Office in Cape Town; closed during fire danger season (October to

April). Hydrological research centre. Lower section of the valley is dammed.

AVAILABLE LITERATURE: Pamphlet and sketch map issued by the Forestry Branch, available from the Regional Office in Cape Town.

CLIMATE: Winter rainfall area. Summer: showers possible. Winter: snow possible. Dwarsberg holds the record for the highest rainfall in South Africa (3 300 millimetres in one year).

Jonkershoek State Forest is set in one of the most beautiful valleys in southern Africa. A number of footpaths meander through the diverse and attractive montane fynbos, as well as through stands of pine plantation. The reserve thus offers a variety of day hikes of which the Panorama Trail (27 kilometres) is the best known. Many of these footpaths provide mountaineers with access to the Jonkershoek Twins (1 504 m), First, Second and Third Ridge peaks (1 517 m,

1 515 m and 1 516 m respectively), Banghoek Peak (1 526 m), Haelkop (1 384 m), and other summits. The footpaths vary in difficulty with most being easy to follow, but the peaks should be ascended only by mountaineers guided by a competent leader.

A tributary of the Jonkershoek River in Swartboskloof flows into Jonkershoek, and the footpath following the river's course forms one of the legs of the Hottentots Holland section of the Boland Trail (see page 58).

Water is plentiful on most trails and the kloofs are cool and shady; some have spectacular waterfalls, abundant birdlife and large specimens of indigenous trees such as Breede River yellowwood, red alder, Cape beech, ironwood and wild olive.

Tadpoles of the ghost frog, *Heleophryne purcelli*, are found in all the mountain streams and can be identified by their relatively large, pale bodies, and flat heads with sucker-like undersides. The sucker

helps them cling to underwater vegetation and rocks, thereby aiding survival in fast-flowing waters. Large mammals present in the valley include baboon, klipspringer, grey rhebok, grysbok and the introduced eland.

A world-renowned, long-term catchment research programme, emphasizing the influence of plant cover on water supplies and on the ecology, is in progress at Jonkershoek. The reserve is also concerned with the conservation of montane fynbos. Be particularly careful not to pollute.

35. *Helderberg Nature Reserve*

SOMERSET WEST

AUTHORITY-IN-CHARGE: Municipality of Somerset West, P.O. Box 19, Somerset West 7130.

SIZE: 385 hectares.

MAIN ATTRACTIONS: Spectacular views; reintroduced large mammals and endemic birdlife; gardens and natural fynbos.

FACILITIES/AMENITIES: Circular nature walks; visitor's centre; braai area; tea kiosk, open at weekends and on public holidays.

PERTINENT INFORMATION: Day-use area only. Entrance is free for residents of Somerset West; non-residents are charged a fee. Biological control zone for hakea.

AVAILABLE LITERATURE: *Welcome to Helderberg Nature Reserve*, brochure and map.

CLIMATE: Winter rainfall area.

Nature walks at Helderberg offer mountain views, glimpses of wildlife such as springbok, bontebok, steenbok, grysbok and duiker, and a rich endemic birdlife whose existence depends upon the lush, flowering fynbos. The circular walks, located on the lower reaches of the mountain, are colour-coded. The longest is 8,2 kilometres and traverses half the length of the Helderberg up to Disa Gorge, famous for its disa orchids which bloom from December to February. A more exacting walk, along the upper region of the mountain, provides complete ac-

JONKERSHOEK STATE FOREST
ASSEGAAIBOSCH TRAIL
STELLENBOSCH, VARIOUS TRAILS

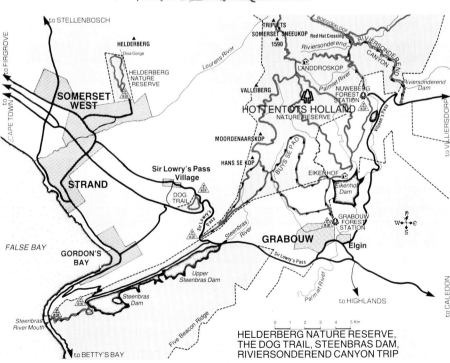

HELDERBERG NATURE RESERVE,
THE DOG TRAIL, STEENBRAS DAM,
RIVIERSONDEREND CANYON TRIP

cess to Disa Gorge. A day walk, below the krantzes of the mountain, has recently been constructed by the Forestry Branch. Mountaineers can also ascend the Helderberg Peak by following Disa Gorge, or via Porcupine Ridge, which avoids all the difficult parts of Disa Gorge. The view from the summit is a sensational 360° sweep, taking in the Cape Peninsula, its bays, the Hottentots Holland Mountains and other western Cape ranges.

Helderberg Nature Reserve is extremely popular, especially among the local residents of Somerset West. Being a fire problem area, visitors are requested not to smoke and to be careful with camp-stoves and cooking fires. Hakea, one of the serious invader plants in the fynbos, is prevalent on the reserve's higher slopes. The winged seeds are released from their cones after a fire, so uncontrolled burns spread hakea plants.

Helderberg Nature Reserve has been chosen by the Department of Agricultural Technical Services as one of the experimental zones for testing the biological control of hakea. In this experiment, hakea seed-eating beetles have been introduced into young stands in the hope that they can contain the spread of this noxious weed.

36. The Dog Trail

SIR LOWRY'S PASS, see also map page 57

AUTHORITY-IN-CHARGE: Western Cape Forest Region, Forestry Branch, Department of Environment Affairs.
SIZE: 85 hectares.
LENGTH: 10 km.
MAIN ATTRACTIONS: Dogs are allowed, and encouraged.
FACILITIES/AMENITIES: Marked footpaths only.
PERTINENT INFORMATION: No permits necessary.
AVAILABLE LITERATURE: Located on *Boland Hiking Trail, Hottentots Holland Section*, map by Peter Slingsby, Mapcape.
CLIMATE: Winter rainfall area.

Let your dog take you for a walk on the Dog Trail. Because so many parks, gardens and nature trails are prohibited to our canine companions, it is refreshing to see a trail designed specifically for dogs. Positioned at the junction of the railway line and Sir Lowry's Pass Village Road, off Sir Lowry's Pass, near Somerset West, the Dog Trail is constructed on 85 hectares of flat terrain offering excellent views of the Helderberg, the Hottentots Holland Mountains, False Bay, Table Mountain and the Peninsula. The trail receives traffic noise from the national highway but the dogs don't seem to mind. The tread is sandy and the 10-kilometre route is a maze of 'paw-paths' which will oc-

cupy dogs for hours; it is also an ideal rambling area for the very young as well as the elderly, and will probably prove popular with joggers, too. No permits are needed; enquiries should be directed to the Forester at Grabouw State Forest, P.O. Box 41, Grabouw 7160; tel. (0240) 2606.

37. Boland Hiking Trail (Hottentots Holland Section)

AND ASSOCIATED WALKS
SIR LOWRY'S PASS/FRANSCHHOEK AND GRABOUW

AUTHORITY-IN-CHARGE: Western Cape Forest Region, Forestry Branch, Department of Environment Affairs*.
LENGTH/DURATION: 55 km/2,5 days; many shorter variations possible.
MAIN ATTRACTIONS: Mountain scenery; wildflowers; natural pools for swimming.
FACILITIES/AMENITIES: Five huts, with bunks and mattresses, each accommodating 30 people per night; safe parking at Nuweberg, Grabouw and Jonkershoek state

forests; toilets and ablution facilities at Nuweberg State Forest.
PERTINENT INFORMATION: Parking is not recommended on Sir Lowry's Pass as there is no supervision and cars have been broken into. The Jonkershoek section of the trail is closed until September 1989. Boegoekloof walks are closed from May to October.
AVAILABLE LITERATURE: *The Boland Hiking Trail (Hottentots Holland Section)*, comprehensive brochure and map; *The Hottentots-Holland Nature Reserve*, pamphlet 316, Fred Kruger, December 1983.
CLIMATE: Winter rainfall area. Warning: the

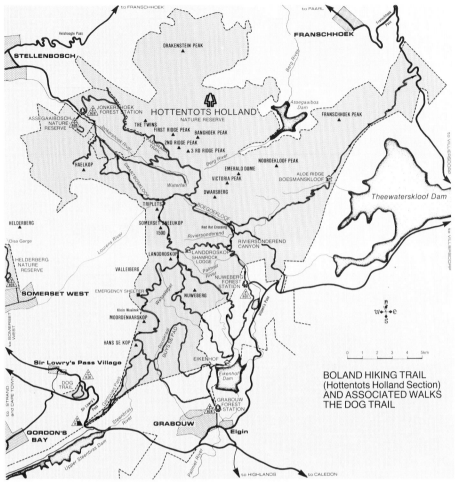

BOLAND HIKING TRAIL
(Hottentots Holland Section)
AND ASSOCIATED WALKS
THE DOG TRAIL

weather on the Hottentots Holland range can be extremely inclement, with thick mists and clouds often blanketing the mountains in both summer and winter. Always be prepared for sudden changes to cold, wet and windy weather conditions; this trail has already claimed several lives through hypothermia. The forester can close the trail at his discretion.

Extending from Sir Lowry's Pass to the Franschhoek Pass, the Hottentots Holland Hiking Trail was the fifth major completed section of the National Hiking Way System. Hikers wind their way through more than 55 kilometres across the beautiful wildflower displays of the Cape fynbos and through kloofs with crystal-clear streams.

Five huts in three locations have been erected. Landdroskop Hut and Shamrock Lodge are at the 23-kilometre mark from Sir Lowry's Pass. They can also be reached via a 19-kilometre footpath from Grabouw State Forest. Eikenhof Hut is situated at the five-kilometre mark from the Grabouw State Forest.

After spending the night at the Landdroskop-Shamrock site (the huts are on the lower slopes of the 1 590-metre Sneeukop), the hiker has the choice of:
1. Walking north around the Somerset-Sneeukop and the Triplets and then descending Swartboskloof into the Jonkershoek State Forest via the former Swartboskloof Nature Reserve which is now included in the larger Hottentots Holland Nature Reserve. The Jonkershoek descent is closed during the fire season (approximately October to the end of March); hikers can then

skirt the Triplets and descend Boegoekloof back to Landdroskop and Shamrock Lodge huts;
2. Returning to Grabouw by way of a 17-kilometre footpath (passing Eikenhof Hut *en route*); or
3. Continuing along the main trail route to Boesmanskloof, where two hiking huts (Boesmankloof and Aloe Ridge) exist, *en route* traversing beautiful rock pools, much appreciated during the hot summer months. Near the second set of huts hikers will discover a long kloof pool – welcome and refreshing after the 17-kilometre traverse. Do not use soap or shampoo to wash in the pool, as detergents destroy the abundant, tiny animal life and lush plant growth in and around these mountain waters.

The final stretch of the Hottentots Holland trail meanders along the shores of the Theewaterskloof Dam and then steeply ascends the slopes of Franschhoek Peak; sufficient height is gained for a beautiful view of Franschhoek and its surrounding farmlands. The trail ends at Jan Joubertsgat Bridge, where parking is provided. The old exit, at the top of the pass, is closed.

Other trail variations and day walks are possible, for example the Rooskraal day walk (15 kilometres), which starts at Sir Lowry's Pass and extends to Rooskraal, passing the historic Gantouw Wagon Tracks and Signal Cannon. The Buys se Pad 20-kilometre circular route starts from the Grabouw forestry office in Worcester Street, Grabouw, and proceeds through the plantation around Buys se Pad, past Rooskraal, and back to the office.

For other variations, consult your Hiking Way map carefully.

As a 'safety precaution' for hikers, an emergency shelter (no amenities) was constructed midway between Sir Lowry's Pass and Landdroskop Hut. Log bridges and stone steps were built to span potential flooded river crossing. Forest guards patrol the reserve, checking that each hiker has a permit for the trail.

The many people who venture on to the Hottentots Holland trail do so with varying motives. Some enjoy its physical challenge.

Others appreciate the opportunity to walk in a botanic and wildlife reserve: enthusiasts will see hundreds of wildflowers, including many showy proteas – a small sample of which have been photographed for the display at Landdroskop Hut. Wildlife lovers may see klipspringer and rhebok, dassie, the ground woodpecker, Cape sugarbird, sunbird, jackal buzzard and possibly even a leopard or puff adder.

Views into the indigenous forest-clad kloofs (such as Wesselsgat) and the views of the coast (such as False Bay from Klein Waainek) are superb.

Being only an hour and a half's drive from Cape Town also contributes to the trail's popularity, so if you seek solitude, avoid this trail over holiday periods and weekends.

38. Steenbras Dam

GORDON'S BAY, see map page 57

AUTHORITY-IN-CHARGE: City of Cape Town.
LENGTH: Nature walks of variable lengths.
MAIN ATTRACTIONS: Beautiful mountain setting; on the walk between the Steenbras River mouth and the dam are some of the largest and most beautiful pools in the area.
FACILITIES/AMENITIES: Gardens; picnic site; sandstone footpaths.
PERTINENT INFORMATION: Permits necessary, obtainable from the Parks and Forest Department, City Engineer's Department, Civic Centre, Hertzog Boulevard, Cape Town 8001.
CLIMATE: Winter rainfall area.

39. Harold Porter National Botanic Gardens

BETTY'S BAY

AUTHORITY-IN-CHARGE: National Botanic Gardens.
SIZE: 188 hectares.
LENGTH: Rod Smitheman Trail: 3 km.
MAIN ATTRACTIONS: Fynbos reserve preserving rare species; mountain and coastal scenery.
FACILITIES/AMENITIES: Rod Smitheman self-guided trail; contour mountain walks; picnic site (at entrance to gardens); nursery and herbarium (closed to the general public); labelled display of plants; toilets.

Opposite page: Boesmanskloof Hut welcomes hikers on the Boland Hiking Trail.
Top: Roella incurva.

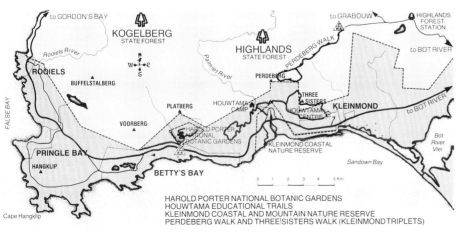

HAROLD PORTER NATIONAL BOTANIC GARDENS
HOUWTAMA EDUCATIONAL TRAILS
KLEINMOND COASTAL AND MOUNTAIN NATURE RESERVE
PERDEBERG WALK AND THREE SISTERS WALK (KLEINMOND TRIPLETS)

PERTINENT INFORMATION: Open daily 08h00-17h00. Entrance is free. Dogs allowed, on leash.
AVAILABLE LITERATURE: *Harold Porter Botanic Gardens, Betty's Bay, C.P.*, comprehensive brochure and map; *Rod Smitheman Trail*, pamphlet.
CLIMATE: Average annual rainfall: 900 millimetres, falling mostly in winter. Annual temperature range: 10-35 °C.

The Harold Porter National Botanic Gardens is a scenic, well-maintained sanctuary for montane and coastal fynbos. Flowers are its main attraction: the red disa blooms in January and the Nerina lily in March. Watch for the sunbirds, sugarbirds and other endemic birdlife attracted to these colourful displays.

The network of trails caters for all levels of interest and fitness. The Rod Smitheman interpretive trail emphasizes plant identification and ecology. Leopard's Kloof, for which an access permit must be obtained from the curator, is especially beautiful. The waterfall and pool are accessible via a short but fairly rough path.

40. Houwtama Educational Trails

KLEINMOND, see map page 59

AUTHORITY-IN-CHARGE: Peter Slingsby, Swamp Daisy Farm, P.O. Box 108, Kleinmond 7195.
DURATION: 3 or 4 days (variable).
MAIN ATTRACTIONS: Conservation awareness programme; Western Cape montane and coastal fynbos; varied mountain, river and sea views; tidal pools and coastal environment; wildlife present but not often seen, except for the endemic birdlife.
FACILITIES/AMENITIES: Primitive campground with shelters and stream water; firewood provided.
PERTINENT INFORMATION: Trails are designed for scholars in Stds. IV to VII. Courses are run *only* for school classes plus

teacher in term time (no exceptions). Schools and/or students must supply their own food, sleeping bags, daypacks and cooking equipment.
AVAILABLE LITERATURE: *Houwtama Environmental Awareness Venture – Field Guide*, booklet; worksheets and sketch maps distributed to students when on trail.
CLIMATE: Winter rainfall area. Strong winds possible.

Houwtama hosts a conservation awareness programme designed for schoolchildren in Stds. IV to VII. Educational trails are led through the foothills of the Kogelberg Wilderness and Kleinmond Coastal Nature Reserve; the camp-site is situated on the banks of the Palmiet River near excellent swimming pools and slides. *Houwtama* is the Hottentot word for 'winding river', the meaning of which becomes clear if you swim upstream into the Kogelberg Mountains.

The terrain is typical of the Western Cape, including sandstone cliffs and ridges, horizontal shale bands, coastal plains as well as rocky and sandy beaches. The fynbos is particularly beautiful in this region and the nectar-feeders such as sunbirds and sugarbirds are very active when the flowers bloom. You also have the chance to spot baboon, grysbok and klipspringer, and possibly the spoor of these as well as the nocturnal porcupine, leopard and other wild cats.

The nature trails are led by Peter Slingsby, South Africa's well-known hiking trail cartographer and a teacher by training. His trails – the objectives of which are to instil in children an awareness and appreciation of the natural environment – do not include vigorous physical trail endurance tests. Rather, they emphasize field studies of vegetation, geology, exotic species and tidal pool, stream and vlei ecology – each tailored specifically to the age, number and capabilities of the participants. The schoolteachers are expected to present pre-course preparations and follow-up programmes.

Various sketch maps and field guides, attractively drawn by Peter Slingsby, are used as teaching aids. Further enquiries should be directed to Peter Slingsby.

41. Kleinmond Coastal and Mountain Nature Reserve

KLEINMOND, see map page 59

AUTHORITY-IN-CHARGE: Municipality of Kleinmond, P.O. Box 3, Kleinmond 7195; tel. (02823) 3030/3090.
SIZE: 343 hectares.
LENGTH: Approximately 14 km of nature trails.
MAIN ATTRACTIONS: Coastal fynbos; views of the Kogelberg and its sandstone cliffs; wide stretch of sea; Palmiet River Lagoon and Kleinriviersvlei; rocky tidal pools.
FACILITIES/AMENITIES: Fairy Glen picnic site.
PERTINENT INFORMATION: Snorkelling is popular, but take care in thick kelp and avoid rough seas. No permits necessary.
AVAILABLE LITERATURE: *Kleinmond 1983*, detailed map with ecological data by Mapcape.
CLIMATE: Winter rainfall area.

42. Perdeberg Walk and Three Sisters Walk (Kleinmond Triplets)

HIGHLANDS STATE FOREST, see map page 59

AUTHORITY-IN-CHARGE: Western Cape Forest Region, Forestry Branch, Department of Environment Affairs.
LENGTH: Perdeberg Walk: 16 km. Three Sisters Walk: 8 km.
MAIN ATTRACTIONS: Montane fynbos; memorable views of mountains, sea and towns.
PERTINENT INFORMATION: Perdeberg Walk: permits necessary, obtainable from Highlands Forest Station, P.O. Box 125, Grabouw 7160, tel (02824) 655; maximum of 36 people per day (maximum of 12 people per group), starting at one-hour intervals. Three Sisters Walk: permits necessary, obtainable from the Municipality of Kleinmond; permits will be left at Kleinmond police station for collection at weekends. The Perdeberg Walk is linked to the Three Sisters Walk by a footpath near Fairy Glen.
CLIMATE: Winter rainfall area.

The Perdeberg Walk is a lovely stroll through well-managed montane fynbos with wildflowers in bloom year-round. A five-kilometre, flat access path near the High-

plant) and the Bot River vlei. The rich natural display of delicate blooms such as painted ladies and China flowers is another highlight of this approximately four-hour ramble, as are the frequently seen rock kestrels, orangebreasted sunbirds and klipspringers.

43. Lebanon State Forest

HOUWHOEK

AUTHORITY-IN-CHARGE: Western Cape Forest Region, Forestry Branch, Department of Environment Affairs.
LENGTH: Old Pass Trail: 4 km. Klein Houwhoek Peak Trail: 8 km (one way).
MAIN ATTRACTIONS: Fynbos vegetation; impressive sea and mountain views.
FACILITIES/AMENITIES: Both trails start at the Houwhoek Inn.
PERTINENT INFORMATION: Old Pass Trail: from the Inn, down the old road to the Bot River. Klein Houwhoek Peak Trail: from the Inn, up the forestry track to the summit. Permits necessary, obtainable from the Forester, tel. (0240) 2638, or from the Inn; 12 people are admitted per permit.
CLIMATE: Winter rainfall area.

44. Riviersonderend Canyon Trip

HOTTENTOTS HOLLAND NATURE RESERVE, see map page 57

AUTHORITY-IN-CHARGE: Western Cape Forest Region, Forestry Branch, Department of Environment Affairs.
LENGTH/DURATION: 17 km/one full day recommended.
MAIN ATTRACTIONS: Spectacular canyon scenery.
FACILITIES/AMENITIES: Changing rooms, toilets and carpark at Nuweberg State Forest.
PERTINENT INFORMATION: Open only in summer (November-February); Boegoekloof walks are closed from May to October. Trip involves compulsory swims, scrambling and jumps into pools. Physically

LEBANON STATE FOREST

0   5   10   15 km

lands forestry office leads walkers to the six-kilometre circular trail on the slopes of Perdeberg (498 m). Critical junctions on the walk are marked by white or yellow footprints. On a clear day Kleinmond, Betty's Bay, False Bay, the Kogelberg and other surrounding peaks and ranges are visible.

Another pleasant trail partially situated in Highlands State Forest is the Three Sisters Walk. This path begins directly behind Kleinmond with a very steep ascent to the Three Sisters Ridge. From the beacon (634 m) the path descends to join an old firebreak, crosses streams of the Palmiet River, passes through lush protea growth and circles back to town past two (disgraceful) quarries.

Magnificent views highlight this trail – they stretch along the coastline from Danger Point (past Hermanus) in the east to Cape Hangklip in the west, and include the Palmiet River and its once-spectacular valley (now dammed by a giant hydro-electric

Opposite page, top: An attractive footbridge in the Harold Porter National Botanic Gardens offers a splendid vista of coastal montane fynbos.

Opposite page, bottom: A dragonfly, a member of the order Odonata.

Above: The challenge of icy water on the Riviersonderend Canyon Trip.

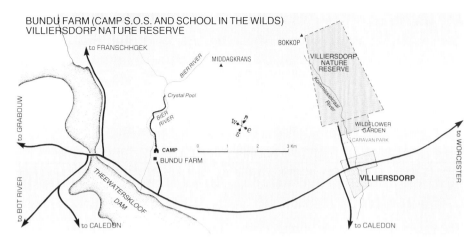

BUNDU FARM (CAMP S.O.S. AND SCHOOL IN THE WILDS)
VILLIERSDORP NATURE RESERVE

weather. Waterproof your pack and camera. Jogging shoes, or similar light footwear with a good sole grip, are recommended. If you are chary of cold water, wear a light woollen shirt or wetsuit jacket. A large part of the canyon remains in shade for most of the day.

45. Villiersdorp Nature Reserve

VILLIERSDORP

AUTHORITY-IN-CHARGE: Municipality of Villiersdorp, P.O. Box 23, Villiersdorp 7170.
SIZE: 35 hectares (to be expanded to 500 hectares).
MAIN ATTRACTIONS: Kommissiekraal River; rich montane fynbos; 60 species of proteas, as well as watsonias and ericas, feature in the wildflower garden.
FACILITIES/AMENITIES: Shade huts; nursery; caravan park with five huts adjacent to the reserve.
PERTINENT INFORMATION: Hiking trails are planned for the area. For information: The Town Clerk, P.O. Box 23, Villiersdorp 7170. November, when the summer annuals bloom, is the best time to visit the wildflower garden (open daily 08h00-17h00).
CLIMATE: Winter rainfall area.

46. Bundu Farm (Camp S.O.S and School in the Wilds)

VILLIERSDORP

AUTHORITY-IN-CHARGE: South African Exploration Society (S.O.S.), P.O. Box 153, Villiersdorp 7170.
SIZE: 160 hectares.
MAIN ATTRACTIONS: Fynbos and mountain scenery.
FACILITIES/AMENITIES: Outdoor education courses; educational holidays for children; bungalows, large halls, kitchen, hot and cold water, electricity and showers; swimming pool; farm animals; camps containing buck and ostriches.
PERTINENT INFORMATION: Trails are run for organized groups only.
AVAILABLE LITERATURE: The Ecology of Bundu Farm, comprehensive booklet by Sue Milton; information leaflet.
CLIMATE: Winter rainfall area.

Bundu Farm hosts outdoor education classes for schoolchildren, youth groups and teacher-trainees, in which accompanied

demanding terrain. Permits necessary, obtainable from The Forester, Nuweberg State Forest, P.O. Box 81, Elgin 7180. Maximum of 24 people admitted per day. The Riviersonderend Canyon is sometimes referred to as Suicide Gorge.
AVAILABLE LITERATURE: The Hottentots-Holland Nature Reserve, Fred Kruger (for ecology); see Boland Hiking Trail (Hottentots Holland Section), map by Mapcape, on which the canyon can be located.

There are many lovely rivers in the Cape but few offer the opportunity for such action-packed adventure as a trip down the Riviersonderend, the upper reaches of which are sometimes referred to as Boegoekloof. Overhangs and cave-like formations, compulsory leaps into long, dark rock pools as well as swims, all contribute to the challenge and growing popularity of the Riviersonderend Canyon Trip.

The best way to approach the canyon is from the Nuweberg Forest Station, where parking and ablution facilities have been constructed for the hikers on the Hottentots Holland Hiking Trail. A permit is necessary to proceed into the Hottentots Holland Nature Reserve. Climb the hiking trail, a jeep

track at this point, until it forks (6 kilometres), then follow the right track which leads to Bosmanskloof Hut. The most straightforward way to enter the kloof is at the bridge named 'Red Hat Crossing', along the main section of the hiking trail. An alternative route is via a path farther upstream in Boegoekloof.

Once in the canyon, you have no choice but to follow the eccentricities of the river itself (8 kilometres). One place is particularly unnerving; I have seen some mighty tough guys shiver in their wet tackies at the 'free-style' jump from about seven metres into a very dark, round rock pool. Be careful: because the water is so dark, you may not be able to see dangerous obstructions such as logs or boulders in it. If the centre is free of such dangers, and after careful negotiation, jump! Then continue down the river, leaving at the weir in the pine plantation near the tarred road, at Viljoen's Pass (3 kilometres). This route requires a full day. If you are pressed for time, or frightened of deep, dark holes, turn around and head upstream. Follow the left tributary which will eventually bring you back to the hiking trail.

Take note: this is not an easy trip. Do not attempt it in cloudy, rainy or threatening

A lovely circular walk has been opened recently on the southern slopes of the Swartberg, just off the national highway (the Garden Route). Starting from the Caledon Wildflower Garden, famous for its annual spring wildflower shows since 1927, this half-day excursion climbs to the crest of the mountain (834 m) through rich fynbos veld where panoramic views of the Swartberg and the Cape folded mountains emerge. With permission from the relevant landowners, hikers can traverse the ridge and climb the higher summits.

48. Vogelgat Private Nature Reserve

KLEINRIVIER MOUNTAINS

AUTHORITY-IN-CHARGE: Vogelgat Nature Reserve (Pty) Ltd (a private company with Dr Ion Williams as director and chairman), c/o Dr I. Williams, 29 Tenth Street, Voëlklip 7203.
SIZE: 602 hectares.
LENGTH: Approximately 30 km of footpaths.
MAIN ATTRACTIONS: Rich montane fynbos; deep pools fed by perennial streams; superb scenery – mountains, river, estuary, sea and coastal towns; abundant birdlife; well-graded footpaths.
FACILITIES/AMENITIES: Three overnight huts, for use by permit holders only; access to herbarium on request.
PERTINENT INFORMATION: South African Natural Heritage Site No. 5. Entry is strictly limited to permit holders and their immediate families; permits, when available, are issued by Dr Williams at a fee of R75 per year. Trespassers are prosecuted.
AVAILABLE LITERATURE: Permit holders receive a map, details of nature walks, lists of plant and bird species to be seen in the reserve, and an annual newsletter.
CLIMATE: Winter rainfall area; prone to mists.

Dr Ion Williams, who purchased Vogelgat in 1969, deserves credit for turning it into one of the finest privately run ecosystem reserves in southern Africa. Spanning an elevation from just above sea level to 800

trails play an integral role as an education technique. Situated at the foot of the Villiersdorp Mountains and near the Theewaterskloof Dam, Bundu Farm comprises rich montane fynbos which attracts small wildlife such as red rock hare, porcupine, dassie, baboon, mongoose, klipspringer and grysbok. The clean Bier River flows through Bundu Farm and attracts birdlife such as bokmakierie, Cape batis and Karoo prinia.

Sue Milton's comprehensive manual, *The Ecology of Bundu Farm*, is an invaluable environmental education publication. You can use the booklet to learn about not only Bundu Farm, but also the whole Western Cape fynbos region.

Field studies for school groups are held weekly for Stds. II to V. School in the Wilds also trains pre- and in-service teachers in the principles and practices of outdoor education. The farm and its facilities can be hired by private and church groups over weekends and public holidays, but they must organize their own activities.

Opposite page, left: The krantz protea, Protea rupicola.
Opposite page, right: Mesembryanthemaceae.
Above: Outdoor education at Bundu Farm.

47. Caledon Nature Reserve and Wildflower Garden

CALEDON

AUTHORITY-IN-CHARGE: Municipality of Caledon, P.O. Box 14, Caledon 7230.
SIZE: 214 hectares (nature reserve); 56 hectares (wildflower garden).
LENGTH/DURATION: 10 km/3-5 hours.
MAIN ATTRACTIONS: Rich indigenous fynbos vegetation; cultivated indigenous trees and wildflowers; panoramic mountain views.
FACILITIES/AMENITIES: Famous annual spring wildflower show; ornamental lake attracts prolific birdlife; tearoom (open in spring flower season only); cloakroom; braai/picnic site; nursery which sells annuals, ericas and vygies; camping at nearby hot mineral springs.
PERTINENT INFORMATION: Bring water as drinking water is scarce on the trail.
AVAILABLE LITERATURE: *Caledon Nature Reserve and Wildflower Garden*, brochure with map by Mapcape.
CLIMATE: Winter rainfall area.

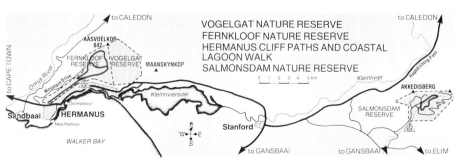

metres, well-constructed footpaths lead through the reserve, up to the highest points. Apart from the beauty of the kloofs, rock pools and mountain slopes, unsurpassed views are obtained of Walker Bay, coastal towns and Kleinriviersvlei. The fynbos is lush and constant vigilance has prevented invasive alien vegetation from gaining a hold.

About 700 species of plants, many of them rare, endangered or endemic to the area, have been found in the reserve so far. For this reason Vogelgat was recognized and declared a National Heritage Site in 1985.

Each season witnesses its particular blooms. In July a sticky green heath, *Erica coccinea* var. 'inflata' covers the north-facing rocky scree. In spring, magnificent displays of *Erica aristata* and *E. holosericea* may be seen, as well as the yellow proteaceous plants *Aulax umbellata* and *Leucadendron xanthoconus*. In summer, tall strands of *Brunia albiflora*, with its strong smell of coffee, bloom in damp swampy places. One of the more unusual plants found in Vogelgat is the giant flycatcher, *Roridula gorgonias*. Once insects are trapped by this plant, a small beetle feeds among them without itself being caught.

Among the 80 species of birds observed in the region is a pair of black eagles. Although not often seen, grysbok, klipspringer and rhebok live in these mountains, as do baboons, otters, snake-like whip lizards, frogs and toads.

The paths are well signposted and the names of stations in the detailed itineraries of walks are clearly marked.

Vogelgat is bounded on the west by the Fernkloof Nature Reserve and on the east by the Maanskyn Reserve. It is hoped that this large tract of preserved fynbos will secure a viable gene pool for the preservation of its unique flora.

49. Fernkloof Nature Reserve

HERMANUS, see map page 63

AUTHORITY-IN-CHARGE: Municipality of Hermanus, P.O. Box 20, Hermanus 7200.
SIZE: 1 446 hectares (to be expanded).
LENGTH: 40 km of footpaths; 4,5-km nature trail.
MAIN ATTRACTIONS: Coastal montane fynbos; 92 species of birds; views of Kleinrivier Mountains, lagoon, sea and coastal towns.
FACILITIES/AMENITIES: Self-guided nature trail; visitor's centre (botanical displays and literature); interpretive centre (botanical lectures, shows and displays); herbarium, open to the public on Monday mornings and Friday afternoons (approximately 2 500

specimens); guided trails for organized groups on request; one hut (which is being upgraded) with two beds and mattresses, and pots and pans.
PERTINENT INFORMATION: Hikers must carry camp-stoves as no fires are allowed. Book by phoning the officer-in-charge at (02831) 22985 or (02831) 22700. No entrance or hut fees are charged, but donations, especially in the form of equipment such as pots, torches and candles, are welcomed.
AVAILABLE LITERATURE: *Fernkloof Nature Trail*, concise information sheet (appropriate for school-age users) explaining the 'stations' along the trail; *Fernkloof Nature Reserve*, brochure and map by Peter Slingsby, published by the Hermanus Botanical Society.
CLIMATE: Winter rainfall area; sea mists are possible year-round.

Fernkloof Nature Reserve is a pleasant, well cared-for area concentrating on the preservation of unspoilt montane coastal fynbos. A 4,5-kilometre nature trail runs on a gentle gradient from the interpretive centre. The footpaths sprawl over 40 kilometres, varying from very easy to steep gradients. Zigzag paths lead to the mountain peaks.

Situated in an open kloof in the western region of the Kleinrivier Mountains above Hermanus, the reserve spans an elevation from 63 metres above sea level to 842 metres on Aasvoëlkop, its highest point. The Fernkloof Advisory Board is extending the boundary to the high water mark so that coastal vegetation and the cliff paths are given adequate protection and management.

The views of the mountains, Hermanus and the sweep of Walker Bay are impressive. The lovely floral composition of the reserve attracts endemic bird species such as orange-breasted sunbirds, Cape sugarbirds and rock thrushes. Baboons, klipspringers and other mammals are present, but not readily seen.

Hikers who wish to stay overnight in the reserve may do so in Galpin's small, simple hut. The hut, which can accommodate two (four at a squeeze), is reached after a relatively strenuous two-hour walk following a

well-signposted route from the parking lot via Galpin's Kop. Fires are not allowed, so hikers must carry camp-stoves with them to the hut and, since no toilets are provided, you are expected to display proper outdoor toilet etiquette and bury all human waste.

50. Hermanus Cliff Paths and Coastal Lagoon Walk

HERMANUS, see map page 63

AUTHORITIES-IN-CHARGE: Municipality of Hermanus, P.O. Box 20, Hermanus 7200; Hermanus Publicity Association.
LENGTH: 27 km of nature trails, plus minor paths.
MAIN ATTRACTIONS: Flowers; sweeping sea views; coastal boulder headlands; sandy beaches.
FACILITIES/AMENITIES: Footpaths.
PERTINENT INFORMATION: To be incorporated into the Fernkloof Nature Reserve.
AVAILABLE LITERATURE: Contact the Hermanus Publicity Association.
CLIMATE: Winter rainfall area.

51. Salmonsdam Nature Reserve

NEAR STANFORD, see map page 63

AUTHORITY-IN-CHARGE: Department of Nature and Environmental Conservation, Cape Provincial Administration.
SIZE: 834 hectares.
MAIN ATTRACTIONS: Fynbos reserve with reintroduced mammals; attractive kloof; 124 bird species.
FACILITIES/AMENITIES: Nature walks;

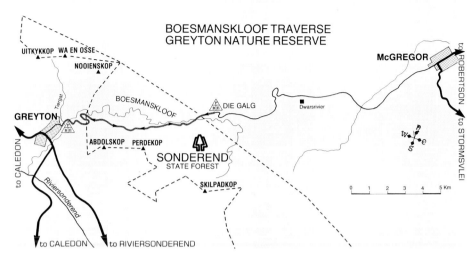

BOESMANSKLOOF TRAVERSE
GREYTON NATURE RESERVE

cottages, camping site, ablution block and fireplaces.
AVAILABLE LITERATURE: *Salmonsdam Nature Reserve*, information pamphlet and map; checklists.
CLIMATE: Winter rainfall area.

Salmonsdam Nature Reserve is situated in typical fynbos 18 kilometres from Stanford, or 33 kilometres from Hermanus and 60 kilometres from Caledon. It is not well known and most people seem unaware of the nature trails following paths and dirt roads radiating from the camping area along both sides of the Keeromskloof. From these paths mammals such as grysbok, springbok, steenbok and klipspringer are often seen, and more than 124 bird species have been recorded. This reserve is recommended for fynbos studies, bird-watchers and as a relaxing retreat with pleasant rambles.

52. Greyton Nature Reserve

GREYTON

AUTHORITY-IN-CHARGE: Municipality of Greyton, P.O. Box 4, Greyton 7233.
SIZE: 2 220 hectares.
MAIN ATTRACTIONS: Steep, southern slopes of Riviersonderend Mountains (rugged peaks such as Uitkykkop, Perdekop and Abdolskop, and deep ravines); proteas and other attractive montane fynbos; klipspringer, grysbok and grey rhebok.
FACILITIES/AMENITIES: Municipal camping site near boundary of the reserve on Riviersonderend, with hot water (if bookings are made in advance), shower and toilets; swimming and canoeing in the river is popular; two boarding houses in Greyton, the Greyton Lodge and Post House.
PERTINENT INFORMATION: Part of the hiking trail from McGregor passes through

the reserve (see the Boesmanskloof Traverse). Nature walks are planned. Elevation span: 240-1 465 m. Fire swept through the reserve in February 1987, so obtain further information from the town clerk before you plan your trip.
AVAILABLE LITERATURE: Contact the Town Clerk, Municipality of Greyton.
CLIMATE: Average annual rainfall: 600-900 millimetres, falling mostly in winter (April to September). Average annual temperature range: 8-20 °C.

53. Boesmanskloof Traverse

RIVIERSONDEREND MOUNTAINS

AUTHORITY-IN-CHARGE: Western Cape Forest Region, Forestry Branch, Department of Environment Affairs★.
LENGTH/DURATION: 15,8 km/4-5 hours (one way).
MAIN ATTRACTIONS: Spectacular, rugged mountain scenery; Cape fynbos flowers; large rock pools and waterfalls.
FACILITIES/AMENITIES: None; private accommodation available at either end of the trail.
PERTINENT INFORMATION: Permits necessary, obtainable from The State Forester, Sonderend State Forest, P.O. Box 128, Robertson 6705. Trail may be closed at times due to soil tests. Fire swept across the trail in February 1987, so obtain further information from the forester before you plan your trip.
AVAILABLE LITERATURE: *Boesmans Kloof*, information sheet.
CLIMATE: Winter rainfall area.

An old track, upgraded to a fine hiking trail, winds through the only gap in the rugged Riviersonderend mountain range. Now known as the Boesmanskloof Traverse, this

route between McGregor and Greyton has become one of the most popular trails in the Western Cape. Highlights include views of the majestic Riviersonderend Mountains, their steep gorges and the Greyton and McGregor valleys; scenic waterfalls; and the lovely Cape wildflowers. Water is abundant in large rock pools.

Physically the trail requires a reasonable degree of fitness as it continuously ascends, descends and contours the slopes of Boesmanskloof, but the traverse requires only 4-5 hours to complete, which leaves plenty of time for swimming and enjoying the views. At present there are no overnight facilities. There is, however, a municipal camp-site in Greyton.

A delightful way to do the trail is to begin at McGregor, walk to Greyton, stay the night at the quaint Post House (tel. (02822) 9995), and return to McGregor the following day.

Note: The trail at McGregor ends at a dirt road, 15 kilometres from the town.

54. Bredasdorp Mountain Reserve

BREDASDORP

AUTHORITY-IN-CHARGE: Municipality of Bredasdorp, P.O. Box 51, Bredasdorp 7280.
SIZE: 800 hectares (86-hectare wildflower garden).
LENGTH: 20 km of nature trails.
MAIN ATTRACTIONS: Wildflower garden containing, among other flowering plants endemic to this area, the Bredasdorp lily; views from Bredasdorp to the Indian Ocean; coastal renosterveld and fynbos.
FACILITIES/AMENITIES: Footpaths; resting shelters.
PERTINENT INFORMATION: Entrance is free.
CLIMATE: Winter rainfall area.

Opposite page, left: Ericaceae.
Opposite page, right: A chameleon, family member of a group of slow-moving arboreal lizards.

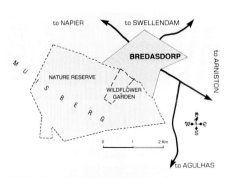

BREDASDORP MOUNTAIN RESERVE

55. *De Hoop Nature Reserve and Potberg Environmental Education Centre*

NEAR BREDASDORP

AUTHORITY-IN-CHARGE: Department of Nature and Environmental Conservation, Cape Provincial Administration.
SIZE: 18 000 hectares (to be expanded).
LENGTH/DURATION: Vlei Trail: 6 km/ 2 hours. Potberg Trail: 4 km/1 hour to summit. Coastal Trail: variable.
MAIN ATTRACTIONS: De Hoop vlei (excellent birdlife); Potberg, with eroded limestone cliff formations and treed kloofs; coastal environment (rich intertidal life; high, windswept sand dunes); southern right whales; 228 species of birds; De Hoop farmstead, a national monument.
FACILITIES/AMENITIES: Hiking and nature trails as well as picnic and braai areas are being planned; education centre accommodating 60 students, with laboratory and visitor's centre; rondavels at De Hoop, each accommodating 8 people, with kitchen facilities, ablution blocks, toilets and fireplaces; education centre at Koppie Alleen, on the coast, accommodating organized groups of up to 30 people.

PERTINENT INFORMATION: The De Hoop-Potberg complex is in the process of development. Permits necessary, obtainable at the gate. The objective of the education centre is to provide formal environmental education courses, therefore casual visits by individual members of the public are restricted so as not to conflict. Water must be carried on trails.
AVAILABLE LITERATURE: *De Hoop Provincial Nature Reserve and Potberg Environmental Centre*, comprehensive brochure and map; information pamphlet; checklists; *African Wildlife*, Vol. 37, No. 1, January/February 1983 (special issue on De Hoop).
CLIMATE: Average annual rainfall: 450 millimetres, falling mostly in winter. Summer: warm and dry, although strong south-east winds may bring rain. Winter: cold and wet, north-west winds.

Covering 18 000 hectares, the De Hoop-Potberg complex embraces widely varying terrains: a large vlei; 13 kilometres of sandy and rocky coastline with diverse intertidal pools and shifting sand dunes reaching 90 metres in height; unspoilt strandveld; calcareous ridges and kloofs; and Potberg, the winter rainfall breeding centre for the endangered Cape vulture. These varying habitats support a wealth of wildlife including bontebok, Cape mountain zebra, eland, grey duiker, steenbok, baboon, blackbacked jackal, marsh mongoose, mice, over 200 species of birds, snakes (especially puff adder,

cobra and skaapsteker), angulate tortoises, mountain agamas, scorpions, peripatids and large dung beetles. The intertidal community is also very diverse and the beachcomber or snorkeller is likely to encounter octopuses, sea urchins, sea anemones, rockpool fishes, snails and whelks, to name but a few of the more common life forms. Southern right whales and dolphins are sometimes seen close inshore.

The emphasis of the reserve is on outdoor recreation and environmental education courses for schoolchildren and organized groups. Self-guided nature trails, all physically undemanding, are located in each major ecosystem in the reserve: the montane coastal fynbos, the vlei and the coast.

To enhance the value of your experience at this reserve, I suggest the following:
☐ always carry binoculars to enable you to see as much of the wildlife as possible
☐ always wear boots to protect against poisonous snakes
☐ snorkel in the larger tidal pools but avoid swimming or diving in the rough waters of the open reef area
☐ explore the sand dunes; they are lovely at early light or in the late afternoon and are favoured by small buck, birdlife such as blue cranes and flocks of wattled starlings, and even blackbacked jackals. Photographers and artists will find this a particularly challenging area.

The Potberg Environmental Education Centre is not open to the public. However, organized groups can apply for conservation

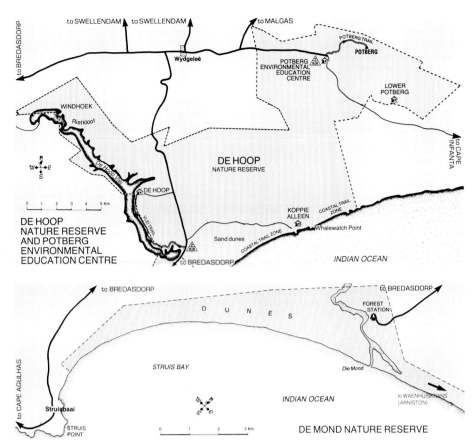

DE HOOP
NATURE RESERVE
AND POTBERG
ENVIRONMENTAL
EDUCATION CENTRE

DE MOND NATURE RESERVE

56. *De Mond Nature Reserve*

BREDASDORP

AUTHORITY-IN-CHARGE: Western Cape Forest Region, Forestry Branch, Department of Environment Affairs.
SIZE: 301 hectares.
MAIN ATTRACTIONS: Beach and estuary; coastal fynbos and milkwood forest; seabirds and other seashore and estuarine life.
FACILITIES/AMENITIES: Fishing, with permit.
PERTINENT INFORMATION: Day use only. Entrance is free. Permit necessary, obtainable from The State Forester, De Mond Nature Reserve, P.O. Box 277, Bredasdorp 7280; tel. (0284) 42170.
AVAILABLE LITERATURE: Included in *Wilderness Areas and Nature Reserves*, information sheets issued by the Forestry Branch.
CLIMATE: Winter rainfall area. October to March is the best season to visit.

As a result of the Forestry Branch's efforts to keep the river mouth open, De Mond is a classic example of an estuary in motion. All the physical, chemical and biological components are present – the ocean, sand bars, beach dunes, intertidal zone, river, salinity variations, and plants and animals capable of tolerating great changes in salinity. Research on the management of drift-sand communi-

courses and accompanied trails. Each application is considered on an individual basis and all courses are run to suit the objectives, ages and background of the group involved.

In the years between the publication of *Everyone's Guide to Trailing and Mountaineering in Southern Africa* and this updated edition, De Hoop Nature Reserve rose from a poorly publicized and little-known provincial reserve to become one of southern Africa's most prominent conservation issues. The Potberg Environmental Education Centre was officially opened in February 1983 and less than a month later Armscor's (the quasi-government Armaments Corporation) intention to develop a missile-testing facility in the south-western Cape was revealed by the press. Despite public pressure opposing Armscor's presence in the Arniston/Cape Infanta area, the decision to incorporate this vital conservation region was a *fait accompli*.

Concern is high over the fate of De Hoop's rich and varied birdlife (De Hoop is recognized internationally for its important wetlands habitat); characteristic fynbos (which is largely limestone-dependent and includes floral species found nowhere else in the winter rainfall area, in addition to specific endemics in Potberg); the unique De Hoop Guano Cave (with its 150 000 bats of five species); the single most important winter calving ground of South Africa's southern right whales; and the winter breeding colony of the Cape vulture. Facilities such as the hiking trail have also been left

in abeyance due to the problem of public access.

However, there are many ways to look at every problem. A committee appointed to do an environmental impact study on the effect of Armscor's planned activities in De Hoop's ecosystem concluded that 'multiple use of this diverse natural area as both a proclaimed nature reserve and a weapons test range will be possible without undue prejudice to either cause, provided the conditions stipulated in this report are met and honoured'. Hence, the future of De Hoop lies with Armscor and the meticulous monitoring of that organization's activities. The amateur naturalist and trailist can do his share by walking the areas that remain open to the public and keeping out a watch-dog eye for changes, both positive and negative.

Opposite page: Exploring an intertidal pool at De Hoop Nature Reserve. The reserve complex embraces widely diverse terrains, including 13 kilometres of sandy and rocky coastline. This area became one of southern Africa's most prominent conservation issues when Armscor announced its intention of developing a missile-testing site here.

Below left: Schoolchildren on one of De Hoop's environmental education courses.

Below right: Beach dunes at De Mond Nature Reserve.

Above: Taking a break on the Swellendam Hiking Trail.

Opposite page, top: A spectacular view along the Cape folded mountains from the Boosmansbos Wilderness Area.

Opposite page, centre: Pelargonium magenteum.

as hermit crabs, mussels, snails and octopuses, estuarine fish, various high-level tidal plants such as *Salicornia*, over 25 species of dune plants, small antelope such as duiker, and 20 species of birds, including the Caspian tern, curlew, ringed plover and Cape sugarbird.

The beauty of De Mond lies in its unspoilt nature. There is no intrusion by waterskiers, sand buggies or trail bikes – not the case in nearby Walker Bay, Hermanus.

57. Swellendam Hiking Trail

SWELLENDAM

AUTHORITY-IN-CHARGE: Western Cape Forest Region, Forestry Branch, Department of Environment Affairs★.
LENGTH/DURATION: 74 km/6 days; shorter variations are possible.
MAIN ATTRACTIONS: Mountain scenery and fynbos; ravines with indigenous forests.
FACILITIES/AMENITIES: Six overnight huts with bunks, mattresses and lanterns; firewood at two huts only (Koloniesbos and Wolfkloof); safe parking at the forest station; picnic site at Hermitage.
PERTINENT INFORMATION: The hiking trail is located in the Marloth Nature Reserve, declared in 1981. Stoves are essential. Warning: the Vensterbank route must be avoided in rain, strong winds and mist, and by those afraid of heights.
AVAILABLE LITERATURE: *Swellendam Hiking Trail*, comprehensive brochure and map.
CLIMATE: Winter rainfall area, but sudden weather changes are always possible and rain can be expected at any time. The northern slopes of the mountains are drier and warmer than the southern slopes. June to December, snow possible.

ties and the prevention of spreading drift-sands is being conducted.

Within this unique and vulnerable ecosystem, you are free to ramble, swim, bird-watch, fish (once you have obtained a permit), paint and photograph. Some hikers choose to walk along the coast to Waenhuiskrans (Arniston) or Struisbaai. In one short visit, I saw marine invertebrates such

The Swellendam Trail, often said to be one of the most beautiful hiking trails in the Cape, was the first National Hiking Way System trail to follow a 360° route, thereby returning hikers to the starting point on the final day of the trail. It offers numerous alternative or shorter routes if six days of hiking is too long for you and, as a result, the trail is very popular on weekends and public holidays. When I planned the trail, I walked the entire route in three days and ended completely exhausted; however, by staying overnight at each hiking hut, walking time is reduced to four to six hours per day, offering more time to relax, absorb the scenery or swim in the rock pools of the kloofs.

Kruispad, near Proteavallei Hut, and the Vensterbank route (see Pertinent Information) provide short-cuts over the mountain, thereby eliminating the western sec-

SWELLENDAM HIKING TRAIL

to MONTAGU
Scheepersrus
to BARRYDALE
NOOITGEDACHT
Twistniet
GOEDGELOOF
MIDDELRIVIERBERG
PROTEAVALLEI
MISTY POINT 1710
LEEURIVIERBERG
VENSTERBANK
MARLOTH NATURE RESERVE
to WORCESTER
Kruispad
BOSKLOOF
ONE O'CLOCK PEAK
12 O'CLOCK PEAK
11 O'CLOCK PEAK
WOLFKLOOF
Hermitage
10 O'CLOCK PEAK
FOREST STATION
KOLONIESBOS
Buffeljags Dam
SWELLENDAM
to MOSSEL BAY
to CAPE TOWN
BONTEBOK NATIONAL PARK
0 1 2 3 4 5 Km

BOOSMANSBOS WILDERNESS AREA

WITBOOISRIVIER
BOOSMANSBOS WILDERNESS AREA
GROOTBERG
BOOSMANSBOS
HELDERFONTEIN
Palmiet River
DWARSBERG
Bobbejaanskloof
Saagkuilkloof
BLOMBOS
HORINGBERG
SPITSKOP
NOUKRANS PEAK
KOPBERG
Barend Koen Road
FOREST STATION
GROOTVADERSBOS
Heuningneskloof
KLEIN-KOPBERG
to HEIDELBERG
0 1 2 3 4 5 Km

tion. These alternatives provide impressive views but are recommended only to shorten your hike.

On each day of the Swellendam Trail, stretches of shadeless fynbos alternate with cool, indigenous forested kloofs. The southern and northern Langeberg slopes offer far-reaching views of the Swellendam Valley, including the Bontebok National Park and the Robertson Valley respectively. Other trail sections provide the sensation of being in a secluded wilderness. The diversity of changing landscapes and the colourful flowers of the rich montane fynbos are highpoints. In November the slopes of the mountain are blanketed with ericas in different shades of pink.

Middelrivierberg, Leeurivierberg, Misty Point (1 710 m), Twelve o'clock, One o'clock and Ten o'clock peaks, as well as others, are encircled by the trail and are

popular with mountaineers. Climbers must apply to the Forestry Branch for permits to ascend peaks which do not form part of the hiking trail. Misty Point is a particularly treacherous ascent because, as its name indicates, it becomes rapidly and frequently shrouded in mist.

For hikers with an insatiable appetite to explore, there are numerous paths into some of the densely forested kloofs such as Wolf-kloof, Duiwelsbos, Koloniesbos and Wamakersbos. These paths also make fascinating day excursions, especially in hot, sunny summer weather.

58. Boosmansbos Wilderness Area

GROOTVADERSBOS STATE FOREST

AUTHORITY-IN-CHARGE: Western Cape Forest Region, Forestry Branch, Department of Environment Affairs*.
SIZE: 14 200 hectares.
LENGTH: 70 km of footpaths and gravel roads.
MAIN ATTRACTIONS: Large relic of indigenous kloof forest; Cape fynbos in dramatic mountain terrain.
FACILITIES/AMENITIES: Two sets of small

huts; old jeep road and circular route.
PERTINENT INFORMATION: Permits necessary, obtainable from The Forester, Grootvadersbos State Forest, P.O. Box 109, Heidelberg 6760. Maximum of two groups per day (maximum of 12 people per group) admitted. Cooking on camp-stoves only.
AVAILABLE LITERATURE: *Boosmansbos Wilderness Area*, information sheet with sketch map issued by the Forestry Branch.
CLIMATE: Borders on the winter and all-year rainfall areas. May to July, December and January are dry months. May to July, dry mountain winds. October to April, best hiking season.

About 300 kilometres east of Cape Town, between Heidelberg and Swellendam, in the Langeberg Mountains, exists a rugged forest reserve not very well known to the general public. Declared the Forestry Branch's seventh wilderness area in 1978, Boosmansbos Wilderness Area, within the Grootvadersbos State Forest, is an excellent place to hike up peaks with far-reaching views, explore one of the larger remaining indigenous Cape forest patches in the fynbos ecological zone and enjoy the many flowering species which blanket the mountain slopes.

Specifically, climbers can scramble to the summits of the highest peaks, Grootberg (1 637 m), Horingberg (1 496 m) and Nou-krans Peak (1 452 m). Hikers can walk to Helderfontein Hut, an old stone 'manage-

ment' hut, ascending and descending via Saagkuilkloof (13 kilometres) and Bobbejaanskloof (14 kilometres) respectively, exploring Boosmansbos *en route*.

For a longer and more fascinating alternative to the Saagkuilkloof path, try the Grootberg-Horingberg Trail. This footpath could be one of the most scenically dramatic in the Cape folded mountains. Approximately 30 kilometres long, it ascends from Helderfontein Hut on the north-facing slope of the Grootberg, traverses the mountains in a southerly direction with views of rich kloof forests below, and descends the south-facing slope of Horingberg in a series of zigzags. Not often used, the path is indistinct in places; it is also drawn incorrectly on the forestry sketch map, so ask the forester to clarify the route for you.

Boosmansbos is one of the larger relics (125 hectares) of indigenous kloof forest in Cape montane fynbos. Located on the slopes of Grootberg, it contains impressive specimens of stinkwood, yellowwood, Cape holly, white alder (wit-els), red alder (rooiels), beech and candlewood, in addition to a patch of mountain cypress (one of the few indigenous softwoods in South Africa) growing on an adjoining ridge. The descent into the deep ravines of indigenous forest is steep but worthwhile. Once under the canopy, you are enveloped by a completely different atmosphere to that on the fynbos-covered slopes. The forests are dark, cool and moist. Two uncommon birds recently recorded here are the Knysna woodpecker and the martial eagle.

On the slopes of the reserve, *Protea repens* and *P. longiflora* are abundant, while *Leucadendron pubibracteolatum* occurs in the vleis. Generally, the southern slopes which receive rain year-round house a different flora to that growing on the drier northern slopes. Baboons and dassies are frequently seen, and keen observers may also spot bushbuck in the forest, or grey rhebok, klipspringer

Above left and right: In the Boosmansbos Wilderness Area.

Right: Fynbos in the Simonsberg.

Opposite page: Hiking in the fynbos-rich Langeberg range.

and grysbok, as well as birds such as the Cape bulbul, doublecollared sunbird and redwinged starling.

Be prepared to walk in the veld off the paths, as the existing footpaths and tracks were originally constructed for patrol purposes; you will find some interesting peaks, forests and kloofs off the main routes.

59. Heidelberg Wildflower Garden

HEIDELBERG

AUTHORITY-IN-CHARGE: Municipality of Heidelberg, P.O. Box 12, Heidelberg 6760.
SIZE: 8 hectares.
MAIN ATTRACTIONS: Coastal renosterveld.
FACILITIES/AMENITIES: None.
PERTINENT INFORMATION: Coastal renosterveld is a rare veld type endangered by wheat cultivation.
CLIMATE: Winter rainfall area.

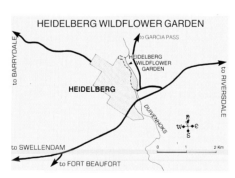

60. Garcia State Forest

RIVERSDALE

AUTHORITY-IN-CHARGE: Western Cape Forest Region, Forestry Branch, Department of Environment Affairs*.
SIZE: Approximately 12 000 hectares.
MAIN ATTRACTIONS: 'Sleeping Beauty' (mountain outline); rich montane fynbos.
FACILITIES/AMENITIES: Two sets of stone huts available for hikers, but no amenities provided; 62 km of footpaths.
PERTINENT INFORMATION: Permits necessary, obtainable from The Forester, Garcia State Forest, P.O. Box 87, Riversdale 6970; tel. (02932) 32.
CLIMATE: Winter rainfall area. October to March, best hiking months.

Garcia State Forest, 10 kilometres northwest of Riversdale and 40 kilometres east of the Boosmansbos Wilderness Area, lies on the high Langeberg range. In these mountains you will discover the flowering fynbos communities endemic to the Riversdale area. An interesting hike is to climb the southern slopes of the Langeberg, over Sleeping Beauty (1 343 m) and down the northern slopes to the Tolhuis. The vegetation changes dramatically: the great variety of flowering fynbos species, extensive pine plantations and an indigenous shrub-like forest on the moist southern slopes, give way on the drier northern side to bushes and other plants characteristic of the Karoo. Along the forested banks of the Meul River a new footpath leads into the Langeberg foothills. This is an interesting route to follow if you wish to study birdlife.

Garcia State Forest, a water catchment area and plantation, is not developed for visitors; the two sets of huts on either side of the range are actually small stone shelters for

the forestry staff, and are available for hikers if not being used by forestry officials. Eight to 10 people can squeeze into each set. The 62 kilometres of footpaths through the reserve can be used by hikers; obtaining water is not a problem, although good swimming pools are scarce.

The reserve, set in an area once inhabited by Bushmen, is traversed by Garcia Pass, part of the provincial road between Riversdale and Ladismith.

61. *Pauline Bohnen Nature Reserve*

STILBAAI, see Regional Map page 38

AUTHORITY-IN-CHARGE: Municipality of Stilbaai, P.O. Box 2, Stilbaai 6785.
SIZE: 1 407 hectares.
MAIN ATTRACTIONS: Small buck such as grysbok and duiker; birdlife.
FACILITIES/AMENITIES: Limited tracks and paths only.
PERTINENT INFORMATION: This reserve was donated by Mrs Pauline Bohnen and is being developed for public use.
AVAILABLE LITERATURE: Included in annual reports of the Department of Nature and Environmental Conservation.
CLIMATE: Winter rainfall area.

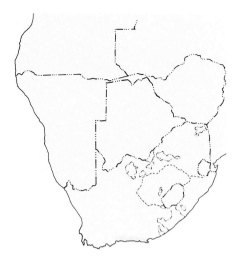

SOUTHERN CAPE

Bordered by the Gouritz River mouth in the west, and Port Elizabeth and the Sundays River in the east, graduating into the dry Karŏo on its north, and washed by the Indian Ocean on its south, the Southern Cape is a delightful, well-developed recreational area. The southern slopes of the Cape folded mountains harbour tall fynbos and indigenous dense forest. These mountains are cut by south-north dramatic passes and interlaced by a myriad long-distance National Hiking Way trails, nature walks and appealing coastal rambles.

The coastal temperate forests of the Southern Cape owe their existence to the broad mountain belt of the Outeniqua range. Known as the Cape Fold, these mountains and their narrow subparallel chains form an impenetrable barrier to humid air moving in off the sea. Rain-heavy clouds gather and eventually discharge themselves over the south-facing slopes which form a sharp divide between the moist coastal belt and the dry Karoo plains to the north.

This year-round moisture, plus plentiful sunlight and small diurnal and seasonal temperature variations provide ideal conditions for six forest types, varying from 'dry' forest to 'moist' and 'wet' types, all characteristic of the Southern Cape. Hikers on steep northern and north-western slopes will encounter 'dry' forest. Trees have a scrub-like appearance. Thorny bushes such as num-num, *Carissa bispinosa*, are common. Moving on to plains and hills, trees grow up to 30 metres high. These 'high forests' harbour many species such as stinkwood, yellowwood, white pear, candlewood and ironwood, in addition to a densely vegetated forest floor. In deep, perennially damp kloofs and gorges, the 'wet' forest predominates. Trees such as red and white alders, Cape beech, stinkwood, tree-fuschia and Cape holly reach heights of about 15 metres, amidst a dense undergrowth of ferns.

The Southern Cape lies within a continuous rainfall zone (rain occurs at any time of the year). The highest falls occur from September to April, varying from 700 to 800 millimetres per year at the coast, to 1 100 to 1 300 millimetres in the mountains. There is an obvious drop in temperature with increasing altitude from the coast to the mountain peaks. The average daily minimum temperature in July is 7,4 °C, contrasting with an average daily maximum of 24,5 °C in January. Snow falls sporadically on the mountains between June and August.

The unique 'berg wind' is prominent during winter. It occurs when air from cold inland areas of high pressure flows down the escarpment to areas of low pressure along the coast. The descending air heats by compression and as the temperature rises, relative humidity becomes very low. A few hours of exposure to these winds is sufficient to desiccate vegetation and ground cover, thus creating conditions extremely conducive to fire. Between May and September is the most hazardous period. Trailists heed the warning!

ECOLOGICAL ZONE: EASTERN
EVERGREEN TEMPERATE FOREST

62. Ruitersbos Forest Walks

MOSSEL BAY

AUTHORITY-IN-CHARGE: Southern Cape Forest Region, Forestry Branch, Department of Environment Affairs.
LENGTH/DURATION: 9,3 km/3,5 hours (shorter variations possible); other walks in the vicinity.
MAIN ATTRACTIONS: Rare and endangered flowering species; indigenous forest; pools and waterfalls.
FACILITIES/AMENITIES: Horses allowed on the property of Eight Bells Mountain Inn; trees on walk labelled with their national tree list numbers.
PERTINENT INFORMATION: Permits necessary, obtainable from Eight Bells Mountain Inn.
AVAILABLE LITERATURE: *Ruitersbos Forest Walks*, sketch map.
CLIMATE: Continuous rainfall area.

The Ruitersbos Forest Walks, coupled with a stay at Eight Bells Mountain Inn, is a wonderful treat during a visit to the Southern Cape. Several short walks through indigenous forest and plantation can be combined for a day's excursions into the Ruitersbos Forest area. These trails are well-marked, and have stone bridges across rivers and aids such as rope and cemented steps at steep rocky areas. About 25 rare and endangered flowering species such as *Disa bodkinii*, a black orchid, and *Acrolophia ustulata* occur in this confluence of Western and Southern Cape floras.

A short, attractive walk is around Protea Hill (access via the forestry rugby field). For the more ambitious, drive to the top of Rob-

inson Pass (where there is parking) and walk the well-graded path. This leads in a westerly direction for about 1,5 hours, and climbs over the mountain, offering magnificent views and rich fynbos. This path is actually the beginning of a new hiking trail, on which some of the overnight stops will be caves.

The Eight Bells Mountain Inn (415 m) is a friendly, country-style hotel accommodating visitors in Knysna-style log cabins. It is situated in the foothills of the Outeniqua Mountains, and at the foot of the Robinson Pass. The Inn was once part of the outspan between Oudtshoorn and Mossel Bay. It provides an excellent base for day walks in the vicinity. On the property there are short

strolls known as the Eight Bells Rooster Trails.

For trailists who would like a taste of the sea, the 13,5-kilometre Mossel Bay Walk is nearby. Starting from Bat's Cave at Cape St. Blaize and stretching to Dana Bay, the trail is fairly level and ideal for families. Following the 30-metre contour line above the high water mark, trailists can enjoy the rock pools, birdlife such as oystercatchers, cormorants, crowned plovers, night owls and black korhaans, and karroid-type fynbos. Angling, diving, swimming and braaiing are other ways to enjoy this trail. The booklet available from the Mossel Bay Municipality, the authority-in-charge of this walk, supplies more information.

Left: Lunch stop in the scenic Robinson Pass area.

Above: Many refreshing streams lace the forests along the Ruitersbos Forest Walks.

Opposite page: A hiker takes a break after climbing Matthew Peak near George. The Outeniqua Hiking Trail winds its way along the lower slopes.

63. Outeniqua Hiking Trail

GEORGE

AUTHORITY-IN-CHARGE: Southern Cape Forest Region, Forestry Branch, Department of Environment Affairs.

LENGTH/DURATION: Approximately 140 km/8 days (many shorter variations possible). Circular day walk: 20 km.

MAIN ATTRACTIONS: Indigenous forest and montane fynbos; elephants in the Rondebossie area; relics of the gold rush near Millwood.

FACILITIES/AMENITIES: Nine huts, each accommodating 20 or 30 people, with bunks, mattresses, fireplaces and firewood.

PERTINENT INFORMATION: Voortrekker Hut has been built to shorten the second day of the route. Farleigh Hut is now an office, and hikers are accommodated in a nearby house. There is a circular day walk in Bergplaas State Forest.

AVAILABLE LITERATURE: *The Outeniqua Hiking Trail*, second edition, comprehensive brochure and map.

CLIMATE: Continuous rainfall area. Snow and frost are possible during June, July and August. Mists are possible throughout the year.

The Outeniqua Hiking Trail had a long-standing reputation of being one of the most difficult in South Africa because of the relatively long distances between huts, and the steep gradients, especially on the first two days. Yielding to public pressure, the Forestry Branch has added Voortrekker Hut, 17 kilometres from Tierkop, which shortens the second day by five kilometres. Other changes, such as the 17-kilometre path from Witfontein to Tierkop on the first day, have been made to shorten the trail route. Also, alternatives to the main trail, such as beginning at Kleinplaat, are possible. Consult the second edition of the map for an accurate plan of the revised Outeniqua trail.

The first four days of the trail take hikers through extensive areas of montane fynbos. The Southern Cape is situated in the year-round rainfall belt which contributes to the fact that, generally, its fynbos has fewer species than that of the winter-rainfall Western Cape. This can be an advantage for the beginner botanist, because the more common species, less cluttered by other plants, stand out and are easier to identify.

October to January (early to midsummer) is the best time to see fynbos in flower; February to May are perhaps the poorest months. Unfortunately, two species you are sure to notice are *Hakea sericea* and *Pinus pinaster*, both alien invaders.

The latter half of the trail passes through indigenous forests and many trees are la-

OUTENIQUA HIKING TRAIL, WOODVILLE WALK, GROENEWEIDE FOREST WALK, TERBLANS NATURE WALK, KRANSHOEK COASTAL NATURE WALK, GOUDVELD STATE FOREST, GARDEN OF EDEN, DIEPWALLE STATE FOREST, THE ELEPHANT WALK

belled with their national tree list numbers. The booklet *National List of Trees*, as well as the NHWS brochure, lists these numbers with tree names.

In general, forests are classified according to canopy height, species, ground cover and undergrowth, in addition to other technical characteristics. Each type is adapted to its respective moisture regime: 'wet' on high plateaux with a 6-20 metre-high broken canopy, 'moist' on lower slopes and plateaux with a 16-30 metre-high dense canopy, and 'dry' near the coast and on lower plateaux.

After descending the trail, you reach the Elephant Walk (see page 80). Although spoor is often seen, there is only a remote possibility of spotting one of the endangered Knysna elephants. Birds and snakes are plentiful, and antelope species readily seen by hikers include bushbuck, klipspringer, grey rhebok, Cape grysbok and blue duiker.

For enthusiasts not having the time to walk the entire Outeniqua Hiking Trail but still wishing to experience these mountains, I suggest the circular day walk in the Bergplaas State Forest. Most of this 20-kilometre trail follows the route of the Outeniqua Hiking Trail. Ask the forester for permission to drive to Kleinplaat Hut, a converted forester's house in a forestry village. The trail can be walked either clockwise or anticlockwise; I recommend the latter because I feel it is nicer to save the plantation roads for the end of the day. Prolific fynbos wildflowers, and views of the Duiwelsberg and the Klein Langkloof Valley, plus a lunch stop at Langberg Hut, are the highlights of this excursion.

64. *Woodville Walk*

NEAR GEORGE, see map page 75

AUTHORITY-IN-CHARGE: Southern Cape Forest Region, Forestry Branch, Department of Environment Affairs.
DURATION: Approximately 30 minutes.
MAIN ATTRACTIONS: The 'Big Tree' (Outeniqua yellowwood).
FACILITIES/AMENITIES: Picnic sites.
PERTINENT INFORMATION: The Big Tree is a 1 000-year-old living fossil.
AVAILABLE LITERATURE: Information sheets and maps available from the Forestry Branch, and from the Publicity Association of George and Knysna.
CLIMATE: Continuous rainfall area.

Above: An alternative to the Outeniqua Hiking Trail is the one-day circular walk in Bergplaas State Forest; wildflowers are a highlight on this excursion.

Opposite page: The elegant bushbuck found in forest thickets and dense bush in the Southern Cape are shy and elusive. However, if attacked, they can be very dangerous. Listen for their loud, clear bark.

65. *Groeneweide Forest Walk*

SAASVELD, NEAR GEORGE, see map page 75

AUTHORITY-IN-CHARGE: Southern Cape Forest Region, Forestry Branch, Department of Environment Affairs.
LENGTH/DURATION: Nature walks of 7 km/2,5 hours; 11 km/4 hours; and 15 km/5,5 hours.
MAIN ATTRACTIONS: Indigenous 'moist' forests; trees labelled with their national tree list numbers; natural swimming pool.
FACILITIES/AMENITIES: Picnic site.
PERTINENT INFORMATION: Cars can be parked at Saasveld, a training college for foresters, 10 km from George.
AVAILABLE LITERATURE: *Groeneweide Walk*, brochure and map available from the Forestry Branch.
CLIMATE: Continuous rainfall area.

66. *Wilderness Lake Area*

GARDEN ROUTE (BETWEEN GEORGE AND KNYSNA)

AUTHORITY-IN-CHARGE: National Parks Board.
LENGTH: Kingfisher Trail: approximately 12 km.
MAIN ATTRACTIONS: Juxtaposition of sea, lake, estuarine and mountain scenery; three types of lakes in close proximity; rich birdlife, especially waterbirds.
FACILITIES/AMENITIES: Circular nature walk; wilderness camp with five

2-bedroomed chalets, caravan park and shop; angling, canoeing, windsurfing, sailing, waterskiing and pedal boating.
PERTINENT INFORMATION: This area is not a national park but was placed under the aegis of the National Parks Board to control uncoordinated development around the lakes. A circular hiking trail with huts and a canoe trail are planned. Netting is not allowed, angling with rod and reel only.
AVAILABLE LITERATURE: *Kingfisher Trail*, brochure and map; *Wilderness Lakes*, brochure; *South Africa's National Parks*, booklet.
CLIMATE: Moderate with occasional hot days. No frost. Wind is common. Average annual rainfall: 800 millimetres, falling mostly in September, October, February and March.

The Kingfisher Nature Trail is the first of a complex of hiking and canoeing trails in the Wilderness National Lake Area, an area bounded on the south by the Indian Ocean and in the north by the Outeniqua Mountains. At present the National Parks Board controls the Touw River Estuary, the Wilderness Lagoon, the Serpentine, Eilandvlei (including Dromedaris Island), Langvlei, and the terrain as far as the western side of Rondevlei. Although many water-orientated sports, including angling, have always been very popular here, the Kingfisher Trail offers the naturalist a marked footpath to ex-

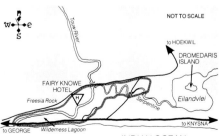

WILDERNESS LAKE AREA

plore one of the most important wetland systems in southern Africa.

Principally a trail for the rambler interested in bird-watching, aquatic life and marine-influenced vegetation (reeds, sedges and rushes), the Kingfisher Trail winds over beach and dune, along the floodplain of the twisting Serpentine waterway, and next to steep wooded slopes of the temperate forest. Binoculars and identification books should be carried. Seventy-nine of South Africa's 95 water-bird species are found here as well as many colourful forest species such as the Knysna loerie and Narina trogon.

67. *Bushbuck Trail*

FEATHERBED NATURE RESERVE, KNYSNA

AUTHORITY-IN-CHARGE: Mr William M. Smith, P.O. Box 31648, Braamfontein 2017.
SIZE: 70 hectares.
LENGTH: 5 km (2,5 km can be ridden on a motorized trailer).
MAIN ATTRACTIONS: Spectacular views of coastal environment; wildlife and flora, including milkwood trees; beach-comber caves; history.
FACILITIES/AMENITIES: Teas and meals are provided; group tours are arranged on request; swimming is pleasant off the reserve's beaches.
PERTINENT INFORMATION: The reserve can be reached only by water; private barge operators provide transport. Standard tour size, 10-40 people; smaller and larger parties can be catered for. Educational walks for children can be arranged. No age limits, ideal for very young and old. Open all year. For trail bookings: The Trail Organizer, Featherbed Nature Reserve, P.O. Box 1245, Knysna 6570; tel. (0445) 21233.
AVAILABLE LITERATURE: *The Featherbed Nature Reserve, The Western Head, Knysna and the District of Knysna, Past and Present*, by Martin Hatchuel.
CLIMATE: Continuous rainfall region. East-facing slope provides protection from westerly storms.

The Bushbuck Trail in the Featherbed Nature Reserve is a trail for tourists rather than mountaineers, and is also a popular educational walk for schoolchildren. Situated in the very scenic south-east corner of Knysna's Western Head, this small private reserve offers a diverse experience in a short space of time.

You can reach the trailhead, the Featherbed Bay Beach, via a private boat or on one of the two barges operating on the Knysna Lagoon. These barges are run by Southern Seas Charter from the jetty next to the Knysna Railway Station, and Lightley's Holiday Cruisers from the road bridge

BUSHBUCK TRAIL

where the national road crosses the Knysna Lagoon.

Refreshments are available on arrival. Then visitors are given a choice whether to walk the first 2,5 kilometres, rising 120 metres from sea level, or ride a motorized trailer. The 2,5-kilometre descent along the coast is for walking only. Here, on the Bushbuck and Old Rocket paths, the trail leader expounds on the ecology and history of the surrounding area.

Walking under the shade of milkwoods, the picturesque views of the sea, lagoon and coastline capture your attention. Short visits are made to the Western Head where rockets were used to fire ropes to shipwrecked sailors, and to beach-comber caves.

About 100 species of birds are present as well as small game such as Cape bushbuck, blue duiker and klipspringer. An enclosure

allows children to see grey rhebok and giant east Cape mountain tortoises.

A traditional South African braai awaits walkers on their return. I feel this trail is ideal for visitors to South Africa (and South Africans visiting their own country), families of varied ages, and the elderly who want to be 'pampered' while enjoying a day in the wilds.

68. Terblans Nature Walk

GOUNA STATE FOREST, KNYSNA, see map page 75

AUTHORITY-IN-CHARGE: Southern Cape Forest Region, Forestry Branch, Department of Environment Affairs.
LENGTH/DURATION: 6,5 km/2-3 hours.
MAIN ATTRACTIONS: Indigenous 'moist' forest; trees labelled with their national tree list numbers.
FACILITIES/AMENITIES: Picnic sites; swimming area.
PERTINENT INFORMATION: No permits required, but visitors must sign the book at the picnic site. Open 06h00-18h00. This walk was formerly known as the Bushpig Nature Walk.
AVAILABLE LITERATURE: *Terblans Nature Walk*, brochure, map and tree list issued by the Forestry Branch.
CLIMATE: Continuous rainfall area with the heaviest falls occurring in September, November and March. Temperate climate in general, but with occasional hot berg winds.

The Terblans Nature Walk, located just north of Gouna Forest Station, meanders through the heart of the Southern Cape's spectacular indigenous forest. Looping away from the Grootdraai picnic site and then back, this undulating walk is not strenuous and is therefore ideal for families with small children as well as reasonably fit, elderly people. Hikers familiar with the Outeniqua Hiking Trail will recognize that the Terblans Nature Walk is situated just south of Rondebossie, the last hut on the trail.

The forests blanketing these lower mountain slopes lie 250-350 metres above sea level and, classified as 'moist' and 'medium moist' types, comprise tall (approximately 18-30 metres), densely growing indigenous trees such as Outeniqua yellowwoods, real yellowwoods, ironwoods, stinkwoods and boekenhouts. Pine plantations also occur along the trail.

The most commonly seen animal in the forest is the bushbuck, but really fortunate hikers will see the gregarious bushpig feeding on bulbs, fruit, grass, insects or carrion. Although the Southern Cape forests contain fewer than 50 typical forest-dwelling bird

species, hikers may see the crowned eagle which preys on monkeys and small antelope, or the African goshawk, the main predator of forest birds. More easily heard than seen are the olive thrush and chorister, and Cape and starred robins. The beautiful Rameron pigeon and Knysna loerie are also present.

69. Kranshoek Coastal Nature Walk

HARKERVILLE STATE FOREST, see map page 75

AUTHORITY-IN-CHARGE: Southern Cape Forest Region, Forestry Branch, Department of Environment Affairs.
LENGTH/DURATION: 9,4 km/approximately 3 hours.
MAIN ATTRACTIONS: Coastal cliff scenery, fynbos and coastal indigenous forest; birdlife.
FACILITIES/AMENITIES: Picnic and viewing sites; swimming; Harkerville Youth Centre nearby for school or university students.
PERTINENT INFORMATION: Permits not required, but visitors must sign the registration book at Kranshoek picnic site.
AVAILABLE LITERATURE: *Kranshoek Nature Walk*, brochure, map and tree checklist issued by the Forestry Branch.
CLIMATE: Continuous rainfall area with the heaviest falls occurring from September to April. Harkerville Forest Station has an average annual rainfall of 960 millimetres.

Between Noetzie and the Robberg Peninsula, approximately 32 kilometres from Knysna, the Kranshoek Coastal Nature Walk with its numerous vantage points overlooking densely wooded ravines, and

sheer cliffs dropping into the sea, offers that perfect blend of scenery which makes the Otter Trail, about 75 kilometres to the east, so popular. Swimming is possible both in the warm Indian Ocean and in the clear, mountain-fed rivers, while woodland canopies and the varied terrain, from stony beaches to sandstone headlands, also add to the pleasure of this ramble.

A large part of this walk is located in 'dry' coastal forest – one of the major forest types in the Southern Cape. Growing on the shallow, dry soils of the lower plateau and near the coast, these dense, scrubby woodlands contain many thorny shrubs. The floor beneath the tree canopy is strewn with dry leaf litter, making fire an ever-present hazard.

Groups engaged in scientific and educational studies especially related to conservation or production forestry, are allowed to book the nearby Harkerville Youth Group Centre, an overnight facility for 42 people.

The Harkerville Hiking Trail, which is a 40-kilometre/two-day circular route planned for completion in 1988, will start at the Harkerville Youth Group Centre. The large swimming pools in the Wit River (on the second day) will be just one of the attractions of this forested coastal hike. Contact the Regional Director of the Southern Cape Forest Region for details.

Above: A view towards the Indian Ocean on the Kranshoek Coastal Nature Walk shows the densely wooded ravines and steep cliffs which characterize the Southern Cape coast.

Opposite page, top: You can cross the Goukamma estuary via the swinging footbridge which connects the parking area to the rolling dunes in the western section of the Goukamma Nature Reserve.

Opposite page, centre: On the new, circular seven-kilometre nature walk in the Goukamma Nature Reserve, trailists experience rich, wildflower-blanketed dunes, far-reaching views of the Goukamma River estuary and possible sightings of bontebok and eland.

70. Goukamma Nature Reserve

KNYSNA

AUTHORITY-IN-CHARGE: Department of Nature and Environmental Conservation, Cape Provincial Administration.
SIZE: 2 230 hectares
MAIN ATTRACTIONS: Beautiful sandy and rocky coastline and estuarine scenery; freshwater lake; oyster beds; diverse birdlife (including water-birds) and small antelope; reintroduced mammals, including bontebok and eland.
FACILITIES/AMENITIES: Fireplaces and picnic sites near river; 48 km of footpaths;

angling in sea, Goukamma River and Groenvlei.
PERTINENT INFORMATION: Permits necessary, issued free of charge. Beach is dangerous for swimming (rip currents). Trailists should carry water and be wary of snakes in forest areas. Take precautions against mosquitoes in forest areas at dusk.
AVAILABLE LITERATURE: Sketch map available from the Department; included in annual reports of the Department of Nature and Environmental Conservation.
CLIMATE: Continuous rainfall area.

Goukamma is a lovely coastal sand dune and freshwater lake complex lying between Knysna and Sedgefield. I find the tranquillity of this 13-kilometre stretch of sandy beach with occasional rocky outcrops most appealing, and the sand dunes, clothed in coastal renosterveld and shrub forests containing milkwood trees, a welcome retreat from the crowded beaches in the Knysna forest region.

Some 48 kilometres of footpaths lead the trailist from the Goukamma River in the eastern section of the reserve to the oyster beds along the beach, then up over fynbos-covered dunes, and down to the freshwater Groenvlei. Once, when following this route myself, I was rambling over the high ridges of the stable dune complex when I suddenly came upon a small family group of recently reintroduced bontebok. Their startled yet curious expressions at my rude intrusion remain distinct in my mind's eye.

The newest trail is a circular, approximately seven kilometre/2-3 hour walk. Starting at the footbridge on the western side of the Goukamma estuary, this well-constructed footpath leads up and over vegetated dunes and through coastal forests. The wildflowers and sea views are fantastic. A short diversion

leads to the sea; plans are to extend this walk westwards.

Groenvlei, originally an estuary, is now cut off from the sea by high dunes and is fed by rainwater and freshwater springs. Almost completely fringed with reedbeds, it provides an ideal habitat for a great many of the 75 bird species in the area. The vlei and the equally bird-rich lower reaches of the Goukamma River also make a very pleasant canoeing environment.

A fable about the lake tells of a beautiful young maiden who lives alone in a palace deep beneath Groenvlei's waters. When darkness approaches she grabs anyone foolish enough to venture on the surface and takes him to her palace for company. No one has ever returned, perhaps explaining why Goukamma is open for day use only!

Finally, I draw your attention to a few dangers that are certainly more real. Although the altitude in the reserve varies only 200 metres from sea level to the high dunes, the hot summer sun and sandy trail tread make walking more taxing than would be expected – so carry water at all times. Before setting out, all beach walkers should check the tide table carefully as it is easy for the unwary to be stranded by an incoming tide.

71. Goudveld State Forest

NEAR KNYSNA, see map page 75

AUTHORITY-IN-CHARGE: Southern Cape Forest Region, Forestry Branch, Department of Environment Affairs.
MAIN ATTRACTIONS: Old Millwood Village site and cemetery; indigenous forest (three main types); bushbuck, baboon, vervet monkey, blue duiker, lynx and leopard; crowned eagles, Narina trogons and Knysna loeries.
FACILITIES/AMENITIES: Picnic sites; natural bathing pools; short nature walks at Krisjan se Nek, Jubilee Creek and Mine Tunnels; Die Kelders forest walk (1-2 hours) to large pools and dripping overhangs.
PERTINENT INFORMATION: Before the discovery of the richer goldfields at Barberton and on the Witwatersrand,

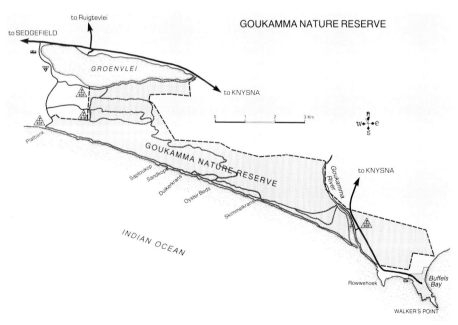

GOUKAMMA NATURE RESERVE

to Ruigtevlei
to SEDGEFIELD
GROENVLEI
to KNYSNA
Platbank
GOUKAMMA NATURE RESERVE
Saptoukop
Sandkop
Dukerkrans
Oyster Beds
Skimmelkrans
Goukamma River
to KNYSNA
INDIAN OCEAN
Rowwehoek
Buffels Bay
WALKER'S POINT
0 1 2 3 Km

Goudveld was a thriving gold-mining area. The town of Millwood sprang up and prospered briefly between 1888 and 1889. Today, its main street is a plantation road lined with blue gums and fruit trees. A section of the Outeniqua Hiking Trail (see page 75) passes through this ghost town. Day visitors can walk 8 km from Goudveld State Forest to Millwood, but must remember that Millwood Hut is solely for the use of hikers on the Outeniqua Trail.

AVAILABLE LITERATURE: *Recreation Facilities*, issued by the Publicity Association of George and Knysna.
CLIMATE: Continuous rainfall area.

72. *Garden of Eden*

NEAR KNYSNA, see map page 75

AUTHORITY-IN-CHARGE: Southern Cape Forest Region, Forestry Branch, Department of Environment Affairs.
MAIN ATTRACTIONS: Indigenous forest.
FACILITIES/AMENITIES: Picnic sites.
AVAILABLE LITERATURE: *The Garden Route*, map by Peter Slingsby, Mapcape.
CLIMATE: Continuous rainfall area.

73. *Diepwalle State Forest*

NEAR KNYSNA, see map page 75

AUTHORITY-IN-CHARGE: Southern Cape Forest Region, Forestry Branch, Department of Environment Affairs.
MAIN ATTRACTIONS: The 'Big Tree' (Outeniqua yellowwood); fynbos and indigenous forest; Spitskop Lookout site.
FACILITIES/AMENITIES: Short nature rambles; four picnic sites: Dal van Varings ('Valley of Ferns'), Velbroeksdraai, Ysterhoutrug and Diepwalle (Grootboom).
PERTINENT INFORMATION: The Ysternek Mountain Fynbos Reserve is located in the Diepwalle State Forest.
AVAILABLE LITERATURE: *Outeniqua Hiking Trail*, brochure; *Recreation Facilities*, issued by the Publicity Association of George and Knysna.
CLIMATE: Continuous rainfall area.

Above: The steep descent into Die Kelders in the Goudveld State Forest is well worth the effort. Large swimming holes, waterfalls and shady indigenous forest alive with bird calls await the weary hiker. The Die Kelders forest walk is in the vicinity of the Outeniqua Hiking Trail.

74. *The Elephant Walk*

DIEPWALLE STATE FOREST, see map page 75

AUTHORITY-IN-CHARGE: Southern Cape Forest Region, Forestry Branch, Department of Environment Affairs.
LENGTH/DURATION: 18,2 km/6,5 hours (shorter alternative routes are possible).
MAIN ATTRACTIONS: Indigenous forests (three main types); eight 'big' trees (Outeniqua yellowwoods); Knysna elephants; birdlife.
FACILITIES/AMENITIES: Nature trail with picnic sites.
PERTINENT INFORMATION: Permits necessary, obtainable free of charge from Diepwalle State Forest, Private Bag X85, Knysna 6570.
AVAILABLE LITERATURE: *The Elephant*

Walk, comprehensive brochure and map; tree list; *The Knysna Elephants and their Forest Home*, by Margo Mackay, Knysna Centre, Eastern Province Branch of the Wildlife Society of Southern Africa, P.O. Box 1000, Knysna 6570.
CLIMATE: Average annual rainfall: 1 200 millimetres, falling mostly between September and April. Continuous rainfall area.

People often ask me: 'What happens if I see an elephant on the Elephant Walk?' And I reply: 'Quickly take its picture, then step out of its way.' However, my answer is not as facetious as it may sound for, if you do see one, consider yourself extremely fortunate as this small herd of three elephants, intensively studied to ensure its survival in an ever-dwindling habitat, comprises the last of the 'uncaged by game reserve' elephants in South Africa.

And although the Diepwalle State Forest, where the walking tours begin and end, is in Knysna elephant terrain, the hiker is far more likely to see bushbuck, blue duiker, baboon and vervet monkey, a large variety of birdlife including the Narina trogon, crowned eagle and gymnogene, and possibly the boomslang, the most common snake in the area. You cannot help but notice some of the finest specimens of stinkwood, yellowwood, red and white alder, Cape beech and other indigenous forest trees in the region.

The Elephant Walk is physically very easy and remains flat to gently sloping most of the way. A whole day is recommended to fully appreciate this circular nature trail. Take your lunch with you; there are picnic sites at the halfway point. Fires may be made at the approved sites only.

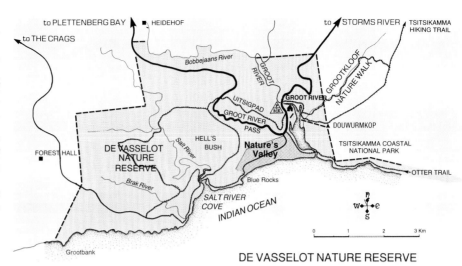

DE VASSELOT NATURE RESERVE

75. Robberg Nature Reserve

PLETTENBERG BAY, see map page 82

AUTHORITY-IN-CHARGE: Department of Nature and Environmental Conservation, Cape Provincial Administration.
SIZE: 160 hectares.
MAIN ATTRACTIONS: Diverse coastal scenery; varied plant and littoral life; excellent angling and bird-watching area.
FACILITIES/AMENITIES: Footpaths; private camp-site nearby.
PERTINENT INFORMATION: Water supply is unreliable, availability depends on rainfall. Warning: freak waves and ocean surges near rocky outcrops can occur.
AVAILABLE LITERATURE: A Fisherman's Map, printed by the Angling Club of Plettenberg Bay.
CLIMATE: Continuous rainfall area.

Robberg, 'mountain of seals', has always been popular with anglers for its fine fishing and intertidal life. As a result, a network of old fishermen's walks exists from the carpark to Cape Seal, a distance of about 4,5 kilometres. Circular routes can also be followed which will take you to all the viewpoints on this mountain peninsula. When exploring the intertidal life and rocky promontories, watch out for freak waves, especially in rough weather. Drownings have occurred here.

A factor contributing to Robberg's ecological interest is the distinction between its southern and northern sides. The southern aspect is exposed to strong wave action on outlying reefs, while the northern side has deep and sheltered waters. North-facing slopes are more arid and therefore have a more open vegetation than the closed canopied, south-facing slopes. The prevailing winds are so intense that sand from the dunes linking Robberg with the mainland is often blown right over the peninsula.

The Nelson Bay Cave, rich in artefacts and fossils from early Upper Pleistocene

times, is proof that prehistoric man thrived on the peninsula. Birds dependent on Robberg's marine and terrestrial life include Cape gannets, crowned eagles, black oystercatchers, Cape dikkops, swift terns, spotted eagle owls, giant kingfishers, ground woodpeckers, black sunbirds and tchagra shrikes. Dassies and Cape grey mongoose are also present. The very fortunate trailist may spot humpback whales wallowing in the surf.

76. Keurbooms River Nature Reserve

PLETTENBERG BAY, see map page 82

AUTHORITY-IN-CHARGE: Department of Nature and Environmental Conservation, Cape Provincial Administration.
SIZE: 760 hectares.
LENGTH: 5 km.
MAIN ATTRACTIONS: Riverine forest with prolific birdlife.
FACILITIES/AMENITIES: Keurbooms River Public Resort – chalets, cottages, caravan and camping sites; footpath to picnic sites.
PERTINENT INFORMATION: Speedboating is prohibited on the upper reaches of the river (legislation to this effect is being passed). A 20-km circular trail is planned.
AVAILABLE LITERATURE: Included in annual reports of the Department of Nature and Environmental Conservation.
CLIMATE: Continuous rainfall area.

If you enjoy a peaceful holiday in a tranquil setting, camp under the yellowwoods along the banks of the Keurbooms River, in the lower foothills of the Tsitsikamma Mountains. Then canoe upstream with your senses alert for the cry of the fish eagle, a sight of bushbuck, blue duiker or grysbok drinking at the river's edge, the rattling of high branches by vervet monkeys and a glimpse of the sensational colours displayed

by the Knysna loerie and the Narina trogon. Alight from your canoe in the Keurbooms River Nature Reserve, picnic at one of the newly cleared sites and then walk along the nature trail cut into the dense forest on the steep riverine slopes.

77. De Vasselot Nature Reserve

KEURBOOMS RIVER AND BLOUKRANS STATE FOREST

AUTHORITY-IN-CHARGE: Tsitsikamma Forest Region, Forestry Branch, Department of Environment Affairs.
SIZE: 2 561 hectares.
MAIN ATTRACTIONS: High indigenous forest; colourful fynbos flowers; rocky coastline; deep river gorges and ravines; wilderness environment.
FACILITIES/AMENITIES: Groot River camp-site for both public and youth groups; 8 nature trails.
PERTINENT INFORMATION: Permits necessary, obtainable from The Forester, Bloukrans State Forest, Private Bag X530, Humansdorp 6300; tel. (04457) 6710. The Tsitsikamma Hiking Trail (see page 82) traverses part of the reserve.
AVAILABLE LITERATURE: De Vasselot Nature Reserve, notes as well as geological, trail and vegetation sketch maps issued by the Forestry Branch.
CLIMATE: Continuous rainfall area. Average annual rainfall: 1 011 millimetres, falling mostly between April and the end of July. Warm and humid climate with an average maximum monthly temperature of 18 °C. Dry winter mountain winds from the north and north-west bring high temperatures. December to March and June to September are the fire hazard seasons.

Within the De Vasselot Nature Reserve, which forms part of the Tsitsikamma Forest environment near Nature's Valley, are eight short nature walks ranging from 1,3 to 4,1 kilometres each way. To fully appreciate this lovely area, I suggest you do several of the walks in sequence, following the sketch map issued by the Forestry Branch.

These trails pass through varied plant communities, each hosting a wide variety of animals. Knysna-type, high indigenous forest contains, in addition to majestic tree specimens, 25 species of ferns, aloes, lilies and orchids as well as birds such as the Knysna loerie, olive woodpecker, sombre bulbul, paradise flycatcher and the slender forest canary.

Dry scrub forest occurring along the coast and southern parts of the reserve differs appreciably in species composition from the high forests in the central and western reserve and along the Groot River. These dry forests contain trees with intriguing names such as bastard lightning bush, dune koko tree, common poisonbush and bush-tick berry. Bird-watchers along the coast may be fortunate enough to observe the Cape gannet, black oystercatcher, giant kingfisher and fish eagle.

Coastal plateau fynbos is plentiful, with ericas, sugarbushes, mimetes, pincushions, everlastings, the king protea and hundreds of other colourful flowers attracting the nectar-feeding Cape sugarbird, orange-breasted sunbird and lesser doublecollared sunbird. Grey duiker, blue duiker, bushbuck and grysbok are also abundant in the De Vasselot Nature Reserve, as are baboons, vervet monkeys and three species of mongoose. Listen for the 'screaming' call of the tree hyrax, a relative of the rock dassie but which has nocturnal and arboreal habits.

At several places the walks, demarcated by white footprints, cross the Brak, Salt and Groot rivers. The water from these rivers is deliciously potable despite its deep red colour, which is caused by natural organic substances in the soils through which the rivers drain. The paths provide views of the sensational Groot River Pass and deep ravines which contribute to the reserve's rugged wilderness atmosphere. Traversing the eastern section of the De Vasselot Nature Reserve is the Tsitsikamma Hiking Trail.

At the most eastern point of Uitsigpad, on the banks of the Groot River near Nature's Valley and the sea, is a public and group overnight facility providing 45 camping sites, fireplaces, ablution blocks and toilets, cold water taps, rubbish bins and firewood (for sale). Youth groups which perform conservation-orientated projects such as footpath maintenance or eradication of exotic plants are allowed to camp free of charge. Members of the public and youth groups who do not do conservation work are charged a nominal fee. Youth groups can book for the Groot River camp-site through the Forestry Branch at Humansdorp. Others must book through the forester at Bloukrans

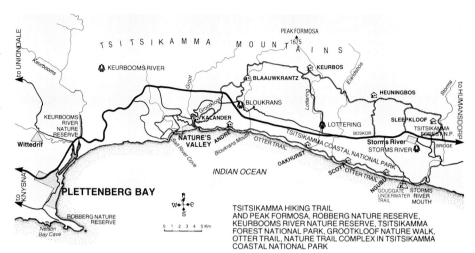

TSITSIKAMMA HIKING TRAIL
AND PEAK FORMOSA, ROBBERG NATURE RESERVE,
KEURBOOMS RIVER NATURE RESERVE, TSITSIKAMMA
FOREST NATIONAL PARK, GROOTKLOOF NATURE WALK,
OTTER TRAIL, NATURE TRAIL COMPLEX IN TSITSIKAMMA
COASTAL NATIONAL PARK

State Forest. Ramblers intending to walk any of the De Vasselot trails must also obtain permits from the Bloukrans State Forest.

78. Tsitsikamma Hiking Trail and Peak Formosa

NATURE'S VALLEY

AUTHORITY-IN-CHARGE: Tsitsikamma Forest Region, Forestry Branch, Department of Environment Affairs*.
LENGTH/DURATION: 61 km/5 days, 4 nights. Several variations suitable for weekend excursions possible; can be walked in conjunction with the Otter Trail (see opposite page), thereby making a 10-day loop.
MAIN ATTRACTIONS: High, humid indigenous forest; flowering Cape fynbos; tree ferns.
FACILITIES/AMENITIES: Five huts, each accommodating 30 people, with bunks, mattresses and fireplaces.
PERTINENT INFORMATION: Parking available at Groot River camp-site, Storms River, Bloukrans and Lottering State Forest offices, and Boskor sawmill. Beware of flash floods while crossing rivers, and waterproof your bags. Hikers must overnight in huts for which they are booked. Ticks are prevalent.
AVAILABLE LITERATURE: *Tsitsikamma Hiking Trail – Otter Trail*, comprehensive brochure and map.
CLIMATE: Similar to the Otter Trail, but snow is possible in June, July and August.

Beginning at Kalander Hut on the Groot River at Nature's Valley and terminating at the Storms River mouth, the Tsitsikamma Hiking Trail winds in and out of high, humid indigenous forests, Cape fynbos and plantations. The trail is situated on both the lower and higher plateaux, farther inland that the Otter Trail but below the Tsitsikamma Mountains. Fast-running, clean rivers, subject to rapid flooding, flow over the plateau to the sea; waterproof bags should be carried at all times.

The Tsitsikamma Hiking Trail is an easily negotiated hike; no day's stretch is longer than 17 kilometres, thus allowing leisurely walking and plenty of time to enjoy and appreciate the environment. The high humid forests, reaching a height of 18 to 30 metres, grow on shale formations; trees are labelled with their national tree list numbers. The fynbos, found on quartzite soils, differs from that of the winter-rainfall Western Cape in that it contains only those species that will tolerate year-round rainfall. An advantage, however, is that the less dense bush makes identification of specific plants easier for the amateur botanist. To take full advantage of the flowering season, hike in early to midsummer; February to May is the poorest time.

Except for coastal and marine creatures which are obviously absent on the Tsitsikamma trail, wildlife is similar to that encountered on the Otter Trail.

Towering above the Tsitsikamma Hiking Trail in Lottering State Forest stands Peak Formosa (1 675 m). It rises ruggedly above the Tsitsikamma range, forming the head of Lottering, Bloukrans, Krakeel and Louterwater valleys. On its northern slopes a dry and sparse fynbos community grows, sharply contrasting with the dense indigenous forest and thick fynbos on its higher-rainfall, southern aspect.

Several routes ascend Formosa, with those from the north being shorter and more direct. Once you reach the top you can see the entire coast from Storms River to Plet-

Opposite page, left: the crane flower or bird-of-paradise, Strelitzia reginae.

Opposite page, right: Otter Trail hikers must cross the Bloukrans River at low tide.

tenberg Bay, Cockscomb and Mac peaks on the northern horizon, an array of ridges, valleys and smaller mountains to the east and the peaks near George and Oudtshoorn to the west. Beware of winter snows, and the mists that roll in from the sea at midday and rapidly cover the mountain ridges. Only experienced mountaineers should venture into this area; no amenities are present and any routes are only rough mountain tracks.

79. *Tsitsikamma Forest National Park*

NATURE'S VALLEY

AUTHORITY-IN-CHARGE: National Parks Board.
DURATION: Three 15-90 minute nature trails.
MAIN ATTRACTIONS: Indigenous coastal high forest; the 'Big Tree'; birdlife.
FACILITIES/AMENITIES: Lumber museum at Paul Sauer Bridge; camping and caravan sites; café and restaurant.
AVAILABLE LITERATURE: *A Guide to the Tsitsikamma Forest National Park*, brochure with sketch map.
CLIMATE: Continuous rainfall area.

Sometimes confused with the Tsitsikamma Coastal National Park, the smaller Tsitsikamma Forest National Park is located on the northern side of the Garden Route (N2), to the west of Storms River. Noted for its indigenous coastal forest, the park hosts three short, easy rambles.

The Big Tree Trail (15 minutes) features stinkwood and ironwood trees and the Big Tree, a 36,6 metre-tall yellowwood.

The Bush Pig Trail (90 minutes) meanders through forest and fynbos; the fifth day

of the Tsitsikamma Hiking Trail follows part of the Bush Pig Trail.

The Tree Fern Trail (60 minutes) features a fallen giant yellowwood, tree ferns and an old saw pit.

The trails also provide interesting rambling asides to the longer hiking trails in the area.

80. *Grootkloof Nature Walk*

NATURE'S VALLEY

AUTHORITY-IN-CHARGE: Tsitsikamma Forest Region, Forestry Branch, Department of Environment Affairs.
LENGTH: 10 km.
MAIN ATTRACTIONS: Indigenous forest and montane fynbos.
FACILITIES/AMENITIES: Parking available at Kalander Hut; Groot River camp-site.
PERTINENT INFORMATION: A section of the nature walk forms part of the Tsitsikamma Hiking Trail (see opposite page).
AVAILABLE LITERATURE: *Tsitsikamma Hiking Trail*, brochure and map.
CLIMATE: Temperate. Rain is possible all year but falls mainly in March, August, October and November. Dry south-easterly winds blow mainly during May and June, and can be accompanied by moisture-laden sea mists. Snow is possible in June, July, August and September. Average maximum winter temperature is 18 °C, but this can be higher when the hot berg wind blows.

The Grootkloof Nature Walk, which coincides with the beginning of the Tsitsikamma Hiking Trail, is a lovely looping walk through both Southern Cape fynbos and high indigenous forests. Ramblers follow a

five-kilometre path through leucadendrons, ericas, pelargoniums and other attractive fynbos species before leaving the hiking trail and circling back through Grootkloof's shady indigenous forest. Naturalists who wait patiently in the forest may be rewarded, as bushbuck, grysbok, blue duiker and over 30 species of elusive forest birds can be seen. More information on the plants and animals of this region is given in the entry on the Tsitsikamma Hiking Trail.

81. *Otter Trail*

TSITSIKAMMA COASTAL NATIONAL PARK, STORMS RIVER

AUTHORITY-IN-CHARGE: National Parks Board.
LENGTH/DURATION: 41 km/5 days.
MAIN ATTRACTIONS: Rugged coastal scenery with tidal pools rich in marine life; Cape coastal indigenous forests and fynbos.
FACILITIES/AMENITIES: Log huts with toilets, fireplaces and firewood: two huts per site, each hut accommodating 6 people, with mattresses on bunk beds.
PERTINENT INFORMATION: The Bloukrans River must be crossed by wading or swimming; waterproof your backpack and check the tide table to determine low water. Although the Otter Trail can be walked in conjunction with the Tsitsikamma Hiking Trail, providing a loop walk, they must be booked separately – the Otter Trail through the National Parks Board, and the Tsitsikamma Hiking Trail through the Forestry Branch in Humansdorp.
AVAILABLE LITERATURE: *Otter Trail – Tsitsikamma Hiking Trail*, comprehensive brochure and map issued by NHWB; *The Otter Trail*, brochure and map issued by the National Parks Board.

CLIMATE: Temperate. Rain is possible all year but falls mainly in March, August, October and November. Dry south-easterly winds blow mainly during May and June, and can be accompanied by moisture-laden sea mists. Hail and frost can occur, but are uncommon. Winter is hot with dry berg winds. Average maximum winter temperature is 18 °C but 38 °C has been recorded during winter berg wind conditions.

South Africa's first organized hiking trail and a perennial favourite, the Otter Trail winds from the Storms River mouth along the coast to the Groot River estuary at Nature's Valley on the park's western boundary. Its popularity stems from its unbeatable coastal scenery, indigenous forest, and the short daily stretches which make hiking possible for backpackers of limited ability and experience, including families and even trailists of suspect fitness.

The Otter Trail, built and run by the National Parks Board, is demarcated with the otter emblem or splashes of white paint in rocky areas, instead of the more usual white footprints.

The Otter Trail's route follows the shore, and ascends 200 metres to the coastal plateau where necessary. It funnels through thick canopy forest and crosses streams and rivers. Although the stretches between overnight shelters are short (the longest day's hike is only 14 kilometres), some of the slopes are steep. However, there is enough time to walk slowly, study the flora, snorkel in the tidal pools and observe birds and other wildlife. The National Parks Board insists that hikers sleep at every hut, otherwise bookings become confused.

Some of the features of the trail include cave middens left by strandlopers, the Guano Cave, and waterfalls; coastal forests with a wealth of Outeniqua yellowwood, stinkwood, saffronwood, elder, Cape beech and white milkwood; large marine mammals such as dolphins, seals and whales; dassies (on the cliffs); bushbuck, grysbok, blue duiker, baboon and vervet monkeys in the forests; and spoor of bushpig, leopard, the Cape clawless otter and klipspringer. A total of 210 species of birds has been recorded – these include 35 seabirds such as the black oystercatcher, sooty shearwater and the Arctic skua.

To avoid disappointment, especially during peak holiday seasons, it is essential to book well in advance. It is best to contact the National Parks Board first (tel. (012) 44-1100) to work out dates with the booking clerks.

Above: Protea rupicola *growing on Saptoukop.*

Opposite page, top: One of the many scenic waterfalls in the Langkloof.

Opposite page, bottom: Water uintjies are a main ingredient in a Cape Malay stew.

82. *Nature Trail Complex*

TSITSIKAMMA COASTAL NATIONAL PARK, see map page 82

AUTHORITY-IN-CHARGE: National Parks Board.
LENGTH: 5 nature trails, each less than 3 km.
MAIN ATTRACTIONS: Rugged coastal scenery with tidal pools rich in marine life; Cape coastal indigenous forest and fynbos; underwater trail.
FACILITIES/AMENITIES: Cottages, caravan- and camp-sites; restaurant.
AVAILABLE LITERATURE: *Tsitsikamma Coastal National Park,* brochure; field guides to park (see page 340).
CLIMATE: Temperate. Winter: hot with dry berg winds; average maximum winter temperature is 18 °C but 38 °C has been recorded during winter berg wind conditions. Rain is possible throughout the year but falls mainly in March, August, October and November. Dry south-easterly winds blow mainly during May and June, and can be accompanied by damp sea mists. Hail and frost occur, but are uncommon.

The Tsitsikamma Coastal National Park is one of South Africa's most beautiful coastal reserves. Here, huge waves breaking on rugged cliffs, richly endowed intertidal pools, high humid indigenous forests and lower coastal forests create a diverse, scenic venue for the five short walks within the developed park complex. All follow easy gradients, and each is less than three kilometres in length. They are the Blue Duiker Trail (the longest), the Loerie Trail (about a kilometre), the Mouth Trail (about two kilometres) and, on the east side of the Paul Sauer Bridge, the very short Look-out Trail and Dead End Trail.

A unique trail with interpretive plaques placed underwater has also been set out in a bay west of Goudgate. Here, trailists equipped with snorkels and masks can experience the fascinating world of submarine animals and plants. Although scuba gear is ideal, its use is restricted to divers with an SAUU third-class diving certificate.

The most popular trail in this park, and indeed one of the most popular in the whole of South Africa, is the 41-kilometre Otter Trail (see page 83).

83. *Langkloof-Garden Route Cycle Trail*

COLESBERG TO GEORGE

AUTHORITY-IN-CHARGE: Trailblazers.
DURATION: 9,5 days.
MAIN ATTRACTIONS: Spectacular mountain passes and valleys; coastal scenery; high indigenous forests.
FACILITIES/AMENITIES: Camping accommodation; tarmac roads; all transport, equipment and food provided; cost of tour does not include cycle hire, therefore trailists are welcome to use their own bicycles.
PERTINENT INFORMATION: Maximum of 18 people per group. Either racing (thin-tyre) or all-terrain (fat-tyre) bicycles can be used. A back-up vehicle lifts cycles up main escarpments; riding is mainly downhill, so trail requires only moderate fitness.
AVAILABLE LITERATURE: Brochures available from Trailblazers.
CLIMATE: Southern Cape: continuous rainfall area. Karoo: summer rainfall area.

Combining the drier regions of South Africa (the Karoo) with the lush Southern Cape forests, this cycle tour blends dramatic mountain passes with productive and scenic

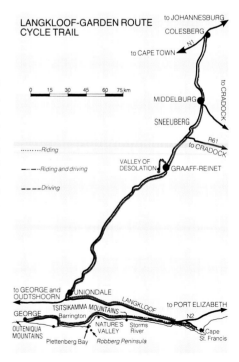

apple farming lands, dramatic coastal scenery and cool, high forests.

After camping at Colesberg in the Karoo on the first night, cyclists ride down through the passes of the Renosterberg and Sneeuberg to Graaff-Reinet and the Valley of Desolation. Back-up vehicles transport trailists to Uniondale, where they start the 120-kilometre stretch down the Langkloof, famous for its apple and citrus farms. The coastal areas visited include Cape St. Francis, the Tsitsikamma Mountains, Storms River bridge and Storms River mouth. Nature's Valley provides the venue for a scenic camp before cyclists move to Plettenberg Bay, the Robberg Peninsula and Goukamma. The trail ends at George after cycling the back road via Barrington, along the slopes of the Outeniquas.

84. Cockscomb, Baviaanskloof and Formosa State Forests

PATENSIE TO WILLOWMORE

AUTHORITY-IN-CHARGE: Tsitsikamma Forest Region, Forestry Branch, Department of Environment Affairs★.
SIZE: Baviaanskloof Forest: 142 000 hectares.
MAIN ATTRACTIONS: Vast, dramatic wilderness; deep kloofs negotiable on foot; large specimens of Willowmore (Baviaanskloof) cedar, *Widdringtonia schwarzii*; rock pools; wildlife.
FACILITIES/AMENITIES: Caves and footpaths only.
PERTINENT INFORMATION: 70 000 hectares of this forest area may be declared a Wilderness Area in the near future. 75 per cent of the proposed wilderness will fall in the Kouga Mountains. The three forest stations serving this area are, for the southern area of the Kouga Mountains, Formosa State Forest, P.O. Box 117, Joubertina 6410, tel. (04272), ask for 169; Baviaanskloof State Forest, Private Bag X203, Willowmore 6680, tel. (04942), ask for 469; and, for the eastern area of the Kouga Mountains, Cockscomb State Forest, P.O. Box 218, Patensie 6335, tel. (04232), ask for 270. Access is restricted. This area is for experienced hikers. Always carry maps and compass. Open fires are prohibited.
AVAILABLE LITERATURE: 'Baviaanskloof – Een Van Ons Mees Afgesonderde Valleie', *Flying Springbok*, March 1983.
CLIMATE: Border of continuous and summer rainfall areas. Sea-facing mountains receive more rain than inland range.

The Baviaanskloof and Kouga mountains merge into a tough, vast and wild region

which is similar to, but not as dramatic as, the Cedarberg in the Western Cape, and is more arid. Of all the southern and eastern Cape mountains, these are the most challenging and scenically rewarding, with their deep kloofs and bathing pools, impressive rock faces, high peaks and endless traverses.

It is up to the mountaineer to plan his adventure carefully using topographic maps and conferring with the foresters for advice. Private land is usually crossed to reach the mountain catchment government-owned land, so it is important to make arrangements with the relevant farmers. The local people are very friendly, helpful and knowledgeable about footpaths, caves and wildlife in the area.

The most prominent peaks are Saptoukop (1 714 m) in the Kouga Mountains, and Mac (1 562 m) in the Baviaanskloof Mountains. Saptoukop, in the west, has a faint, beaconed path leading to its summit, a steady ascent although technically a walk. Mac dominates the eastern extremity of its range. Scrambling and walking up kloofs and ridges brings you to the summit from which you can see the Steytlerville Flats to the north and the rugged, broken country of the lower Kouga foothills to the south. Separating the Baviaanskloof Mountains from the Cockscomb and Groot Winterhoek Mountains is the Groot River Valley.

However, 'peak bagging' is not essential to fully enjoy this area. The exploration of its kloofs is equally rewarding. Fine old specimens of *Widdringtonia schwarzii*, 30 metres in height, can be found only in remote rocky ravines, where neither fire nor woodcutter has reached. The most impressive stand occurs in Doringkloof, in the shadow of Kougakop (1 719 m). A new path ascends to Kougakop's summit.

Attractive proteas such as *Protea eximia*, *P. rupicola*, *P. grandiceps*, *P. tenax*, *P. vogtsiae* and *P. intonsa* occur in the fynbos veld, while the Geranium family (pelargoniums) line the river banks. Water uintjies (*Aponogeton* spp.) sometimes float on the surface of still ponds. These flowers are a well-known flavouring in the Cape Malay stew known as 'waterblommetjiebredie'.

Careful investigation of krantzes, ponds and vegetation reveals birds such as black cuckoo-shrikes, black crakes, Cape reed warblers, African sedge warblers, bluebilled firefinches, redbreasted sparrowhawks, peregrine falcons and black eagles. Duiker, klipspringer and baboon are plentiful. Fishing yields black bass, eel and other freshwater species.

Bushmen once inhabited these kloofs, and their paintings can be seen in many of the overhangs.

Access to the southern slopes of this area is via Langkloof, the citrus-growing heartland, while the northern slopes can be reached from the Patensie-Willowmore road, itself a spectacular scenic drive.

available locally; 'St. Francis Bay – South Africa's Little Venice', Paul Moorcroft, *Flying Springbok*, March 1986, page 27.
CLIMATE: Average annual rainfall: 660 millimetres. Winter months bring rain and cloudy weather. Spring (September and October) and autumn (March and April) bring heavy downpours. Wind is common throughout the year.

85. St. Francis Bay and Cape St. Francis Nature Reserve

HUMANSDORP

AUTHORITY-IN-CHARGE: St. Francis/Kromme Trust, 9 George Road, St. Francis Bay 6312. Nature reserve: Department of Nature and Environmental Conservation, Cape Provincial Administration.
SIZE: Nature reserve: 36 hectares.
LENGTH: Nature walk from Cape St. Francis lighthouse to St. Francis Bay: approximately 6 km.
MAIN ATTRACTIONS: Scenic coastline, rich marine life and birdlife; middens; fishing; small mammals; shipwrecks; lighthouse; unique township resort.
FACILITIES/AMENITIES: Fishing, boating and snorkelling; braai areas; restaurant in township.
PERTINENT INFORMATION: Longer walks do exist, but they cross private ground; the permission of the landowner must be obtained; large groups should contact the St. Francis/Kromme Trust.
AVAILABLE LITERATURE: *St. Francis/Kromme Trust, 1985*, booklet with maps, ecological information and flower checklists,

ST. FRANCIS BAY AND CAPE ST. FRANCIS NATURE RESERVE

LOERIE DAM NATURE RESERVE

Above: The Cockscomb, Baviaanskloof and Formosa state forests are rich in wildflowers. Here, pincushions grow in abundance near the Saptoukop peak.

Opposite page: To visit Emerald Pool in the Groendal Wilderness Area, hikers sleep in a large cave and then descend the steep footpath into the kloof below. This view is from the lower slopes of Strydomsberg.

86. Loerie Dam Nature Reserve

HANKEY

AUTHORITY-IN-CHARGE: Nature Conservation Section, Dias Divisional Council, P.O. Box 318, Port Elizabeth 6000.
LENGTH/DURATION: 5 km/2-3 hours.
MAIN ATTRACTIONS: Scenery (mountains, fynbos and bush flora); perennial streams; Loerie Dam.
FACILITIES/AMENITIES: Timber hut, accommodating 20 people, for hikers; canoes and punting.
PERTINENT INFORMATION: This is a developing reserve; contact the Dias Divisional Council for the latest information on educational programmes, etc.
AVAILABLE LITERATURE: In process of being compiled.
CLIMATE: Summer rainfall area.

87. Groendal Wilderness Area

NEAR UITENHAGE

AUTHORITY-IN-CHARGE: Eastern Cape Forest Region, Forestry Branch, Department of Environment Affairs*.
SIZE: 21 793 hectares.
MAIN ATTRACTIONS: Deep forested ravines; Emerald Pool, and other rock pools; fynbos-type vegetation and valley bushveld; antelope and forest bird species; Bushman paintings in natural rock shelters.
FACILITIES/AMENITIES: Patrol paths and footpaths only; labelled tree specimens; showers at forest station; caves available for shelter.
PERTINENT INFORMATION: Permits necessary, obtainable from Groendal State Forest, Poste Restante, Uitenhage 6230. Vehicles and pack animals prohibited. No fires allowed.
AVAILABLE LITERATURE: *Groendal Wilderness Area* and *Blindekloof and Emerald Pool in the Groendal Wilderness Area*, information sheets and sketch map issued by the Forestry Branch; located on Government Printer's 1:50 000 maps '3325 CB Uitenhage North' and '3325 AD Kirkwood'.
CLIMATE: Average annual rainfall: 500-800 millimetres, falling mostly in summer. Weather unpredictable.

The south-eastern Cape is not as richly endowed with unexploited rugged mountain terrain as some other regions of South Africa. However, eight kilometres from Uitenhage, in the Groot Winterhoek range, lies a stretch of almost inaccessible ravines, vertical rock faces, natural cave shelters, impenetrable valley bushveld, fynbos and indigenous forest where leopards and caracal are, on occasion, still seen. This mountainous area, well-known to old-time farmers who resisted Bushman raids, and known to mountaineers for its challenges such as the highest peak, Strydomsberg (1 180 m), was given wilderness conservation status in 1976.

The Groendal Wilderness Area has numerous well-marked footpaths and patrol tracks which mountaineers may use, but you are not restricted to them. However, at relatively low elevations (314-630 metres) the

dense form of valley bushveld vegetation makes hiking on routes other than prepared trails almost impossible.

One of the popular destinations for hikers is Emerald Pool, a 4-5 hour walk from the forest station. (It is advisable to carry water *en route* to the final kloof and pools.) The pool is situated in a deep gorge. There is a large cave in the steep-sided walls of the gorge offering overnight shelter. From this cave to the top of Strydomsberg peak you must be prepared to walk for about 3-4 hours on an overgrown, scratchy path. Heat exhaustion is a possible hazard in summer, especially if the berg wind blows.

Although the steepest southern slopes in the area have higher and more moist fynbos communities, where *Leucadendron eucalyptifolium* and *Protea neriifolia* species are conspicuous, short fynbos – characterized by the common pincushion, salignum conebush and large-leaved sugarbush, and interspersed with *Themeda triandra* grass – is the most common floral community blanketing these mountains. Over 60 species of veld and forest trees such as yellowwood, stinkwood, fig, sugarbush, alder, currant, holly, saffron, guarri, pomegranate, assegai and cabbage tree are also present; many are labelled with their national tree list numbers so don't forget your *National List of Trees* booklet or the Forestry Branch's information brochure.

Among the bushveld, fynbos and forested kloofs live grey duiker, grysbok, bushbuck, blue duiker, chacma baboon, bushpig and the Knysna loerie. Other animals which hikers may be fortunate to see are the yellowbilled and black ducks, grey rhebok and mountain reedbuck.

The entire wilderness area is a catchment for the Swartkops River whose tributaries have cut impressive, deep ravines in the consolidated river gravel sands and mud, and higher folded and fractured quartzitic formations. The Groendal Dam, which sup-

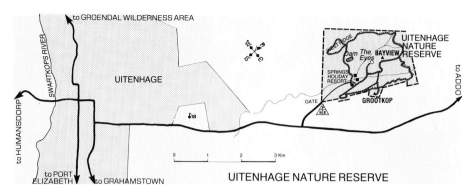

UITENHAGE NATURE RESERVE

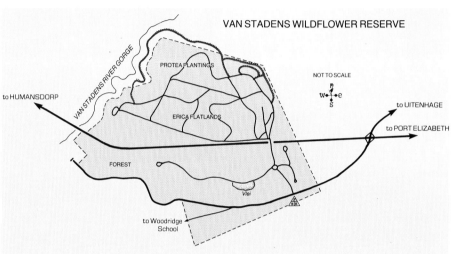

VAN STADENS WILDFLOWER RESERVE

plies Uitenhage's industrial and domestic water, and some small private properties are also situated within the wilderness area.

This area is believed to have been the last refuge of the Bushmen between the Gamtoos and Kei rivers. Some of their paintings still remain.

88. *Uitenhage Nature Reserve*

UITENHAGE

AUTHORITY-IN-CHARGE: Municipality of Uitenhage, P.O. Box 45, Uitenhage 6230.
SIZE: 396 hectares.
MAIN ATTRACTIONS: Tropical and temperate plant and animal life; birdlife; freshwater springs ('The Eyes').
FACILITIES/AMENITIES: Footpaths; guided tours to the springs are conducted each weekday, except Thursday, at 15h00 and on weekends and public holidays at 14h00 and 16h00; small enclosure for animals, and an aviary; Springs Pleasure Resort with bungalows, caravan sites, swimming pool and playground; access to herbarium on request.
PERTINENT INFORMATION: Permits necessary, obtainable from The Supervisor, Springs Holiday Resort, Uitenhage (for

whites) and The Director of Parks, Buxton Avenue, Uitenhage (for blacks). Open 08h30-19h00 (October to March), 08h00-17h30 (April to September).
AVAILABLE LITERATURE: *Uitenhage Nature Reserve*, brochure and map.
CLIMATE: Summer: dry and warm. Winter: mild. Rainfall: variable.

Emphasizing vegetation and its associated bird and small mammal life, the trails in the Uitenhage Nature Reserve offer gentle, pleasant strolls over a variety of undulating terrains. Three wide, circular paths, requiring from 40 minutes to three hours to complete, lead the rambler through thick valley bushveld as well as karroid shrub and grassland. These plant communities, noted for their inclusion of both tropical and temperate species, support small antelope such as bushbuck, grysbok, steenbok and duiker. The veld is also home to bushpig, porcupine and more than 100 bird species, including a number of waterfowl which are attracted to an old concrete dam converted into a 'pan'.

Plant-lovers will enjoy the variety of angiosperms, including many representatives of the Compositae, Liliaceae and Crassulaceae families. June to the end of August, the aloe blooming season, is recommended for visits. Interesting trees, such as white milkwood, sneezewood, wild olive and the Karoo boer-bean are also present in this reserve. The north- and west-facing slopes, being drier and warmer, naturally support the more succulent-type plants such as spek-boom and euphorbia.

In addition to following the footpaths, a visit to 'The Eyes' freshwater springs is worthwhile. Here, approximately 3,6 million litres of water bubble out of the ground each day and many birds and small animals are attracted to the resultant lush 'oasis' vegetation. Uitenhage is able to use the natural fountains for its water supply as the reserve is located only seven kilometres from the town.

From a look-out tower along the trail, ramblers can see the coastal mountains, the Winterhoek Mountains, the Suurberg and the coastline of Algoa Bay.

The public resort within the nature reserve, offering single and double bungalows and caravan sites, is popular with local residents, so book well in advance of holiday seasons.

89. Van Stadens Wildflower Reserve

PORT ELIZABETH

AUTHORITY-IN-CHARGE: Dias Divisional Council.
SIZE: 400 hectares.
LENGTH/DURATION: River Walk: 2 km/1 hour. Forest Walk: 2 km/1 hour.
MAIN ATTRACTIONS: Forested riverine slopes; expansive mountain views; protea plantings; indigenous flowering plants; dams attract water-birds.
FACILITIES/AMENITIES: Circular trails and tracks; information centre; display shelter featuring flowers in bloom; picnic sites; swimming pools in Van Stadens River.
PERTINENT INFORMATION: Permits not required, except for groups of more than 20 people. 73 hectares of ground was added to the reserve in December 1986, and walking trails are planned in this area.
AVAILABLE LITERATURE: *Van Stadens River Wildflower Reserve and Bird Sanctuary*, comprehensive booklet and sketch map; *Van Stadens Wildflower Reserve*, brochure.
CLIMATE: Variable; year-round rainfall.

Located 40 kilometres from Port Elizabeth on the east bank of the Van Stadens River, the Van Stadens Sanctuary was declared a reserve for the conservation of Alexandria forest and the eastern Cape fynbos, in addition to the protection and propagation of proteas and other indigenous flora.

Attractive chiefly to the botanically and ornithologically orientated rambler, tracks on level to gently sloping terrain criss-cross erica flatlands and plantings of *Protea nerii-folia*, and lead to vantage points overlooking forested gorges. Table Mountain sandstone soils support ground orchids, succulents and

annuals in addition to cultivated and forest species. The forests along the southern slopes and river are transitional between the more western Knysna flora and the more tropical vegetation to the east. February to August is the main flowering season.

Birdlife flourishes within the forests and on the vleis: the sombre bulbul, Narina trogon, paradise flycatcher and forest canary are just some of the 102 recorded species. The reserve also hosts colourful butterflies and a population of small mammals which includes grysbok, blue and grey duiker and bushbuck.

For detailed lists, descriptions and sketches of natural vegetation, trees, shrubs, butterflies, snakes, birds and mammals, and the regulations pertaining to the area, obtain the useful booklet on the reserve, published by the Dias Divisional Council.

A hiking trail winds along the Van Stadens River, the latest details of which can be obtained from the Dias Divisional Council.

90. Maitland Mines Nature Reserve

PORT ELIZABETH, see map page 90

AUTHORITY-IN-CHARGE: Dias Divisional Council.
SIZE: 127 hectares.
LENGTH/DURATION: 3,2 km/2 hours.
MAIN ATTRACTIONS: Coastal forest and bush; birdlife; beach with tremendously high dunes.
FACILITIES/AMENITIES: Picnic sites; trees along the trail labelled with their national tree list numbers; angling; Maitland Camping Site at the Maitland River mouth.
PERTINENT INFORMATION: Entrance by permit, to be completed at the first information box (see below). Scholars are

encouraged. Do not drink water from the small stream of the Van Stadens River, which passes the picnic spot near the entrance to the reserve.
AVAILABLE LITERATURE: *The Maitland Mines Nature Trail*, guide; plant and bird checklists; environmental education material.
CLIMATE: Summer rainfall area.

In the Maitland Mines Nature Reserve a nature trail winds through the almost impenetrable and very valuable coastal forest which flanks the lower Maitland River and its mouth. There is also an old wagon road to the lead mines which were worked towards the end of the last century. The hilly terrain, fine beach areas and large sand dunes are all popular with nature ramblers. Birdlife is plentiful because of the secluded nature of the reserve as well as an abundance of natural food, and typical of the area are the emeraldspotted wood dove, African hoopoe, paradise flycatcher, forest canary and Knysna loerie.

As part of its contribution to environmental education, the Dias Divisional Council has designed a very popular self-guided trail, at strategic points along which information boxes have been placed. The visitor removes a sheet of paper, on which there appears a sketch of the immediate area, from the box. Numbers on the sketch relate to information supplied on the sheet. Ecological topics discussed on this trail include natural cycles, succession, soil and soil erosion, bird observation, aesthetical values, animals and territorial behaviour, habitats and niches, and the forest and canopy levels. The 'what-to-do' section is particularly geared for groups of children accompanied by a teacher.

91. Sardinia Bay and Sylvic Marine and Nature Reserves

PORT ELIZABETH, see map page 90

AUTHORITIES-IN-CHARGE: Municipality of Port Elizabeth; Dias Divisional Council.
SIZE: Sardinia Bay: 320 hectares. Sylvic: 78 hectares.
MAIN ATTRACTIONS: Coastal walking; coastal flora.
FACILITIES/AMENITIES: Picnic sites; bridle paths.
PERTINENT INFORMATION: Fishing is not permitted. A minimum of two people per

Opposite page: Aloe sp. growing in the kloof below Saptoukop.

Above: The skeletal remains of a praying mantid, an insect of the order Mantodea.

party recommended on weekdays during office hours.

AVAILABLE LITERATURE: Included in general tourist brochures issued by the Port Elizabeth tourist office.

CLIMATE: Summer rainfall area.

These two small reserves lying between Schoenmakerskop and Sea View offer pleasant rambling along a seven-kilometre stretch of shoreline. The coastal vegetation varies from the dense scrub mantling the stable dunes, to the relatively sparse covering of pioneer species on the unstable dunes, to the isolated plant communities along the rocky shore. Among the plants, vygies, red-hot pokers, taaibos and everlastings can be readily identified, while the fortunate hiker will perhaps also spot small antelope, vervet monkeys and otters, as well as guineafowl and francolins.

Remember that the species in the reserve are protected – do not take them home as dying souvenirs.

92. *Cape Recife Nature Reserve*

PORT ELIZABETH

AUTHORITY-IN-CHARGE: Municipality of Port Elizabeth.

SIZE: 336 hectares.

LENGTH: Variable walking opportunities, approximately 10 km.

MAIN ATTRACTIONS: Coastal landscape; rock angling; prolific birdlife; varied and abundant intertidal marine life; Cape Recife lighthouse.

FACILITIES/AMENITIES: Footpaths and bird hides are planned; potable water available at points.

PERTINENT INFORMATION: Permits for vehicle access necessary, obtainable at the Beach Manager's office in Happy Valley; beach walkers do not need a permit.

AVAILABLE LITERATURE: Included in general tourist brochures issued by the Port Elizabeth Publicity Association.

CLIMATE: Summer rainfall area.

In the area from the Gamtoos River to Cape Recife, the southernmost tip of Algoa Bay, lie four nature reserves – Cape Recife Nature Reserve, Maitland Mines Nature Reserve, and Sardinia Bay and Sylvic Marine and Nature Reserves (see page 89). The walking potential is great and embraces not only trails in the reserves themselves, but also the full sweep of this lovely, unspoilt coastline. Drought-resistant Alexandria forest blankets part of this region and has a fascinating range of trees, particularly the spectacular coastal coral tree and the yellowwood. These coastal forests are surrounded

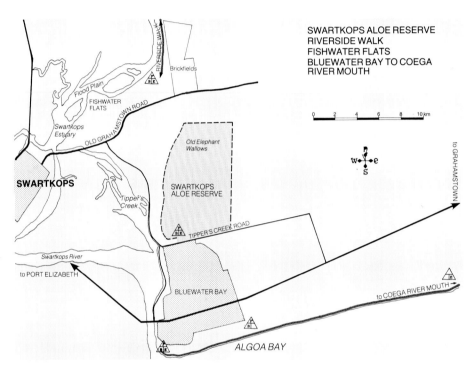

by drier valley bushveld vegetation. Coastal fynbos also occurs in this area. A permit must be obtained, if necessary, from the authority-in-charge of the area in which you wish to walk.

A favourite with anglers, Cape Recife's sandy beaches which link rocky foreshores to scrub-covered dunes of the mainland make the peninsula a popular rambling venue.

The birdlife is particularly worth studying, as wader, bush, pond and seashore species are present in abundance. Many, such as the South African shelduck, flamingo, maccoa duck, and Cape and redbilled teal, are attracted by the sewage settling ponds of the nearby water reclamation scheme. Besides black oystercatchers, other rarities include the crab plover, redshank and knot. Cape Recife is one of the main wader concentration points in Algoa Bay, and, in addition to those already mentioned, turnstones, Ethiopian snipes, greenshanks and whimbrels can be seen. Cape gannets and cormorants are seen offshore, while the coastal scrub vegetation is alive with sombre bulbuls, Karoo robins, tchagra shrikes, wattled starlings and streakyheaded seedeaters.

The peninsula also hosts small mammals such as grey and blue duiker, bushpig, the

Above: Trees on the Bushbuck Nature Trail are labelled with their national tree list numbers.

Opposite page: In the Suurberg National Park.

Cape clawless otter, water, grey and yellow mongoose and the vervet monkey.

Beachcombers and snorkellers can enjoy the tidal pools and broken rocky foreshores with their communities dominated by mussels, oysters and redbait. Perlemoen are also present.

The Cape Recife lighthouse is the oldest original lighthouse on South Africa's coast, and one of the few still manually staffed. It functions to warn ships off Recife Point and Thunderbolt Reef, a graveyard of ships; the last wreck was the *Patti* in 1976.

93. *Bushbuck Nature Trail*

ISLAND FOREST STATION, PORT ELIZABETH

AUTHORITY-IN-CHARGE: Eastern Cape Forest Region, Forestry Branch, Department of Environment Affairs.
LENGTH/DURATION: 16 km/7 hours (variations possible).
MAIN ATTRACTIONS: Alexandria-type forest; birdlife (50 species recorded to date); small mammals; sea views.
FACILITIES/AMENITIES: Picnic sites with fireplaces; trees labelled with their national tree list numbers; water tank on trail.
PERTINENT INFORMATION: Permits necessary, obtainable from the forester between 07h00 and 17h15. Horse-riding is allowed on forestry roads but not on footpaths.
AVAILABLE LITERATURE: *Bosbok Walk*, brochure and map; bird and tree checklist.
CLIMATE: Average annual rainfall: 750 millimetres. Rain falls all year but is heaviest in winter.

The most popular day walk on the National Hiking Way System, the Bushbuck (Bosbok) Nature Trail starts from the forester's house at the Island Forest Station near Sea View, 25 kilometres from Port Elizabeth. It winds through and around indigenous forest on a vegetated 282 metre-high dune. Forty fine tree specimens, including hard pear, white Cape beech, Cape cherry and Outeniqua yellowwood, are marked with their national tree list numbers. Remember to take your *National List of Trees*, however, as the information sheet issued by the Forestry Branch does not list these numbers. The plant life of the region provides a fine example of what is known botanically as Alexandria forest, a xerophytic form of the more verdant tropical coastal forest to the northeast and the coastal bush of Natal and the Transkei. Within this forest, you have an excellent chance of seeing bushbuck and the Knysna loerie, both secretive species, and possibly vervet monkeys, grey duiker, black

cuckoos and scalythroated honeyguides as well.

Birdsong is literally everywhere. Once, by following the series of loud 'kok, kok, kok's' of the Knysna loerie, I was rewarded by the unusual sight of a family group feasting in a wild fig tree.

The Bushbuck Nature Trail also takes the hiker through stands of *Pinus radiata* and crosses a number of plantation roads, all of which provide easy exits to terminate your walk if necessary. A look-out tower can be climbed for views as far as Jeffrey's Bay and Cape St. Francis.

The entire trail is on gently undulating terrain and is physically undemanding. The only readily available water is a reservoir on the trail, 10 kilometres from the trailhead.

94. *Swartkops Aloe Reserve*

PORT ELIZABETH

AUTHORITY-IN-CHARGE: Municipality of Port Elizabeth.
LENGTH: Circular walk: approximately 1,5 km.
MAIN ATTRACTIONS: Old elephant wallows; Addo-type bushveld, brilliant red aloes; views of the sea, city and mountains beyond Uitenhage.
FACILITIES/AMENITIES: Footpath only.
PERTINENT INFORMATION: Locally, the reserve is called Tipper's Creek Aloe Reserve. Access is via a gate off Tipper's Creek Road, behind the public tennis courts.
AVAILABLE LITERATURE: Included in *Walks*

and Hikes in the Port Elizabeth and Eastern Cape Region, package obtainable from the Municipality of Port Elizabeth.
CLIMATE: Summer rainfall area.

95. *Suurberg National Park*

PORT ELIZABETH

AUTHORITY-IN-CHARGE: National Parks Board.
SIZE: 21 000 hectares.
LENGTH/DURATION: Doringnekkloof Walk: 11 km/4 hours. Zuurberg Walk: 2,5 km/ 1 hour.
MAIN ATTRACTIONS: Wild, broken terrain with pleasant kloofs, pools and forested ravines; rare plants (Suurberg cushionbush and Suurberg cycad); large game species (to be introduced).
FACILITIES/AMENITIES: Two circular trails; rest camp and longer trails are planned; accommodation at the Suurberg Inn.
PERTINENT INFORMATION: For information: The Game Ranger, Suurberg National Park, Private Bag X6052, Port Elizabeth 6000; tel. 04252, ask for 106.
AVAILABLE LITERATURE: Brochure planned; located on Government Printer's topographic maps '3325 BC Coerney' and '3325 BD Paterson'.
CLIMATE: Year-round rainfall, with most falling between September and March. Thunderstorms are frequent. Snow, hail and frost occur, but are rare.

Local mountaineers have long been familiar with the footpath in the Sundays River catchment area, a wild, broken terrain, previously the Suurberg State Forest but now under the authority of the National Parks Board. This new park, north of Port Elizabeth and Addo, is open for the exploration of its kloofs, krantzes and peaks rising 250-970 metres above sea level. There are at present two circular footpaths but the Parks Board plans to expand these recreational facilities. Until such time as overnight facilities are constructed, visitors can stay in the pleasant Suurberg Inn (book in advance), just across the road from the entrance to the park.

Suurberg National Park is composed of folded quartzites, sandstones and shales of the Witteberg Series (Cape System), and tillites and shales of the slightly younger Dwyka Series (Karoo System), both belonging to the Paleozoic Era.

Grasses dominate the peaks and their upper slopes, while the valleys are wooded with dry scrub. In these vegetation zones two rare plants, the Suurberg cushionbush and the Suurberg cycad, were discovered.

Kudu, bushbuck, blue duiker, grysbok, water leguan and Knysna loerie are found in the forest and ravines while mountain reedbuck, grey rhebok and baboon can be seen on the broken terrain of the mountain slopes. Mountain zebra, buffalo and the Addo elephant will be introduced.

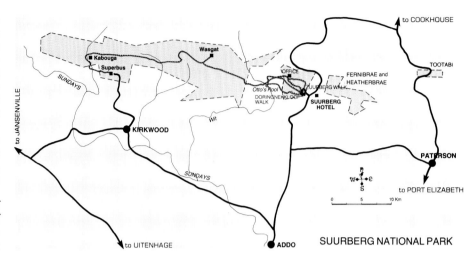

SUURBERG NATIONAL PARK

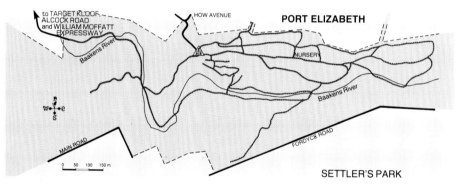

PORT ELIZABETH

SETTLER'S PARK

96. Settler's Park

PORT ELIZABETH

AUTHORITY-IN-CHARGE: Municipality of Port Elizabeth.
SIZE: 54 hectares.
MAIN ATTRACTIONS: Indigenous vegetation and botanical displays; excellent birdlife; tortoises, leguans and small mammals.
FACILITIES/AMENITIES: Footpaths with benches; display centre featuring flowers in bloom; toilets and tap water.
PERTINENT INFORMATION: Venue for Port Elizabeth Bird Club meetings. River water is not potable.
AVAILABLE LITERATURE: *Settler's Park, Port Elizabeth*, colour brochure and map; *Settler's Park*, included in the municipality's trail package.
CLIMATE: Summer: hot with heavy rains. Winter: mild and dry. Wind and light rains are common throughout the year.

Settler's Park, a large open kloof framing the Baakens River in Port Elizabeth, is one of the Republic's most interesting urban green areas. Several paths contour the reserve or lead you around dams, wide, tree-planted lawns, bright flowers and into the Baakens River Gorge. The Port Elizabeth Parks and Recreation Department has constructed an extremely pleasant 5,5-kilometre nature trail from Target Kloof to Mangold Park, at the William Moffatt Expressway. The path follows the valley floor, crossing and recrossing the river by 'stepping stones' or drifts.

Energetic hikers can extend their walk along the Baakens River Valley beyond Settler's Park. The official trail extends from the vicinity of 7th Avenue in Walmer to 'The Dip', the causeway crossing of the river which is an extension of 3rd Avenue in Newton Park. However, the valley can be walked as far as Circular Drive, Walmer, in the vicinity of Frame's Drift. Note that the numerous river crossings are hazardous after heavy rains.

The principal botanic value of Settler's Park lies in its location as the meeting point of four vegetation types: the subtropical flora of the summer rainfall area, fynbos, grasslands of higher altitudes, and karroid vegetation. This diverse flora attracts a fascinating array of birdlife, especially exciting because of its close proximity to the city centre. Paradise flycatchers, Knysna loeries and malachite kingfishers are a few of the more colourful species.

Guided tours can be arranged with the curator.

Left: Exploring the Wit River Valley.

Opposite page, top: The historic building housing the Port Elizabeth public library is a feature on the Donkin Heritage Trail.

Opposite page, bottom: Arum lily, Zantedeschia aethiopica.

PERTINENT INFORMATION: The trail starts at
the Port Elizabeth Tourist Information
Bureau in Library Building on Market
Square.
AVAILABLE LITERATURE: *Heritage Trail*,
guide book, obtainable from the Port
Elizabeth Publicity Association Tourist
Bureau.
CLIMATE: Summer rainfall area.

99. *Fishwater Flats*

PORT ELIZABETH, see map page 90

AUTHORITY-IN-CHARGE: Municipality of
Port Elizabeth.
MAIN ATTRACTIONS: Swartkops River
floodplain; interesting plant life.
FACILITIES/AMENITIES: None.
PERTINENT INFORMATION: Walk during
spring and at low tide for the most
interesting ecology.
AVAILABLE LITERATURE: Included in *Walks
and Hikes in the Port Elizabeth and Eastern
Cape Region*, package obtainable from the
Municipality of Port Elizabeth.
CLIMATE: Summer rainfall area.

100. *Bluewater Bay to Coega River Mouth*

PORT ELIZABETH, see map page 90

AUTHORITY-IN-CHARGE: Municipality of
Port Elizabeth.
LENGTH/DURATION: 10 km/2,5 hours each
way (variations possible).
MAIN ATTRACTIONS: Beaches; views of St.
Croix Island; Coega River estuary;
flamingos.
FACILITIES/AMENITIES: Parking area on
Bluewater Bay beach (starting point).
PERTINENT INFORMATION: St. Croix Island
is a 12-hectare reserve which protects the
sensitive breeding environment of the
endangered jackass penguin; the reserve is
closed to the public.
AVAILABLE LITERATURE: Included in *Walks
and Hikes in the Port Elizabeth and Eastern
Cape Region*, package obtainable from the
Municipality of Port Elizabeth.
CLIMATE: Summer rainfall area.

97. *Riverside Walk*

PORT ELIZABETH, see map page 90

AUTHORITY-IN-CHARGE: Municipality of
Port Elizabeth.
LENGTH/DURATION: From the brick fields to
Perseverance and back: 14 km/2,5 hours
(variations possible).
MAIN ATTRACTIONS: River banks, changing
riverine scenery; wooded hills; interesting
plant life.
FACILITIES/AMENITIES: Cars can be parked
outside the gates of the brick factory; the
trail follows a jeep track.
PERTINENT INFORMATION: This route is
often taken by Zwartkops Trust for its
annual public walk to encourage
conservation awareness.
CLIMATE: Summer rainfall area.

98. *Donkin Heritage Trail*

PORT ELIZABETH, see map page 90

AUTHORITY-IN-CHARGE: Historical Society
of Port Elizabeth, 7 Castle Hill, Port
Elizabeth 6001.
LENGTH/DURATION: 5 km/2,5 hours.
MAIN ATTRACTIONS: 37 places of historical
interest in the Old Hill area of Port
Elizabeth; monuments and parks.

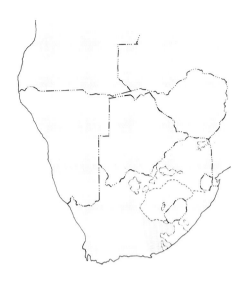

EASTERN CAPE

From the Sundays River in the west, along the Indian Ocean to the Kei River in the east, and north to the Orange River, lies a diverse and recently discovered trailing land: the Eastern Cape. Ciskei, west of the Kei River and sometimes referred to as part of the 'Border Area' because of the 18th-century border clashes between British pioneers and Xhosa-speaking tribes, is now an independent republic.

The Eastern Cape boasts a myriad nature trails along its gentle beaches edged with tall, bush-covered dunes, urban trails through historic towns, guided trails in reserves of valley bushveld, rich with wildlife, and walks through remnants of evergreen moist forests appearing as isolated pockets on its higher mountain escarpments. The widely varying terrain is one of the last strongholds, outside of protected game reserves, of South Africa's wildlife.

Classified as a summer rainfall area, thunderstorms and/or long periods of misty rain are frequent from September to March. Winters are usually crisp and clear with snowfalls possible at higher altitudes in the Amatolas, Stormberg mountains and Barkly Pass area. However, the Eastern Cape is every bit as unpredictable as the Western Cape, and has the reputation of often combining all four seasons in a single day.

ECOLOGICAL ZONES: EASTERN
EVERGREEN TEMPERATE FOREST,
EASTERN GRASSLAND, COASTAL
BUSH AND SUBTROPICAL FOREST.

101. The Alexandria Trail

ALEXANDRIA

AUTHORITY-IN-CHARGE: Eastern Cape Forest Region, Forestry Branch, Department of Environment Affairs★.

LENGTH/DURATION: 37 km/2 days, 1 night; possibility of a one-day extension in the future.

MAIN ATTRACTIONS: Alexandria dunefield, one of the largest active coastal dunefields in the world; coastal dune forest (impressive specimens and rich birdlife); Damara tern, the rarest seabird breeding in South Africa.

FACILITIES/AMENITIES: Base hut with 12 bunks and mattresses, braai, ablutions with hot and cold running water and flush toilets; hiking hut with 12 bunks and mattresses, rainwater; trees labelled with their national tree list numbers.

PERTINENT INFORMATION: The restored

EASTERN CAPE

0   15   30   45   60 75 km

Above: Ascending the coastal dunefield on the first day of the Alexandria Trail.

Opposite page, top: Climbing the fireman's ladder on the Alexandria Trail.

Opposite page, bottom left: Near Kenton-on-Sea.

Opposite page, bottom right: Dias Cross Historical Monument (1488).

private cottage at the 5-km mark can be used by youth groups, with permission from the farmer. No fires allowed at hut; use camp-stoves. Fires can be made on the beach below the high water mark. Ticks can be a nuisance.

AVAILABLE LITERATURE: Brochure and map in process of being compiled; 'Unique Alexandria Trail Opened', *Forestry News*, March 1986.

CLIMATE: Average annual rainfall: 800 millimetres, falling mostly in spring and autumn. Strong winds along the coast, especially in the afternoons.

Ideal for the beginner hiker, the Alexandria Trail (opened in late 1985) has proven a very popular addition to the National Hiking Way System. This two-day circular coastal forest trail is relatively easy; running shoes can be substituted for heavy boots.

A unique feature of the trail is the traverse across the Alexandria dunefield, which, at 120 km^2, is one of the largest active coastal dunefields in the world, and the largest in South Africa. Less than 10 000 years old, this field is still expanding. The highest dune has been recorded at 140 metres.

The dunefield is approached on the first day after emerging from an impressive dune forest where the larger tree specimens such as common wild (Natal) fig, coast erythrina, yellowwood and white ironwood are seen. Also *en route* to the coast, the hiker descends into the beautiful Langevlakte Valley with its green, rolling farmlands.

At the old farmhouse, panelled with wide, yellowwood planks, are the ruins of a chic-ory drying oven from the 1920s. The farmer encourages youth groups to use his farm as an environmental education base camp.

To enable the hiker to find his way across the mountains of sand to the hiking hut, the Forestry Branch has placed tall posts in the dunes. The hut is situated at Woody Cape; weary hikers can relax on the verandah and gaze over the sea at Bird Island, the flocks of gannets and schools of dolphins (binoculars are strongly recommended). Water is lim-ited so I suggest spending an afternoon ex-ploring the beach and its freshwater springs. Signposts lead hikers down the cliffs on a unique fireman's ladder. A half-hour walk westwards will find you on a sandy beach where you can ride the waves in the luke-warm waters of the Indian Ocean. Look for the middens of strandlopers along the coast. Examine the dense blooms of microscopic plants, fed by sub-surface waters rich in nu-trients such as nitrogen, in the surf. And, if you are not too tired after your braai on the beach or dinner at the hut, you can search for a kangaroo-like mouse, the hairy-footed gerbil, endemic to these dunes.

The second day gives the hiker further opportunity to explore the boulder-strewn coast. After turning inland, the trail arrives at the 'lekkerboom', a large yellowwood with a hole in its trunk which provided water to weary travellers of old, trekking from Alexandria to Nankoos.

Having completed this walk, you should be cognizant that the South African govern-ment has chosen Woody Cape as one of two possible sites for a nuclear power plant!

102. Dias Cross

NEAR KENTON-ON-SEA

AUTHORITY-IN-CHARGE: Eastern Cape Forest Region, Forestry Branch, Department of Environment Affairs.
LENGTH/DURATION: 10 km/2 hours (round trip).
MAIN ATTRACTIONS: Dias Cross historical monument (1488); Alexandria State Forest; coastal scenery and dunes.
FACILITIES/AMENITIES: Parking and toilets at the Bushman's River mouth.
PERTINENT INFORMATION: From Dias Cross, it is possible to continue walking west to Cannon Rocks (another 1-2 hours), but this stretch of beach is not as interesting as that from the Bushman's River mouth to Dias Cross.
CLIMATE: Summer rainfall area.

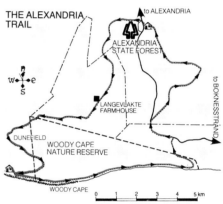

THE ALEXANDRIA TRAIL

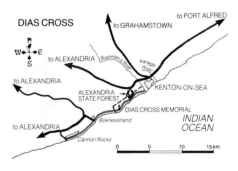

DIAS CROSS

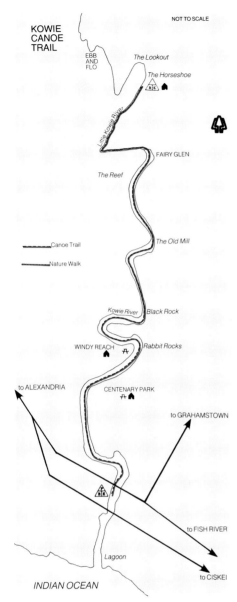

KOWIE CANOE TRAIL

NOT TO SCALE

EBB AND FLO

The Lookout

The Horseshoe

Little Kowie River

FAIRY GLEN

The Reef

The Old Mill

Canoe Trail

Nature Walk

Kowie River — Black Rock

WINDY REACH — Rabbit Rocks

to ALEXANDRIA

CENTENARY PARK

to GRAHAMSTOWN

to FISH RIVER

Lagoon

to CISKEI

INDIAN OCEAN

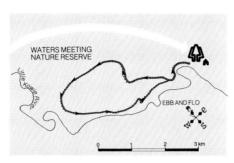

WATERS MEETING NATURE RESERVE

Little Kowie River

EBB AND FLO

0 1 2 3 km

103. Kowie Canoe Trail

PORT ALFRED

AUTHORITIES-IN-CHARGE: Eastern Cape Forest Region, Forestry Branch, Department of Environment Affairs★; Municipality of Port Alfred, tel. (0464) 41140.

LENGTH/DURATION: Canoe Trail: 21 km to camp-site/approximately 3 hours; 25 km to Ebb and Flo. Nature Trail: 12 km/ approximately 3 hours.

MAIN ATTRACTIONS: The only self-guided canoe/hiking trail combination in South Africa; birdlife.

FACILITIES/AMENITIES: Forestry camp-site with water, toilet, open-covered cooking shelter, braai area and rubbish containers; canoes are obtainable from the Kowie River Control officer.

PERTINENT INFORMATION: Day trippers without forestry permits may camp only in sites at Windy Reach or Centenary Park. Canoeing with the tidal flow is strongly recommended.

AVAILABLE LITERATURE: *Kowie Canoe Trail*, leaflet.

CLIMATE: Summer rainfall area.

The Kowie Canoe/Hiking Trail is South Africa's only self-guided combination of this kind. There are other organized canoe and walking adventures, but they are guided by conservation officers. Canoes can be rented at the Kowie River mouth, or canoeists can use their own equipment. I strongly recommend that participants canoe upstream on an incoming tide and downstream on the outgoing tide.

Many birds, such as the giant and pied kingfishers, yellowbilled duck, Egyptian goose, sandpiper, greenshank, sacred ibis, whitebreasted and reed cormorants, mousebird, Knysna loerie and fish eagle, can be seen from the canoe.

In warm and windless weather the 25-kilometre stretch of river to the forestry camp-site is a pleasant, flat-water, 3-hour paddle, negotiable by anybody who is capable of manoeuvring a canoe on a lake or dam. However, in a strong wind the experience can be ghastly. The river grows treach-

erous, with white-caps and swells. If you discover yourself in rough waters, waterproof your gear and tie the bags to the canoe, wear life jackets, and canoe close to shore. Do not hesitate to wait out the storm on land or to 'walk' your canoe in shallow waters.

With a permit from the King William's Town forestry office, canoeists may camp at the Horseshoe Camp-site (bring a tent), and spend the afternoon of the first day or the morning of the second rambling on the pleasant, marked forestry trail in the Waters Meeting Nature Reserve. The trees are labelled with their national tree list numbers.

Bring a second pair of running shoes or boots for the hike, and a sun-screen lotion for the canoe ride. Lastly, don't forget to waterproof your gear in strong plastic bags, tied at the openings.

104. Thomas Baines Nature Reserve

GRAHAMSTOWN

AUTHORITY-IN-CHARGE: Department of Nature and Environmental Conservation, Cape Provincial Administration.

SIZE: 1 013 hectares.

DURATION: 2-3 days, 1-2 nights.

MAIN ATTRACTIONS: Large mammal and birdlife populations; valley bushveld vegetation.

FACILITIES/AMENITIES: Guided trails; game-viewing from motor cars; picnic area with toilets and rubbish bins.

PERTINENT INFORMATION: At present, guided trails are available for organized groups only; trailists provide their own food and equipment. Venue for Enviro-Venture courses.

AVAILABLE LITERATURE: Reserve brochure with map; included in annual reports of the Department of Nature and Environmental Conservation.

CLIMATE: Average annual rainfall: 682 millimetres, falling mostly in spring and autumn.

Fifteen kilometres south-west of Grahamstown lies the Thomas Baines Nature Reserve, a popular day-use retreat for those interested in game-viewing, bird-watching and picnicking. The reserve is composed largely of valley bushveld and grassy fynbos vegetation. About 170 species of birds have been recorded and a noteworthy effort is underway to re-establish large indigenous mammals such as eland, buffalo, bontebok, black wildebeest and white rhinoceros. Trailists may also encounter impala, mountain reedbuck and many smaller animals. Some of these animals (namely bontebok, black wildebeest, white rhinoceros and impala) were introduced by local authorities prior to

Above: Canoeing on the Kowie River in the Waters Meeting Nature Reserve.

Opposite page: The striking horseshoe of the Kowie River.

the Cape Provincial Administration acquiring the reserve. Therefore, a number of species that are not historically indigenous to this area are found here. These populations have been retained as they are readily observable and make good subjects for study by pupils on educational outings.

To increase the educational value of the reserve, its nature conservation officer runs guided trails for organized groups, mainly from schools and youth organizations. All participants are responsible for their own gear, food and carrying their own backpacks. Although each trail is specifically planned to suit the participating group, they usually run for two days and one or two nights. Contact the officer-in-charge of the reserve in advance to make arrangements.

In addition to these trails, Enviro-Venture uses the reserve as a venue for its environmental education courses (for information on Enviro-Venture, see the Valley Bushveld Trail in the Andries Vosloo Kudu Nature Reserve, page 100).

105. 1820 Settlers Wild Flower Garden

GRAHAMSTOWN

AUTHORITY-IN-CHARGE: Department of Nature and Environmental Conservation, Cape Provincial Administration.
SIZE: 61 hectares.
MAIN ATTRACTIONS: Flora indigenous to those areas of the Eastern Cape where the British settled; the botanical garden, the first to be established by the British in the Cape Colony.
FACILITIES/AMENITIES: Footpaths; Douglas Reservoir and Hamilton Dam stocked with mullet and black bass; fishing allowed, no permit necessary.
AVAILABLE LITERATURE: *1820 Settlers Wild Flower Garden, Grahamstown*, issued by the Department of Nature and Environmental Conservation, and the Grahamstown Publicity Association.
CLIMATE: Summer rainfall area.

Short, pleasant rambles through the 1820 Settlers Wild Flower Garden reveal a number of interesting features which commemorate the arrival of British immigrants in the area. For example, the garden displays indigenous plant life of the eastern Cape regions where the British first settled, as well as an old, typically English garden of 150 years ago.

Various historical buildings such as the 1820 Settlers National Monument, Fort Selwyn and the Old Provost lie within these surroundings, as well as military graves of those who died in the early nineteenth century Frontier Wars. The garden is also re-

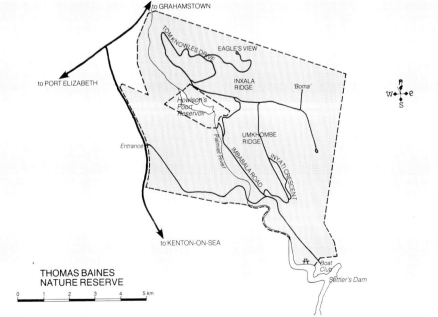

THOMAS BAINES NATURE RESERVE

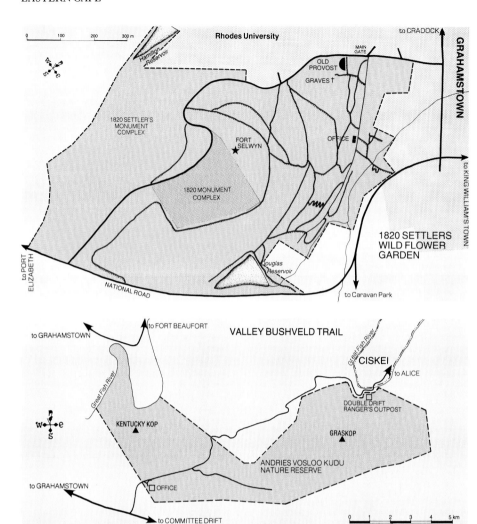

nowned for housing one of South Africa's best collections of gymnosperms, where, in addition to indigenous cycads, these cone-bearing plants are represented by species from all over the world including Brazil, Norfolk Island, the Mediterranean, Europe and Great Britain.

106. Valley Bushveld Trail

ANDRIES VOSLOO KUDU NATURE RESERVE, GRAHAMSTOWN

AUTHORITY-IN-CHARGE: Department of Nature and Environmental Conservation, Cape Provincial Administration.
SIZE: 6 493 hectares.
MAIN ATTRACTIONS: Large mammals and plentiful birdlife (185 species); diverse habitats consisting of dense succulent shrub, humid lowlands, open uplands, riverine communities and woodlands; Double Drift Fort and other historical buildings.
FACILITIES/AMENITIES: Depending on the weather and the trailist's preference, the

following options are available: base camp trail; overnight camp *en route*; bush camp with no facilities; overnight accommodation in old homestead with beds, shower, etc; full pack trail; daypack trail (light travel).
PERTINENT INFORMATION: The Valley Bushveld Trail is variable in length and duration. Maximum of 7 people allowed per trail. Trailists must complete an indemnity form before embarking on a trail.
AVAILABLE LITERATURE: Reserve brochure, trail brochure, application form and indemnity form obtainable from The Officer-in-Charge, Andries Vosloo Kudu Nature Reserve, Private Bag 1006, Grahamstown 6140; tel. (0461) 7909.
CLIMATE: Average annual rainfall: 435 millimetres, falling mostly in March, April, September and October. Temperatures up to 42 °C have been recorded.

As a result of the genuine enthusiasm displayed by the nature conservation officers of the Andries Vosloo Kudu Nature Reserve, trailists have the opportunity to participate on an accompanied interpretive hike in the heart of the Great Fish River valley bushveld.

The reserve preserves the Fish River scrub vegetation (in excess of 400 plant spe-

cies to date) and its associated wildlife. Trailists walk through rolling hills, open uplands, dense thickets, wide riverbeds and forested gorges. The Umkiwane Gorge, noted for its forest-type vegetation, high cliffs and 12 metre-high waterfall, is particularly impressive.

Within these diverse habitats, trailists are likely to see kudu (there are about 500 in the reserve), springbok, warthog, blue and grey duiker, eland, steenbok, red hartebeest, blesbok, baboon, bushbuck and, more rarely, buffalo. Cable and high-voltage electric fencing contain the black rhinoceros, the most endangered large animal in Africa at present, introduced for the first time into a Cape provincial reserve in May 1986.

Over 185 bird species have been recorded. The most commonly seen are those typical of the central Karoo such as the Cape dikkop, black korhaan, ostrich and Karoo scrub robin, and forest inhabitants such as Knysna loeries, forest weavers and olive woodpeckers.

Predators are represented by the black-backed jackal, lynx, aardwolf and clawless otter, as well as the black eagle and fish eagle.

The number of reptile species to date totals 21. This includes the African python, which was introduced as part of the reserve's policy to keep the area in its natural state.

The historically minded will appreciate the preserved buildings dating back to the mid-1800s. These include a crumbling stone fort, part of the defence line along the Great Fish River which at one time served as the border between the Cape Colony and the Xhosa-speaking tribes. A stone-wall 'inn', and 'gun-looped' residences and outbuildings which were once quarters for a British garrison, are now the reserve's office and stores.

The Valley Bushveld Trail requires participants to be in good physical shape and able to carry their own food, clothing and gear, most of which must be provided by the trailists themselves. School parties and youth organizations are therefore well suited, and the trails are adapted to the specific interests of each group.

In addition to the trails run by the Department of Nature and Environmental Conservation, the reserve serves as a venue for Enviro-Venture, an organization which provides pre-arranged environmental awareness courses for groups, about four times a year. The programme is a combined effort of the Albany Museum and the Wildlife Section of the Dias Divisional Council. These courses are usually run for schoolchildren of specific age groups and are advertised in the press and at schools. The duration of each course is two and a half days and the fee includes transport and food.

The turn-off to the reserve is reached 24 kilometres from Grahamstown on the Fort Beaufort Road, just before Fort Brown and the Great Fish River. From here, signboards will direct you a farther four kilometres to the reserve entrance gates. Take the first turn-off to the right after proceeding through the gates. This will take you to the main complex, where trailists should report on arrival.

107. Ecca Pass Nature Reserve

GRAHAMSTOWN

AUTHORITY-IN-CHARGE: Dias Divisional Council.
SIZE: 134 hectares.
LENGTH/DURATION: Approximately 3 km/ 2 hours.
MAIN ATTRACTIONS: Historical significance (A.G. Bain Memorial); valley bushveld ecology; geology; kudu and dassies; birdlife.
FACILITIES/AMENITIES: Well-marked footpaths with plants representative of valley bushveld, labelled; information plinths; picnic area; rubbish bins.
PERTINENT INFORMATION: No permits necessary. No entrance fees. Carry water (there is no water on the trail). Beware of snakes.
AVAILABLE LITERATURE: *Ecca Nature Reserve*, information brochure and map; brochures available from the Grahamstown Publicity Association.
CLIMATE: Summer rainfall area.

The Ecca Pass Nature Reserve is an impressive environmental education project of the Dias Divisional Council and the Grahamstown Branch of the Wildlife Society of Southern Africa. Through the use of information plinths and a trail guide, on an easily negotiable nature walk with labelled plants, the essence of the historical, geological and ecological significance of the Ecca Pass is brought to the visitor's attention.

Geologically famous for preserving the reptilian fossils of *Mesosaurus*, the Ecca Pass area is also partially composed of Dwyka tillite (glacial deposits over 280 million years old). Identical deposits occur in the land masses of South America, Antarctic, India and Australia. This supports the continental drift theory, that these lands were once a supercontinent (Gondwanaland) which broke up into smaller continents 190-120 million years ago.

On the northern horizon of this reserve lies the Winterberg Escarpment. This prominent feature is composed of resistant doleritic (ironstone) dikes, sills and sheets whose summits form the Great Winterberg Peak, Katberg mountains, Elandsberg, Gaika's Kop, Hogsback Mountains and Amatolas.

The reserve's western boundary, Queen's Road, is an historical wagon road leading

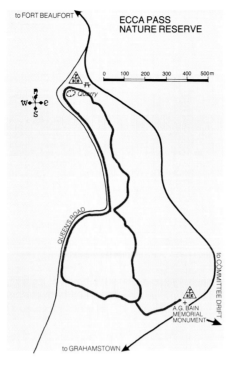

north from Grahamstown. Completed in about 1845, it was one of the first major engineered roads in the eastern Cape, if not in South Africa. It was constructed by Andrew Geddes Bain, the renowned road-builder and geologist. He discovered the fossil reptiles in the Beaufort sediments while constructing Queen's Road, and this was later recognized in the erection of the A.G. Bain Memorial Monument, which marks the entrance to the reserve. A section of one of the nature trails follows Queen's Road.

The two nature trails, the Dassie and Strelitzia trails, which form a figure-of-eight, fall into the Fish River scrub veld type, a variant of valley bushveld. Fish River scrub is also found on the nearby Double Drift Hiking Trail (see page 154) and in the Andries Vosloo Kudu Nature Reserve (see page 100). This vegetation is stunted as a result of low rainfall and shallow soils. Trees, such as the sneezewood, which normally grow to heights of 20 metres in evergreen montane mist-belt forest (such as in the Amatolas), are mere shrubs in valley bushveld. Many popular food species of the kudu, such as spekboom, are labelled. The trailist must look carefully on the ground for identification plaques.

During the day, the rambler is likely to see a wide variety of bush-dwelling birds, the dassie colony near the quarry, rock leguans and possibly kudu, bushbuck and duiker. I almost trod on a large puff adder: although the Ecca Pass Nature Reserve is a small educational day-use area, it is not without the hazards and excitement of the wilderness.

Located only 15 kilometres from Grahamstown on the road to Fort Beaufort, the reserve was not signposted when I visited it in May 1986. Watch for the A.G. Bain Monument near the Committee Drift turn-off. If you approach from the Grahamstown side, look for the sign indicating Ecca Pass.

108. Bosberg Nature Trail

SOMERSET EAST

AUTHORITY-IN-CHARGE: Municipality of Somerset East, P.O. Box 21, Somerset East 5850.
DURATION: Approximately 6 hours (2 days once hut is completed).
MAIN ATTRACTIONS: Magnificent views of Somerset East and Karoo landscape; rare veld type and forest relics; birdlife; Kebe's Cave; game camp.
FACILITIES/AMENITIES: Information hut;

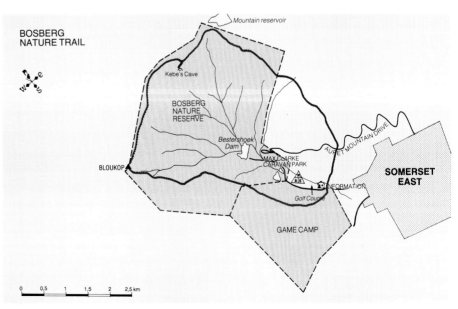

hiking hut planned, to accommodate a minimum of 10 people; Max Clarke Caravan Park; Bestershoek picnic site; children's playground.

AVAILABLE LITERATURE: In process of being compiled; located on Government Printer's topographic map '3225 DA Somerset East'.

CLIMATE: Summer rainfall area. Spring is the most favourable hiking season.

The Bosberg Nature Trail is a magnificent circular walk on the slopes of Bloukop, above Somerset East, in the Bosberg Nature Reserve. Starting from the information hut at the entrance to the nature reserve, hikers ascend the trail to Auret Mountain Drive and then continue upwards through rare dohne-type vegetation (a dense, sour grassveld). The track also passes through relic patches of indigenous forest, rich in yellowwood and wild olive, which provide a valuable habitat for bushbuck and many bushdwelling birds.

Looking back towards Somerset East from the Bloukop ridge, the views are superb, while the forward landscape suddenly gives way to the waves of flat-topped koppies so typical of the Karoo. The large municipal dam on the flat summit is a good spot to observe waterfowl. Gymnogenes, jackal buzzards and other raptors soar above the ridge in search of prey, and Stanley's bustards are often seen marching purposefully among grass tussocks.

From the ridge the trail leads to Kebe's Cave, where clear, cold running water rewards those hikers willing to crawl into its maw (remember to take a torch). A hiking hut accommodating at least 10 people will be built between the reservoir and the cave. From Kebe's Cave, the trail climbs to the Bloukop beacon (1 622 m), down along a south-eastern ridge, and then returns to the information hut, passing through the game camp.

Contact the town clerk for permission to walk and for the latest information on the trail's progress.

109. *Mountain Zebra Trail*

MOUNTAIN ZEBRA NATIONAL PARK, CRADOCK

AUTHORITY-IN-CHARGE: National Parks Board.

LENGTH/DURATION: 25,6 km/2,5 days, 2 nights.

MAIN ATTRACTIONS: Large animals, including the endangered mountain zebra; rugged scenery; mountain drives; Karoo vegetation; Bushman paintings.

FACILITIES/AMENITIES: Mountain Zebra Trail: two huts with bunks and mattresses,

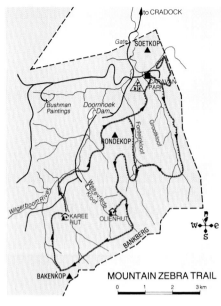

MOUNTAIN ZEBRA TRAIL

0   1   2   3 km

fireplace and water; picnic site and part-rock, part-concrete swimming hole. Mountain Zebra National Park: 20 two-bedroomed chalets; caravan park; restaurant/shop; swimming pool; conference/information hall.

PERTINENT INFORMATION: Water must be carried on the trail (two litres per person per day is recommended).

AVAILABLE LITERATURE: *Mt. Zebra National Park*, with addendum, *Mt. Zebra Trail*, brochure and sketch map; *A Guide to the Mountain Zebra National Park*, Hans Groblar and Anthony Hall-Martin, National Parks Board, 1982.

CLIMATE: Summer: mild to hot. Winter: cold, sunny days and very cold nights, snow on high ridges.

As you approach the Mountain Zebra National Park, the endlessly flat topography of the Cape midlands abruptly gives way to the grand and rugged Bankberg. Set out along the northern slopes of these mountains, the Mountain Zebra Trail passes through typical Karoo midland vegetation – a transitional zone between the succulent-dominated veld of the arid Great Karoo to the west and the wetter grasslands to the east.

The trail begins at the National Parks Board's office, where guide books and cool-drinks can be purchased and cars left safely in the shade. On the first day (9,2 kilometres) the trail ascends the slopes of Grootkloof, passing a huge rock that broke off from a high krantz in 1976. One of the highlights of this first leg is the forest near the rock-slide, which rings with birdsong. The day ends with a descent into Fonteinkloof, to Olienhut. The hut has a total of twelve bunks in two rooms with an outdoor cooking area in between, piped water, a cold shower, toilet and braai area.

I suggest an early start on the second day (9,2 kilometres) in order to ascend the slopes of the Bankberg in the shade. On one

trip to the plateau I breakfasted near eland, mountain zebra, baboon and mountain reedbuck; later I saw Cape vultures, springbok, black wildebeest, klipspringer and ostrich. The second day ends at Karee Hut.

The final day of the hike (7,2 kilometres) is a short walk returning to the park's office. This homeward stretch has been altered: now, instead of following the game-viewing drive, it goes through the veld.

Lack of water and the summer heat are the only factors which make the Mountain Zebra Trail physically demanding. Each day's hike is short in length, and this not only allows leisurely ascents of the steep slopes, but also gives the trailist plenty of time to watch for game.

110. *Commando Drift Nature Reserve*

TARKASTAD

AUTHORITY-IN-CHARGE: Department of Nature and Environmental Conservation, Cape Provincial Administration.

SIZE: 5 983 hectares (including the 951-hectare Commando Drift Dam).

MAIN ATTRACTIONS: Karroid plains, sandstone and dolerite krantzes, wooded watercourses and dolerite koppie veld; birdlife, including wildfowl; large game; Commando Drift Dam.

FACILITIES/AMENITIES: Guided trails on request; the recreation area has three huts with basic accommodation for 4 people each, mattresses and bunks, toilets and cold showers (visitors must provide their own bedding and cooking utensils); braai facilities, no firewood; watersports are permitted, and a boat slipway exists; safe parking.

PERTINENT INFORMATION: Angling is at present confined exclusively to carp. Camping and caravanning is allowed within the recreation area. The nearest shop is 37 km away at Tarkastad, so visitors must bring all their provisions.

AVAILABLE LITERATURE: *Commando Drift Nature Reserve*, brochure and map.

CLIMATE: Summer rainfall area. Summer temperatures vary between 15 and 42 °C; winter temperatures vary between -4 and 28 °C. Frost is to be expected from April to mid-September. Strong north and north-west winds blow from July to September.

In this remote wilderness reserve, one of the conservation priorities is resting the veld from prior mismanagement due to farming and overgrazing. The Karoo midland-type vegetation has been invaded by false karroid broken veld where hardier but less productive elements have replaced the pure grassveld. Karoo gold, sweet thorn, cross berry and blue bush represent the most common flowering trees and shrubs.

The main feature of the reserve, the Commando Drift Dam, is popular with both boating enthusiasts and bird-watchers. Egyptian goose, shelduck, yellowbilled duck, southern pochard, black duck, redknobbed coot, redbilled teal, spurwinged goose and fish eagle are commonly observed. The waterfowl habitat is enhanced by the four rivers which flow into the dam: the Elands, Tarka, Paling and Vlekpoort.

Indigenous animals are being introduced in small numbers and include Cape mountain zebra, kudu, blesbok, springbok, steenbok, grey duiker and black wildebeest.

No set hiking route has yet been laid out, but prospective hikers can choose between two alternatives if they want to visit the reserve. They can make prior arrangements to go on an accompanied trail, or be provided with a map of the area and proceed on their

own. Canoeing around the dam is particularly attractive. No overnight huts exist apart from those in the recreation area. However, trail groups may overnight within the reserve, providing they are fully equipped. The officer-in-charge insists that all arrangements are made well in advance by writing to him at P.O. Box 459, Cradock 5880 (tel. (0481) 3925).

111. Blanco Private Nature Reserve and Guest Farm

TARKASTAD

AUTHORITY-IN-CHARGE: Mr P.J. Ryan, P.O. Box 50, Tarkastad 5370.
SIZE: 1 700 hectares.
MAIN ATTRACTIONS: Birdlife attracted to the dam (marabou stork, spurwinged goose and redbilled teal); ostriches, eagles and vultures; wildlife, including zebra, black wildebeest, blesbok, waterbuck, eland, red hartebeest and impala.
FACILITIES/AMENITIES: Rambling, climbing and horse-riding; resort facilities (golf, bowls, tennis, squash and a swimming pool); cottages and restaurant.
PERTINENT INFORMATION: Known for its invigorating climate, the guest farm attracts people with respiratory ailments. Martha and Mary peaks can be climbed with permission from the farmer, Alan Porter of 'Hill and Dale', tel. 04582, ask for 1612.
AVAILABLE LITERATURE: *Blanco Farm Holiday Resort*, brochure issued by owners.
CLIMATE: Summer rainfall area.

Above: The author beneath Martha Peak.

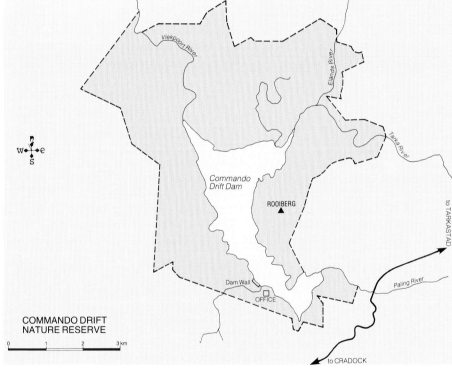

COMMANDO DRIFT
NATURE RESERVE

0   1   2   3 km

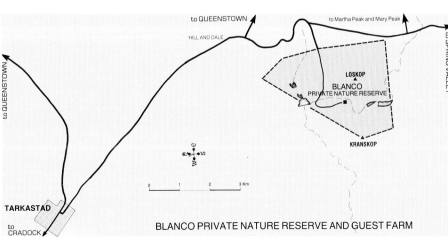

BLANCO PRIVATE NATURE RESERVE AND GUEST FARM

112. Hogsback State Forest and Auckland Nature Reserve

HOGSBACK

AUTHORITY-IN-CHARGE: Eastern Cape Forest Region, Forestry Branch, Department of Environment Affairs.

MAIN ATTRACTIONS: Indigenous forests and waterfalls; birdlife and monkeys; peak climbing; wild berries; rock-climbing; tranquil, resort-type atmosphere.

FACILITIES/AMENITIES: Marked footpaths; horses for hire; three hotels, forestry campsite and numerous private cottages to let; trading store, post office and petrol (limited hours).

PERTINENT INFORMATION: Permits necessary, obtainable from Hogsback Forest Station; permits for walks in Ciskei which start at the Tyume River necessary, obtainable from Hogsback Forest Station or one of the three hotels in Hogsback.

AVAILABLE LITERATURE: *Exploring Hogsback (The Piggy Book)*, Hogsback Inn; *All About Hogsback*, visitor's guide by E.W. Holliday; *Forestways and Falling Water*, J.J.T. Cook (all available at Hogsback hotels and supermarket); 'Hogsback' by Jaynee Levy, *The Motorist*, Second Quarter, 1986; *A Brief Guide to Hogsback*, available at King's Lodge; located on Government Printer's topographic map '3226 DB Seymour'; sketch map of Ciskei walks and trails available from the Ciskei Department of Tourism and Aviation.

CLIMATE: Summer: mild to warm days, mist and rain common. Winter: sunny days, cold nights, snow possible.

I lived in and explored the Hogsback for more than four years, and I recommend this area as prime rambling country. It always frustrates me to see tourists walking only up and down the main gravel road, for Hogsback State Forest, Auckland Nature Reserve and the adjoining Zingcuka Forest (Ciskei) offer a myriad unforgettable day excursions. There are 'piggy walks', 'blue crane walks' (Ciskei), peaks to climb and historic sites and waterfalls to visit. The keen hiker can combine many short walks into an all-day excursion.

The dense, indigenous evergreen forest, with its primeval atmosphere, is rich in yellowwood, white stinkwood, knobwood, white ironwood, underbush, sneezewood and Cape chestnut. The call of the Knysna loerie and the chattering of the samango monkey echo through the valleys and moist slopes below the Hogsback plateau.

The South African Forestry Branch and the Ciskei Forestry Department maintain a complex of walks here, marked with hogs, blue cranes and other symbols. It is essential to obtain the booklet, *Exploring Hogsback*, and the sketch map of the reserve, in order to orientate yourself in these forests.

For a pleasant, 3-4 hour walk, enter the Auckland Nature Reserve near King's Lodge. Descend through the forest to the Big Tree, a 36 metre-high Outeniqua yellowwood estimated to be 800 years old.

Then carry on to the Madonna and Child Waterfall on the Tyume River, accessible from both South Africa and Ciskei. Backtrack to near the Big Tree (perhaps after a side-trip to the Bridal Veil Falls). Return to King's Lodge on Wolfridge Road, and then the main Hogsback road.

Another 'piggy walk' combination, this one lasting about two hours, and running above the level of the main road, starts at the Oak Avenue picnic site. Proceed down Forest Drive, detour to the Kettlespout Falls, and return along the contour path. Shorter walks include the 'Military Path' (through indigenous forest, stretching from the little library to the Alice-Hogsback road below King's Lodge), and the very short excursion from the picnic site to the 39 Steps Waterfall.

Almost everyone is keen to climb Tor Doon (1 565 m), a minor summit overlooking the forest station, where a 360° eagle's-eye view of Hogsback and its environs unfolds. Below the peak stands a plaque and traces of the earth embankments of Fort Michell, bearing testimony to the border clashes during the 1800s.

I suggest the following full-day excursion for the ambitious hiker: starting at Gaika Road, enter the state forest plantation area (with a permit) and climb Gaika's Kop (1 963 m). Follow the firebreak to the rocky summit, scrambling to the beacon. Gaika's Kop is Hogsback's most prominent peak, named from the Xhosa *Ntab'egqira* (the doctor's or diviner's mountain), and not for the chief Gaika as is usually assumed. From its flat summit, you can see as far north as Hangklip (above Queenstown), and south over the Hogsback Peaks to the sea. Descend Gaika's Kop via the opposite, less steep side, cross the valley of plantations and ascend Tor Doon. Return following the piggy signs through indigenous forest to either the forest station or the picnic site.

Hiking on the Hogsback grassland plateau and peaks affords far-reaching views, sitings of jackal buzzard, and a chance to see Cape rock hyrax (dassies). The wildflowers in season are exquisite, especially the hair-bells (*Dierama* spp.). Between December and February, the ubiquitous *Rubus* bramble bears its inexhaustible tasty supply of sweet blackberries. At other times, its thorny stems tear at one's flesh, eliciting mumbled curses from walkers who stray off the path.

The other popular hiking peaks include Elandsberg (2 017 m) and the famous Hogsbacks (1 836 m, 1 824 m and 1 937 m). A new Ciskeian day walk (16 kilometres) starting at the Tyume River, near Hobbiton, ascends Hogsback One. These peaks are responsible for this area's name. The three ridged summits suggest the bristly-backed wild hogs (pigs) which roam the local forests at night.

While hiking in spring and summer, be on the alert for puff adder, boomslang and cobra. Thunderstorms are frequent and mist can envelop the peaks and valleys within minutes, even after the clearest of morning skies. Always hike with a raincoat, jersey, map and water bottle.

A 2-3 day circular National Hiking Way trail has been suggested for the Hogsback State Forest. Contact the Forestry Branch at King William's Town for the latest details.

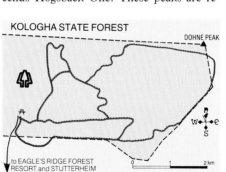

KOLOGHA STATE FOREST

DOHNE PEAK

to EAGLE'S RIDGE FOREST RESORT and STUTTERHEIM

0   1   2 km

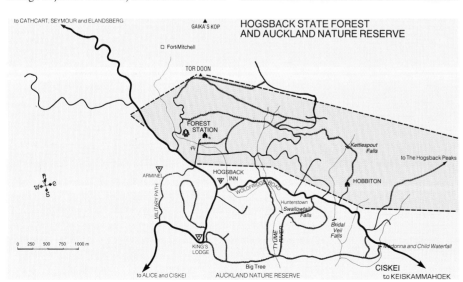

HOGSBACK STATE FOREST AND AUCKLAND NATURE RESERVE

to CATHCART, SEYMOUR and ELANDSBERG

GAIKA'S KOP

Fort Mitchell

TOR DOON

FOREST STATION

ARMINEL

MILITARY PATH

HOGSBACK INN

WOLOFRIDGE ROAD

Kettlespout Falls

to The Hogsback Peaks

HOBBITON

Hunterstown

Swallowtail Falls

TYUME RIVER

Bridal Veil Falls

KING'S LODGE

Big Tree

Madonna and Child Waterfall

CISKEI

to KEISKAMMAHOEK

to ALICE and CISKEI   AUCKLAND NATURE RESERVE

0 250 500 750 1000 m

113. Kologha State Forest

STUTTERHEIM

AUTHORITY-IN-CHARGE: Eastern Cape Forest Region, Forestry Branch, Department of Environment Affairs.
DURATION: Half-day nature trails.
MAIN ATTRACTIONS: Indigenous evergreen forests and wildlife; grassveld; pine plantations.
FACILITIES/AMENITIES: Picnic and braai sites; four circular walks marked with eagle pictograms.
PERTINENT INFORMATION: The Kologha Hiking Trail (see page 106) ends in the Kologha State Forest.
AVAILABLE LITERATURE: Sketch map.
CLIMATE: Summer rainfall area.

Opposite page, top: Moonrise over Gaika's Kop at Hogsback.

Opposite page, bottom: The popular Madonna and Child Waterfall on the Tyume River.

Above left: 'Piggy signs' indicate the walks in the Hogsback State Forest.

Above right: Snow blanketing a forest walk.

114. Kologha Hiking Trail

STUTTERHEIM

AUTHORITY-IN-CHARGE: Eastern Cape Forest Region, Forestry Branch, Department of Environment Affairs.
LENGTH/DURATION: 34,6 km/2 days, 1 night.
MAIN ATTRACTIONS: Gubu Dam and hiking hut; Kubusie Crest view; indigenous forest; De Fin oak tree.
FACILITIES/AMENITIES: One hut with four rooms and 30 bunks, verandah, cooking shelter and ablution block with showers.
PERTINENT INFORMATION: Eagle's Ridge Hotel is within walking distance from the end of the trail, and the hotel will arrange transport back to your car.
AVAILABLE LITERATURE: *Kologha Hiking Trail*, notes with checklists, to be replaced by brochure and map.
CLIMATE: Summer rainfall area; thunderstorms are common.

If ever I was homesick for my native northern American woods, it was at the Gubu Dam hiking hut on the Kologha Hiking Trail. Set among pine and pin oak trees on a steep slope above the dam (which, from the verandah, looks like a natural lake because the dam wall is not in view), this weatherboard cabin is reminiscent of an American log house. Mr C.J. Rance and the late Mr J.D. Lentz, well-known local sawmillers, generously donated the timber, without which the five-star hiking hut could not

have been constructed. The ducks and herons on the water and the duiker browsing in the oaks add atmosphere to the setting.

The old De Fin oak tree, seen on the first day in the Isidenge Forest, is a feature of the trail. Kubusie Crest and Rooikrans (both on the second day) have magnificent views of Gubu Dam, Keiskammahoek Valley (Ciskei), King William's Town and the Kologha Forest. But the nicest section of the trail for me was the final descent past several waterfalls, old sawpits and magnificent yellowwoods. Rather than completing the trail at the old Kologha Forest Station (7 kilometres from Stutterheim), I recommend walking to the Eagle's Ridge Hotel (1 kilometre farther). The hotel will arrange transport back to Isidenge Forest Station.

This trail will be lengthened by one day when funds become available.

115. King William's Town Nature Reserve

KING WILLIAM'S TOWN

AUTHORITY-IN-CHARGE: Municipality of King William's Town, P.O. Box 33, King William's Town 5600.
SIZE: 68 hectares.
MAIN ATTRACTIONS: Valley bushveld (thorny plants such as sweet thorn, witolienhout, cabbage tree, euphorbia, wild olive and camphor bush).
FACILITIES/AMENITIES: Nature trails along constructed footpaths.
CLIMATE: Summer rainfall area.

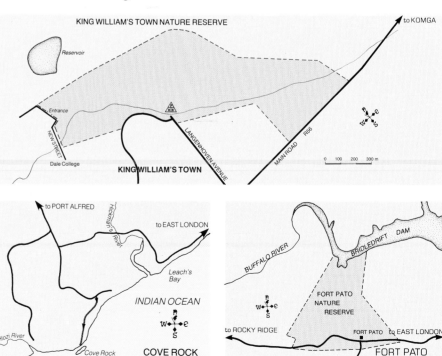

Top: The De Fin oak tree.
Above: The Gubu Dam hiking hut.
Opposite page, left: The bloubos, Diospyros lycioides.
Opposite page, right: Umtiza Nature Reserve.

116. *Cove Rock*

EAST LONDON

AUTHORITY-IN-CHARGE: Municipality of East London, P.O. Box 984, East London 5200.
MAIN ATTRACTIONS: Many species of seabirds and waders along this stretch of coastline; dramatic rock formations.
FACILITIES/AMENITIES: Parking area.
PERTINENT INFORMATION: Best time to visit is during low tide when there is little or no wind. Watch out for freak waves.
AVAILABLE LITERATURE: Included in *Nature Walks around East London*, booklet by Graham Bell-Cross, obtainable from the Greater East London Publicity Association.
CLIMATE: Summer rainfall area.

117. *Fort Pato Nature Reserve*

EAST LONDON

AUTHORITY-IN-CHARGE: Eastern Cape Forest Region, Forestry Branch, Department of Environment Affairs★.
SIZE: 676 hectares.
LENGTH/DURATION: 6 km/2 hours.
MAIN ATTRACTIONS: Indigenous forest; open grassland.
FACILITIES/AMENITIES: Trail is marked with white footprints.
PERTINENT INFORMATION: The reserve borders on the Bridledrift Dam. Permits necessary, obtainable from The Forester, East London Coast State Forest, P.O. Box 5185, Greenfields 5208.
CLIMATE: Summer rainfall area.

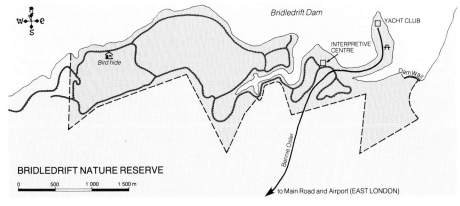

BRIDLEDRIFT NATURE RESERVE

118. *Bridledrift Nature Reserve*

EAST LONDON

AUTHORITY-IN-CHARGE: Municipality of East London, P.O. Box 984, East London 5200.
LENGTH: Seven nature trails, varying from 1,3 km to 7,5 km.
MAIN ATTRACTIONS: Birdlife; Bridledrift Dam.
FACILITIES/AMENITIES: Bird hide; overnight hut, picnic area, water, toilets and braai; yacht club and canoes; interpretive centre.
AVAILABLE LITERATURE: Trails map.
CLIMATE: Summer rainfall area.

119. *Umtiza Nature Reserve*

EAST LONDON

AUTHORITY-IN-CHARGE: Eastern Cape Forest Region, Forestry Branch, Department of Environment Affairs★.
SIZE: 560 hectares.
LENGTH: Trail 1: 1,5 km. Trail 2: 2,5 km. Trail 3: 6 km.
MAIN ATTRACTIONS: Eastern Cape valley bushveld; blue duiker, samango monkey and tree hyrax; Buffalo River; remains of Fort Grey.
FACILITIES/AMENITIES: Nature trails; trees labelled with their national tree list numbers.
PERTINENT INFORMATION: Located in the Buffalo Pass area. Permits necessary, obtainable from The Forester, East London Coast State Forest, P.O. Box 5185, Greenfields 5208. The reserve used to be called Fort Grey, but has been renamed after the umtiza tree, a protected species confined mainly to the forests and kloofs along the Buffalo River.
AVAILABLE LITERATURE: Tree list; included

UMTIZA NATURE RESERVE

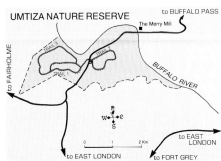

in *Nature Walks around East London*, booklet by Graham Bell-Cross, obtainable from the Greater East London Publicity Association.
CLIMATE: Summer rainfall area.

120. *Amalinda Fish Station and Nature Reserve*

EAST LONDON

AUTHORITY-IN-CHARGE: Department of Nature and Environmental Conservation, Cape Provincial Administration.
SIZE: Nature reserve: 134 hectares.
MAIN ATTRACTIONS: Birdlife, including waterfowl; rare reedbuck, eland, blesbok and blue duiker; riverine forest and gently rolling hills; warm-water fish species.
FACILITIES/AMENITIES: Nature trails along

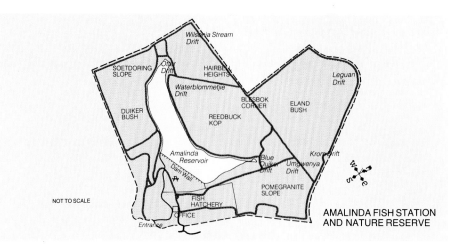

AMALINDA FISH STATION AND NATURE RESERVE

(map labels): Wilsonia Stream Drift, SOETDORING SLOPE, Otter Drift, HAIRBELL HEIGHTS, Waterblommetjie Drift, Leguan Drift, DUIKER BUSH, BLESBOK CORNER, ELAND BUSH, REEDBUCK KOP, Amalinda Reservoir, Blue Duiker Drift, Umgwenya Drift, Krom Drift, Dam Wall, POMEGRANITE SLOPE, NOT TO SCALE, FISH HATCHERY, OFFICE, Entrance

roads and firebreaks; walks around the dam and over forested hills in the nature reserve; picnic area with braais; canoeing on the reservoir.

PERTINENT INFORMATION: Angling is allowed in the Amalinda Reservoir, which is stocked with kurper, black bass, mullet, carp, catfish (barbel) and eel; an angling licence (obtainable from the Receiver of Revenue) and a permit (obtainable from the reserve office) are required. The fish hatchery is open on weekdays only, 08h00-16h00. For information: The Senior Officer, Amalinda Fish Station, P.O. Box 3084, Cambridge 5206.

AVAILABLE LITERATURE: Included in *Nature Walks around East London*, booklet by Graham Bell-Cross, obtainable from the Greater East London Publicity Association.

CLIMATE: Summer rainfall area.

121. *Potter's Pass Wildflower Reserve*

EAST LONDON

AUTHORITY-IN-CHARGE: Municipality of East London, P.O. Box 984, East London 5200.

MAIN ATTRACTIONS: 70 flowering species.

PERTINENT INFORMATION: Watch out for vagrants between Potter's Pass and the lighthouse.

AVAILABLE LITERATURE: Included in *Nature Walks around East London*, booklet by Graham Bell-Cross, obtainable from the Greater East London Publicity Association.

CLIMATE: Summer rainfall area.

Above: A feature on the East London Urban Trail is the Art Gallery.

Opposite page, top: Luxury chalets in the Bosbokstrand Private Nature Reserve.

Opposite page, centre: Indigenous coastal forest lines the estuary at Bosbokstrand.

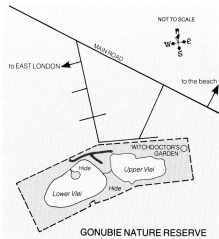

GONUBIE NATURE RESERVE

(map labels): NOT TO SCALE, MAIN ROAD, to EAST LONDON, to the beach, 'WITCHDOCTOR'S GARDEN', Hide, Upper Vlei, Lower Vlei, Hide

122. *The Urban Trail*

EAST LONDON

AUTHORITY-IN-CHARGE: Municipality of East London, P.O. Box 984, East London 5200.

MAIN ATTRACTIONS: History of East London: the harbour, buildings, architecture, museums and monuments.

FACILITIES/AMENITIES: Four self-guided routes.

PERTINENT INFORMATION: The trail guide is an invaluable aid, full of historical information, maps and sketches.

AVAILABLE LITERATURE: *The Urban Trail*, trail guide published by the Greater East London Publicity Association.

CLIMATE: Summer rainfall area.

123. *Nahoon River Estuary*

EAST LONDON

AUTHORITY-IN-CHARGE: Municipality of East London, P.O. Box 984, East London 5200.

MAIN ATTRACTIONS: Estuary mud flats; rich birdlife and marine life; strelitzias, cycads and mangrove trees.

FACILITIES/AMENITIES: Rock angling.

PERTINENT INFORMATION: At high tide, the mouth of the Nahoon River cannot be crossed by wading.

AVAILABLE LITERATURE: Included in *Nature Walks around East London*, booklet by Graham Bell-Cross, obtainable from the Greater East London Publicity Association.

CLIMATE: Summer rainfall area.

124. *Gonubie Nature Reserve*

EAST LONDON

AUTHORITY-IN-CHARGE: Municipality of Gonubie, P.O. Box 20, Gonubie 5256.

SIZE: 8 hectares.

MAIN ATTRACTIONS: Waterfowl on two vleis; 130 species of birds; breeding crowned cranes; trees and flowers; 'Witchdoctor's Garden', medicinal local plants.

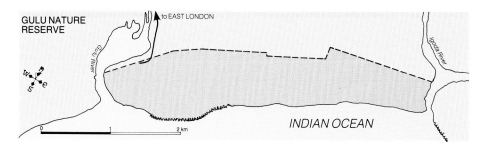
GULU NATURE RESERVE

(map labels): to EAST LONDON, Gulu River, Igoda River, INDIAN OCEAN, 0, 1, 2 km

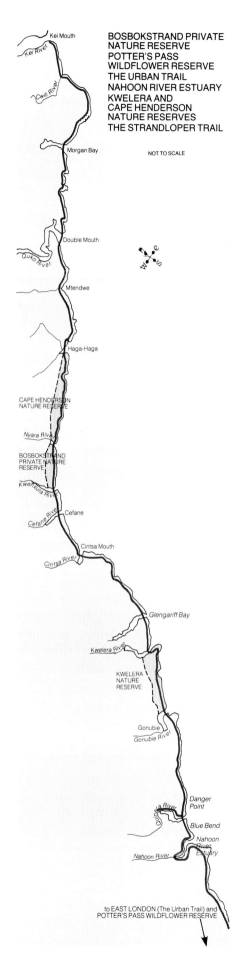

BOSBOKSTRAND PRIVATE
NATURE RESERVE
POTTER'S PASS
WILDFLOWER RESERVE
THE URBAN TRAIL
NAHOON RIVER ESTUARY
KWELERA AND
CAPE HENDERSON
NATURE RESERVES
THE STRANDLOPER TRAIL

NOT TO SCALE

Kei Mouth
Kei River
Cwili River
Morgan Bay
Double Mouth
Quko River
Mtendwe
Haga-Haga
CAPE HENDERSON
NATURE RESERVE
Nyara River
BOSBOKSTRAND
PRIVATE NATURE
RESERVE
Kwenkura River
Cefane River   Cefane
Cintsa Mouth
Cintsa River
Glengariff Bay
Kwelera River
KWELERA
NATURE
RESERVE
Gonubie
Gonubie River
Quinera River
Danger
Point
Blue Bend
Nahoon
River
Estuary
Nahoon River

to EAST LONDON (The Urban Trail) and
POTTER'S WILDFLOWER RESERVE

FACILITIES/AMENITIES: Observation hides.
PERTINENT INFORMATION: Open on
Monday afternoons, or by arrangement with
the municipal office.
AVAILABLE LITERATURE: Included in *Nature
Walks around East London*, booklet by
Graham Bell-Cross, obtainable from the
Greater East London Publicity Association;
bird checklist.
CLIMATE: Summer rainfall area.

125. *Gulu, Kwelera and Cape Henderson Nature Reserves*

EAST LONDON TO MORGAN BAY

AUTHORITY-IN-CHARGE: Eastern Cape
Forest Region, Forestry Branch,
Department of Environment Affairs★.
SIZE: Gulu Nature Reserve: 350 hectares.
Kwelera Nature Reserve: 200 hectares.
Cape Henderson Nature Reserve: 240
hectares.
MAIN ATTRACTIONS: Extensive unspoilt
dune forests, grasslands, steep farmlands
and rocky cliffs; surf and sandy beaches;

abundant birdlife; small mammals.
FACILITIES/AMENITIES: Double Mouth
camp-site (south of Morgan Bay); picnic
sites; fishing; bathing beaches.
PERTINENT INFORMATION: The reserves
form part of the 2 000-hectare East London
Coast State Forest; part of the Strandloper
Trail (see page 110) runs through these
nature reserves.
AVAILABLE LITERATURE: *The Strandloper
Trail: Kei Mouth to East London*, booklet
obtainable from the Greater East London
Publicity Association, or the Wildlife
Society of Southern Africa (Border Branch).
CLIMATE: Summer rainfall area.

126. *Bosbokstrand Private Nature Reserve*

HAGA-HAGA

AUTHORITY-IN-CHARGE: Mr C. Nolte, P.O.
Box 302, Randfontein 1760; tel. (011) 696-
1442. On-site manager, tel. 04372, ask for
Mooiplaas 4512.
SIZE: 205 hectares.
MAIN ATTRACTIONS: Walks in indigenous
coastal forest; estuary and beach.

FACILITIES/AMENITIES: Self-contained luxury chalets, camp-site, caravan park, ablution block and small store.
AVAILABLE LITERATURE: Leaflet available on request.
CLIMATE: Summer rainfall area.

Bosbokstrand is a delightful private nature reserve tucked away in indigenous forest, behind the Bay of Cape Henderson, 70 kilometres east of East London. Known as a fisherman's paradise, ramblers can also enjoy a day of trail walking. Large antelope have been introduced. The upper reaches of the estuary divide into pleasant rivulets, very rich in birdlife. The luxury chalets and camp-site can accommodate hikers on the Strandloper Trail.

127. The Strandloper Trail

EAST LONDON, see map page 109

AUTHORITY-IN-CHARGE: Land above high water mark: Divisional Council of Kaffraria, P.O. Box 320, East London 5200, and Eastern Cape Forest Region, Forestry Branch, Department of Environment Affairs.
LENGTH: 93 km.
MAIN ATTRACTIONS: Coastal scenery: middens, shipwrecks, forests, dunes, sand and surf, and rock formations; birdlife.
FACILITIES/AMENITIES: Hotels and camp-sites *en route*.
PERTINENT INFORMATION: Permits to enter forestry land necessary, obtainable from The Forester, Fort Grey, East London 5200, otherwise no permits needed. Overnight camping on beaches is prohibited. Carry a tide table.
AVAILABLE LITERATURE: *The Strandloper Trail: Kei Mouth to East London*, booklet obtainable from the Greater East London Publicity Association, or the Wildlife Society of Southern Africa (Border Branch).

The coastal walk from the Kei River (Transkei's southern border with South Africa) to East London has always existed, but the publication of the highly informative booklet, *The Strandloper Trail*, helped to popularize this exciting and informal hike.

Serious hikers may wish to tackle the entire 93-kilometre stretch at one time, sleeping at the various hotels, resorts and camp-sites *en route*, or the walk can be done as several shorter excursions. Whichever way you choose, carry the trail booklet at all times as an excellent guide to the river crossings and accommodation, and the shipwrecks, bird-life and rock formations to be seen.

The Strandloper Trail traverses a magnificent stretch of coast, with rugged rocky

scenery and a history of wrecks – *Margaret, Nossa Sewhora, Da Atalaia* and *Santo Alberto*, among others. The hiker is in constant company of terns, kelp gulls, cormorants and waders. There are several river mouths – the Quko River at Double Mouth, Kwenxura, Cefane, Cintsa, Bulura and Nahoon – which should be crossed with caution, preferably at low tide, or at the turn or beginning of an incoming tide. If, when you finish the walk at East London, 'coastal hike fever' is still with you, you can continue south towards the Shipwreck Trail (see page 156) in Ciskei.

128. Ocean View Guest Farm

KOMGA

AUTHORITY-IN-CHARGE: Mr and Mrs M von Plato, P.O. Komga 4950; tel (04372) 2603.
SIZE: 260 hectares.
DURATION: Approximately 8 hours of trail walking.
MAIN ATTRACTIONS: Indigenous riverine forest; coastal views; birdlife (200 species); informal country atmosphere.
FACILITIES/AMENITIES: Three fully furnished cottages (2 with cooking facilities), each accommodating 2-4 people; camp-site; firewood for sale; option of eating at the main house or bringing your own food.
PERTINENT INFORMATION: Dogs are allowed, if obedient. Ticks can be a nuisance.
AVAILABLE LITERATURE: *Ocean View Guest Farm and Caravan Park*, leaflet; trail map available on request.
CLIMATE: Summer rainfall area.

Mr and Mrs Von Plato are nature lovers who have generously opened their farm to others who share their interest in natural history and rambling. Not only have they converted three cottages on the farm for public use, they also welcome visitors to dine with their family.

Within the bounds of the farm, nature rambles through unique high riverine forest and grasslands, and to dams and watercourses, have been constructed. Botanical and ornithological specialists in particular are attracted to the wide diversity of unique species.

Because the forest captures the mist, its composition contains many tropical elements. On request, Mrs Von Plato will lead trails and point out orchids, cycads and eagles' nests, as well as describe practical uses for the sneezewood, ironwood, red beech, white gardenia and other indigenous trees. Some of the animals you could see include bushbuck, blue duiker, samango monkey,

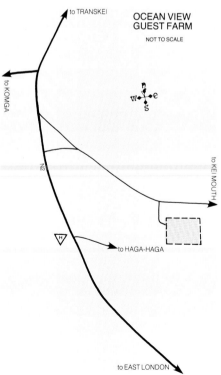

to TRANSKEI

OCEAN VIEW
GUEST FARM

NOT TO SCALE

to KOMGA

to KEI MOUTH

N2

to HAGA-HAGA

to EAST LONDON

tree hyrax, Stanley's bustard, crowned and crested eagles, and the ground hornbill.

Only 29 kilometres by road to Kei Mouth and Morgan Bay (both on the Strandloper Trail, see opposite page), and approximately one hour by car from King William's Town and East London, Ocean View is conveniently situated for a weekend or relaxing holiday. The clearest weather occurs in winter (May to August); flowers are at their best in late winter and spring, and the birdlife excels from September to November.

129. Black Eagle Wilderness Trail

QUEENSTOWN

AUTHORITY-IN-CHARGE: Department of Nature and Environmental Conservation, Cape Provincial Administration, P.O. Box 563, Queenstown 5320, in conjunction with Mr Robin Halse, Carnarvon Estates, owner of the Black Eagle Private Nature Reserve.
LENGTH/DURATION: Approximately 40 km/3 days, 2 nights (variable).
MAIN ATTRACTIONS: Wilderness area in the rugged Andriesberg; prolific birdlife as well as viewing of large and small game; unique educational programme principally for underprivileged children.
FACILITIES/AMENITIES: Environmental education centre, features include talks/slides/field demonstrations on nature conservation; accommodation under two large canvas tents; lecture and kitchen facilities available in a wooden bungalow; toilet facilities; natural rock swimming pools; food and utensils supplied by trail authorities on request; sleeping bags provided on request; conservation pamphlets provided.
PERTINENT INFORMATION: Courses usually run from noon on Friday to noon on Sunday; extension of time by special arrangement, for example during school holidays. Minimum of 12 and maximum of 22 people allowed per trail (more people

allowed by special arrangement only).
AVAILABLE LITERATURE: *Black Eagle Wilderness Trail*, booklet including history, list of species and map; pamphlets and posters issued by the Department of Nature and Environmental Conservation.
CLIMATE: Summer (October to early April): warm days and pleasant, cool evenings. Winter (early April to September): cold, frost and snow common. This area is renowned for its healthy climate.

The Black Eagle Wilderness Trail is a commendable venture initiated by the Lion's Club of Queenstown, who raised the first funds for this programme. It is now operated by the Department of Nature and Environmental Conservation of the Cape Province, in conjunction with Mr R. Halse, owner of the Black Eagle Private Nature Reserve on which the trail is situated. The adjoining Annanwater Private Reserve, owned by Mr George Stretton, is also used.

Both private nature reserves, which total approximately 15 000 hectares in extent, are located in the Andriesberg range, about 20 kilometres east of Sterkstroom. Here, the mountain slopes and broad valleys are covered mainly by grassveld and shrubs – a terrain which lends itself well to trails. Many of these lead to the peaks and gorges where the hiker may catch sudden glimpses of the black eagle, bateleur or Cape vulture soaring high on thermals.

Owing to the fine conservation practices of its owner, the Black Eagle Private Nature Reserve is well stocked with larger mammals such as springbok, black wildebeest, bles-

bok, eland, mountain reedbuck, grey rhebok, impala and fallow deer (exotic). There are also many smaller animals such as squirrels, mongooses and hares, in addition to the prolific birdlife.

The objectives of this trail programme are to allow underprivileged children contact with an unspoilt natural environment and to teach them basic conservation values. In so doing, participants are provided with a worthwhile and memorable experience. To this end, therefore, nature conservation officers spend considerable time during the trail interpreting the environment in the children's home language. Aspects of conservation such as erosion, poaching, indigenous and exotic animals and plants and the food web are discussed as examples of each are encountered.

All trail facilities, including food and sleeping bags, are offered to underprivileged children free of charge, while the more privileged groups are subject to a levy.

Opposite page: The Eastern Cape coast offers endless stretches of beach hiking. The 93-kilometre coastal walk from the Kei River to East London, the Strandloper Trail, is one of the more exciting. It can be walked as a whole or broken up into several shorter excursions.

Above: Ciskeian students are guided on a trail in the Black Eagle wilderness. The objectives of this trail are to allow underprivileged children contact with an unspoilt, natural environment and to teach them basic conservation values. Different aspects of conservation are discussed.

130. *Madeira Guided Trails*

LAWRENCE DE LANGE NATURE RESERVE, QUEENSTOWN

AUTHORITY-IN-CHARGE: Town Engineer's Department, Municipality of Queenstown, P.O. Box 135, Queenstown 5320.
SIZE: 818 hectares.
LENGTH: 4 or 10 km, according to arrangement.
MAIN ATTRACTIONS: Attractive views of gorges, valleys and Queenstown; large mammals and prolific birdlife; tamboekie thorn (localized endemic).
FACILITIES/AMENITIES: Picnic and camping sites.
PERTINENT INFORMATION: The camping site is for trailists; casual users are accepted on application. Walks are allowed under supervision only. Maximum of 12 people allowed per trail.
AVAILABLE LITERATURE: In process of being compiled.
CLIMATE: Summer: warm days, cool evenings. Winter: cold; frost and snow are common.

Responding to public requests, the Queenstown Municipality runs overnight, accompanied walks through the Lawrence de Lange Nature Reserve and surrounding mountains. Trails offer possible sightings of kudu, mountain reedbuck, zebra, eland, bushbuck, duiker, black wildebeest, gemsbok, red hartebeest, blesbok, springbok, steenbok, impala and ostrich.

The reserve itself is situated on the slopes of Madeira Mountain, and the vegetation is principally grassveld, aloes, cycads and acacia. Of special interest is the tamboekie thorn, *Erythrina acanthocarpa*, a dense thorny shrub whose prickly large seedpods give this plant its name. Localized to the Queenstown district, the tamboekie thorn is rumoured to be a cure for skin cancer.

There are two trail routes which differ in character. The longer, some 10 kilometres, is suitable for fit hikers as it ascends to the summit of Madeira Mountain. The more leisurely, four-kilometre game-viewing walk leads through the reserve's lower regions.

Because of the high concentration of game, all walks are accompanied by a conservation officer. They begin early in the morning in order to see as much game as possible. Details can be obtained on request from the Town Engineer's Department of the Municipality of Queenstown.

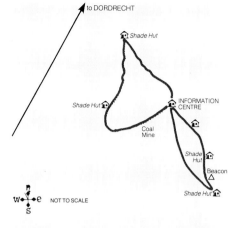

KOOS RAS NATURE TRAIL

131. *Koos Ras Nature Trail*

KOOS RAS NATURE RESERVE, STERKSTROOM

AUTHORITY-IN-CHARGE: Municipality of Sterkstroom, P.O. Box 25, Sterkstroom 5425.
SIZE: 280 hectares.
LENGTH: Approximately 6 km.
MAIN ATTRACTIONS: Game, including chamois, kudu, eland, zebra, blesbok, rhebok, impala, springbok, wildebeest and ostrich; historical coal mine dating back to 1887; white rocks spelling 'Sterkstroom' against mountain, dating back to 1913.
FACILITIES/AMENITIES: Rest camp with chalets and ablution blocks; drinking water; parking at start of trail in rest camp.
PERTINENT INFORMATION: Facilities are being developed.
AVAILABLE LITERATURE: Planned.
CLIMATE: Summer: hot with rain. Winter: long and cold, frost possible.

132. *The Ecowa Hiking Trail*

ELLIOT

AUTHORITY-IN-CHARGE: Municipality of Elliot, P.O. Box 21, Elliot 5460.
LENGTH/DURATION: 40,8 km/3 days, 2 nights; can be split into one-, two- and three-day routes.
MAIN ATTRACTIONS: Scenery of the southern Drakensberg, the Gatberg, and large sandstone caves; Noah's Ark Forest; ouhout stands; birdlife.
FACILITIES/AMENITIES: Two huts (details not finalized).
PERTINENT INFORMATION: The trail crosses

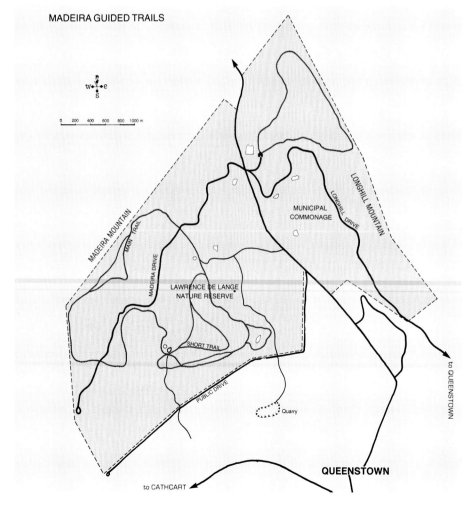

MADEIRA GUIDED TRAILS

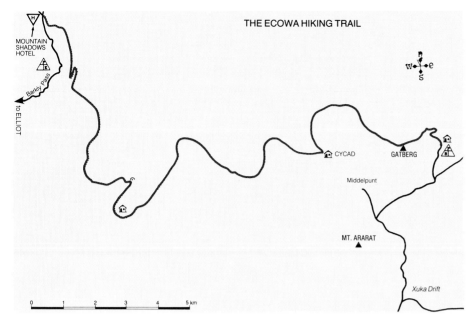

THE ECOWA HIKING TRAIL

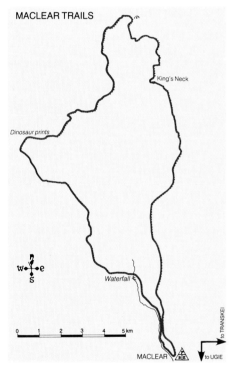

MACLEAR TRAILS

pearance which is common on the lower slopes of the Drakensberg and in the Transvaal Highveld.

In general, the endless vistas of wind- and water-eroded cave sandstones, black eagles, kestrels and secretarybirds soaring overhead, Xhosa kraals and grass-covered slopes (watch out for snakes in spring), contribute to the attraction of the relatively unexplored southern Drakensberg midlands.

133. Maclear Trails

MACLEAR

AUTHORITY-IN-CHARGE: Municipality of Maclear, P.O. Box 1, Maclear 5480; tel. (045322) 25 or 3.
LENGTH/DURATION: Approximately 34 km/2 days; trails lasting between 1 and 5 days are also available.
MAIN ATTRACTIONS: Southern Drakensberg mountains; waterfalls; flora; Bushman paintings; dinosaur prints; trout fishing.
FACILITIES/AMENITIES: Hikers sleep in caves or empty farmhouses, or they can bring their own tents; the trail begins and ends at Maclear Caravan Park.
PERTINENT INFORMATION: The cave accommodates about 20 people. Guided trails must be arranged a month in advance. There are no limits on numbers or ages of participants.
AVAILABLE LITERATURE: Trail brochure planned; located on Government Printer's 1:50 000 topographic maps '3028 CD Tsitsana' and '3128 AB Maclear'.
CLIMATE: Summer rainfall area.

134. Mountain Shadows Walks

BARKLY PASS

AUTHORITY-IN-CHARGE: Mountain Shadows Hotel, P.O. Box 130, Elliot 5460; tel. 0020 Barkly Pass 3.
LENGTH/DURATION: Viewpoint Trail: 4,8 km/1-2 hours. Vulture's Roost Trail: 6,4 km/2-3 hours. Camel Rock Trail: 7,6 km/2-3 hours. Castle Rock Trail: 10,4 km/3-4 hours. Shadow Mountain Trail: 14,8 km/5-7 hours.
MAIN ATTRACTIONS: Spectacular mountain scenery, embracing southern Drakensberg ranges and cave sandstone ramparts, with caves, overhangs and arches; game-viewing on foot (mountain reedbuck, grey rhebok,

Above: Asparagus virgatus.

15 private farms. The appointed leader is held accountable for any problems (eg. flower-picking, breaking trees, fires). Maximum of 10 hikers admitted.
AVAILABLE LITERATURE: In process of being compiled; located on Government Printer's topographic maps '3127 BB Barkly Pass', '3127 BD Elliot', '3128 AA Ugie' and '3128 AC Xuka Drift'.
CLIMATE: April to August: cold to very cold, snow possible. September to November: wet and cold at times. December to March: hot and pleasant.

Although the exact route and details of the Ecowa Hiking Trail were not finalized by the time this book went to print, enough of the trail existed to realize that it could be a winner!

When I arrived in Hogsback in 1983, I was thrilled to be included in the Border Outdoor Adventure Association's (B.O.A.A. or Hiking Club of East London) recce of the now-named Ecowa (Xhosa for 'mushroom') Hiking Trail. For hikers who do not feel ready for the Drakensberg proper, here is a taste of what it is all about: high altitudes, magnificent rock and wind-blown sandstone formations, and deep kloof forests. For those who have visited the Drakensberg, you will be astonished that so much exists so far south, a definite attraction for Eastern Cape enthusiasts.

It is a privilege to walk over private land, and when doing so in the north-eastern Cape, one wonders how this area escaped proclamation as a landscape reserve. The trail begins in sight of the unique Gatberg, 'the mountain with the hole'. It runs north of Noah's Ark Forest, a rich evergreen kloof forest better viewed from afar than while bushwacking within! Falie's Cave is an enormous work of natural art, as are the forest stands of *Leucosidea sericea* (ouhout, oubos or umChiohi), a gnarled tree of ancient ap-

springbok, blesbok and baboons).
FACILITIES/AMENITIES: All trails are colour-coded; parking, refreshments, meals and accommodation at Mountain Shadows Hotel.
PERTINENT INFORMATION: All trails are on privately owned land. No open fires. allowed. Do not litter. Carry water on all trails. Two-day (and longer) backpacking hikes, especially along the sandstone escarpment, using the caves for overnighting, are possible. Carry warm clothing in winter.
AVAILABLE LITERATURE: Information sheet and map showing walks, obtainable from the hotel.
CLIMATE: Summer: warm to hot, mists and rain likely, cool nights. Winter: clear, sunny days, cold nights; frost common, snow possible.

135. Rhodes Hiking Trail

RHODES

AUTHORITY-IN-CHARGE: For information: The Manager, Rhodes Hotel, P.O. Box 21, Rhodes 5582; tel. 04542 (Barkly East), ask for 9203 or 9906.
DURATION: 1-5 days.
MAIN ATTRACTIONS: Ben Macdhui (highest

mountain in the Cape); waterfalls and trout streams; birdlife; flowers in spring and summer.
FACILITIES/AMENITIES: Rhodes Hotel can be used as a base; old farmhouses and ski hut; skiing in winter if there are good snowfalls; trout fishing.
PERTINENT INFORMATION: The route is not marked; obtain 1:50 000 Government Printer's maps '3027 DB Ben Macdhui', '3027 DD Rhodes', '3028 CA Naudesnek' and '3028 CC Eland Heights'. The trail is on private land.
AVAILABLE LITERATURE: Promotional brochures, available from Rhodes Hotel.
CLIMATE: Summer rainfall area; winters are very cold (temperatures drop to -10 °C), snow is frequent.

The north-eastern Cape, a wedge of mountainous terrain bordered by Transkei and Lesotho, is often referred to as the 'Little Switzerland' of South Africa. Part of the southernmost Drakensberg, the 'bulge' is well known to South African skiers, wilderness trekkers, trout fishermen and tourists who crave the midwinter landscape around Lady Grey, Barkly East, Maclear, Rhodes, Ugie, Elliot, Indwe and Dordrecht. For the hiker, Ben Macdhui (3 001 m) offers a stiff but rewarding walk to its summit. You pass waterfalls, delight in far-reaching vistas over Transkei and have the opportunity to collect agate-rich rocks.

Rhodes Hotel has designed a hiking trail which begins at the historic hotel and, although hikers need not stay there, all enquiries are best made with the manager. The trail, which is over private farmland, is not marked, so hikers should navigate with the 1:50 000 maps available from the Government Printer.

Day hikers can drive 10 kilometres from Rhodes and then walk up the valley to Ham-

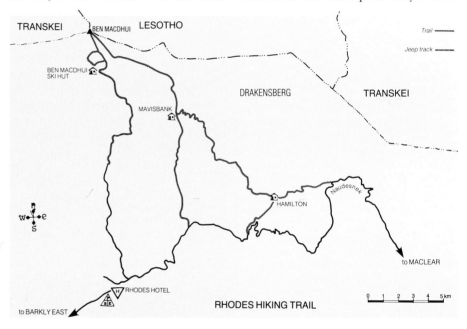

ilton and beyond to Naudesnek, which, at 2 740 metres, is the highest mountain pass in the Republic. This day trip can be extended into two days by sleeping at Hamilton, a two-bedroom farmhouse with two mattresses, table and chairs, paraffin lamps and stream water nearby.

Another two-day option is a strenuous hike up Ben Macdhui from Rhodes (1 800 m), overnighting at the ski hut. The hut has bunks and mattresses, and must be booked through Paul Sephton (tel. 04542, ask for 2440). If this hut is unavailable, there is another one, but with no facilities. Hikers return the following day.

Alternatively, Rhodes Hotel will supply (at a cost) a Land Rover to the ski hut. Hikers can then ascend Ben Macdhui and walk south-east towards the old farmhouse at Mavisbank. Note that this house has no doors, but does have a roof, and firewood is provided. Hikers return the following day.

Longer routes of up to five days can be planned. All hikers are warned to prepare themselves for severe winter weather, including freezing temperatures and snow. Remember, too, that the altitude is relatively high, which moderates spring and summer temperatures, and causes breathlessness in the unacclimatized.

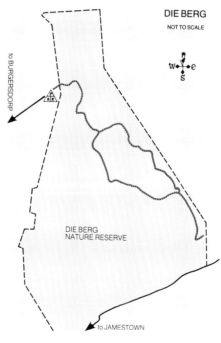

DIE BERG

NOT TO SCALE

to BURGERSDORP

DIE BERG
NATURE RESERVE

to JAMESTOWN

Opposite page, left: A cave in the Barkly Pass area.
Opposite page, bottom: At the summit of Ben Macdhui.
Above: Die Berg, above Burgersdorp.

136. Die Berg

BURGERSDORP

🚶 🚶

AUTHORITY-IN-CHARGE: Municipality of Burgersdorp, P.O. Box 13, Burgersdorp 5520.
SIZE: 411 hectares.
LENGTH: 7 km.
MAIN ATTRACTIONS: Large game readily visible; wilderness atmosphere above a town; rugged, scenic Karoo-like terrain.
FACILITIES/AMENITIES: Marked footpath; two rondavels, each accommodating 10 hikers, with toilet facilities.
PERTINENT INFORMATION: Carry water; rugged terrain necessitates sturdy footwear.
AVAILABLE LITERATURE: In process of being compiled.
CLIMATE: Winter: cool, dry, sunny days and cold nights. Summer: hot days; thunderstorms are common.

Die Berg Nature Reserve is what I like to refer to as 'pocket wilderness'. Rising steeply above the historic little town of Burgersdorp, Die Berg is part of the Stormberg range. Not far above the hum of the town you can retreat into wild, rugged terrain and feel miles away from it all.

The reserve may appear to be a flat-topped plateau from a distance but once on top, the landscape is surprisingly diverse. The nature trail winds through grassy plateau, rugged and dry kloofs, bush-dotted slopes and rocky outcrops of dolerite boulders. Wild olive and cabbage trees and broom karee, *Rhus erosa*, are conspicuous, as are the large game species introduced by the municipality: hartebeest, wildebeest, blesbok, springbok, zebra, duiker and vaal rhebok. Dassies are also plentiful.

Burgersdorp High School has been given the responsibility of planning and marking the trails, which when completed will be two short walks. The reserve is reached on an unpaved road between the old cemetery and the waterworks. Permission from the municipality must be obtained in order to visit the reserve.

137. Oviston Nature Reserve

VENTERSTAD

AUTHORITY-IN-CHARGE: Department of Nature and Environmental Conservation, Cape Provincial Administration.
SIZE: 13 000 hectares.
MAIN ATTRACTIONS: Indigenous large game; Hendrik Verwoerd Dam; birdlife (141 species).
FACILITIES/AMENITIES: Guided trails for educational groups, on request and by prior arrangement only; tarred game-viewing roads; picnic spots; angling facilities; no overnight accommodation, except on the guided trails.
PERTINENT INFORMATION: Entrance is free. Open on weekends and public holidays. The reserve extends from Bethulie Bridge in the east to the dam wall in the west. Hikers are advised to wear gaiters to guard against

scratchy grass seeds. For information: The Officer-in-Charge, Oviston Nature Reserve, P.O. Box 7, Venterstad 5990, tel. 055332, ask for 21.
AVAILABLE LITERATURE: Reserve pamphlet, with map; included in annual reports of the Department of Nature and Environmental Conservation; *Trees and Larger Shrubs of Three Karoo Nature Reserves*, booklet available from the Department.
CLIMATE: Summer rainfall area.

138. Doornkloof Nature Reserve

COLESBERG

AUTHORITY-IN-CHARGE: Department of Nature and Environmental Conservation, Cape Provincial Administration.
SIZE: 10 000 hectares.
MAIN ATTRACTIONS: Extremely rugged and scenic terrain; dolerite koppies and deep wooded kloofs; P.K. le Roux Dam and Seekoei River; large mammals.
FACILITIES/AMENITIES: Guided walks for organized groups; hiking trail planned, with shelters; game-viewing from vehicle; picnic sites and fishing areas; canoeing allowed on dam.
PERTINENT INFORMATION: Experienced backpackers can hike in this reserve on their own; guided trails are for education groups and must be arranged in advance with the Officer-in-Charge, Doornkloof Nature Reserve, P.O. Box 23, Vanderkloof Dam 8771, tel. 05852, ask for 1303. Hikers should wear gaiters to keep grass seeds out of their boots. Water from the river and dam should be purified before drinking.
AVAILABLE LITERATURE: Trail brochure and map; included in annual reports of the Department of Nature and Environmental Conservation; *Trees and Larger Shrubs of Three Karoo Nature Reserves*, booklet; located on Government Printer's

topographic maps '3025 AC Kooffontein', '3024 BB Joubertsgat' and '3024 BD Ventersvlei'.
CLIMATE: Average annual rainfall: 350 millimetres, falling mostly in March and April. Summer maximum temperature: 42 °C. Winter minimum temperature: -10 °C.

If you are attracted to the Karoo wilderness and are physically fit, a self-designed backpacking trek in Doornkloof Nature Reserve is an ideal holiday.

Until the hiking trail with shelters is completed, backpackers can roam at will the

10 000 hectares of rugged dolerite koppies, densely wooded kloofs, and dam and riverine banks. The reserve officer, who leads trails for organized groups such as schools or clubs, will also assist private parties by designing a trail route. Hiking can be combined with canoeing on the P.K. le Roux Dam and fishing at designated sites in the Seekoei River. Camping along the gentle inlets of the river and dam is particularly lovely.

The presence of large expanses of water tremendously enhances the birdlife. Fish eagles, kingfishers, goliath herons, spoonbills

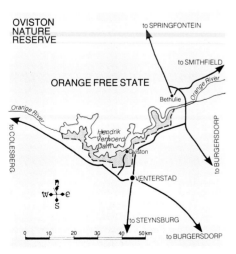

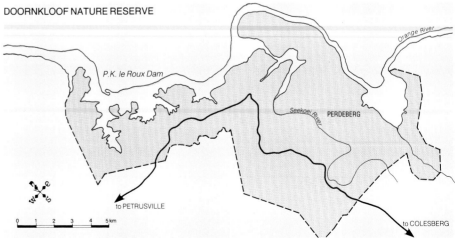

DOORNKLOOF NATURE RESERVE

and ducks feed in shallow bays. Although the reintroduction of a diverse selection of large animals is being planned (the veld is being rested at present), hikers can now see mountain reedbuck, kudu, duiker, steenbok, baboon and vervet monkey. Most of the larger floral species, classified as false upper Karoo veld, are identified in the Department's booklet, *Trees and Larger Shrubs of Three Karoo Nature Reserves*. Rolfontein (see page 130) and Oviston (opposite page) are considered Doornkloof's sister reserves.

Grasses are also common and hikers should wear gaiters and non-woollen socks to guard against the sharp seed dispersal mechanisms which scratch one's legs. The terrain is very rough, so sturdy hiking boots are a must. I also suggest boiling the water from the dam and the river, although my hiking party drank it without mishap.

Opposite page: Rhipsalis *sp.*

Above: Experienced hikers can explore on foot the 10 000 hectares of rugged dolerite koppies and densely wooded kloofs of the Doornkloof Nature Reserve, a beautiful Karoo wilderness. Canoeing is permitted on the P.K. le Roux Dam.

KAROO AND NORTHERN CAPE

Karoo is the Hottentot word for 'dry' – and dry is the principal characteristic of this region. Comprising the Great and Little Karoo, it covers the Cape Province, excluding the moister sea-bordering and mountainous western, southern and eastern parts.

The Great Karoo is a plateau lying 600-900 metres above sea level and is situated between the Great Escarpment and the Cape folded mountains. The Little Karoo lies between the mountains surrounding the Great Karoo, and the coastal plain. To the east and north-east, the Upper Karoo merges imperceptibly into the highveld of the Orange Free State.

Most of the trailing opportunities present themselves as relatively short hiking trails run by the National Parks Board, guided trails in Cape provincial nature reserves and botanical gardens displaying flora typical of this climatic zone, and rambles in small municipal reserves and private resorts. The trails expose hikers to fascinating natural sculptures such as the Cango Caves; the rugged, forbidding Swartberg; the basalt towers of the Valley of Desolation; flat-topped, basalt-capped koppies; and the thundering cataracts of the Augrabies Falls.

Both the Department of Nature and Environmental Conservation of the Cape Provincial Administration and the National Parks Board have reintroduced into their reserves viable populations of indigenous game such as white rhino, red hartebeest, black wildebeest, springbok, eland and mountain zebra, all of which allow close encounters on the varied hiking trails.

Climatic conditions are extreme. Violent thunderstorms bring rain, especially in March and April. Days are warm to hot, but

night temperatures plummet very low, sometimes to well below freezing during winter. Most nights are clear, due to the high elevation and low humidity of this region.

ECOLOGICAL ZONES: SEMI-DESERT AND KAROO, ACACIA SAVANNAH OR KALAHARI

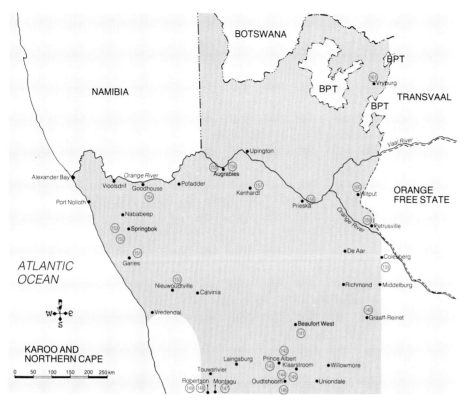

KAROO AND
NORTHERN CAPE

0   50   100   150   200 250 km

140. Karoo Nature Reserve

GRAAFF-REINET

AUTHORITY-IN-CHARGE: Department of Nature and Environmental Conservation, Cape Provincial Administration.
SIZE: 14 300 hectares.
MAIN ATTRACTIONS: Valley of Desolation; Spandaukop and the Drie Koppe; Vanrhyneveld's Pass Dam; typical Karoo landscape with reintroduced large mammals.
PERTINENT INFORMATION: Permits necessary, obtainable from The Officer-in-Charge, Karoo Nature Reserve, P.O. Box 349, Graaff-Reinet 6280. Water must be carried on all walks and hikes (at least two litres per person per day is recommended).
AVAILABLE LITERATURE: *Karoo Nature Reserve*, comprehensive brochure and map.
CLIMATE: Summer: hot with rain, mostly in the form of thunderstorms. Winter: cool days, cold nights.

The Karoo Nature Reserve, located near the history-steeped and architecturally restored town of Graaff-Reinet, is often confused with the Karoo National Park beyond Beaufort West. Both reserves are conservation achievements initiated through the fundraising efforts of the South African Nature Foundation. Once a land of flourishing wildlife in a healthy semi-desert environment, the area of the Karoo Nature Reserve – actually the old municipal commonage surrounding Graaff-Reinet – was saved from becoming a barren tract of overgrazed and over-utilized veld by the Cape's Department of Nature and Environmental Conservation. The Department's efforts are rejuvenating the reserve to a near-original natural state containing healthy indigenous plant and animal communities.

This diverse reserve spans an altitude from 784 metres to 1 565 metres and ecom-

139. Little Karoo Cycle Trail

COLESBERG TO GEORGE

AUTHORITY-IN-CHARGE: Trailblazers.
DURATION: 9,5 days.
MAIN ATTRACTIONS: Dramatic mountain passes of the Little Karoo.
FACILITIES/AMENITIES: Camping accommodation; tarmac roads; all transport, equipment and food provided; cost of tour does not include cycle hire, so trailists are welcome to use their own bicycles.
PERTINENT INFORMATION: Maximum of 18 people per group. Either racing (thin-tyre) or all-terrain (fat-tyre) bicycles can be used. A back-up vehicle lifts cycles up main escarpments; riding is mainly downhill so the trail requires only moderate fitness.
AVAILABLE LITERATURE: Brochures available from Trailblazers.
CLIMATE: Summer rainfall area.

The passes of the Little and Great Karoo are too dramatic to appreciate fully by touring in a motorcar. Their sharp turns, steep sides and fascinating geology demand time to savour both man's architecture and nature's sculptures. The Little Karoo Cycle Trail

provides the opportunity to experience this area in a relaxed and fun-filled manner.

From Colesberg, where the cyclists camp on the first night, the trail runs through the passes of the Renosterberg and Sneeuberg to Graaff-Reinet and the Valley of Desolation. Travelling southwards, cyclists drive and ride to Willowmore and then through the Gwarriepoort Pass in the Slypsteenberg, and between the Swartberg and Kammanasieberg ranges to Oudtshoorn.

Proceeding to the hamlet of Prince Albert by vehicle and cycle, trailists then ride along the banks of the Groot River through the imposing Meiringspoort Pass, and camp at De Rust. The last dramatic ride takes cyclists along the slopes of the Outeniqua Mountains to George.

Participants will be transported back to Johannesburg if they wish.

Opposite page, top: Spandaukop, seen from the Valley of Desolation.

Opposite page, bottom: In the Valley of Desolation, near Graaff-Reinet.

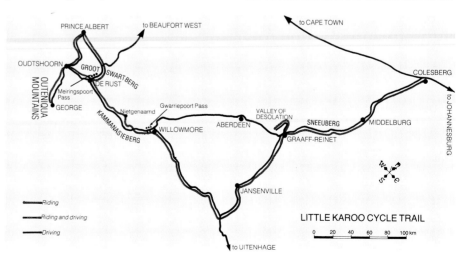

LITTLE KAROO CYCLE TRAIL

0   20   40   60   80   100 km

reedbuck; and the medium-altitude, bush clump savannah, a community of wild olives, karee and white stinkwood interspersed with grasses, which is favoured by the Cape mountain zebra. A small herd of these animals has been introduced from Cradock's Mountain Zebra National Park (see page 102) in the hope that the Karoo Nature Reserve's population will grow and contribute to saving this species – one of the most endangered on earth. Thus far, they are increasing very satisfactorily.

People wishing to walk through the reserve must obtain a permit from the Department of Nature and Environmental Conservation's office in Graaff-Reinet. Walks accompanied by a nature conservation officer within the wilder, more rugged portions of the reserve are available on request, but the officer-in-charge must be notified well in advance.

I suggest the following routes for unaccompanied rambles:

1. Around the Vanrhyneveld's Pass Dam where birdlife is particularly prolific. Greater flamingo, South African shelduck, Cape teal, whitebreasted cormorant and grey heron are common, while mammals such as the Cape clawless otter, water mongoose, bateared fox, kudu and springbok can also be seen. Hides are present.

2. On to the plateau overlooking the Valley of Desolation, with its impressive views of the basalt pillars, caves and other rock formations, as well as possible glimpses of vervet monkeys, reedbuck, steenbok, black eagles and other animals.

3. Up Spandaukop (1 316 m), a steep cone topped with dolerite. This climb, although it takes no more than an hour, is strenuous because of the eroded shale slopes. Only one fairly easy route, among precipitous rock cliffs, leads to the summit. Special permission to climb here must be obtained from the officer-in-charge of the reserve.

4. Along the old jeep track, passing the only natural springs in the reserve. This route offers views of the surrounding landscape with possible sightings of springbok, black wildebeest, blesbok, mountain zebra and small antelope.

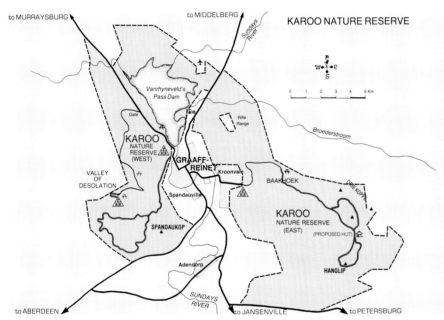

KAROO NATURE RESERVE

passes the unique basalt pillars of the Valley of Desolation (a national monument); the impressive peaks and cliffs of Spandaukop, Hanglip and the Drie Koppe; deep kloofs and natural springs; Vanrhyneveld's Pass Dam; as well as rare and endangered plants and animals. Fossil remains bear testimony to the dinosaurs that trampled through the long-gone swamps of prehistory, while artefacts and, more recently, history books speak of man's involvement in the area from the Early Stone Age to the present day.

Although often hot and seemingly barren, the sere Karoo veld is in fact alive with creatures, both large and small. Look for hunting spiders, dung beetles, cicadas, mountain and angulate tortoises, and rock leguans, but be cautious, as scorpions, Cape cobras, puff adders and other snakes are also present. Some of the more conspicuous grassland birds are the crowned guineafowl,

redwing francolin, secretarybird, ostrich, kori bustard and Karoo korhaan, while chanting goshawks and martial and black eagles may also be seen occasionally.

The mountain vegetation of the Karoo Nature Reserve comprises large areas of succulents dominated by the spekboom which imparts the characteristic dusty-green colour to the veld. This plant is a major food for browsing animals and provides an ideal habitat for the kudu, a secretive and beautiful large antelope which demands silence and patience from the would-be observer. The three other major types of vegetation found in the reserve are the Karoo flora of the plains where true Karoo plants such as composites, mainly aromatic bushes, thorny succulent scrubs and aloes thrive; the high altitude grasslands referred to by Acocks as Karroid-*Merxmuellera* Mountain Veld, and favoured by klipspringer and mountain

141. Springbok Trail

KAROO NATIONAL PARK, BEAUFORT WEST

AUTHORITY-IN-CHARGE: National Parks Board.

LENGTH/DURATION: 40 km/2,5 days, 2 nights.

MAIN ATTRACTIONS: Rugged Karoo mountain landscape; large mammals reintroduced to the area.

FACILITIES/AMENITIES: Two huts with bunks and mattresses, water, firewood, fireplaces, toilets and rubbish bins.

PERTINENT INFORMATION: Maximum of 12 people per night. Water must be carried (two litres per person per day is recommended). The trail has been altered to run anticlockwise through the park, to shorten the first day's hike from 17 to 10 kilometres.

AVAILABLE LITERATURE: *The Springbok Trail – Karoo National Park*, information sheet issued by the National Parks Board; *The Karoo National Park, Beaufort West*, G. de Graaff and others, published by the National Parks Board, 1979.

CLIMATE: Subject to climatic extremes with marked day/night and seasonal temperature fluctuations. January daily average minimum and maximum temperatures: 16 and 32 °C; July daily average minimum and maximum temperatures: 5 and 18 °C. March and April: main rainy season but rain is possible at any time, usually accompanied by thunderstorms. June to August: snow and frost possible. August: strongest winds.

For a feeling of the Great Karoo as the trekboers experienced it, hike the Springbok Trail. The Karoo mountains are harsh, rugged and starkly beautiful, especially in early morning and late afternoon. The Springbok Trail winds up steep shale slopes and along doleritic plateaux, through kloofs, and across dry stream beds and wildlife-rich plains. Like the mountains of the Karoo, the trail is rough and steep in places, the unstable shale slopes and the stony ground being difficult to negotiate. Once the vast plateau is reached, however, walking is level and pleasant.

Precautions must always be taken against the blazing Karoo sun and water must be carried at most times of the year. I was fortunate to hike the trail just after the 'Laingsburg floods' in January 1981: the rivers were high, the waterfalls dramatic and everywhere the shale slabs glistened with moisture. These conditions are, however, most unusual.

The naturalist will be fully occupied identifying the many species of Karoo bush and the many 'LBJs' in the avian-rich river thickets. (For non-birders, LBJ stands for 'little brown jobs' – small brown birds diffi-cult to identify in the field.) Mountain reedbuck, duiker, steenbok, hare, dassie and baboon are common, while the observant hiker is also likely to spot mountain zebra, red hartebeest, black wildebeest, gemsbok, springbok and kudu. Common kestrels and other predators can occasionally be seen wheeling overhead. The invertebrate life, especially the large beetles, spiders and grasshoppers, is equally fascinating.

The two overnight facilities are unusual – they are built from local stone in the style of 100- to 150-year-old Karoo-type huts and blend well with their mountain backdrop. Both huts have two small rooms with six beds each and a central section with a fireplace. Chemical toilets are provided.

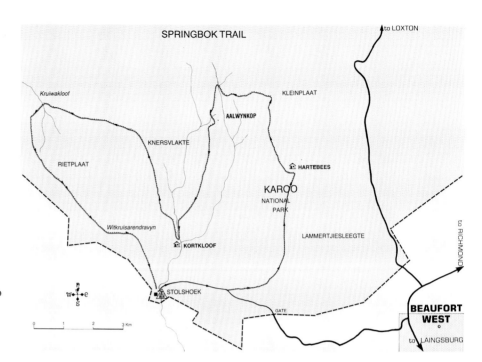

SPRINGBOK TRAIL

SWARTBERG HIKING TRAIL

142. Swartberg Hiking Trail

OUDTSHOORN/PRINCE ALBERT, GROOT SWARTBERG

AUTHORITY-IN-CHARGE: Southern Cape Forest Region, Forestry Branch, Department of Environment Affairs★.

LENGTH/DURATION: 84 km/5 days, 4 nights; shorter variations (3 circular routes) are possible.

MAIN ATTRACTIONS: Spectacular sandstone formations; wildflowers in fynbos and

Karoo veld; historical monument; Swartberg Pass.

FACILITIES/AMENITIES: Gouekrans Hut (proposed); Bothashoek Hut (converted forester's house) with 30 bunks and mattresses, no washing facilities but natural pool close to hut, and outdoor toilets; Ou Tol Hut (converted forester's house) with 30 bunks and mattresses, flush toilet and bath.

PERTINENT INFORMATION: Carry drinking water (available at huts) when hiking between huts.

AVAILABLE LITERATURE: Brochure and map in process of being compiled; located on Government Printer's 1:50 000 topographic map '3322 AC Cango Caves'.

CLIMATE: Average annual rainfall: 572 millimetres, falling mostly in March and November; thunderstorms are common. Average annual rainfall on southern slopes: 742 millimetres. Average annual rainfall on northern slopes: 447 millimetres. Average maximum temperature in January: 31 °C. Average minimum temperature in July: 3 °C. Snow falls five to six times per year, on average, from June to September. Best hiking months, August and September.

The Groot Swartberg, a spectacular, twisted and contorted mass of Table Mountain sandstone, was opened to the hiking public in late 1987. Lying mostly between 2 000-3 000 metres above sea level, the hiking trail traverses rocks that are 250 million years old, formed during the Cretaceous Period. Since then nature's forces – rain, wind and earth movements – have sculpted these once flat-lying sediments into a landscape not easily rivalled by those on other trails. The impressive diversity and richness of Cape fynbos and Karoo flora on these slopes is an enigma to science. The soil is poor in nutrients and shallow, and the slopes are steep. Yet *Protea*, *Leucadendron*, *Erica*, *Watsonia*, *Gladiolus*, *Disa*, *Haemanthus* and many lesser known, rare plants abound.

Animal life is also interesting. Colourful lizards delight the trailist, while eleven species of snakes keep you alert for these sunbathers on rocks and paths. The rarer birds include the booted eagle, martial eagle, Cape eagle owl, Victorin's warbler and Protea seedeater. Sunbirds and sugarbirds, rock jumpers and black eagles are often spotted. Mammals most likely to be seen by the hiker include the dassie, klipspringer and baboon, although leopards, otters, jackals, aardvarks, kudu, steenbok, grysbok and vaal rhebok are also present.

The Swartberg Hiking Trail divides into the Cango, Swartberg Pass and Prince Albert sections. The Cango section begins at the Cango Caves near Oudtshoorn; the Swartberg section starts at Ou Tol Hut on top of the Swartberg Pass; and the Prince Albert section starts at Scholzkloof near Prince Albert, where parking is available. Alternatively, you can start at De Hoek, the same place hikers start the De Hoek Nature Walk. From these points, you can choose your trail route.

The following approximate times can be used to plan your hike:
De Hoek to Gouekrans Hut: 7 hours.
Gouekrans Hut to Bothashoek Hut: 4,5 hours.
Bothashoek Hut to Ou Tol Hut: 4 hours.
Prince Albert (Scholzkloof) to Ou Tol Hut: 5,5 hours.

143. De Hoek Nature Walk

SWARTBERG

AUTHORITY-IN-CHARGE: Southern Cape Forest Region, Forestry Branch, Department of Environment Affairs*.
LENGTH/DURATION: 11,6 km/7 hours.
MAIN ATTRACTIONS: Rugged mountain scenery.
FACILITIES/AMENITIES: De Hoek Holiday Resort, run by the Divisional Council of Klein Karoo-Langkloof.
AVAILABLE LITERATURE: Information sheets and map available from the Forestry Branch or the State Forester, P.O. Box 350, Oudtshoorn 6620, tel. (04431) 3392.
CLIMATE: Average annual rainfall: 750 millimetres, peaking in March and August. Summer: rainy, very hot. Winter: dry, cool to cold, snow possible above 1 200 metres.

The Swartberg is a seemingly endless series of rugged peaks and poorts, crests, cliffs and kloofs, all brightly coloured by red oxides and covered with proteas, heath, tolbos, pincushions, everlastings and other fynbos species, in addition to thorn trees, karroid bushes, aloes and euphorbias. The sense of latent power in these mountains – their quartzitic rock and Table Mountain sandstones moulded into complex, wave-like contortions by unimaginable natural forces – is awesome, and it is not difficult to understand why the area is frequented by mountaineers looking for physically demanding, unusual challenges.

The Swartberg is relatively inaccessible to casual ramblers and therefore the De Hoek Nature Walk, in the southern foothills of this range near the Cango Caves, is a valuable and commendable project. Rising on rugged terrain from about 850 metres to over 1 220 metres, you can expect fairly strenuous walking, but the rewards are well worth the effort. I suggest walking the trail in the cooler parts of the day when dassies, klipspringers, grey rhebok, baboon and even leopard may be observed. The most common birds are the Cape sugarbird, orangebreasted sunbird, rockjumper and black eagle.

144. Cango Caves

OUDTSHOORN

AUTHORITY-IN-CHARGE: Municipality of Oudtshoorn, P.O. Box 255, Oudtshoorn 6620.
LENGTH: Approximately 3,5 km of natural subterranean corridors.
MAIN ATTRACTIONS: Stalactite and stalagmite formations in one of the world's most spectacular caves.
FACILITIES/AMENITIES: Guided walks; natural structures lit by coloured spotlights; restaurant, bar and café; crèche; kennels, as animals are not allowed in the caves.
PERTINENT INFORMATION: The caves are humid, so light clothing is recommended. Guided tours are available during January, February, April and December, daily and hourly 08h00-17h00 inclusive, and the remainder of the year daily at 09h00, 11h00, 13h00 and 15h00. Seventy steps must be climbed to reach the cave entrance, but in

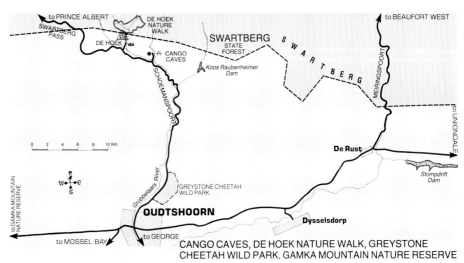

CANGO CAVES, DE HOEK NATURE WALK, GREYSTONE CHEETAH WILD PARK, GAMKA MOUNTAIN NATURE RESERVE

other respects the walk is not difficult. An entrance fee is charged.
AVAILABLE LITERATURE: Information brochure on sale at the office; *Cango Caves*, AA Bulletin TBE-K3.

Gouged out of the Groot Swartberg, the Cango Caves are a spectacular wonder of limestone eroded by carbonic acid to form stalactite and stalagmite structures, caverns and corridors.

A small section of the subterranean complex is open to the general public and the guided tours through these chambers are immensely popular and have educational value. Most of the unexploited caves, however, are not open to inexperienced cavers; they are dangerous to explore without prior know-how and appropriate equipment.

145. *Greystone Cheetah Wild Park*

OUDTSHOORN, see map page 123

AUTHORITY-IN-CHARGE: Barron's Greystone Cheetah Wild Park, P.O. Box 146, Oudtshoorn 6620; tel. (04431) 6014.
MAIN ATTRACTIONS: Close-up exposure to a great variety of animals; park is set on historic site; views of the Little Karoo.
FACILITIES/AMENITIES: Walking paths; motorcar roads; shop and refreshments; Cango Caves Motel across the road.
PERTINENT INFORMATION: Open daily 07h30-17h30.
AVAILABLE LITERATURE: *Barron's Greystone Cheetah Wild Park*, brochure.
CLIMATE: Summer days are very hot.

Readers may think that the privately owned Greystone Cheetah Wild Park is an incongruous entry in this book. However, I visited the park late in the afternoon and again in the early morning, before the swarm of motorists arrived. I left my car at the entrance and walked the gravel roads and game tracks to enjoy the many and unusual captive and wild mammals and birds in the park.

Some of the species indigenous to South Africa include cheetah (you can pet them under supervision), blesbok, zebra, blue wildebeest, red duiker, steenbok, springbok, mountain reedbuck, bushbuck, rhebok, gemsbok, lynx, porcupine, bateared fox, jackal, baboon, mountain tortoise, angulate tortoise and blue crane. Other animals include Australian birds, camels, the rhea and other birds from South America. Many of the 'non-dangerous' species roam freely and visitors can walk cautiously among them. In fact, when the Greystone Cheetah Wild Park was first opened, motor vehicles were not admitted. However, the

manager noticed that too many people objected to walking so he opened the gravel roads to vehicles.

In addition to game-viewing, I recommend a stroll to the top of Tafelkop from where Oudtshoorn and the picturesque valley of the Little Karoo can be seen. The park is set on sandstone hills, quarried between 1860 and 1914 by Scottish masons. The stone from this historic site was used in the construction of the nearby 'feather palaces' and public buildings.

The combination of an outing to Greystone Cheetah Wild Park and the Cango Caves makes for a very interesting day.

146. *Gamka Mountain Nature Reserve*

OUDTSHOORN, see map page 123

AUTHORITY-IN-CHARGE: Department of Nature and Environmental Conservation, Cape Provincial Administration.
SIZE: 9 428 hectares.
LENGTH/DURATION: Nature Trail: approximately 15 km. Guided Trail: approximately 26 km/2 days, 1 night.
MAIN ATTRACTIONS: Cape mountain zebra and small game; birdlife; geological features, ravines and associated vegetation.
FACILITIES/AMENITIES: Parking area, toilet and hand basins; tented overnight camp can be provided; Calitzdorp Spa 10 km from the reserve, with restaurant, chalets, caravan park and swimming pool.
PERTINENT INFORMATION: Permits necessary, obtainable from the officer-in-

charge of the reserve. The two-day trail must be booked in advance. Maximum of 10 people per trail; minimum of 6 adults per two-day trail. Hikers must carry all equipment plus water, but do not have to carry tents. Sturdy boots are essential. For bookings and information: The Officer-in-Charge, Gamka Mountain Nature Reserve, Private Bag X21, Oudtshoorn 6620, tel. (04431) 367.
AVAILABLE LITERATURE: Included in annual reports of the Department of Nature and Environmental Conservation.
CLIMATE: Average annual rainfall: 250 millimetres (400-500 millimetres on the summit), falling mostly in winter (May to October), but summer precipitation is possible. Average temperature range: 5-25 °C. Prevailing winds: south-east in summer, north-west in winter. Hot summers, mild winters. Autumn and spring are the best hiking seasons.

The Department of Nature and Environmental Conservation of the Cape claims that the Gamka Mountain Nature Reserve, with its multitude of plants, is one of the most unspoilt of all their reserves. Covering 70 per cent of the reserve is false macchia, while succulent mountain scrub (spekboomveld) and mountain renosterveld are present on the lower northern and southern slopes. In addition, succulent Karoo vegetation occurs on the northern plain. Hence, hikers can experience many attractive species belonging to the protea, erica and restio families, as well as *Elyptropappus* spp. and spekboom. These plants survive in the sandy, shallow soils of this relatively dry area, 35 kilometres from Oudtshoorn.

The reserve protects several small game species such as klipspringer, common and blue duiker, steenbok, grysbok and grey rhebok, in addition to baboon, dassie, caracal and Cape grey mongoose. However, the Cape mountain zebra is the rarest animal and the principal reason why this reserve was established in 1970. The black and booted eagles are among the 90 recorded bird species.

The geology of the reserve is another attractive feature. Bakenkop (1 100 m), the highest peak, forms part of the Gamkaberg-Rooiberg range, which in turn is part of the Cape folded mountains. Although the Gamkaberg is rounded by gentle slopes near the summit, its northern slopes are deeply incised by impressive steep-sided ravines.

While it is not developed for tourism, the Gamka Mountain Nature Reserve encourages hikers. Walkers can follow a footpath in a deep kloof, whose gradual slope offers an easy five- to six-hour ramble. Alternatively, the officer-in-charge offers a two-day guided trail. On the first day, the route rises from 350 to 1 100 metres over about 15 kilometres. Hikers are advised to wear sturdy footwear and are reminded that all their water must be carried, as streams are not dependable in this arid region.

A tented camp-site can be erected if requested in advance.

147. Montagu Mountain Reserve

MONTAGU

AUTHORITY-IN-CHARGE: Municipality of Montagu, P.O. Box 24, Montagu 6720.
SIZE: 1 200 hectares.
LENGTH/DURATION: Bloupunt Hiking Trail: 15,6 km/6-9 hours. Cogman's Kloof Hiking Trail: 12,1 km/3-6 hours. Lover's Walk: 2,2 km/1 hour.
MAIN ATTRACTIONS: Narrow gorges formed by coastward-flowing streams; transitional zone between Cape fynbos and Karoo vegetation; wildflowers; waterfalls, caves and views; black eagles, dassies and klipspringers.
FACILITIES/AMENITIES: Nature walks and hiking trails in mountain kloofs; Donkerkloof Hut, with two rooms for 6 people each, supplying wood stoves indoors for heat and cooking, braai area and washing-up facilities, ablution block with toilets, hand basins, shower, and hot and cold water; limited overnight camping allowed in vicinity of hiking hut; hot springs

Opposite page: Coloured spotlights highlight the spectacular cave formations in the Cango Caves, near Oudtshoorn. There are approximately 3,5 kilometres of subterranean corridors in this cave system, which is gouged out of the Groot Swartberg.

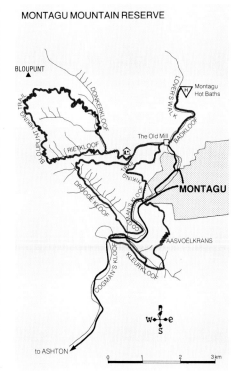

MONTAGU MOUNTAIN RESERVE

with caravan park; hotel with casual and time-share units; picnic sites at Kleurkloof; hot and cold baths in radioactive spa (19 mach units); nature garden (11 hectares, in Montagu South) offering walks through the largest vygie collection in the world, bird-watching hides, and tea on Tuesday mornings from June to October (best flowering season).
PERTINENT INFORMATION: For information, bookings and permits: Montagu Information Office, Bath Street, Montagu 6720; tel. (0234) 42471.
AVAILABLE LITERATURE: *Bloupunt Hiking Trail, Montagu*, brochure and map.
CLIMATE: Average annual rainfall: less than 300 millimetres; mild Karoo-type weather.

The Municipality of Montagu deserves praise for reconstructing this unique reserve after the infamous 'Laingsburg floods' virtually demolished all facilities in 1981.

Several kloofs within the Montagu Mountain Reserve are accessible for short walks and hikes. The loveliest stroll is Lover's

Walk, through Badkloof, which links the hot springs and hotel resort to Montagu. Birdlife, baboon, klipspringer and dassie abound on the steep, cave-dotted mountain slopes. Branching from Badkloof is Donkerkloof, which leads up to a nek on Bloupunt (1 304 m).

Two new trails start at the Old Mill. The Bloupunt Hiking Trail climbs Bloupunt via Rietkloof and descends via Donkerkloof. From the summit of Bloupunt the towns of Montagu and Ashton can be seen, as well as Robertson, McGregor and Bonnievale in the distance. Small pools in Donkerkloof, passed on the descent, provide relief from the heat. Hikers sleep in a comfortable stone hut with reed ceilings and cast-iron stoves. The hut, located only 1 300 metres from the parking area, blends beautifully into the surroundings. The second part of the trail (the Cogman's Kloof hike) explores Drooge Kloof and Cogman's Kloof. More trails into Kleurkloof and over Aasvoëlkrans are planned.

148. Dassieshoek Nature Reserve

ROBERTSON

AUTHORITY-IN-CHARGE: Municipality of Robertson, P.O. Box 52, Robertson 6705.
SIZE: 865 hectares.
MAIN ATTRACTIONS: Mountain renosterveld and fynbos in kloofs and on the Langeberg; waterfalls.
FACILITIES/AMENITIES: Constructed footpaths; picnic/braai complex; toilets; chalets, flats, rondavels, cabins, caravan and camping sites at Silverstrand Resort, Breede River.
PERTINENT INFORMATION: Located 15 km north of Robertson. Large numbers of birds attracted to picnic site. Open sunrise to sunset. Permits necessary, obtainable at the gate.
AVAILABLE LITERATURE: Brochure, available from the town clerk.
CLIMATE: Summer: hot days, cool nights. Winter: cool days, cold nights.

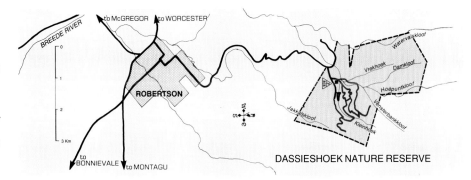

DASSIESHOEK NATURE RESERVE

150. Nieuwoudtville Nature Reserve

AUTHORITY-IN-CHARGE: Municipality of Nieuwoudtville, Voortrekker Street, Nieuwoudtville 8180.
SIZE: 66 hectares.
MAIN ATTRACTIONS: Spring flora and endemic species; dolerite koppies; views of the Bokkeveld.
FACILITIES/AMENITIES: Picnic site and parking; footpaths.
PERTINENT INFORMATION: The reserve is open all the time.
AVAILABLE LITERATURE: Included in annual reports of the Department of Nature and Environmental Conservation.
CLIMATE: Summer: hot days, cool nights. Winter: cool days, cold nights.

151. Namaqualand Coast Trail

AUTHORITY-IN-CHARGE: National Parks Board.
LENGTH: Approximately 80 km.
MAIN ATTRACTIONS: Wild, isolated coastal scenery; birdlife.
FACILITIES/AMENITIES: Huts planned.
PERTINENT INFORMATION: The trail, which is still in the planning stages, will run from the Groen River, north to the Spoeg River.
AVAILABLE LITERATURE: In process of being compiled.
CLIMATE: Summer: hot days, cool nights. Winter: cool days, cold nights.

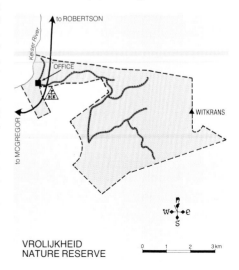

VROLIJKHEID NATURE RESERVE

149. Vrolijkheid Nature Reserve

ROBERTSON

AUTHORITY-IN-CHARGE: Department of Nature and Environmental Conservation, Cape Provincial Administration.
SIZE: 1 827 hectares.
MAIN ATTRACTIONS: Karroid broken veld; succulents, especially vygies, are colourful in spring; large and small mammals as well as birdlife.
FACILITIES/AMENITIES: Centre for problem animal research and teaching of control techniques (tours on request); permit necessary, obtainable at the reserve's main office.
AVAILABLE LITERATURE: *Nature Conservation in the Cape*, booklet; included in annual reports of the Department of Nature and Environmental Conservation.
CLIMATE: Drier part of the winter rainfall area.

Vrolijkheid Nature Reserve is primarily a research centre where the control of animals such as blackbacked jackals, vagrant dogs, members of the cat family, rodents and dassies (in other words, those animals which cause farm losses by preying on livestock or destroying crops) is studied.

The reserve attracts nature lovers who enjoy wandering on tracks through interesting habitats. Sweet thorn and large reedbeds dominate the banks of the Keiser River, while the hill slopes are covered with bitterbos, renosterbos and kraalbos. Succulents and karroid shrubs characterize the open veld. Fauna is varied: 146 recorded bird species, 43 mammal species (the antelope include gemsbok, black wildebeest, blesbok, springbok, grey duiker and grey rhebok), 23 reptile species, eight amphibian species and five fish species are found here.

152. Namaqualand Daisy Cycle Trail

SPRINGBOK

AUTHORITY-IN-CHARGE: Trailblazers.
DURATION: 9,5 days.
MAIN ATTRACTIONS: Namaqualand flowers; west coast semi-desert mountain vistas and long passes; quaint seaside villages.
FACILITIES/AMENITIES: Camping accommodation; tarmac and gravel roads; all transport, equipment and food provided; cost of tour does not include cycle hire, so trailists are welcome to use their own bicycles.
PERTINENT INFORMATION: The trail is run only when the Namaqualand flowers are in bloom, generally at the end of August and the beginning of September. Maximum of 18 people per group. All-terrain (fat-tyre) bicycles recommended. A back-up vehicle lifts cycles up main escarpments; riding is mainly downhill so trail requires only moderate fitness.
AVAILABLE LITERATURE: Brochures available from Trailblazers.
CLIMATE: Winter rainfall area, but rainfall is minimal. Fog in cool seasons. Strong sea breezes. Hot berg winds in winter. Hot summers.

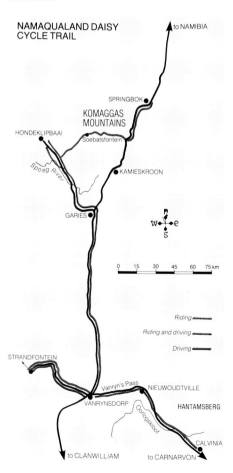

NAMAQUALAND DAISY CYCLE TRAIL

Cycling through a carpet of flowers is a unique way to view the Namaqualand show that nature puts on every spring.

From Springbok and the copper mines, the trail runs through Kamieskroon and over the Komaggas Mountains. The route offers picturesque valleys and steep, winding passes that sweep down to the strandveld. Moving on to Soebatsfontein, cyclists pass the route of the old Copper Road transporters. If rains have been good, flowers cover the veld, their names a festival of the Nama and Afrikaans languages – t'netjie, langbeen, t'nouvroubos, varkieskrol and many more. The strandveld gives way to the coast, diamond diggings, and the quaint village of Hondeklipbaai, once a bustling seaside resort and gateway to the copper mines. Turning east, trailists ride through vast flower-covered flats (in season), past Wallekraal and over the Spoeg River, then on to Garies and Vanrynsdorp. Vehicles lift cyclists up Vanryn's Pass into Nieuwoudtville. The trail then runs through the Oorlogskloof, and on to Calvinia in the Hantamsberg, where it ends.

153. Ian Myers Nature Walk

HESTER MALAN NATURE RESERVE, SPRINGBOK

AUTHORITY-IN-CHARGE: Department of Nature and Environmental Conservation, Cape Provincial Administration.
SIZE: 6 576 hectares.
LENGTH: 4 km, 5,5 km and 7 km (circular).
MAIN ATTRACTIONS: Namaqualand broken veld, famous for spring display of wildflowers; dome-shaped and rugged rocky hills; kokerbooms; Hartmann's zebra, springbok, gemsbok, klipspringer and other antelope.
FACILITIES/AMENITIES: 7-km circular game-viewing drive; picnic and braai facilities at the beginning and end of the circular trail; toilets and water; exhibition of Namaqualand succulents housed at the office complex.
PERTINENT INFORMATION: The reserve is open for day use only; no overnight accommodation available. Visitors using the hiking trail in summer should walk during the cooler parts of the day. For information: The Officer-in-Charge, Hester Malan Nature Reserve, Private Bag X1, Springbok 8240, tel. (0251) 21880.
AVAILABLE LITERATURE: Information guide planned; located on Government Printer's 1:50 000 topographic maps '2917 DB Springbok' and '2918 DA Kaip'.
CLIMATE: Average annual rainfall: 162 millimetres, falling mostly between May and

IAN MYERS NATURE WALK

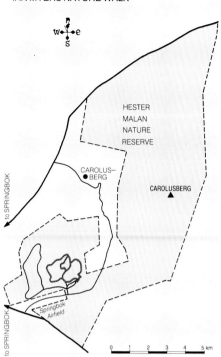

September. Average minimum temperature: 11 °C. Average maximum temperature: 23 °C.

Located only 16 kilometres from Springbok in the north-eastern Cape, near Namibia, is the attractive Hester Malan Nature Reserve. Noted for its strikingly beautiful seasonal variation in density and composition of wildflowers, the Namaqualand broken veld type will thrill plant enthusiasts.

During the light winter rains, ephemerals (short-lived plants) cover the reserve. These include Dimorphotheca polyptera, Osteospermum amplectens, O. hyposeroides and Arctotis fastuosa. The reserve also protects endemic species such as Gladiolus salteri and a Spiloxene species. The attractive kokerboom is common on some of the hills.

Animal life is also plentiful and easily spotted along the Ian Myers Nature Walk. Endangered species include the Hartmann's mountain zebra, aardwolf and honey badger. Springbok and gemsbok have been re-introduced but 31 mammal species, including klipspringer, baboon, Cape fox and steenbok, occur naturally. Of the 47 recorded bird species, ostrich, black eagle, Karoo korhaan, spotted dikkop and ground woodpecker are frequently seen. Smaller animal life such as the armadillo lizard, rock agama and Namaqualand padloper should not be overlooked.

No major rivers or streams run through the rocky hills, or across the sandy plains

Opposite page: A lynx, Felis caracal, in the Vrolijkheid Nature Reserve, a centre for problem animal research.

and rugged plateau, so carry water, and during summer plan to walk in the early morning and late afternoon. The Ian Myers Nature Walk is for leisurely enjoyment and observation. It is named in memory of the late Ian Myers, a keen naturalist who spent 30 years exploring the area and leading groups in Namaqualand.

154. Richtersveld Canoeing Trail

GOODHOUSE

AUTHORITY-IN-CHARGE: Trailblazers.
DURATION: 9,5 days
MAIN ATTRACTIONS: Remote, often desolate scenery; deep ravines; plentiful fast water with small rapids.
FACILITIES/AMENITIES: Food and Indian-style canoes supplied (kayaks available on request); transport from Johannesburg supplied; no facilities; camping on river banks.
PERTINENT INFORMATION: Maximum of 18 people per group. Moderate fitness required; previous exposure to canoeing recommended but not essential.
AVAILABLE LITERATURE: Brochures available from Trailblazers.
CLIMATE: Very dry and hot.

The most leisurely way to explore the !Garieb, or Great River, is in Trailblazer's five metre-long, stable Indian canoes. Discovered by the Bushmen and Hottentots, this river (more commonly known as the Orange) meanders 2 000 kilometres from its source in Lesotho to the deserts of western South Africa. Its route is diverse. Sometimes the river slashes through steep gorges, sometimes it slinks past large islands on which bandits of old took refuge. In other areas, man has tamed the Great River and taken its water for irrigation schemes.

Starting at Goodhouse in northern Bushmanland, canoeists negotiate fast-flowing water and small rapids. Three days later, at Vioolsdrif (where the Springbok-Windhoek road crosses the river), supplies are replenished. After 160 kilometres (five days of paddling), the trail terminates at the irrigation settlement at Aussenkehr.

The river both above and below Vioolsdrif is flanked by rugged and picturesque country, with deep ravines and kloofs, tortuous sand river gorges, vast boulder-strewn slopes and knife-edge ridges. The grey, black and brown surroundings are broken only by the green strip of river bank.

Opposite page, top: The Klipspringer Hiking Trail traverses an arid mountain landscape.
Opposite page, bottom: On the Orange River.

155. Klipspringer Hiking Trail

AND SHORT NATURE RAMBLES
AUGRABIES FALLS NATIONAL PARK

AUTHORITY-IN-CHARGE: National Parks Board.
SIZE: 9 000 hectares.
LENGTH/DURATION: 37 km/3 days, 2 nights (to be extended in length, and to 3 nights).
MAIN ATTRACTIONS: Augrabies Falls and Gorge; river landscape; semi-desert wildlife.
FACILITIES/AMENITIES: Hiking trail: two huts with bunks, mattresses, toilets, braai facilities, firewood and water; maximum of 12 people per night. General park facilities: interpretive centre, rest camp with fully equipped huts, caravan site with ablution facilities, shop and restaurant.
PERTINENT INFORMATION: A sun hat and water bottle are vital on the trail. Beware of snakes.
AVAILABLE LITERATURE: *Klipspringer Hiking Trail/Augrabies Falls National Park*, brochure with map; *Augrabies Falls National Park*, brochure containing general information, issued by the National Parks Board; checklists (*Mammals of Augrabies Falls National Park, Birds of Augrabies Falls National Park* and *Amphibians, Reptiles and Fishes of Augrabies Falls National Park*); *The Augrabies Falls National Park*, AA Bulletin TBE-K2, containing general information.
CLIMATE: Summer: very hot. Winter: very cold. Spring and autumn are the best hiking seasons.

Undoubtedly the falls themselves are the main attraction of the Augrabies Falls National Park and its walks and trails. For here, set against a dramatically barren landscape, the tumbling, muddy-brown waters of the Orange River have eroded the solid granite bedrock into a deep ravine, sculpting in the process a remarkable array of rock formations and potholes.

The main falls are 56 metres high, but in total the river drops 191 metres, placing it among the largest cataract-type waterfalls in the world. The entire gorge is 18 kilometres long, and the roaring of water plunging, whirling and swirling over such a great distance lends credence to the name Augrabies, a corruption of a Bushman phrase meaning 'place of great noise'.

Ramblers with limited time can take the very easy 2,5-kilometre path to view the gorge and Twin Falls, Arrowhead and Ararat Rock. The Klipspringer Hiking Trail, which is popular with the physically fit, also passes the falls: this arduous, three-day trail holds other rewards, as an alert hiker could spot colourful lizards basking on the sun-baked rocks, as well as klipspringers, mon-

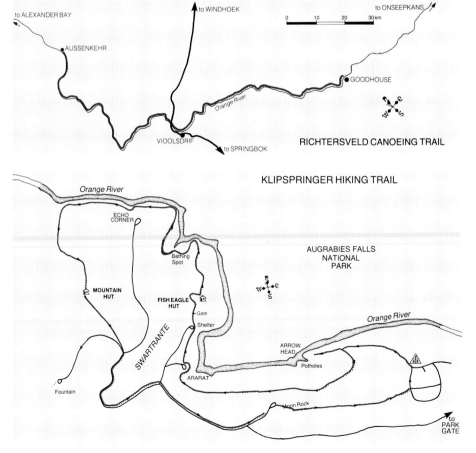

keys, baboons, steenbok, wild cats and their spoor. The extended trail will incorporate the rhinoceros and big game area.

In sharp contrast to the dry, euphorbia- and tree aloe-dominated semi-desert veld, the banks of the Orange River are thickly wooded with bush willows, olives, karee and sweet thorns. Within both vegetation types birdlife is plentiful, including fish eagles, bustards, dikkops, plovers, finches, wagtails, swifts and many bush-dwelling birds. And nowhere in South Africa have I seen as many rock hyrax (dassies) as on the granite slopes of Augrabies.

It is best to plan your hiking times for early morning and late afternoon in order to maximize both comfort and chances of spotting wildlife.

156. Orange Gorge Kayak Trail

AUGRABIES

AUTHORITY-IN-CHARGE: The Rivermen.
DURATION: 7 days.
MAIN ATTRACTIONS: Stark, arid granite mountain landscape; birdlife along the river, especially fish eagles and goliath herons; challenge of shooting rapids; scenic camps along the river banks; Ritchie Falls and Orange Gorge.
FACILITIES/AMENITIES: All kayaking equipment, first aid, food and communal camping gear is supplied; trail is led by competent guides.
PERTINENT INFORMATION: Take as little personal gear as possible as packing space in the kayak is limited. Orange River water should be purified or boiled before drinking. The trail is suitable for beginners. Everyone must obey the guides at all times.
AVAILABLE LITERATURE: Brochures available from The Rivermen; see Klipspringer Hiking Trail (opposite page) for checklists of the area.
CLIMATE: Hot, sunny days with temperatures reaching 50 °C; cool nights. Rain is rare.

If you are looking for a change from hiking, sensational mountain scenery, the solitude of a wilderness experience, and some adrenaline-pumping moments, the privately run, guided Orange Gorge Kayak Trail is a must.

Although no previous kayaking experience is necessary, this is not a trip for the faint-hearted. Competent guides provide a day's instruction which includes the teaching of paddling strokes, ferry gliding, capsize drill and how to shoot rapids, and then each individual is responsible for paddling his kayak during the five and a half day trip.

Long, flat stretches are broken by fast-flowing ripples and small to medium-sized rapids which grow larger as the days pass. There are always participants willing to take down the kayak of anyone who wishes to walk around a rapid. An entirely different set of muscles from those exercised in backpacking is used: my fingers, hands, upper arms, neck and lower back got quite a workout. Portaging in the gorge also requires upper body strength.

'Deep-Heat' is strongly recommended, as is a good sunscreen lotion for your face and upper body. Alternatively, a long-sleeved, collared shirt and a broad-brimmed sunhat worn under a helmet will guard against sunburn. To protect my feet against rocks and twigs while walking on land or in the river, I wore a pair of running shoes at all times; however, the men with large feet found this impossible as their feet in tackies did not fit into the kayak. In this case, a pair of diving booties is ideal.

The trail brochure contains a checklist of personal 'wet' and 'dry' kit that you should take. Bring as little as possible and pack carefully: all dry kit (such as night clothes, sleeping bag and toiletries) must be stuffed into one small waterproof bag. Items which are great assets but rather costly include un-derwater cameras, waterproof binoculars and torches.

The route followed on the Orange Gorge trip is scenically spectacular. Situated in Bushmanland and semi-desert, on the border of South Africa and Namibia, the muddy Orange with its greened, lush banks snakes through barren, decomposing granite mountains. The river itself is diverse: flat, wide stretches flow into a maze of islands which reminded me of the Florida Everglades. Along the banks fish eagles and goliath herons are plentiful. Other birds spotted from the kayak include blackheaded and grey herons, malachite kingfishers, whitebreasted and reed cormorants, darters and black eagles. Baboons bark from the summits of mountains, vervet monkeys play in riverine treetops and occasionally an otter or snake swims across the river.

In the late afternoon you have the opportunity to hike up a mountain peak, explore dry kloofs where animal spoor is found and hardy plants survive, and look down at the mighty Orange River. Near the end of the trip the Orange Gorge steepens and most take the 'chicken run'; only the experts can shoot the gorge. However, a morning is

ORANGE GORGE KAYAK TRAIL

spent exploring on foot, marvelling at the tremendous force and scouring power of the water, which has sculpted great potholes and rock boulders. Dead fish and vegetative debris high on rock ledges attest to the level of the water at peak flood periods.

A portage is made around the gorge and kayaks are put in below Ritchie Falls. The paddle up to the falls is the scenic highlight of the trip. A myriad dashing martins plays in the great spray of water as the Orange tumbles 50 metres into potholed rocks.

The final adrenalin-pumping exercise is shooting 'Big Bunny', a long and turbulent Class III rapid. To my dismay, I capsized and became separated from my kayak, crashed into several rocks and, gasping for breath, was tossed in the furious waves, spun in the funnels and dropped down big holes. The guide was present at the end of the ordeal to help me to shore when I emerged blue, bruised and shocked, and with a tremendous respect for the power of rushing water.

Everyone (in our case, 10 trailists and three guides) agreed that the time spent on the Orange was an all-encompassing experience. All our concentration was on the teamwork needed to make this trail a success.

After completing the Orange Gorge Kayak Trail, I recommend allowing a day to relax and explore Augrabies Falls National Park. If you have enough energy, you can walk the Klipspringer Hiking Trail (see page 128).

The Rivermen run guided canoe and kayak trails in various parts of southern Africa. It is best to write for their latest brochures and itineraries.

Above: Shooting a rapid on the Orange River.

157. Kokerboom Trail

KENHARDT, see Regional Map page 120

AUTHORITY-IN-CHARGE: Municipality of Kenhardt, Kenhardt 8900.
LENGTH: 4 km.
MAIN ATTRACTIONS: Kokerbooms; sociable weaver nests; wildflowers.
FACILITIES/AMENITIES: Parking is available at the trailhead.
PERTINENT INFORMATION: The trail is located 8 km from Kenhardt, south-west of the town. Carry water. Most of the trail is situated on a private farm.
AVAILABLE LITERATURE: No brochure or map has been printed.
CLIMATE: Extremely dry region. May and June are best months for viewing flowers.

158. Doringberg Hiking Trail

(name to be finalized)

PRIESKA

AUTHORITY-IN-CHARGE: Municipality of Prieska. Until trail has been fully developed, contact Mundus van Niekerk, P.O. Box 34, Prieska 8940.
LENGTH/DURATION: 24 km/1 day and 20 km/1 day.
MAIN ATTRACTIONS: Panoramic views;

beautiful gorges; geologically interesting formations; variety of plants and birdlife; wildlife, including springbok, duiker, steenbok, jackal, lynx, baboon, kudu and vervet monkey.
FACILITIES/AMENITIES: Overnight huts accommodating 20 people, planned.
PERTINENT INFORMATION: Huts are located at the beginning and end of the trail. Trails run over private property.
AVAILABLE LITERATURE: 1:50 000 maps and brochure in process of being compiled.
CLIMATE: Summer: extremely hot, thunderstorms common. Winter: cold.

159. Rolfontein Nature Reserve

P.K. LE ROUX DAM ON THE ORANGE RIVER

AUTHORITY-IN-CHARGE: Department of Nature and Environmental Conservation, Cape Provincial Administration.
SIZE: 7 000 hectares.
MAIN ATTRACTIONS: Windswept grassy plains with dolerite koppies and wooded kloofs; large and small game; P.K. le Roux Dam with abundant waterfowl when it is full.
FACILITIES/AMENITIES: Pied Barbet Trail (self-guided educational trail, approximately 2 km); camp with 4 tents, each accommodating 6 adults or 10 children, with basic cooking, toilet and washing facilities; picnic area; limited motorcar routes with viewing points; Douglas Hey Limnological

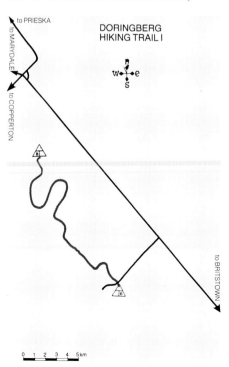

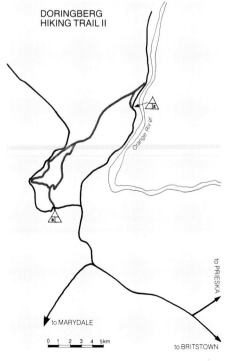

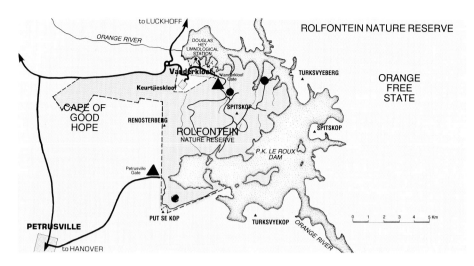

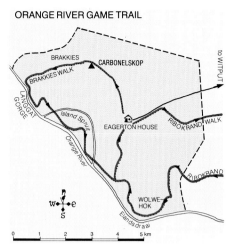

Research Station and small public display of reserve's ecology; angling for yellowfish, catfish and carp; watersports are permitted; Vanderkloof Municipal Caravan Park, nearby.

PERTINENT INFORMATION: For information: The Officer-in-Charge, Rolfontein Nature Reserve, P.O. Box 23, Vanderkloof Dam 8771, tel. 0020 Vanderkloof 160.

AVAILABLE LITERATURE: *Rolfontein Nature Reserve*, brochure and map; *Trees and Larger Shrubs of Three Karoo Nature Reserves*, booklet.

CLIMATE: Average annual rainfall: 430 millimetres, falling mostly in summer. Summer: hot and dry, frequent thunderstorms. Winter: cold and dry. Temperature varies between 16 and 40 °C during the day and -2 and 15 °C at night. April to mid-October, frost possible. September to December, strong north and north-west winds.

As a result of its remote location on the southern banks of the P.K. le Roux Dam on the Orange River, 13 kilometres from Petrusville and 189 kilometres from Kimberley, Rolfontein is one of the least known Cape provincial nature reserves. Yet it is one of the most valuable, for its windswept grassy plains, interspersed with rugged dolerite koppies and heavily bushed river courses, support growing herds of game species such as eland, red hartebeest, black wildebeest, gemsbok, blesbok, kudu and Burchell's zebra. In addition, smaller mammals such as mountain reedbuck, springbok, steenbok, grey duiker, bateared fox, vervet monkey and baboon are found. Cheetah, brown hyaena and white rhinoceros have also been introduced in an attempt to recreate the original ecosystem.

Vegetation is the typical grassveld of the Orange River mountainous region, but also includes false upper Karoo veld. The latter poses a serious ecological threat; because of past mismanagement of the veld, such as overstocking and soil erosion, the hardier but less productive Karoo species have invaded and replaced the pure grassveld.

Sweet thorn, swarthaak, bluebush and camphor bush are some of the more common flowering trees and shrubs.

Within this stark, rugged landscape, the man-made P.K. le Roux Dam has created a habitat for hundreds of waterbirds. Many quiet inlets and bays are now inhabited by South African shelduck, yellowbilled duck, spurwinged geese, Egyptian geese and fish eagles. In the reserve, two hundred bird species have been identified to date. Other animals include cobras and puff adders, rock and water leguans, the dainty frog and two toad species. Hikers may also come across flint tools from the Early Stone Age. Samples are displayed at the Douglas Hey Limnological Research Station.

The company of a conservation officer is no longer available on the walking trails. However, the two-kilometre self-guided Pied Barbet educational trail leads trailists to points of ecological interest, each marked along the path and explained in a pamphlet. Trees along the route are also labelled. Trailists are accommodated in a tent camp with basic facilities. As these facilities are still being developed, visitors should contact the staff in advance to make arrangements.

160. Orange River Game Trail

WITPUT

AUTHORITY-IN-CHARGE: P.F. Roux, P.O. Witput 8740; tel. (0020) Belmont 1222.
SIZE: 2 881 hectares.
LENGTH: Brakkies Walk: 14 km. Ribokrand Walk: 17 km.
MAIN ATTRACTIONS: Orange River; remote wilderness of the northern Cape; large game species; waterfowl and other birdlife.
FACILITIES/AMENITIES: Nature rambles and hiking trails; hiking hut (Eagerton house) accommodating 15 people, with toilet facilities, braai and firewood.

PERTINENT INFORMATION: Bring your own utensils, food and bedding. No dogs allowed.
AVAILABLE LITERATURE: Brochure with sketch map.
CLIMATE: Summer rainfall area.

161. Vryburg Hiking Trail

VRYBURG

AUTHORITY-IN-CHARGE: Municipality of Vryburg, P.O. Box 35, Vryburg 8600.
LENGTH/DURATION: Trail 1: 19 km. Trail 2: 27 km. Can be combined into a two-day hiking trail.
MAIN ATTRACTIONS: The Lost City (ruins which compare with the Zimbabwe Ruins); birdlife and wildlife.
FACILITIES/AMENITIES: Hikers overnight at the Swartfontein Recreation Resort.
PERTINENT INFORMATION: The trail begins at the youth camp on Brussels farm. Hikers must arrange for transport to the Swartfontein Recreation Resort at the end of the first day's walk.
AVAILABLE LITERATURE: Trail map.
CLIMATE: Summer rainfall area.

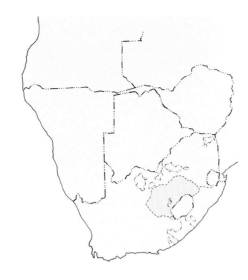

ORANGE FREE STATE
AND QWA-QWA

The Orange Free State, situated in the high-veld of the central plateau, is one of South Africa's four provinces. Although today the Free State comprises largely farmland, it was known in the past for its vast scenarios of waving grasslands teeming with huge herds of game.

While there is only a handful of trails in the Orange Free State, authorities and resort owners are beginning to realize the magnetic potential of their province. The mountainous eastern section bordering on Lesotho and often referred to as the 'Little Switzerland' of the Republic, and more recently the southern area along the Orange River, are particularly attractive to trailists.

The Free State has a temperate climate similar to the Transvaal Highveld: warm, cloudless summer mornings followed by afternoon thunderstorms, and cool, dry winters with very cold nights.

ECOLOGICAL ZONE: HIGHVELD

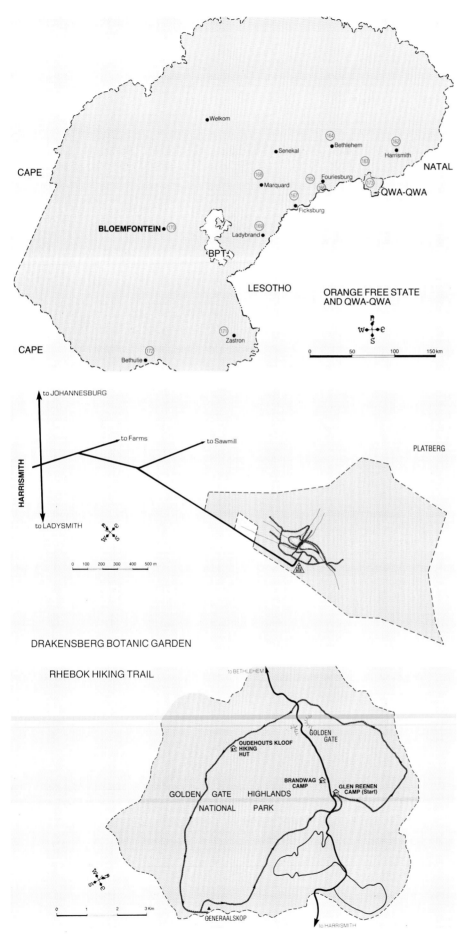

ORANGE FREE STATE
AND QWA-QWA

DRAKENSBERG BOTANIC GARDEN

RHEBOK HIKING TRAIL

162. Drakensberg Botanic Garden

HARRISMITH

AUTHORITY-IN-CHARGE: Municipality of Harrismith, P.O. Box 43, Harrismith 9880.
SIZE: 114 hectares.
MAIN ATTRACTIONS: Over 1 000 species of Drakensberg flora, labelled with scientific names, within cultivated area of the garden; 100 recorded species of birds; many small mammals, including grey duiker and dassie.
FACILITIES/AMENITIES: The Bush Trail (self-guided trail) and other walks; nursery and herbarium, closed to the public; information centre; toilets.
PERTINENT INFORMATION: Entrance is free. Open 08h00-17h00. Dogs allowed, on leash.
AVAILABLE LITERATURE: *The Bush Trail*, booklet with map; map of popular walks; *Drakensberg Botanic Garden, Harrismith, Orange Free State*, brochure and map; *Preliminary checklist of birds of the Drakensberg Botanic Garden; Common grasses of the Drakensberg; Karee species of the Drakensberg*.
CLIMATE: Summer: hot with frequent thunderstorms. Winter: cold with severe frosts; snow possible.

Several popular walks, ranging from 20 minutes to an hour, on easy to medium gradients through floral displays and natural vegetation, provide a good botanical introduction for Drakensberg hikers and mountaineers. The Bush Trail, a one-kilometre self-guided educational trail, winds through typical montane belt vegetation, from the valley to the base of the basalt cliffs at the edge of the Little 'Berg.

The Drakensberg Botanic Garden is located at the foot of the Platberg, five kilometres from Harrismith.

163. Rhebok Hiking Trail

GOLDEN GATE HIGHLANDS NATIONAL PARK

AUTHORITY-IN-CHARGE: National Parks Board.
SIZE: 6 241 hectares (may be expanded).
LENGTH/DURATION: 30 km/2 days.
MAIN ATTRACTIONS: Mountain scenery (situated 1 500-2 750 metres above sea level); reintroduced wildlife; birdlife; fresh mountain air; interesting geological formations.
FACILITIES/AMENITIES: Rhebok Hut, accommodating 18 people, with gas lamps, a

HOUTKOP HIKING TRAIL

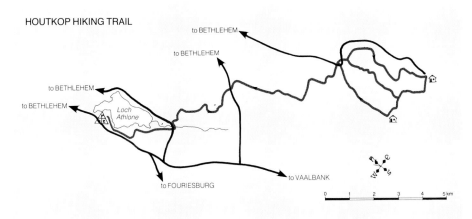

to BETHLEHEM
to BETHLEHEM
to BETHLEHEM
to BETHLEHEM
Loch Athlone
to FOURIESBURG
to VAALBANK

0 1 2 3 4 5 km

two-plate gas stove, cooking utensils and washing facilities, a protective reed 'boma' with braai facilities and firewood, and potable stream water nearby (borehole water available in winter); Glen Reenen and Brandwag rest camps with camping, caravanning, huts, a lodge and horses for hire; environmental education centre and youth hostel.
PERTINENT INFORMATION: Hikers must be fit and older than 10 years. The latest time to start walking the trail from Glen Reenen is 08h00, and during summer walking should start at 07h00.
AVAILABLE LITERATURE: *The Rhebok Trail*, information sheet, issued by the National Parks Board; *Ribbok Wandelpad – Golden Gate – Rhebok Trail*, brochure including sketch map, and mammal and bird list, issued by the National Hiking Way Board; *List of Interesting Geological Sites – Rhebuck Trail* and frog checklist, available from Golden Gate's information centre.
CLIMATE: Pleasant and invigorating. Summer: cool to moderate with rain; heavy thunderstorms and lightning can occur in the late afternoon; can become very hot during midday. Winter: cold, snow

common; mist can become thick at times; sudden drops in temperature with sleet occur frequently.

The Rhebok Hiking Trail climbs Generaalskop (2 757 m), and provides a panoramic view of Lesotho and the Orange Free State. This rugged, mountainous area is well-endowed with streams, kloofs and waterfalls, all traversed by the hiking trail.
Starting at the Glen Reenen Rest Camp, the first leg of the trail winds 15 kilometres (7 hours) to Oudehouts Kloof where the overnight hut is scenically situated next to a stream. The climb up Generaalskop on the second day is strenuous; the 1 000-metre ascent takes about 3,5 hours, followed by a two-hour return to the base.
Indigenous wildlife, which includes eland, black wildebeest, blesbok, springbok and zebra, was once prolific in this northeastern highland region of the Orange Free State and has been reintroduced to the park. Hikers may also spot grey rhebok, mountain

Above: On the Rhebok Hiking Trail.
Right: The Little Caledon River.

ORANGE FREE STATE AND QWA-QWA

reedbuck and oribi. Birdlife is plentiful – the black eagle, jackal buzzard and various waterfowl species can readily be seen, while the rare lammergeyer (bearded vulture) may be seen occasionally.

164. Houtkop Hiking Trail
BETHLEHEM

AUTHORITY-IN-CHARGE: Hoogland Wildlife Society, P.O. Box 582, Bethlehem 9700; tel. (01431) 32800 or 35732.
LENGTH/DURATION: 37 km/2 days, 1 night.
MAIN ATTRACTIONS: Birdlife, including waterfowl on dams, weavers and Cape vultures; indigenous flora, including proteas and wildflowers; rhebok and hyrax; ridges offering panoramic views of undulating grasslands.
FACILITIES/AMENITIES: Two overnight sites (windshelter near old farm, and shed); water available; Loch Athlone Holiday Resort at the start of the trail; parking; bungalows for hire.
PERTINENT INFORMATION: This is an easy trail, ideal for beginners and families.
AVAILABLE LITERATURE: Contact the Hoogland Wildlife Society.
CLIMATE: Summer rainfall area, often in the form of thunderstorms. Winter: sunny, dry, cool days and cold nights; frost possible.

165. Brandwater Hiking Trail
FOURIESBURG

AUTHORITY-IN-CHARGE: Municipality of Fouriesburg.
LENGTH/DURATION: Approximately 65 km/ 5 days, 4 nights.
MAIN ATTRACTIONS: Salpeterskrans, largest sandstone overhang in the southern hemisphere; overhangs used as overnight

135

sites; views of the Maluti, Rooiberg and Witteberg ranges; historic Anglo-Boer War interest; hartebeest shelter and other old farm buildings; Little Caledon Valley.

FACILITIES/AMENITIES: The trail begins and ends at Meiringskloof (parking and camping); a hiking lodge is planned; each overnight site has only bush toilets and water; fires are discouraged.

PERTINENT INFORMATION: Circular trail; longest trail in the Orange Free State, mostly over private land. Carry at least one litre of water daily. For information: Rev. J. Mostert, P.O. Box 24, Fouriesburg 9725, or Mr J. van Eeden, P.O. Box 86, Fouriesburg 9725.

AVAILABLE LITERATURE: Brochure and sketch maps; located on Government Printer's 1:50 000 topographic maps '2828 CB Clarens', '2828 AD Jordaan River' and '2828 CA Fouriesburg'.

CLIMATE: Average annual rainfall: 750 millimetres. Summer: pleasant days with afternoon thunderstorms; cool nights. Winter: sunny, cool, dry days; cold to very cold nights; frost possible.

The Brandwater circular hiking trail, the 'gem' of the Orange Free State's trails, is superlative in many respects.

Located on what was once referred to as the Brandwater Basin (the land surrounded by the Witteberg, Rooiberg and Maluti Mountains), the Brandwater Hiking Trail is the longest trail in the Free State; it features the largest sandstone overhang in the southern hemisphere; with the exception of a seven-kilometre stretch, it is entirely over private farmland; and it was initiated, motivated and constructed by two energetic and enthusiastic citizens of Fouriesburg, Rev. Joseph Mostert and Jap van Eeden, a farmer.

With no previous experience in developing trails, these two young men accomplished a task that large government organizations often cannot realize. Their route planning is excellent: each day brings experiences of new and exciting aspects of the eastern Free State. The trail is within the capabilities of moderately fit hikers and children but is also challenging for the experienced backpacker. Contours are closely adhered to. The overhanging sandstone caves selected for overnight points are close to water, scenically situated, and deep enough to protect against rain and wind. The trail is well signposted with yellow metal arrows on yellow poles, and yellow stiles over fences. Blue arrows mark water points and yellow arrows with black stripes indicate alternative routes (to avoid stream crossings).

Starting at Meiringskloof (2 000 m), where cars can be parked safely, the trail rises out of the deep, dark gorge on an eight metre-high steel ladder, similar to that found at Mont-Aux-Sources (see page 174). After seven kilometres on a four-wheel drive

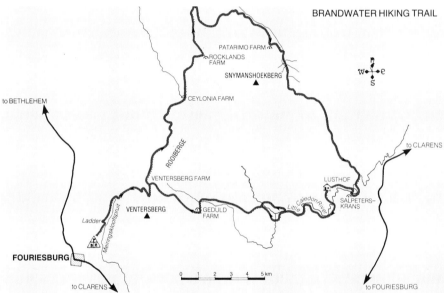

BRANDWATER HIKING TRAIL

track, tea can be enjoyed at Ventersberg Farm, in the grounds shared by an old ox-wagon. Cattle, maize and wheat production are the farming objectives of this area. Note the Basotho farm-workers' houses in the vicinity, as they are very attractive. Leaving municipal ground, the route ascends the Rooiberg to the first overnight spot, a cave situated at 1 879 metres, on the farm Ceylonia. This large, deep overhang shelters sheep, so hikers will need a groundsheet or space blanket to place over the insulating droppings. Water drips over the lip of the cave. The shrubs are alive with rock pigeons, canaries, buntings and other birdlife. Walking time to the cave from the start of the trail is about five hours.

The second day begins with a descent to Rocklands farm where there are water tanks from which hikers can wash. Rocklands is one of the oldest farms in the eastern Free State. The markers then lead to a fascinating cave with a very low, overhanging roof.

Deep inside you can see excavations where clay pots containing the remains of babies were buried. The trail continues down Wilger's Valley to the farmhouse and then along a magnificent valley overshadowed by tremendous mushroom-shaped krantzes. The day ends at a cave on the farm Patarimo. This cave once sheltered a group of Boers in hiding during the Anglo-Boer War. Water is located 100 metres below in the river. (Walking time on the second day is approximately four hours.)

The third day is the most exciting. The route crosses Snymanshoekberg (2 454 m), the second-highest mountain in the Free State. The highest point reached on the gentle ascent is 2 193 metres. The descent on the southern side is long and hard on the knees but worth the effort, as this is the only area on the trail that offers a wilderness-like character. Descending through the 'agate zone', hikers are likely to see specimens of attractive quartz, chalcedony and chert.

Distant views emerge of the Free State's highest mountain, Generaalskop (2 757 m), in the Golden Gate Highlands National Park. Secretarybirds and vaal rhebok feed in the tall grass and black ducks fly over the Caledon River.

As you rise over a ridge, you are suddenly confronted by the Salpeterskrans, the largest sandstone overhang in the southern hemisphere. After a steep descent and a rocky crossing of the Little Caledon River, you can explore Salpeterskrans Cave with its many artefacts, as people come from as far away as Malawi to offer gifts to the fertility gods. Three kilometres farther on, along the lovely poplar-lined Little Caledon, lies Lusthof, an empty stone farmhouse which serves as the overnight hut. (Hikers spend five hours walking on the third day.)

The fourth day begins on 'the highway', a gentle, flat cow path in the narrow and very pretty gorge formed by the Little Caledon River. With an early start, the cave on the farm Geduld can be reached by lunchtime. A stream with pools is crossed and although this cave is also near the maize fields, its opening faces stained sandstone cliffs, steep slopes and a small stream greened with lilies.

The final day completes the loop. Hikers walk above the cave, over the steep northeastern ridge of Ventersberg (2 262 m), and rejoin the jeep track. The fifth day was shortened (approximately three hours' walking time) to allow hikers to reach their cars by midday.

The planners of the Brandwater Hiking Trail hope to incorporate alternative routes in the future, and provide a short, two-day loop for beginners and families.

166. Wynford Holiday Farm

FOURIESBURG

AUTHORITY-IN-CHARGE: Wynford Holiday Farm, Private Bag, Fouriesburg 9725; tel. 014332, ask for 1803.
SIZE: Approximately 200 hectares.
DURATION: A variety of trails, requiring from half an hour to 3 hours.
MAIN ATTRACTIONS: Bald ibis breeding colony; rock/cave adventures; sandstone rock krantz 'sculptures'; Caledon River walks; Agate Terrace; Bushman paintings (porpoises); the Castle; views of Basotho village life.
FACILITIES/AMENITIES: Guided or self-guided walks; horses for hire (guided or self-

Opposite page: The Salpeterskrans, a highlight on the Brandwater Hiking Trail.

Above right: A guided walk under sandstone krantzes at Wynford Holiday Farm.

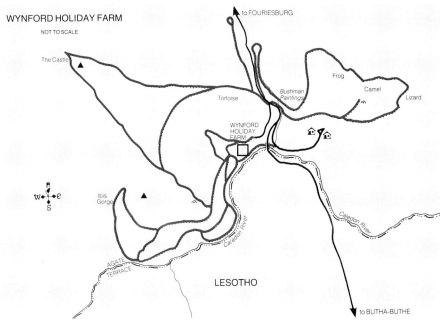

guided rides); resort facilities, including tennis courts, swimming pool, bowling green, cottages and dining-room.

PERTINENT INFORMATION: The resort is located at 2 000 metres above sea level. The terrain is rugged, so sturdy boots are recommended. For rock/cave adventures, wear old clothes.

AVAILABLE LITERATURE: Promotional brochures; trail guide.

CLIMATE: Summer rainfall area. Winter: sunny, cool days; cold nights; frost common, snow possible. June, July and August are the best months for hiking.

Wynford Holiday Farm offers the adventurer and fun-seeker an exciting variety of trails, rock/cave scrambles and natural wonders. I was astonished during my visit to see the many fascinating areas discovered by Roy Langford, the energetic and friendly host. Roy leads trails for guests to all his discoveries on a regular but not scheduled basis. With the trail guide or directions from the Langfords, the hiker can also explore on his own. Self-guided markers are planned for many routes.

The most unusual of Roy's trails are the rock/cave adventures which have intriguing names such as Cleft Rock Crawl, Rock Rabbit Ramble, The Tunnel, The Labyrinth, Micky Mouse House, Monkey Jol and Slippery Slide. Each requires a sense of humour, a daring personality and agility, and holds the prospect of getting muddy and dirty or wearing out your clothes, so old clothes that don't inhibit your movements are essential. These adventures, competently guided by Roy Langford, are for both the young and the old (even if the old just listen and watch).

The longer trails lead to fascinating sites such as the Castle (a real but uncompleted castle in the midst of the grasslands above the sandstone krantz), Ibis Gorge (the bald ibis breeding colony), Rock Pigeon Cave

and Bat Cave, Rainbow Rock and Red Cliff Ravine (where towering red cliffs curve over your head). Tranquil, easy strolls along the poplar-lined Caledon River, the border between the Orange Free State and Lesotho, are also popular. These offer views of traditional Basotho village life on the opposite bank, and Agate Terrace. Near the resort's entrance is an unusual Bushman painting depicting several porpoises.

The sandstone krantzes above the resort have been carved by wind and water into sculptures resembling a tortoise, a lizard, a frog and a camel. Walks to each are possible.

Although a popular venue in its own right, Wynford Holiday Farm makes a fine retreat for recuperating from the five-day Brandwater Hiking Trail (see page 135).

167. Imperani Hiking Trail

FICKSBURG

AUTHORITY-IN-CHARGE: Municipality of Ficksburg, P.O. Box 116, Ficksburg 9730; tel. (0563) 2122/3/4.

LENGTH/DURATION: Approximately 22 km/2 days, 1 night (the trail can be walked in 6-7 hours using a light pack).

MAIN ATTRACTIONS: Sandstone overhangs; krantzes; magnificent views of the distant Malutis; birdlife.

FACILITIES/AMENITIES: Overnight hut accommodating 16 people; Meulspruit Pleasure Resort can be used as a base camp (camping and caravanning, ablution block, and thatched shelter).

PERTINENT INFORMATION: The trail lies approximately 1 800 metres above sea level. The terrain is rough in parts, so boots are recommended. Famous Cherry festival in November; cherry blossom time from September to October.

AVAILABLE LITERATURE: Brochure with map.

CLIMATE: Average annual rainfall: 760 millimetres, falling mostly in summer in the form of thunderstorms and, sometimes, violent hail storms. Winter: sunny, dry, cool days and cold nights; frost is common.

The Municipality of Ficksburg, in conjunction with the Department of National Education, has developed a scenic hiking trail covering the entire circumference of Imperani Mountain, with an optional loop on Camel Ridge.

The Imperani Hiking Trail is an invigorating way to experience Ficksburg's scenic grandeur. 'Imperani' is a Basotho word meaning 'mountain of many', and for the hiker it does offer many attractions.

The circular trail starts and ends at the new Meulspruit Pleasure Resort, where a

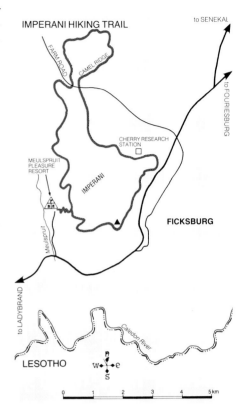

steep ascent takes the hiker past Bushman paintings to the grand sandstone overhangs of Imperani. (The scenery here reminds me of the Golden Gate Highlands National Park.) Continuing in a northerly direction on Imperani's west-facing slopes, the trail winds below krantz level over some rough terrain. As you approach the old government plantation on the plateau, now used as grazing commonage, the tread is much easier. Much time is spent walking in a mixed exotic conifer forest. When the trail turns to the north-east, magnificent views of the Maluti Mountains emerge.

An optional loop descends the mountain, crosses a tarred road and ascends Camel Ridge. Impressive caves, far-reaching views and lovely poplar- and willow-lined streams make this section worthwhile. Returning to Imperani, a steep descent into a kloof adds

interest before the trail winds back under majestic weathered sandstone krantzes.

Wildlife is scarce although dassie, red rockrabbit, vaal rhebok, wild cat, porcupine, jackal and meerkat make their home on Imperani. Big-game introductions are planned. Birdlife is a constant companion: rock pigeon, redwing francolin, guineafowl and orangebreasted rockjumper are commonly seen.

I completed the trail in one long day with a light pack, but the provision of an overnight hut makes the route ideal for families and the less fit. Although water is available, I recommend carrying some, as the sources are far apart. When I walked the trail in June, the snow-capped Malutis were magnificent in the crisp, clear air. However, the town clerk reminded me to return in spring for the unique cherry blossom season.

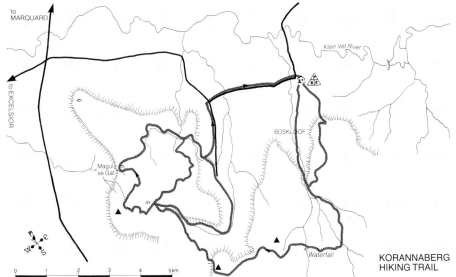

KORANNABERG HIKING TRAIL

168. The Korannaberg Hiking Trail

MARQUARD

AUTHORITY-IN-CHARGE: The Wildlife Society, P.O. Box 11187, Universitas, Bloemfontein 9321.
LENGTH/DURATION: 32 km/2 days, 1 night. Two one-day circular trails are also available.
MAIN ATTRACTIONS: Variety of landscapes; weathered sandstone caves with Bushman paintings; intriguing rock formations; approximately 150 species of birds; vistas of the Orange Free State and Maluti Mountains; wildflowers.
FACILITIES/AMENITIES: Base hut with shower, bath, toilet and limited firewood; overnight camp-site at a huge cave with veld toilet, firewood and water; trees labelled with their national tree list numbers.
PERTINENT INFORMATION: Try to reach the base hut before dark. Carry water (minimum one litre per person per day). Maximum of 25 people per day allowed on the trail. An extended trail, over three to four days, is planned. The famous old homestead once leased to Sir Abe Bailey, and located at the foot of the mountain, is being restored. An interpretive centre is planned.
AVAILABLE LITERATURE: Die Koranna-Voetslaanpad, comprehensive brochure with map and numbered tree list; 'The

Opposite page, top: 'The tortoise', one of the sandstone krantzes on Wynford Holiday Farm, viewed from the Little Caledon River.

Opposite page, bottom: A view of the more rugged parts of the Free State, on the Imperani Hiking Trail.

Above: The Imperani Hiking Trail is particularly pretty in autumn.

Korannaberg Trail: Orange Free State',
Caravan and Outdoor Life, November 1986.
CLIMATE: Average annual rainfall: 500
millimetres, peaking between January and
March. Summer: hot days with
thunderstorms common in the afternoons.
Winter: cold and dry. Best hiking months
are September, October, February, March
and April.

The Korannaberg Hiking Trail is the product of an enthusiastic group of Wildlife Society members belonging to the local Marquard Branch. They deserve congratulations
for their efforts in laying out an unusual
trail, providing more variety and physically
challenging terrain than you might expect to
find in the Orange Free State.

The starting point, 30 kilometres from
Excelsior (or 48 kilometres from Marquard),
is difficult to find in the dark, so obtain the
sketch map and plan to arrive before sunset.
The base hut, a comfortable farmhouse with
a pleasant view of the Free State, provides
basic amenities such as tap water, toilets,
shower, firewood and a limited number of
mattresses, but no beds.

The first day's 17-kilometre walk is the
more difficult of the two days and includes
flat bushy areas rich in birdlife, steep ascents necessitating boulder scrambling in a
ravine well-endowed with streams and
waterfalls, and plateau trekking among interesting koppies, over farmland and past

*Above: The stone hiking hut is visible from the slopes
of the Platberg on the Steve Visser Nature Walk in
Ladybrand. This 15-kilometre trail, one of only a
handful of trails in the Orange Free State, begins at
the Leliehoek Pleasure Resort, which is situated
against the sandstone krantz of the Platberg. The
resort offers all modern facilities.*

stone overhangs. The overnight site is a
magnificent cave consisting of two large
'rooms' separated by a stone pillar and sheltered behind natural bush.

The shorter second day (15 kilometres)
leads the hiker through fields of wildflowers, past koppies and Bushman paintings to
Magul se Gat. Do not forget your torch if
you wish to explore this unique rock tunnel
and cave.

The Korannaberg is located in a transitional zone between a dry and a wet climate,
which results in a wide variety of plant life:
grassland on mountain plateau, riverine
forest, and fynbos. Birdlife includes endangered species such as the black and martial
eagles and the Cape vulture.

The entire hiking trail is situated in the
approximately 7 000-hectare Korannaberg
Conservancy, privately owned by a number
of farmers. Founded in 1985, it is expanding
as more farmers join the conservancy. Day
visitors are welcomed, provided that a permit is obtained in advance. Two one-day
trails are available for day use. The hiking
trail will be extended in the near future by

young members of the Land Service
Movement in Bloemfontein.

The conservancy, although open throughout the year, reserves the right to close temporarily if the need arises.

169. Steve Visser Nature Walk

LADYBRAND

AUTHORITY-IN-CHARGE: Municipality of
Ladybrand, Private Bag X11, Ladybrand
9745.
LENGTH/DURATION: 15 km/2 days; shorter
walks are possible.
MAIN ATTRACTIONS: Maluti Mountain
scenery; Bushman caves; indigenous trees
and shrubs; history.
FACILITIES/AMENITIES: Mountain hut with
40 beds, accessible by motor car; Leliehoek
Pleasure Resort (start of trail) with camping
and caravanning, and modern facilities.
AVAILABLE LITERATURE: *Ladybrand*,
brochure issued by the municipality; *Steve
Visser Wandelpad*, information brochure
available at the resort.
CLIMATE: Average annual rainfall: 700
millimetres. Pleasant summers, cold
winters.

Ladybrand is located in the shadows of the
Platberg, near the Lesotho border. Informal
nature rambles, bridle paths, and the 15-
kilometre Steve Visser trail radiate from
Leliehoek Pleasure Resort.

The overnight stone house in Mauershoek
(Nursery's Hoek), provided by the munici-

STEVE VISSER
NATURE WALK

to BLOEMFONTEIN

to FICKSBURG

LADYBRAND

MAUERSHOEK

LELIEHOEK
PLEASURE RESORT

PLATBERG

'The Stables'

to MASERU

0   1   2   3   4   5 km

pality for hikers, is most popular with large groups. The trail can easily be walked in one day, and hikers can enjoy the amenities of Leliehoek Pleasure Resort or the stone house before or after their walk. Several historic sites, which lend interest to this walk, are passed on Platberg's slopes. Mauershoek itself was the first inhabited settlement of Ladybrand, and Jacob Mauer was the first person to live here. The second part of the trail passes 'The Stables', a giant crevice against the mountain slope in which the Boers hid their horses during the Basuto War of 1858.

Birdlife is rich: rock kestrels play among the cliffs and rock thrushes and redfaced mousebirds feed on the slopes below. Some of the common plants include ouhout, *Leucosidea sericea*; a sweet-scented heath, *Erica caffra*; white stinkwood, *Celtis africana*; wild olive, *Olea africana*; wag-'n-bietjie or buffalo thorn, *Ziziphus mucronata*; and the very distinctive fine-leaved karee, *Rhus erosa*.

The trail is marked with painted white arrows on rocks, many of which are fading or peeling. Because the soil is shallow and rocky, no well-defined path has been constructed. Sometimes I felt that the trail was a 'treasure hunt', searching for arrows, which detracted from its enjoyment. Views over Ladybrand and beyond are excellent. However, the trail does not lend itself to seclusion: motor cars, fences, wires, towers and whistles are often seen or heard.

There is no potable water *en route* so I suggest you carry a litre.

170. *Orange Free State National Botanic Gardens*

BLOEMFONTEIN

AUTHORITY-IN-CHARGE: National Botanic Gardens.
SIZE: 45,4 hectares.
MAIN ATTRACTIONS: Peaceful setting; display of Orange Free State flora; 110 species of grasses from the Orange Free State, grouped in grass gardens and labelled with their scientific names; collection of South African karees (*Rhus* spp.); 55 tree species; 110 recorded bird species; Iron Age Sotho dwelling site.
FACILITIES/AMENITIES: Nursery and herbarium, closed to the public; teas provided on Sunday afternoons; surplus plants available for sale on the first Friday afternoon of each month; braai facilities.
PERTINENT INFORMATION: Open daily 07h30-16h00. Dogs allowed, on leash. Situated 1 300-1 400 metres above sea level.
AVAILABLE LITERATURE: *Orange Free State Botanic Gardens*, comprehensive brochure

and map; bird and tree checklists available on request.
CLIMATE: Average annual rainfall: 564 millimetres. Temperature range: -6 to 34 °C. Summer: high temperatures and thunderstorms. Winter: low temperatures (average July minimum 0,3 °C) and frost.

The main attraction of the Orange Free State National Botanic Gardens is the complex of short, easily negotiated, self-guided nature walks which emphasize plants and historical features. The duration of the walk around the three koppies is approximately 1,5 hours.

The garden is situated in typical central Orange Free State terrain: dolerite koppies separated by valleys and dry watercourses. Distinct vegetation types grow in the valleys and kloofs, on grassed plains and on Karoo koppies and their wooded slopes. A useful feature of the gardens is that some of the koppie flora, in addition to that in the cultivated garden, is labelled. A visit to trails such as these can enhance appreciation and understanding of nature when hiking in wilder environments. Conducted trails for schoolchildren are available on request.

171. *Mayaputi Gorge Canoeing Trail*

ZASTRON

AUTHORITY-IN-CHARGE: Trailblazers.
DURATION: 6 days.
MAIN ATTRACTIONS: Remote, often desolate scenery; deep ravines; plentiful fast water with small rapids.
FACILITIES/AMENITIES: Food and Indian-style canoes supplied (kayaks available on request); transport from Johannesburg supplied; no facilities; camping on river banks.
PERTINENT INFORMATION: Maximum of 18 people per group. Moderate fitness required; previous exposure to canoeing recommended but not essential.
AVAILABLE LITERATURE: Brochures available from Trailblazers.
CLIMATE: Summer rainfall area.

The most leisurely way to explore the !Garieb, or Great River (more commonly

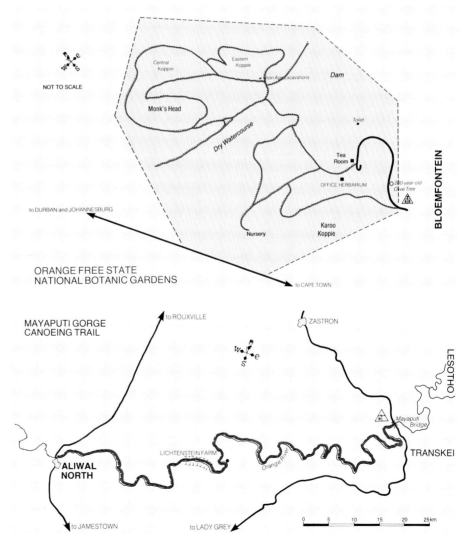

172. Tussen-die-Riviere Game Farm

BETHULIE

AUTHORITY-IN-CHARGE: Nature Conservation Branch, Office of the Provincial Secretary, Orange Free State Province, P.O. Box 517, Bloemfontein 9300.

SIZE: 22 000 hectares.

LENGTH/DURATION: Middelpunt Trail: 8,6 km/3 hours. Klipstapels Trail: 10 km/ 3-4 hours. (Proposed trail: 6,5 km/ 2-3 hours.)

MAIN ATTRACTIONS: Large variety of game such as kudu, zebra, eland, blesbok, steenbok, impala and springbok; confluence of Orange and Caledon rivers; Klipstapels (rock formations).

FACILITIES/AMENITIES: Overnight accommodation at Hunter's Camp, consisting of 5 shelters with reed 'bomas', braais and wood, and a central ablution block with showers, toilets and wash basins, hot and cold water; another site with shelters is planned; office with displays of wildlife, orientated towards hunting; game-viewing roads and picnic sites.

PERTINENT INFORMATION: The reserve is closed for hikers during the hunting season (May to August), so the trails are open only in the summer. Entrance permits are issued at the gate, walking permits are not required. Walkers are advised to carry water, and to wear gaiters to protect their legs from grass seeds. No dogs allowed.

AVAILABLE LITERATURE: Map available at the gate.

CLIMATE: Summer rainfall area, mostly in

known as the Orange River), is in Trailblazer's stable, five metre-long, Indian-style canoes.

Discovered by the Bushmen and Hottentots, this river meanders 2 000 kilometres from its source in Lesotho to the deserts of western South Africa. Its route is diverse. Sometimes the river slashes through steep gorges, sometimes it slinks past large islands on which bandits of the last century once took refuge. In other areas, man has tamed the Great River and taken its water for irrigation schemes.

The guided trail begins at Mayaputi Bridge, close to the Lesotho border. The river soon enters a deep gorge cut into basalt. Although the current is strong, the rapids are small and easy to run. Before reaching Aliwal North after four days (110 kilometres) of paddling, canoeists experience stretches of open water and deep ravines near the farm Lichtenstein. Some excellent examples of Bushman paintings, including the well-known 'hippopotamus' painting, are found in caves along the route.

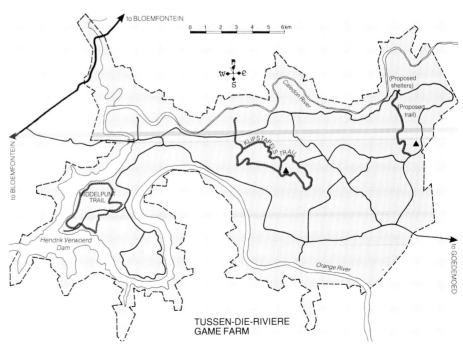

TUSSEN-DIE-RIVIERE GAME FARM

the form of thunderstorms. Strong winds and cold nights are possible year-round.

Although the Tussen-die-Riviere Game Farm was developed to cater for the South African hunter, three valuable nature trails have been laid out for hikers visiting the reserve during the summer (non-hunting season). Although relatively unknown, each of these trails has exciting attributes and is well worth walking.

Because of its large size, scenic Karoo splendour and development for hunting, Tussen-die-Riviere supports large populations of diverse and readily observable game species: springbok, blesbok, red hartebeest, black and blue wildebeest, steenbok, impala, mountain reedbuck, gemsbok, kudu, zebra, eland and white rhino. Spotting these majestic herds or spooking a solitary antelope while walking can be a thrilling experience.

The Middelpunt Trail on the reserve's well-watered western boundary is physically easy as it meanders along the banks of the Orange and Caledon rivers, and offers the trailist the opportunity to spot waders and larger water-birds. The Klipstapels Trail, situated in the middle of the reserve's vast 22 000 hectares, has a unique attraction: in an approximately two square-kilometre area

lies a field of eroded basalt pillars, each block precariously balanced on its base. This natural phenomenon resembles the stone cairns of the Matobos in Zimbabwe. The third and shortest trail (not yet completed during my Easter 1986 visit) is situated in the mountainous eastern section.

Several species of long grass and thorny annuals possessing seeds with sharply pointed dispersal mechanisms are common in the reserve; gaiters with boots are highly recommended footwear. Woollen socks should be avoided as they collect seeds in abundance. Hikers should carry binoculars and water.

Opposite page, top: The precariously balanced 'klipstapels' are an unusual erosional formation in the Tussen-Die-Riviere Game Farm.
Opposite page, centre: The Middelpunt Trail meanders along the banks of the Orange and Caledon rivers.
Above: The Mont-Aux-Sources area in Qwa-Qwa.

QWA-QWA

Qwa-Qwa, a small homeland belonging to the South Sotho people, is situated on land which was once part of the Orange Free State. Bordered by Lesotho and the Maluti Mountains on its south-west, the Royal Natal National Park and Natal on its south-east, and the eastern Orange Free State on its north, it is an attractive mountainous area where the Basotho pony is the national means of conveyance. Mountaineering, wilderness trekking and skiing attract trailists to Qwa-Qwa. The Witsieshoek Mountain Resort, situated very close to the Royal Natal National Park, is a well-known base for many hikes.

There are no border formalities for entrance into Qwa-Qwa at present, but trailists planning extensive hikes should get permission from the Secretary for the Interior, Qwa-Qwa Government, Private Bag, Witsieshoek 9870.

The climate is similar to the rest of the Drakensberg region: summer rainfall, mostly in the form of thunderstorms, and dry, sunny but very cold winters when snow is possible.

ECOLOGICAL ZONE: DRAKENSBERG

173. Qwa-Qwa Conservation Area

SOUTHERN QWA-QWA

AUTHORITY-IN-CHARGE: Nature Conservation Section, Department of Agriculture and Forestry, Private Bag X816, Witsieshoek 9870.
SIZE: Approximately 30 000 hectares.
MAIN ATTRACTIONS: Striking mountain scenery; birdlife; South Sotho culture.
FACILITIES/AMENITIES: Three one-day trails; Witsieshoek Mountain Resort; camping site; picnic site; hikers' huts; trout fishing.
PERTINENT INFORMATION: Hiker's hut located at end of mountain from Witsieshoek does not require bookings; it accommodates 10 people on a 'first come, first served' basis.
AVAILABLE LITERATURE: *Drakensberg North: Mt. Aux Sources to Cathedral Peak*, map number 1 by Peter Slingsby, Mapcape, compiled by the Forestry Branch, Department of Environment Affairs; *Isen Report*, comprehensive report on Qwa-Qwa, compiled by the University of the Orange Free State.
CLIMATE: Summer: warm temperatures with high rainfall occurring as thunderstorms and mist; weather can change very rapidly. Winter: very cold, snow possible on high mountains.

Between the Lesotho/Free State and Free State/Natal escarpments lies a very mountainous area. Owned by several tribes in Qwa-Qwa and scheduled for expansion, this conservation area offers a wilderness terrain for hikers and mountaineers. Due to unpredictable weather, a harsh climate and diffi-

cult terrain, it can be dangerous if you are unprepared. However, for experienced trailists, Qwa-Qwa's conservation area is open throughout the year. Permits can be obtained from the Nature Conservation Section or the Witsieshoek Mountain Resort.

The Maluti Mountains, Drakensberg Amphitheatre, Mont-aux-Sources, Sentinel, Broome Hill, Elands River and Mahai Falls are scenic attractions familiar to Drakensberg mountaineers. Although wildlife is scarce in these harsh conditions, grey rhebok and baboons are often spotted, and bearded and Cape vultures, black eagles and jackal buzzards command the skies.

Three day-walks are available, in addition to large expanses of explorable wild terrain.

Two trails start from the Witsieshoek Mountain Resort, which offers chalets and a restaurant. The full day's hike to Mont-aux-Sources includes the chain ladder near the end of the trail (see page 174), and there is a small hiker's hut halfway, at the carpark. The Metsi Matso Trail, a half day's walk, leads north from the Witsieshoek Mountain Resort, ending near the Swartwater Dam. Trout fishing and an overnight hut accommodating 10 people are available at the end of this walk. On the western side of the conservation area, a one-hour walk leads from Monontsha Village to the huge sandstone Wetsi's Cave, where picnic facilities are available. A camping site for hikers is planned for 1988.

Opposite page, left: A near-vertical chain ladder aids hikers on their way to Mont-Aux-Sources in the Qwa-Qwa Conservation Area.

Opposite page, right: Daily life in Qwa-Qwa near Witsieshoek Mountain Resort.

Above: Approaching Mont-Aux-Sources from Witsieshoek.

CISKEI

Ciskei, formerly part of the Eastern Cape, gained its independence in December 1981. Although small in area (its 10 000 km² area is about the size of the state of Delaware in the USA), Ciskei is large in ecological diversity. Spanning an elevation from sea level to 2 000 metres, Ciskei incorporates 64 kilometres of pristine beaches and 11 tidal estuaries; coastal plains; the indigenous forest-clad Amatola and Katberg ranges, plentiful in mountain streams and wildlife; the semi-arid Great Fish River Valley; and the high Karoo-like northern plateau.

The President of Ciskei, realizing that trails are a growing tourist attraction worldwide and that Ciskei's natural diversity and beauty could be delicately exploited, devoted a quasi-government division to trails development, under the auspices of the Ciskei Tourist Board (now the Department of Tourism and Aviation).

You can easily spend two to three weeks hiking in Ciskei: each trail reveals different scenery, from sand and surf to rock krantzes, with varying veld types and animal and plant associations.

Despite Ciskei's large population, backpackers are assured of a wilderness-like or solitary experience. All the major trails are located in game, forest or coastal reserves, minimizing contact between villagers and backpackers. Tribal life is viewed from afar or when driving to and from the trailhead.

All hiking trails in Ciskei are marked with stylized blue cranes on white rectangular backgrounds. The blue crane (*indwe*) is Ciskei's national bird. The hiker follows the direction in which the crane's beak points.

Ciskei is a friendly land, and border posts have been eliminated. Although it is sug-

gested that you carry identification (passport or Book of Life) while travelling in Ciskei, no visas or entry formalities are necessary.

Ciskei falls into a summer rainfall region, where late afternoon thunderstorms are frequent. Winter months (June to September) are clear, crisp and cool, with temperatures dropping sharply at night, and sometimes to below freezing at the higher altitudes. Snow is possible in the mountains, although it seldom lasts long. Thick mist can occur at any time, but especially in the warmer months.

ECOLOGICAL ZONES: COASTAL BUSH, EASTERN EVERGREEN TEMPERATE FOREST, KAROO

147

174. Tsolwana Game Park

NEAR WHITTLESEA

AUTHORITY-IN-CHARGE: Division of Wildlife Resources and Parks, Ciskei.

SIZE: 17 000 hectares.

MAIN ATTRACTIONS: Tsolwana Mountains and Swart Kei River Valley, a rugged Karoo-type topography with magnificent mountain scenery, broad vistas and valley plains; abundant and readily observable game (48 species); 117 species of birds, including ostrich, woollynecked stork, Cape vulture, martial and fish eagles, Stanley's bustard and giant kingfisher; Bushman caves and paintings.

FACILITIES/AMENITIES: Guided wilderness trails led by professional officers and/or game scouts, lasting from several hours to several days, tailored to fit personal or group requirements; rock climbing on Tafelberg; day and night vehicle game-viewing excursions; hunting under the supervision of professional guides, in season (April to August); trout fishing; bush camp, accommodating 10 people on wilderness or pony trails, with cabins, bunks and mattresses, hot and cold water, braai area, 'boma' and lecture area; another camp at Moddervlei is planned; Thorn Camp, with site for tents and caravans, wood, water and toilets (showers planned); self-catering luxury lodges (Indwe and Otterford); game ranch where visitors live with professional staff and their families; store selling Tsolwana curios, skins, venison and biltong; tribal dances and braais can be arranged for a minimum of 10 people (or R150); vehicles, horses and fishing rods for hire.

PERTINENT INFORMATION: Tsolwana is a unique and highly successful multi-use venture which incorporates African rural communities into a tourist development programme for hikers, outdoor enthusiasts and hunters. Details on rifle and bow-hunting can be obtained directly from the park. Walking trails are conducted from September to March, and when the park is not utilized by hunters. For bookings: The Director, Tsolwana Game Park, P.O. Box 87, Tarkastad 5370, tel. (04582) 5402. Visitors must provide their own food on trails, and at camp-sites and self-catering lodges. Lodges accommodate eight to 10 people, and only one party is booked per night at each lodge. Rock climbers require permits.

AVAILABLE LITERATURE: Pamphlets, price lists, and animal and plant lists available on request; located on Government Printer's 1:50 000 topographic maps '3226 AB Tarkastad (second edition)', '3226 BA Poplar Grove' and '3226 BC Hackney'.

CLIMATE: Average annual rainfall: 500

millimetres, falling mostly as showers and thunderstorms in summer (October to March). Dry, sunny and cold winters, snow possible. Semi-arid region. Temperatures in January: average daily maximum 30-33 °C; average daily minimum 15 °C. Temperatures in July: average daily maximum 17 °C; average daily minimum 0 °C.

Rising 1 877 metres above sea level is a conically shaped hill named Tsolwana, Xhosa for 'sharp little one', formerly known as Spitzkop. Just north of the Tsolwana range is Tafelberg, the massive flat-topped plateau (1 965 m) edged with dolerite cliffs and visible from many vantage points in Ciskei and the Eastern Cape. Between the two peaks lies a plateau teeming with animal life.

On foot, this seemingly flat plateau is riddled with valleys, cliffs, caves, gulleys and wooded hollows. The southern slopes of the Tsolwana range end in the upper Swart Kei River Valley, once a land inhabited by Bushmen, but now by farmers who breed racehorses and Jack Russell terriers, and irrigate large fields. Sections of these farms

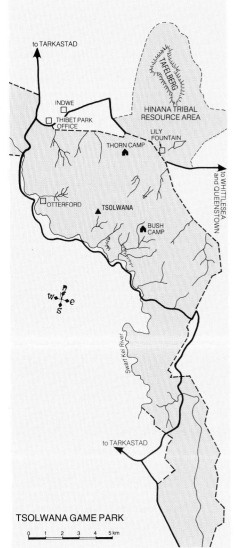

TSOLWANA GAME PARK

0 1 2 3 4 5km

have recently been incorporated into the game park.

Clothing this magnificent topography are three vegetation systems: subdesert (Karoo dwarf shrub), temperate (fynbos and grassland) and arid savannah (thornveld). Wildflowers are abundant during the rainy season, creating a colourful spectacle on the green hills and plains. Waterfalls and streams run in numerous lightly wooded kloofs during times of strong rains.

But Tsolwana's most attractive feature to the trailist is the privilege of walking unrestricted in a natural wonderland, and being guaranteed observation of many game species. On the plateau there are large herds of wildebeest, red hartebeest, gemsbok, eland, springbok, impala and blesbok. Bateared fox, steenbok, grey duiker, striped ground squirrel, scrub, Cape and red hares, blackbacked jackal, Cape fox and banded mongoose can be observed by the keen eye. The game rangers will also point out white rhino, giraffe and red lechwe. On the mountain slopes watch for mountain zebra, mountain reedbuck, vaal rhebok, baboons and dassies. There is also an unusual dassie colony that inhabits old antbear holes. At night on game drives you might see serval, caracal, wild cat, aardwolf, zorilla, genet, otter, five species of mongoose, spring hare and porcupine, in addition to the large antelope. Species not indigenous to southern Africa (fallow deer, mouflon sheep, barbary sheep and Himalayan tahr) roam freely among the other animals.

Marked hiking trails have not been built in Tsolwana; rather a complex of game paths and four-wheel drive gravel roads is followed by professional game rangers and scouts who accompany hikers on all excursions. These men have an incredible ability to spot animals, many of which are invisible to the untrained eye. The professional guides are highly experienced and knowledgeable, not only about Tsolwana's flora and fauna, but also about its history, archaeology, and unique management policy.

Trails are tailored to suit the party's interests and fitness level. Groups usually consist of one to 10 people but larger school, youth or club groups can be accommodated with prior arrangements. Trails run from casual 2-3 hour game-viewing walks to two- and three-day hikes covering all Tsolwana's wildlife habitats and peaks. Experienced rock climbers are welcome to scale the impressive dolerite cliffs of Tafelberg but must be fully equipped. All-terrain (fat-tyre) bicycles are allowed in the park, but cyclists are required to sign an indemnity form.

The scenically situated bush camp on the northern slopes of the Tsolwana Mountains

Opposite page: The white rhino is one of over 48 mammal species that may be seen on one of the guided excursions at the unique Tsolwana Game Park, near Whittlesea.

looks into the southern mountain range. Hikers can drive or walk to the camp. Photographers are strongly advised to carry a powerful telephoto lens. A second bush camp, on the southern slopes of the mountains, is planned.

Day walkers who prefer not to 'rough it' can stay at one of two luxurious self-catering lodges and take short or full-day walks, and/or vehicular day and night excursions. Alternatively, visitors can stay in the game ranch house with the professional staff.

Why is Tsolwana unique? The answer lies in the park's farsighted and practical application to the problem that 'there is no room in Africa for inedible scenery': Tsolwana provides tangible proof that it exists for the benefit of the Ciskeian people, and is not just a playground for the leisurely, privileged minority. This is done through numerous avenues. Firstly, all products from cropped or hunted animals (and not taken by the hunter) are sold directly to the local people, without wholesalers and retailers exploiting prices. Furthermore, all revenue from the park goes to the Ciskei Agricultural Corporation.

But even more important is the Hinana Tribal Resource Area which lies north of Tsolwana and incorporates much of Tafelberg and its lower slopes. This is a fully fenced game area stocked with suitable indigenous and exotic animals and owned entirely by the local tribe. All revenue from hunting, except licence fees, is channelled directly back to the tribe (not the government). These funds are used to better the tribal infrastructure, such as for schools and health projects. Tribal domestic stock is allowed to graze this area during winter months, and the gathering of wood and medicinal herbs is permitted. Poaching in the tribal area virtually does not exist because the tribesmen regard the game as their rightful property. Tribal courts deal with poachers, and punishments are severe, sometimes involving replacement of poached game with equal numbers of domestic stock.

The Hinana Tribal Resource Area has proved itself such a great success that five new resource areas in Ciskei have been planned . . . and these areas will also be sites for future recreational trails.

175. Katberg/Readsdale Mountain Complex

BALFOUR

AUTHORITY-IN-CHARGE: Department of Forestry, Ciskei.
DURATION: Nature walks: 1-4 hours (if combined, can take one day). Hiking trail: 2 or 3 days (in process of being constructed). Mountain bicycle trails: several hours to one

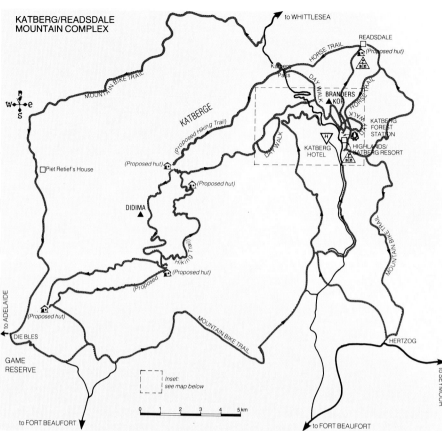

day. Horse-riding trails: half an hour to one day.

MAIN ATTRACTIONS: Readsdale wilderness-like area; Katberg escarpment, rich indigenous forest, cool mountain streams and waterfalls; excellent birdlife; bushbuck, baboons, samango monkeys and small antelope; wildlife introductions are planned.

FACILITIES/AMENITIES: Highlands/Katberg Resort (P.O. Box 40, Balfour, Ciskei; tel. 040452, ask for 1002), with furnished rondavels, gas cooking facilities, utensils and refrigerators (ablution facilities are separate); self-contained chalets with private toilets and showers; camping and caravan sites; horses for hire (the hiring of mountain bicycles is planned); tennis courts, swimming pool, bowling green, recreation and communal room; shop. Katberg Hotel, with large forested grounds, offering walks, horses for hire, swimming pool, tennis courts, golf course and other resort facilities. Two hiking huts are planned; mountaineers can camp in the area with a permit from the forestry office; picnic sites; scenic drives.

PERTINENT INFORMATION: Republic of Ciskei received the Katberg State Forest from South Africa in 1987; this is a developing area, so check with the Ciskei Tourist Department for progress on the hiking and other trails.

AVAILABLE LITERATURE: *Hiking Trails and*

Above: On the Katberg Hiking Trail.
Opposite page: On the Amatola Hiking Trail.

Nature Walks in Ciskei, general information brochure; *Walks and Hikes at Katberg*, information sheet with sketch map; *Highlands/Katberg Holiday Resort: Ciskei*, brochure; *Katberg Hotel*, brochure; located on Government Printer's topographic maps '3226 BC Hackney (second edition)' and '3226 DA Healdtown (second edition)'.

CLIMATE: Summer rainfall area. Thunderstorms and mist are common. Winter days are warm and sunny, the nights cold; snow is possible on the mountains.

The Katberg forest area has long been popular for its lovely short walks and guided horse rides on the forested slopes below the dramatic krantzes of the escarpment. The Republic of Ciskei controls the Katberg Forest and the adjoining rugged mountain terrain to its east, commonly referred to as the Readsdale area. Under the direction of the Ciskei Tourist Department, this area is being developed as a trailing mecca for ramblers, backpackers, mountaineers, horse-riders and mountain bicycle enthusiasts.

The existing nature walks have been cleared and re-marked, and new ones are being constructed. Work on a three-day hiking trail is in progress. This trail can be walked in a two-day circular loop, starting from the Highlands/Katberg Resort, or as a three-day linear trail to Mpofu Game Park (see opposite page). The long-term plan is to connect the Katberg Hiking Trail to the Amatola Hiking Trail with a four-day link via Hogsback and the slopes of the Elandsberg.

Hikers may walk sections of the Katberg Hiking Trail as they are completed. Progress reports can be obtained from the Ciskei Tourist Department in Bisho.

Horse-riding trails are tailored to suit the skills, experience and wishes of the riders. The 30-60 minute ride through the lower Katberg Forest is a tradition, but longer rides with 'bush braais' can be arranged by contacting the manager of the Highlands/Katberg Resort. A popular trail is up the Katberg Pass, down the path that leads to Readsdale, through exquisite mountain scenery, and along a pony trail through grazing veld and indigenous forest.

Mountain bicycles ('all-terrain' bicycles) are fat-tyred, 12-18 geared machines with straight handlebars and cantilever brakes. They offer stability, toughness and ease of handling on non-paved mountainous tracks.

Although trails will be mapped out, the cyclist is free to ride his own route. Plantation roads, often through shady indigenous forest with sparkling streams, are particularly pleasant during hot summer days. Surprisingly, you will see more wildlife when travelling on a bicycle than when walking through the forest.

The Katberg is part of the greater Winterberg range. Peaks such as Branderskop (1 531 m), above the forest station, and Didima Peak (1 829 m) to its west, are particularly lovely during the infrequent snowstorms.

Mountain fynbos, grassland and indigenous forest flourish on the slopes below the krantzes. Fine examples of white ironwood, assegai, lemonwood, yellowwood, tree-fuchsia and many other indigenous trees are present. In addition to the exotic pine plantations, remnants of early experimental plots dating back to 1883 have left majestic deodars (a Himalayan cedar, *Cedrus deodara*), redwoods and oaks.

Within the Katberg Forest, bushbuck are often seen. Vervet and samango monkey, baboon, duiker and porcupine are common. The birdlife is also rich: crowned hornbill, Knysna loerie, swee waxbill, grey cuckooshrike, yellow canary, chorister robin, blackheaded oriole, jackal buzzard, Cape robin and doublecollared sunbird are just some of the more common sightings.

176. *Mpofu Game Park*

BALFOUR

AUTHORITY-IN-CHARGE: Division of Wildlife Resources and Parks, Ciskei.
SIZE: 7 200 hectares.
DURATION: Guided and self-guided nature trails and hikes: 1-2 days. Guided pony trails: 1-2 days.
MAIN ATTRACTIONS: Large game species; scenic surroundings; numerous veld types (Dohne veld, false thornveld and valley bushveld) in a small area; forested kloofs.
FACILITIES/AMENITIES: Hiking hut planned; camp-site.
PERTINENT INFORMATION: The Mpofu Game Park is a developing reserve, so contact the Division of Wildlife Resources and Parks for the latest details. Trails operate from mid-August to the end of March (non-hunting season). Ten people per day are permitted on the guided trails; eight people per day are permitted on the pony trails.
AVAILABLE LITERATURE: Proposed; located on Government Printer's 1:50 000 topographic map '3226 DA Healdtown'.
CLIMATE: Average annual rainfall: 560 millimetres, falling mostly in summer.

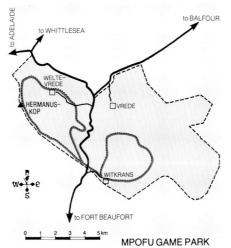

MPOFU GAME PARK

177. *The Amatola Hiking Trail*

(INCLUDING THE EVELYN VALLEY AND ZINGCUKA LOOP TRAILS) AMATOLA MOUNTAINS

AUTHORITY-IN-CHARGE: Department of Forestry, Ciskei.
LENGTH/DURATION: Amatola Trail: 105 km/6 days, 5 nights. Evelyn Valley Loop Trail: 27 km/2 days, 1 night. Zingcuka Loop Trail: 36 km/2 days, 1 night. Hikes varying from one to six days are also possible.
MAIN ATTRACTIONS: Indigenous forests,

rich in yellowwoods; birdlife and buck, endangered giant earthworms and golden moles; numerous waterfalls and bathing pools; mountain wildflowers; edible wild berries (in season); spacious views; relics of forestry and Frontier War history; the Hogsback peaks; traditional Xhosa-style hut accommodation.

FACILITIES/AMENITIES: Clearly marked trail; five hiking trail lodges; Evelyn Valley Lodge, a converted forester's house; traditional thatched-roof huts at Cata and Mnyameni; large lean-to at Dontsa and prefabricated houses at Zingcuka; all lodges are near perennial streams and have toilets and fireplaces, bunks and mattresses; parking at Maden Dam, Dontsa, Cata and Zingcuka forest stations; assistance for groups, with transport, can be arranged;

trout fishing, with permit and licence.

PERTINENT INFORMATION: The six-day Amatola Hiking Trail is strenuous, and should be attempted only by backpackers who are physically fit and wearing well broken-in boots; for others, the shorter variations are recommended. Water is plentiful, except between Evelyn Valley and Dontsa. Winter days and berg winds create fire hazards, so do not smoke and do not make fires that could spread at overnight sites. Be prepared for sudden drops in temperature, and rain or snow; do not hesitate to use one of the many trail exits if the weather turns bad, and ask the foresters for help if necessary. For information: Ciskei Department of Tourism and Aviation.

AVAILABLE LITERATURE: Included in *Ciskei*

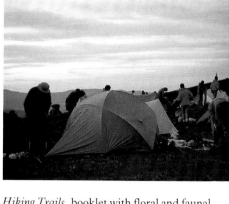

Hiking Trails, booklet with floral and faunal checklists; *The Amatola, Pirie and Sandile Hiking Trail Guide* (covers Evelyn Valley Loop only of the Amatola Trail), in colour with map; *Available and Projected Hiking Trails and Nature Walks in Ciskei*, general information brochure; *The Amatola Hiking Trail*, topographic map; located on Government Printer's 1:50 000 topographic maps '3227 CB Stutterheim', '3227 CA Keiskammahoek' and '3226 DB Seymour'.

CLIMATE: Average annual rainfall: 1 000-2 000 millimetres, falling mostly in summer (October to March). Driest months: June and July. Coldest month: July. Hottest month: February. Frost possible: June, July and August. Mist common in spring and summer. Brief snowfalls possible.

Ranking among southern Africa's top mountainous forest-clad walks is the new 105-kilometre Amatola Hiking Trail. The Amatolas are a deceptive range – the hiker must fully immerse himself in their dense yellowwood forests and spacious plateaux, with their enormous specimens of indigenous trees, spectacular waterfalls, cool, clear bathing pools and rushing trout streams, to fully appreciate their beauty.

From the plateaux and forest openings in the Amatolas, views extend from the Karoo to the sea, encompassing the greater part of Ciskei, Hogsback and beyond.

The topography of the Amatola Trail varies dramatically from approximately 518 metres above sea level at Maden Dam to 1 880 metres on Geju Plateau. The soils vary with the altitudes and are derived from sandstones of the Beaufort Series, limestone and shales. Many of the krantzes consist of dolerite. The Beaufort soil series of the Upper Karoo System was formed during the Triassic to Lower Jurassic periods.

The Evelyn Valley is drained by tributaries of the Buffalo River. However, the greater part of the trail is drained by tributaries of the Keiskamma River which flows into the Indian Ocean at Hamburg.

About a third of the trail runs through indigenous, climax-type high forest which has a tall, extensive canopy reaching up to 30 metres in height. The canopy and the sub-canopy are so dense that they exclude sunlight from the lower levels, resulting in little

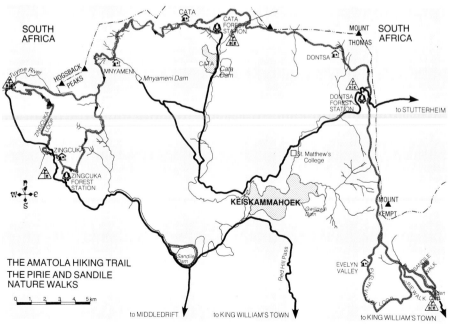

THE AMATOLA HIKING TRAIL
THE PIRIE AND SANDILE
NATURE WALKS

or no undergrowth. Shrub-like bush and grassland also occur. Fynbos or macchia grows in rocky areas on the mountain peaks.

The Amatolas span an area rich in cultural history. Frontier pioneers were responsible for the many villages, mission stations, graveyards and churches nestling in the shadow of the escarpment. The people who lived in the fertile Keiskammahoek Valley and the slopes above placed heavy demands on the forest until demarcation began in 1883. Maize cultivation, uncontrolled pasturing of cattle, hunting, and burning of forest and grassland in accordance with shifting agricultural practices have exerted powerful pressures on the local environment. Evidence of 19th and early 20th century forest exploitation – the so-called 'timber square', trestle bridge and the first steam-powered sawmill – are found on the Pirie Walk.

In the past, the rich valleys of the Amatolas have sheltered elephant and other large game, which attracted hunters from the Cape colony; an ivory trade thrived until late in the 1820s. Nowadays the hiker will not see this kind of wildlife, but duiker, samango monkey, baboon, bushbuck and

178. The Pirie and Sandile Nature Walks

MADEN DAM

AUTHORITY-IN-CHARGE: Department of Forestry, Ciskei.
LENGTH/DURATION: Pirie Walk (circular): 9 km/1 day. Sandile Walk (return on the same path): 8 km/1 day.
MAIN ATTRACTIONS: Indigenous evergreen forest, rich in yellowwoods and birdlife; interesting historical forestry and Frontier War artefacts; Sandile's Cave with its spectacular view.
FACILITIES/AMENITIES: Parking and picnic sites at Maden Dam; information hut at the beginning of the trails.
PERTINENT INFORMATION: Trailists wishing to explore Sandile's Cave do so at their own risk; prior caving experience is recommended, and strong torches and ropes are essential. The Pirie Walk is very easy. For information and bookings: Ciskei

Department of Tourism and Aviation.
AVAILABLE LITERATURE: *The Amatola, Pirie and Sandile Hiking Trail Guide*, with map.
CLIMATE: Average annual rainfall: 928 millimetres, falling mostly in summer. Driest months: April to September. Coldest months: May to August. Temperature range: 9-31 °C.

Early 19th century woodcutters and foresters were quick to realize the great potential of Pirie for commercial timber. As far back as 1819, trees were felled from this area to build Fort Willshire, on the banks of the Keiskamma River. Wood was then taken by settlers for pioneering necessities.

In 1853 the Pirie Forests were declared royal reserves, along with others in the catchments of the Tyume, Keiskamma and Buffalo rivers. However, injudicious hunting of game and felling of trees continued, including cuttings and clearings for military operations. (In 1879, 554 cubic metres of yellowwood sold for about R737; compare this with the average price of R612 for one cubic metre of yellowwood obtained at timber auctions in Knysna today!)

During 1897 Mr J.E. Howse was granted the sole right to extract wood from the Pirie Forest. To facilitate exploitation, he built a railway line and timber chute, using lemonwood (*Xymalos monospora*) for the sleepers and coffee bitterberry (*Strychnos henningsii*) for the construction of the bridge over Hut-

Opposite page, top: Sunrise at the old Cata camp-site on the Amatola Hiking Trail.

Opposite page, centre: A refreshing swim after the long day's hike to Cata Hut.

Left: Golden guinea, Helichrysum argyrophyllum.

Centre: Syselbos, Plumbago auriculata.

Below: An old trestle bridge on the Amatola Hiking Trail.

bushpig are common. The samango monkey and tree hyrax reach the southernmost limit of their distributions here. Birdlife is abundant in the Amatolas, with Cape parrots, green twinspots and Gurney's sugarbirds being the avian specialities. The Knysna loerie with its prominent red wing flashes and raucous 'kok, kok, kok' call is delightfully common. The underground-dwelling giant golden mole and giant earthworm (growing to nearly 2,5 metres in length) are found here, as well as a rare fish, *Barbus trevelyani*, which lives in the streams of the upper Keiskamma. The Hogsback frog and the Amatola toad are also special to this region.

The planners of the Amatola Hiking Trail, aware that even the most enthusiastic hiker does not often have six continuous days at his disposal, have provided numerous exit and entrance link paths from various forest stations. This means that the trail can be done in a series of shorter walks, or in two loop trails (in the Pirie and Zingcuka forests) located at either end of the trail.

chin's River. Howse extracted 0,04 million cubic metres of wood from 16 500 trees (worth about R27 000 at that time) from 1910 to 1917.

The Pirie Walk follows the route of the railway from Howse's mill site over the trestle bridge to the old timber square where the train was loaded.

Only restricted exploitation of indigenous trees takes place in the forest today. The Ciskei government, in keeping with its policy of protecting valuable flora, has proposed that a large part of the forest be declared a nature reserve.

The Pirie Forest contains the grave and cave of Sandile, the legendary Ciskeian warrior and Paramount Chief of the amaRharhabe. Sandile succeeded to the chieftainship of the Rharhabe section of the Xhosa people at the age of nine years, after his father died in 1829. Chief Sandile led his tribe in the Frontier Wars of 1846-7, 1850-3 and 1877-8. His shrewd and brave fighting tactics presented a major problem to the British forces attempting to safeguard the ever-expanding colonial borders.

There are varying tales of how Sandile was killed, but in reality he was shot by a group of Captain Lonsdale's volunteers in May 1878 in the dense forests of Pirie above the present Maden Dam. A few days previously, while being pursued by the British and Colonial forces, Chief Sandile had hidden in a deep cave at the foot of what is now Sandile's Krantz. It is this cave to which the Sandile Walk leads.

Top left: The Amatola trail is marked with blue cranes, the Pirie nature walk with yellow ones.
Top right: Maden Dam, seen from the Pirie Forest.
Right: Ntaba Ka Ndoda national amphitheatre.
Opposite page, top: A wilderness hike in Ciskei along the Great Fish River.
Opposite page, centre: The Double Drift Hiking Trail runs along this huge horseshoe.

179. Sandile Dam Walk

NEAR KEISKAMMAHOEK, see Regional Map page 148

AUTHORITY-IN-CHARGE: Department of Nature Conservation, Ciskei.
MAIN ATTRACTIONS: Sandile Dam (fishing and watersports); mountain scenery; excellent birdlife and flora; Ciskeian tribal life.
FACILITIES/AMENITIES: Camping site, caravan park and chalets planned.
PERTINENT INFORMATION: A nature walk and boat trip are planned. This is a developing area, so contact the Ciskei Tourist Department for the latest details.
AVAILABLE LITERATURE: Brochure planned; see also *Available and Projected Hiking Trails and Nature Walks in Ciskei*, pamphlet.
CLIMATE: Summer rainfall area.

180. Ntaba Ka Ndoda

NEAR KEISKAMMAHOEK, see Regional Map page 148

AUTHORITY-IN-CHARGE: Department of Forestry, Ciskei.
MAIN ATTRACTIONS: Ntaba Ka Ndoda national amphitheatre; historical grave; sacred mountain; birdlife; the Peace Forest (semi-evergreen dry forest).
FACILITIES/AMENITIES: The amphitheatre serves as a venue for conferences, lectures and meetings; ample parking.
PERTINENT INFORMATION: A circular day walk, as well as a cultural museum in the area, is planned by the National Monuments

Council; contact the Ciskei Tourist Department for the latest details.
AVAILABLE LITERATURE: Brochure planned; see also *Available and Projected Hiking Trails and Nature Walks in Ciskei*, pamphlet.
CLIMATE: Summer rainfall area.

181. The Double Drift Hiking Trail

ALICE

AUTHORITY-IN-CHARGE: For bookings and information: Division of Wildlife Resources and Parks, Ciskei.
LENGTH/DURATION: 54 km/3 days, 2 nights or 2 days, 1 or 2 nights.
MAIN ATTRACTIONS: Wildlife (kudu, bushbuck, bushpig, jackal, vervet monkey); planned big-game introductions; birdlife, especially water-birds on the Great Fish River; unique Fish River scrub vegetation; dramatic river valley scenery, horseshoe bends and krantzes; traditional Xhosa-style accommodation; historic fort.
FACILITIES/AMENITIES: Clearly marked trail; trees and shrubs labelled with English,

Afrikaans and scientific names, and national tree list numbers; two thatched, traditional Xhosa hiking lodges; Mbabala Lodge, furnished, with 10 beds and bedding, maid service and television; parking at Double Drift and Mbabala Lodge.

PERTINENT INFORMATION: The Fish River Valley can become very hot, so do not overexert yourself, and carry plenty of water. Do not attempt this trail under flood conditions. Boil or purify water from the Fish River. Small cooking fires, made from driftwood, are permitted. This trail will be run as a guided trail once potentially 'dangerous' large mammals have been introduced.

AVAILABLE LITERATURE: Included in *Ciskei Hiking Trails*, booklet with floral and faunal checklists; *Available and Projected Hiking Trails and Nature Walks in Ciskei*, general information brochure; located on Government Printer's 1:50 000 topographic maps '3326 BB Breakfast Vlei' and '3226 DD Alice'.

CLIMATE: Average annual rainfall: less than 500 millimetres; mist is a major contributor of precipitation. Winter months (June, July and August) bring the lowest temperatures and rainfalls. Frosts can occur. Summer months are very hot, with January's average maximum temperature being 38 °C.

The Great Fish River, with its rushing rapids, natural pools, flat water and gentle flood plains rich with duck, geese and otters, forms the boundary between Ciskei and South Africa.

Its arid, hot climate where only the toughest plants survive is not an environment which appeals to everyone. However, hikers and nature lovers who walk the trail on the river bank and plateau, through Fish River scrub and past historic forts and farmland, will know a Ciskei that has not changed much since the frontier wars.

Succulent bush and thornveld species such as spekboom, *Portulacaria afra*, the favoured food of the kudu; euphorbia, particularly *Euphorbia bothae*, the cactus-like plant with poisonous milk latex; aloes, with their impressive flower spikes; and sweet thorn, *Acacia karroo*, support a thriving bird and wildlife population. However, the 2-3 metre-high bush presents a nightmare to backpackers. The hiking trail therefore follows the banks of the river, or old wagon tracks and paths cut into the thicket.

Geologically, the trail lies on the Karoo Sequence which underlies about 84 per cent of Ciskei. This means that the soils originate from shales, mudstone, siltstones and sandstones.

Kudu, bushbuck, bushpig, baboon, jackal, monkey, tortoise and water-birds thrive at Double Drift. This area is planned as an exciting game reserve where buffalo, rhino and other spectacular stock will be reintroduced and a lodge, education centre and riverside cottages will be constructed.

Guided trails will eventually replace the self-guided walks.

It is possible to walk the 54 kilometres of trail in two or three days. Hikers choosing the two-day option must allow eight hours of walking time each day, but need carry only a daypack. They can stay overnight at Mbabala Lodge (book the previous night and leave overnight gear and food at the lodge). From here, drive to Double Drift and follow the trail upstream. The trail returns hikers to the lodge by dusk. The second day's loop returns to Double Drift.

The three-day hike also starts at Double Drift. The first overnight outspan is at the confluence of the Fish and Kat rivers, a beautiful spot with abundant wildlife and river scenarios. The second overnight is below the old farm Grootdraai, on a grassy flat plain next to the river. Here the Fish River provides bathing in refreshing potholes at the end of the day's hike.

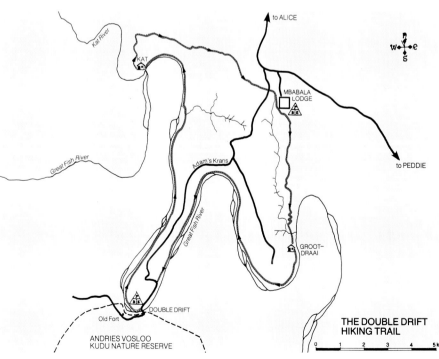

THE DOUBLE DRIFT HIKING TRAIL

182. The Shipwreck Hiking Trail

MPEKWENI AND HAMBURG

🚶 🚶

AUTHORITIES-IN-CHARGE: Department of Forestry, Ciskei. Division of Wildlife Resources and Parks, Ciskei.
LENGTH/DURATION: 64 km/1-4 days; variations possible.
MAIN ATTRACTIONS: Unspoilt stretches of wild, sandy shores and surf; rich coastal bush; beautiful estuaries; birdlife; excellent angling; accessible entry points.
FACILITIES/AMENITIES: Hiking, rambling, rock and surf angling, bird-watching, spear-fishing, canoeing, boardsailing, surfing, camping, hotel and resort life; hikers can camp anywhere on the beach (excluding military zones) for a nominal fee; hikers' lodges planned; Hamburg Hotel (P.O. Hamburg, Ciskei, tel. (0020) Hamburg 4); Mpekweni Marine Resort (P.O. Box 66, Bisho, Ciskei, tel. (0403) 613126); Hamburg Camp-site (Hamburg Corporation, P.O. Box 90, Bisho, Ciskei, tel. (0020) Hamburg 16 during office hours); Kiwane bungalows,

enquiries to the Ciskei Tourist Department.
PERTINENT INFORMATION: Fires made from driftwood are permitted, provided they are made in the sand, away from vegetated dunes. The military location between the Gqutywa and Umtana river mouths should be traversed only during the day, below the high water mark. Full water discipline is vital as fresh water is available only at resorts, organized camp-sites and holiday townships. For information: Ciskei Department of Tourism and Aviation.
AVAILABLE LITERATURE: Included in *Ciskei Hiking Trails*, booklet with floral and faunal checklists; *Available and Projected Hiking Trails and Nature Walks in Ciskei*, brochure available from Ciskei Tourist Department; located on Government Printer's 1:50 000 topographic maps '3327 AC Prudhoe', '3327 AD Hamburg' and '3327 BA and BC Kidd's Beach'.
CLIMATE: The Ciskei coast is generally clear, with blue skies and small variations in daytime temperatures; the average coastal temperature is 18 °C. Rain falls mainly in summer (October to March), but be prepared for rain and/or wind throughout the year.

The Ciskei coast, extending from the Great Fish River mouth, beyond the Keiskamma estuary to the Ncera River, boasts a unique wilderness character. The 64 kilometres of coast can be walked in either direction in three or four days, or can be tailored to choice. Combined with the Transkei Wild Coast, Strandloper and Alexandria trails, the Shipwreck Trail forms a link in a unique coastal hiking paradise.

Walking distances between major points are given here for planning purposes. Remember that coastal walking, especially at low tide, is generally faster than on mountainous terrain.
Great Fish River to Ncera River: 64 km.
Great Fish River to Mpekweni: 11,5 km.
Mpekweni to Bira River: 11 km.
Bira River to Keiskamma River: 20 km.
Keiskamma River to Chalumna River: 10,5 km.
Chalumna River to Ncera River: 11 km.
(Ncera River to East London: 29 km).

My favourite areas along this coastline are the Great Fish River mouth, Mpekweni, the Bira and Gqutywa estuaries and the beach between Hamburg and Chalumna.

The rock sculptures at the mouth of the Great Fish River are worthy of exploration. Numerous wave- and wind-eroded tunnels and caves have been carved out of the head-land, which played a significant role in Cis-

keian history. It served as the port captain's office from 1846 to 1848 when soldiers disembarked and supplies destined for Fort Peddie were offloaded in Waterloo Bay. In order to protect landing operations, Fort Albert was established at Old Woman's River, now a very attractive picnic site.

The Great Fish River mouth and lagoon between the Boy Retief bridge and the river mouth teems with birdlife. Cape teal and other ducks breed here. Yellowbilled ducks, pochards, and Egyptian and spurwinged geese are often seen, while stilts, whimbrels, greenshanks and smaller migratory waders are numerous.

Mpekweni's estuary, once a quiet fisherman's hideaway, is now the site of the new Mpekweni Marine Resort, a very attractive hotel complex offering watersports such as boardsailing.

Bira mouth is a place of immense charm. It was here, many years ago, that the *Grosvenor* survivors, trekking to civilization, were confronted by a herd of bathing elephant. On its eastern side is a dangerous ridge of rocks called Madagascar Reef, where the steamer *Madagascar* came to grief in 1858, and the *Ben Holden* in 1934. The sailing ship *Elizabeth* has the dubious honour of being the first wreck at this spot, in 1839. To get a good view of Madagascar Reef, climb the hill to the east of the settlement.

It is an easy walk from Bira to Gqutywa River mouth, a beautiful unspoilt area, and easily crossed. The coastline is open, with high forest-covered sand dunes set well away from the sea. Both oystercatchers and whitefronted sandplovers can be seen breeding here in season.

The Keiskamma River estuary is extremely rich in birdlife, as is the adjacent

coastal bush. It is also one of the best fishing grounds on the whole coast. The small town of Hamburg originated as one of the many German settler villages established along the southern bank of the Keiskamma in the 1850s.

The wildest area of the Shipwreck Trail lies between the Keiskamma estuary and the Chalumna. Its forested dunes are being developed as a game reserve and large mammals have been reintroduced. The rocky stretches are rewarding to shell collectors. The size and variety of the mussels found here is legendary.

The Shipwreck Trail is within the capabilities of any reasonably healthy person.

Hikers can exchange heavy mountain boots for lighter boots, or a sturdy pair of running or walking shoes (going barefoot is not recommended). Sunglasses, sunhats and sunscreen lotion are essential for those who are sensitive to sun and wind. A fishing rod would be a logical extra on this coastal walk.

Opposite page: The headlands of the Great Fish River, and the beginning of the Shipwreck Hiking Trail.

Top: The Shipwreck trail offers endless stretches of pristine beach.

Centre: Hikers take time to explore an old fishing vessel on the Shipwreck Hiking Trail.

157

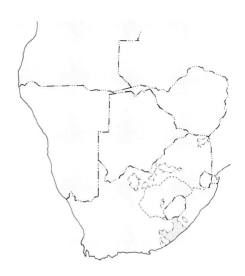

TRANSKEI

Transkei, a Xhosa republic which gained independence from South Africa in October 1976, is situated south of both Natal and Lesotho. Transkei is a relatively large (45 000 km²) land – it is twice the size of Israel and larger than the Netherlands. Natural features clearly delineate Transkei's boundaries – the Kei River in the west, the Drakensberg Mountains in the north, the Umtamvuna River in the north-east and the 280-kilometre Wild Coast in the south.

Large rivers (the Umzimvubu, Umtata, Bashee and Great Kei) incise the land from north-west to south-east, contributing to Transkei's undulating and broken landscape. Although Transkei spans an altitude from sea level to 2 400 metres (where it borders on the Drakensberg in Lesotho), only the coast has thus far been developed for trailing. The country's highlands with their deep valleys and great ridges offer trailing potential for the adventurous explorer, while the coast's rugged cliff-faces, breathtaking estuarine valleys edged by dense, tangled forests and grassy fields, perfect mangrove communities, wide, bleached-white beaches, and rich tidal marine life make for one of the most ideal coastal hiking venues in the world.

Major entrances to Transkei have border posts. South Africans must show either their passport or Book of Life, while aliens must produce a valid passport and visa (obtainable at the gate or in advance for a small fee). Aliens must remember to have a re-entry visa for returning to South Africa.

Transkei falls into the summer rainfall area. Over the coastal plain, rainfall ranges from 750 to 1 400 millimetres annually, with most falling during the summer (October to

March). March is the wettest month, February the driest. Winter skies are crystal-clear, while summers can be cloudy to overcast. The average daily coastal maximum temperature is 23,2 °C, the minimum is 16,7 °C. Climate and vegetation become more tropical as you move northwards.

ECOLOGICAL ZONES: COASTAL BUSH AND SUBTROPICAL FOREST, EASTERN GRASSLANDS

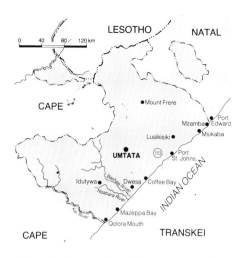

183. Transskei Hiking Trail: The Wild Coast

👣 🚶

AUTHORITY-IN-CHARGE: Department of Agriculture and Forestry, Nature Conservation Section, Private Bag X5002, Umtata, Transkei.

LENGTH/DURATION: 280 km/approximately 25 days. The trail is divided into five 3-6 day sections.

MAIN ATTRACTIONS: One of Africa's most dramatic coastlines: sandy and rocky beaches, coves, lagoons, cliffs, rock formations in the sea and mangrove swamps; intertidal life and birdlife; fishing.

FACILITIES/AMENITIES: Along those sections of the coast opened as a hiking trail: huts accommodating 12 people, with water, bunks and mattresses, tables and benches, and fireplaces (no wood). *En route*: hotels, nature reserves with accommodation, hamlets, small trading stores, and clusters of private cottages; fishermen's tracks run from the main road to the coast.

PERTINENT INFORMATION: Hikers wishing to walk along sections of the coast with no established trails must obtain a permit, free of charge, from the Secretary of the Department of Agriculture and Forestry. Always carry your passport, permits and a tide table. Always carry water, and do not drink from rivers and estuaries without first boiling or purifying the water. Hikers must respect the local population – never take local produce without permission from the villagers. Roads can be extremely difficult to negotiate after heavy rains. Watch for thieving along the coast. Be warned: estuaries host sharks. Never cross an estuary at the mouth during an outgoing tide.

AVAILABLE LITERATURE: *Transkei Hiking Trail: Port St. Johns to Hole in the Wall*, brochure with map; *Transkei Hiking Trail: Mtamvuna River (Port Edward) to Mzimvubu River (Port St. Johns)*, brochure with map; *Transkei Hiking Trail: Coffee Bay to Mbashe River*, published for the Natal Branch of the Wildlife Society of Southern Africa by A.C. Braby, P.O. Box 731, Durban 4000, and also available from the Authority-in-Charge; for trails not yet established use the Government Printer's 1:50 000 topographic

Below: The German ship which ran aground on the southern sector of the Wild Coast.

Opposite page, top: Setting up a wilderness camp on the Transkei Wild Coast.

Opposite page, bottom: The Magwa Falls were particularly impressive during the Transkei floods of 1978.

maps, which can be purchased from the Surveyor-General's Office, Department of Local Government and Land Tenure, Private Bag X5031, Umtata 5100, Transkei; 'The Transkei Hiking Trail', *Great Outdoors*, January 1984; 'Wildcoast North Hiking Trail', *Great Outdoors*, May/June 1984; 'Bomvanaland Trail', *Great Outdoors*, April 1985.

CLIMATE: Summer rainfall area.

'Umtata – Floods in Transkei'
'Port St. Johns has been cut off from the outside world by what have been described as the worst floods in the Wild Coast's history . . . Flooding between Port St. Johns and Port Grosvenor has cut off 60 people on a walking tour of the area . . . 400 millimetres of rain fell in 36 hours . . . landslides and rockfalls have taken a heavy toll . . .'
(Newspaper headlines, 25 April 1978)

That formed part of my experience on the Wild Coast. Despite floods, hardship, adventure, wind, cold and fear, we finally managed to return all 40 children and 20 adults safely to Pretoria. I hiked on to complete the expedition.

The Wild Coast, riddled with the well-worn footpaths of both livestock and people, is not wild through lack of human settlement – on the contrary, Xhosa villages dot the hillsides all along the coast from Port St. Johns southwards. Its reputation stems rather from the numerous ships and lives that have been claimed along the dangerous coastline.

The Wild Coast is the only wilderness trip on which I was able to buy a Coke *en route*; it is also the only wilderness experience during which I was visited by a helicopter, adopted by a stray dog, honoured by the local women for swimming across shark-infested estuaries, saved by two brothers from drowning in mud and befriended by a huge Transkeian sheriff on a beautiful white horse! At

the cost of a pair of running shoes and a handful of sweets, his 1,3 metre-tall son carried my 1,3 metre-tall backpack across the incredible black pebble beach near Brazen Head.

The region explored by coastal mountaineers lies between the Umtamvuna River (Port Edward) and the Great Kei River, with the most popular stretches being between Port Edward and Port St. Johns (approximately 110 kilometres), and between Port St. Johns and Hole-in-the-Wall (approximately 170 kilometres). The former area, the less-populated Pondoland Wild Coast, is rugged, with sensational coastal rock formations and deeply incised river gorges. The latter stretch, on the other hand, provides gentler terrain, mangrove swamps, lovely scenery and more settlements.

A marked hiking trail, with traditional Xhosa-style accommodation, runs along the entire stretch of the coast. In 1983, the five-day stretch from Port St. Johns to Coffee Bay (approximately 100 kilometres) was completed. Camps along the route are located at 12-kilometre intervals at Silaka Nature Reserve, Mngazana, Mpande, Hluleka Nature Reserve, Ngcibe and Coffee Bay. The second part, opened in late 1985, runs from Coffee Bay to Cwebe Nature Reserve at the mouth of the Bashee (Mbashe) River (Bomvanaland) with huts at Coffee Bay, Mhlahlane, Amanzimyama (Mbiza), Xora and the Bashee River mouth. It takes four days to walk. (Note that two sets of huts exist in the caravan park at Coffee Bay; one is for hikers finishing the walk from Port St. Johns, the other for those starting the walk to Bashee. There are also huts at Bashee for those who wish to stay over on completion of the latter trail. These are less than a kilometre from the hotel.)

The newest sections of trail, from north to south, are the three-day stretch from Mzamba near Port Edward to Msikaba River, with camps at Mzamba, Mnyameni,

Mtentu and Msikaba; a six-day hike from Msikaba River to Agate Terrace (Port St. Johns), with camps at Lambasi Bay, Myekane and Ingo, and elsewhere; and five days from Nqabara Estuary (the southern border of the Dwesa Nature Reserve) to north of the Great Kei River at Qolora Mouth, with overnight stops at Nqabara Point, Shixini Point, Mazeppa Point, Cebe and Kobonqaba.

If you get lost and cannot find the markers on the trail, stay close to the coast and ask the locals for directions to stores, river mouths and beaches. They are very helpful and will lead you on the often perplexing network of paths through the thick indigenous bush.

Some noteworthy features of the coast from Port Edward south to Port St. Johns include fossil beds visible at low tide near the Mzamba River; narrow stretches of creamy beaches south of Port Edward; the rare endemic Pondoland palm (also known as Pondoland coconut) on the north banks of the Mtentu and Msikaba rivers; the fishermen's shacks at Lupatana which face huge breakers that easily challenge those of the Tsitsikamma Coast; Waterfall Bluff, a sen-

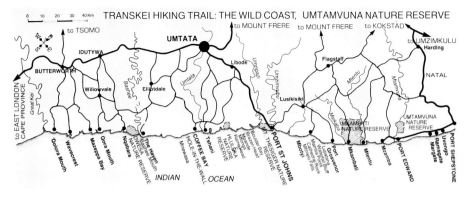

TRANSKEI HIKING TRAIL: THE WILD COAST, UMTAMVUNA NATURE RESERVE

sational waterfall where you can walk between the waters plummeting directly into the sea, and the cliff; Mamba Pools, behind Waterfall Bluff; Cathedral Rock and the Castle, two of the most unusual erosional features in the sea that you are likely to come across; and Mfihlelo Falls, an approximately 160-metre waterfall, reputed to be the highest in the world flowing directly into the ocean.

Farther south, between Port St. Johns and Hole-in-the-Wall, I found the following quite fascinating: the Table Mountain sandstone cliffs of Port St. Johns; the very lovely Mpande Bay; the extensive dolerite intrusion named Brazen Head, south of Mngazana; Hluleka, a nature reserve with plenty of waterfowl on the river; the resort at Coffee Bay; and, just a bit farther south, the famous Hole-in-the-Wall, where a deep rumbling sound is caused by heavy surf further eroding the weathered-out hole.

All along the coast, tidal estuaries are fringed by one of the world's most valuable ecosystems, the mangrove swamps. In Transkei the mangroves reach their southern limit of tolerance, and this is borne out by patchy stands of trees which may be of a single species. Grossly exploited and misunderstood by man, mangrove ecosystems are actually unparalleled as nursery areas for marine fish fry and invertebrates. These swamps are the breeding grounds of mullet, grunter, stumpnose, perch, kob, springer, prawns and crabs. Associated with or dependent on the swamps is a diverse bird population: the fish eagle, whitebacked night heron and tiny mangrove kingfisher, to name a few.

Other vegetation zones along the Wild Coast include coastal grasslands which have a lawn-like appearance as a result of heavy grazing by domesticated stock, valley bushveld occurring in the larger river valleys, and coastal forests, including dune and swamp forests.

Here are a few suggestions and hints which you may find useful: when you have to cross an estuary, walk upstream first and head directly across the stream. By the time you reach the far shore, the current will have carried you to near the mouth. Always cross during incoming tides. Swimming across estuary mouths while wearing your pack is dangerous and foolish: rather float it in front of you or accept 'ferry rides' from the local youths.

For the less adventurous hiker wishing to overnight where specific facilities exist, there are three nature reserves. Mkambati (with a lodge, cottage and rondavels, canoeing and horse-riding), north of Port St. Johns between the Msikaba and Mtentu rivers, contains the Pondoland palm. Hluleka, 30 kilometres south of Port St. Johns, offers fully furnished log cabins, each accommodating five to eight people. At Dwesa, south of Coffee Bay, rustic log cabins that blend well with the forest environment can be rented, and hikers can also camp. This is a particularly lovely reserve, comprising a large indigenous forest, rolling coastal grasslands, rivers and estuaries. Mammals include eland, blesbok, buffalo, hartebeest, warthog, blue and grey duiker, bushbuck and rhinoceros. Dwesa is worth visiting

even if you terminate your hiking tour at Hole-in-the-Wall, and there are many interesting paths within the reserve for day rambles.

Camp-sites charging tariffs but offering no facilities exist at Mazeppa Bay, Xora Mouth, Mpande, Mpame, Mnyameni, Lupatana, Mkweni, Mbotyi, Ntambalala, Mzpuzi, Mbolompo, Shixini and Kobonqaba.

Left: The Hluleka Nature Reserve, which forms part of the Transkei Hiking Trail.

Above: Traditional Xhosa-style huts on the Wild Coast.

Opposite page: The rock-hewn 'castle' on the sea's edge, seen from the Transkei's Wild Coast trail.

Those at Cebe Mouth, Coffee Bay, Dwesa and Msikaba have ablution blocks, and the last-mentioned, a small bungalow. Port St. Johns has camp-sites with ablution blocks at First and Second Beach. In addition, there are hotels along the coast at Bashee Mouth, Mazeppa Bay, Qolora Mouth, Wavecrest, Coffee Bay, Port St. Johns, Umngazi Mouth and Qora Mouth. This information is likely to alter with time so I suggest you obtain a copy of the *Accommodation Guide for Tourists in Transkei*, issued by the Department of Commerce, Industry and Tourism in Umtata. Another useful publication which also details the hiking trails is the *Transkei Official Tourist Guide*, published by Industrial Newsmen (Pty) Ltd, and also available from the Department of Commerce, Industry and Tourism.

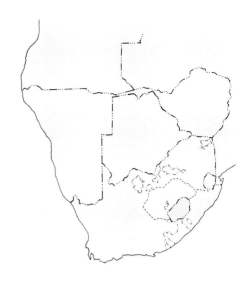

LESOTHO

Lesotho gained its independence from Great Britain in 1966. Often referred to as the 'kingdom in the sky', Lesotho is relatively unexplored and undeveloped. The adventurous hiker is sure to be excited by the mountaineering and trailing freedom offered in this rugged terrain. The 'average' trailist can discover, on horseback, the rich cultural heritage of the Basotho people.

All visitors to Lesotho must be in possession of a valid passport; some nationals, other than South African citizens, may also need visas. Non-South African passport holders must remember to obtain a re-entry visa for returning to South Africa. Liquor and military-like or camouflage clothing should never be carried across the border.

Lesotho is a land of winter sunshine. Cloudless warm days and crisp, cold nights (often with frost) prevail from May to September. Winter also brings snow, not only in the high Malutis but also in the lowlands. (Unseasonal snow can fall at any time of the year.) Be prepared for the intense winter cold. Summer is the rainy season, with more than 85 per cent of the annual rainfall occurring between October and April, often as thunderstorms.

ECOLOGICAL ZONE: DRAKENSBERG

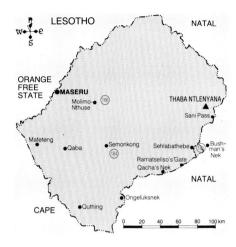

184. Lesotho

AUTHORITY-IN-CHARGE: Permits to walk through Lesotho are obtainable from the Lesotho Tourist Board, P.O. Box 1378, Maseru 100. Inform the Board of proposed dates of visit and places you intend visiting; the Board then promises to inform the relevant authorities (chiefs, district co-ordinators, police and others). As a matter of courtesy, hikers must inform the chiefs on arrival in their village(s) or area(s) of jurisdiction.

SIZE: 30 300 km².

MAIN ATTRACTIONS: Remote mountain scenery and traditional tribal life; waterfalls.

FACILITIES/AMENITIES: Bridle trails used by rural people; country stores selling beer, cooldrinks and other supplies; youth hostels; camping at the side of mountain roads is permitted.

PERTINENT INFORMATION: There are few restrictions on travel, except in the diamond-mining areas around Letšeng-la-Terae. Do not pick or eat village farm produce without permission. Drink water only from springs or remote mountain streams, and purify water obtained near villages or temporary settlements. Take ample provisions from home (stores are dotted throughout the mountains but supplies are limited). Do not import liquor. Do not take across the border or wear military or camouflage clothing.

AVAILABLE LITERATURE: Maps are obtainable from the Department of Lands, Surveys and Physical Planning, P.O. Box 876, Maseru 100; all maps must be applied for well in advance (in fact, it is best to buy them in Maseru); the two 1:250 000 maps which cover the whole country are excellent but do not have sufficient detail for hikers; the sixty 1:50 000 topographic maps provide comprehensive coverage of the country but are not always reliable; the new maps are good but the old maps omit place names, roads and tracks and make no distinction between permanent villages and seasonal

kraals; many prominent members of the Mountain Club of South Africa lead trips to Lesotho and have information in their private files or in the MCSA library; *Motoring in Lesotho*, AA Bulletin MNE-7, has excellent coverage on roads and driving conditions which they state 'necessitate the utmost care'.

CLIMATE: Summer rainfall area. Very cold winters; snow possible.

Although Lesotho has no organized hiking trails or camp-sites (except for their well-known horse-riding treks), the Lesotho Tourist Board has informed me that plans are already underway for the establishment of such trails. In the meantime, hikers are free to plan their own routes, ensuring that they abide by the conditions detailed under Pertinent Information.

Geologically, Lesotho is similar to the Natal Drakensberg (see page 30). Many footpaths and roads are located on dolerite dykes running through the sandstone escarpment. The cave sandstone forms huge overhangs or rock shelters, rich in Bushman art, and provides handy shelter for local herdsmen (and hikers). The youngest rock layer, the basalt, which formed from cooled volcanic

lava flows, still covers three-quarters of the country, dividing naturally into five main ranges, each with prominent peaks, 2 500-3 000 metres high. The seemingly endless network of footpaths, bridle paths and rough vehicle tracks that criss-cross the highlands, allows access to these summits and provides inexhaustible and exciting hiking opportunities.

1. The Drakensberg range, from the Malibamatso River source to Ramatseliso's Gate: running along Lesotho's eastern border, this range includes Thaba Ntlenyana, meaning 'nice little mountain'. . . an ironic description, for although the peak appears as a low hill on the high moorland plateau, at 3 482 metres it is the highest in southern Africa. The 'hill' is only five kilometres from the escarpment edge and, from the Natal side, its summit can be easily reached by walking; the panoramic view of the Natal escarpment and half the province is spectacular.

Sani Top (or Sani Pass), described in detail on page 182, can be reached by a path from Koma-Koma Bridge on the Orange (or Senqu) River. Hikers walk from village to village in an easterly direction, asking assistance from local villagers. The well-travelled

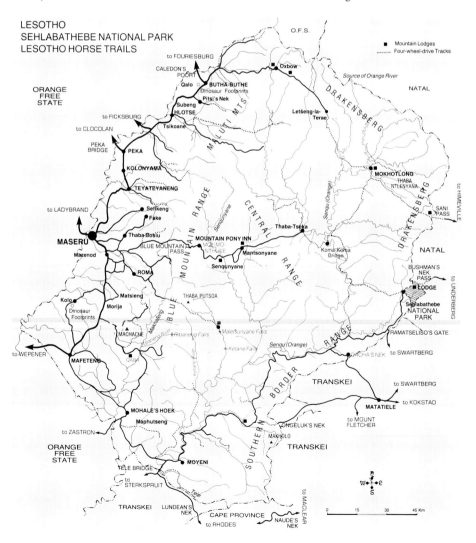

rounding peaks. The ascent of Machache Mountain is via a 15-kilometre walk from the agricultural station at Machache, 45 kilometres from Maseru.

Another day's outing from Maseru is the beautiful area in the foothills of the Malutis, where Ha Khotso rock paintings are found. The road passing the agricultural training college ends at a deep ravine; a guard lives in a little rondavel near the river (when it is not in flood) and he will show you these 500-year-old paintings of blue cranes, antelope and feline predators as well as Bushman hunters and dancers. You can also walk to the paintings from the Toll House on the mountain road from Maseru. There is a camp-site and hotel here. Ask the locals for route directions.

Lesotho's world-famous alluvial deposits contain the fossilized bones and footprints of the most recent and largest dinosaurs. These fossils, found in the red beds and cave sand-stones, have been unearthed in varied habitats – streambeds, flat outcrops of sandstone, on the sides of boulders which have fallen from higher krantzes and even in roofs of overhanging caves.

The red beds, formed in the Upper Triassic Period, are the only areas – apart from adjoining parts of South Africa, and parts of China and Brazil – where dinosaur bones have been found. The best known and accessible sites are at Qalo near Butha-Buthe; Subeng and Tsikoane near Hlotse; Morija and Matsieng; Kolo; Maphutseng near Mohale's Hoek; and Moyeni.

Botanically, Lesotho is a grassland with wooded mountain valleys hosting trees such as the Cape willow and wild olive. Aloes are common: a most intriguing species is the spiral aloe found on steep basalt slopes in the higher reaches of the Malutis. There are some excellent specimens growing on the plateau above Maletsunyane Falls.

As in most populated and rural African lands, the larger species of wildlife have

horse trail (occasionally used by four-wheel drive vehicles), which runs along the river from Koma-Koma Bridge to Qacha's Nek, is another scenic and interesting trek. At Qacha's Nek you are quite likely to see blanketed horsemen trading with local storekeepers. The well-worn tracks are regularly used by the Basotho and although you will undoubtedly get lost at times, you will find the local people most friendly and often willing to act as temporary guides.

2. The southern border range, from Ramatseliso's Gate to the Tele River source: Makholo Mountain (2 899 m) is frequently climbed and is accessible from the Ongeluks Nek track. A new southern perimeter road, linking the lowlands of Lesotho with the south-east corner of the rugged Qacha's Nek and Quthing districts, will facilitate inland travel.

3. The central range, between the Senqu and Senqunyane rivers: the giant Highland

Water Scheme will open up new areas in this hitherto relatively inaccessible region. (See 'True Freedom for Lesotho' in *Southern Africa Today*, March 1987.)

4. The Blue-Grey Mountain range (often simply referred to as the Blue Mountains), Thaba Putsoa, between the Senqunyane and Makhaleng rivers: D. Ambrose in his *Guide to Lesotho* (third edition, Winchester Press, 1983) states that Thaba Putsoa (3 097 m) offers the finest panoramic view in Lesotho and that in this area the Cape vulture, jackal buzzard, black eagle and lammergeyer can all be seen on the same day. The ascent of the mountain is detailed in his guide book. The many caves with their impressive Bushman paintings are a feature of this range.

5. The front range, or Maluti Mountains, which forms the background of peaks seen from Lesotho's lowlands: Machache (2 885 m) is one of its best-known mountains and offers spectacular views of sur-

Above left: The Maletsunyane Falls (192 metres) are the highest single falls in southern Africa.

Above right: Near Ongeluks Nek, the access to Makholo Mountain (2 899 metres), a frequently climbed peak of the southern border range. The low-lying ground is Transkei.

been exterminated. The grey rhebok and mountain reedbuck have survived and they, along with jackal, baboon, caracal, spotted genet and other small mammals and rodents, populate this area. Birdlife is prolific: the 265 recorded species include the yellow-breasted pipit, bearded vulture (or lammergeyer), bald ibis and giant kingfisher. Be on the lookout for dangerous snakes such as the puff adder, spitting cobra and rhombic night adder.

185. Sehlabathebe National Park

RAMATSELISO'S GATE, see map page 166

AUTHORITY-IN-CHARGE: Ministry of Agriculture, Conservation Division, National Parks, P.O. Box 24, Maseru 100.
SIZE: 6 500 hectares.
MAIN ATTRACTIONS: Scenic landscape, including fascinating rock shapes; rare plants, endemic fish, mountain birds and reintroduced game; trout fishing; Bushman paintings and stone shelters.
FACILITIES/AMENITIES: Mountain lodge providing luxury accommodation for 12 people; park hostel providing simple accommodation for 8 people; unlimited number of sites for camping; research station for visiting scientists.
PERTINENT INFORMATION: Bookings for the lodge and hostel: Sehlabathebe Lodge Reservations, Lesotho National Parks, Ministry of Agriculture, P.O. Box 24, Maseru 100, tel. (0501) 23600. For both lodge and hostel, visitors must provide their own bedding and food. All payments at Sehlabathebe National Park should be made in cash. Until the road to the park is upgraded, four-wheel drive vehicles are essential. From Maseru, flights are available

to Ha Paulus airstrip, and arrangements can be made for transport to the lodge (contact Air Lesotho, P.O. Box 861, Maseru 100). Hikers can walk for five to six hours from Bushman's Nek to the park.
AVAILABLE LITERATURE: General references on Lesotho; 'Sehlabathebe Nature Reserve', *Great Outdoors*, August 1985; *Motoring in Lesotho*, AA Bulletin MNE-7; *Drakensberg South: Garden Castle, Boesmansnek Sehlabathebe*, map number 6 by Peter Slingsby, Mapcape, compiled by the Forestry Branch, Department of Environment Affairs.
CLIMATE: Summer rainfall area. Cold winter nights, snow possible.

Lying at an average altitude of 2 400 metres, but rising to nearly 3 000 metres at the Natal/Lesotho border, and located on the south-west side of the Drakensberg escarpment, is Sehlabathebe, Lesotho's first national park. The scenery is spectacular – only the difficult access to the park keeps the number of visitors low. This fact is a definite attraction for solitude-loving backpackers.

Serving as the upper catchment for the Tsoelikana River, Sehlabathebe National Park consists largely of sub-alpine grassland, dominated by three peaks, Baroa-ba-Bararo ('the three Bushmen'). Sandstone wind- and water-eroded caves, arches and pools are a photographer's playground. There are numerous pools for refreshing swims, and both the Leqooa and the Tsoelikana rivers are well known for their rainbow trout. The tiny minnow, *Oreodaimon quathlambae*, is endemic to the Tsoelikana catchment area. Overhead, the rare lammergeyer commands the skies.

Snakes are generally not found in highland regions and are therefore uncommon in the park. A dangerous exception, however, is the mountain adder, and climbers must be especially alert for this reptile. Its neurotoxic venom, unusual for adders as their venom is chiefly cytotoxic and haemotoxic,

paralyses the eye muscles, temporarily blinding the victim. Recovery usually occurs without treatment.

Backpackers should realize that here, as in the rest of Lesotho, rivers in flood present potential hazards, especially impeding east-west progress in the summer rainy season. Be prepared.

186. Lesotho Horse Trails

MOLIMO NTHUSE, see map page 166

AUTHORITIES-IN-CHARGE: Lesotho Tourist Board, P.O. Box 1378, Maseru 100; Basotho Pony Breeding and Marketing Programme, P.O. Box 1027, Maseru 100.
DURATION: Variable: from two hours to 12 days and 11 nights.
MAIN ATTRACTIONS: Unique, sure-footed Basotho ponies; remote mountain scenery and tribal life.
FACILITIES/AMENITIES: Variable: consult your tour guide; fully-inclusive trails (with shelters and food) are available; all trails provide ponies, pack bags and guides.
PERTINENT INFORMATION: Packing space is limited, so take as little as possible; backpacks are not practical.
AVAILABLE LITERATURE: Colour brochures and price lists available from the Lesotho Tourist Board.

Riding carefree in the saddle on my sure-footed pony, who was sweating and puffing up the Rasebetsane Pass in Thaba Putsoa (the Blue Mountains), I thought to myself, 'This is the perfect trail for the harrassed, uptight businessman: it offers total isolation from urbanization, and a chance to experience the philosophical attitude of the rural people'. Requiring neither riding proficiency nor physical fitness (but good health

and a flexible, adaptable outlook), the Lesotho Horse Trails are an 'easy' way to see the inner mountain kingdom, a virtually inaccessible area which, in the past, was open only to intrepid mountaineers, missionaries, Peace Corps workers and those in four-wheel drive vehicles.

The Lesotho Tourist Board co-ordinates and arranges trails for tourists in conjunction with the Basotho Pony Breeding and Marketing Programme, which has a pony trekking centre at Molimo Nthuse ('God help me') Pass, one hour's drive from Maseru. Private trailing organizations such as Trailblazers will book trips inclusive of food, and spare you the sometimes-difficult communication link-ups with the centre. Trips range from short, mid-morning rides, to 12 days and 11 nights for the more ambitious. The ponies, originally from Javanese stock, have a long-standing reputation for being hardy, well-trained, good-natured and reliable. The guides handle the horses well.

Riders 'camp' at night in traditional thatched huts in local villages, sometimes even in the chief's home. Local lodges are also used. I suggest bringing a small camping mattress and a warm sleeping bag, in addition to informal warm clothing, riding jeans and boots, a bathing costume, sun-screen lotion, a sun hat and small change for cooldrinks and beer. Remember that all gear is packed in saddlebags and these offer less space than backpacks. Do not wear a day-pack while riding; not only are they awkward, but straps tear loose as a result of jolting during trots and gallops across open veld.

The horse-riding trail I experienced began at the Makhaleng River ('river of aloes') at Fraser's Lodge, Qaba, and passed Ribaneng Falls (92 m), Ketane Falls (124 m) and Le-Bihan or Maletsunyane Falls (192 m), terminating at Semonkong with a 20-minute 'plane flight back to Maseru. Four to six hours of riding a day was just enough; the side trips to view the falls and stretch our legs were welcomed, as were the lunch stops along rivers and waterfalls, where ample swimming time was allocated.

Maletsunyane Falls, the highest single falls in southern Africa, are a spectacular sight. The river tumbles 192 metres over a basalt cliff in a single drop. The clouds of mist and spray are responsible for the popular name Semonkong or 'place of smoke'. Fit and ambitious hikers have time to descend 350 metres along a very steep and indistinct path to the foot of the waterfalls and attempt a swim in the icy pool. (The herd of goats on the steep cliffsides look stranded in their precarious home.) It is fun to explore this gorge, but leave yourself time for the steep ascent.

The Lesotho Horse Trails are a unique experience, not only because of the ponies and the scenery, but because the trails are run by the Basotho and not expatriates, and so display to the tourist much of the country's culture and outlook. You will see the Basotho dressed in their traditional blankets, families sleeping on cowskins, and perhaps pass a herdboy playing the *lesiba*, a woodwind and string musical instrument believed to bring contentment to grazing cattle. Hikers should insist that their guide organizes local foods, Sotho dishes such as wild spinach, wheat samp, sorghum bread, steamed bread and Joala beer.

To fully enjoy this trip, tourists must come with an open mind, prepared to relax, observe and be as friendly and flexible as the Basotho themselves.

Opposite page, left: Cooling off under one of the many waterfalls passed on the Lesotho pony trek.
Opposite page, right: Ongeluks Nek.
Above: Riding a Basotho pony is one of the best ways to experience 'the roof of Africa'.

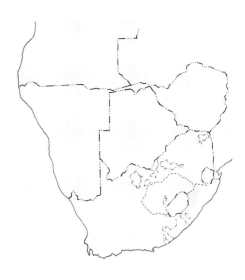

NATAL DRAKENSBERG

Quathlamba, a barrier of upward-pointing spears, is the Zulu name for the craggy pinnacles that form the most spectacular section of the Great Escarpment, southern Africa's watershed. No less apt is the Dutch-derived epithet meaning 'mountain of the dragon', for the forbidding, jagged peaks seem a natural domain for these fabled creatures.

The Natal Drakensberg, the highest mountains in South Africa and noted for their magnificent buttresses and peaks and the numerous trails which traverse the lower slopes, have a magnetic attraction for mountaineers and trailists. Here, the summer heat is tempered by altitude, and the very cold winters cap the peaks in snow.

ECOLOGICAL ZONE: DRAKENSBERG

187. Holkrans Hiking Trail

NEWCASTLE

AUTHORITY-IN-CHARGE: Mr and Mrs D.C.P. van Niekerk, P.O. Box 2734, Newcastle 2940; tel. (03435) 600.

SIZE: 1 206 hectares.

LENGTH/DURATION: 17,5 km/2 days, 1 night (may be extended).

MAIN ATTRACTIONS: Drakensberg sandstone formations such as overhanging cliffs with waterfalls; indigenous forests with numerous labelled tree specimens; plentiful clear freshwater streams, especially in the rainy season; birdlife and small buck; rock tunnel at overnight camp.

FACILITIES/AMENITIES: Base camp with 30 bunkbeds and mattresses, showers, toilets, hot and cold water, braai and firewood, iron pots and electric lights; overnight camp either under overhang with toilets, firewood, iron pots, grills and water from stream, or at the trail hut.

AVAILABLE LITERATURE: *Holkrans Trail*, brochure with sketch map and tree list; located on Government Printer's

Above: The Holkrans Hiking Trail is a relatively low-altitude Drakensberg experience.

Opposite page: The hand-painted Bushman trail markers on the Holkrans trail.

TRANSVAAL

SWAZILAND

ORANGE FREE STATE

⑱ Newcastle

● Dundee

● Ladysmith

QWA-QWA

⑱

⑱

Bergville ●

⑲ ⑲

⑲ ● Winterton

● Weenen

⑲ ● Estcourt

● Mooi River

● Rosetta

LESOTHO

⑲ ⑲

⑲ ⑲ ● Himeville

⑲ ⑲ ● Underberg

⑲ ⑲

TRANSKEI

⑳

● Kokstad

TRANSKEI

INDIAN OCEAN

NATAL DRAKENSBERG

0 20 40 60 80 100 km

topographic maps '2729 DC Mont Pelaan' and '2729 DD Newcastle'.
CLIMATE: Average annual rainfall: 1 000 millimetres, falling mostly in summer. Winter nights are cold but days are warm and sunny.

The Holkrans Hiking Trail is a lovely day and a half ramble through the lower Drakensberg mountains, at an altitude of less than 2 000 metres. Hikers walk through indigenous forests, under sandstone krantzes with their small waterfalls, and across grasslands where baboons, grey duiker, mountain reedbuck and a variety of birds, such as the secretarybird, can be observed. This is an easy trail, recommended for the beginner hiker and especially suitable for school and youth groups. The only demanding stretch is the first two kilometres, which is a climb from the base hut to the rock band.

The facilities offered reflect the personal touch of the owners of the trail, the Van Niekerks, who developed this trail to share with others the beauty of their farm. Electric lights at the base hut facilitate arrival in the dark the night before you begin hiking. The overnight camp offers accommodation under an overhang or in a new, thatched hut. Unlike Drakensberg trails run by South African Forestry authorities, the Van Niekerks allow campfires and provide all necessary amenities. And, most unusual, Mrs Van Niekerk herself painted all trail markers, which depict Bushmen with arrows.

188. Royal Natal National Park

BERGVILLE

AUTHORITY-IN-CHARGE: Natal Parks Board.
SIZE: 8 094 hectares.
LENGTH: 130 km of paths.
MAIN ATTRACTIONS: Free-standing peaks create spectacular mountain scenery; the Amphitheatre, a crescent-shaped rock wall; Mont-aux-Sources, forming the continental divide; the Tugela Falls (850 m); yellowwood forests; Bushman paintings; bird-watching; game-viewing; trout hatchery.
FACILITIES/AMENITIES: Numerous footpaths; guided walks and wildlife films; visitor centre and curio shop; camping and caravan sites; Tendele Camp with 13 bungalows and two self-contained cottages; hotel within park, night access allowed; Mont-aux-Sources Hotel close to park; horse-riding available at Rugged Glen; picnic sites with braai; trout hatchery.
PERTINENT INFORMATION: There is a border post between South Africa and Lesotho at the summit of the Namahadi Pass, so hikers should carry passports and health documents. Permits necessary for climbing. Camping is allowed in designated areas only; for bookings: The Officer-in-Charge, Mahai

Camp-site, P.O. Box Mont-aux-Sources 3353. Access via Bergville.
AVAILABLE LITERATURE: *Royal Natal National Park*, fully comprehensive booklet with sketch map, issued by the Natal Parks Board; *Mont-aux-Sources*, 1:20 000 map obtainable from the Natal Parks Board; *Drakensberg North: Mt. Aux Sources to Cathedral Peak*, map number 1 by Peter Slingsby, Mapcape, compiled by the Forestry Branch, Department of Environment Affairs; *Otto's Walk*, trail booklet; *Royal Natal National Park*, pocket brochure; *The Self-guided Trails of the Natal Parks Board*, issued by the Natal Parks Board.
CLIMATE: The area receives 85 per cent of its rainfall between October and March; annual rainfall varies from 1 778 millimetres on the escarpment to 1 040 millimetres on the north-east boundary. Summer mornings are usually clear. Thunderstorms are common.

Adding to the dramatic beauty which makes the Drakensberg one of southern Africa's natural wonders is the Amphitheatre, an eight-kilometre stretch of the escarpment wall which gives an unobstructed view of the great range of altitude in this area (1 340 to 3 048 metres). Here, too, the Tugela Falls drop 850 metres in five clear leaps (with a main vertical section of 183 metres), the river eroding the escarpment edge.

Plant life in the park is particularly rich, and in the Natal Parks Board's booklet nine

HOLKRANS HIKING TRAIL

ROYAL NATAL NATIONAL PARK

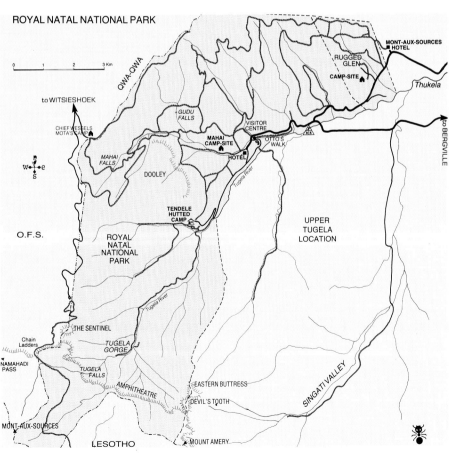

communities are detailed. Contributing to the floral wealth are a number of factors such as the large range in altitude with varied topography, high rainfall, and uninterrupted periods of stability which encourage the process of evolution.

Mammals most commonly observed are baboon, mountain reedbuck, black wildebeest, blesbok and dassies, while among the birds, black eagles, bearded vultures, Cape vultures and jackal buzzards can be seen.

Bushmen are believed to have survived in this region until 1878; their paintings remain in four major sites which are easily accessible and are described in the park's booklet.

Within this exciting area, 31 walking and horse-riding routes, ranging in length from three to 45 kilometres (a round-trip), are an open invitation to hikers of all fitness levels. The walks start from the hotel, campground or picnic site and some include short chain ladders to help the less agile over difficult places. It is worthwhile obtaining the Natal Parks Board's booklet on the Royal Natal National Park as it describes all the walks. I have included three to illustrate the diversity offered.

Otto's Walk

Beginning at the visitor centre, Otto's Walk is a three-kilometre, one-hour nature trail for which a very informative printed trail guide is available from a self-help box at the trailhead. This valuable educational guide provides an excellent introduction to the park by describing its ecological features,

emphasizing geological history, the forest and its inhabitants, and man's centuries-old association with the area.

Tugela Gorge

The spectacular scenery of the Tugela Gorge path deserves a full day devoted to it. Starting from the carpark near the entrance to Tendele Camp, the footpath is clearly signposted. The first section winds along the contours of the slope above the Tugela River, through yellowwood forested valleys and protea savannah. The path then merges with the river and boulder-hopping becomes necessary. I recommend a change from boots to jogging shoes to increase your agility. Farther up the gorge you have a choice of climbing a sturdy, man-made ladder up a rock face or wading through a wet tunnel. The tunnel is spectacular and worth negotiating, but in times of high water it is sensible to waterproof your gear. All along the path the surrounding scenery of the Amphitheatre and views of the Tugela Falls are superb.

Mont-aux-Sources

The climb up Mont-aux-Sources (3 282 m) can be accomplished in one very long day, but a one- or two-night hiking trip is more rewarding. If you have only a day, however, drive through Qwa-Qwa via Phuthaditjhaba (Witsieshoek) to the end of the mountain road. Permits are obtainable at the gate, about 10 kilometres from the end of the road. A hut is available for hikers. Bunkbeds are provided, but there are no other fa-

cilities. There is no charge and no advance bookings can be made.

A steep two-hour walk, with chain ladders (100 rungs) to ease the ascent, brings you to the summit. The longer, more exciting routes require rock-climbing or backpacking and camping out.

One suggestion is the 22,5-kilometre path (each way) leading from the end of the road in the Royal Natal National Park via the Mahai Falls trail. Once on top of the escarpment, a path with stunning mountain views leads to Mount Amery (3 143 m).

189. Upper Tugela Location

(SINGATI VALLEY AND
NTONJELANA-MNWENI-IFIDI
VALLEYS)
NORTHERN DRAKENSBERG

AUTHORITY-IN-CHARGE: Department of
Development Aid, P.O. Box 384, Pretoria
0001.
SIZE: 97 378 hectares.
MAIN ATTRACTIONS: The Saddle, Rockeries,
Mnweni Cutback and other prominent
escarpment buttresses and peaks; Mnweni
Needles (free-standing peaks); Orange River
source.
FACILITIES/AMENITIES: Caves provide the
only shelter, but hikers may find those at
lower altitudes inhabited by local tribesmen.
PERTINENT INFORMATION: Permission to
enter must be obtained from the Director-
General of the Department of Development
Aid. The Little 'Berg region has a fairly
large rural population and both the land and
the roads are in a poor state. Main access via
Bergville.
AVAILABLE LITERATURE: *Drakensberg North:
Mt. Aux Sources to Cathedral Peak*, map
number 1 by Peter Slingsby, Mapcape,
compiled by the Forestry Branch,
Department of Environment Affairs; the
scientific report *Towards a Plan for the
Tugela Basin*, E. Thorrington-Smith *et al*,
Natal Town and Regional Planning Report
No. 5, Pietermaritzburg, 1960; located on
Government Printer's 1:50 000 topographic
maps '2829 CC Cathedral Peak', '2828 DD
Mont-aux-Sources', '2828 DB Witsieshoek'
and '2829 CA Oliviershoek'.
CLIMATE: Summer rainfall area. Winters are
cold and dry.

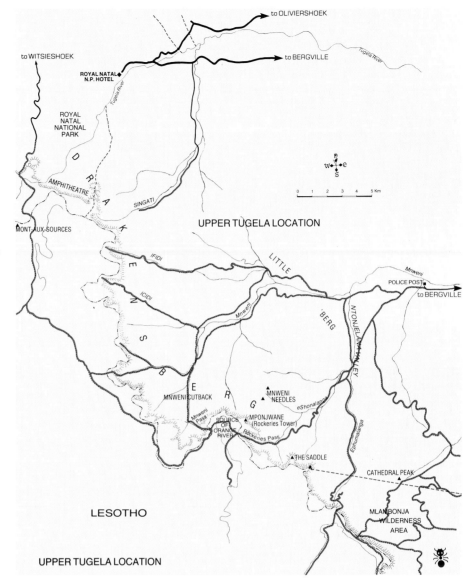

UPPER TUGELA LOCATION

This remote corner is noted for its myriad
impressive buttresses and spires, but while
these present fine challenges to the mountaineer and climber, the area is infrequently
traversed because of its inaccessibility and
lack of facilities. There are some cave shelters, but these cannot be relied on as the
chances are that most of them will be occupied by shepherds or local families. Tents,
therefore, are a prerequisite for those intent
on tackling this mountaineering zone.

Rambling in the lower reaches, the Little
'Berg, is not very rewarding as these parts
are relatively heavily populated, making it
difficult to achieve the sense of privacy so essential to a hiking experience. Furthermore,
and more seriously, the number of people
attempting to eke out an existence, coupled
with poor farming techniques – especially
overgrazing – and the denuding of the countryside for firewood, has led to considerable
erosion. This deteriorated ecology is a very
serious problem, especially because of the

region's importance as a major catchment
area. Not surprisingly, wildlife is scarce.
Beyond these rather barren foothills, however, any initial disappointment is more
than compensated for by the towering rock
faces of the main escarpment.

Several rough paths lead to the top. I suggest that you either follow the Mnweni Cutback, emerging at the source of the Orange
River, or take the Rockeries Pass, starting in
the Ntonjelana Valley and following the
eShonalanga tributary. Although these are
the easiest of the numerous ascents, both
take a full day from the Upper Tugela police
post.

The escarpment ascent is a walk – albeit
strenuous – and the traverse along its edge is

*Opposite page, top left: The krantzes of the
Amphitheatre at the head of the Tugela Gorge.*
Opposite page, top right: The Tugela River Valley.
*Opposite page, below: The descent from Mont-Aux-
Sources.*
Left: Autumn in the Mnweni Valley.

magnificent (see D. Dodd's *Cradle of Rivers* for a detailed route description). The free-standing peaks are a different proposition, however, and should remain the domain of experienced mountaineers. These sharply pointed spires, pinnacles, pillars, columns and other rocky projections are fine examples of the sculpturing forces of nature and are aptly described by the Zulu word *Mn-weni*, meaning 'the place of fingers'.

190. Cathedral Research Area and Mlambonja Wilderness Area

(CATHEDRAL PEAK NATURE RESERVE)
NORTHERN DRAKENSBERG

AUTHORITY-IN-CHARGE: Natal Forest Region, Forestry Branch, Department of Environment Affairs★.

MAIN ATTRACTIONS: Cathedral Peak, the Bell, Outer and Inner Horn and other prominent peaks; Organ Pipes Pass and Camel Ridge; the Little 'Berg (contour path); Mike's Pass (the only drive to the top of the Little 'Berg); Ndedema Gorge (natural forest and rock art); easily accessible region; extensive rock-climbing opportunities.

FACILITIES/AMENITIES: Cathedral Peak Hotel (commercial hotel with horses for hire); camp-site in the nature reserve; all-weather surface access road; picnic sites on Mike's Pass; Cathedral Peak Education Centre, a centre for environmental education run by the Department of National Education, accommodating 50 people in rondavels, with ablution facilities and kitchen.

PERTINENT INFORMATION: Relatively heavily used mountaineering/hiking region. Note: in 1982, the northern section of the nature reserve, approximately 6 000 hectares in extent, was proclaimed the Mlambonja Wilderness Area; the remainder of the area is now called the Cathedral Research Area. Permits necessary, obtainable from the forester; advance applications are preferred. During the winter fire season, the research area is closed to those members of the public who do not have special permission. Trailists are not permitted to stay overnight in caves which contain Bushman paintings, unless they are shown on the Mapcape map. The trail up Masongwane Valley is used for education; there are no restrictions on party size. Access via Winterton.

AVAILABLE LITERATURE: Well covered by general Natal Drakensberg references;

CATHEDRAL RESEARCH AREA AND MLAMBONJA WILDERNESS AREA MDEDELELO WILDERNESS AREA

Cathedral Peak worksheets and comprehensive teacher's guide, available from the Natal Education Department, Educational Field Studies section; *The Cathedral Area*, R.O. Pearse, 1:32 000 map, obtainable at Cathedral Peak Hotel and the Forestry Branch at Cathedral Peak, showing all walks; *Drakensberg North: Cathedral Peak to Injasuti*, map number 2 by Peter Slingsby, Mapcape, compiled by the Forestry Branch, Department of Environment Affairs.

The Cathedral Peak region stretches to the Mdedelelo Wilderness Area, also administered by the Forestry Branch. Because of its well-worn and accessible trails and the popular Cathedral Peak 'base hotel', this region is one of the prime mountaineering sections of the 'Berg.

Cathedral Peak (3 004 m), accessible via a path from the hotel, is a free-standing mountain. This full day's strenuous trek, including rock scrambling, is well worth the effort, as from the summit the panoramic view of the entire northern Drakensberg, from Mont-aux-Sources to Champagne Castle, is magnificent. Other prominent free-standing peaks of the Cathedral range include the Bell (2 930 m), the Inner Horn (3 005 m) and the Outer Horn (3 006 m), Chessmen (2 987 m), Mitre (3 023 m) and the Twins (2 899 m). Each requires at least 'C' scrambling skills or advanced rope climbing.

If you intend hiking to the escarpment, follow the Mlambonja River, starting at the hotel, or ascend Camel Ridge, which leads you to Cleft Peak (3 281 m).

A third alternative is via Organ Pipes Pass, an ascent I well recall. After a long,

hot trek through the Little 'Berg, we pitched camp on the contour path at the foot of the pass – a less-than-ideal site but nowhere around was better. The night was not restful – I was rudely awoken in the early hours by a rather aggressive herd of Basotho cattle and, still tired and sunburnt from the previous day, we began our steep hike up the escarpment. My discomfort was soon dispelled, however, by the sheer beauty of our surroundings and I felt guilty testing the echoing reputation of the numerous rock spires giving the pass its name – not wanting to disturb the silent world of some of the Drakensberg's most prominent and most photographed peaks. Beautiful as they undoubtedly are, they are equally uncompromising, a fact borne out by the number of climbing parties that have come to grief on the brooding rock faces.

'Classic' mountaineering traverses can be completed either on the escarpment, a scenically superb but strenuous trip lasting several days, or along the footpath of the Little 'Berg. The traverse on the Little 'Berg follows the 2 000-metre contour path, starting at the Cathedral Peak Hotel and ending two days (40 kilometres) later at the Injasuti Valley. This hike is easier than the escarpment traverse and enables you to appreciate the wildlife, Bushman art and the forested river valleys you pass *en route*. D. Dodds, in his book *Cradle of Rivers*, describes the way in detail.

Ramblers will find numerous short walks described in the hotel's brochure. The hotel itself is usually filled with exhausted climbers relating the hair-raising accounts of their first assaults on the famous free-standing peaks.

191. Mdedelelo Wilderness Area

(CATHKIN PEAK AREA)
NORTHERN DRAKENSBERG

AUTHORITY-IN-CHARGE: Natal Forest Region, Forestry Branch, Department of Environment Affairs★.
SIZE: 29 000 hectares (including Cathedral Peak State Forest).
MAIN ATTRACTIONS: Cathkin Peak (3 149 m), Monk's Cowl (3 234 m), Champagne Castle (3 378 m) and Intunja Mountain (2 408 m); Leslie's Pass and Nkosazana Cave; Bushman caves and paintings; wildlife; Little 'Berg contour path.
FACILITIES/AMENITIES: Forestry camp-site in Monk's Cowl State Forest; footpaths and bridle paths; hotels and private accommodation in the vicinity; Champagne Castle Hotel, closest hotel to the mountain (horses for hire and bridle paths); Dragon Peaks Park caravan complex (horses for hire, day rambles to the Sunken Forest and the Sphinx); Cathkin Park Lake Hotel (paths to Fern Forest, Grotto waterfalls and other sights); El Mirador (arranges hikes and horses for hire); The Nest (provides horse-riding); Mountain Splendour caravan and camp-site complex.
PERTINENT INFORMATION: Access via Winterton. Entrance by permit only. No fires permitted. Hikers may overnight only in those caves shown on the Mapcape map.
AVAILABLE LITERATURE: Covered in general

Opposite page: Hikers ascending the grasslands en route *to the plateau in Cathedral Peak Nature Reserve.*

Above: After a long, hard walk, hikers emerge at the top of Leslie's Pass.

Right: A freak Easter snowstorm surprised these (fortunately) well-prepared mountaineers in the Mdedelelo Wilderness Area in the northern Drakensberg.

references on the Natal Drakensberg; located on Government Printer's topographic maps '2829 CC Cathedral Peak', '2829 CD Zunckels', '2929 AB Champagne Castle' and '2929 AA Champagne Castle-West'; *Drakensberg North: Cathedral Peak to Injasuti*, map number 2 by Peter Slingsby, Mapcape, compiled by the Forestry Branch, Department of Environment Affairs.

Reflecting on my mountaineering adventures, I recall not only scenery and wildlife, but also the experiences I have in an area. Gray's Pass was my first confrontation in Africa with snow, and the Nkosazana Cave, near its summit, was my introduction to the enthusiastic, highly dependable and knowledgeable leaders of the MCSA, and their colleagues.

Starting off from the forestry office in brilliant Easter sunshine, clad in only a cotton shirt and shorts, I was totally unprepared for what lay ahead. Twenty kilometres farther on and 2 000 metres higher, after being near-blinded by wind-driven snowflakes, I was shivering uncontrollably and struggling to follow my companion's footprints which were moulded step-like into the rapidly forming deep drifts on the steep upper reaches of the pass.

The Nkosazana Cave, 'conveniently' situated just at the top of the pass – wet from drips and puddles as it was – and great quantities of hot soup and tea, saved me from the onslaught of hypothermia. Obviously none of the MCSA members thought there was anything unusual about the freak storm, neither did they struggle to reach the escarpment for, if they had, I doubt whether they would have been quite so high-spirited later that night!

The escarpment traverse was magnificent. Drakensberg mountaineers who never see the peaks and slopes blanketed with snow, glistening in the moonlight, miss one of the 'Berg's most elegant features. On an escarpment traverse, Ship's Prow to the south provides a relatively easy descent. I have also used Leslie's Pass in the Giant's Castle Area, which makes a five-day trip possible.

The free-standing peaks of this wilderness area, especially Cathkin and Monk's Cowl, are impressive landmarks and very difficult rock climbs – graded E (difficult to very difficult) through to G (very severe), with some routes requiring mechanical aids. Cathkin, named *Mdedelelo* by the Zulus, which means 'make room for him', implying a bully, is the peak after which the wilderness area is named. The most unusual peak is Intunja (2 408 m), meaning 'eye', a reference to the huge hole in its summit basalt. From Gray's Pass, non-rock climbers can ascend Champagne Castle (3 377 m), which is part of the main escarpment.

The contour path mentioned under the Cathedral Peak Nature Reserve (see page 176) traverses this wilderness area, ending at Injasuti Valley in the Giant's Castle Game Reserve. The southern boundary peak, 'Old Woman Grinding Corn' (2 986 m), separates the two reserves on the escarpment.

192. Spioenkop Public Resort Nature Reserve

WINTERTON

AUTHORITY-IN-CHARGE: Natal Parks Board.
SIZE: 4 562 hectares.
MAIN ATTRACTIONS: 400-hectare game park; historical areas; the Spioenkop Discovery Trail; aloes in bloom.
FACILITIES/AMENITIES: Educational programme including guided trail in game park and to battlefields; museum, launch tours and horse rides; Ntenjwa Bush Camp, four A-frame thatched structures accommodating 8 people altogether, with stretchers, sleeping bags, hot and cold showers, refrigerator, gas stove and cooking utensils; wildlife films shown during peak visiting periods; chalets, caravan and tent sites; picnic sites; watersports on dam, and land sports available.
PERTINENT INFORMATION: Take your own food and drink. The bush camp is a 10-km walk from the hutted camp.
AVAILABLE LITERATURE: *The Battle of Spioenkop*, booklet; *The Discovery Trail*, trail guide; *The Battle of Spioenkop*, trail guide in process of being compiled; *Spioenkop Public Resort*, pocket brochure; *Self-guided Trails of the Natal Parks Board*, pocket brochure (all issued by the Natal Parks Board).
CLIMATE: Summer rainfall area.

Spioenkop Public Resort Nature Reserve is a valuable environmental education work-study area, with ranger-naturalists and historians present to assist teachers who wish to use it as an outdoor classroom. Three guided trails are available at present, and these can be combined to form a programme lasting a day and a half.

The Spioenkop Discovery Trail is an overall introduction to the ecology of the region. It is really three trails in one. The first is marked with yellow arrows and is a two-hour educational walk. The second trail (3-4 hours) is marked with red arrows and extends trail one to include the shoreline of the Spioenkop Dam. The third and longest trail (the Aloe Trail), marked in green, extends 10 kilometres to the Ntenjwa Bush Camp.

The guided game trail offers rare, exciting opportunities to experience at close range large animals such as white rhino, black and blue wildebeest, kudu and eland. The history trail takes hikers to the battlefield of Spioenkop. If you are interested in Anglo-Boer War history, the museum, located near the resort's office, is worth a visit.

193. Giant's Castle Game Reserve

MOOI RIVER

AUTHORITY-IN-CHARGE: Natal Parks Board.
SIZE: 34 284 hectares.
MAIN ATTRACTIONS: Mountaineering, hiking, rambling, rock-climbing, ice-climbing and horse-riding; excellent wildlife and bird-watching area; 140 recorded bird species, including the lammergeyer (bearded vulture); stone bird hide from which cliff-dwelling species can be viewed; high concentration of Bushman rock art; brown and rainbow trout fishing, with licence and permit.
FACILITIES/AMENITIES: Fifty kilometres of trails (Bushman's River Trail, Skyline Trail, Hillside Forest Trail and Injasuti Valley

Trail are educational trails with interpretive brochures; the others are walks and hikes); horse-riding trails (two, three or four days, and morning rides) for which horses and riding equipment, sleeping bags, groundsheets, cooking and eating utensils, are provided; three mountain huts and three caves for hikers; two hutted base camps (Giant's Castle and Injasuti); one luxurious lodge accommodating seven people (Giant's Lodge); two camping areas; picnic sites.

PERTINENT INFORMATION: For prolonged school visits, camp-sites are available at the Hillside camping ground, adjoining the reserve; visitors must provide their own food and drink. Mountain huts and caves must be booked, and hikers are not permitted to stay overnight in caves containing Bushman paintings. Horse-riding trails: only accomplished riders are advised to apply; caves can be used for overnighting; no trails are run during July and August; trails depart from the Hillside camp; maximum of 8 people allowed per trail (minimum age 12 years); participants must supply their own food. Access via Estcourt and Mooi River.

AVAILABLE LITERATURE: *Walks of the Giant's Castle Game Reserve*, amended list of 20 walks with descriptions and durations, but no maps; *Giant's Castle Game Reserve*, trails booklet available from the Natal Parks Board; *Giant's Castle Game Reserve*, map showing paths, by J.C. Simpson, obtainable at the camp office; *Wilderness Trails*, available from the Natal Parks Board; *Drakensberg Central: Injasuti, Giant's Castle, Highmoor*, map number 3 by Peter Slingsby, Mapcape, compiled by the Forestry Branch, Department of Environment Affairs; *Giant's Castle Game Reserve*, AA Bulletin TBE-N1; good coverage in all books and brochures pertaining to the Natal Drakensberg.

CLIMATE: Summer rainfall area. Cold winters, snow possible.

First impressions are very often the most lasting . . . and certainly this generalization is accurate regarding my introduction to the Giant's Castle Game Reserve. When I visited the 'main caves' in the reserve, the clear visual evidence of the everyday lives and the culture of the Bushmen who, until the mid-1800s, had lived there continuously for many centuries, left an indelible impression on me. It was this experience that has greatly enhanced my appreciation of all the Bushman art and caves I have subsequently visited while hiking throughout southern Africa. Today, the 'main caves', together with taped information and a life-sized display, are part of the Bushman's River Trail, a self-guided, three-kilometre nature walk. This two-hour stroll, in conjunction with its booklet, provides an excellent introduction

Opposite page: Ship's Prow Pass, a relatively easy descent on an escarpment traverse.

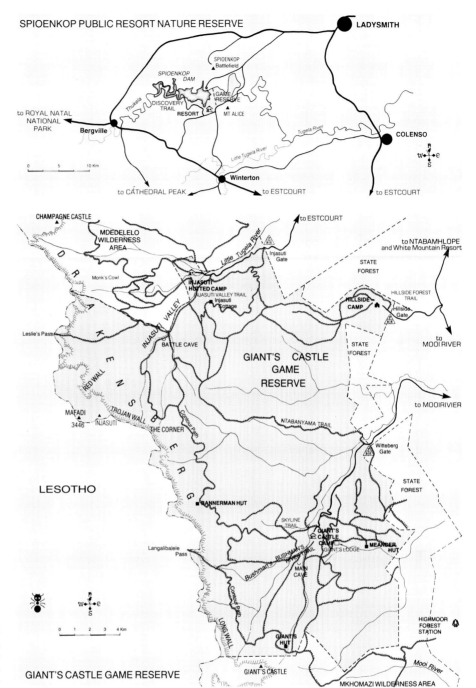

to the geology, vegetation and history of the Giant's Castle Game Reserve.

The Natal Parks Board has recently added three new and valuable educational walks to this reserve: the Skyline Trail, which is a 10-kilometre walk starting one kilometre from the camp office; the Hillside Forest Trail, a two-hour walk through one of the few remaining high-altitude forests in the Natal Drakensberg; and the Injasuti Valley Trail, a six-hour walk through the Injasuti Valley, with its dense indigenous forests, rich in berg hard pear (mountain olinia) and yellowwoods, and with its tree ferns growing alongside cascading mountain waters. On these walks you learn many fascinating facets of ecology, such as why the ants on the

trail are named 'cocktail ants', why soils differ in colour, where the birth control pill originates, how ghost frogs climb waterfalls, which Giant's Castle plant is used during theatrical shows, the origin of ox-bow lakes, who lives in 'Old Man's Beard', and the astonishing fact that man has polluted 99 per cent of the earth's fresh water.

In addition to the self-guided trails, there is an array of further walking and hiking opportunities in the reserve. For example, a round-trip of 30 kilometres (a full day's excursion from the camp office) will take you to Giant's Castle Peak (3 314 m). Another 30-kilometre route follows a high-level (2 300-2 400 metres) contour path running below and along the escarpment, on which

the Giant's Castle and Bannerman huts are situated.

Injasuti Dome, at 3 409 metres the second-highest point in South Africa, can, depending on the route, be negotiated with or without ropes. Furthermore, mountaineers can ascend the escarpment summit via several passes (not easy!) and then explore three long unbroken rock walls – the Red, Trojan and Long walls.

Irwin, in his *Field Guide to the Natal Drakensberg*, considers the Giant's Castle region to be the best area in the Drakensberg for game- and bird-watching. It is a well-founded opinion and visitors to the reserve are likely to see eland, grey rhebok, oribi, mountain reedbuck, black wildebeest and blesbok – in fact, most of the wildlife present in the Drakensberg occurs in the Giant's Castle Game Reserve. The interesting bird-life includes the black stork, and the predatory black and martial eagles, lanner falcon and lammergeyer.

194. Kamberg, Loteni and Vergelegen Nature Reserves

SOUTHERN AND CENTRAL DRAKENSBERG

AUTHORITY-IN-CHARGE: Natal Parks Board.
SIZE: Kamberg: 2 232 hectares. Loteni: 3 984 hectares. Vergelegen: 1 159 hectares.
MAIN ATTRACTIONS: Rainbow and brown trout fishing; self-guided trails, including trail for the physically handicapped in Kamberg Nature Reserve; rambling, swimming and horse-riding; large game animals.
FACILITIES/AMENITIES: Kamberg: The Mooi

River self-guided trail; hutted camp with five 2-bed bungalows, a 6-bed cottage, a farmhouse accommodating 10 people, picnic site, trout hatchery and trout fishing.
Loteni: The Eagle self-guided trail; hutted camp with 12 bungalows, 2 self-contained cottages, rustic cottage accommodating 10 people, camp-site, Settler's Homestead Museum and picnic site. Vergelegen: camp with two 5-bed self-contained cottages.
PERTINENT INFORMATION: 1 September to 30 April is trout season (fishermen need both a provincial angling licence and a daily angling permit). Take your own food and drink. Permits are necessary to walk in the adjoining forestry reserves. Booking for camp-site at Loteni: The Camp Superintendent, Loteni Nature Reserve, P.O. Box 14, Himeville 4585. Road to Vergelegen subject to flooding from December to February.
AVAILABLE LITERATURE: *Walks and Climbs*

of Kamberg Nature Reserve, description of seven walks with map, issued by the Natal Parks Board; *Mooi River Trail, Kamberg Nature Reserve*, trail guide; *The Eagle Trail (Loteni Nature Reserve)*, trail guide; *Kamberg Nature Reserve, Loteni Nature Reserve* and *Vergelegen Nature Reserve*, pocket brochures; *Settler's Homestead Museum*, booklet; *Drakensberg South: Vergelegen, Cobham, Garden Castle*, map number 5, and *Drakensberg Central: Highmoor, Mkhomazi, Loteni*, map number 4 by Peter Slingsby, Mapcape, compiled by the Forestry Branch, Department of Environment Affairs; *Some Natal Game and Nature Reserves*, AA Bulletin TBE-N7.
CLIMATE: Summer rainfall area.

In the foothills of the Drakensberg, the Little 'Berg, these three pleasant nature reserves attract trout fishermen, nature ramblers, solitude-seekers and naturalists. I

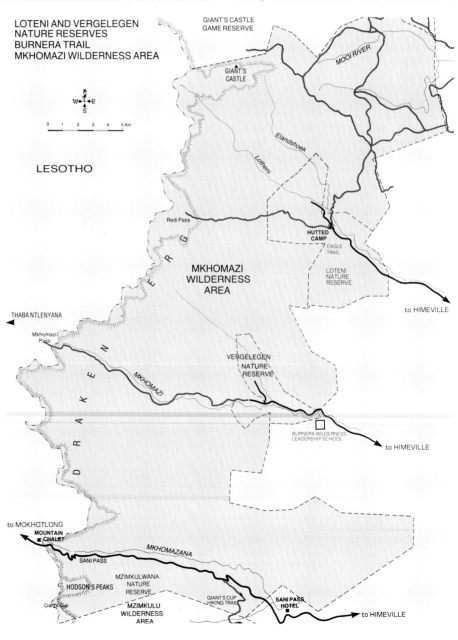

LOTENI AND VERGELEGEN
NATURE RESERVES
BURNERA TRAIL
MKHOMAZI WILDERNESS AREA

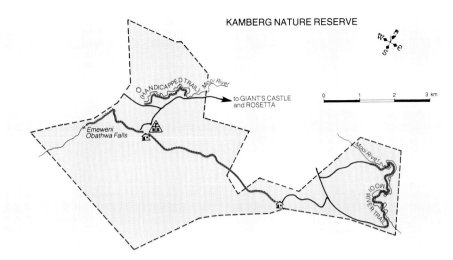

KAMBERG NATURE RESERVE

Emeweni
Obathwa Falls

(HANDICAPPED TRAIL) Mooi River

to GIANT'S CASTLE
and ROSETTA

Mooi River

MOOI RIVER TRAIL

0   1   2   3 km

spent days enjoying the rivers and streams, studying the birds, searching for antelope and admiring the backdrop of the sensational high peaks of the great Drakensberg. From Vergelegen Nature Reserve, Thaba Ntlenyana (3 482 m), the highest mountain in southern Africa, is visible.

The four-kilometre Mooi River self-guided trail in the Kamberg Nature Reserve consists of the main trail as well as three one-kilometre loops, each taking approximately two hours to complete. It is one of the few trails in southern Africa planned for the physically handicapped: the trail is level and firm, so that it can be easily negotiated by those in wheelchairs.

The newer 12-kilometre circular Eagle Trail in Loteni helps to focus the walker's attention on human history, as well as the geological, botanical and ecological processes working in the reserve. It offers magnificent views of the Drakensberg and should be allocated six hours to be fully appreciated.

195. Burnera Trail

HIMEVILLE

AUTHORITY-IN-CHARGE: Wilderness Leadership School.
DURATION: Two-day (weekend) guided trail.
MAIN ATTRACTIONS: Little 'Berg ecology.
FACILITIES/AMENITIES: Accommodation in old farmhouse; transport, food and all equipment, except sleeping bags and daypacks, provided.
PERTINENT INFORMATION: Maximum of 9 people per group. Burnera Wilderness Leadership School borders the Vergelegen Nature Reserve (Natal Parks Board).
AVAILABLE LITERATURE: *Wilderness Trails: Wilderness Leadership School*, brochure.
CLIMATE: Summer rainfall area.

Opposite page: Descent to Giant's Castle Reserve.

196. Loteni Hiking Trail

KWAMEHLENYATI NATURE RESERVE, MKHOMAZI STATE FOREST, NEAR LOTENI

AUTHORITY-IN-CHARGE: Natal Forest Region, Forestry Branch, Department of Environment Affairs★.
LENGTH/DURATION: 15 km one way/2 days, 1 night.
MAIN ATTRACTIONS: Beautiful scenery ranging from forest to grassland, and protea grassveld; prominent rock formations including the sandstone cliff along Surprise Ridge; good views of Giant's Castle Peak; wildlife, including eland, baboon and mountain reedbuck; birdlife; flora.
FACILITIES/AMENITIES: Two huts, one at each end of the trail.
PERTINENT INFORMATION: This trail is proposed but not opened as of 1987. Huts are planned. The name of the trail may be changed.
AVAILABLE LITERATURE: Planned; *Drakensberg Central: Highmoor, Mkhomazi,*

Loteni, map number 4 by Peter Slingsby, Mapcape, compiled by the Forestry Branch, Department of Environment Affairs (shows trail area but not trail itself).
CLIMATE: Summer rainfall area.

197. Mkhomazi and Mzimkulu Wilderness Areas and Mzimkulwana Nature Reserve

SOUTHERN DRAKENSBERG, see also map page 182

AUTHORITY-IN-CHARGE: Natal Forest Region, Forestry Branch, Department of Environment Affairs★.
SIZE: Mkhomazi: 54 000 hectares. Mzimkulu: 28 340 hectares. Mzimkulwana: 22 751 hectares.
MAIN ATTRACTIONS: Rugged mountain scenery; Sani Pass; Rhino's Horn; Hodgson's Peaks; skiing.
FACILITIES/AMENITIES: Mountain chalet at the top of Sani Pass; hotels in the foothills (Sani Pass Hotel, Drakensberg Gardens Hotel, Bushman's Nek Hotel).
PERTINENT INFORMATION: Permits necessary, obtainable (for a maximum of 10 people per party) from The State Forester, Mkhomazi Wilderness Area, P.O. Himeville 4585; for Mzimkulu and Mzimkulwana, apply to The State Forester, Cobham, P.O. Himeville 4585, in advance, or collect your permit at the entry gates between 07h00 and 17h00 (open until 22h00 on Fridays). No fires allowed. Hikers may stay overnight only in those caves marked on the Mapcape map.
AVAILABLE LITERATURE: *Drakensberg South: Vergelegen, Cobham, Garden Castle* and *Drakensberg Central: Highmoor, Mkhomazi,*

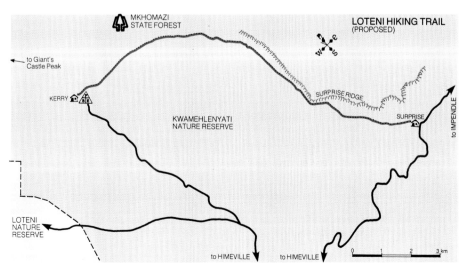

MKHOMAZI
STATE FOREST

LOTENI HIKING TRAIL
(PROPOSED)

to Giant's
Castle Peak

KERRY

KWAMEHLENYATI
NATURE RESERVE

SURPRISE RIDGE

SURPRISE

to IMPENDLE

LOTENI
NATURE
RESERVE

to HIMEVILLE   to HIMEVILLE

0   1   2   3 km

Loteni, map numbers 5 and 4 by Peter Slingsby, Mapcape, compiled by the Forestry Branch, Department of Environment Affairs.
CLIMATE: Summer rainfall area.

My feelings for this region are probably best expressed in the following excerpt from a 'Report on the Drakensberg Hike', written for the then-Directorate of Forestry soon after my arrival in South Africa in 1975.

'It is extremely difficult to relate the experience of such a hike in writing, as it incorporates a total involvement of the mind, the body and the soul. Geomorphological forces create a landscape of stark columnar basalt extrusions over sandstone in a most forbidding manner; the wind blows fiercely through narrow passes; water tumbles down cliffs as waterfalls converge into rivers; and whitenecked ravens scold at the unusual invasion of their formidable domain. The weather changes quickly and unexpectedly, and one's body shifts from perspiring and burning under the intense rays of the sun, to shivering under the shade of the clouds, to feeling the pain of hail and the discomfort of heavy rains – all of which can be experienced within the same afternoon. To an American such as myself, who has spent the majority of her hiking experiences in glaciated landscapes of the northern temperate, boreal and arctic country, the steep, V-shaped valleys, the lack of cirque lakes, and the sight of Basotho cloaked in robes, armed with primitive hunting weapons and accompanied by dogs is, in itself, an adventure comparable to none.'

The Mkhomazi Wilderness Area is bordered in the north by Giant's Castle Game Reserve (see page 178) and in the south by the Sani Pass. Within the Little 'Berg section of this area lie the Natal Parks Board's reserves, Loteni and Vergelegen, which are described on page 180. The Mzimkulu Wilderness Area and the Mzimkulwana Nature Reserve stretch southwards from Sani Pass to Bushman's Nek.

The most conspicuous peak of the region is Rhino's Horn (3 051 m), which protrudes from the escarpment. It can be walked via Mashai Pass, but more skilled mountaineers will find Rhino's E-F grade climbs very challenging. Rising from the escarpment to the south of the top of the pass are Hodgson's Peaks (3 244 m and 3 256 m). Both can also be ascended by walking.

Hikers in the region are likely to come across the cairn, dating from the mid-1800s, which marks the grave of Thomas Hodgson. At that time the southern Drakensberg was the scene of a bitter, drawn-out struggle between white pastoralists and Bushmen who reacted to the diminution of their hunting grounds by rustling the farmers' livestock. It was during one of the many skirmishes of these times that Hodgson, a farmer, was accidentally shot by one of his comrades.

The wilderness areas of the southern Drakensberg are not as well known as the northern region; paths are few and far between, the country appears wilder, the scenery more rugged and even the Little 'Berg seems more spectacular. It is a vast and remote region – a true wilderness with countless challenges for the really ambitious backpacker. This rugged region also boasts southern Africa's highest mountain, Thaba Ntlenyana (3 482 m, in Lesotho), and the highest motor road, the Sani Pass (2 877 m).

Tracing the upper valley of the Mkomazana River, the incredible Sani Pass follows a 20-kilometre tortuous route from the luxurious Sani Pass Hotel at its foot to the Drakensberg escarpment, and continues for 50 kilometres into the Black Mountains to the remote village of Mokhotlong, 'the place of the baldheaded ibis'. The pass is regularly travelled by Basotho horsemen leading pack mules and donkeys laden with trade goods. And the only alternative to walking or riding is a four-wheel drive vehicle or trail bike, for the route up into the mountains, which is flanked by precipitous cliffs, river cascades, gorges and caves, is far beyond the capabilities of the ordinary motor car. After driving the entire pass in a Land Rover, often reversing several times at the many steep hairpin turns and manoeuvring around pack animals and hikers, I was not sure whether to marvel at the incredible track, the mechanics of the Land Rover, or the spectacular scenery. At the top of the escarpment (2 900 m) is a shack, licensed to sell liquor, where mountaineers can find accommodation. During winter, snows frequently lie deep and make the added effort of taking skis well worthwhile. But whatever the season, don't forget your money, passport and vaccination certificate, as the head of the Sani Pass marks the border between South Africa and Lesotho.

If you wish to enjoy this region without having to climb laden with heavy packs, hike the Giant's Cup section of the Drakensberg Hiking Trail. This hiking trail begins at the foot of the Sani Pass and extends to Bushman's Nek, traversing the easier gradients of the 'Berg's foothills *en route*.

MZIMKULU WILDERNESS AREA
MZIMKULWANA NATURE RESERVE
DRAKENSBERG HIKING TRAIL,
GIANT'S CUP SECTION

198. Drakensberg Hiking Trail, Giant's Cup Section

SOUTHERN DRAKENSBERG

AUTHORITY-IN-CHARGE: Natal Forest Region, Forestry Branch, Department of Environment Affairs★.
LENGTH/DURATION: 68 km/5 days (2-, 3- or 4-day variations are possible).
MAIN ATTRACTIONS: Historical areas and interesting caves; rock pools for swimming; 135 species of birds; flowering plants; fishing for rainbow and brown trout.
FACILITIES/AMENITIES: Five huts, each accommodating 30 people, with bunks, mattresses, tables and benches.
PERTINENT INFORMATION: Camp-stoves are essential; fires are allowed at two huts only. Parking available at Pholela, Swiman and Bushman's Nek. Note: the environmentally based land-use plan operating in the Natal Drakensberg concentrates hiking in the trail zone, a belt ranging in altitude from approximately 1 770 metres to 1 970 metres, which includes the region of open grassland, wooded protea savannah and forest growing on soils derived from the Upper Beaufort Series of the Karoo System; above the trail zone, in the 'Wilderness Heart Zone', mountaineering and more strenuous hiking is available.
AVAILABLE LITERATURE: *Drakensberg Hiking Trail, Giant's Cup*, comprehensive brochure and map; *Drakensberg South: Vergelegen, Cobham, Garden Castle* and *Drakensberg South: Garden Castle, Boesmansnek, Sehlabathebe*, map numbers 5 and 6 by Peter Slingsby, Mapcape, compiled by the Forestry Branch, Department of Environment Affairs.
CLIMATE: Usually unpredictable.

When you think of hiking in the Drakensberg, you immediately conjure up images of a very difficult trail full of ascents on steep passes. However, the Giant's Cup section of the Drakensberg Hiking Trail is nowhere near as formidable.

Starting on the Sani Pass road, near the Sani Pass Hotel (Sani Pass is the highest pass in South Africa), the Giant's Cup trail heads south to Bushman's Nek, a Lesotho/South African border post. Because the gradient remains flat to gentle the entire way, with only a few short, steep sections, and because all five days are less than 14 kilometres each, this trail is one of the physically easier hikes in the NHWS. This was done purposely in order to allow those less fit and less adventurous than the 'Drakensberg mountaineer' an opportunity to experience this lovely natural area. Besides the rugged mountain backdrop with views of famous peaks such

COLEFORD NATURE RESERVE
HOWICK TOWN TRAIL
DOREEN CLARK NATURE RESERVE
AMATIKULU NATURE RESERVE
OCEAN VIEW GAME PARK
MVUBE TRAIL
MAPELANE NATURE RESERVE
UBIZANE GAME RANCH

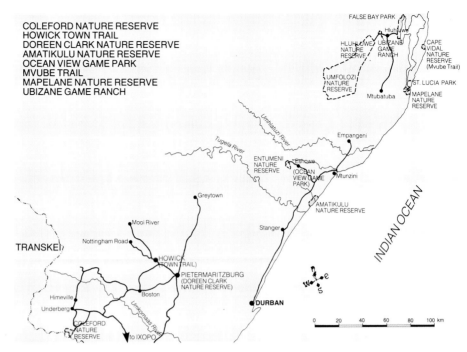

as Hodgson's (3 244 m and 3 256 m), Rhino's Horn (3 051 m), Wilson's (3 276 m) and Devil's Knuckles (3 028 m), a wide variety of plants and animals make this a fascinating section of the Natal Drakensberg.

Proteas bloom in February and March, while other plants flower at various times throughout the year. Trees are labelled with their national tree list numbers. Among the variety of wildlife found in this area, eland, bushbuck, grey duiker, oribi, common and mountain reedbuck, grey rhebok, water mongoose, the bearded vulture, black and martial eagles and the secretarybird are the most commonly seen.

199. Coleford Nature Reserve

UNDERBERG

AUTHORITY-IN-CHARGE: Natal Parks Board.
SIZE: 1 272 hectares.
MAIN ATTRACTIONS: Black wildebeest, blesbok and red hartebeest; antelope enclosures.
FACILITIES/AMENITIES: Hutted camp with six rest huts, five bungalows, two 3-bed cottages, a communal lodge, kitchens and ablution block; rainbow trout fishing; nature trails; guided horse trail through antelope enclosure with game guide (three-hour morning ride, one-hour afternoon ride); horses for hire.
PERTINENT INFORMATION: Bring your own food and drink.
AVAILABLE LITERATURE: *Coleford Nature Reserve*, pocket brochure.
CLIMATE: Summer rainfall area.

200. Mount Currie Nature Reserve

KOKSTAD

AUTHORITY-IN-CHARGE: Natal Parks Board.
SIZE: 1 541 hectares.
MAIN ATTRACTIONS: Grey rhebok, mountain reedbuck and other species; national monument (Adam Kok laager site, and cemeteries).
FACILITIES/AMENITIES: Old cattle tracks and paths can be used by ramblers until new paths are constructed; camping site with hot and cold water; picnic sites; Crystal Dam, stocked with trout, bass and bluegill.
PERTINENT INFORMATION: This is a developing reserve. For bookings: The Officer-in-Charge, Mount Currie Nature Reserve, P.O. Box 378, Kokstad 4700; tel. (0372) 3844 during office hours. Fishing is allowed, with a licence and permit. Open sunrise to sunset.
AVAILABLE LITERATURE: *Mount Currie Nature Reserve*, pocket brochure.
CLIMATE: Summer rainfall area.

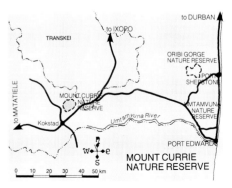

MOUNT CURRIE NATURE RESERVE

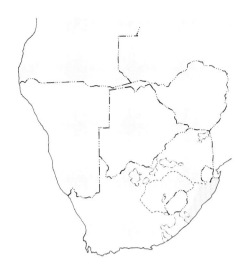

NATAL AND KWAZULU

Natal, or the Garden Province, which also incorporates the territory under the government of the KwaZulu homeland, stretches from the northern border of Transkei to the southern border of Swaziland and Mozambique, bounded on the west by Lesotho, the Orange Free State and the Transvaal and on the east by the Indian Ocean.

Although Natal is South Africa's smallest province, its diversity of trailing opportunities is immense, and the quality of environmental education-type trails and interpretive centres is commendable. This province attracts mountaineers to the high Drakensberg; naturalists who concentrate on wilderness trails in game reserves and self-guided trails and historic routes in the Natal midlands; and seaside ramblers who love roaming the coast and its estuaries with their forested sand dunes and prolific waterbird populations. (No visas are required for entry into KwaZulu.)

Climate varies dramatically with altitude and terrain throughout Natal. In general, Natal and KwaZulu are subtropical. The coast in summer is hot and humid, but tempered by sea breezes. The inland summer heat is tempered by altitude. In winter, the coast is mild to warm which contrasts with the very cold and often snow-capped 3 000 metre-high Drakensberg.

ECOLOGICAL ZONES: EASTERN GRASSLANDS, DRAKENSBERG, COASTAL BUSH AND SUBTROPICAL FOREST

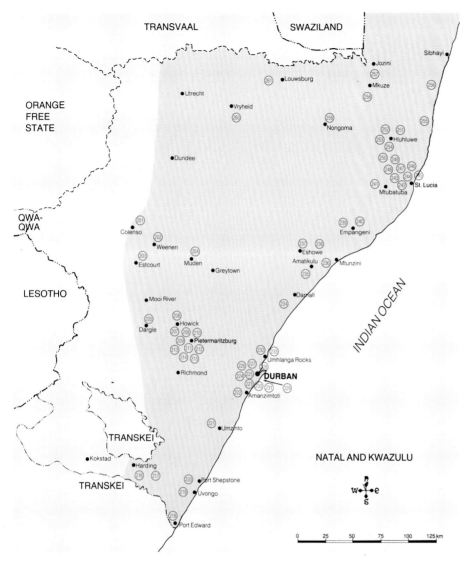

TRANSVAAL

SWAZILAND

Sibhayi

ORANGE
FREE
STATE

● Utrecht
(261) ● Louwsburg
● Jozini
(257)
● Mkuze
(256)
(258)

● Vryheid
(260)
(255)

QWA-
QWA

● Nongoma
(259)
(252) (251)
(253) ● Hluhluwe
(254)
(250) (249)
(248) (247) (246)
(243) (244)
(241) (242) ● St. Lucia
● Mtubatuba

Colenso ●
(201)
(202)
● Weenen
(203)
● Estcourt
(204)
● Muden
(239) (240)
● Empangeni
(237) (238)
● Eshowe
Amatikulu ●
(236) ● Mtunzini
(235)

LESOTHO

● Dundee

● Greytown

INDIAN OCEAN

● Mooi River
(234) ● Darnall

(205)
Dargle ●
(206)
● Howick
(207) (208) (210)
(209) ● Pietermaritzburg
(213) (211) (212)
(214) (215)
(232) (233)
Umhlanga Rocks
(226) (225)
● Richmond
(223) (231) ● DURBAN
(222) (230)
● Amanzimtoti

NATAL AND KWAZULU

(221) ● Umzinto

TRANSKEI

● Kokstad
● Harding
(216) (217)
(220) ● Port Shepstone
(219) ● Uvongo
TRANSKEI

● Port Edward
(218)

0 25 50 75 100 125 km

W N E S

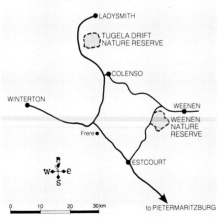

TUGELA DRIFT NATURE RESERVE
WEENEN NATURE RESERVE

● LADYSMITH
TUGELA DRIFT
NATURE RESERVE
● COLENSO
WINTERTON ●
WEENEN ●
WEENEN
NATURE
RESERVE
Frere ●
● ESTCOURT
W N E S
0 10 20 30km
to PIETERMARITZBURG

Opposite page: The zebra, a member of the horse family, is restricted to Africa, inhabiting plains and savannahs, and sometimes mountainous areas. It is a regular drinker and is seldom found at any great distance from water. Look out for its distinctive stripes in Natal's nature reserves.

---

to numbered stops along the trail and graphic displays, not only interprets but brings to life the military engagements that took place in the area.

202. Weenen Nature Reserve

WEENEN

AUTHORITY-IN-CHARGE: Natal Parks Board.
SIZE: 3 661 hectares.
MAIN ATTRACTIONS: Large mammals; 100 species of birds.
FACILITIES/AMENITIES: Two self-guided trails; caravan and camping sites; bush camp; curio shop; picnic sites with braais; bass and bream fishing in two dams.
PERTINENT INFORMATION: For booking camping and caravan sites: The Officer-in-Charge, Weenen Nature Reserve, P.O. Box 122, Weenen 3325.
AVAILABLE LITERATURE: Trail guides.
CLIMATE: Summer rainfall area.

Located in the Natal midlands, the undulating Weenen Nature Reserve is covered in thornveld, excellent habitat for the larger introduced game species such as white and black rhino, red hartebeest, giraffe, kudu, eland, common and mountain reedbuck, zebra, bushbuck, grey duiker and steenbok.

Two educational walks, the three-hour Amanzimyama Trail and the Reclamation Trail, concentrate on anti-erosion work and damaged veld reclamation. Considering that 30 years ago the whole reserve was barren, and that it now supports a healthy big-game population, you can appreciate the hard labour and time devoted to this remarkable veld recovery programme.

203. Old Furrow Trail

MOOR PARK NATURE RESERVE, ESTCOURT

AUTHORITY-IN-CHARGE: Natal Parks Board.
SIZE: 264 hectares.
MAIN ATTRACTIONS: Acacia thornveld; angling, especially for scaly fish; reintroduced large antelope and other game animals.
FACILITIES/AMENITIES: Self-guided trail; picnic site; education centre with 80 beds.
PERTINENT INFORMATION: Moor Park Nature Reserve and the adjacent Wagendrift Public Resort Nature Reserve form a major environmental education area. Talks by Natal Parks Board officials can be arranged.
AVAILABLE LITERATURE: Old Furrow Trail, trail booklet; Teacher's Information Pamphlet

201. Tugela Drift Nature Reserve

COLENSO

AUTHORITY-IN-CHARGE: Natal Parks Board.
SIZE: 98 hectares.
MAIN ATTRACTIONS: Louis Botha Trail; Boer military history and Colenso battlefields; views of the Tugela River.
FACILITIES/AMENITIES: Self-guided trail; picnic site.
PERTINENT INFORMATION: Day use only.
AVAILABLE LITERATURE: *Natal Parks Board: Tugela Drift Nature Reserve: Louis Botha Trail*, trail guide.
CLIMATE: Summer rainfall area.

History buffs will enjoy the relatively short Louis Botha Trail, laid out in a battleground of the Second Anglo-Boer War and named after the general who commanded the Boer troops in this area. The lively commentary of the Natal Parks Board trail guide, linked

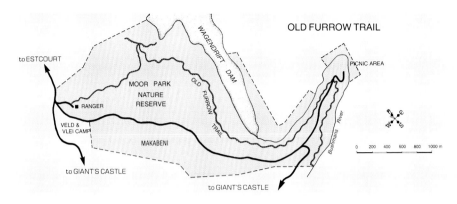

OLD FURROW TRAIL

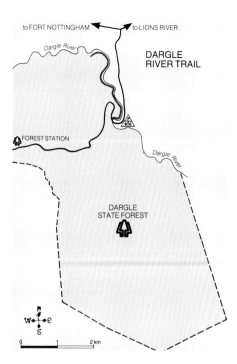

DARGLE RIVER TRAIL

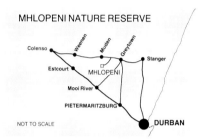

MHLOPENI NATURE RESERVE

No. 1; The Self-guided Trails of the Natal Parks Board, general information pocket brochure (all issued by the Natal Parks Board).
CLIMATE: Summer rainfall area.

The Old Furrow self-guided trail is a short, easy walk and is particularly suited to school groups. The ramble runs parallel to an old furrow irrigation system laid over a century ago by the Moor family, who also donated these lands to the Natal Parks Board for preservation as a nature reserve.

Interpretive displays are strategically placed along the route, while the trail booklet describes aspects of the park's environment and history, emphasizing vegetation, tree types and the ecology of the Bushman's River.

204. Mhlopeni Nature Reserve

MUDEN

AUTHORITY-IN-CHARGE: Mr R. Alcock, Mhlopeni Nature Reserve, P.O. Box 386, Greytown 3500; tel. (03346) 722.
SIZE: 807 hectares.
MAIN ATTRACTIONS: Iron and Stone Age sites with artefacts; a variety of game, including zebra, blesbok, impala, bushbuck, duiker, mountain reedbuck and oribi; education centre and museum;

historical trails and sites, including Zulu kraals of Boer War vintage.
FACILITIES/AMENITIES: Accommodation in thatched huts and rondavels: Nshozi, with two large rondavels accommodating up to 8 people; Umvumvu, camp for up to 12 people; Mphafa, with two smaller huts accommodating up to 4 people; Inkonka, a school camp for up to 40 children, with field education centre. All camps have hot water, showers, toilets, fully equipped kitchens and 'bomas' with braai areas. Picnic sites for day visitors.
AVAILABLE LITERATURE: Newsletters and brochures available on request, including *Mhlopeni Nature Reserve, a Reserve for Nature Lovers*.
CLIMATE: Summer rainfall area.

In the early 'seventies Mhlopeni was a desolate valley eroded to red sands and occupied by squatters. A project to save the region and return it to the 'peaceful valley of white rocks' of its Zulu name was undertaken by SACCAP (the South African Council for Conservation and Anti-Pollution) with the encouragement of the Natal Parks Board. Their diligent attention to rehabilitation has been amply rewarded – schemes such as grass habitat management, a reservoir complex, wildlife reintroductions, and the installation of an anti-poacher unit have transformed the valley into a valuable natural area and educational facility.

There are trails all over the reserve, and visitors can wander at will enjoying game-viewing, bird-watching and the fauna and flora of the rugged terrain. People from all walks of life and of all ages visit Mhlopeni, as do school and university groups, which are offered lectures on conservation, backed by physical participation. In projects such as donga reclamation, erecting fences, eradica-

tion of noxious weeds, etc., a trophy is awarded annually to the school that does the most work in the restoration of the environment.

On the mountain trails, activities include game-viewing and swimming in the natural potholes eroded from the solid white rocks. Flora includes a wealth of aloes, euphorbias, white stinkwood and many varieties of thornbush. If you are vigilant, you may find some Iron and Stone Age artefacts.

Mhlopeni is owned by devoted private conservationists. The warden conducts guided tours to various areas of interest, including climbs to the nest of a black eagle (where the hide is a mere three metres from the nest itself), the Iron and Stone Age sites, and the wagon trails.

205. Dargle River Trail

DARGLE

AUTHORITY-IN-CHARGE: Natal Forest Region, Forestry Branch, Department of Environment Affairs★.
LENGTH: 6 km round-trip.
MAIN ATTRACTIONS: Swimming and fishing; beautiful scenery; variety of birdlife; bushbuck and duiker.
FACILITIES/AMENITIES: Picnic site at start of trail.
PERTINENT INFORMATION: The Dargle River Trail was opened in November 1986.
AVAILABLE LITERATURE: Located on Government Printer's 1:50 000 topographic map '2930 CA Merrivale'.
CLIMATE: Summer rainfall area.

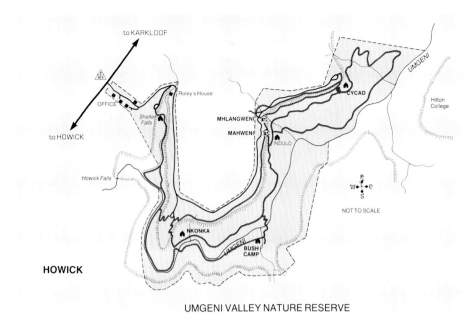

UMGENI VALLEY NATURE RESERVE

206. *Umgeni Valley Nature Reserve*

HOWICK

AUTHORITIES-IN-CHARGE: Wildlife Society of Southern Africa (Natal Branch); Umgeni Valley Project, P.O. Box 394, Howick 3290, tel. (03321) 393.
SIZE: 656 hectares.
MAIN ATTRACTIONS: Scenic walks through varied terrain; large and small mammals; over 200 species of birds.
FACILITIES/AMENITIES: Environmental education centre where intensive courses are run regularly for a wide variety of groups, from pre-primary to tertiary; facilities are also open to self-guided groups or individuals; casual day visitors are welcomed; rustic camps consisting of two or more bungalows, with kitchen, showers, flush toilet and firewood; guest cottage equipped with beds, linen, towels, crockery, cutlery, gas, fireplace and firewood; holiday trails are run on a regular basis, and include the Wild Coast hike, cycling trails and a canoeing course.
PERTINENT INFORMATION: Access to hutted camps is by foot, about 25 minutes' walk from the carpark. Ticks are prevalent at certain times of the year.

Right: The magnificent Howick Falls, which plunge 111 metres over dolerite rock into the gorge, feature in the Umgeni Valley Nature Reserve and on the Howick Town Trail.

Opposite page: You can enjoy sailing, water-skiing, canoeing and power-boating on Lake Midmar in the Midmar Public Resort Nature Reserve, while for the more sedentary, angling is permitted.

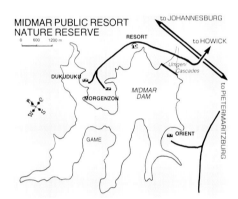

MIDMAR PUBLIC RESORT NATURE RESERVE

AVAILABLE LITERATURE: *Umgeni Valley Project Prospectus*, booklet and map; *A Guide to Umgeni*, brochure.
CLIMATE: Summer rainfall area.

The Umgeni Valley Nature Reserve is important as it is one of South Africa's few 'outdoor' education centres where intensive environmental courses are run by experienced field officers, most of whom are qualified teachers. The setting is ideal – located only 30 kilometres from Pietermaritzburg and close to Howick, the reserve borders 10 kilometres of the Umgeni River, immediately below the scenic Howick Falls which plunge 111 metres over dolerite cliffs into the gorge.

Habitats are diverse, ranging from regions of bushveld harbouring big game such as zebra, wildebeest, nyala, impala, eland, bushbuck and grey duiker, to cliffs topped by grassland plateaux hosting blesbok, mountain reedbuck and oribi. Birdlife ranges from tiny warblers to magnificent black, crowned and martial eagles.

The Karkloof Education Park, used in conjunction with the Umgeni Valley Nature Reserve, is a farm in the Karkloof Mountains, endowed with heavily wooded indig-

enous forest, gorges, animals such as samango and vervet monkeys, dassies and tree hyraxes, as well as the impressive forest loerie, trumpeter hornbill and Narina trogon.

Courses for schoolchildren, as well as for university students, are run regularly. When the reserve is not being used for these courses, trailists can sign up for conducted trails or ramble unaccompanied along the maze of footpaths that criss-cross the valley.

207. *Howick Town Trail*

HOWICK, see map page 183

AUTHORITY-IN-CHARGE: Geography Department, University of Natal, P.O. Box 375, Pietermaritzburg 3200.
MAIN ATTRACTIONS: Historic buildings and older areas of Howick; Howick Falls viewing site.
FACILITIES/AMENITIES: Those present in the town.
PERTINENT INFORMATION: Especially useful

for teachers, as trail guide asks stimulating questions.
AVAILABLE LITERATURE: *Howick Town Trail*, brochure with sketch maps available from the Geography Department, University of Natal.
CLIMATE: Summer rainfall area.

208. Midmar Public Resort Nature Reserve

LAKE MIDMAR, HOWICK

AUTHORITY-IN-CHARGE: Natal Parks Board.
SIZE: 2 831 hectares.
MAIN ATTRACTIONS: Antelope; waterfowl; watersports (sailing, boardsailing, water-skiing, canoeing, power-boating); angling.
FACILITIES/AMENITIES: Chalets, cabins, tent and caravan sites, café, playground, tennis, squash, bowls and horse-riding; launch tours.
AVAILABLE LITERATURE: *Midmar Public Resort*, issued by the Natal Parks Board; *Midmar Public Resort Nature Reserve, Natal*, AA Bulletin TBE-N3.
CLIMATE: Summer: hot. Winter: mild days, cold nights.

Midmar, as with most public resorts, is orientated more towards sporting than environmental activities. However, the Natal Parks Board offers launch trips which follow the shores of the game park and provide close-up views of white rhino, zebra, eland,

impala, blesbok, springbok, blue wilde-beest, red hartebeest and reedbuck.
Waterfowl frequenting the inlets and bays of the dam can be observed if you ramble along the shore, and at spots such as the Umgeni Cascades. These cascades, which should more properly be called rapids, are particularly impressive when in flood. The surrounding natural vegetation teems with birdlife, a feature being the kingfishers which include South Africa's largest (the giant) and smallest (the pygmy) species.

209. Natal National Botanic Garden

PIETERMARITZBURG

AUTHORITY-IN-CHARGE: National Botanic Gardens.
SIZE: 49 hectares.
MAIN ATTRACTIONS: The old garden with its exotic tree collection; the indigenous garden

which features plants of Natal; flowers bloom year-round; birds (57 species have been recorded).
FACILITIES/AMENITIES: Walk through indigenous forest; constructed paths; education centre and teaching garden run by the Natal Provincial Administration, Education Department, for primary schools; tearoom, open daily except Tuesdays; toilets.
PERTINENT INFORMATION: Open 08h00-18h00. Entrance is free. Dogs allowed on leash. Public transport from main bus station.
AVAILABLE LITERATURE: *Natal Botanic Garden, Pietermaritzburg*, comprehensive pamphlet and map.
CLIMATE: Summer: hot and humid, thunderstorms, some mist and drizzle. Winter: dry and cold to mild, with occasional frosts. Temperature range: -2 to 40 °C. Average annual rainfall: 1 000 millimetres.

Situated in a deep bend of the Dorpspruit, on the Swartkops Valley side of Pietermaritzburg, the Natal National Botanic Gar-

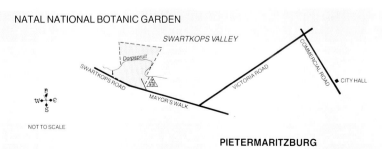

NATAL NATIONAL BOTANIC GARDEN

SWARTKOPS VALLEY

Dorpspruit

SWARTKOPS ROAD

MAYOR'S WALK

VICTORIA ROAD

COMMERCIAL ROAD

CITY HALL

NOT TO SCALE

PIETERMARITZBURG

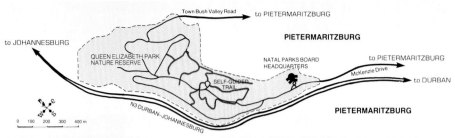

QUEEN ELIZABETH PARK NATURE RESERVE

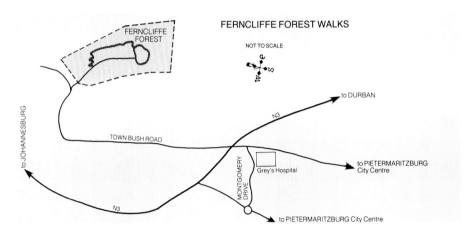

FERNCLIFFE FOREST WALKS

den provides a first-class educational introduction to the flora of Natal. Walks of approximately one hour in duration follow laid-out paths through an area of mistbelt forest, and provide panoramic views of the Swartkops Valley. Of special interest is the plane tree avenue, planted in 1908, which is magnificent throughout the year.

210. Queen Elizabeth Park Nature Reserve

PIETERMARITZBURG

AUTHORITY-IN-CHARGE: Natal Parks Board.
SIZE: 93 hectares.
MAIN ATTRACTIONS: Small but comprehensive selection of game animals; aviary; indigenous flora and plant nursery.
FACILITIES/AMENITIES: Self-guided trail; walks for schoolchildren; picnic sites and braais; Douglas Mitchell Centre (headquarters of the Natal Parks Board, tel. (0331) 51514, 51530, 51554/5/6/9, for all park reservations); bookstore; curios.
PERTINENT INFORMATION: Due to extensive building operations, the self-guided trail has been closed temporarily.
AVAILABLE LITERATURE: *Queen Elizabeth Park Trail*, guide and sketch map; *Queen Elizabeth Park Nature Reserve*, pocket brochure; *The Self-guided Trails of the Natal Parks Board*, general information brochure; *Teacher's Information Pamphlet No. 3* (all issued by the Natal Parks Board); *A Visit to Queen Elizabeth Park*, worksheets available from the Natal Education Department.
CLIMATE: Summer rainfall area.

The Queen Elizabeth Park's self-guided trail is an easy, short educational walk through the grounds of the Natal Parks Board's headquarters. Although only a kilometre long, the trail passes paddocks of game animals, aviaries, snake pits, ponds, gardens and trees. All of these are described in the trail booklet, and the trees are tagged for identification purposes.

Outdoor study trips and guided trails within the 93-hectare reserve are offered by the education officer at specific times. Details are available from the Natal Parks Board.

For those trailists wanting an unstructured walk, visitors are encouraged to ramble anywhere on the numerous paths in the vicinity.

211. Ferncliffe Forest Walks

PIETERMARITZBURG

AUTHORITY-IN-CHARGE: Municipality of Pietermaritzburg, P.O. Box 31, Pietermaritzburg 3200.
SIZE: 250 hectares.
DURATION: Seven trails, each less than one hour.
MAIN ATTRACTIONS: Urban green pocket; ngongoni vegetation (tropical affinity); birdlife; waterfalls; views of Pietermaritzburg; bat cave.
FACILITIES/AMENITIES: Constructed trails.
PERTINENT INFORMATION: The reserve lies 12 km by road north-west of the city hall. It is located 140 m above sea level. For information: The Director of Parks and Recreation, Municipality of Pietermaritzburg.
AVAILABLE LITERATURE: *An Introduction to Ferncliffe Forest*, booklet with bird checklist, maps and trail guide.
CLIMATE: Annual average rainfall: 1 100 millimetres.

212. Green Belt Trails

PIETERMARITZBURG

AUTHORITY-IN-CHARGE: Municipality of Pietermaritzburg, P.O. Box 31, Pietermaritzburg 3200.
LENGTH: Several trails, more than 20 km in total.
MAIN ATTRACTIONS: Plantations, streams and birdlife; city views; historical significance; abandoned railroad and tunnel.
FACILITIES/AMENITIES: Trails are marked with a system of logos; parking at World's View and Wylie Park.
PERTINENT INFORMATION: Trails are for walking or horse-riding only; no motorized vehicles are permitted.
AVAILABLE LITERATURE: *Pietermaritzburg Green Belt Trails*, brochure and map; brochures obtainable from the Pietermaritzburg Publicity Association, P.O. Box 25, Pietermaritzburg 3200.
CLIMATE: Summer rainfall area.

More than 20 kilometres of Green Belt Trails, providing scenic natural history and historical interest, have been constructed on Pietermaritzburg's north-eastern escarpment which rises 350 metres above the city. Large parts of these trails, all marked by white painted rocks with appropriate colour emblems, run through pine and wattle forests owned by the Pietermaritzburg Corporation.

One of the most exciting trails (the World's View Trail) follows the route of the Voortrekkers and offers a panoramic view of both the city and its surrounding countryside. In contrast, the Upper Linwood Trail follows the abandoned railroad of the 1916 main railway line, passing through an old tunnel *en route*.

It is planned to increase the number of trails and link them via pathways along stream courses to a series of urban walks.

Opposite page: The oldest surviving house in Pietermaritzburg, featured on the town trail.

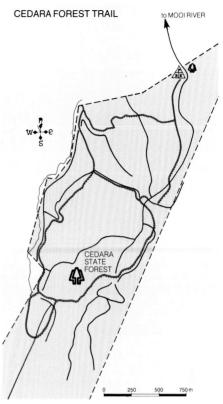

to MOOI RIVER

CEDARA STATE FOREST

0 250 500 750 m

213. Pietermaritzburg Town Trails

PIETERMARITZBURG

AUTHORITY-IN-CHARGE: Municipality of Pietermaritzburg, P.O. Box 31, Pietermaritzburg 3200.
DURATION: Six walks, each approximately one hour.
MAIN ATTRACTIONS: Civic, commercial and residential buildings in various styles; national monuments.
FACILITIES/AMENITIES: Those present in the city.
AVAILABLE LITERATURE: *Pietermaritzburg*

Town Trails, trails guide; *Pietermaritzburg City Centre Walk*, leaflet; brochures obtainable from the Pietermaritzburg Publicity Association, P.O. Box 25, Pietermaritzburg 3200.
CLIMATE: Summer rainfall area.

Pietermaritzburg's city centre holds an uncommon interest, for despite its growing central business district (CBD), an historic core of colonial buildings not only stands, but is functional and plays an integral part in the CBD. Hence, the CBD exhibits a pleasantly rare character with its maze of courtyards, arcades and lanes set aside for pedestrians. Well known for its fine Victorian buildings which are elaborately described in the trail's accompanying booklet, you should also appreciate the Indian mosques and temples and the Zulu medicine ('muti') shops.

214. Doreen Clark Nature Reserve

PIETERMARITZBURG, see map page 183

AUTHORITY-IN-CHARGE: Natal Parks Board.
SIZE: 5 hectares.
MAIN ATTRACTIONS: Indigenous evergreen forest.
FACILITIES/AMENITIES: Walk through forest; picnic sites.
PERTINENT INFORMATION: The reserve is

relatively undeveloped at present. It can be explored on foot only.
AVAILABLE LITERATURE: Included in the Natal Parks Board's brochures.
CLIMATE: Summer rainfall area.

215. Cedara Forest Trail

CEDARA STATE FOREST, PIETERMARITZBURG

AUTHORITY-IN-CHARGE: Natal Forest Region, Forestry Branch, Department of Environment Affairs.
LENGTH: 10 km (or 5-km circular walk).
MAIN ATTRACTIONS: Tranquillity of pine plantations; old Voortrekker route; 80-year-old, and older, deodar trees.
FACILITIES/AMENITIES: Educational trail with observation points; picnic and braai area; fishing permitted in dams.
PERTINENT INFORMATION: Roads must be crossed with care as they are used by heavy-duty forestry lorries.
AVAILABLE LITERATURE: *Cedara Forest Trail*, guide and map.
CLIMATE: Summer rainfall area.

Originally planned to offer people from Pietermaritzburg a venue for rambling and relaxation, the Cedara Forest Trail has been extended and improved so that it is now a valuable environmental education experi-

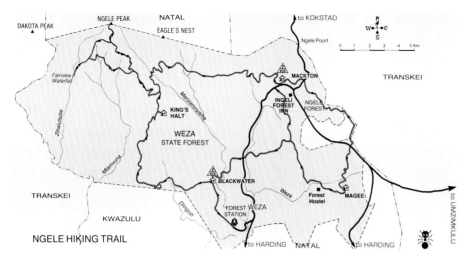

NGELE HIKING TRAIL

Africa, as well as grey duiker, common reedbuck, grey rhebok and baboon, and samango and vervet monkeys, are easily identified. With the necessary licence, trout fishing is allowed.

The trail offers an optional and strenuous 880-metre ascent of Ngele Mountain with views of East Griqualand, Transkei and the sea, as well as an optional six-hour circular walk following an easy gradient to Fairview Waterfall.

ence for students of the Land Service Movement (a state-aided conservation youth movement) and local schools. The trail guide concentrates on Voortrekker history and forest ecology.

Covering 670 hectares, the Cedara State Forest contains trees from a variety of countries, including Australia, the Himalayas, Japan, Mexico, the Mediterranean area, Britain, Europe, North Africa, China and the USA. These experimental specimens were planted in 1903, when the plantation was started.

216. Ngele Hiking Trail

WEZA STATE FOREST, HARDING

AUTHORITY-IN-CHARGE: Natal Forest Region, Forestry Branch, Department of Environment Affairs.
LENGTH/DURATION: Circular route: approximately 60 km/4 or 5 days. A shorter route (50 km/3 days) is available. Many other variations, including a weekend circular route.
MAIN ATTRACTIONS: Indigenous forest; bushbuck, samango monkey and birdlife; trout fishing; Ngele Mountain and Fairview Waterfall; largest state-owned plantation in South Africa.
FACILITIES/AMENITIES: Four huts, each accommodating 30 people, with bunks, mattresses, tables, benches, stove, firewood and toilets.
PERTINENT INFORMATION: Trails may be closed during fire season (August to October). Ticks are prevalent.
AVAILABLE LITERATURE: *Ngele Hiking Trail*,

Opposite page, top: The Umtamvuna Gorge, which forms the border between Transkei and Natal.

Opposite page, bottom: The dense riverine rain forests of the Umtamvuna have a magical quality.

comprehensive brochure and map.
CLIMATE: Average annual rainfall: 1 000-1 500 millimetres, falling mostly in summer. November to March, thunderstorms and mist common. May to August, dry season. Winter: mist, frost and snow are common on Ngele Mountain. In general the climate is cool and subject to rapid change.

The Ngele Hiking Trail is a physically undemanding walk located within the Weza State Forest (the largest man-made forest in South Africa) near Harding in southern Natal. It winds in and out of an indigenous forest boasting yellowwood, lemonwood, knobwood and stinkwood; grasslands with attractive wildflowers; and plantations grown for veneer logs and softwood timber.

Birdlife is very good but, as in all dense forests, more easily heard than seen. Some of my favourites include the black duck, usually found on running waters; the long-crested eagle, which feeds on rodents; and the chorister robin, which often sits in treetops, mimicking other bird calls. One of the largest populations of bushbuck in South

217. Lorna Doone Forest Hostel and Trails

WEZA STATE FOREST, HARDING

AUTHORITY-IN-CHARGE: Natal Forest Region, Forestry Branch, Department of Environment Affairs.
LENGTH: Dassie Trail: 5 km. Hoopoe Trail: 6 km. Bushbuck Trail: 9,5 km.
MAIN ATTRACTIONS: Forest management practices; indigenous forest.
FACILITIES/AMENITIES: Three self-guided educational trails; Lorna Doone Hostel, accommodating 40 people, with wooden bunks, mattresses, benches, tables, stove and ablution facilities.
PERTINENT INFORMATION: Bring your own food, bedding and cooking utensils.
AVAILABLE LITERATURE: *Lorna Doone Forest Hostel and Trail*, booklet with map; accompanying trail guides; 'Things to Do' brochure.
CLIMATE: Summer rainfall area.

The three self-guided educational trails laid out in the Weza State Forest are intended

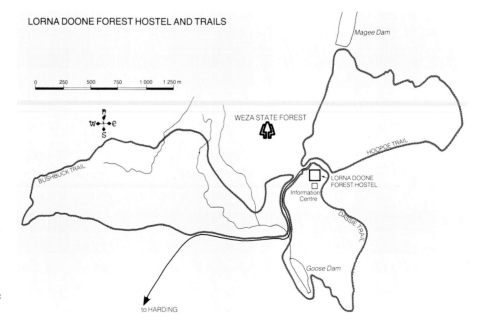

LORNA DOONE FOREST HOSTEL AND TRAILS

for school, youth and other groups interested in conservation. The Bushbuck Trail takes you through a stinkwood forest, rich in large yellowwood and wild quince species. On the Hoopoe Trail, trees from California, Japan and Mexico grow in attractive groves.

The shortest trail, the Dassie Trail, traverses the pine plantation, and visits Goose Dam and an elite tree. This tree has a white band indicating that it has been selected by forestry tree-breeding specialists as a specimen showing above-average growth, stem straightness, wood quality and branch pattern. Grafts from 'elite tree' parents improve seed, which grows faster than other trees, and results in straighter stems and lighter crowns than those of trees grown from unselected seed.

Guides produced for these trails provide valuable and detailed descriptions of forest management practices, trees, ecology, wildlife habitats and species, and activities for scholars. The Lorna Doone Trails are a commendable environmental education project.

The Ngele Hiking Trail (see opposite page) is also located in the Weza State Forest.

218. Umtamvuna Nature Reserve

PORT EDWARD, see map page 162

AUTHORITY-IN-CHARGE: Natal Parks Board.
SIZE: 3 257 hectares.
MAIN ATTRACTIONS: Steep-sided forested gorge, botanically rich with many endemic species; plentiful, clear streams; far-reaching, spacious views; magnificent sandstone koppies.
FACILITIES/AMENITIES: Complex of day walks; game scouts available with prior

arrangement; toilets and parking; access to herbarium on request. Research hut available on request; contact The Officer-in-Charge, Umtamvuna Nature Reserve, P.O. Box 25, Port Edward 4295; tel. (03930) 383.
PERTINENT INFORMATION: At present, day use area only. No fishing permitted. Open sunrise to sunset. No dogs allowed. River difficult to cross in rains.
AVAILABLE LITERATURE: *Umtamvuna*, sketch map; *Beacon Hill*, pamphlet; self-guided trail leaflets planned.
CLIMATE: Summer rainfall area; rain can be heavy at times.

On the northern banks of the Umtamvuna River and its magnificent gorge which forms the border between Transkei and Natal, lies a developing and relatively unknown reserve, a paradise for day hikes. The Umtamvuna Nature Reserve is the best example of the eastern coastal sandstone region in South Africa, and the only example of Pongoland coastal highland sourveld under coastal management. The fortress-like koppies and sandstone cliffs, grasslands scattered with wildflowers and dense riverine rain forest with numerous pretty waterfalls tumbling into the gorge have a magical quality.

Over 250 bird species, including Gurney's sugarbirds, crowned eagles, peregrine falcons, and a breeding colony of Cape vultures, and more than 100 species of identified plants, contribute to the biological richness of the area. Some of the protected rarer plants include *Ficus polita (bizanae)*, the wild rubber fig; *Olea capensis*, subsp. 'enervis', the ironwood; *Encephalartos natalensis*, the Natal cycad and *E. villosus*; *Syzygium pondoense*; *Alberta magna*, the Natal flame bush; and *Manilkara nicholsonii*. If lucky, hikers can also observe southern or common reedbuck, blesbok, bushbuck, blue and grey duiker, serval and lynx.

The system of day walks which leads hikers largely in the forest and along the

river is gradually being replaced by three trails: a short, a medium and an all-day trail incorporating all features in the reserve, including both the Bulolo River and the Umtamvuna River gorges. Contact the officer-in-charge for the latest details and the most accurate trails map.

219. Uvongo River Reserve

UVONGO

AUTHORITY-IN-CHARGE: Municipality of Uvongo, P.O. Box 13, Uvongo 4270.
SIZE: 28 hectares.
MAIN ATTRACTIONS: Uvongo Falls (23 m).
FACILITIES/AMENITIES: Several short walks in and around the reserve; picnic sites.
PERTINENT INFORMATION: Two entrances: Edward Avenue for the south bank and Marine Drive for the north bank. Day use area only.
AVAILABLE LITERATURE: *Uvongo River Reserve, A Wildlife Guidebook*, available from the Wildlife Society and local chemists.
CLIMATE: Summer rainfall area.

Man's greed for holiday homes and development as close to the sea as humanly possible has made the Natal south coast a nightmare for the environmental purist. The Uvongo River Reserve is a tiny 'island' of preserved coastline, between the Umzim-

kulu and Umtamvuna rivers, which illustrates how things were before the 'march of progress'.

The Nicholson Trail meanders along the northern slopes of the Ivungu River (from the Zulu word *Evungu*, meaning 'the reverberating roar of the falls'), while the Collett Trail runs along its southern slopes.

The Ivungu River rises in the Murchison range (which includes Oribi Gorge), and at its journey's end plunges over sandstone cliffs into the sea. This is why this Natal river lacks the silty mouth and reed-covered banks characteristic of many others.

Only a remnant of the once-extensive forests remains in this tiny reserve: 116 species of trees and shrubs have been recorded, and many are labelled with their national tree list numbers. The guide book is a must, as many of the common species of trees, birds, fish and frogs are illustrated, and the geology of the area is intricately discussed.

Other walks in the vicinity of the Uvongo River Reserve include the easy Saint's Walk (approximately two kilometres), laid out along the length of the sea front from St. Michael's on Sea to the Uvongo beach, and guided visits to the Skyline Arboretum and Herbarium, two kilometres inland from the coast at St. Michael's on Sea.

220. Oribi Gorge Nature Reserve

PORT SHEPSTONE

AUTHORITY-IN-CHARGE: Natal Parks Board.
SIZE: 1 809 hectares.
MAIN ATTRACTIONS: Deep, forested gorge with 268 species of birds; 35 km of day walks and hiking trails.
FACILITIES/AMENITIES: Hutted camp, at edge of gorge, with six 3-bed bungalows, refrigerator, bedding, cutlery, crockery and braai, and one 7-bed self-contained cottage with electricity, bathroom, toilets and personal chef; ablution block, kitchen where chefs cook your food; outdoor communal braai 'boma'; picnic site and toilets along the river; fishing, with permit and licence; store selling books, etc., but no food.
PERTINENT INFORMATION: Scouts available on request to lead hikers. Visitors must supply their own food and drink. Oribi Gorge Hotel at Fairacres provides spectacular viewing points. Bilharzia may be present in the main river. The river cannot be crossed in flood.
AVAILABLE LITERATURE: *Oribi Gorge Nature Reserve*, pocket brochure; trail map; bird and tree checklists; *Some Natal Game and*

Opposite page, top: The Oribi Gorge.
Opposite page, below: Vernon Crookes Reserve.

Nature Reserves, AA Bulletin TBE-N7; trail guides planned; located on Government Printer's 1:50 000 topographic map '3030 CB Port Shepstone'.
CLIMATE: Average annual rainfall: 570-1 625 millimetres, falling mostly in summer (October to March). July, driest and coldest month. Eastern cliffs (which lie in the direction of the sea) supplement rain with mist; western and central gorge receive more rain than the eastern section.

Oribi Gorge is a spectacular landscape feature located 21 kilometres west of Port Shepstone near the lower south coast of Natal. Here the Umzimkulwana River, a tributary of the Umzimkulu, has carved out of the Oribi and Murchison Falls plateaux a five kilometre-wide and 305 metre-deep gorge, through Table Mountain sandstone right down to granite. The Umzimkulwana River now rests on a bouldery substrate (ideal in parts for boulder-hopping and river crossings) and has short, shallow rapids with a few low waterfalls. However, the impressive sandstone cliff faces bordering the river have dramatic waterfalls such as the Hoopoe and Samango falls.

Bounded by sugar cane, wattle and cattle farms, Oribi Gorge protects over 700 plant species, of which 500 are trees. Coastal forest forms the most extensive vegetation type; however, the plant communities respond to altitude and the nature reserve also boasts evergreen riverine thickets in the riverbed, grasslands on the plateau (note the grass owls which are common here), lithophytic flora on cliffs and rocky areas, and open woodlands with proteas.

Of the many protected animal species, special attention is drawn to the African python, Peringuey's leaf-toed gecko, the black sparrowhawk, Cape vulture, bat hawk, samango monkey, water leguan (nile monitor) and African broadbill. Ironically, the oribi, a small, graceful, rufous-coloured antelope after which the gorge is named, is rare.

Originally there were seven day-walks, which led hikers along the plateau, into the river valley, up and down the gorge and to the falls. Although well constructed, these trails are steep, not circular and are impossible to complete when the river is in flood. A new complex of day-walks, all planned to radiate from the picnic site, and two trail camps providing opportunities for 2-3 day backpacking trips, are planned. (Consult the warden for details.)

One of the new trips involves boulder-hopping upriver in the narrow gorge, past

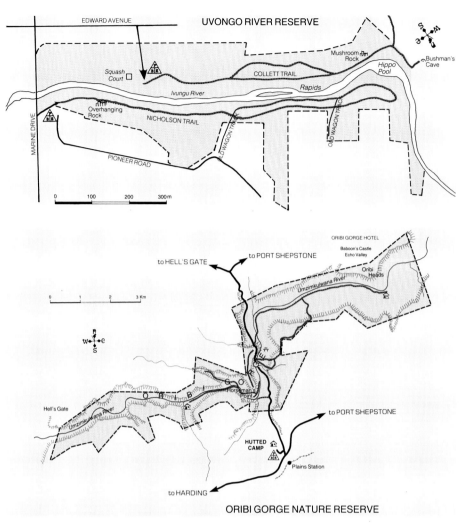

fern caves and forests, while the other, downstream, is through valley bushveld vegetation where the gorge is hotter and wider. People are discouraged from walking off the trails because the going is rough and dangerous. The game scouts warned me that the black mamba and cobra populations are very high, but hikers will be fortunate to catch a glimpse of such beautiful (and deadly) creatures.

After a tough day of physical exertion, well rewarded by magnificent views, waterfalls and solitude in the deep, wilderness-like gorge, I suggest a stroll to the plateau's edge on the Riverside Trail to near the hutted camp, from which you have a commanding view of the entire gorge and can hear the erosive power of the rapids and waterfalls, softened by the birds calling from the canopy of trees. Or, although slightly commercialized, the Oribi Gorge Hotel at Fairacres estate offers superb views of the reddish sandstone cliffs and their eroded formations – Echo Valley, the Pulpit, Oribi Heads, Ola's Nose, Lehr Waterfall, Horseshoe Bend and Baboon's Castle.

221. Vernon Crookes Nature Reserve

UMZINTO

AUTHORITY-IN-CHARGE: Natal Parks Board.
SIZE: 2 189 hectares
MAIN ATTRACTIONS: Coastal forested valleys; grasslands and grazing animals; sea views; rich birdlife and interesting flora.
FACILITIES/AMENITIES: Three self-guided walks and a backpacker's camp are planned. Hutted camp with five rondavels, each containing two double-bed bunks, mattresses and gas lamps, communal kitchen with refrigerator, ablution block with hot water, and braai area (it is planned to extend the camp for 20 people in group accommodation). Nyengelezi Laboratory classroom, for use by schools and universities on request; picnic sites; approximately 15 km of game-viewing drives.
PERTINENT INFORMATION: For booking of rondavels, tel. (03231) 42222. Bring your own sleeping gear, food and drink.
AVAILABLE LITERATURE: *Vernon Crookes Nature Reserve*, information leaflet and map; *Some Natal Game and Nature Reserves*, AA Bulletin TBE-N7; trail guides planned; located on Government Printer's topographic maps '3030 BC and BD Scottburgh'.
CLIMATE: Summer rainfall area. Mist zone.

The Vernon Crookes Nature Reserve is prime rambling territory for people with a keen interest in birds and flora. In the sur-

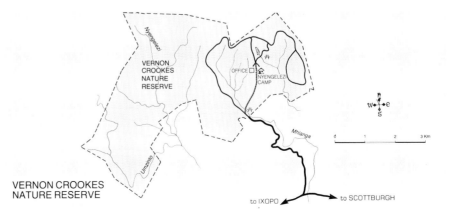

VERNON CROOKES
NATURE RESERVE

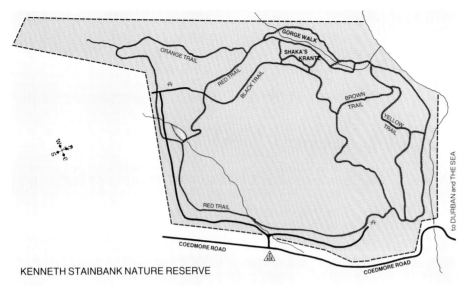

KENNETH STAINBANK NATURE RESERVE

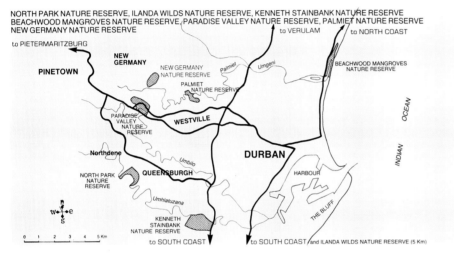

NORTH PARK NATURE RESERVE, ILANDA WILDS NATURE RESERVE, KENNETH STAINBANK NATURE RESERVE
BEACHWOOD MANGROVES NATURE RESERVE, PARADISE VALLEY NATURE RESERVE, PALMIET NATURE RESERVE
NEW GERMANY NATURE RESERVE

rounding sea of pine, eucalyptus and sugar cane, this lovely little area preserves rolling sourveld grasslands interspersed with coastal forested kloofs and thornveld slopes.

Spanning an altitude from 150 to 610 metres above sea level, the reserve is dissected by several fast-flowing streams such as the Mhlanga (meaning Egyptian mongoose) and Nyengelezi (or whitenaped weasel). Birdlife thrives here: the grasslands host widow and bishop birds while spurwinged geese and crowned cranes are seen at the dams, along with larger game such as zebra, nyala, blue wildebeest and eland. Bushbuck and blue and grey duiker live in the forests.

The reserve also contains many large specimens of trees representative of the coastal forest, such as the wild date palm, *Phoenix reclinata*; wild banana, *Strelitzia nicolai*; flat-crown, *Albizia adianthifolia*; umzimbeet, *Millettia grandis*; and common coral tree, *Erythrina lysistemon*. The honey-scented protea, *Protea welwitschii*, which is not that common in Natal, reaches its southernmost point of distribution here.

The traditional Zulu kraals bordering on the reserve are part of the magnificent vistas of coastal forested kloofs and grasslands, and the Indian Ocean can be seen in the distance.

No trails existed when I visited the reserve in December 1985, but three self-guided walks of varying lengths, starting from the picnic site, will be constructed. The walking area is to the east of the road while the western section is a wilderness with only a backpacker's camp and trail (to be constructed).

222. Ilanda Wilds Nature Reserve

AMANZIMTOTI

🚶 🅶

AUTHORITY-IN-CHARGE: Municipality of Amanzimtoti, P.O. Box 26, Amanzimtoti 4125.
SIZE: 14 hectares.
MAIN ATTRACTIONS: Rock faces with aloes; euphorbias; 300 species of birds; 126 species of trees and shrubs; Amanzimtoti River

(*Amanzimtoti* is Zulu for 'so the water is sweet').
FACILITIES/AMENITIES: Labelled trees; hides; marked trails; picnicking is permitted.
PERTINENT INFORMATION: The Wildlife Society runs guided trails on request. No fires allowed. *Ilanda* is the Zulu name for the cattle egret which used to frequent the river reedbeds.
CLIMATE: Sub-tropical. January and February, high humidity. Winter: mild and frost-free; July is the coldest month. Average annual rainfall: 87,4 millimetres, 70 per cent of which falls between October and March.

223. Kenneth Stainbank Nature Reserve

DURBAN

🚶 ♿ 🅶

AUTHORITY-IN-CHARGE: Natal Parks Board.
SIZE: 214 hectares.
MAIN ATTRACTIONS: Coastal forest providing habitat for red and blue duiker; other small mammals, and reintroduced zebra, impala and nyala; prolific birdlife; historic Zulu sites.
FACILITIES/AMENITIES: Six self-guided nature trails; trail for the handicapped; trees labelled with national tree list numbers; picnic sites.
PERTINENT INFORMATION: The Chatsworth second access route has been proposed to pass through the reserve. Since the reserve was donated to the people of South Africa by Mr Kenneth Stainbank, the placing of the road here means that the reserve will revert to Mr Stainbank's heirs and will be lost forever as a conservation area. However, the Wildlife Society of Southern Africa favours the Umhlatuzana or 4a Route, which will have a low impact on the reserve. As yet no date has been set for the opening of the route; people who are interested in this controversy should contact The Senior Naturalist, Kenneth Stainbank Nature Reserve, P.O. Box 53048, Yellow Wood Park 4011, tel. (031) 42-1125.
AVAILABLE LITERATURE: *The Kenneth Stainbank Nature Reserve*, map; *The Self-guided Trails of the Natal Parks Board*, general information pocket brochure.
CLIMATE: Typical of Durban's climate (average annual rainfall: over 1 000 millimetres; average temperature: 20-22 °C), but with a greater temperature range. Thunderstorms are common. 70 per cent of rain falls in summer.

The Natal Parks Board considers the Kenneth Stainbank Nature Reserve to be one of

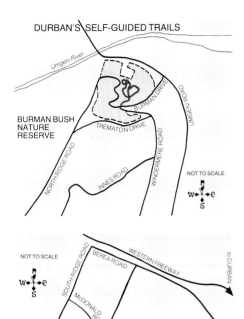

DURBAN'S SELF-GUIDED TRAILS

Umgeni River

BURMAN BUSH
NATURE
RESERVE

BURMAN DRIVE

UMGENI ROAD

TREMATON DRIVE

NORTH RIDGE ROAD

WINDERMERE ROAD

INNES ROAD

NOT TO SCALE

NOT TO SCALE

DURBAN'S
SELF-GUIDED TRAILS
PIGEON VALLEY PARK

BEREA ROAD

WESTERN FREEWAY

SOUTH RIDGE ROAD

McDONALD ROAD

GEORGE V AVENUE

KING ROAD

PRINCESS ALICE AVE.

MANNING ROAD

to DURBAN

to DURBAN

DURBAN'S SELF-
GUIDED TRAILS

NOT TO SCALE

BOUNDARY PATH

BAMBOO TRAIL

YELLOWWOOD TRAIL

Entrance

to North Coast Road

LOTHIAN ROAD

to NORTHWAY

SEATON PARK

to Manfred Road

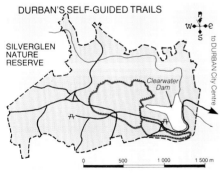

DURBAN'S SELF-GUIDED TRAILS

SILVERGLEN
NATURE
RESERVE

Clearwater
Dam

to DURBAN City Centre

0   500   1 000   1 500 m

its major educational areas. Located only 9,5 kilometres from the Durban city centre and 6,5 kilometres from the sea, the reserve offers students an ideal, easily accessible venue for ecological studies.

Six self-guided trails, each 30-60 minutes in duration, branch off from the main trail,

an approximately two-hour circular walk. All are cut through coastal forest vegetation and grassveld where trailists can observe bushbuck, blue and red duiker, impala, giraffe, zebra and nyala, in addition to small mammals, birds, reptiles and insects. The routes, varying from easy to strenuous, are mapped.

The 600-metre Kenneth Stainbank Special Trail was designed with the assistance of specialists for paraplegics, the blind, the deaf and people confined to wheelchairs, and is one of the few of its kind in South Africa. Even the amenities, such as the parking area, toilet block, and braai and picnic sites, have been designed for use by disabled people. The trail is constructed of concrete with a hand-rail running along its length. There are interpretive displays and a booklet which tell the story of the reserve, its importance to the people of South Africa and how it functions ecologically, with emphasis on coastal forests and grassland.

Guided group trails may be requested.

224. North Park Nature Reserve

NORTHDENE, DURBAN

AUTHORITY-IN-CHARGE: Natal Parks Board.
SIZE: 52 hectares.
MAIN ATTRACTIONS: Coastal lowland forest on the northern bank of the Umhlatuzana River; abundant birdlife; wildlife, including bushbuck, blue and grey duiker, and banded mongoose.
FACILITIES/AMENITIES: Network of footpaths; braai and picnic facilities.
PERTINENT INFORMATION: Day use area only. For information: The Officer-in-Charge, North Park Nature Reserve, P.O. Box 288, Kloof 3640.
AVAILABLE LITERATURE: Included in the Natal Parks Board's brochures.
CLIMATE: Summer rainfall area.

225. Durban's Self-guided Trails

DURBAN MUNICIPAL AREA

AUTHORITY-IN-CHARGE: City of Durban.
PERTINENT INFORMATION: In recent years the Durban Department of Parks, Recreation and Beaches has done a commendable job of developing a series of short, self-guided educational trails through urban green pockets. Each trail is described in a printed guide consisting of attractive colour maps, directions to reserves,

diagrams, checklists and detailed ecological coverage for the amateur enthusiast. For information: The Director, Department of Parks, Recreation and Beaches, P.O. Box 3740, Durban 4000.
AVAILABLE LITERATURE: Self-guided Trails in Durban, booklet including information on Burman Bush Nature Reserve (Hadeda, Pithi and Umgeni trails), Pigeon Valley Park (the Elm Trail), Seaton Park, Silverglen Nature Reserve, the Umbilo River Trail, the ARC Trail, Virginia Bush Nature Reserve, and common butterflies of Durban.
CLIMATE: Summer rainfall area.

Burman Bush Nature Reserve

Located in this reserve are the Hadeda Trail (180 metres), the Pithi Trail (500 metres) and the Umgeni Trail (1 kilometre). The reserve boasts good bird and plant life, trees bearing their national tree list numbers, picnic sites, toilets and a resource centre. It is open from 07h00 to 16h30 (other times by appointment in writing to the Director) and no permits are required. No dogs are allowed. The Umgeni Trail leaflet and the colour map, Burman Bush: Trail/Wandelpad will be helpful on the self-guided trails.

Pigeon Valley Park

On the 500-metre Elm Trail, ramblers will walk through remnant forest with Natal white stinkwood (Celtis mildbraedii) and, in winter, may see the spotted thrush. There is a picnic area (no fires are permitted) and toilets in the park. It is open from 07h00 to 16h30 (other times by appointment in writing to the Director). No permits are needed. No dogs are allowed.

Seaton Park

The 6-hectare Seaton Park boasts interesting tree species, some of which are not found in other reserves around Durban; abundant birdlife, including the African goshawk; and peaceful and relaxing walks, including the Yellowwood Trail (300 metres), the Bamboo Trail (200 metres) and the Boundary Path (400-500 metres). There are observation points, trees bearing their national tree list numbers, toilets and a children's play area in the park.

Silverglen Nature Reserve

The 3,5-4 kilometre Silverglen Trail winds through what are probably the best preserved coastal bush and grasslands in the Durban metropolitan area. The reserve has a resource centre, a picnic site and a nursery for growing medicinal plants. Fishing and wind-powered boating or sailboarding are allowed on the reservoir.

Umbilo River Trail

This 3-5 kilometre trail runs along the banks of the river and canal, and through the fingers of steep land running up the valleys off the river. The trail is to be extended to the borough boundary. The ARC (Awareness,

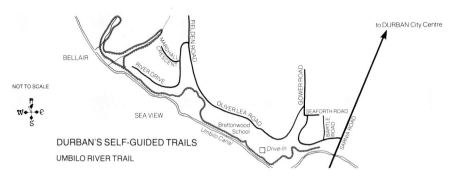

BELLAIR

NOT TO SCALE

FIELDEN ROAD

MARSHALL CRESCENT

RIVER DRIVE

OLIVER LEA ROAD

SEA VIEW

Brettonwood School

Umbilo Canal

Drive-In

GOWER ROAD

SEAFORTH ROAD

BARTLE ROAD

SARNIA ROAD

to DURBAN City Centre

DURBAN'S SELF-GUIDED TRAILS

UMBILO RIVER TRAIL

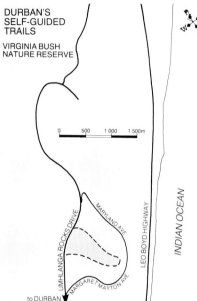

DURBAN'S SELF-GUIDED TRAILS

VIRGINIA BUSH NATURE RESERVE

0   500   1 000   1 500m

UMHLANGA ROCKS DRIVE

MARYLAND AVE

MARGARET MAYTON AVE

LEO BOYD HIGHWAY

INDIAN OCEAN

to DURBAN

Recreation, Conservation) Trail, which runs for 2,5-3 kilometres, forms the start of the M.O.S.S. Umbilo Trail for the Greater Durban area.

Virginia Bush Nature Reserve

Because of the edge effect created by bush clumps, birdlife abounds in the 38-hectare Virginia Bush Nature Reserve. Specialities include the bush shrike and the crested guineafowl. A brochure is available at the reserve, which also has an information board. The 1,5-kilometre Virginia Bush self-guided trail runs through this reserve.

226. Beachwood Mangroves Nature Reserve

DURBAN, see map page 196

AUTHORITY-IN-CHARGE: Natal Parks Board.
SIZE: 76 hectares.
MAIN ATTRACTIONS: Last remaining mangrove swamp of any size on the Natal coast south of the Tugela River; sand dunes.
FACILITIES/AMENITIES: Nature conservation

education centre near Durban city centre; work study environment for Department of Biological Sciences of the University of Natal; no accommodation.
PERTINENT INFORMATION: Guided trails can be arranged with the Natal Branch of the Wildlife Society of Southern Africa.
AVAILABLE LITERATURE: Included in the Natal Parks Board's general brochures.
CLIMATE: Summer rainfall area.

227. Paradise Valley Nature Reserve

DURBAN, see map page 196

AUTHORITY-IN-CHARGE: Municipality of Pinetown, Pinetown 3600.
SIZE: 28 hectares.
MAIN ATTRACTIONS: Coastal forest on the banks of the Umbilo River; bushbuck and blue and grey duiker.
FACILITIES/AMENITIES: Picnic sites; short walks.
PERTINENT INFORMATION: Located beneath the N3 (North) freeway. For information: The Officer-in-Charge, Paradise Valley Nature Reserve, P.O. Box 288, Kloof 3640.
AVAILABLE LITERATURE: Included in the Natal Parks Board's brochures.
CLIMATE: Summer rainfall area.

228. Palmiet Nature Reserve

WESTVILLE, DURBAN, see also map page 196

AUTHORITY-IN-CHARGE: Borough of Westville, P.O. Box 39, Westville 3630.
SIZE: 60 hectares.
MAIN ATTRACTIONS: Rugged gorge with dense riverine forest and grassy, bush-covered slopes; 145 recorded bird species; over 150 species of indigenous trees.
FACILITIES/AMENITIES: Nature and guided trails; picnic site with braai facilities; use as an environmental area is encouraged.
PERTINENT INFORMATION: This reserve is linked to the Durban Metropolitan hiking trail network (see page 197). The Palmiet Trail extends south-west to the Westville Park Trail, north-west to the New Germany Nature Reserve, and east to Durban (the Burman Bush and Beachwood Mangroves nature reserves) via the Umgeni River. The reserve is managed by a committee of the Wildlife Society of Southern Africa.
AVAILABLE LITERATURE: *Palmiet Nature Reserve, Self-guided Trails*, by C. Schoute-Vanneck; worksheets for schools.
CLIMATE: Summer rainfall area.

Although only 60 hectares in extent, the Palmiet Nature Reserve, 11 kilometres from Durban, allows an interesting day's exploration for enthusiastic naturalists. Several trails descend the grassy, bush-covered slopes into dense riverine forests along the Palmiet River. These trails, steep in places, give views of the Natal sandstone reddish-brown cliffs, towering 80 to 100 metres above the riverbed.

The reserve contains over 150 species of indigenous trees, and 145 bird species have been recorded in the diversified habitat – bush shrikes, sunbirds and Natal robins are

PALMIET NATURE RESERVE

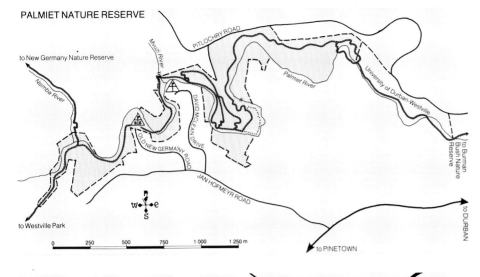

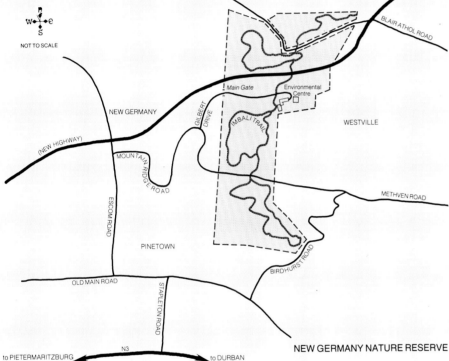

particularly well represented. The booklet on sale from the ranger should be purchased to increase your appreciation of the reserve: it describes the Palmiet's birds, insects, mammals, trees, vegetation communities and geology, and includes a map.

On the first Sunday of every month, the Natal Branch of the Wildlife Society runs a free, half-day guided walk. It is very popular as it caters for all ages and fitness levels. Breakfast trails (in the summer) and sunset trails (in the winter) are also organized.

Opposite page: Crossing a well-constructed hiker's bridge in the Paradise Valley Nature Reserve, situated on the banks of the Umbilo River.

Right: The steel ladder which descends to Cuckoo Corner on the Ingweni Hiking Trail is visible from the Durban/Pietermaritzburg freeway.

229. New Germany Nature Reserve

NEW GERMANY, see also map page 196

AUTHORITY-IN-CHARGE: Borough of New Germany, New Germany 3620.
SIZE: 110 hectares.
MAIN ATTRACTIONS: Climax forest mixed with indigenous coastal grassland; rare and unique flower species; excellent birdlife, including waterfowl on small dams; large and small mammals, including zebra, bushbuck, reedbuck and duiker.
FACILITIES/AMENITIES: Environmental education centre, with lecture theatre, museum, reception and restaurant;

indigenous arboretum; picnic sites; Imbali Trail, self-guided by brochure or guided by the Natal Branch of the Wildlife Society, by arrangement (*Imbali* is the Zulu word for 'flowers').
PERTINENT INFORMATION: Research projects on fire management are carried out in the reserve. For information: The Officer-in-Charge, New Germany Nature Reserve, P.O. Box 2, New Germany 3620; tel. (031) 72-2940 or 72-9391.
AVAILABLE LITERATURE: Trail guides.
CLIMATE: Summer rainfall area.

230. Ingweni Hiking Trail

DURBAN

AUTHORITY-IN-CHARGE: M.O.S.S. (Metropolitan Open Space System), Private Bag 9038, Pietermaritzburg 3200.
LENGTH/DURATION: 25 km/2-3 days.
MAIN ATTRACTIONS: Views from the escarpment edge; protea savannah, grassland, cliff communities, forested valleys and waterfalls; wooden ladder; 162 species of birds.
FACILITIES/AMENITIES: Three rustic timber cabins, each accommodating 12 people, with bunks and mattresses.
PERTINENT INFORMATION: Overnight trail led by guide appointed by the Wildlife Society; casual day or half-day trips by

groups or individuals allowed, providing that they do not trespass on private property. For bookings: Wildlife House, 100 Brand Road, Durban 4001; tel. (031) 21-3126. Bilharzia is a hazard.

AVAILABLE LITERATURE: Booklet with map.
CLIMATE: Summer rainfall area.

The Ingweni Hiking Trail is very special. Unlike most South African trails, which are left to government authorities to construct, this trail is a real community development project, the result of the work of enthusiastic students from St. Mary's School, Thomas More School, Pinetown Boys' and Girls' high schools, and Kearsney College, who made themselves responsible for cutting and maintaining sections of the trail, in conjunction with the Wildlife Society and the Lion's Club.

With so much tender loving care being devoted to it, the Ingweni Hiking Trail deserves your support – and you won't be disappointed. This horseshoe-shaped trail runs through the forested river gorges and adjacent grasslands of sandstone formations in the Pinetown/Kloof/Gillitts/Everton subregion of the Greater Metropolitan area of Durban. Following a route of great beauty and natural charm, the trailist passes three lovely waterfalls – Everton, Kloof and Nkutu – and has magnificent views while walking along the edge of the sandstone escarpment on the southern boundary of Kloof, starting at the Cheeseman Nature Reserve. Krantzkloof Nature Reserve, with Nkutu Falls, comprises the last several kilometres of the walk.

Tree ferns and giant *Macaranga* (indigenous wild poplar) trees grow prolifically in the Molweni Valley; the trail even boasts its own species of *Streptocarpus*, *S. molweniensis*, which grows only on the south-facing bank of the Molweni Stream in the Everton riverine forest. Some hikers may decide that the main attraction of this trail is the creosoted pole ladder descending nine metres and crossing a metre-wide crevice in an otherwise sheer krantz!

Note: this trail is one of a series in the Durban Metropolitan Open Space System (now known as M.O.S.S.), a joint project of the Wildlife Society and the Natal Town and Regional Planning Commission. M.O.S.S.'s stated goal is 'to establish and maintain the most efficient open space trail system which will link established and potential conservation areas within metropolitan Durban'.

Above right: The 'leopard-crawl ledge' in Gillitts, on the Ingweni Hiking Trail.

Opposite page, above: Cautious hikers cross the Molweni Stream in the Everton riverine forest on the Ingweni Hiking Trail. Trees and tree ferns grow prolifically in the Molweni Valley.

Opposite page, bottom: Rambling trails delight the day walker in the Krantzkloof Nature Reserve, near Durban.

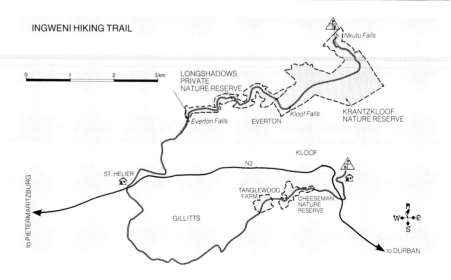

INGWENI HIKING TRAIL

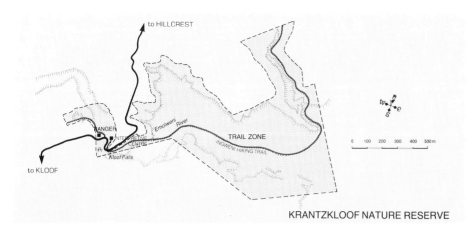

KRANTZKLOOF NATURE RESERVE

231. Krantzkloof Nature Reserve

KLOOF

AUTHORITY-IN-CHARGE: Natal Parks Board.
SIZE: 532 hectares.
MAIN ATTRACTIONS: Well-forested gorge;
Kloof Falls; antelope and birdlife.
FACILITIES/AMENITIES: 20 km of footpaths;
interpretive centre.
PERTINENT INFORMATION: Day use area
only. Guided walks on request. The Ingweni
Hiking Trail (see page 199) runs through the
reserve.
AVAILABLE LITERATURE: *Some Natal Game
Parks and Nature Reserves*, AA Bulletin
TBE-N7; included in Natal Parks Board's
general brochures.
CLIMATE: Summer rainfall area.

Only 27 kilometres from Durban, the
Krantzkloof Nature Reserve serves as a major environmental education centre. A large
rondavel-type building houses natural history displays and has facilities for film
shows. An officer accompanies hikes
through the well-forested gorge cut by the
Emolweni River and its tributaries. A great
number of trees, shrubs and flowers are
present, including *Podocarpus*, *Encephalartos* and various aloes. Naturally occurring
mammals are the bushbuck, grey, red and
blue duiker, bushpig, baboons, vervet mon-

keys and a number of smaller species such as mongoose, dassie and genet. The reserve has abundant birdlife and is a breeding area for birds such as the crowned eagle, Wahlberg's eagle, and the Knysna and purplecrested loeries.

Approximately 20 kilometres of fairly undemanding rambling trails meander through the forest. There is a popular picnic site immediately above the Kloof Falls.

232. The Hawaan Bush

UMHLANGA ROCKS

AUTHORITY-IN-CHARGE: Hulett Sugar Corporation.
SIZE: 65 hectares (40,5 hectares of which are in an unexploited climax state).
MAIN ATTRACTIONS: Unique indigenous coastal forest situated close to a main urban centre; some trees, birds and mammals reach their most southerly distribution in Africa in this forest; pythons.
FACILITIES/AMENITIES: The Natal Branch of the Wildlife Society arranges trails in the forest and lagoon areas.
PERTINENT INFORMATION: Included in the greater Durban Green Belt in the Pietermaritzburg and Durban Regional Guide Plan. For information: the Natal Branch of the Wildlife Society of Southern Africa.
AVAILABLE LITERATURE: Contact the Natal Branch of the Wildlife Society.
CLIMATE: Sub-tropical, with wet, humid summers. Winters are dry and mild. Prevailing winds are north-easterly, while rain-bearing winds are south-westerly.

The privately owned Hawaan Bush, about 16 kilometres north of Durban, on the south bank of the Umhlanga River, is ecologically valuable as it provides a fine example of climax coastal forest. We are indebted to the late Sir Marshall Campbell who had the foresight to set aside and maintain this nature reserve in 1913. The winding tracks, used by wagons to remove timber for fuel to fire the boilers of steam ships and sugar mills, are today the tracks followed by the Wildlife Society during their guided trail outings.

The name 'Hawaan' possibly derives from the language spoken by the Tamil Indian workers in the surrounding canefields, who called the forest *Hawaa*, meaning 'light breeze'. (It could also be derived from the Zulu name for a dancing shield, *Halwana*.)

Although only 65 hectares in extent, the Hawaan Bush forest contains tree species rare elsewhere in South Africa and here many trees, birds and small mammals reach their most southerly distribution in Africa.

THE HAWAAN BUSH
UMHLANGA LAGOON
NATURE RESERVE

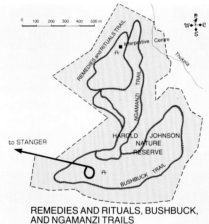

REMEDIES AND RITUALS, BUSHBUCK, AND NGAMANZI TRAILS

It is the only forest in the Republic known to have *Cola natalensis* and *Cavacoa aurea* as dominant species. *Cola natalensis* (or common cola) is well distributed in other Natal forests, but is not common. *Cavacoa aurea* (Natal hickory) is a rare tropical tree of the Euphorbia family, characterized by highly fluted stems and yellow flowers, and known to occur in only two other localities in South Africa. The white stinkwood is also common here. The forest is rich in flowers, and over thirty species of trees and twenty species of liane grow here. The liane contribute to the dense canopy, maintaining the forest microclimate in an area of high winds and salt spray.

The winds tend to blow down the tall trees, which have poor anchorage in the sandy soils. The only canopy trees which remain standing are the *Celtis africana* (white stinkwood) and the *Mimusops obovata* (redmilkwood), probably because their buttress-type roots are deep and firm.

In this unusual forest dwell bushbuck, blue and grey duiker and the rare red duiker, in addition to vervet monkey, bushpig, mongoose and some large specimens of python. The forest also provides the southernmost habitat for the crested guineafowl,

yellowbreasted apalis, white-eared barbet, brownthroated golden weaver and purplebanded sunbird. Intensive ecological studies are being done to determine what factors cause the sharp drop-off of tropical species in the region.

The lagoon and riverine areas support a variety of waders, waterfowl and seabirds, including the fish eagle and osprey.

233. Umhlanga Lagoon Nature Reserve

UMHLANGA ROCKS

AUTHORITY-IN-CHARGE: Natal Parks Board.
SIZE: 26 hectares.
MAIN ATTRACTIONS: The forest provides a habitat for a variety of wildlife such as bushbuck, red and blue duiker and crested guineafowl; unspoilt beach and dune system; shell midden dating back to 600 AD.
FACILITIES/AMENITIES: Regular guided trails arranged by the Natal Branch of the Wildlife Society of Southern Africa; nature trail constructed by the Natal Parks Board; toilets and picnic site.
PERTINENT INFORMATION: The reserve lies to the north of Umhlanga Rocks and adjacent to Hawaan Bush, but its vegetation differs from that found in Hawaan Bush and its birdlife is more prolific. It is the home of South Africa's internationally known poet, Roy Campbell.
AVAILABLE LITERATURE: Contact the Wildlife Society of Southern Africa; included in *Game and Nature Reserves, Resorts and Parks in Natal*, issued by the Natal Parks Board.
CLIMATE: Summer rainfall area.

234. Remedies and Rituals, Bushbuck, and Ngamanzi Trails

HAROLD JOHNSON NATURE RESERVE, NEAR DARNALL

AUTHORITY-IN-CHARGE: Natal Parks Board.
SIZE: 89 hectares.
LENGTH/DURATION: Remedies and Rituals Trail: 1,8 km/0,5-1 hour. Bushbuck Trail: 7 km/2 hours. Ngamanzi Trail: 5 km/1,5 hours.
MAIN ATTRACTIONS: Coastal vegetation; small antelope; historical monuments nearby.
FACILITIES/AMENITIES: Self-guided interpretive trails; small education centre

with reference collection of natural objects; limited camping and caravanning facilities (prior arrangements are necessary).

PERTINENT INFORMATION: Arrangements for camping and short, guided educational trails: The Officer-in-Charge, Harold Johnson Nature Reserve, P.O. Box 148, Darnall 4480.

AVAILABLE LITERATURE: *Remedies and Rituals Trail* and *Bushbuck Trail*, trail booklets; *Teacher's Information Pamphlet No. 2*; *The Self-guided Trails of the Natal Parks Board*, general information pocket brochure (all issued by the Natal Parks Board).

CLIMATE: Summer rainfall area.

The Remedies and Rituals, Ngamanzi and Bushbuck self-guided trails are short, physically undemanding, educational walks which interpret trees and their uses by the Zulus and early Natal settlers, as well as other ecological features such as the geology and fauna in the reserve.

Although it spans only 89 hectares, the Harold Johnson Nature Reserve encompasses bush-clad slopes of valuable coastal vegetation, which includes such species as

epiphytic orchids. Blue, red and grey duiker, bushbuck and impala, as well as the purplecrested loerie, Narina trogon and forest weaver, can be seen.

The small education centre and the reserve itself are particularly popular with the residents of the nearby town of Stanger.

235. Amatikulu Nature Reserve

AMATIKULU, see map page 183

AUTHORITY-IN-CHARGE: KwaZulu Bureau of Natural Resources.

MAIN ATTRACTIONS: Coastal forest with beautiful large tree specimens; giraffe, zebra and reedbuck; estuary and coast.

FACILITIES/AMENITIES: Bamboo rondavels.

PERTINENT INFORMATION: This is a developing reserve. For information: The Officer-in-Charge, Amatikulu Nature Reserve, P.O. Box 223, Mtunzini 3867.

CLIMATE: Summer rainfall area.

236. Umlalazi Nature Reserve

MTUNZINI

AUTHORITY-IN-CHARGE: Natal Parks Board.

SIZE: 908 hectares.

LENGTH: Mangrove Trail: 2 km. Siyayi River Trail: 3 km. River Mouth Trail: 8 km.

MAIN ATTRACTIONS: Mangrove and dune forests.

FACILITIES/AMENITIES: Eight 5-bed Swiss-type log cabins, fully equipped; 56 tent and caravan sites with full ablution facilities; nature trails and picnic sites; beach (swimming and surfing); fishing permitted; playground with trampoline; film shows during holiday periods.

PERTINENT INFORMATION: Take your own food and drink. Advance booking is recommended for peak seasons. Beach vehicles strictly controlled. No pets permitted. Warning: crocodiles are present in waterways.

AVAILABLE LITERATURE: *Umlalazi Nature Reserve*, pocket brochure, issued by the Natal Parks Board.

CLIMATE: Summer rainfall area.

Situated on the north coast road, 128 kilometres from Durban, Umlalazi Nature Reserve is the perfect venue for the urbanite who wishes to enjoy the beauty of nature in a peaceful setting.

Each of the three short nature trails offers a different experience. The undemanding, two-kilometre walk meanders alongside several species of mangrove, while the slightly longer dune forest walk allows possible glimpses of bushpig, bushbuck, or the red, grey and blue duikers. The longest and most strenuous walk – an eight-kilometre round-trip – follows the Umlalazi River from its la-

Top: The mangrove forest in the Umlalazi Reserve.
Below: The fiddler crab, an inhabitant of mangrove swamps.

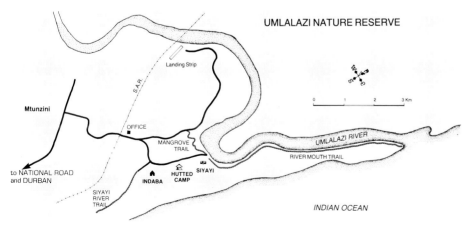

UMLALAZI NATURE RESERVE

goon, through both dune and mangrove forest, to its mouth.

A wide variety of bird species is attracted to the dense coastal vegetation, which includes red and white milkwoods, strangler figs, reeds, rushes and mangroves.

237. Ocean View Game Park

ESHOWE, see map page 183

AUTHORITY-IN-CHARGE: Municipality of Eshowe, Eshowe 3815.
SIZE: 45 hectares.
MAIN ATTRACTIONS: Large and small game; birdlife.
FACILITIES/AMENITIES: Game guard accompanies walkers.
PERTINENT INFORMATION: Open 09h00-12h00, 13h00-17h00.
AVAILABLE LITERATURE: Brochure.
CLIMATE: Summer rainfall area. Cooling breezes bring relief from the humidity.

238. Dlinza Forest Nature Reserve

ESHOWE

AUTHORITY-IN-CHARGE: Natal Parks Board.
SIZE: 203 hectares.
MAIN ATTRACTIONS: Indigenous evergreen forest; antelope; interesting birds and insect life.
FACILITIES/AMENITIES: Walking on limited trail system; Bishop's Seat, an amphitheatre-like clearing where nativity plays are held; picnic and braai sites.
PERTINENT INFORMATION: The reserve borders the Eshowe municipal caravan park.
AVAILABLE LITERATURE: Included in the Natal Parks Board's brochures.
CLIMATE: Summer rainfall area.

239. Nyala Game Ranch

EMPANGENI

AUTHORITY-IN-CHARGE: The Scott-Barnes, c/o Nyala Game Ranch, Private Bag, Empangeni Station 3910.
SIZE: 500 hectares.
MAIN ATTRACTIONS: Large game species, including blesbok, waterbuck, wildebeest, zebra, kudu and nyala; diversified wildlife

and good birdlife; special educational trails and courses.
FACILITIES/AMENITIES: Day and night trails; wildlife can be viewed on foot, from hides and from open vehicles; special education courses for children; education centre. Mbondwe Safari Camp provides rondavels, large lounge, large tents, electric lights, bedding, crockery, cutlery, toilets, hot and cold showers, a resident cook and a swimming pool. Hlati Safari Camp offers the same facilities as Mbondwe but without the lounge and electricity (paraffin and gas lamps supplied). Umvumvu Bush Camp provides rustic huts, tents, beds, bedding, mattresses, utility cooking and eating utensils, water, firewood, a lean-to kitchen, hot and cold showers, long-drop toilets and a resident cook.
PERTINENT INFORMATION: Visitors must provide their own food, unless prior arrangements are made. Maximum of 60 and minimum of 15 schoolchildren per group. Camps are reserved for the sole use of one party, and each camp has its own game guard/cook. Gates open at dawn and close at dusk for day visits.
AVAILABLE LITERATURE: *Nyala Game*

Ranch, general brochure; wildlife checklist; bird checklist; *Trees on Trails, Mbondwe Camp Trail*, guide; *Happiness is Jabulani*, brochure about the Zulu rehabilitation centre (all the above literature is available from the owners of the ranch).
CLIMATE: Average annual rainfall: 700 millimetres. April to September recommended as the best time to visit the reserve. October to March are the best months to study young animals and nesting birds. December to February are the hottest months.

Private game ranches, such as Nyala, are able to offer a variety of activities which most government reserves do not. At Nyala, walking safaris at night, in addition to day trails, supply the opportunity to spot aardwolf, caracal, bush baby, porcupine, hares, rabbits and other nocturnal creatures. Lectures on many aspects of conservation can be arranged for organized groups at the interpretive centre near Mbondwe Camp. Conservation-orientated courses for school and youth groups are also available. A typical course for secondary schoolchildren includes day and night trails, practical soil and

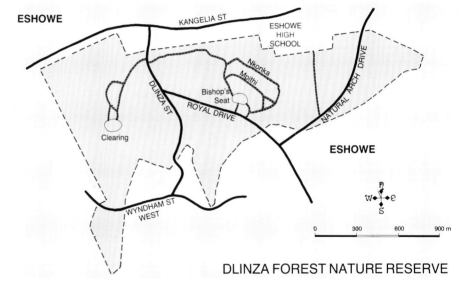

DLINZA FOREST NATURE RESERVE

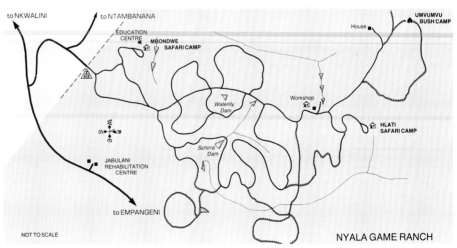

NYALA GAME RANCH

Parks Board; *Some Natal Game and Nature Reserves*, AA Bulletin TBE-N7.
CLIMATE: Summer rainfall area.

The Enseleni Nature Reserve, located 16 kilometres north-east of Empangeni and available for day use only, offers a great deal within a relatively small area. Botanically orientated trailists will enjoy the Swamp Trail, an approximately one-hour ramble through the dense fig tree forests along the banks of the Enseleni River. The vegetation surrounding the smaller streams teems with a wide variety of coastal bush-dwelling birds.

The reserve also offers visitors the opportunity of walking within the 143-hectare game paddock to view reintroduced nyala, blue wildebeest, waterbuck, reedbuck, zebra, grey duiker and bushpig.

water conservation, slide and film shows, lectures and discussions on ecology and game ranching, and visits to the adjoining Jabulani Rehabilitation Centre, where physically handicapped Zulu craftsmen make curios from skins and wood.

Nyala Game Ranch also serves as a venue for ACE, African Conservation Education. ACE, once a project of the Natal Branch of the Wildlife Society, is now run jointly by the Natal Parks Board and the KwaZulu Government. The objectives of the environmental education courses are to demonstrate to Zulu teachers the place of man in the environment and the responsibility he has to care for it properly; and teachers are, in turn, expected to impart their knowledge to their students.

240. Swamp Trail

ENSELENI NATURE RESERVE, NEAR EMPANGENI

AUTHORITY-IN-CHARGE: Natal Parks Board.
SIZE: 293 hectares.
LENGTH/DURATION: 5 km/1 hour or less.
MAIN ATTRACTIONS: Large mammals have been reintroduced; plant and birdlife.
FACILITIES/AMENITIES: Nature trail; picnic sites; botanic garden envisaged.
PERTINENT INFORMATION: Accompanied walks available on request.
AVAILABLE LITERATURE: *Enseleni Nature Reserve*, pamphlet available from the Natal

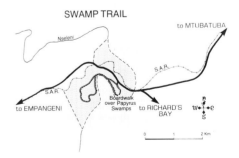

Top: The Nyala Game Ranch specializes in guided, educational walks. The walking safaris which are conducted at night enable trailists to spot nocturnal creatures.

Above: The Swamp Trail runs through the Enseleni Nature Reserve near Empangeni.

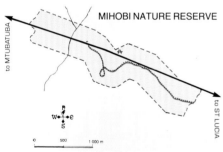

MIHOBI NATURE RESERVE

to MTUBATUBA

to ST LUCIA

w + e
s

0   500   1 000 m

241. Mihobi Nature Reserve

MTUBATUBA

AUTHORITY-IN-CHARGE: Zululand Forest Region, Forestry Branch, Department of Environment Affairs.
SIZE: 565 hectares (to be enlarged).
MAIN ATTRACTIONS: Evergreen indigenous forests; mangrove swamps; endangered bird species.
FACILITIES/AMENITIES: Footpaths; picnic area.
PERTINENT INFORMATION: Permits necessary, obtainable, free of charge, from

The Forester, Dukuduku State Forest, P.O. Box 112, Mtubatuba 3935.
AVAILABLE LITERATURE: Included in the Forestry Branch's *Wilderness Areas and Nature Reserves* information sheet.
CLIMATE: Summer rainfall area, with high humidity. Dry winters.

Mihobi's impenetrable evergreen high forest, situated on the flat coastal Zululand sand dunes, is accessible only by footpaths. Aside from its sense of remoteness, nature enthusiasts will enjoy Mihobi Nature Reserve for its wide range of botanical and bird species.

Evergreen high forests bordered by mangrove swamps create niches for many endangered water and forest birds, as well as raptors. *Acacia karroo*, usually occurring only in grasslands, is present, together with figs, white stinkwood, the rarer Natal white stinkwood, Zulu and small-leaved jackalberry, Natal hickory (which has medicinal properties), and the coast red-milkwood (valuable for consolidating sand dunes and used for boat-building). Other interesting plants include the rare *Clivia miniata* and a variety of tree orchid.

Hikers must be extremely cautious of another rare species – the Gaboon adder. This snake is the largest and most distincti-

vely marked of the African adders. Its geometric 'oriental carpet' colour patterning provides effective camouflage in the dappled light of the forest. It can weigh as much as 8,5 kilograms, and its fangs can grow to five centimetres or more. A bite from such a large snake penetrates deeply into the flesh and a large amount of venom is injected. Wounds are therefore extremely serious; victims require early intravenous antivenom and treatment for shock.

THE ST. LUCIA COMPLEX

CENTRAL ZULULAND

Poised at the edge of the tropical and subtropical climatic zones, the St. Lucia complex teems with plants and animals, all bound within an intricate web of interdependence.

Not surprisingly, St. Lucia provides endless hours of discovery and adventure for the outdoor enthusiast. Within the four reserves of the complex – St. Lucia Game Reserve, St. Lucia Park, False Bay Park and the Eastern Shores Nature Reserve – are hiking

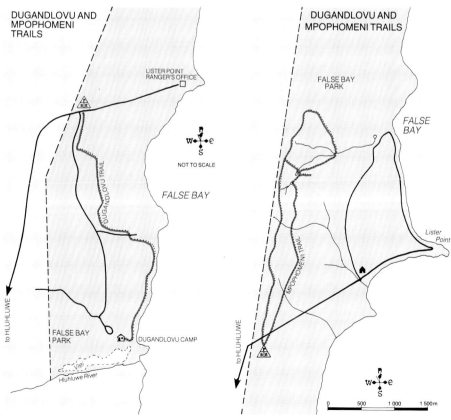

DUGANDLOVU AND MPOPHOMENI TRAILS

LISTER POINT RANGER'S OFFICE

DUGANDLOVU TRAIL

FALSE BAY

NOT TO SCALE

FALSE BAY PARK

DUGANDLOVU CAMP

Vlei

Hluhluwe River

to HLUHLUWE

DUGANDLOVU AND MPOPHOMENI TRAILS

FALSE BAY PARK

FALSE BAY

Lister Point

MPOPHOMENI TRAIL

to HLUHLUWE

0 500 1 000 1 500m

cold water, shower, bush latrine, two small gas cookers, utensils, braai sites and firewood, paraffin lamps and drinking water. False Bay Park: 40 camping and caravan sites along the shoreline. Route indicators (arrows burnt into poles) on the Dungandlovu Trail; trees marked with names and national tree list numbers on the Mpophomeni Trail; other short walks are possible.

PERTINENT INFORMATION: The huts on the Dugandlovu Trail serve as a base camp, and are reached after an 8,5-kilometre walk. Maximum of 16 people admitted per night. Anti-malaria precautions are necessary; ticks and mosquitoes are prevalent. No swimming because of crocodiles. Trails suitable for school groups.

AVAILABLE LITERATURE: *Dugandlovu Trail*, information sheet issued by the Natal Parks Board and the NHWB; *Mpophomeni Trail*, trail guide and map; *False Bay Park*, pocket brochure; bird checklist.

CLIMATE: Summer rainfall area.

The Mpophomeni Trail is located in the northern section of False Bay Park, while the Dugandlovu Trail is laid out in the park's southern section.

The Mpophomeni Trail passes through woodland, sand forest and thicket, the last-named being the intermediate stage between the other two. The trail guide describes the different tree and bird species in each area, emphasizing trees such as the tamboti, marula, black monkey thorn, Zulu podberry, spineless monkey orange, Natal fig, lala palm and others. The sand forest, a low-canopy forest which once extended throughout north-eastern Natal, is the home of South Africa's rarest antelope, the suni.

The Dugandlovu Trail meanders through woodlands and along the shores of Lake St. Lucia. The camp has a superb setting overlooking the Hluhluwe River and floodplain.

Game-viewing and bird-watching on both trails is good. Game includes hippo, bushpig, warthog, zebra, reedbuck, nyala, grey and red duiker, suni and crocodile. Common birds of the sand forest include the paradise flycatcher, goldentailed woodpecker and purplecrested loerie. The birds differ in woodland, where common species are brownhooded kingfishers, puffback shrikes and crested francolins, and also in the thickets, where one is more likely to see tambourine doves, crested guineafowl and the Natal and whitethroated robins.

248. Mziki Trail

EASTERN SHORES STATE FOREST AND NATURE RESERVE, ST. LUCIA COMPLEX

AUTHORITY-IN-CHARGE: Natal Parks Board.
LENGTH/DURATION: 40 km/3 days. Loop trails: 10 km, 10 km and 18 km.
MAIN ATTRACTIONS: The trail covers many of the components of the St. Lucia Complex: open grassland, dune forest, beach, freshwater pans and hippo paths; huge flocks of birds on pans (seasonal).
FACILITIES/AMENITIES: Mount Tabor hut is equipped with bunks, mattresses, table and benches, water, gas cooker, gas lamps, bush shower and toilet; trail markers are yellow

reedbuck spoor on black backgrounds; three loop trails begin at the hut.
PERTINENT INFORMATION: Maximum of 8 and minimum of 4 people per group. The Mziki Trail is part of a trail system planned to link St. Lucia Estuary to Cape Vidal. Anti-malaria precautions are necessary. Carry water.
AVAILABLE LITERATURE: *Mziki Trail*, general information, trail guide and sketch map issued by the Natal Parks Board.

For further information, see The St. Lucia Complex, page 206.

249. Isikhova and Umkhumbe (Red Duiker) NatureTrails

CHARTER'S CREEK, ST. LUCIA COMPLEX, see map page 207

Umkhiwane Trail

FANIE'S ISLAND, ST. LUCIA COMPLEX

AUTHORITY-IN-CHARGE: Natal Parks Board.
LENGTH/DURATION: Isikhova Trail: 7 km. Umkhumbe Trail: 5 km. Umkhiwane Trail: 5 km. Approximately 2-3 hours each.
MAIN ATTRACTIONS: Coastal forest, typical of the western shore of Lake St. Lucia; birdlife such as purplecrested loeries, crested guineafowl, marsh owls and Cape eagle owls (*Isikhova* is Zulu for 'place of owls').
FACILITIES/AMENITIES: Trail guides are used to explain marked points of interest, including individual trees; petrol is available; fishing is permitted. Charter's Creek: hutted camp with a 7-bed cottage, fifteen 2- and 3-bed huts, community lounge, kitchen blocks, laundry, ablution

block, refrigerator and deep freeze facilities, table tennis, swimming pool and playground, braai and picnic sites. Fanie's Island: twelve 2-bed rondavels, fully equipped, with kitchen, ablution block, refrigerator, and deep freeze facilities. Camping and caravan site with hot and cold water; for bookings: The Camp Superintendent, P.O. Box 201, Mtubatuba 3935, tel. (03552) 1431.
PERTINENT INFORMATION: Fanie's Island is a more secluded camp than Charter's Creek. Hippos and crocodiles can be dangerous. Anti-malaria precautions are necessary.
AVAILABLE LITERATURE: *Isikhova Nature Trail*, trail guide concentrating on botanical aspects of the coastal forest ecology; *Umkhumbe Nature Trail, Charter's Creek*, guide; *The Umkhiwane Trail*, guide; *Charter's Creek and Fanie's Island Hutted Camp*, pocket brochure; *The Self-guided Trails of the Natal Parks Board*, general information pocket brochure.
CLIMATE: Summer rainfall area.

For further information, see The St. Lucia Complex, page 206.

250. Nyalazi State Forest

WEST OF ST. LUCIA COMPLEX, see map page 207

AUTHORITY-IN-CHARGE: Natal Forest Region, Forestry Branch, Department of Environment Affairs.
MAIN ATTRACTIONS: Water-birds near St. Lucia Estuary; pelican, flamingo and hippopotamus.
PERTINENT INFORMATION: Permits necessary, obtainable from The Forester, Nyalazi State Forest, Private Bag 7206, Mtubatuba 3935.
CLIMATE: Summer rainfall area.

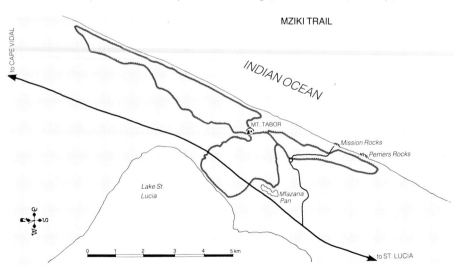

MZIKI TRAIL

UMKHIWANE TRAIL

Above: Along the entire stretch of Lake St. Lucia, adjacent to the sea, range the world's highest forested dunes; the variety of tropical plant and animal life within these dunes is astonishing.

Below: The Wilderness Leadership School leads the White Rhino Trail through the Umfolozi Game Reserve.

251. Umfolozi Wilderness and Primitive Trails and Auto Trail

UMFOLOZI GAME RESERVE

AUTHORITY-IN-CHARGE: Natal Parks Board.
SIZE: 47 753 hectares.
LENGTH/DURATION: Walking trail: 3 days. Auto trail: 67 km/5 hours.
MAIN ATTRACTIONS: Diverse wildlife; 300 species of birds; a trail situated within a 24 000-hectare wilderness area.
FACILITIES/AMENITIES: Wilderness trails;

'primitive' trails; self-guided auto trail; short walks from Mpila Camp (prior arrangement with the camp superintendent necessary); bush camps, used as base camps for wilderness trails, may be hired when trails are not operating; Mpila Hutted Camp with twelve 3-bed rest huts; Msinda Hutted Camp with six 3-bed huts; hide at rhino drinking pan; picnic site on Mpila Hill.
PERTINENT INFORMATION: Visitors must provide their own food and drink. Maximum of 6 and minimum of 4 people per trail (minimum age 16 years). Anti-malaria precautions are necessary; ticks are prevalent. Certain items of equipment (backpack, sleeping bag, water bottles, cutlery, groundsheet) can be hired. Trails run from March to November. For information: The Camp Superintendent, Umfolozi Game Reserve, P.O. Box 99, Mtubatuba 3935.
AVAILABLE LITERATURE: *Wilderness Trails*, issued by the Natal Parks Board; *The Hluhluwe/Umfolozi Complex*, booklet, Natal Parks Board; *Umfolozi Game Reserve*, pocket brochure; *Umfolozi Mosaic*, auto trail guide.
CLIMATE: Average annual rainfall: 750 millimetres, falling mostly during the hot summer. Winter is temperate.

This reserve lies between, and stretches beyond, the White and Black Umfolozi rivers from which it takes its name. The vegetation, thickest along river courses, is composed largely of short trees. White and black rhino, waterbuck, nyala, kudu, buffalo, giraffe, cheetah, lion and crocodile, as well as other smaller animals and a diverse birdlife, can be observed.

Umfolozi is a Zulu word embracing the essential qualities displayed by the leader of a span of oxen – courage, strength and patience. Certainly the name is appropriate for this park as it, too, is a leader in its field. To the ecologist and environmental educationalist the name calls to mind a number of worthwhile ventures in nature conservation, but none could have won as much public

UMFOLOZI WILDERNESS AND PRIMITIVE TRAILS AND AUTO TRAIL

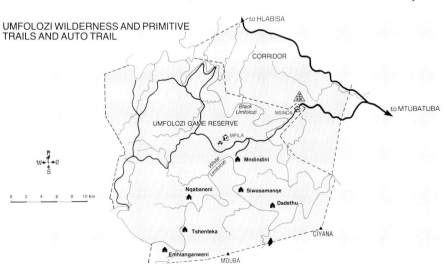

relationships which occur in the Umfolozi wilderness. Alphabetical markers, which correspond to letters on the map and the text in the trail guide, are placed along the route. History, ecology, trees, birds, management policy, geography and, of course, the wildlife of the reserve, are covered in this self-guided auto trail.

252. White Rhino Trail

UMFOLOZI GAME RESERVE, see map page 207

AUTHORITY-IN-CHARGE: Wilderness Leadership School.
DURATION: 5 days for adults, 6 days for scholars.
MAIN ATTRACTIONS: Abundant wildlife, including prolific birdlife; historical Zulu traditions.
FACILITIES/AMENITIES: Transport, canoes, rucksacks, tents, sleeping bags, groundsheets, meals and utensils are provided.
PERTINENT INFORMATION: Maximum of 6 people per trail (minimum age 15 years). Anti-malaria precautions are recommended. Water must be purified before drinking.
AVAILABLE LITERATURE: *Wilderness Trails, Wilderness Leadership School*; *Prospectus*; *Background to the Natural History of Zululand*, J.M. Freely (all available from the Wilderness Leadership School); *The Motorist*, Second Quarter, 1985, pages 36-7.
CLIMATE: Summer rainfall area.

Operating in the Umfolozi Game Reserve in Zululand, this well-run and educationally valuable trail incorporates big-game viewing (including the wealth of water-based fauna, such as crocodiles and hippopotamus, and water-birds) and Zulu history. Courses begin and end in Durban, from where trailists are transported to the reserve.

253. Mbhombe Forest Trail and Auto Trails

HLUHLUWE GAME RESERVE, see map page 207

AUTHORITY-IN-CHARGE: Natal Parks Board.
SIZE: 23 067 hectares.
LENGTH/DURATION: Mbhombe Trail: 30 minutes (within camp area). 'Northern 40' drive: 40 km/3 hours. Southern Auto Trail: 3 hours.
MAIN ATTRACTIONS: Plentiful and varied wildlife, including black and white rhino,

---

sympathy as the determined and successful bid to save the white rhino from extinction.

In conjunction with the nearby Lake St. Lucia Reserve, Umfolozi is also the birthplace of the first South African wilderness trail, and Ian Player, an erstwhile Natal Parks Board ranger and prominent conservationist, is often credited with the wilderness trail concept: 'I knew in the wilderness areas we had resources that were vital to the well-being of the people of the world. These were like a foundation that they could return to for nourishment; a spiritual recreation, something desperately needed in the twentieth century.'

Player founded the Wilderness Leadership School in 1957, and one of his field officers, Clive Walker, the conservationist and famous wildlife artist, founded Educational Wildlife Expeditions in 1975. Rangers who lead their trails are inspired by their love of nature and the firm belief that the only way man will prevent himself from de-stroying the fragile web of life of which he is part and on which he is so dependent, is to understand nature's balance and respect it.

The Umfolozi Wilderness Trails are led through the old hunting ground of Shaka, founder and king of the Zulu nation during the nineteenth century. The first night and optional last night are spent in the base camp, while the other two nights are spent under canvas in the wilderness area. Trailists must provide their own food, which is carried between camps by donkeys.

The 'primitive' trail combines the features of a wilderness trail with a hiking trail; in other words, you carry your backpack with food, clothing and equipment, but the route and overnight stops, in caves or bush enclosures, are not standard and are chosen by the accompanying officer. Novice hikers can rent some equipment from the warden.

For the motorist, the Umfolozi Mosaic Auto Trail has been developed to provide insight into the complexity of the inter-

elephant, cheetah and nyala; over 200 species of birds.

FACILITIES/AMENITIES: Self-guided walk and two auto trails; interpretive programmes, including walks, talks, films and slide shows; game-viewing hide; picnic site where visitors may leave their cars; open-air museum, traditional Zulu homestead; shop for curios, books and film.

PERTINENT INFORMATION: Visitors must provide their own food. Ticks are prevalent. Petrol and oil are available at the hutted camp, known locally as 'Hilltop'.

AVAILABLE LITERATURE: *Mbhombe Forest Trail*, guide book; *The Southern Auto Trail*, detailed ecological guide; *The Northern 40, Self-guided Drive*, detailed ecological guide; *The Hluhluwe/Umfolozi Complex*, booklet; *Hluhluwe Game Reserve*, pocket brochure.

CLIMATE: Average annual rainfall: 800 millimetres, falling mostly during the hot summer. Winter is mild to cold.

Hluhluwe, established in 1897, along with the Umfolozi and St. Lucia game reserves, is the oldest existing wildlife sanctuary in South Africa.

Although Hluhluwe is not used as intensively for walking as other Natal game reserves, the Mbhombe Forest Trail, located at the fringe of the rest camp, is a rewarding, half-hour self-guided walk. Semi-deciduous forest provides the focus for the trail, and the guide booklet points out interesting facts about plants such as *Dalbergia armata*, a thorn climber from whose Zulu appelation *umHluhluwe* this reserve derives its name.

The two self-guided auto trails are a recent introduction to Hluhluwe Game Reserve. Their accompanying trail guides contain a wealth of ecological information which make game-viewing drives infinitely more interesting and educationally valuable.

254. *Ubizane Game Ranch*

HLUHLUWE, see map page 183

AUTHORITY-IN-CHARGE: Ubizane Game Ranch, P.O. Box 102, Hluhluwe 3960.
SIZE: 1 500 hectares.
MAIN ATTRACTIONS: Bushveld; large game.
FACILITIES/AMENITIES: Hunting safaris; walking safaris; night safaris; accommodation available in the luxurious Zululand Safari Lodge.
PERTINENT INFORMATION: Contact the authority-in-charge for further details.
AVAILABLE LITERATURE: Brochure.
CLIMATE: Summer rainfall area.

Opposite page: Impala at a drinking hole in the Hluhluwe Game Reserve.

255. *Sodwana Bay National Park*

NORTHERN ZULULAND, see map page 207

AUTHORITY-IN-CHARGE: Natal Parks Board.
SIZE: 413 hectares.
MAIN ATTRACTIONS: Beach with tidal pools; coastal game fishing; small mammals and abundant birdlife.
FACILITIES/AMENITIES: Paths; open camp-sites (take all your own equipment); ablution blocks, water and petrol; 15-amp electrical outlets for hire; store sells basic food supplies.
PERTINENT INFORMATION: Anti-malaria precautions are necessary; cholera vaccinations are recommended. Booking for camp-sites: The Officer-in-Charge, Sodwana Bay National Park, Private Bag 310, Mbazwana 3974; tel. 0020, ask for Jozini 1102.
AVAILABLE LITERATURE: *Sudwana Bay National Park*, pocket brochure; included in general Natal Parks Board brochures; *Mkuzi and Ndumu Game Reserves and Kosi Bay to Sodwana Bay*, AA Bulletin TBE-N4.
CLIMATE: Summer rainfall area.

Sodwana Bay National Park is a popular holiday resort, especially for coastal game fishing; it is also ideal for casual, undemanding beach and dune rambles, although none of the routes is interpreted. The birdlife is particularly interesting, with such species as Woodwards' batis and Rudd's apalis being present. Observant walkers can spot suni, red and grey duiker, steenbok, reedbuck, bushpig, the Tonga red squirrel and species of mongoose.

The coastal dune forest, the vegetational zone found closest to the shore and lining the estuary, is dominated by Natal strelitzia and wild silver-oak trees. In the early 1950s, in an effort to stabilize the shifting coastal dunes, *Casuarina equisetifolia* trees were planted. These trees, imported from the Far East and Australia, are used for this purpose in many parts of Africa.

Prior to the building of a bridge in 1971/2, a small, very productive black mangrove stand grew farther inland from the coastal dune forest. The bridge proved to be ecologically disastrous, however, as it flooded the mangrove mudflats; low salinities killed the fauna and high water levels killed all but the largest trees. Restoration of the mangrove community by methods such as the removal of sediments, re-establishment of the estuarine topography, removal of invasive sedges growing under the existing mangrove trees and planting of black mangrove seedlings, is being implemented. However, it will take many years of work in this area before the delicate natural balance is restored.

256. *Kosi Bay Nature Reserve*

NGWANASE, see map page 207

AUTHORITY-IN-CHARGE: KwaZulu Bureau of Natural Resources.
SIZE: 20 hectares (the lake system is much more extensive).
MAIN ATTRACTIONS: Kosi Bay lake system, including 247 species of birds, hippo, fish, crocodiles, leatherback turtles, coral reef and mangrove swamps.
FACILITIES/AMENITIES: Open camp-sites with cold water; guided walks by game scouts to forests and mangrove swamps; Turtle Research Station, Natal Parks Board; three-day guided hiking trail with two huts planned.
PERTINENT INFORMATION: For booking of camp-sites: The Officer-in-Charge, Kosi Bay Nature Reserve, P.O. Box 1, Ngwanase 3973 (note: camping is allowed only at camp-sites). Permits necessary, obtainable from The Secretary, Department of the Interior, Private Bag X02, Ulundi 3838 (allow one to two months for reply). Four-wheel drive vehicles essential for sandy roads and river crossings. Zambezi sharks possible in first lake. Beware of walking on hippo paths. Bring your own food and drink. Anti-malaria precautions are necessary. Fishing is allowed only in the second and third lakes and from the camping area.
AVAILABLE LITERATURE: In process of being compiled; contact the KwaZulu Bureau of Natural Resources.
CLIMATE: Summer: warm to hot and humid. Winter: warm. Windy.

For those willing to venture to the remote north-eastern corner of Zululand, a fascinating experience awaits their arrival. Kosi Bay (not a bay but four interlinked, clear, freshwater lakes in close proximity to the shore, the first of which empties into the sea) is a unique mosaic of interdependent ecosystems. The system stretches over 25 kilometres, therefore the nature reserve on the shore of Nhlange, the third and largest lake, is only a small component. The other lakes include Mpungwini, which is the smallest of the four lakes; Sifungwe, which is four times the size of Mpungwini; and Amanzimnyana, which is located 16 kilometres from the estuary.

Kosi Estuary is the southernmost example of thick mangrove woodlands over large areas which include all the mangrove species in South Africa. Guided walks with game scouts have you exploring fig and raffia palm forests, mangrove swamps and marshes and coastal sand dunes with dense bush and milkwood trees. Without a guide, the inexperienced in the bush could just bump into an outraged hippo, and have to struggle through thick, black, glutinous mud in retreat! A three-day guided hiking trail with two overnight huts *en route* is near completion. (Contact the KwaZulu Bureau of Natural Resources for the latest information about the hiking trail.)

The most unusual bird of this area is the palmnut vulture which eats, among other things, the husks of the raffia palm and the oil palm. Another inhabitant of the tidal forest is the tiny mudskipper, an amphibious fish which lives on the roots and low branches of mangrove trees. Its fins are shaped so that it can skip over the water's surface, alternating rapidly between swimming and flying.

Tribal customs are also fascinating to observe. With no appropriate soil to use for housing, all huts are built of reeds, and beautiful waterproof basketware is crafted in place of clay utensils.

257. Ndumu Game Reserve

JOZINI, see map page 207

AUTHORITY-IN-CHARGE: Natal Parks Board.
SIZE: 10 117 hectares.
MAIN ATTRACTIONS: Unique birdlife (416 species), including tropical East African species and abundant aquatic birdlife on pans; large crocodile population; tropical insect species.
FACILITIES/AMENITIES: Five walks guided by game scout (a charge is levied per walk); self-guided trails are being considered; open-vehicle Land Rover tours (mornings, and afternoons until sunset); five hides where motorists can get out of their cars; hutted camp with seven 3-bed rest huts containing refrigerator, ablution block, communal deep freeze in kitchen, store (for books only) and chefs to cook your food; provincial library; talks given on request, with prior arrangement.
PERTINENT INFORMATION: New tarred road until the last 14 km, then road deteriorates to sand. Nearest hotels are 80 km away at Jozini and 100 km away at Mkuze. Ndumu has 100 per cent occupancy rate, so book in advance and confirm before arrival (no camping allowed). Visitors must supply their own food and drink; nearest trading store (with petrol) is 5 km away in the town of Ndumu. No children under 5 years allowed on Land Rover tours, but family tours can be organized; no children under 14 years allowed on walks. Anti-malaria precautions are necessary.
AVAILABLE LITERATURE: *Ndumu Game Reserve*, pocket brochure; *Birds of Ndumu Game Reserve*; tree checklist; *Mkuzi and Ndumu Game Reserves and Kosi Bay to Sodwana Bay*, AA Bulletin TBE-N4.
CLIMATE: Summer rainfall area.

Ndumu, situated in the far north-eastern part of Zululand, on the Mozambique border, is the reserve for the avid bird-watcher. Here, many bird species from East Africa, such as the African broadbill, yellowspotted nicator and white-eared barbet, reach the southernmost limit of their distribution, thereby making the region unique in South Africa. Largely low-lying and well-watered, with numerous pans and the Pongola-Usutu floodplain, Ndumu is also a haven for water-dependent birds such as the black heron, pygmy goose, fish eagle and fishing owl, as well as numerous waders.

Five 5 km/2-3 hour guided walks are located in different habitats, and are geared for bird-watchers, who can ramble slowly through riverine forests and bush, alert for any moving creature. My game guard was able to 'call up' several species, including the Narina trogon and chorister robin.

Ndumu Hill (115 m) is covered with acacia trees. Mammals inhabiting the semi-evergreen scrub forest and swampy grassland of Ndumu include hippopotamus, nyala, bushbuck, impala, grey and red duiker, reedbuck, zebra, white and black rhino, bushpig and suni.

Above left: Although the main attraction of Ndumu Game Reserve is the prolific birdlife, guided trails in the large game habitat also fascinate visitors. Here, the game guard points out a rhino scratching post.

Above right: Open vehicle Land Rover tours complement the guided walks offered in Ndumu Game Reserve. The five walks are located in different habitats and are geared for bird-watchers.

Opposite page: Giraffes in Mkuzi Game Reserve. Although not as well known as the older Natal reserves, Mkuzi offers the opportunity to experience the mood of Africa on the Bushveld Trail.

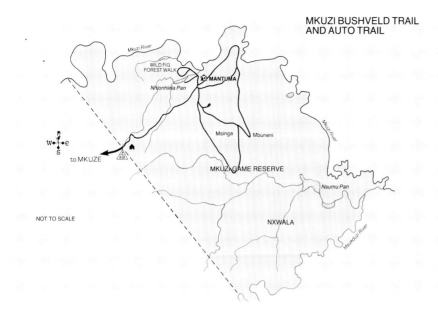

MKUZI BUSHVELD TRAIL
AND AUTO TRAIL

258. *Mkuzi Bushveld Trail and Auto Trail*

MKUZI GAME RESERVE

AUTHORITY-IN-CHARGE: Natal Parks Board.
SIZE: 28 900 hectares.
LENGTH/DURATION: Bushveld Trail: 3 days.
Auto Trail: 57 km.
MAIN ATTRACTIONS: Diverse and plentiful wildlife typical of northern Zululand; approximately 300 species of birds, including plentiful waterfowl; low-lying thornveld and open, park-like country.
FACILITIES/AMENITIES: One-day walks, three-day 'bushveld trail' (run twice a month only) and Auto Trail; trail camps equipped with tents and stretchers, as well as cooking and eating utensils; rucksacks

provided; Mkuzi main camp with fully equipped luxury huts, tent and caravan site; three game-viewing hides (Bube, Msinga and Malibali).

PERTINENT INFORMATION: Visitors must provide their own food (camp cooks are available). Bushveld trails operate from April to the end of October, starting Friday and returning Monday; maximum of 6 and minimum of 3 people per trail (minimum age 16 years). Anti-malaria precautions are recommended.

AVAILABLE LITERATURE: *Mkuzi Game Reserve*, a study of Mkuzi's ecology, issued by the Natal Parks Board; *Around and About Mkuzi*, guide for Auto Trail; *Mkuzi Game Reserve*, pocket brochure; *Mkuzi and Ndumu Game Reserves and Kosi Bay to Sodwana Bay*, AA Bulletin TBE-N4; *Wilderness Trails*, Natal Parks Board information brochure.

CLIMATE: Dry winters.

Although not as well known as the older Umfolozi Wilderness Trail, the Mkuzi Bushveld Trail gives participants the opportunity to experience the mood of Africa; to see large herds of mammals such as blue wildebeest and zebra, and also the rare black and white rhinos. Birdlife is profuse and includes subtropical visitors and migrant waterfowl that are attracted to the large Nsumu Pan.

Walking through Mkuzi, you will notice that it differs from the other nearby game reserves in that it is composed of large, park-like stretches of flat, open country which facilitate game-viewing. Two of the attractive trees in this reserve are the wild wistaria (also known as tree wistaria) and the flame bush. The wild wistaria is deciduous or semi-deciduous and displays beautiful, sweet pea-like, violet-blue flowers among pale green, glossy leaves. In contrast, the flame bush is an evergreen with a crown of

shiny green leaves and sprays of scarlet tubular flowers and scarlet fruits. Acacia and marula trees are also prominent.

In addition to the longer bushveld trails where the trails officer chooses the route and distance, day hikes are available. In the company of a game guard, walks are arranged from Tongaland sand forest with its characteristic trees, along the Mkuzi River and through the wild fig forest to the hilly plains of the Nhlonhlela Pan, where water-associated life, such as crocodile, hippopotamus and water-birds, is abundant. Other

day walks can be arranged to Nsumu Pan to see its hippopotamus and birdlife.

A new addition to Mkuzi Game Reserve is the Auto Trail. Emphasizing trees and the ecology and history of the reserve, the detailed trail guide offers abundant information, making game-viewing drives infinitely more meaningful to the motorist.

259. *Ntendeka Wilderness Area*

NONGOMA

AUTHORITY-IN-CHARGE: Zululand Forest Region, Forestry Branch, Department of Environment Affairs★.

SIZE: 5 230 hectares.

MAIN ATTRACTIONS: Indigenous forest, grassland and savannah; epiphytic orchids and rare plants; birdlife; Ntendeka cliffs.

FACILITIES/AMENITIES: Bridle paths; picnic sites at fringes of wilderness; camping permitted for wilderness users only.

PERTINENT INFORMATION: This wilderness area forms part of Ngome State Forest. Permits necessary, obtainable from The Forester, Ngome State Forest, Private Bag X1306, Vryheid 3100. Maximum of 12 people per overnight group.

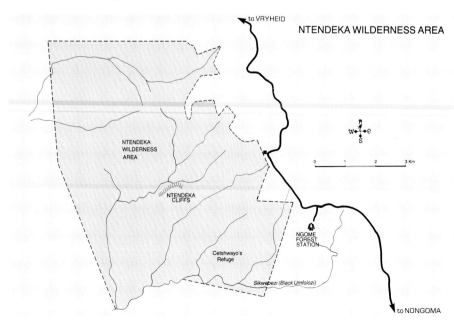

Above: A kudu cow in Mkuzi Game Reserve.

AVAILABLE LITERATURE: *Notes on Ntendeka Wilderness Area, Ngome State Forest, Zululand, 1975*, information sheets, including tree and shrub list, and sketch map, issued by the Forestry Branch.
CLIMATE: Average annual rainfall: 1 000-1 700 millimetres, falling mostly in summer.

Ntendeka's principal conservation value is its indigenous high forest, exceptionally rich in plant life that exhibits strong tropical elements, unusual for an area far from the sea. This tropical environment is created by the interaction of numerous physical factors such as the substantial annual summer rainfall, the cool, moist winds of winter, and the steep south-east-facing forested slopes which receive little frost or sun and are dissected by perennial streams.

Some of the interesting plants to look out for are *Didymochlaena truncatula*, a large fern, with 2,5-metre, dark, glossy green fronds, found in wet, shady kloofs, and the forest tree fern, *Alsophila capensis*. Although the forest tree fern also grows in the Southern Cape, it reaches the unusual height of eight metres only along the streams of Ngome.

Epiphytic ferns, more often associated with tropical jungle, also abound in the forests of the Ntendeka wilderness. Look for them above the ground, on moss-covered tree bark or in humus-filled tree cracks, as these micro-habitats are their sole source of water and nutrients. The area contains other rare species such as terblans (a tree member of the Proteaceae), and endemics such as the Ngome lily; both species have limited distributions. The forest, as well as the lower, tropical grassland and savannah region of the reserve, provide good and varied habitats for many birds, including the bronze-naped pigeon, Narina trogon, purplecrested loerie, longcrested eagle and the endangered bald ibis.

Mammals such as bushbuck, blue and grey duiker and vervet monkey are also prevalent. The area is rich in Zulu history and, prior to 1905, its timber, especially yellowwood, was heavily exploited.

The erosion of Peruvian Ecca sandstones of the Karoo System reveals a dolerite intrusion that forms the impressive Ntendeka cliffs (approximately 1 350 metres). The rock shelter known as Cetshwayo's Refuge,

situated under one of these majestic cliffs, is said to have been the place where Cetshwayo, last independent king of the Zulus, took shelter when fleeing from the British who were eventually to defeat him.

Although this wilderness area is not as well known as some others, nature lovers will be well rewarded by a visit. Several paths lead into the forest from the Ngome Forest Station. Attractive camping spots can be found in the valleys near the streams.

260. *Vryheid Hiking Trail*

VRYHEID, see Regional Map page 186

AUTHORITY-IN-CHARGE: Municipality of Vryheid, P.O. Box 57, Vryheid 3100.
DURATION: 3 days.
MAIN ATTRACTIONS: Game; mountain scenery; Natal Spa (hot springs).
FACILITIES/AMENITIES: Planned.
PERTINENT INFORMATION: This hiking trail is in its developing stages, planned for completion in 1988. The first day will be from Vryheid Berg to Grootgewacht Dam, traversing a game reserve; the second and third days will pass through private land.
AVAILABLE LITERATURE: In process of being compiled.
CLIMATE: Summer rainfall area.

261. *Itala Nature Reserve*

LOUWSBURG, see map page 207

AUTHORITY-IN-CHARGE: Natal Parks Board.
SIZE: 29 651 hectares.
MAIN ATTRACTIONS: Large variety of reintroduced game, including black and white rhinoceros and cheetah; great variety of scenery, including bushveld, grassland, steep-sloped valleys and jointed cliffs; over 300 recorded species of birds.
FACILITIES/AMENITIES: Wilderness trail (3

days, 4 nights); conducted day walks with game scout; self-guided auto trail; two rustic camp-sites with basic amenities (cold taps, flush toilet, kitchen and showers) are being replaced by a large hutted camp of international standards, including a restaurant, swimming pool, hydro and shop, and bush camps next to the river.
PERTINENT INFORMATION: Due to the introduction of dangerous animals, hikers are not permitted to walk on their own. Bring your own food and drink on all trails and to camps (until the restaurant is opened). For bookings: The Warden, Itala Nature Reserve, P.O. Box 42, Louwsburg 3150; tel. (03882) 1413. Anti-malaria precautions are advisable in the low country.
AVAILABLE LITERATURE: *Itala Nature Reserve*, pocket brochure; *Itala Game Reserve – A World on its Own, the Ngubhu Loop Trail.*
CLIMATE: Average annual rainfall: 685-1 170 millimetres, falling mostly in summer. Winters (May to August) can be very cold, with low morning temperatures. Summers can be hot in the valleys.

Located in the Pongola River Valley on the Natal/Transvaal border, Itala is a scenically stunning mosaic of open bushveld, grassed hilltops and highveld, steep, deep valleys, cliff-faces and granite boulder outcrops. Interesting rock formations have been created by the erosion of Karoo sandstone to reveal dolerite dykes and sills which appear as prominent, jointed cliffs.

Elevation spans 250 metres to 1 450 metres above sea level, creating conditions suitable for a wide variety of flora and fauna. With the exception of elephant, buffalo and lion, all the major mammal species are present at Itala. Plans to expand this reserve to 100 000 hectares include the introduction of these three species as well.

Through the wonderland of Itala, the Natal Parks Board runs wilderness trails on demand for three days and four nights. Six people per trail supply only their food and clothes, and sleep in beautiful bush camps along the river. Conducted day trails with armed guards are also available. For motorists, a circular drive of 30 kilometres (three hours) has been provided. When done in conjunction with the trail guide, this gives a fine introduction to the ecology of Itala.

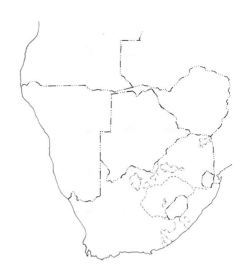

SWAZILAND

Swaziland, one of Africa's few remaining kingdoms, is a constitutional monarchy. Landlocked by Natal, the Transvaal and Mozambique, its 17 363 square kilometres (similar in size to Wales or the American state of New Jersey) contains examples of many African ecosystems: the western mountains of the highveld with their impressive river gorges, valleys and peaks such as Emlembe, the highest at 1 863 metres; rolling grasslands; and bush typical of the lowveld.

At one time, hiking trails for tourists were scarce; however, in the past few years Swaziland's National Trust Commission has been developing game parks and nature reserves such as Malolotja, Mlawula and Mlilwane, where the hiker is 'king'.

All visitors must be in possession of a valid passport, and nationals other than South Africans may require visas. Non-South African passport holders must have re-entry permits to return to the Republic.

Swaziland's temperate climate varies considerably with geographical region. The north-west highlands are cooler than the south-east lowveld. Average temperatures range from 13 °C in winter to 20 °C in summer. Rain and humidity occur throughout the country between November and March; some areas receive up to 2 250 millimetres. The crisp, clear winter days (April to September) are perfect for hiking. Note that bilharzia is a major health hazard and that bathing in rivers, streams and dams at the lower altitudes is not advised.

ECOLOGICAL ZONE: DRY
WOODLANDS

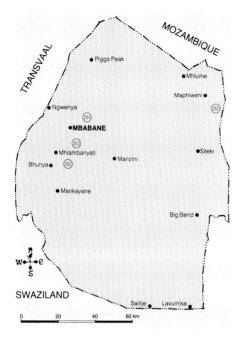

Below right: The River Walk in Meikles Mount follows the banks of the Usutushane River.

Opposite page, top: Mhlane Mountain is particularly attractive for its large granite boulders and the magnificent summit view of the entire Meikles Mount estate and beyond.

Opposite page, bottom: The unique Macobane Furrow Trail in Mlilwane Wildlife Sanctuary follows the historic 26-kilometre aquaduct on the Nyonyane mountains. This trail is along a contour, so it is relatively easy.

262. Meikles Mount

MHLAMBANYATI

AUTHORITY-IN-CHARGE: Murray and Norah Meikle, Meikles Mount, P.O. Box 13, Mhlambanyati, Swaziland.

SIZE: 300 hectares.

MAIN ATTRACTIONS: Indigenous forests and plantations; rare plants; mountain streams and waterfalls; small game and birdlife (92 bird species).

FACILITIES/AMENITIES: Network of footpaths and bridle trails; horses for hire; natural and man-made swimming pools; fishing for yellowfish, bream and catfish; eight fully equipped luxury cottages, serviced, cook and maid provided; small shop selling groceries, meat, dairy products and vegetables; croquet, tennis and badminton courts.

AVAILABLE LITERATURE: *Meikles Mount*, brochure with colour sketch map; bird list loaned on request.

CLIMATE: Average annual rainfall: 1 400 millimetres, falling mostly in summer. Mist common. January and December, hottest months. July and August, coldest and driest months. Refreshingly cool when surrounding areas are hot.

Stretching 1 341 metres from the edge of the Usutushane River (884 m) to the top of The Mountain at World's View, Meikles Mount is a small, secluded country estate offering day ramblers and horse-riders a network of walks and bridle paths varying in length and difficulty.

The estate is located on granite in sour grassveld vegetation, with numerous springs and streams, some clogged by delicate rows of tree ferns. The climate is ideal for tree-growing and the owners have developed many eucalyptus stands on their grounds.

From the summit of World's View or Giant Rock (the steepest walk), the hiker gazes over no less than 75 million pine trees, all belonging to the Usutu Forest, the largest plantation of conifers in the southern hemisphere and the fourth-largest block of plantation in the world. (As you stand in awe overlooking this gigantic man-made forest, you should realize that all these trees will be ground to 100 million tons of pulp per year just to produce paper products!) Do not wander into this forest. Not only are the owners reluctant to allow hikers access, but you stand the chance of getting hopelessly lost among the trees.

The walks on Meikles Mount are varied. Many are shady paths through plantations and firebreaks. My favourite routes include Mhlane Mountain, Floral Tunnel, the River Walk and Secret Valley. Mhlane Mountain is particularly attractive due to the large granite boulders, wildflowers and its magnificent summit view of the entire estate, the Usutushane River and beyond. Floral Tunnel is actually a scramble through a fine pocket of indigenous forest, while the River

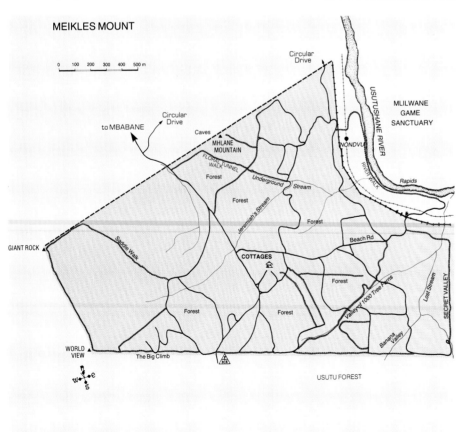

Land-Rover tours; rest camp with four double huts, two family huts and nine traditional grass beehive huts, ablution block with showers, hot and cold water (wooden huts have refrigerators; all have bedding and towels); camp-site, cabin and open-air dormitories; restaurant, with self-service cooking, overlooking the Hippo Haunt (waterhole with prolific birdlife and hippopotamus); open camp-fire all hours; provision and curio shop; established base for the National Environmental Education Programme; Reynolds Memorial Garden (aloes are spectacular); nursery.

PERTINENT INFORMATION: Mosquitoes are a pest; malaria is possible but not prevalent. Main gates open between sunrise and sunset; night gate opened with pass (arrange beforehand).

AVAILABLE LITERATURE: *Mlilwane Wildlife Sanctuary, Swaziland*, brochure; *Mlilwane Wildlife Sanctuary*, map of southern area; *Mlilwane 21 – The Mlilwane Story: A History of Nature Conservation in the Kingdom of*

Walk meanders along the banks of the Usutushane River.

The Mlilwane Wildlife Sanctuary borders the other side of the river and with prior arrangements and instructions from both the owners of Meikles Mount and the Reillys, who own Mlilwane Wildlife Sanctuary, ambitious hikers can spend a day walking from the estate to the reserve. Some of Mlilwane's animals, such as kudu, zebra and buffalo, are seen browsing at Meikles Mount. Also

near the river are the ruins of a 1963 iron ore railroad.

Birds of Meikles Mount are interesting. Some specials include the Ayres hawk eagle, black sparrowhawk, crested guineafowl, redcrested korhaan, buffstreaked chat and the bluemantled flycatcher.

Hikers can expand their walk by exploring the surrounding countryside. Mrs Meikle recommends walking to the Lipholo Dam wall and back (a round-trip of about five hours) or around Mhlane (about two and a half hours). Alternatively, visitors can hire horses and a guide to cover the same routes.

263. *Mlilwane Wildlife Sanctuary*

MBABANE

AUTHORITY-IN-CHARGE: Mlilwane Trust, Mlilwane Wildlife Sanctuary, P.O. Box 33, Mbabane, Swaziland.
SIZE: 4 545 hectares (to be enlarged).
MAIN ATTRACTIONS: Unusual variety of fauna (mixture of both highveld and lowveld species), including endangered animals; impressive variety of birds (roosting birds at the Hippo Haunt are especially attractive); magnificent scenery, especially in the northern wilderness; forest, savannah and grassveld; sacred places; old tin mine; 26-km historic furrow.
FACILITIES/AMENITIES: The Macobane Furrow Trail; the Tree Trail (self-guided); guided walks and hikes; horse-riding with game scouts; backpacking trail planned; interpretive centre, conservation hall, film and slide shows; game-viewing drives;

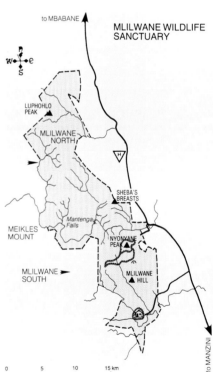

Swaziland and Fund Raising Appeal, by Terence R. Reilly.
CLIMATE: Summer rainfall area (October to April). Winter days are warm, but nights are cool.

Before I met Ted and Liz Reilly, I enjoyed Mlilwane; after several days with this energetic and ambitious couple, I began to appreciate fully Mlilwane Wildlife Sanctuary and its tremendous conservation achievements and contributions to the Swaziland kingdom.

The reserve is divided into two parts: the well-known southern section which abounds

with wildlife, and offers game drives, the Macobane Furrow Trail, the Tree Trail, the unique rest camp with its tame animals and unforgettable waterhole, and an interpretive centre and facilities for the National Environmental Education Programme; and the relative wilderness of the northern section, a rugged area of scenic landscapes and wildlife, best explored on foot.

Mlilwane lies in 'the Valley of Heaven', potentially the most fertile area in Swaziland. The escarpment, which forms part of the reserve, was long ago a turning point of easterly and westerly migrations of game. Spanning an altitude from 660 metres to 1 437 metres, the reserve represents middle-veld and highveld, including montane and riverine forests, valley bushveld, broadleaf savannah and sour grassveld. This adds up to an area capable of supporting a wide variety of game; the animals include white rhino, giraffe, zebra, blue wildebeest, eland, kudu, waterbuck, sable antelope, buffalo,

hippo, crocodile, wild cat, civet cat, leguan and many more.

You can only appreciate the biological diversity of Mlilwane when you learn the incredible story of how each animal was reintroduced into a mixed farming operation: Mlilwane was developed on a family farm, previously so heavily exploited that entire habitats had to be created before wildlife could be introduced. Trees were planted, and effort was devoted to re-establishing a wetlands ecosystem. Indigenous animals, from water scorpions and frogs to impala and kudu, were introduced.

While it has always offered guided walks and horse-riding trails with Swazi game guards, the reserve has recently opened two self-guided educational trails. The Tree Trail is an easy stroll around the camp, used in conjunction with the interpretive centre. Plaques with ecological and botanical descriptions of each indigenous tree take approximately one hour to study.

The Macobane Furrow Trail is named after Ted Reilly's father, James Weighton 'Mickey' Reilly, who was known as 'Macobane' to the Swazis. He mined tin and was the largest employer of industrial labour in Swaziland at the time, providing 800 jobs.

Among his 'impossible' achievements was the building of a 26-kilometre aquaduct on the Nyonyane mountains. The Macobane trail follows this historic furrow, even to the extent that a boardwalk has been built along the face of a precipice where the old furrow flue carried water. The gradient is one in one hundred, so this walk is along a contour and relatively easy. Interpretive stations, tree numbers, telescopes, Bushman caves, abundant large game and views of the old tin workings all add interest to this unusual trail.

For the physically fit, a climb up Nyonyane (1 136 m) with a game scout is highly recommended. The summit offers superb 360° views, including the Sheba's Breasts of Rider Haggard fame. The circular rock piles you encounter are actually remains of Basotho buildings from the time before the Swazis invaded.

For the real wilderness seeker, ask for permission to explore Mlilwane north, where a backpacking trail is planned. This highveld habitat with forests and waterfalls is home to endangered species such as klipspringer, oribi, vaal rhebok, sable antelope and Addo buffalo. Luphohlo Peak, the highest point on Mlilwane, offers a view across Swaziland, from the western border near Redhill to the Lebombo Mountains on the Mozambique border.

The Reillys' energies are ceaseless. They also own Mkhaya, a 7 500-hectare lowveld reserve comprising granite sandveld (a sourveld of mixed broadleaf tree species) and dolerite or sweet acacia veld. Many large game species such as white rhino, wildebeest, nyala, waterbuck and tsessebe have been introduced. And when the Reillys' dreams materialize, this reserve will have a rest camp, guided walks and Land Rover tours. Keen naturalists are welcome to arrange visits to Mkhaya with the Reillys. Remember to carry water while hiking.

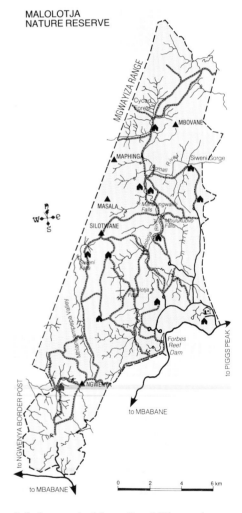

MALOLOTJA NATURE RESERVE

Left: An example of the smaller wildlife spotted on the Macobane Furrow Trail.

Top: The Ngwenya hills in Malolotja Nature Reserve present a strenuous climb to the trailist.

Opposite page, left: Peering into Lion Cavern Mine, reputed to be the oldest in human history.

Opposite page, right: Mhlangampepa Valley.

264. Malolotja Nature Reserve

MBABANE

🥾 🥾

AUTHORITY-IN-CHARGE: Swaziland National Trust Commission, P.O. Box 100, Lobamba, Swaziland.
SIZE: Approximately 18 000 hectares.
MAIN ATTRACTIONS: Magnificent western highveld landscape; complex geology and dramatic mountain scenery; Swaziland's second- and third-highest peaks; breeding colonies of bald ibis and blue crane; 150 species of birds; Malolotja Falls (95 m, the highest in Swaziland); Barberton cycad forest; Komati River Valley; oldest mine in human history (41000 BC).
FACILITIES/AMENITIES: Complex of day walks and backpacking trails (1-7 days'

duration); camp-sites on trails are designated clearings near water; camp-site with 15 sites and braais, thatched ablution block and hot and cold water; camp-site with five A-frame thatched and stone structures with four beds each, outside cooking facilities and ablution block; five fully furnished log cabins, accommodating up to 6 people each, serviced (bring your own bedding, towel and food); interpretive centre; trout fishing, with permit, on Upper Malolotja River and Forbes Reef Dam; 20 km of game-viewing roads; skins and game meat for sale at the office.
PERTINENT INFORMATION: Only one party is booked per trail camp-site per night; sites are small, and hold only one or two tents each. Trails are physically demanding and some require hikers to cross rivers. Backpackers are required to carry a spade, which can be rented from the office, to bury human waste. For information: The Senior Warden, Malolotja Nature Reserve, P.O. Box 1797, Mbabane, Swaziland.
AVAILABLE LITERATURE: *Malolotja Nature Reserve*, brochure and map; bird checklist;

articles in *Great Outdoors*, July 1984 and May 1985; located on Government Printer's topographic map series D.O.S. 435, sheets 2631 AA and 2630 BB (PWD No. 5), edition 6, D.O.S. 1983; *Backpackers' Guide to Trails*, planned.
CLIMATE: Average annual rainfall: 1 525 millimetres, falling mostly in summer. Thunderstorms and mist are common.

Malolotja, spanning an altitude from 615 to 1 800 metres above sea level, is Swaziland's prime hiking reserve, a paradise of highveld and middleveld topography comprising beautiful valleys, broken mountainous terrain, high peaks, plains, plateaux and deep river gorges clothed with forests and grassveld. Some of the outstanding physical features of this area include the Malolotja Falls, the highest in Swaziland, the Mahulungwane Falls and Valley ('the valley of tree ferns'), and two of Swaziland's three highest peaks, Ngwenya (1 829 m) and Silotwane (1 680 m).

Ecologically Malolotja is an essential habitat for nesting colonies of blue cranes and bald ibises, and the locally endangered vaal rhebok, oribi and mountain reedbuck are found here. Malolotja protects many endangered plants such as *Encephalartos laevifolius* (Kaapsehoop cycad), *E. paucidentatus* (Barberton cycad), *E. heenanii* (woolly cycad) and *Kniphofia umbrina* (red-hot poker), and hosts spectacular highveld flora including *Aloe thorncroftii*, *A. chortoliriodes* var. 'boastii' and *Disa intermedia*, a rare orchid.

In addition to being ecologically valuable, Malolotja's geology contributes to its uniqueness. It incorporates a representative sample of the Swaziland System, the oldest sedimentary rocks in the world, which contains the oldest known origin of life on earth – fossils of blue-green algae, estimated at 3,5 billion years old. The southern end of the reserve is rich in haematite-chert ironstones,

mined extensively in recent times for their metallic content and by Stone Age peoples for their red pigment. Lion Cavern Mine, on the west side of Ngwenya, is listed in the Guinness Book of Records as the oldest mine in the world, dating to *c.* 41000 BC.

Malolotja is Swaziland's last true wilderness area and its management policies are geared for walkers. Wilderness trails are marked with stone cairns only and paths are not constructed, but are cleared of bush where necessary. Hikers must sleep in designated tent sites and these, located next to water, are also only cleared of bush.

There are approximately 80 kilometres of trails to choose from, and more than six day walks. All routes must be discussed at the tourist office before setting off. I arranged a seven-day backpacking trip to see the whole of the reserve. I found the backpacking trails extremely physically demanding, although short in length. Take the times given in the literature seriously! All trailists must be able to read a map and navigate in poor weather conditions. Remember, the backpacking area is managed as a wilderness, and minimal tampering with the environment is the policy. I discovered two 'dry' tent sites so I recommend checking with the warden about the water situation when arranging your route.

Each section of the reserve is different. One trail which I found particularly lovely was the walk from Ngwenya Camp, a tent site situated deep in the densely forested foothills of Ngwenya Peak, to Siweni Camp at the foot of Silotwane Mountain. We began in the morning with a very steep, 2,5-hour climb out of Ngwenya Forest. Struggling up through broken, rugged terrain with distant views of rural Swazi homesteads and dense forests in deeply incised kloofs reverberating with the calls of baboons and Knysna loeries, I felt the strains reminiscent of climbing a high Himalayan pass. But once over the ridge, the gentle, almost magical Mhlangampepa Valley unfolded. Highveld rolling grassland was alive with white butterflies feeding on a carpet of yellow daisies. Swarms of alpine swifts feasted on these butterflies while wildebeest, blesbok and mountain reedbuck grazed on young green grass shoots. A pair of mating blue cranes danced in the grass and Stanley's bustards called from afar.

The stream bed is delineated by a thin green line of tree ferns which dance in and out of the shadows dropped by cumulus clouds high overhead; the wind creates a changing mosaic of patterns on these gentle slopes; and on the horizon, the distant Barberton Mountains with their formidable peaks and gorges disappear into the haze.

The next morning I climbed Silotwane, Swaziland's third-highest peak, an exhilarating experience that I highly recommend. Once on top, a 360° view of the entire reserve, reaching into the Barberton Mountains of the Transvaal, unfolds. From the summit you can really appreciate the park's rugged topography, and the views of the Siweni and Malolotja Falls and the Komati River Valley are spectacular. In fact, your entire backpacking route can be traced. A pair of blue cranes flew below me while I was standing there; top-lit by the sun, they appeared as a sleek set of silver-winged jets.

In direct contrast to the southern section of the park is the more rugged and relatively unexplored northern section. To reach these mountains the Komati River Valley (615 m), a hot, lowveld area of winding river and gorge, must be crossed. Remember to waterproof your pack if you have to cross the river in the rainy season. The cycad forest on the Mgwayiza range, with specimens reaching seven metres high, is a highlight of this region where only fit trailists should attempt the steep spurs between the deeply incised, forested kloofs.

265. Mlawula Nature Reserve

(INCORPORATING MLAWULA, MBULUZI, NDZINDZA AND SIMUNYE NATURE RESERVES)
MHLUME

AUTHORITY-IN-CHARGE: Swaziland National Trust Commission, P.O. Box 100, Lobamba, Swaziland.
SIZE: Approximately 18 400 hectares.
MAIN ATTRACTIONS: Unique Lebombo Mountains; views over Mozambique; endangered plant species (Lebombo ironwood, *Androstachys johnsonii*, found in dry forest) and locally endangered animal species; 'vulture restaurant' (where mammal carcasses are dumped) and hide; 300 species of birds; large game species; Rhyolithic rockface communities and dramatic topography (gorges, pools, caves and rapids); archaeology (artefacts of Stone Age peoples).
FACILITIES/AMENITIES: Guided walks and Land Rover tours on request; canoeing and fishing with permit (bring your own equipment); interpretive centre at the gate; archaeological interpretive walk in Timphisini area planned; two camp grounds with thatched shelters, ablution blocks and hot and cold water; hutted camp planned; network of self-guided trails; backpacking trail planned.
PERTINENT INFORMATION: For information and bookings: The Officer-in-Charge, Mlawula Nature Reserve, P.O. Box 312, Simunge, Swaziland; tel. (0194) 38239. Beware of crocodiles and bilharzia in rivers. Ticks are prevalent. Anti-malaria precautions are advised from October to May. Birdlife is best from September/October to December.
AVAILABLE LITERATURE: *Mlawula Nature Reserve*, map and information brochure; *Tree Checklist: Mbuluzi Nature Reserve*; *Vertebrate Checklist: Mbuluzi Nature Reserve*; *Bird Checklist: Mbuluzi Nature Reserve*; *Trails Guide: Mbuluzi Nature Reserve*; *Mbuluzi Nature Reserve Newsletter*; other publications planned.
CLIMATE: Hot summers, with rain. Warm winters. Humid.

Mlawula, Mbuluzi, Ndzindza and Simunye nature reserves are managed as a unit, and present to the trailist an excitingly rich lowveld and Lebombo Mountain wilderness in eastern Swaziland, on the Mozambique border. This area has the distinction of possessing the earliest known record of our species, *Homo sapiens*, dating back 110 000 years.

Mlawula is an interesting area, archaeologically and ecologically. Along the riverbeds of the Lebombo Mountains, Early Stone Age tools, one million years old (and older), have been discovered. In the lowveld, evidence of Middle Stone Age people exists. Many of these sites are protected and an archaeological trail is planned.

Ecologically the reserve offers a diverse topography ranging from 76 metres at the eastern end of the Mbuluzi gorge to 573 metres above sea level in Ndzindza in the Lebombo Mountains. Dry thorn savannah in the west blends into coastal moist thickets in the east. The diversity of vegetation types produces a habitat where a great variety of animals thrive, including unusual coastal birds such as the yellow weaver, African broadbill, crested guineafowl, golden-rumped tinker barbet, nicator and gorgeous bush shrike, and dry savannah species such as the grey loerie, marico sunbird and Bennett's woodpecker. Game animals also abound.

The bush clump grassland plateau, an area to be developed with walking trails near an escarpment overlooking Mozambique, supports oribi, zebra, duiker, wildebeest and mountain reedbuck. Waterbuck are found mainly on Mbuluzi, and Ndzindza is important for supporting locally endangered species such as samango monkey, spotted hyaena, Sharpe's grysbok and the fishing owl. Ndzindza also protects endemic floral species such as *Encephalartos umbuluziensis*,

Above: The crocodile pool in the Timphisini area of Mlawula Nature Reserve.

Opposite page: Hiking in Mbuluzi Nature Reserve.

Aloe keithii and *Euphorbia keithii* (Swazi euphorbia). Hippopotamus and crocodile occur in the two perennial rivers, the Mbuluzi River on the northern boundary and the Mlawula River in the west.

The self-guided trails, such as the three-kilometre Mathewu Trail near the Mbuluzi River, were rebuilt after cyclone Demoina demolished the warden's enthusiastic efforts. These trails are accompanied by a guide book comparing the geology, botany and animal life of the area, before and after the cyclone. The huge horseshoe in the Mbuluzi River is particularly scenic when viewed from a height on the Mathewu Trail. The reserve is also in the process of constructing more day walks and overnight backpacking trails (contact the officer-in-charge for details). However, interested people are encouraged to walk wherever they wish (except along game-viewing roads). It is the hiker's responsibility to take care near potentially dangerous animals such as crocodiles and hippos on the river banks.

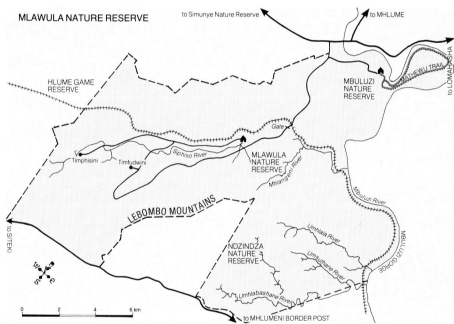

MLAWULA NATURE RESERVE

to Simunye Nature Reserve
to MHLUME
to LOMAHASHA
MATHEWU TRAIL
HLUME GAME RESERVE
MBULUZI NATURE RESERVE
Gate
Timphisini
Timfudwini
Siphiso River
MLAWULA NATURE RESERVE
Mhlangeni River
Mbuluzi River
LEBOMBO MOUNTAINS
Umhlala River
MBULUZI GORGE
NDZINDZA NATURE RESERVE
Umsuthane River
to SITEKI
Umhlabashane River
to MHLUMENI BORDER POST
0 2 4 6 km

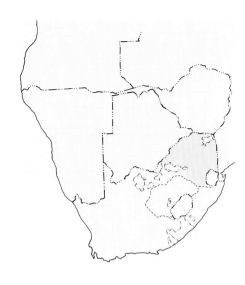

NORTHERN AND EASTERN TRANSVAAL, LEBOWA AND KANGWANE

The Northern and Eastern Transvaal comprise vast areas of South Africa's northernmost province. This region includes the land of baobab, acacia and mopane trees known as the Lowveld, bordered on the north by the Limpopo River and on the east by Mozambique; and the large stretch of high land north and east of Pretoria which includes the Waterberg, Wolkberg, Magoebaskloof area, Soutpansberg and Transvaal Drakensberg. The Highveld forms this region's southern border and the Kalahari its western border.

Venda, Bophuthatswana and Lebowa once formed part of the Transvaal. Venda

and Bophuthatswana are now independent states, while Lebowa operates as an independent homeland.

Facilities and amenities for trailists abound in the Northern and Eastern Transvaal. Guided 'big game' trails are plentiful in the Lowveld, and in the Kruger National Park and adjoining, privately run game reserves. A plethora of constructed hiking ways along scenic mountains and through forests and woodlands has been developed under the auspices of the National Hiking Way Board, the Transvaal Provincial authorities and private enterprise. The rambler will delight in the numerous short walks through indigenous forest, bushveld and wetlands, while the mountaineer is well catered for within the magnificent Wolkberg Wilderness and Transvaal Drakensberg areas. Overnight facilities offer a wide variety of choice, from sleeping under the stars below the Wolkberg range, to bunkbeds in the historic gold-miner's hut on the Prospector's Hiking Trail, and luxurious chalets in the Mount Sheba Resort.

Climate is predictable in the Northern and Eastern Transvaal, except in the mountains, which dictate their own weather. Generally, summer (October to March) is hot and rainy, while winter (May to September) is cool, dry and sunny during the day and cold and clear at night.

ECOLOGICAL ZONE: DRY
WOODLANDS

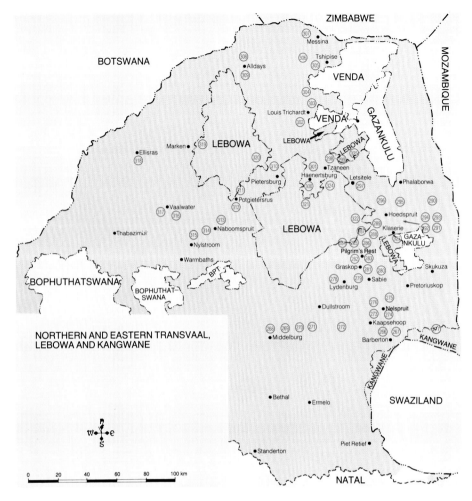

NORTHERN AND EASTERN TRANSVAAL,
LEBOWA AND KANGWANE

266. Gold Nugget Hiking Trail

BARBERTON

AUTHORITY-IN-CHARGE: Makhonjwa
Conservation Foundation, P.O. Box 221,
Barberton 1300.
LENGTH/DURATION: 37 km or 44 km/
2-3 days.
MAIN ATTRACTIONS: The trail gives insight
into the rugged, adventurous life of early
Barberton gold miners; old mines and their
associated buildings; Barberton mountain
scenery.
FACILITIES/AMENITIES: Agnes Top Hut (an
old miner's house), where water, shower,
toilets, bunks for 20 people, firewood and a
braai place are provided. Lone Tree Hill
Hut (an old fort), where toilets, shower,
tank water, bunks for 20 people, firewood
and a braai place are provided. Cars can be
left at the municipal caravan park or police
station.
PERTINENT INFORMATION: Hikers must be

*Opposite page: The Cycad Trail is named for the
endemic cycads discovered en route.*

10 years or older. This is a circular trail. To
complete the trail in two days, you must
walk an extra 3 km on the second day, from
Lone Tree Hill Hut to Barberton. Water
should be carried.
AVAILABLE LITERATURE: *The Gold Nugget
Trail*, information sheet with sketch map,
issued by the Barberton Publicity
Association.
CLIMATE: Summer rainfall area. Winter is
the best hiking season. July, average low
temperature: 9 °C. January, average high
temperature: 28 °C.

Hiking trails in South Africa took on an
added dimension with the opening of the
Gold Nugget trail. This is a two- or three-
day hike which winds along old bridle paths,
and past historical gold mines and relevant
sections of Barberton and its surroundings,
all filled with the romance and spirit of adventure of a bygone era.
   The historical emphasis of the trail is unusual, but there is much also to hold the attention of the naturalist, for along the trail a
variety of *Aloe* and *Protea* species, flowering
plants such as the Barberton daisy and
Pride-of-De-Kaap, and indigenous trees
such as the African ebony, tamboti, sausage
tree, mobola plum, lowveld chestnut,
Transvaal red-milkwood and lowveld cabbage tree will be encountered. *Lonchocarpus*

capassa, or the rain tree, is mentioned in
Thomas Baines' *Goldfield Diaries* and was
well known to the early miners. The so-
called 'rains' shed by the tree during the hot
months before the authentic rains break are
in fact produced by the frothy-foamed
nymphs of the frog-hopper. This Hemiptera
insect, *Ptyelus grossus*, sucks sap from the
tree and ejects pure water as droplets, or
'rain'.
   Birdlife is equally fascinating because the
Barberton area is a complex ecotone environment where a blend of highveld, lowveld
and Drakensberg species coexist.
   This trail is not recommended for beginners or unfit hikers. The first day covers a
distance of 14 kilometres and takes approximately eight hours to walk. The second day,
a distance of 20 kilometres along the Sad-
dleback Ridge of the Makhonjwa Mountains, can also be covered in about eight
hours, and is equally strenuous. As there
can be no guarantee that water will be available on the route, it is essential to carry
water with you.
   One of the highlights of the trail is Rim-
er's Creek, which is explored on the third
day (10 kilometres). Here, in this erstwhile
hive of mining activity, the original Barber's
Reef and other workings can be seen, along
with the old Guard House which was built
during the Anglo-Boer War and is now a national monument.
   The first day of the trail coincides for a
short way with the Fortuna Mine Rotary
Nature Trail. Slight changes to the trail may
occur, as an open-air mining museum is being developed in the area.

267. Fortuna Mine Rotary Nature Trail

BARBERTON

AUTHORITY-IN-CHARGE: Makhonjwa
Conservation Foundation, P.O. Box 221,
Barberton 1300.
LENGTH/DURATION: 2 km/1,5-2 hours.
MAIN ATTRACTIONS: Large variety of trees;
views of De Kaap Valley and Barberton;
man-made tunnel.
FACILITIES/AMENITIES: 100 labelled
indigenous trees; circular walk.
PERTINENT INFORMATION: A strong torch is
necessary in the tunnel. No fires are
permitted.
AVAILABLE LITERATURE: *Barberton Tunnel
Hiking Trail*, information sheet and sketch
map, available from the Barberton Publicity
Association.

The Rotary Club that initiated this short, attractive, easy walk deserves praise for its
imagination. The route passes through the
Barberton Indigenous Tree Park with its

100 labelled lowveld trees and shrubs, meanders across hill slopes, through gorges and through a 75-year-old tunnel. Built to transport gold-bearing ore from the Fortuna Mine to the Mill, the 600-metre tunnel cuts through 3 400 million-year-old rock, the earth's oldest. A strong torch is essential to enable you to negotiate the tunnel.

It is planned to expand this trail to include other tunnels, as well as an outdoor mining museum. The first day of the Gold Nugget Hiking Trail coincides for a short way with the Fortuna Mine Rotary Nature Trail.

268. Middelburg Hiking Trail

MIDDELBURG, see Regional Map

AUTHORITY-IN-CHARGE: Private youth project.
DURATION: Approximately 4-6 days.
MAIN ATTRACTIONS: Highveld/middleveld ecotone; rocky riverine environment; cycads; birdlife; steenbok, hippopotamus, crocodile and baboon.
FACILITIES/AMENITIES: To be decided.
PERTINENT INFORMATION: The trail will begin at Botshabelo (see page 230) and end at Loskop Dam (see page 231). For information: National Hiking Way Board.
AVAILABLE LITERATURE: Planned.
CLIMATE: Summer rainfall area.

269. Baboon, Cycad, Tarentaal and Suikerbos Hiking Trails

MIDDELBURG

AUTHORITY-IN-CHARGE: Mr P.C. Oberholzer, P.O. Box 1326, Middelburg 1050; tel. (01321) 23764.
LENGTH/DURATION: Baboon Trail: 22 km/2 days, 1 or 2 nights. Cycad Trail: 14 km/1 day, 1 optional night. Tarentaal Trail: 8 km/1 day. Suikerbos Trail: 15 km/1 day.
MAIN ATTRACTIONS: Olifants River scenery; rare, endemic cycads and other indigenous flora; prolific birdlife.
FACILITIES/AMENITIES: Five huts at each of the three sites, with drinking water, veld toilets, fireplaces and firewood, but no bunks; although the huts are large, only one party is booked per hut per night; horse-riding can be arranged.
PERTINENT INFORMATION: Swim at your own risk; river water may have bilharzia. Ticks are prevalent. Beware of snakes.

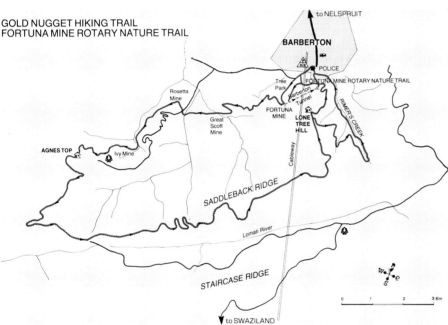

GOLD NUGGET HIKING TRAIL
FORTUNA MINE ROTARY NATURE TRAIL

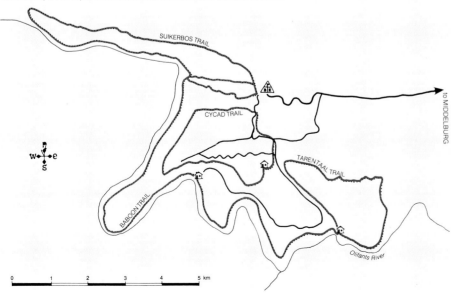

BABOON, CYCAD, TARENTAAL AND SUIKERBOS HIKING TRAILS

AVAILABLE LITERATURE: *Cycad Trail*, information sheet and map.
CLIMATE: Summer rainfall area. Days are very hot. Spring is the best hiking season.

Located 15 kilometres from Middelburg, between the Loskop Dam Public Resort and Fort Merensky, is a complex of privately run hiking and nature trails.

The 14-kilometre Cycad Trail is situated at the top of the ravine through which the Olifants River flows. The trail is physically easy as it winds over flat terrain, through thick indigenous bush, under overhanging trees and around rocky formations, revealing beautiful views of the Olifants River and surrounding area. The Cycad Trail is so-named from the Waterberg cycad and the Olifants River cycad, two species endemic to the area. Cycads, a rare group of trees whose origins date back 300-200 million years, are protected in South Africa and Zimbabwe.

The Cycad Trail ends near the start of the Baboon Trail, a route of 22 kilometres which provides a convenient weekend hike as you can walk to the halfway point, overnight there, and return to your car the following day. It is a more difficult hike than the Cycad Trail as there is a lot of climbing up and down large rocks on steep slopes. Much of the trail is located at the bottom of the ravine and on the banks of the Olifants River.

The Suikerbos Trail winds towards Loskop on the upper plateau with dramatic views of the Olifants River, and returns to the starting point via the river bank.

The shortest trail, the Tarentaal, gives the hiker a taste of both river and plateau.

On all trails the variety of proteas, aloes, cycads, fruiting shrubs and large trees in the bushveld-type vegetation provides habitat for a wide diversity of birds, as well as small antelope, the ubiquitous baboon, vervet monkeys, leopards, hyaenas and bateared foxes, and three types of snakes – mambas, puff adders and cobras.

Top: The Olifants River forms a dramatic backdrop to the Baboon Trail.

Above: A toktokkie beetle of the Tenebrionidae family, seen on the Baboon Trail.

Opposite page: On the Loskop Dam Nature Trail.

270. Klein Aasvoëlkrans, Botshabelo and Oorbietjie Nature Walks

MIDDELBURG

AUTHORITY-IN-CHARGE: Municipality of Middelburg, P.O. Box 14, Middelburg 1050; tel. (01321) 23897.
LENGTH/DURATION: Klein Aasvoëlkrans Nature Walk: 12 km/8 hours. Botshabelo and Oorbietjie nature walks: 4 hours each.
MAIN ATTRACTIONS: Klein Olifants River Valley; rare plants; cycads; large mammals, including black wildebeest; wide variety of wildlife; Fort Merensky, a national monument; South Ndebele village, an open-air museum; Botshabelo, a restored mission station.
FACILITIES/AMENITIES: Circular trail marked with white footprints; overnight accommodation available in youth hostels (toilets, showers, kitchen, stoves,

refrigerators and braai facilities) and family rondavel; no mattresses supplied.
PERTINENT INFORMATION: Bilharzia is present, and swimming in the river is not recommended. Sufficient drinking water must be carried (2 litres per person per day is recommended in summer). Gates open 08h00-18h00.
AVAILABLE LITERATURE: *Wandelpaaie-Hiking Trails*, brief information sheet with sketch map; 'Botshabelo' by Danie Stoltz, *Flying Springbok*, September 1985.

The 12-kilometre Klein Aasvoëlkrans circular walk, beginning and ending at Botshabelo, is rich in bushveld atmosphere. Winding through the Klein Olifants River Valley, the trail abounds with birdlife, small antelope such as oribi, grey rhebok, duiker, steenbok and klipspringer, and baboons and vervet monkeys. Sadly, despite the trail's name, which means 'small vulture cliff', there are no vultures left in the vicinity. (The cliff earned its name from the tribal legend that the missionaries threw their old and sick horses over it to feed the vultures.)

The endemic Olifants River cycad grows within a plant community which hosts an interesting diversity of indigenous trees and shrubs. Ramblers can walk the entire eight-hour trail or opt for a shorter loop, the Oorbietjie Nature Walk, which will return them to the parking area in approximately four hours.

The Botshabelo Nature Walk, situated just north of the Klein Aasvoëlkrans trail, is yet another option. This four-hour ramble on the escarpment surrounding Botshabelo offers, in addition to the natural features seen on the Klein Aasvoëlkrans trail, views of Fort Merensky, Botshabelo (a Sotho word meaning 'place of refuge') village and the South Ndebele village.

271. Loskop Dam Nature Trail

NEAR MIDDELBURG

AUTHORITY-IN-CHARGE: Overvaal Resorts.
LENGTH/DURATION: 6 km/2 hours.
MAIN ATTRACTIONS: Flora; birdlife; scenic views of Loskop Dam and the Olifants River Valley and farmlands.
FACILITIES/AMENITIES: Constructed trail marked with footprints; trees labelled with their national tree list numbers, scientific, Afrikaans and English names; accommodation and full resort facilities available at the public resort, across the road.
PERTINENT INFORMATION: Circular trail. No water *en route*. Trail markings are confusing, so carry a sketch map. Trail begins opposite the entrance to the public resort, which is well signposted. For information: The General Manager, Loskop Dam Public Resort, Private Bag X1525, Middelburg 1050; tel. 0020, ask for Damwal 2.
AVAILABLE LITERATURE: Sketch map, available at the office of the public resort.
CLIMATE: Summer rainfall area. Hot summers; cool winters.

272. Elandskrans Hiking Trail and Nature Walk

WATERVAL-BOVEN

AUTHORITY-IN-CHARGE: Municipality of Waterval-Boven, P.O. Box 53, Waterval-Boven 1195.
DURATION: 2-day circular hiking trail or 1-day nature trail.
MAIN ATTRACTIONS: South Africa's first hiking trail to include a train ride *en route*; waterfalls; indigenous trees; historical monuments.
FACILITIES/AMENITIES: One overnight hut; Elandskrans Holiday Resort at the trailhead

(chalets, flats, caravan sites); natural swimming pools on trail; trees labelled with their national tree list numbers.
PERTINENT INFORMATION: Maximum of 28 people per group per hiking hut. For bookings: The Manager, Elandskrans Holiday Resort, P.O. Box 53, Waterval-Boven 1195.
AVAILABLE LITERATURE: Sketch map issued by the Municipality of Waterval-Boven.
CLIMATE: Summer rainfall area.

In a lush setting of waterfalls and bushveld, the Elandskrans Hiking Trail is South Afri-

ca's first and only trail to include a train ride *en route*. On the morning after the 14,5-kilometre walk to the overnight hut, hikers board the SAR passenger train, which leaves Waterval-Onder daily at 10h10, for a thirty-minute journey to Waterval-Boven. The train winds through two tunnels in the Elands Pass and skirts the historic five-arch bridge, the 90 metre-high Elands River Falls and the abandoned 400 metre-long NZASM (Nederlandsche Zuid-Afrikaansche Spoorwegmaatchappij) tunnel. The tunnel was built in 1892/3 as part of the railway company's line from Lourenço Marques (now

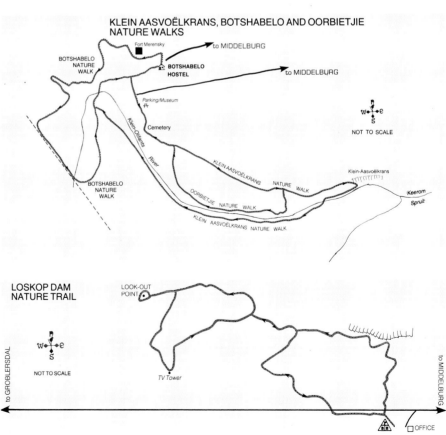

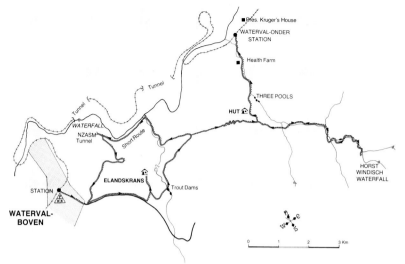

ELANDSKRANS HIKING TRAIL AND NATURE WALK

protecting rare plants such as the Kaapsehoop cycad; grassveld on mountain tops with excellent birdlife, including the endangered blue swallow.

FACILITIES/AMENITIES: Three hiking huts (two are restored forestry quarters; the overnight facility at the starting point is an old train coach).

PERTINENT INFORMATION: The trail is in the form of a figure-of-eight, with Berlin (the starting point) in the centre. Situated mainly on the plateau, it is a physically fairly easy route. The building of this trail was made possible by a very generous grant from the Gold Fields Foundation, P.O. Box 1167, Johannesburg 2000.

AVAILABLE LITERATURE: Sketch map and brochure until NHWB printed maps become available.

CLIMATE: Summer rainfall area.

Maputo) to Pretoria, to free the Transvaal Republic from economic dependence on the surrounding British colonies.

Once at Waterval-Boven, hikers walk only 1,5 kilometres to return to the Elandskrans Holiday Resort. The trail tariff includes the train fare and the overnight hut accommodation. Resort accommodation is extra.

The Elandskrans trail is accessible for day walks via a modified circular route. Trailists begin at the holiday resort, pass the bridge and NZASM tunnel and return to the resort via the old Waterval-Onder motor car pass.

273. Kaapsehoop Hiking Trail

BERLIN

AUTHORITY-IN-CHARGE: Southern Transvaal Forest Region, Forestry Branch, Department of Environment Affairs.

LENGTH/DURATION: 4 days/approximately 50 km.

MAIN ATTRACTIONS: Indigenous forests

274. Sudwala Caves and Walks

NELSPRUIT

AUTHORITY-IN-CHARGE: Sudwala Vakansiebelange (Edms) Bpk, P.O. Box 30, Schagen 1207; tel. 0131232, ask for 3913.

LENGTH: 609-metre walk in caves. Four other walks of 2 km, 2 km, 6 km and 12 km.

MAIN ATTRACTIONS: Caves: large natural amphitheatre with limestone formations; collenia fossils. Walks: river, cliffs, kloofs, forests and sinkhole; trees labelled with their national tree list numbers.

FACILITIES/AMENITIES: Guided tours through the caves; caves adjoin the Dinosaur Park (an open-air museum); Sudwala holiday resort and restaurant.

PERTINENT INFORMATION: Guided tours through caves daily from 08h30 to 16h30; special six-hour Saturday tour to more remote chambers. Permits for 6-km and 12-km walks necessary, obtainable from the restaurant.

AVAILABLE LITERATURE: *Sudwala Walks and Hiking Trails*, brochure; *The Sudwala Caves and Dinosaur Park*, AA Bulletin TBE-T4.

CLIMATE: Summer rainfall area. Within the caves the temperature remains a steady 17 °C year-round, controlled naturally by an unknown source of cool, fresh air.

The Sudwala Caves, a huge network of interlinking chambers, lie within the Mankelekele Mountain which overlooks the valley of the Houtbosloop River, a tributary of the

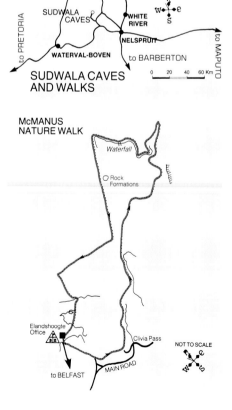

Opposite page: The Riverside Trail in the Lowveld National Botanic Garden runs along the banks of the Crocodile River.

Crocodile. The name Sudwala comes from the Swazi renegade who showed the caves to early European settlers in the area. Rainwater percolating through surface cracks in the dolomitic massif has, through the ages, eroded the mountain into an extraordinary succession of vast subterranean halls. Weirdly shaped stalagmites and stalactites fill the caves, and are specially illuminated, some with coloured lights that prevent the formation of algae.

Spectacular as these are, it is the collenia fossils that are most fascinating. These ancient algae were vital in the development of life as they contributed to the original supply of atmospheric oxygen, and their petrified remains can be clearly seen embedded in the ceiling of the caves.

Visitors to the caves also have the opportunity to walk along one of four colour-coded nature trails. The longest trail climbs 500 metres above the restaurant, through the sinkhole and past the rainforest and caves, and then circles back to the starting point.

275. McManus Nature Walk

NELSPRUIT

AUTHORITY-IN-CHARGE: The Management Forester, Sappi, P.O. Box 141, Machadodorp 1170; tel. 013242, ask for 1630.
LENGTH/DURATION: 19 km/7 hours.
MAIN ATTRACTIONS: Views of the Lowveld; rock formations; proteas; waterfalls and pools.
FACILITIES/AMENITIES: Parking and toilets at start of trail.
PERTINENT INFORMATION: Permission to use the trail must be obtained in advance from The Forester, Elandshoogte Plantation, c/o Sappi Forests, P.O. Box 1011, Nelspruit 1200. The trail is open only between November and June; closed the

rest of the year due to fire hazards. An extension to the trail and new trails are planned.
AVAILABLE LITERATURE: *McManus Hiking Trail*, information sheet with sketch map; comprehensive information booklet planned.
CLIMATE: Summer rainfall area.

276. Lowveld National Botanic Garden

NELSPRUIT

AUTHORITY-IN-CHARGE: National Botanic Gardens.
DURATION: Approximately 1,5 hours.
MAIN ATTRACTIONS: Indigenous flora of the Crocodile River Valley; 500 plant species, including many lowveld trees; birdlife (245 recorded species); spectacular 'pothole' waterfalls.
FACILITIES/AMENITIES: Self-guided trail; developed gardens; information office; toilets.
PERTINENT INFORMATION: Bilharzia is present in the river. Detours must be used if the river is in flood. Be wary of the slippery rocks at the water's edge.
AVAILABLE LITERATURE: *Riverside Trail, Lowveld Botanic Garden, Nelspruit*, trail booklet.
CLIMATE: Summer rainfall area. Very pleasant winter climate.

Within the Lowveld National Botanic Garden, the Riverside Trail along the banks of the Crocodile River highlights the plant life of the region. The trail booklet singles out and illustrates interesting species and includes a list of the most prominent plants found along the trail. This short, physically undemanding trail is especially recommended as it will enhance your experiences on the longer hiking trails in this region.

277. Trails in KaNgwane

TRANSVAAL, see Regional Map page 228

AUTHORITY-IN-CHARGE: KaNgwane National Parks Board, P.O. Box 1330, Nelspruit 1200.
LENGTH: 50 km of canoe trails; variable self-guided and guided trails are planned.
MAIN ATTRACTIONS: Songimvelo Game Reserve (60 000 ha); headwaters of the Komati River.
FACILITIES/AMENITIES: Planned.
PERTINENT INFORMATION: The KaNgwane National Parks Board is in its embryonic stage; trails will open in 1988; canoe trails will operate only in the summer months.
AVAILABLE LITERATURE: Planned.
CLIMATE: Summer rainfall area. Hot summers, cool winters.

278. Gustav Klingbiel Nature Reserve

LYDENBURG

AUTHORITY-IN-CHARGE: Municipality of Lydenburg, P.O. Box 61, Lydenburg 1120.
SIZE: 2 200 hectares.
MAIN ATTRACTIONS: Large game species; over 100 bird species; rich variety of flora; archaeological ruins from the Late Stone Age.
FACILITIES/AMENITIES: One interpretive

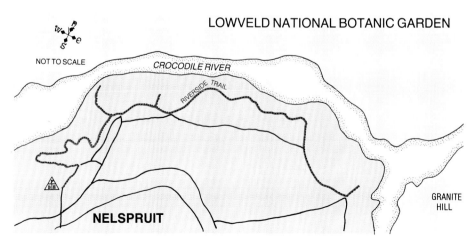

LOWVELD NATIONAL BOTANIC GARDEN

NOT TO SCALE

CROCODILE RIVER

RIVERSIDE TRAIL

NELSPRUIT

GRANITE HILL

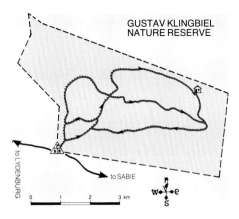

walk; two nature walks; one hiking trail; overnight cottage.

PERTINENT INFORMATION: Trails are in the process of being developed; contact the town clerk for the latest details.

AVAILABLE LITERATURE: None.

CLIMATE: Average annual rainfall: 650 millimetres.

279. Fanie Botha Hiking Trail

SABIE

AUTHORITY-IN-CHARGE: Eastern Transvaal Forest Region, Forestry Branch, Department of Environment Affairs.

LENGTH/DURATION: 79 km/5 days; numerous shorter variations possible.

MAIN ATTRACTIONS: Old pine plantations interspersed among indigenous forests; rich bird and butterfly life; views over the escarpment.

FACILITIES/AMENITIES: Five huts with bunks, mattresses and cooking pots; 30 people per night can be accommodated.

PERTINENT INFORMATION: The trail officially stops at God's Window, but you can continue, following either a four-kilometre route to Watervalspruit Hut on the Blyderivierspoort Hiking Trail, or 1,5 kilometres to Paradise Camp, a private estate. Water should be carried, especially during the dry months (May to September); one litre per person per day is recommended. Lighting facilities are not provided; hikers must supply their own candles and lamps.

AVAILABLE LITERATURE: *Fanie Botha Hiking Trail, Eastern Transvaal*, comprehensive brochure and map.

CLIMATE: Summer rainfall area. July to September, dry, fire season. August to April, lightning. September to April, misty months. October to March, hottest months. May to October, frost and snow.

Given only a couple of weeks to prove that a hiking trail could be established in the East-ern Transvaal, a forestry officer braved blisters and exhaustion to establish this route in 1973.

Named after the then-Minister of Forestry, the Fanie Botha Hiking Trail became the first of the many NHWS trails that will eventually form a continuous chain throughout South Africa. When I hiked the trail in 1975, it was physically strenuous – however, numerous route changes, additional huts and alternative endpoints now make the trail a reasonable challenge for all physically capable backpackers.

Although the Fanie Botha Hiking Trail runs primarily through the pine plantations so characteristic of the Eastern Transvaal, patches of indigenous forest and open grassveld are also traversed. Views of the adjoining Lowveld, from the Drakensberg escarpment, are spectacular. The whole area is particularly rich in birdlife – the Knysna loerie, blue crane, scarletchested sunbird, paradise flycatcher and black eagle are among the species readily seen. Hikers have also reported sightings of mammals such as oribi, grey rhebok, klipspringer, bushbuck, duiker, baboons and vervet monkeys. Take care not to tread on the unusual rain frog, a stocky little amphibian which puffs itself up if alarmed. Seen only after heavy rains, the frog feasts on wingless termites searching for mates after their nuptial flight. Butterfly enthusiasts will also find much of interest here.

Consult the Hiking Way map carefully to decide where to leave the trail, park your car at one of these suggested places and then make your way back to Ceylon State Forest to sleep in the base hut the night before you begin the trail. On the first day (20,7 kilometres) the trail passes through plantations and indigenous forest and then ascends Mount Anderson to Hartebeestvlakte Hut. Complaints that this stretch was too long and steep resulted in the construction of Maritzbos Hut, only 8,1 kilometres from Ceylon.

What is now the third day (19,4 kilometres to Mac-Mac Hut following the mountain ridge) affords the best views. If necessary you can return to Ceylon via a plantation path leading on to the Loerie Nature Walk.

Day four offers two alternative routes: the first choice is via Mac-Mac Pools (22,3 kilometres), the second via Stanley Bush Hill or the Bonnet (13 kilometres). The latter

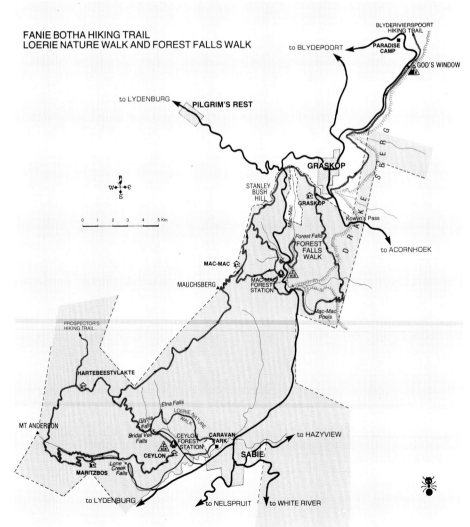

FANIE BOTHA HIKING TRAIL
LOERIE NATURE WALK AND FOREST FALLS WALK

280. Loerie Nature Walk and Forest Falls Walk

EASTERN TRANSVAAL

AUTHORITY-IN-CHARGE: Eastern Transvaal Forest Region, Forestry Branch, Department of Environment Affairs.
LENGTH/DURATION: Loerie Nature Walk (two starting points): circular route from caravan park, 16 km; circular route from forest station, 11 km. Forest Falls Walk: 4 km/1,5 hours (circular).
MAIN ATTRACTIONS: Waterfalls, indigenous forests, plantations, scenic views and natural caves.
FACILITIES/AMENITIES: Safe parking at forest station; picnic site at the start of the Forest Falls Walk; municipal caravan/camping park on Loerie Nature Walk; Tweefontein Forest Hostel for youth groups.
PERTINENT INFORMATION: Registration for both nature walks necessary; for Loerie

choice is easier, full of historical interest, and it avoids the tourist-infested Mac-Mac Pools.

The final day (14,5 kilometres) differs in scenery from all the rest and is, in my opinion, the most picturesque. Weathered rock formations and views of the Lowveld dominate this home stretch. Officially the Fanie Botha Hiking Trail ends at God's Window, but if you have made bookings on the Blyderivierspoort Hiking Trail, walk on!

Above left: The Fanie Botha Hiking Trail was the first trail to be developed in the National Hiking Way System.
Above right: Although the Fanie Botha Hiking Trail runs primarily through pine plantations, patches of indigenous forest and open grassveld are also traversed.
Left: A view of Mount Anderson on the Fanie Botha Hiking Trail.

Nature Walk, at Ceylon Forest Station; for Forest Falls Walk, near Mac-Mac Forest Station.
AVAILABLE LITERATURE: *Fanie Botha Hiking Trail: Eastern Transvaal*, comprehensive brochure and map on which the routes are indicated by dots; *Loerie Nature Walk*, brochure and map; *Forest Falls Nature Walk*, brochure and map.
CLIMATE: Summer rainfall area. July to September, dry, fire season. August to April, lighting. September to April, misty months. October to March, hottest months. May to October, frost and snow.

To experience indigenous high forests and intensive state afforestation schemes, ramble the Loerie and Forest Falls nature walks. The high-point of the Forest Falls Walk is the impressive, broad waterfall where the Mac-Mac River tumbles 56 metres into a rock pool. A smaller waterfall and the graves of gold-rush miners can be visited via a short, easy 400-metre walk from the tarred road.

The Loerie Nature Walk passes the famous Bridal Veil Falls, so-named because of the delicate manner in which rocky protrusions deflect the water to form a veil-like cascade. The route also leads to the spectacular Glynis and smaller Alida falls. A new route deviation leads to the Elna Falls. The route includes beautiful views of the Sabie area and also passes impressive natural caves.

Both trails pass through *Pinus taeda, P. elliottii* and *P. patula* plantations. These pleasant strolls are, of course, much easier than the Fanie Botha Hiking Trail. Nevertheless, I suggest you purchase the *Fanie Botha Hiking Trail: Eastern Transvaal* brochure or the new Mapcape map brochures, also issued by the Forestry Branch, as they include a comprehensive description of the human, forestry and natural history surrounding the Forest Falls and Loerie Nature walks.

281. Blyderivierspoort Hiking Trail

GRASKOP

AUTHORITY-IN-CHARGE: Eastern Transvaal Forest Region, Forestry Branch, Department of Environment Affairs.
LENGTH/DURATION: 65 km/5 days (variations possible).
MAIN ATTRACTIONS: Views of the Blyde River Canyon; historical area; geological features; diversity of plant life.
FACILITIES/AMENITIES: Four huts equipped with bunks, mattresses, cold water ablutions, fireplaces, cooking utensils and firewood.
PERTINENT INFORMATION: The hut inside Blydepoort Public Resort has been replaced with another outside the resort, with a separate entrance. Maximum of 30 people per group. Information centre at Bourke's Luck (headquarters of the Blyderivierspoort Nature Reserve). Supervised parking available at Bourke's Luck Potholes, God's Window and Swadini Public Resort. Gates at Bourke's Luck and God's Window open 07h00-17h00; hikers for Watervalspruit should not leave God's Window later than 15h00. As the trail ends at Swadini (no overnight hut), it is necessary to leave a

Opposite page, top: The turmoil of rushing water grinding pebbles into Black Reef quartzites has created the jumble of Bourke's Luck Potholes.

Opposite page, bottom: The classic view of the Blyde River Canyon seen from the Blyderivierspoort Hiking Trail.

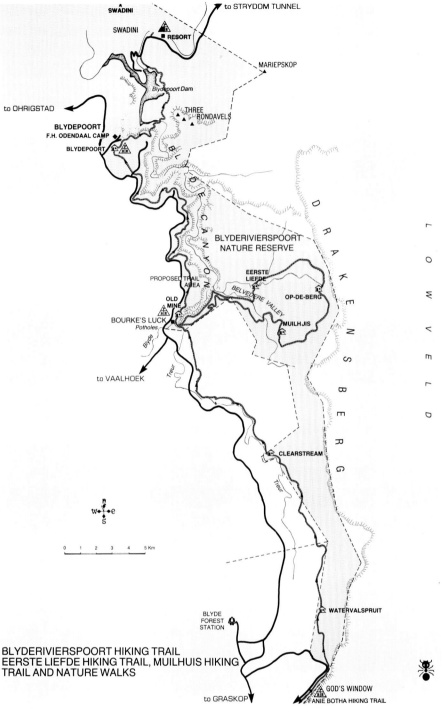

BLYDERIVIERSPOORT HIKING TRAIL
EERSTE LIEFDE HIKING TRAIL, MUILHUIS HIKING
TRAIL AND NATURE WALKS

vehicle at this point in order to return to the start (hitch-hiking is lengthy and involved). Note that hikers are not permitted to walk back to Blydepoort, but must complete their hike at Swadini. Anti-malaria precautions are recommended. Ticks are prevalent. Water between Old Mine and Blydepoort is not potable.
AVAILABLE LITERATURE: *The Blyderivierspoort Hiking Trail* (third edition), comprehensive brochure and map.
CLIMATE: Summer rainfall area. June to September, coolest and driest period; frost possible. September to April, mists are common. Winter is a good time to hike,

except that the view is sometimes clouded by smoke from veld fires; if you hike during April and May you can avoid the 'smoky' season and heavy rains.

If you have never hiked before and are deciding which NHWS trail to do first, I suggest you try this one. The distances between the huts are relatively short (5,8 kilometres, 13,6 kilometres, 13,5 kilometres, 18,3 kilometres and 15 kilometres respectively) and the gradient of the trail is very easy.

The Blyderivierspoort Hiking Trail offers excellent opportunities for nature study, and the comprehensive trail brochure elaborates on aspects of the ecology likely to be encountered on each of the consecutive hiking stages. Plant life is extremely diverse and, depending on aspect and altitude, varies from elements typical of Cape mountain flora to tropical vegetation. The trail also enables you to see, if you are alert and lucky, baboons, vervet monkeys, samango monkeys and bushbabies – the full range of South Africa's primate wildlife. All three species of South African loerie thrive here – the Knysna loerie, purplecrested loerie and grey loerie.

The Transvaal Division of Nature Conservation, the Public Resorts Board, the Forestry Branch and several private owners and estates contributed land, money, facilities, know-how and management to make this trail a success. From God's Window (where the Fanie Botha Hiking Trail terminates) at the southern end of the Blyderivierspoort Nature Reserve, it stretches northwards, partly across privately owned land through the Blyde State Forest and then again across the reserve to Swadini in the Lowveld.

The only long stretch (18,3 kilometres) is between Old Mine and Blydepoort, but it is not difficult. Trailists often complain that this section is within sight of the road. Unfortunately, this was necessary to keep the trail within the boundaries of the reserve. Don't look at the road – the views into the canyon and over the Belvedere Valley and the Lowveld are far more exciting!

282. Morgenzon Hiking Trail

PILGRIM'S REST

AUTHORITY-IN-CHARGE: Eastern Transvaal Forest Region, Forestry Branch, Department of Environment Affairs.
LENGTH/DURATION: 36,4 km/2,5 days, 2 nights (variations possible).
MAIN ATTRACTIONS: Lovely mountain scenery – inland tropical forest and typical grassveld vegetation; wildlife is similar to

MORGENZON HIKING TRAIL

that on the Fanie Botha Hiking Trail (see page 234).

FACILITIES/AMENITIES: Single hut (double-storey house) with bunks, mattresses, pots, toilet, water and a braai area; rondavel with bunks and mattresses; together, the hut and rondavel can accommodate 30 people per night.

PERTINENT INFORMATION: Streams are dry in winter so water must be carried. Fires are allowed only at the hut. Parking is available at Morgenzon State Forest.

AVAILABLE LITERATURE: Information sheet and map, available from the Forestry Branch; *Prospector's Hiking Trail*, map by Mapcape.

CLIMATE: Summer rainfall area. May to August, minimum temperatures and driest months. June, coldest and driest month. July to September, extreme fire season. August to April, lightning possible. September to April, hail and mist are possible but rarely last long.

Dramatic escarpment topography, rocky outcrops, slopes greened by extensive plantations, and inland tropical forests interspersed with sour bushveld, provide a natural mosaic which attracts hikers to the Eastern Transvaal thoughout the year . . . in growing numbers. And once the Fanie Botha Hiking Trail had proved successful, foresters in the Eastern Transvaal started to examine the wealth of potential extensions, link-ups and variations.

The Morgenzon Hiking Trail lies eight kilometres from the quaint historical town of Pilgrim's Rest, a national monument. This trail is shorter than the Fanie Botha Hiking Trail but has equally attractive scenery. It also provides an excellent opportunity to see oribi: search the long grass plains carefully and listen for the antelope's distinctive soft whistle and sneezing. The Oribi Vlaktes is an obvious region in which to look for these antelope, as well as grey rhebok and birds such as Swainson's francolin, red-collared widows and bronze mannikins.

The trail, constructed as a figure-of-eight, consists of three relatively short days of walking. The first day, from the forest station to Excelsior Hut, is a 13-kilometre (approximately six-hour) walk; the second day is a 15-kilometre (also about six hours) loop back to the hut, and includes an optional five-kilometre circular route to Eldorado Ridge. The last day's hike is 8,4 kilometres (approximately 2,5 hours) and returns to the forest station.

Black Hill (2 079 m), the highest peak in the region, is passed on the first day. (I suggest you have lunch below its lookout tower,

Right: Damp and shady indigenous forest in the Mount Sheba Nature Reserve.

Opposite page, left: Old mining equipment at Beta-North Mine.

Opposite page, right: Pilgrim's Rest.

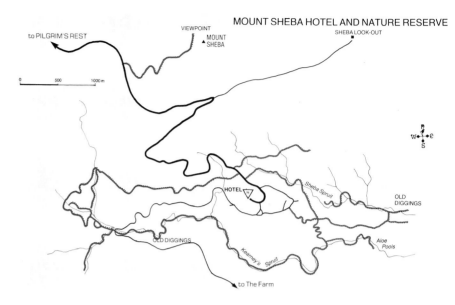

MOUNT SHEBA HOTEL AND NATURE RESERVE

at the stream.) The view is impressive: you can see all the way to the Wolkberg, Strydpoort and the Waterberg. Note also the Cape fynbos in the gully – a small remnant of past wider distribution.

In order to link the Morgenzon Hiking Trail to the Fanie Botha Hiking Trail and the Blyderivierspoort Hiking Trail, the Prospector's Hiking Trail was opened in 1983.

283. *Mount Sheba Hotel and Nature Reserve*

PILGRIM'S REST

AUTHORITY-IN-CHARGE: Mount Sheba Hotel, P.O. Box 100, Pilgrim's Rest 1290; tel. 0131532, ask for 17.

SIZE: 500 hectares.

MAIN ATTRACTIONS: Conservation-orientated atmosphere; indigenous forests; waterfalls; antelope and small mammals; rich birdlife; 110 species of trees.

FACILITIES/AMENITIES: Nature trails; horses for hire; trees labelled with their national tree list numbers; three-star hotel with luxury suites, cottages, conference facilities and swimming pool; time-share cottages available; airstrip.

AVAILABLE LITERATURE: General brochures; maps; descriptions of nature walks, flora and geology; tree and bird checklists.

CLIMATE: Average annual rainfall: 1 250-1 500 millimetres, falling mostly in summer. Mist zone.

I include the Mount Sheba Hotel and Nature Reserve because I am impressed by the management's commendable environmental conscience and the beautifully laid-out nature trails.

The climax forest, one of the last remaining stands of indigenous Drakensberg growth, typifies the vegetation which grew in this area many hundreds of years ago. Some trees, such as yellowwoods and ironwoods, have been estimated to be 1 500 years old. Fifty-two plant families, comprising 110 tree specimens, have been identified, not counting the numerous species of ferns, mosses, forest creepers and parasitic figs which flourish in the damp and shady forest.

The well-written booklet, *Mount Sheba*, gives details of 10 nature trails, each less than six kilometres in length, and most of them physically undemanding. Located on a 1 600-2 200 metre plateau in a spectacular bowl of mountains in the Transvaal Drakensberg above Pilgrim's Rest, overlooking the Lowveld, the Mount Sheba complex provides a great venue to relax and celebrate your hiking achievements.

284. Rambler's Trails and Bridle Trails

PILGRIM'S REST

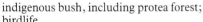

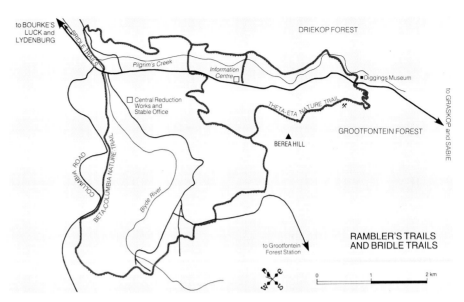

RAMBLER'S TRAILS AND BRIDLE TRAILS

AUTHORITIES-IN-CHARGE: Rambler's Trails: Pilgrim's Rest Museum. Bridle Trails: The Head Equestrienne, Works Department, Transvaal Provincial Administration, Private Bag X516, Pilgrim's Rest 1290.
LENGTH/DURATION: Beta-Columbia nature trail: approximately 10 km. Theta-Eta nature trail: approximately 10 km. Guided trails: 6 hours. Single bridle trail: 6 km/ 1 hour. Double bridle trail: 12 km/2 hours.
MAIN ATTRACTIONS: Historical interest (old gold mines, Old Graveyard, Theta gas chimney and ore-bin); scenic surroundings;

indigenous bush, including protea forest; birdlife.
FACILITIES/AMENITIES: Nature trails: toilet facilities and tap water available at Beta Mine and the Diggings Museum. Double bridle trail: cross-country jumps, six horses. Accommodation in Pilgrim's Rest available at the Royal Hotel, cottages and camp-sites.
PERTINENT INFORMATION: Nature trails: guides are available (during school holidays on Mondays, Wednesdays and Fridays, and out-of-season by prior arrangement for groups of 10 or more people); lunch is provided on guided trails and does not have to be carried; guided trails start at 09h00; maximum of 20 people per trail; permits are necessary; children under five years are not permitted; minors must be accompanied by an adult; for information, contact The Information Centre, Pilgrim's Rest Museum, Private Bag X519, Pilgrim's Rest 1290. Double bridle trail: for experienced

riders only; maximum of six riders per trail; trails should be booked at least a day in advance; children under 16 years are not permitted; all trails are accompanied by the head equestrienne and are under her supervision. Information centre open daily 09h00-16h30.
AVAILABLE LITERATURE: Trail brochures; bird, mammal and tree checklists; maps.
CLIMATE: Summer: fairly hot; thunderstorms common in the afternoon. Winter: mornings are very cold, days are warm; rain infrequent.

Within the historical monument and proclaimed nature reserve of Pilgrim's Rest is a complex of nature and bridle trails, the nature trails guided on request. Although the Pilgrim's Rest area of the Eastern Transvaal is known for its scenic countryside, these trails, which are laid out on the farm Ponieskrantz (once the centre of the district's

gold-mining industry), are also valuable for their historic interest.

Both the Beta-Columbia and the Theta-Eta nature trails visit the Old Graveyard, the Theta gas chimney and the Theta ore-bin. The Beta-Columbia trail also visits Brown's Hill Mine, Beta Mine and Beta-North Mine, and affords the rambler excellent views of the area from Columbia Hill. The Theta-Eta trail visits various sections of the Theta Mine, Theta cable station, the Diggings Museum, Eta open-cast mine and the New Graveyard, and provides excellent views from Berea Hill. Each of these sites and many more are described in the trail guides.

If trailists are particularly keen, guides can be requested. The guides are museum staff who are familiar with the local mining history. Guided tours allow greater access to the mines.

The nature trails are physically fairly easy walks, carefully planned so that steep hills are negotiated when the trailist is fresh, in the morning and after the lunch stop.

The bridle trails are maintained and administered by the Transvaal Department of Works. They follow the Blyde River in a northerly direction from the Joubert Bridge. The river crossings and bushveld scenery are the main attractions on these trails. Besides the address listed above, enquiries can also be made at the stable's office, just inside the gates of the Reduction Works.

285. Prospector's Hiking Trail

PILGRIM'S REST

AUTHORITY-IN-CHARGE: Eastern Transvaal Forest Region, Forestry Branch, Department of Environment Affairs.
LENGTH/DURATION: 69 km or 55,3 km/ 5 days, 4 nights.
MAIN ATTRACTIONS: Unique hiking huts; Pilgrim's Rest (national monument); 1 000th kilometre plaque; old mines.
FACILITIES/AMENITIES: Four overnight huts, each accommodating 30 people, with fireplaces, firewood, cooking pots, bunks, mattresses, water, latrines and rubbish containers.
PERTINENT INFORMATION: Ticks can be a nuisance. Water from the Blyde River must be purified before drinking.
AVAILABLE LITERATURE: *Prospector's Hiking Trail*, brochure and map by Mapcape.
CLIMATE: Summer rainfall area, lightning storms common. May to September, snow and frost possible. July to September, extreme fire season.

The Prospector's Hiking Trail has something of everything: some of the Fanie Botha and Morgenzon trails, Pilgrim's Rest (an historic South African mining town), two hiking huts donated by mining companies, the plaque to commemorate the 1 000th kilometre of the National Hiking Way System, and eastern Transvaal ecology – pine and eucalyptus plantations, grassveld, proteaveld, wooded valleys, wild horses, oribi and other antelope, and rich birdlife.

Relative to the other National Hiking Way trails, the Prospector's is fairly easy, although I did not think so at the time – I had the misfortune to walk this trail with a stress fracture, during the official opening in 1983. Perhaps that is why I so well remember Sacramento Creek Hut, donated by Transvaal Gold Mining Estates (Rand Mine Properties) and situated in the valley under wild fig trees. I reached this hut three hours after sunset, but the pain in my leg dissipated fast when I was exposed to the high spirits prevailing at the trail's inauguration.

Since several options and circular routes are available, study the map carefully to plan the course you will follow.

286. Echo Caves

OHRIGSTAD

AUTHORITY-IN-CHARGE: National Monuments Council.
LENGTH: 6 subterranean chambers; 200 metres of trails open to the public.
MAIN ATTRACTIONS: Dolomite caves, with stalactites and stalagmites, once used by local tribes as a refuge; unique echo effect when stalactites are tapped.
FACILITIES/AMENITIES: Guided tours; the Museum of Man; motel at the caves.

PERTINENT INFORMATION: Stabbing knives and other historical objects to be found in the caves. The Museum of Man displays skeletons; the museum is located in a shelter decorated with Bushman paintings, near the entrance to the caves. Caves open daily 08h00-17h00.
AVAILABLE LITERATURE: *Tourist Attractions – Lydenburg and Surroundings*, issued by the Municipality of Lydenburg.
CLIMATE: Summer rainfall area.

287. Eerste Liefde Hiking Trail, Muilhuis Hiking Trail and Nature Walks

BOURKE'S LUCK POTHOLES, BLYDE RIVER CANYON, see map page 236

AUTHORITY-IN-CHARGE: Division of Nature Conservation, Transvaal Provincial Administration.
LENGTH/DURATION: Eerste Liefde Hiking Trail: 22 km/2 days. Muilhuis Hiking Trail: 40 km/4 days.
MAIN ATTRACTIONS: See Blyderivierspoort Hiking Trail, page 236.
FACILITIES/AMENITIES: Eerste Liefde Hiking Trail: 1 hut. Muilhuis Hiking Trail: 2 huts (Muilhuis and Op-de-Berg). At trail huts, bunkbeds, mattresses and toilets are provided. Stream water is potable. All huts except Op-de-Berg provide firewood and a braai place. At Bourke's Luck, overnight huts are available to hikers, with beds, mattresses, open-air showers, toilets, fireplaces and firewood.
PERTINENT INFORMATION: Maximum of 10 people per group; only one group allowed on any one trail at a time. No fires (except camp-stove) permitted at Op-de-Berg Hut. Rubbish tins provided. Permits necessary, obtainable from the Nature Conservation office at Bourke's Luck. Eerste Liefde Hiking Trail is often referred to as the

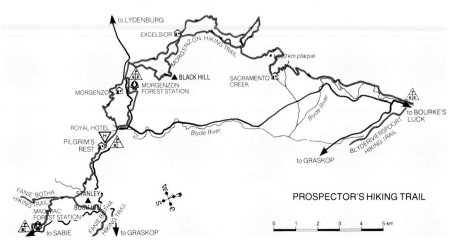

PROSPECTOR'S HIKING TRAIL

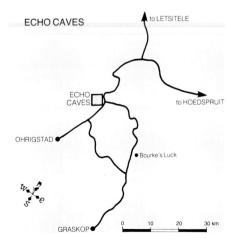

northerly track, the Eerste Liefde trail, continues as an approximately three-hour walk to the overnight hut near a rock pool on the Belvedere River, edged between montane forest and grassland. This stream is free of bilharzia and its water is potable.

The southern track, the Muilhuis Hiking Trail, was laid at a higher altitude than the Eerste Liefde trail. Two overnight huts are provided: Muilhuis, an old stable located in montane grassveld, and Op-de-Berg, eight kilometres farther on, situated on the edge of montane woodland. These trails are now linked, so that the extended trail system consists of one-, two-, three- or four-night circular loop trails, with no 'back-tracking'.

288. Kadishi Valley Trail System

BLYDE RIVER CANYON

AUTHORITY-IN-CHARGE: Division of Nature Conservation, Transvaal Provincial Administration.
LENGTH: Kadishi Trail: 2 km. Leopard Trail: 5 km. Loerie Trail: 3 km.
MAIN ATTRACTIONS: Tufa waterfalls; rock formations in canyon; diverse vegetation types.
FACILITIES/AMENITIES: Public resort offering a variety of facilities, including a small information centre; horses for hire.
PERTINENT INFORMATION: For a description of the Blyde River Canyon, see previous trail. No smoking permitted on trails. Check

Yellowwood Trail; Muilhuis Hiking Trail is often referred to as the Protea Trail or Op-de-Berg Trail. For bookings and information: The Information Officer, Blyderivierspoort Nature Reserve, P.O. Bourke's Luck 1272; tel. 0020, ask for Bourke's Luck 15.
AVAILABLE LITERATURE: *Blyderivierspoort Hiking Map Series 3*, Mapcape map, no text, available from the Transvaal Provincial Administration; *Blyderivierspoort Hiking Trail*, brochure and map (trails are dotted), available from the Forestry Branch; information sheets available from the Division of Nature Conservation, Transvaal Provincial Administration.
CLIMATE: Summer rainfall area. June to September, coolest and driest period; frost is possible. September to April, mists are common. Winter is a good time to hike, except that the view is sometimes clouded by smoke from veld fires; if you hike during April and May you can avoid the 'smoky' season and heavy rains.

Those intrepid old-timers who wrote detailed route descriptions in the early mountaineering journals would turn in their graves to see the present profusion of access routes into the Blyde River Canyon. But even the most fanatical mountaineer could not reasonably expect such a spectacular region to remain forever the jealously guarded domain of a few elite outdoorsmen. Today the Transvaal Provincial Administration's Division of Nature Conservation provides nature walks, hiking trails and an informative interpretive centre at Bourke's Luck Potholes, all of which provide the non-mountaineer with the opportunity to study this region with relative ease.

The Blyde River, from its source on the Transvaal escarpment to its eventual conflu-

ence with the Treur, is central to the trail's environment. The turmoil of rushing water, trapping and grinding pebbles into the soft substrata of Black Reef quartzites, has created a surrealistic jumble of potholes, arches and pools known as Bourke's Luck Potholes, named after a nearby worked-out gold mine. These rock formations are accessible to the casual rambler via a complex of paths and footbridges. From the potholes, the river tumbles through its time-gouged canyon, 600 metres below the escarpment plateau.

The new Bourke's Luck Potholes interpretive trail (0,5 km/1 hour) and the five-kilometre Bushman Nature Trail, both starting from Bourke's Luck, are recommended as an introduction to this area. Also of interest is the *Bourke's Luck Potholes Visitor Centre* booklet, explaining exhibits within the visitor centre.

The Blyderivierspoort Hiking Trail traverses from the south to Bourke's Luck, where hikers spend their third night at Old Mine Hut before walking north towards Blydepoort Public Resort.

Bourke's Luck is also the start of two shorter trails, the Muilhuis and Eerste Liefde hikes. These are routed east of the potholes, along the wall of the canyon through grassveld, bushveld, montane and gallery forest. The diversity of vegetation is mainly the result of the range of microclimates within the canyon system. Wildlife is also plentiful and among the ferns, cycads, wild figs, mobola plums and orchids, you may spot baboons, rhebok, duiker and klipspringer on the krantzes. The bald ibis, a threatened species, as well as the Knysna, purplecrested and grey loeries, are found here.

From the potholes the trail leads eastwards and soon forks in two. The more

Opposite page: Mac-Mac Pools.
Top: The Muilhuis and Eerste Liefde hiking trails start at the fascinating Bourke's Luck Potholes.
Above: The tufa waterfalls with their delicate, vegetation-fringed pools are a unique feature on the Kadishi Valley Trail System.

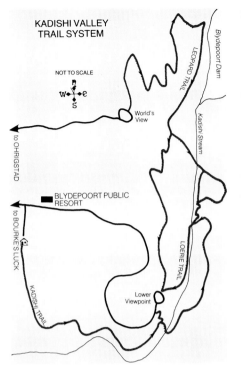

KADISHI VALLEY
TRAIL SYSTEM

NOT TO SCALE

World's View

to OHRIGSTAD

BLYDEPOORT PUBLIC
RESORT

to BOURKE'S LUCK

LEOPARD TRAIL

Blydepoort Dam

Kadishi Stream

LOERIE TRAIL

KADISHI TRAIL

Lower Viewpoint

to TZANEEN

SYCAMORE TRAIL

SYBRAND VAN NIEKERK
PUBLIC RESORT

MARIEPSKOP TRAIL

SWADINI NATURE TRAILS

NOT TO SCALE

WATERFALL TRAIL

PENINSULA TRAIL

SWADINI
INTER-
PRETIVE
CENTRE

in at the office of the F.H. Odendaal Public Resort.

AVAILABLE LITERATURE: Information booklet and *Blyderivierspoort Hiking Trail*, map and brochure (trail route is indicated by dots), both available from the Division of Nature Conservation, Transvaal Provincial Administration; trail guide, issued by the University of the Witwatersrand; A4 maps available at reception at the F.H. Odendaal Public Resort.

CLIMATE: Summer rainfall area. June to September, coolest and driest period. September to April, mists are common (trails are treacherous in mist). June to September, frost is possible. Winter is a good time to hike, except that the view is often clouded by veld fire smoke; by hiking in April and May you can avoid the 'smoky' season and heavy rains.

Several short nature walks which can be treated as one trail emanate from a vantage point near Blydepoort's F.H. Odendaal Public Resort, an extensive recreational complex where horses can be hired. From the trailhead, probably the most popular look-out point in the region, the panoramic views of the canyon are spectacular. Most conspicuous are the 'hut-like' quartzitic rock formations known as the Three Rondavels – shaped by wind and water, these famous 'triplets' rise some 700 metres from

Opposite page, top: A grey heron (near the water) and a bateleur, seen together in the Kruger National Park.

Opposite page, bottom: The Burchell's zebra is a common sight on the Olifants Trail, which operates in the central district of the Kruger National Park.

the canyon floor. Farther to the north lie the famous mountaineering challenges of Mariepskop (1 944 m) and Swadini (1 575 m), often described as sentinels guarding the entrance to the canyon.

The Kadishi Trail (also known as the Tufa Trail), which derives its name from a small plateau stream that drops very steeply into the canyon to merge with the Blyde River, is a two-kilometre nature walk on the steep slopes of the Kadishi Valley. A trail guide, available from either the Department of Botany or the Department of Geography and Environmental Studies of the University of the Witwatersrand, helps tremendously in identifying the diverse plant life. The trail passes near the ruins of an iron smelter and ancient settlements as well as through several vegetation 'zones' as it descends into the canyon. Fig, wild pear, cabbage trees and stamvrug abound as you follow the route downwards, whereas the ascent, on the drier, warmer side of the valley, exhibits trees such as wild olive, sumach bean and sandalwood.

The highlight of the Kadishi Trail is the rockface over which the waterfall tumbles. These rocks are composed of tufa, a calcium carbonate deposit which is carried by the stream from its origin in the dolomite mountains on the escarpment. These porous deposits overlying quartzite are particularly evident along a short walk near the start of the Kadishi Trail. The delicate fern-fringed pools are a feature of this trail. The Kadishi Trail has an interpretive booklet which is available from the Transvaal Provincial Administration.

Other nature trails in the Kadishi Valley, the Loerie Trail and the Leopard Trail, wind through lovely indigenous forest and

offer views of the Blydepoort Dam, a refuge for hippopotamus, crocodile, otter, waterbirds and fish. The Leopard Trail is the longest, running from the upper to the lower viewpoint. The Loerie Trail is circular, beginning from the lower viewpoint and running next to the stream.

289. Swadini Nature Trails

BLYDERIVIERSPOORT NATURE RESERVE, NEAR KLASERIE

AUTHORITY-IN-CHARGE: Division of Nature Conservation, Transvaal Provincial Administration.

LENGTH/DURATION: Sycamore Trail: 1,4 km/30 minutes. Waterfall Trail: 1,9 km/45 minutes. Peninsula Trail: 2,3 km/1,5 hours. Mariepskop Trail: 2-3 hours, depending on route.

MAIN ATTRACTIONS: Views of Blydepoort Dam; rock formations of the eastern Transvaal Drakensberg escarpment; ecology of mixed sour bushveld and lowveld riverine forest-flora; birdlife; geology; waterfalls.

FACILITIES/AMENITIES: Swadini information and interpretive centre, Sybrand van Niekerk (Overvaal) Public Resort, offering accommodation, restaurant and full resort facilities.

PERTINENT INFORMATION: For Sybrand van Niekerk Public Resort: The General Manager, Overvaal Sybrand van Niekerk, P.O. Box 281, Hoedspruit 1380. Permits necessary for the Mariepskop Trail, obtainable from the control gate on the road to the dam.

AVAILABLE LITERATURE: Trail guides and maps available at Swadini interpretive centre; *Sycomorus Trail*, interpretive booklet; *The Story of Swadini*, interpretive booklet; *Peninsula Interpretive Trail*, booklet.

CLIMATE: Summer rainfall area. June to September, coolest and driest period; frost is possible. September to April, mists are common. Winter is a good time to hike, except that the view is sometimes clouded by smoke from veld fires; if you hike during April and May you can avoid the 'smoky' season and heavy rains.

The new Swadini interpretive centre was opened in 1982, in the vicinity of the Blydepoort Dam. In conjunction with this centre, four relatively short nature walks are offered, some with interpretive booklets which give the visitor a fine overall introduction to the Blyde River area.

The Sycamore Trail is an easy, short walk which follows the Blyde River, starting at Sybrand van Niekerk's Chalet 53 and ending at its shop. Trees are labelled and the interpretive booklet describes the veld types and their management, the geology of the Swadini Buttress with its sheer quartzite cliffs, the lowland riverine forest, the invasion of exotic plants, and other interesting ecological points. The Waterfall Trail is also a very easy walk, starting near the bridge opposite the Nature Conservationist's office. It follows the stream to the waterfall and returns on the same route.

The Peninsula and Mariepskop trails require good walking shoes. The Peninsula Trail follows the Ohrigstad branch of the dam from the interpretive centre while the Mariepskop Trail is a circular route along the foothills of Mariepskop. The latter is the longest trail of the four, and the only one requiring a permit.

290. *Kruger National Park Wilderness Trails*

EASTERN TRANSVAAL

AUTHORITY-IN-CHARGE: National Parks Board.
DURATION: 2 days, 3 nights.
MAIN ATTRACTIONS: One of the greatest game sanctuaries in the world.
FACILITIES/AMENITIES: Shelter, food, rucksacks, eating utensils, water bottles, sleeping bags and stretchers provided.
PERTINENT INFORMATION: Trailists meet at the relevant rest camp at 15h00 on Mondays or Fridays and return to the camp after breakfast on the final morning. Maximum of 8 people per trail (age limit 12-60 years). Reduced rates for school and student parties. Bookings accepted a year in advance (proof of booking must be shown at the park gate); costs do not include admission and transport to the park. Anti-malaria precautions are necessary.
AVAILABLE LITERATURE: *Wilderness Trails in the Kruger National Park*, fully comprehensive brochure issued by the National Parks Board.
CLIMATE: Subtropical. Summer: hot, humid, rainy; temperature range: 20-30 °C. Winter: more popular hiking season; warm, dry days and cool to cold nights; temperature range: 12-22 °C.

Wolhuter Trail (southern section of the park)
Named in honour of the legendary Harry Wolhuter (famous for killing a lion with a sheath knife in 1903) and his son, also called Harry, who were both in charge of the southern Kruger Park when they worked for the National Parks Board, the Wolhuter Trail, started in 1978, was the park's first wilderness trail.

This trail operates in the far southern section of the park, an area characterized by

granite outcrops and *Combretum* lowveld savannah. Although this region is not known for its large herds of game because of the denser and more hilly habitat, the south has a wide variety of rarer mammal species such as roan, sable, reedbuck and oribi. This area is also the chosen habitat of the white rhino. These animals are encountered regularly by trail parties. Larger predators, such as lion, cheetah, leopard and wild dog, also occur here. A good cross-section of the avifaunal population of the park is spotted on this trail.

The base camp accommodates trailists in wood and thatched A-frame huts which have replaced the original tents. Parties meet at the Skukuza rest camp for a short briefing by the ranger who accompanies them, and then travel to the permanent bush camp, a 1,5 hour drive.

Olifants Trail (central section of the park)
Operating in the central district of the park, the camp is situated on the southern banks of the Olifants River, near its confluence with the Letaba. Except for the areas in the immediate vicinity of the river, this region is flatter than the south. Consequently, one can expect to encounter more of the large-herd species such as zebra, wildebeest and buffalo, and also their predators. Elephant, crocodile and hippo are commonly encountered, and the birdlife is prolific along the river. Baobab and yellow fever trees dominate the floodplains, and the savannah areas of the central district are typical of Africa.

Participants for this trail report at Letaba rest camp, where they are met by the ranger, and then depart for the base camp, a 1,5 hour drive.

Nyalaland Trail (northern section of the park)
This trail is a must for bird-watchers. Trailists meet at the Punda Milia reception office, from where they are transported north (1,5 hours) to the permanent hutted base camp. The huts, constructed under majestic kudu-

berry trees so that they blend unobtrusively with their surroundings, are situated along the Madzaringwe Spruit, eight kilometres south of the Mutale/Levubu River confluence in the wildest of all the wilderness areas of the park.

The terrain is essentially sandstone, with mopane scrub dominating the area. Elephant, hippo and crocodile are common in the vicinity of the Levubu, but the outstanding feature of this region is the staggering diversity of birdlife. Rare plants and wildlife abound among the sandstone koppies. The plants include aloes such as the Zimbabwe aloe (*Aloe excelsa*) and Wylliespoort aloe (*Aloe angelica*), and *Euphorbia rowlandii*. The Natal red hare, yellowspotted dassie, racquet-tailed and broadbilled rollers and

rough-scaled dark-girdled lizard are representative of the wildlife population.

Bushman Trail (south of the Wolhuter Trail, southern section of the park)
The Kruger Park trails are so popular that in recent years a fourth trail, the Bushman Trail, has been established. It is located in the southernmost section of the park, an area rich in recently discovered Bushman rock art, for which the trail was named. The base camp is situated in a secluded valley, surrounded by granite-domed koppies, an hour's drive from the luxurious Berg-en-Dal camp.

Trailists meet at the Berg-en-Dal reception office and travel by Land Rover to the permanent hutted bush camp, attractively

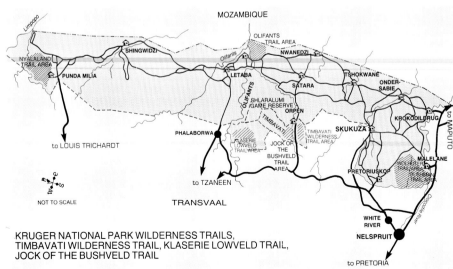

KRUGER NATIONAL PARK WILDERNESS TRAILS,
TIMBAVATI WILDERNESS TRAIL, KLASERIE LOWVELD TRAIL,
JOCK OF THE BUSHVELD TRAIL

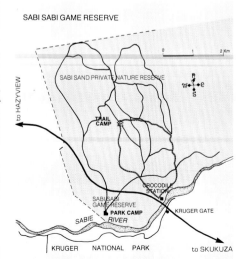

constructed in wood and thatch. Much time is spent exploring the slopes looking for paintings. The surroundings are very similar to those on the Wolhuter Trail, so the same mammal and bird species are seen.

Ox-wagon Trail

The Ox-wagon trail is proposed by the National Parks Board as a long-term project. These unique treks will follow the old transport road from Lydenburg to Delagoa Bay, used from 1877 to 1892. Hikers will travel alongside or in the ox-wagons, and overnight in traditional outspans with historically authentic accommodation. Contact the National Parks Board for details.

291. Sabi Sabi Game Reserve

BORDERING THE KRUGER
NATIONAL PARK

AUTHORITY-IN-CHARGE: Privately owned.
SIZE: Sabi Sand Private Nature Reserve: 72 000 hectares.
LENGTH: Variable guided trails.
MAIN ATTRACTIONS: Rich bushveld ecology; 200 species of game; 450 species of birds.
FACILITIES/AMENITIES: Two luxurious lodges, swimming pool and curio shop; open Land Rover and night safaris.
PERTINENT INFORMATION: Overnight trails in the bush by arrangement. Take precautions against bilharzia, malaria and ticks. Sabi Sabi Game Reserve falls within the Sabi Sand Private Nature Reserve. For bookings: P.O. Box 1170, Johannesburg 2000; tel. (011) 833-7481.
AVAILABLE LITERATURE: *Sabi Sabi Game Reserve*, brochure.
CLIMATE: Average annual rainfall: 575 millimetres. April to the end of October, best time for walking.

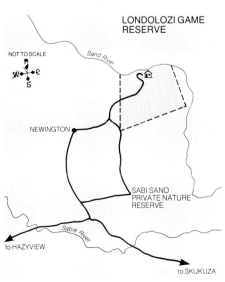

292. Londolozi Game Reserve

BORDERING THE KRUGER
NATIONAL PARK

AUTHORITY-IN-CHARGE: John and Dave Varty, 26 Stanley Avenue, Auckland Park 2092.
SIZE: 18 000 hectares.
MAIN ATTRACTIONS: Rich bushveld ecology; 200 species of game; 450 species of birds.
FACILITIES/AMENITIES: Guided trails of various lengths; luxurious main camp on the Sand River, with swimming pool; comfortable bush camp on the Sand River; open Land Rover safaris by day and night.
PERTINENT INFORMATION: Anti-malaria precautions necessary. Londolozi Game Reserve falls within the Sabi Sand Private Nature Reserve.
AVAILABLE LITERATURE: *The Londolozi Experience* and other brochures.
CLIMATE: Average annual rainfall: 575 millimetres. April to the end of October, best time to walk.

Opposite page: An impala (left) and a steenbok browse in the Kruger National Park.

Top: A stately group of waterbuck greets hikers on one of the Kruger National Park's guided wilderness trails. Eight people are permitted on each of the trails in this great game sanctuary.

Right: A vervet monkey watches a group of trailists from a treetop in the Kruger National Park.

293. *Timbavati Wilderness Trail*

TIMBAVATI GAME RESERVE, see map page 244

G 🚶 🚶

AUTHORITY-IN-CHARGE: B. Jones, P.O. Box 790, Pinetown 3600.
SIZE: 70 000 hectares.
DURATION: 5 days, 4 nights.
MAIN ATTRACTIONS: Lowveld ecology, including big game; 240 species of birds; day trails and night game-viewing drives.
FACILITIES/AMENITIES: Base camp with elevated wooden huts, hot showers and long-drop toilets; on all trails, food, utensils, bedding (optional) and camping equipment, when necessary, are provided.
PERTINENT INFORMATION: Trail party size is limited to 8-10 people unless otherwise arranged. Anti-malaria precautions are necessary.
AVAILABLE LITERATURE: *Timbavati Wilderness Trails*, brochure available from Esmé Weldon, P.O. Box 790, Pinetown 3600; tel. (031) 78-3347.
CLIMATE: Average annual rainfall: 400-500 millimetres, falling mostly in summer in the form of thunderstorms. Summer: days are very hot. Winter: days are warm, nights are cold.

Within one of the world's largest private game reserves, former Natal Parks Board and Timbavati game ranger Brian Jones leads wilderness trails catering for all interests and abilities. On the 'primitive' trails, designed to appeal to the hardiest trailists, participants set off at an easy pace from a canvas camp, with their backpacks fully equipped for sleeping out. The 'normal' trails, on the other hand, are more suited to those who wish to return to base camp every evening, while visitors who prefer *not* to walk much can observe the daily drama of the bush from a hide. A special feature of the game reserve is a night excursion in a four-wheel drive vehicle equipped with

Top: A reedbuck rests in the shade.

spotlights to pick out the more elusive, nocturnal creatures such as porcupine, antbear, civet cat and leopard.

On wilderness trails such as these, seeing a pride of lions – the largest carnivore in Africa – is always a thrill. At Timbavati watch specifically for white lions, as it was in this reserve that the trio of now much-publicized white lions was discovered.

Apart from its lions, Timbavati contains the world's largest concentration of giraffe, and endangered species such as the wild dog, cheetah, brown hyaena and Cape vulture. Trailists can also see sable antelope, white rhino, wildebeest, zebra, buffalo, elephant, impala, kudu and a wealth of birdlife. The ranger might also show you a poacher's deserted camp, the spoor and den of an unseen creature or, perhaps, a baboon spider or puff adder.

294. *Klaserie Lowveld Trail*

KLASERIE PRIVATE NATURE RESERVE, see map page 244

G 🚶

AUTHORITY-IN-CHARGE: Educational Wildlife Expeditions.
SIZE: 60 000 hectares.
DURATION: 5 days, including transfers to and from Johannesburg.
MAIN ATTRACTIONS: Typical Lowveld ecology, bordering on the Kruger National Park.
FACILITIES/AMENITIES: Fully equipped camps, with food, utensils, gas refrigerator, sleeping bags, stretchers, mattresses, linen, camping equipment, tents, showers and toilets.
PERTINENT INFORMATION: Maximum of 8 people per trail. Trails depart on Thursdays at 06h00 from Johannesburg throughout the year. Anti-malaria precautions are necessary.
AVAILABLE LITERATURE: Contact Educational Wildlife Expeditions for their latest brochures; 'Lion and Elephant Trail', M. Blignaut, *Great Outdoors*, No. 24, March 1982.

Several unfenced private game reserves border the Kruger National Park. Many of the owners run wilderness trails, some of which, notably those such as the Klaserie Lowveld Trail founded by Clive Walker, are of a high quality.

A camp with tents provided is aesthetically located on the bank of the Klaserie River. Guided by an armed field officer, trailists walk in the late afternoon and early morning, relaxing at camp during the heat of the day. Night trails involve driving in a four-wheel drive vehicle with a mounted spotlight, in search of nocturnal

animals. The typical big wildlife species – elephant, lion, rhino, buffalo, wildebeest, zebra, giraffe, leopard, cheetah and hyaena – as well as the smaller creatures of the bush, are all likely to be encountered on a nocturnal sortie.

295. *Jock of the Bushveld Trail*

HANS HOHEISEN PRIVATE GAME RESERVE, see map page 244

G 🚶

AUTHORITY-IN-CHARGE: Wilderness Leadership School.
DURATION: 5 days for adults, 6 days for children.
MAIN ATTRACTIONS: Eastern Transvaal Lowveld ecology in its 'original' state; big game and prolific birdlife.
FACILITIES/AMENITIES: Transport, canoes, rucksacks, tents, sleeping bags, groundsheets, meals and utensils are provided.
PERTINENT INFORMATION: Anti-malaria precautions are recommended. Minimum age, 15 years. Water must be sterilized before drinking.
AVAILABLE LITERATURE: *Wilderness Trails, Wilderness Leadership School; Prospectus* (both available from the Wilderness Leadership School).

The venue for the Wilderness Leadership School's Jock of the Bushveld accompanied trail is the 20 000-hectare Hans Hoheisen Private Game Reserve, a remnant of the original Transvaal Lowveld, next to the Kruger National Park, on the Timbavati River. In this environment, the trailist is given the opportunity of seeing most of South Africa's large animals.

The trail for adults begins and ends at White River or Nelspruit, while the trail for scholars begins and ends in Johannesburg.

296. *Selati Ox-Wagon Trails*

MICA TO GRAVELOTTE

G 🚶

AUTHORITY-IN-CHARGE: H.L. Hall and Sons, Ltd., P.O. Mataffin 1205; tel. (01311) 52061 (mornings only).
SIZE: 12 000 hectares.
LENGTH: 8-15 km per day.
MAIN ATTRACTIONS: Ox-wagons; bushveld in the Selati River Valley; abundant birdlife; indigenous trees; sable and other antelope; evening camp-fires.
FACILITIES/AMENITIES: Ox-wagons carry

gear and are handled by a guide who also sets up and breaks camp, loads wagons and prepares meals; tents, accommodating four people each, are provided; couples must share tents or bring their own; mattresses, meals, light refreshments, beer, wine and large dust bags for personal gear are provided; accommodation is at fixed base camps with hot showers and bush toilets.
PERTINENT INFORMATION: The hike is mainly on foot through the Ermelo Ranch game farm; you can ride the wagon instead of walking, but the ride is bumpy. For privacy, bring your own tent; sleeping bags are not provided. Trails operate from 1 April to 30 September, departing on Thursday between 15h30 and 17h00 and returning on Sunday afternoon. Maximum of 20 and minimum of 12 people allowed per trail (minimum age 8 years; at least 8 people per trail must be over 12 years old). Anti-malaria precautions are recommended. The trails are also known as 'Hall's Ox-wagon Trails'.
AVAILABLE LITERATURE: Brochure available on request.
CLIMATE: Summer rainfall area. Hot summer days, cool winter nights.

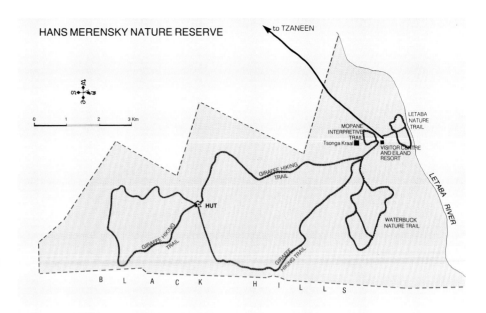

HANS MERENSKY NATURE RESERVE

SELATI OX-WAGON TRAILS

297. Hans Merensky Nature Reserve

LETSITELE

AUTHORITY-IN-CHARGE: Division of Nature Conservation, Transvaal Provincial Administration.
SIZE: 5 288 hectares.
LENGTH: Mopane Interpretive Trail: 1,12 km. Letaba Nature Trail: 7 km. Waterbuck Nature Trail: 11 km. Giraffe Hiking Trail: 37 km.
MAIN ATTRACTIONS: Mopane and *Combretum* veld; large game; prolific birdlife; rare animals; 'Tsonga Kraal'.
FACILITIES/AMENITIES: Picnic sites on the Letaba Nature Trail; overnight hut on the Giraffe Hiking Trail with beds and cooking shelter; information centre; labelled trees on trails; Eiland Resort with mineral baths,

rondavels, caravan park, swimming pools, tennis courts and picnic sites.
PERTINENT INFORMATION: Midsummer days are hot and walking is taxing; hats are recommended. Do not drink stream or river water as bilharzia is present. All permits and bookings must be obtained at the visitor centre; only one group (maximum of 10 people) allowed at one time on the Giraffe Hiking Trail; during peak periods, minimum of 3 people per group. For information: The Officer-in-Charge, Hans Merensky Nature Reserve, Private Bag X502, Letsitele 0885.
AVAILABLE LITERATURE: Information booklet with maps; *Mopane Interpretive Trail*, guide, issued by the Division of Nature Conservation.
CLIMATE: Summer: very hot. Winter: pleasantly mild, best time to hike.

The Transvaal Division of Nature Conservation deserves congratulations for providing walking trails through the lovely Hans Merensky Nature Reserve, which is situated near the Kruger National Park on the southern banks of the Great Letaba River. Before these trails were initiated, visitors could experience the reserve only by means of an organized bus tour; not, in my opinion, the best way to appreciate nature.

The reserve was originally established in 1954 to protect sable, roan and other rare lowveld antelope. The lush mopane veld supports a very diverse wildlife, however, and other animals such as giraffe, bushbuck, waterbuck, impala, grey duiker, zebra, blue wildebeest, tsessebe and leopard are also common. Game-viewing is especially rewarding during the dry winter months when the vegetation dies back and many animals may be seen drinking at the waterholes along the Waterbuck Nature Trail. On the Letaba Nature Trail, particularly when using the picnic sites on the river banks, hikers

must keep a wary eye out for hippos and crocodiles. Needless to say, swimming is strictly prohibited!

The attractive bushveld trees in the park include species such as marula, knob thorn, mopane, rock fig, wild syringa and the candelabra tree. These provide an ideal habitat for a wealth of bush-dwelling birds. The Great Letaba River also attracts the white-browed coucal, fish eagle and fishing owl. Frogs such as the grey tree frog are plentiful, despite the reserve's low rainfall.

The shortest walk in the reserve is the Mopane Interpretive Trail (a circular route starting and ending at the visitor centre), the ecology of which is described in a brochure. The Letaba Nature Trail is a leisurely stroll in the northern part of the reserve, from the Eiland Resort through the dense riverine bush of the Letaba River. The Waterbuck Nature Trail, also beginning and ending at the visitor centre, takes approximately four leisurely hours and includes a hide to view animals drinking from the dam. The Giraffe Hiking Trail gives the hiker an option of a two- or three-day route in the large southern part of the reserve, and includes excellent views of the Black Hills (the series of dolerite hills on the eastern boundary) over the Lowveld towards the Drakensberg.

While visiting the Hans Merensky Nature Reserve, allow yourself sufficient time for a walk around the 'Tsonga Kraal', a village reconstructed as an open-air 'living' museum. Here a chief and his wives demonstrate aspects of traditional Tsonga life such as building techniques; dances accompanied by Tsonga drums, kudu horns and single string instruments; salt-making; basketry; and wood-working. The kraal itself is made entirely of indigenous materials – the mopane framework is held together with mopane bark, walls and floors are made from antheap clay, and paint pigments are derived from the minerals in the soil.

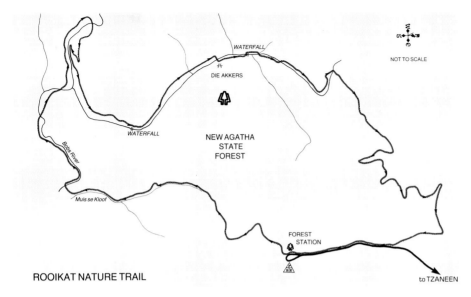

ROOIKAT NATURE TRAIL

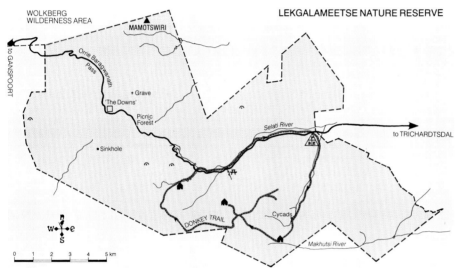

LEKGALAMEETSE NATURE RESERVE

298. Rooikat Nature Trail

TZANEEN

AUTHORITY-IN-CHARGE: Northern Transvaal Forest Region, Forestry Branch, Department of Environment Affairs.
LENGTH/DURATION: 11 km/5 hours (3-km walk also available).
MAIN ATTRACTIONS: Indigenous forest and plantation; impressive backdrop of the Wolkberg; swimming in the Bobs River.
FACILITIES/AMENITIES: Die Akkers: picnic sites, fireplaces and toilets, located at the sixth kilometre.
PERTINENT INFORMATION: Circular trail. Walkers must start out before 10h00. Permits necessary, issued free of charge between 06h00 and 16h00 by The Forester, New Agatha State Forest, Private Bag 4009, Tzaneen 0850, tel. (015236) 22347.
AVAILABLE LITERATURE: *Rooikat Nature*

Walk, brochure and map issued by the Forestry Branch.
CLIMATE: Subtropical. Average annual rainfall: 1 600 millimetres, falling mostly between January and March. Summer (October to April): mist occurs frequently, especially at an altitude of approximately 1 200 metres. Winter (June to September): dry, sunny and cold; frost possible. Average annual temperature: 20-22 °C. July to October, winds are strong and dry. Prevailing winds are south-easterly, cool and moderate.

In South Africa, dense, jungle-like forest is associated mainly with the southern coastal region; however, it also grows profusely in some parts of the northern Transvaal. The New Agatha State Forest, 18 kilometres from Tzaneen, preserves such patches of natural forest, and here the Rooikat Nature Trail winds through 11 kilometres of lush, evergreen woodlands along the Bobs River.

The trail is named after the rooikat, the Afrikaans name for the caracal or African lynx, a large, long-eared, reddish-fawn cat.

Being nocturnal, the lynx is seldom seen by hikers, although its spoor may be found. Bushbuck, duiker, baboon, vervet and samango monkey are easier to spot, as are the water leguans. Hikers should be on the alert for mambas, berg adders and grass snakes.

Much of this relatively easy walk passes through indigenous forest, where many of the trees are numbered; you will see trees such as the forest cabbage tree in moist wooded ravines, and the Natal mahogany and matumi, both of which are shaped into dug-out canoes by local tribesmen. The final four kilometres lead you through plantation before returning to the carpark.

299. Lekgalameetse Nature Reserve

TZANEEN

AUTHORITY-IN-CHARGE: Department of Development Aid, P.O. Box 384, Pretoria 0001.
SIZE: 19 500 hectares.
MAIN ATTRACTIONS: Wild mountainous terrain with gorges, rivers and forests; open bushveld to tropical montane forests; rare birdlife; endemic butterflies in the Malta Forest.
FACILITIES/AMENITIES: Seven fully furnished log cabins, accessible by vehicle; five braai/picnic sites with modern ablution block, and forest-riverine walks; luxurious guided donkey trail with permanent tented camps; bridle trails, hiking and nature walks planned.
PERTINENT INFORMATION: For information

and permits: The Chief Conservator, Lekgalameetse Nature Reserve, Private Bag 408, Trichardtsdal 0890. The reserve is to be transferred to Lebowa. A public road suitable for four-wheel drive vehicles only traverses the reserve.

AVAILABLE LITERATURE: Brochures and maps planned; located on Government Printer's 1:50 000 maps '2430 AA The Downs' and '2430 AB Ofcolaco'.

CLIMATE: Average annual rainfall: 800-1 100 millimetres, falling mostly between November and March. Average annual temperature range: 7,5 °C (July) to 30 °C (January). Mist occurs frequently above 1 100 metres.

Located south-east of the Wolkberg Wilderness Area on the Transvaal Drakensberg escarpment, 40 kilometres south of Tzaneen, Lekgalameetse is a spectacular mountainous reserve. Amphitheatres, krantzes, steep-sloped peaks and river gorges dominate the east. The plateau is eroded in a series of basins separated by mountain peaks. Towards the south-east, the flatter terrain is dolomite

with low cliffs, caves and sinkholes, the largest of which is 87 metres deep and five metres in diameter!

Numerous rivers, including the Selati and Makhutsi, and tributaries of the Ngwabitsi, endowed with beautiful waterfalls and deep pools, dissect both Lowveld sour bushveld and north-eastern mountain sourveld, the two major veld types found here. The Lowveld sour bushveld consists of woodland with tall grassveld. Some of the dominant trees include kiaat (*Pterocarpus angolensis*), round-leaved kiaat (*Pterocarpus rotundifolius*), mobola plum (*Parinari curatellifolia*), mitzeerie (*Bridelia micrantha*) and bushwillow (*Combretum collinum*). Belts of dense forest occur along the rivers. The north-eastern mountain sourveld consists of a mosaic of grasslands, woodlands and forests. Several protea species are found here.

The indigenous forests occur in isolated pockets, often on steep slopes. These forests house an impressive selection of flora and birdlife. Epiphytic orchids, ferns and mosses are plentiful in the higher moist forests and some very impressive trees are

found. One of the biggest Outeniqua yellow-woods in the Transvaal (it has a diameter of 1,8 metres at chest height) is found here.

Elevation ranges from 720 metres to the top of Mamotswiri ('mother of mist') Mountain, 1 838 metres above sea level.

The reserve is noted for its endemic and rare butterfly species, including some not yet described, in addition to rare and restricted forest birds, and a frog and several plant species endemic to the Transvaal escarpment. Fauna includes mountain reedbuck, bushbuck, duiker, klipspringer, baboon, vervet and samango monkey and blackbacked jackal. Leopard, caracal, serval and honey badger occur in small numbers. Small-spotted genet, civet, porcupine, lesser bushbaby (nagapie) and greater bushbaby (bosnagaap) are often seen or heard at night. Birds are less plentiful here than in the Low-

Opposite page: Hikers' cabins in Lekgalameetse Nature Reserve.

Above: Lekgalameetse Nature Reserve, once referred to as 'The Downs'.

veld, but some interesting species occur in the evergreen forests. The Knysna and purplecrested loeries and Narina trogon can be seen, while several robin species, the southern boubou and the gorgeous bush shrike can be heard in the undergrowth.

Lekgalameetse was once referred to as 'The Downs' after the historical and well-known farm located on a grassy plateau above the Lowveld. Orlando Baragwanath, also known as the Copper King, was the first settler on The Downs. He arrived there in 1904 and died in 1973 at the age of 102. His impressive avocado farms, bought by the state, can be still be seen. A portion of indigenous forest, locally known as the Picnic Forest, was regularly used as a church in the past for wedding ceremonies and Christmas Eve services.

At present facilities for visitors include seven fully furnished log cabins situated deep in riverine forest on the banks of the Makhutsi River, with a semi-natural swimming hole. Day visitors can enjoy the braai and picnic sites, and short walks to the Selati River with its lovely pools and waterfalls. Part of the proposed hiking trail link to be built by Lebowa, from the Blyde River Canyon to the Wolkberg, will cross the reserve, as will numerous other walking and pony trails.

One of the more exciting is the donkey trail. This guided 'luxury' walk will include donkeys, food, cooks and furnished tented camps with hot showers. In four days (three nights), eight trailists at a time will be taken up the Wolfspruit to experience some of Lekgalameetse's highlights: riverine forests, gorges with cycads growing on the cliffs, interesting geological formations and magnificent views over the Lowveld. Horse owners will be delighted to know that bridle trails are also planned where participants are encouraged to bring their own horses. Old farmhouses will be used for overnight accommodation.

Until Lekgalameetse Nature Reserve is fully developed for hikers, organized groups such as mountain clubs can apply for wilderness permits from the Chief Conservator.

300. *Wolkberg Wilderness Area*

HAENERTSBURG

AUTHORITY-IN-CHARGE: Northern Transvaal Forest Region, Forestry Branch, Department of Environment Affairs★.
SIZE: 17 390 hectares.
MAIN ATTRACTIONS: Very rugged terrain (elevation ranges from 795 to 2 050 metres); deep, densely forested ravines; endangered wildlife.
FACILITIES/AMENITIES: No overnight facilities in the wilderness area; camp-site with ablution block for hikers at Serala entry point; footpaths.
PERTINENT INFORMATION: Access point (approximately 400 km from Johannesburg) via Haenertsburg at Serala Forest Station only. Permits necessary, obtainable from The Forester, Serala State Forest, Private Bag, Haenertsburg 0730. Fires are prohibited; camp-stoves are necessary. Maximum of 60 day visitors; maximum of 10 people per overnight group; maximum of 60 overnight visitors.
AVAILABLE LITERATURE: *The Wolkberg Wilderness Area*, by C.J. Esterhuyse, January 1986, Pamphlet 361, issued by the Forestry Branch; *The Wolkberg Wilderness Area*, information pamphlet with sketch map, issued by the Forestry Branch; 'The Wolkberg Wilderness Area', *Great Outdoors*, August 1984.
CLIMATE: Ranges from subtropical to semi-arid. Summer (October to April): rainfall varies from 500 to 1 350 millimetres; mist occurs frequently, especially at approximately 1 200 metres. Winter (June to September): dry, sunny and cold; frost possible. July to October, winds are strong and dry. Prevailing winds are south-easterly, cool and moderate. Average annual temperature: 20-22 °C.

Mountains with real wilderness character are rare in the Transvaal. The Wolkberg, part of the northern Drakensberg and Strydpoort ranges, with its great, vertical quartzite krantzes, countless kloofs, cool, deep and densely forested ravines, massive buttresses and folded and interlocking spurs, was appropriately proclaimed a wilderness area in October 1977.

The 'cloudy mountain', a valuable catchment area, produces clear, silt-free water. Many streams in steep ravines flow to the

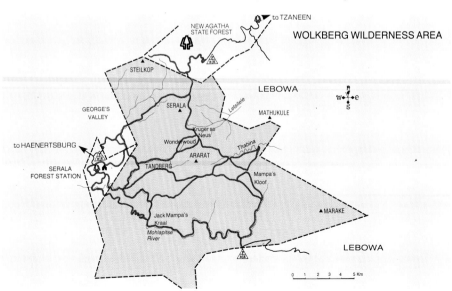

Mohlapitse River, a tributary of the Olifants. The entrance to the Mohlapitse River is through a magnificent gorge flanked by perpendicular, aloe-covered cliffs. Smaller branches of the Letaba River, the Thabina (the 'river that dances with happiness') and the Letsitele, also originate in the Wolkberg. These rivers, with their sensational waterfalls and potholes, are refreshing after a long, tough hike.

The steep, quartzitic cliffs of the Black Reef Series resting on granite gneiss formations provide impressive landmarks. Serala (Krugerskop), at 2 050 metres the highest peak in the Wolkberg, is neighboured by Steilkop (1 900 m), Marake (1 790 m) and Ararat (1 853 m), which is situated on the Tandberg (alternatively called the Knuckles or the Apostles), a well-known feature. Although mountaineers are free to travel anywhere within the wilderness, the Forestry Branch warns that only experienced rock-climbers should venture on the route from the Serala plateau over Kruger se Neus through Wonderwoud Forest and over the Tandberg.

The Wolkberg has the grass-covered slopes typical of the region, referred to by Acocks (1975) as 'North-Eastern Mountain Sour Veld'. Savannah-type bushveld occurs on the southern, drier slopes where you will find trees such as Transvaal beech and teak, marula and common wild pear. The indigenous high forest pockets found in deep, wet valleys host species such as the Outeniqua and real yellowwoods, wild fig, lemonwood, cheesewood, wild peach and Cape beech.

Marijuana, or dagga, also flourishes in the Wolkberg and is, indirectly, held responsible for the scarcity of wildlife in the region. Before the area was 'cleared out' during the 1950s in an almost military-style operation, dagga growers abounded in the remote ravines and lived off the game. But blame must also be levelled at the many farmers whose over-enthusiasm for hunting took its toll. Happily, however, the balance of wildlife is gradually being restored and today you once again have the chance of seeing klipspringer, grey rhebok, mountain reedbuck, duiker, bushbuck, genet, otter, lynx, and vervet and samango monkeys, and if extremely lucky, leopard and brown hyaena. Watch out for berg adders, puff adders, mambas and pythons. The Wolkberg is rich in birdlife; my favourites include the hamerkop, bat hawk, black eagle, lilacbreasted roller, blackcollared and pied barbets, pearlbreasted swallow and crested francolin.

No experienced mountaineer should miss exploring the Wolkberg. It is the ultimate experience after participating on the numerous hiking ways in the vicinity.

301. Magoebaskloof Hiking Trail

TZANEEN

AUTHORITY-IN-CHARGE: Northern Transvaal Forest Region, Forestry Branch, Department of Environment Affairs.
LENGTH/DURATION: Dokolewa section: 36 km/2 or 3 days, 2 or 3 nights. Grootbosch section: 50 km/3 days, 2 or 3 nights.
MAIN ATTRACTIONS: Evergreen indigenous mountain forest (largest in the Transvaal); pine plantations; tallest eucalyptus trees in South Africa; 'huilklip' (a unique rock with acoustic properties and tribal significance).
FACILITIES/AMENITIES: Dokolewa section: three huts, each equipped with fireplaces, firewood, three-legged pots, bunks, mattresses, water and toilets. Grootbosch section: two shelters with water from mountain stream, toilet, fireplace and firewood; base hut at De Hoek Forest Station.
PERTINENT INFORMATION: Hiking groups are limited to 30 people per day on the Dokolewa section and 12 people per day on the Grootbosch section; however, if more than eight people book on the Grootbosch section, four of them must carry their own tents. The hike is strenuous, and is designed for fit people; children under 12 years are not permitted. Grootbosch section: overnight accommodation is spartan shelters in the forest, near a clear stream.
AVAILABLE LITERATURE: Information sheets with map; colour brochure and map in process of being compiled.
CLIMATE: Summer rainfall area.

The Magoebaskloof Hiking Trail is one of the most beautiful in the Transvaal. When completed, it will link the Wolkberg to Magoebaskloof by way of George's Valley, and then stretch into the exquisite Duiwelskloof forests.

The three sections of the trail are George's Valley (New Agatha State Forest to the Ma-

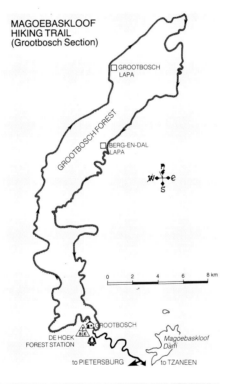

MAGOEBASKLOOF HIKING TRAIL (Grootbosch Section)

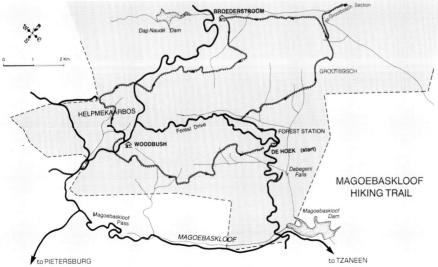

MAGOEBASKLOOF HIKING TRAIL

Opposite page: Cool, densely wooded ravines in the Wolkberg Wilderness Area.
Left: The Wolkberg Wilderness Area.

goebaskloof Hotel), which was not yet open at the time of writing; Grootbosch (circular tent route in the De Hoek State Forest); and Dokolewa (the circular route in the De Hoek and Woodbush state forests).

The rugged, forest-clad mountains in the northern Transvaal are a mosaic of dense montane evergreen forest and plantation dissected by fast-flowing streams and rivers. The Magoebaskloof area preserves possibly the best remaining example of high forest in the Transvaal, with typical tree species including yellowwood, bastard stinkwood, forest elder, tree fern and wild peach. Many animals find shelter in this thickly wooded region, including leopard, samango monkey, grey and red duikers, longcrested and crowned eagles, the bat hawk and other rarely seen species.

On the first day of the Dokolewa section, which is also the most strenuous of the three days, the trail passes through the Transvaal's largest indigenous forest – Grootbosch – before descending to Broederstroom Hut. Just before this hut, watch for the oak forest planted by Lionel Phillips in the 1930s. On the easier second and third days, you climb to the escarpment for magnificent views of indigenous forest in the valley below. *En route* to Woodbush Hut, next to the arboretum, you hike through a stand of *Eucalyptus grandis*, the tallest trees in the country. These massive trees are certainly impressive – just try to wrap your arms around one of the trunks!

The final day is a 10-kilometre stretch which returns to De Hoek Hut through forest on Magoebaskloof's northern slopes.

The entire circular trail is an easy route, recommended for beginner hikers and families.

The most strenuous trail, the Grootbosch section, branches off the circular route after the first ten kilometres. Winding through the Grootbosch indigenous forest, you eventually follow the summit of the northern spur of the Drakensberg range, where views over the Mooketsi Valley are magnificent. Forest scenery and beautiful waterfalls feature on the third day. The Grootbosch trail is one of the first National Hiking Way trails offering simple shelters and a tent site for accommodation instead of hiking huts with bunks and mattresses.

302. Ben Lavin Nature Reserve

NEAR LOUIS TRICHARDT

AUTHORITY-IN-CHARGE: Transvaal Branch of the Wildlife Society of Southern Africa, P.O. Box 5003, Delmenville 1403.
SIZE: 2 519 hectares.
LENGTH: Tabajwane Trail: 8 km. Fountain Trail: 4 km. Waterbuck Trail: 3 km. Tshumanini Springs Trail: 5 km.
MAIN ATTRACTIONS: Sweet and mixed bushveld vegetation; 54 mammal species, including large game; 250 recorded bird species; archaeological sites.
FACILITIES/AMENITIES: Four walking trails; camping and caravan sites; huts and lodges with firewood, linen, crockery, cutlery and refrigerators; trees labelled with their national tree list numbers; game-viewing hides; game-viewing night drives.
PERTINENT INFORMATION: Visitors may walk anywhere in the reserve. For bookings: Ben Lavin Nature Reserve, P.O. Box 782, Louis Trichardt 0920; tel. (01551) 3834.
AVAILABLE LITERATURE: *Ben Lavin Nature*

Reserve, brochure, map, mammal, bird and tree lists, available from the Wildlife Society or at the gate.
CLIMATE: Summer rainfall area.

The Ben Lavin Nature Reserve is a game reserve project of the Wildlife Society. It is situated only 12 kilometres south-east of Louis Trichardt in beautiful bushveld country, and is therefore a convenient recreation venue for townsfolk and can be easily visited by hikers in the Northern Transvaal, Venda and Lebowa.

The four circular trails in the Ben Lavin Nature Reserve lead off from the game-viewing drives, but the reserve's greatest advantage, especially for bird-watchers, is the freedom to walk where you please. The trails vary from one and a half to four hours in duration.

The Tabajwane Trail offers superb views of the surrounding bushveld and the Soutpansberg range, as well as possible sightings of game at waterholes, wallows and dams. Drinking water should be carried on this trail. The Fountain Trail meanders along the banks of the Doring River, through lush riverine vegetation where bushbuck, nyala, reedbuck and leguan are often encountered. To see kudu, impala and waterbuck, follow the Waterbuck Trail to the Waterbuck, Steenbok and Marsh dams. The 'wildest' trail, the Tshumanini Springs Trail, lies in the northern part of the reserve, and whereas the other three trails begin at the camp, this one starts from Zebra Dam. Chances of seeing warthog, kudu, impala and zebra are good.

303. Soutpansberg Hiking Trail

(BETWEEN LOUIS TRICHARDT AND LEVUBU)
NORTHERN TRANSVAAL

AUTHORITY-IN-CHARGE: Northern Transvaal Forest Region, Forestry Branch, Department of Environment Affairs.
LENGTH/DURATION: 91 km/5 days (shorter 2-, 3- and 4-day variations possible, as well as an 18 km/1 day circular walk).
MAIN ATTRACTIONS: Over 400 species of birds; indigenous forests; Venda villages.
FACILITIES/AMENITIES: Four huts, each accommodating 30 people, with bunks and mattresses, three-legged pots and fireplaces; information display centre at Hanglip State Forest.
PERTINENT INFORMATION: The trail is physically difficult. Anti-malaria precautions are recommended. Ticks are prevalent. Bilharzia occurs in some streams.
AVAILABLE LITERATURE: *Soutpansberg Hiking Trail, Northern Transvaal* (second

edition), comprehensive brochure and map. CLIMATE: Summer: hot with rain. Winter: cold to temperate. November to March, heaviest rains and mist. April to October, best months for hiking.

In September 1975, having been in South Africa not even a week, I was rushed off to the Soutpansberg Hiking Trail, to attend its inauguration. At that time I found the trail to be physically quite challenging. The altitudes, ranging from 950 to 1 500 metres, the elaborate parties given by the Forestry Branch, and my too-heavy, too-small, American climbing boots which caused an outbreak of blisters, all contributed to a laborious hike!

Other impressions which stand out vividly among my memories of this trail are the glimpses of Venda villages through the mist; the prolific birdlife, much of which is difficult to see in the thick forest vegetation; the

vervet monkeys and their childlike antics; the diversity of scenery and vegetation; Sandfontein Hut, which resembles twin ski chalets; skeletal remains of a leopard kill; and the view towards the 'sacred mountain of the baboons'.

It was on this trail that I learned of a planning problem specific to African trails – the white footprints painted on rocks as route markers often 'disappear' as a result of baboons turning over the rocks in their search for beetles and scorpions.

In general, the Soutpansberg Hiking Trail is one of the more difficult in the system; the distances each day require early starts and steady walking, especially in winter. Starting at the Hanglip Forest Station, the first day (13,5 kilometres) entails a gradual climb through pine plantation and indigenous forest. Views from Hanglip Hut are exceptional. If you prefer a two-day circular walk, you can return to the office on a different, seven-kilometre route. However, on the longer trail, the second day (19,2 kilometres) winds through bushveld and private farms and ends at Sandfontein Hut. The

Opposite page: Setting off on the first day of the Magoesbaskloof Hiking Trail.

Above: Sandfontein Hut, the second night's stopover on the Soutpansberg Hiking Trail.

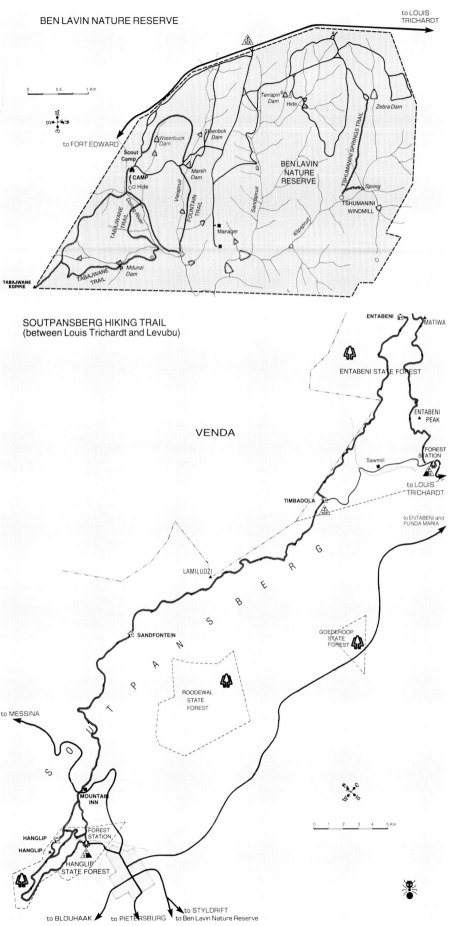

253

third and fourth days (22,1 and 18,1 kilometres respectively) are the most difficult because of the steep gradients of the paths. Both overnight huts, Timbadola and Entabeni, are converted houses. Kabelbaan Hut splits the fourth day into two shorter sections. The last day (18 kilometres) once again traverses indigenous forest until the final descent through a plantation to the Entabeni Forest Station.

304. Soutpansberg Hiking Trail (Entabeni Section)

NORTHERN TRANSVAAL

AUTHORITY-IN-CHARGE: Northern Transvaal Forest Region, Forestry Branch, Department of Environment Affairs.
LENGTH/DURATION: 52 km/4 days (shorter 2- and 3-day variations also possible).
MAIN ATTRACTIONS: Indigenous forests and plantation; 400 species of birds; views of Venda.
FACILITIES/AMENITIES: Circular walk; four huts (including base hut) accommodating 30 people, with fireplaces, firewood, big cooking pots, bunks and mattresses, water and toilets.
PERTINENT INFORMATION: The 2- and 3-day routes are for reasonably fit hikers.
AVAILABLE LITERATURE: *Soutpansberg Hiking Trail (Entabeni Section)*, brochure and map.
CLIMATE: Summer: hot with rain. Winter: cold to temperate. November to March, heaviest rains and mist. April to October, best months for hiking.

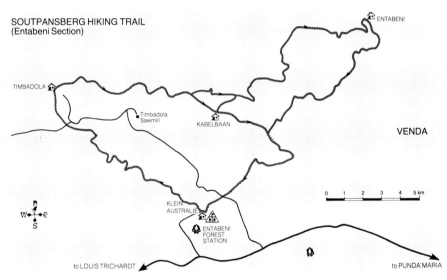

SOUTPANSBERG HIKING TRAIL
(Entabeni Section)

As an easier alternative to the longer Soutpansberg Hiking Trail, trailists may opt for the Entabeni Section, a four-day circular walk. With the exception of the 19-kilometre fourth day, each day covers only 10-12 kilometres. However, for those hikers wanting a more strenuous workout, two- and three-day circular routes with longer distances are also available.

The Entabeni hiking trail is situated in the north-east part of the 'classic' Soutpansberg trail, within similar forest types. In fact, Timbadola Hut and Kabelbaan Hut are shared by both trails (the latter hut only if hikers wish to shorten the fourth day, between Timbadola and Entabeni huts). The hiker passes through beautiful indigenous, semi-deciduous forest, such as that in the Ratombo Nature Reserve (on the first day), *Eucalyptus* and pine plantations, evergreen

Top: A hiker on the Soutpansberg Hiking Trail looks out towards the 'sacred mountain of the baboons'.

indigenous forest and, on the fourth day, an attractive stand of old *Sequoia sempervirens*, the American coastal redwood.

Far-reaching views, encompassing the holy mountain of Venda's Lamando tribe, are highlights of this pleasant route, as are the opportunities for swimming.

305. Baobab Hiking Trail

HONNET NATURE RESERVE, TSHIPISE, see map page 256

AUTHORITY-IN-CHARGE: Overvaal Resorts.
LENGTH/DURATION: 25 km of hiking and nature trails. Guided horse trails: 4 hours.
MAIN ATTRACTIONS: Baobab trees; large game species; plentiful birdlife; ruins built in the same style as the Zimbabwe Ruins.

FACILITIES/AMENITIES: Hiking hut accommodating 10 people, with bunks and mattresses, water, braai facilities, grids, pots, crockery and reed-covered shower; trees labelled with their national tree list numbers.
PERTINENT INFORMATION: The trail is located in the Honnet Nature Reserve, and can be walked in one day; hikers can walk the trail unaccompanied or with a guide. Braais and other meals can be arranged by the resort staff at extra cost, which saves carrying food to the hut. Carry water. An extension of the trail to 51 km across neighbouring farms is planned. *Tshipise* means 'the mountain that explodes', after the mineral spring with temperatures of up to 55 °C, which has its source here. For information: The General Manager, Overvaal Tshipise, P.O. Box 4, Tshipise 0901.
AVAILABLE LITERATURE: *Overvaal Tshipise*, brochure.
CLIMATE: Summer rainfall area.

306. Greater Kuduland Safaris

TSHIPISE, see Regional Map page 228

AUTHORITY-IN-CHARGE: Greater Kuduland Safaris, P.O. Box 1385, Louis Trichardt 0920.
SIZE: 10 000 hectares.
DURATION: Morning game walks. 3- to 5-day walking trails.
MAIN ATTRACTIONS: Large game in mopane woodland, including kudu, impala, blue wildebeest, gemsbok, nyala, red hartebeest, buffalo, eland, waterbuck, zebra, white rhino, leopard and cheetah; klipspringer and dassies; 200 species of birds, including nesting black eagles.
FACILITIES/AMENITIES: Guided game trails; canoeing on dam; base camp accommodating 14 people in luxurious air-conditioned bungalows with fresh linen, hot showers and baths, lounge and dining room and lapa for braaiing; Madindi and Ma'bako bush camps.
PERTINENT INFORMATION: The reserve is located 5 km from Tshipise Hot Springs Resort. Anti-malaria precautions are recommended. Trails are tailored to suit the needs and interests of visitors.
AVAILABLE LITERATURE: *Greater Kuduland Safaris: Photographic and Hiking Safaris*, brochure and tariff list.
CLIMATE: Summer rainfall area.

Greater Kuduland Safaris cater both for those wanting a relaxed holiday, and for hikers wishing for a more strenuous walk of several days' duration.

You can sleep in a luxury camp and participate in a sunrise game trail at a leisurely pace. Afternoon activities are optional and include bird-watching and game drives.

Alternatively, you can choose a three- to five-day guided walking trail and sleep in bush camps. Madindi camp is set in hilly terrain near natural potholes, giant baobab trees and ancient Venda war and burial grounds. Ma'bako camp is situated in an area of huge, wind-eroded sandstone caves.

307. Messina Nature Reserve

MESSINA, see map page 256

AUTHORITY-IN-CHARGE: Division of Nature Conservation, Transvaal Provincial Administration.
SIZE: 3 898 hectares.
MAIN ATTRACTIONS: Baobab trees (some of which have been declared national monuments) and other indigenous trees and shrubs (over 350 species in mopane veld); 12 species of large game, including sable antelope, nyala, giraffe and blue wildebeest; ancient geological formations in the Sand River; endangered, restricted and rare flora and fauna.
FACILITIES/AMENITIES: Two nature trails; self-guided vehicle route with picnic site.
PERTINENT INFORMATION: This is a developing reserve; contact The Officer-in-Charge, Messina Nature Reserve, P.O. Box 78, Messina 0900, for details and brochures.
AVAILABLE LITERATURE: Planned.
CLIMATE: Average annual rainfall: 350 millimetres, falling mostly in summer. Average annual temperature range: 17-29 °C.

308. Limpopo Wilderness Hiking Trail

ALLDAYS

AUTHORITY-IN-CHARGE: Mr Theo Swart, P.O. Box 5, Alldays 0909, tel. (01554) 464; or P.O. Box 33024, Glenstantia 0010, tel. (012) 98-3979.
SIZE: 8 500 hectares.
LENGTH/DURATION: 35 km/3,5 days (variations of 1; 2; 2,5 and 3 days possible).
MAIN ATTRACTIONS: Limpopo River, with its great variety of indigenous trees and rich birdlife; game such as crocodile, hippopotamus, bushbuck, waterbuck, impala, klipspringer and kudu.
FACILITIES/AMENITIES: Three camp-sites with 'bomas', long-drop toilets, cold water and firewood; a trained guide is available for any group exceeding eight people.
PERTINENT INFORMATION: Trails are organized to suit trailists' interests and abilities. No restriction on number of people. Roads to base are good throughout the year. Trails operate throughout the year. Anti-malaria precautions are necessary. Trailists must take their own food. Trailists may not cross the border into Botswana.
AVAILABLE LITERATURE: *Limpopo Wilderness Hiking Trail*, brochure and map.
CLIMATE: Summer rainfall area. Hot in summer, cool to cold in winter.

To really get the feeling of being in the bush, where there is little sign of human intrusion and the environment is absolutely unspoilt, walk the Limpopo Wilderness Hiking Trail. The trail is physically not very demanding, and the distances between overnight camps vary between five and ten kilometres. The short distances covered each day encourage trailists to observe the bush and spend time at the permanent pools in the river where numerous bird species, some rare, can be seen. Crocodiles and bushbuck are also plentiful here. In addition to wildlife, ancient ruins and mines can be seen.

309. Langjan Nature Reserve

ALLDAYS

AUTHORITY-IN-CHARGE: Division of Nature Conservation, Transvaal Provincial Administration.
SIZE: 4 800 hectares.
LENGTH: 50 km of walks (variable).
MAIN ATTRACTIONS: Brak River riverine ecology; indigenous trees; Kalahari atmosphere with gemsbok and 13 other species of large game; prolific birdlife.
FACILITIES/AMENITIES: Walking trails; vehicular tours; bush camp with four carpeted huts providing beds, cooking place, cold showers and pit latrines.
PERTINENT INFORMATION: For bookings: The Officer-in-Charge, Langjan Nature Reserve, P.O. Box 15, Vivo 0924. The bush camp lies outside the reserve.
AVAILABLE LITERATURE: Information sheet and map issued by the Division of Nature Conservation.
CLIMATE: Average annual rainfall: 470 millimetres, falling mostly in summer. Summer daytime temperature maximum: 39 °C. Winter night-time temperature minimum: 5 °C. Frost is not common.

In the remote north-western Transvaal bushveld lies an ecologically interesting reserve, 25 kilometres south of Alldays.

Through the relatively flat and featureless landscape runs the Brak River, often dry

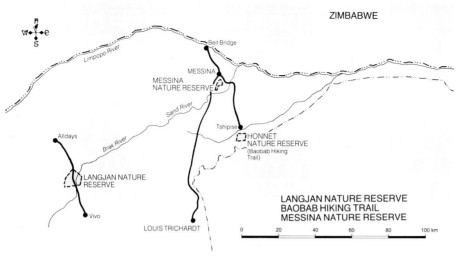

LANGJAN NATURE RESERVE
BAOBAB HIKING TRAIL
MESSINA NATURE RESERVE

PIETERSBURG MUNICIPAL GAME RESERVE

PERCY FYFE NATURE RESERVE

with standing pools of water. On one side of the Brak, the vegetation is mainly sweet grassveld, while on the opposite bank trees grow in dense profusion. Large buffalo-thorn and palm trees shade the river banks, while marulas (famous for their intoxicating fruits), tambotis (infamous for their poisonous milky latex) and knob thorns (well-known by their conspicuous knobbly prickles) are also common.

The unusual aspect of Langjan's ecology is the Kalahari influence which enables gemsbok, red hartebeest and ostrich to thrive here. Blue wildebeest, bushbuck, eland, giraffe, kudu, impala, zebra, sable antelope and waterbuck, along with a great variety of birds, can also be identified.

Trailists are allowed to walk on the extensive gravel road system, although no specific route is marked. All hikers must be out of the reserve by dark, or sleep in the bush camp which is located outside the game area.

310. Pietersburg Municipal Game Reserve

PIETERSBURG

AUTHORITY-IN-CHARGE: Municipality of Pietersburg, P.O. Box 111, Pietersburg 0700.
SIZE: Approximately 2 000 hectares.
LENGTH/DURATION: 40 km/2 days in total (12-km game reserve trail, 28-km semi-urban trail).
MAIN ATTRACTIONS: 15 species of antelope; white rhinoceros; grave of the late Right Honourable Tom Naude; Ethnological Museum; tree park.
FACILITIES/AMENITIES: Caravan park with ablution block, shady sites, tarred roads and electricity; fully equipped chalets

accommodating six people (no food provided).
PERTINENT INFORMATION: Open 07h00-18h00 September to March, 08h00-15h00 April to August; reserve stays open longer for walkers than for motorists. Permits necessary, obtainable at the entrance to the reserve at Union Park. This is one of the largest municipal reserves in the Transvaal.
AVAILABLE LITERATURE: Map issued with permit.
CLIMATE: Summer rainfall area. Minimum temperature: 8 °C. Maximum temperature: 28 °C.

311. Percy Fyfe Nature Reserve

POTGIETERSRUS

AUTHORITY-IN-CHARGE: Division of Nature Conservation, Transvaal Provincial Administration.
SIZE: 3 032 hectares.
MAIN ATTRACTIONS: Breeding of roan, tsessebe and sable antelope; nine other game species; granite koppies and grasslands; euphorbias, resurrection plants and other interesting indigenous plants; prolific birdlife.
FACILITIES/AMENITIES: Nature trails; patrol roads open for walking only; camping area with kitchen, ablution block and hall; self-guided vehicle tours through roan camp between 08h00 and 17h00.
PERTINENT INFORMATION: Visitors may walk through the tsessebe and sable camps. Swimming is prohibited. For bookings: The Officer-in-Charge, Percy Fyfe Nature Reserve, Private Bag X2535, Potgietersrus 0600; tel. (01541) 5678.
AVAILABLE LITERATURE: Percy Fyfe Nature Reserve, information brochure.
CLIMATE: Summer rainfall area.

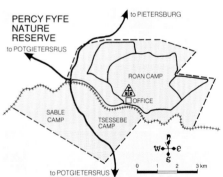

312. National Zoological Gardens

POTGIETERSRUS, see Regional Map page 228

AUTHORITY-IN-CHARGE: National Zoological Gardens of South Africa, P.O. Box 170, Potgietersrus 0600.
SIZE: 1 200 hectares.
MAIN ATTRACTIONS: Wildlife breeding centre, therefore many species of indigenous animals, including the black rhino, are found here; bushveld trees labelled with

their national tree list numbers.
FACILITIES/AMENITIES: Guided walks planned; accommodation at the Park Hotel (all facilities plus swimming pool) or camping and caravan site in Potgietersrus.
PERTINENT INFORMATION: This is a game and nature reserve specializing in the breeding of animals for zoos in South Africa and abroad.
AVAILABLE LITERATURE: *National Zoological Gardens of S.A., Nature Reserve and Game Breeding Centre, Potgietersrus*, booklet with sketches of animals, tree checklist and map.
CLIMATE: Summer rainfall area.

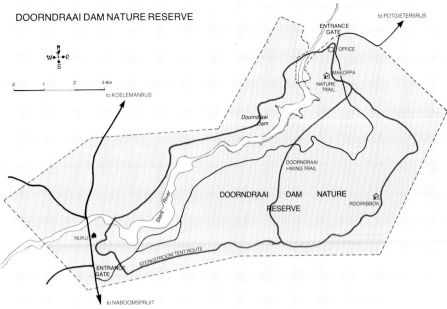

DOORNDRAAI DAM NATURE RESERVE

313. Doorndraai Dam Nature Reserve

NABOOMSPRUIT

AUTHORITY-IN-CHARGE: Division of Nature Conservation, Transvaal Provincial Administration.
SIZE: 7 790 hectares.
LENGTH/DURATION: Doorndraai Hiking Trail: 19 km. Sterkstroom tent route: 30 km. Dam Wall Nature Trail: approximately 3 hours. Wilderness Leadership School guided trail: 2 days.
MAIN ATTRACTIONS: The reserve specializes in the protection of rare species, especially sable, roan and tsessebe; 13 additional large-game species; birdlife is excellent on the dam; sour bushveld vegetation; views over the Springbok Flats; kloofs and waterfalls; hilly terrain; the reserve is located in the foothills of the Waterberg.
FACILITIES/AMENITIES: Doorndraai Hiking Trail: Rooiribbok overnight hut and Makoppa base hut, each with two bedrooms (five beds with mattresses in each), outside eating place, tables, benches, cooking pots, buckets, paraffin lamps, braai place and

firewood, bush toilets. Sterkstroom tent route: Nuku overnight camp with braai area, bush toilet, cold shower and tent site. Wilderness Leadership School guided trail: food and camping equipment are supplied; transport between the reserve and Johannesburg is provided. Dam Wall Nature Trail has trees labelled with their national tree list numbers. Fishing and boating is allowed on Doorndraai Dam. Two self-guided vehicle tour routes.
PERTINENT INFORMATION: Hats recommended when walking in summer. One group with a maximum of 10 people allowed per night at overnight sites, and one adult (over 18 years old) is required per group on self-guided trails; bookings can be made not more than 6 months in advance. If the dam is full, hikers on the Sterkstroom tent route must swim across the dam's inlet at the beginning of the second day. Wilderness Leadership School guided trail: each trailist must provide his own sleeping bag; maximum of 6 people permitted on trail (minimum age 12 years); departure point in Johannesburg is arranged to suit individuals or the group, and is best confirmed at time of booking; trails for school or youth groups available by special arrangement; trail operates on weekends only. The Dam Wall Nature walk is easy. Bilharzia is possible in the dam. Changes to the trail network may occur, so consult the officer-in-charge before your visit. For information: The Officer-in-Charge, Doorndraai Dam Nature Reserve, P.O. Box 983, Potgietersrus 0600.
AVAILABLE LITERATURE: *Doorndraai Dam Information for Walkers*, with map; information sheet available from the Wilderness Leadership School.
CLIMATE: Summer is hot; winter is cold.

Located in the foothills of the Waterberg, the 7 790-hectare Doorndraai Dam Nature

Reserve is hillier than Nylsvley Nature Reserve (see page 258). The sour bushveld vegetation, comprising trees such as boekenhout, wild olive and wild syringa, is home to reintroduced tsessebe (southern Africa's swiftest antelope) and sable antelope, as well as duiker, steenbok, kudu, klipspringer, mountain reedbuck, leopard and baboon. Although its birdlife is not as abundant as Nylsvley's, Doorndraai's dam attracts water-birds, while predators such as the fish eagle, Wahlberg's eagle, martial eagle and hawks can often be seen soaring overhead.

314. Mosdene Private Nature Reserve

NABOOMSPRUIT

AUTHORITY-IN-CHARGE: Mrs M.E.R. Galpin, Mosdene Private Nature Reserve, P.O. Box 28, Naboomspruit 0560; tel. (012072) 2030.
SIZE: 5 421 hectares.
MAIN ATTRACTIONS: One of the best bird-watching areas in the Transvaal (400 species); ecological study centre.
FACILITIES/AMENITIES: Camp-site; cottage, sometimes for hire.
PERTINENT INFORMATION: Arrange visit telephonically, in advance. Subject to summer rainfall flooding – extreme care should be exercised when driving on wet roads. Visitors must remove all rubbish.
AVAILABLE LITERATURE: *Mosdene Private Nature Reserve*, brochure; *Birds of Mosdene*

Above: It is difficult to miss the prominent flower of the Haemanthus *sp. in the Percy Fyfe Nature Reserve.*

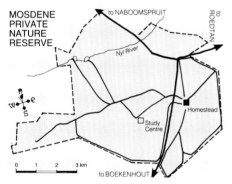

Nature Reserve, Naboomspruit, 1971, by W.R. Tarboton, available from the University of Cape Town.
CLIMATE: Average annual rainfall: 610 millimetres, falling mostly in summer.

To the ecologist, Mosdene Private Nature Reserve (known among local people as Galpin's Farm) is synonymous with birds – 400 species, or almost half the total number of species found in all of South Africa, have been recorded here. It is possible to see approximately 125 species in a weekend, if you take bird identification very seriously. Amateurs can do well by joining Witwatersrand Bird Club outings which frequent this area.

Operated as a cattle ranch (be cautious of ticks), Mosdene protects other large mammals such as kudu, blesbok, reedbuck, steenbok, duiker, brown hyaena and jackal. (Early one morning, when I set off to enrich my bird list, I was confronted by the sight of numerous jackals on the road.)

Several veld types (open vlei, tamboti veld, sand and thornveld) occur in juxtaposition, housing a fine diversity of indigenous trees. The vegetation, in conjunction with the annual flooding of the Nyl River, contributes to the fertility and diversity of avian species. Many academics have recognized the farm as a unique ecological study centre

and have come from as far afield as California and London to study all aspects of the veld, from blue-green algae to parasitic birds.

The owners are justifiably very strict with visitors. Take precautions against getting bogged down on wet roads, and remember to remove, not bury, your litter.

315. *Nylsvley Trail*

NYLSVLEY NATURE RESERVE

AUTHORITY-IN-CHARGE: Wilderness Leadership School. Nature reserve managed by the Division of Nature Conservation, Transvaal Provincial Administration.
DURATION: 2 days.
MAIN ATTRACTIONS: Natural beauty of the Nyl River floodplain with its prolific

birdlife; roan antelope, tsessebe and other large animals.
FACILITIES/AMENITIES: Food and camping equipment are supplied; transport between the reserve and Johannesburg is provided.
PERTINENT INFORMATION: Each trailist must provide his own sleeping bag. Maximum of 6 people permitted on trail (minimum age 12 years). Departure point in Johannesburg is arranged to suit individuals or the group, and is best confirmed at time of booking. Trails for school or youth groups available by special arrangement. Trail operates on weekends only.
AVAILABLE LITERATURE: Information sheet available from the Wilderness Leadership School; *Wilderness Trails, Wilderness Leadership School*, brochure.
CLIMATE: Summer: rainy and warm. Winter: dry and cool to cold. Spring and summer, best seasons for bird-watching.

In keeping with the philosophy of the Wilderness Leadership School, trail groups are purposely kept small so that each trailist receives individual attention. Participants are regarded as those who will very likely be making future policies for land-use and thus, to quote from a WLS publication, they must be made aware 'that man is part of the whole, not a puppet-master pulling the strings from the outside'. With these objectives in mind, the trail facilities are as primitive as possible – tents are provided only in the case of rain and trailists participate in all camp chores and activities.

Ecology provides the trail focus, with emphasis on the history and culture of past inhabitants of the trail area, the reserve's natural history, and the wilderness concept. Night watches are an integral part of each trail experience.

The 3 100-hectare Nylsvley Nature Reserve which straddles the Nyl River is world-famous for its birdlife. Apart from embracing the largest natural vlei in the Transvaal, which in itself attracts a myriad

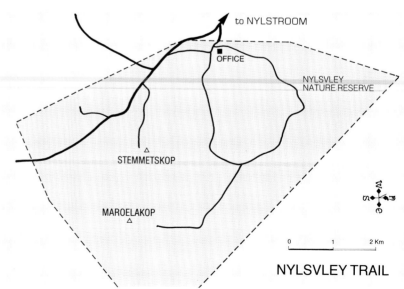

NYLSVLEY TRAIL

water-birds, the surrounding bushveld, rich in wild fruit trees such as marula, stamvrug and sour plum, creates a bird haven in which 400 species have been recorded. The southern 700 hectares of *Burkea africana* sandveld is the study area for the South African Savanna Ecosystem Research Project.

316. Lapalala Wilderness Weekend Trails

NEAR VAALWATER, WATERBERG

AUTHORITY-IN-CHARGE: Educational Wildlife Expeditions (EWE), P.O. Box 645, Bedfordview 2008.
SIZE: 13 753 hectares.
DURATION: 2,5 days; 4-day trails available for schoolchildren.
MAIN ATTRACTIONS: Wild bushveld in the

Opposite page: Mosdene Private Nature Reserve is a place for serious bird-watchers.
Above: Autumn in the Waterberg.

Waterberg mountains; Bushman paintings; antelope and prolific birdlife; white rhino, sable and roan; bilharzia-free rivers; separate trails for adults and children.
FACILITIES/AMENITIES: Trail prices are inclusive of transport to and from Johannesburg, food, accommodation and literature. Four camps in the reserve: Tambuti Camp, accommodating 8 people per night; Marula Camp, accommodating 6 people per night; Mukwa Camp, accommodating 2 people per night; Tshwene Camp, accommodating 8 people per night. All camps are equipped with beds, refrigerators, cutlery, crockery, stoves, showers and toilets. These camps can be hired by groups who wish to walk in the reserve but not by those on organized wilderness trails. The reserve provides a service to schools by way of film and slide shows, and talks. Fishing and canoeing are permitted.
PERTINENT INFORMATION: People hiking within the reserve, but not on organized wilderness trails, must take their own food. Light aircraft can land at Lapalala if advance arrangements are made. Maximum of 10 children per trail (minimum age 9 years); class group bookings of more than 10 scholars may be arranged on request. Vehicles are not permitted in Lapalala.

LAPALALA WILDERNESS WEEKEND TRAILS

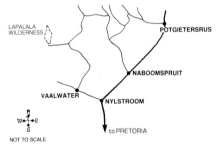

AVAILABLE LITERATURE: Contact EWE for their latest brochures, posters and booklets; *Sanctuary*, quarterly publication.
CLIMATE: Summer rainfall area; warm to hot. Winter days are warm and sunny, nights are cold.

Within a four-hour drive from Johannesburg, via Vaalwater, you can find yourself on a two and a half day weekend wilderness trail under the guidance of trained field staff. From Friday afternoon (13h30) until Sunday night (18h00) you explore a lovely wild area of fast-flowing, bilharzia-free rivers, stark mountain landscapes, and thick bushveld hosting the beautiful roan and sable antelope, nyala, kudu, zebra, impala,

baboon, leopard, blackbacked jackal and brown hyaena. Many smaller creatures, including a considerable bird population, are also present.

Separate trails are run for adults and children. The children's trail, accommodating 8-10 children, is subsidized by the Wilderness Trust. The Trust is 'an independent organization founded with the objectives of teaching young people, of any race, colour or creed, concepts of conservation, ecology, the protection and appreciation of wild creatures, wild areas and the natural resources of our southern African environment' (EWE brochure).

The trails cater for both privileged and underprivileged youngsters. Their camp, consisting of a large bungalow and tent situated on a stream bank, is named Munadu; the adult camp, Umdoni, consists of two-person tents equipped with mattresses, camp beds, sleeping bags and other 'bush' conveniences.

Although the privately owned Lapalala Wilderness hosts large antelope and predators, the emphasis on both trails is environmental awareness and man's responsibility to conserve his natural heritage.

317. Gold River Game Resort

VAALWATER

AUTHORITY-IN-CHARGE: Pieter Baard, P.O. Box 14064, Verwoerdburg 0140; tel. (012) 62-2334 during office hours, (012) 64-5188 after hours. Resort, tel. (015352) 3212.
SIZE: Approximately 4 000 hectares.
DURATION: 1-3 days (variable).
MAIN ATTRACTIONS: Abundant wildlife, including various types of antelope, giraffe

and birds in their natural bushveld habitat; Bushman paintings.
FACILITIES/AMENITIES: Main camp: six chalets, each accommodating 6 people, with bathrooms and cooking space with utensils; one luxury house, accommodating 7 people; dormitories for youth groups; lapas for braaiing; swimming pool, trampoline, dam with boats and recreation hall. Wooden Camp and Fountain Camp: huts accommodating 35 hikers, with beds and mattresses, warm showers, toilets, lapas and a kitchen with crockery, cutlery, gas fridge and gas stove. Wood for braaiing is available at all camps.
PERTINENT INFORMATION: A knowledgeable guide is provided for each group to lead the way to where game may be found, and to point out the different kinds of animals and plants. The group is expected to supply its own and its guide's meals. Advance bookings must be made.
AVAILABLE LITERATURE: *Gold River Game Resort*, brochure; located on Government Printer's 1:50 000 map '2328 CC Blinkwater'.
CLIMATE: Summer rainfall area.

Situated about 300 kilometres north of Pretoria, the privately owned Gold River Game Resort is an ideal getaway for a family or group to return to the peace of nature. The resort is well-stocked with wildlife; nyala, hartebeest, gemsbok, kudu, impala, zebra, roan antelope, eland and abundant smaller buck, as well as giraffe, jackal, serval, lynx and leopard contribute to the reserve's reputation of being one of South Africa's most densely populated nature reserves.

Visitors can stay at the main camp where they can swim, fish, canoe or go for short

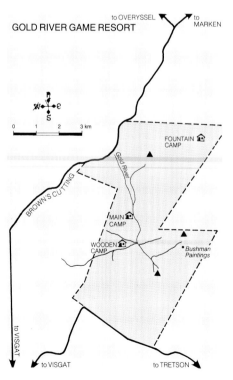

GOLD RIVER GAME RESORT

guided trails or Land Rover drives through the reserve. Alternatively, they can go on longer walks to one of the hikers' camps. These two camps are located in opposite directions from the main camp; Wooden Camp is two kilometres away, Fountain Camp about 10 kilometres. Most hikers walk to the camp, where they leave their heavy packs, and go game-viewing with the guide. A lookout platform is located a few kilometres from Wooden Camp. Hikers can also visit the Bushman paintings, found about five kilometres from the main camp.

Small groups can arrange Land Rover tours at night.

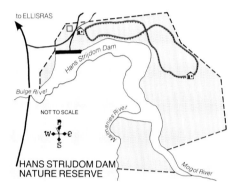

HANS STRIJDOM DAM NATURE RESERVE

318. Hans Strijdom Dam Nature Reserve

ELLISRAS

AUTHORITY-IN-CHARGE: Division of Nature Conservation, Transvaal Provincial Administration.
SIZE: 4 632 hectares (800-hectare fenced game area).
LENGTH: 6 km and 12 km.
MAIN ATTRACTIONS: Roan antelope, Sharpe's grysbok and other game; hilly and mountainous terrain with savannah vegetation.
FACILITIES/AMENITIES: Nature walks; overnight huts, one at the beginning of the trail and one at an overnight point; fishing and pleasure-boating permitted on dam.
PERTINENT INFORMATION: Located 900-1 150 metres above sea level. Water is not potable; bilharzia is possible. For information: The Officer-in-Charge, Hans Strijdom Dam Nature Reserve, P.O. Box 473, Ellisras 0555.
AVAILABLE LITERATURE: Information sheet and map.
CLIMATE: Summer: very hot. Winter: mild, best time to hike.

Top: Straddling the Nyl River, Nylsvley Nature Reserve protects more than 400 species of birds.

Opposite page: Lebowa has contrasting, diverse and richly endowed natural scenic assets, many of which are being developed as reserves.

LEBOWA

Lebowa, a self-governing homeland, is divided into 11 units which are bordered by the Transvaal (South Africa), Venda, Gazankulu and KwaNdebele. Despite its small size (21 830 km²), Lebowa has contrasting, diverse and richly endowed natural scenic assets, many of which are being conserved and developed as reserves with nature, educational and hiking trails. Mountain masses rising out of bushveld; sheer cliffs, home to the Cape vulture and bald ibis; indigenous high forests rich in yellowwoods; the largest number of cycads growing in one locality in the world; the dramatic Drakensberg escarpment; the game-rich grassy highveld; and fantasy-like tufa streams are some of the attractions contributing to the popularity of Lebowa's trails.

No special permission is required to travel through Lebowa providing you stay on national roads, and visit recreational areas, resorts or towns; to enter onto tribal lands, special arrangements must be made with the local magistrate.

Lebowa shares its climate with the Transvaal: a wet, hot summer and a dry, cool winter when hiking opportunities excel.

ECOLOGICAL ZONE: DRY
WOODLANDS

319. Haakdoorndraai Nature Reserve

MARKEN

AUTHORITY-IN-CHARGE: Department of Agriculture and Environmental Conservation, Lebowa.
SIZE: 4 542 hectares.
MAIN ATTRACTIONS: Mixed bushveld with lovely trees, including paperbark albizia (*Albizia tanganyicensis*), paperbark commiphora (*Commiphora marlothii*), marula, fig, combretum and tamboti; diverse birdlife, including black eagles, African hawk eagles, blackbreasted snake eagles, lilacbreasted rollers and brown snake eagles; large mammal life, including eland, kudu, impala, red hartebeest, zebra and waterbuck; interesting caves and shelters with unusual Bushman paintings, smelting furnaces, granaries and other artefacts; unique conglomerate geology; flat-topped koppies with cliffs rising 300 m vertically from the bushveld, in the eastern section; reed-lined river.
FACILITIES/AMENITIES: Nature walks planned; public camp-site with bungalows, youth camp, picnic sites and information centre planned.
PERTINENT INFORMATION: A public road

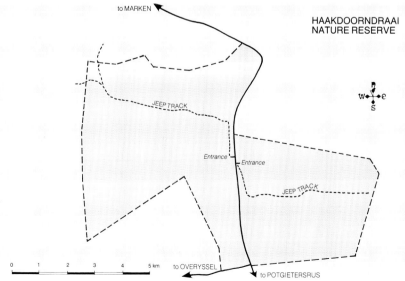

to MARKEN

HAAKDOORNDRAAI
NATURE RESERVE

JEEP TRACK

Entrance — Entrance

JEEP TRACK

0 1 2 3 4 5 km

to OVERYSSEL

to POTGIETERSRUS

divides the reserve into an eastern and a western section. The name of the reserve is to be changed. Rough terrain, so wear sturdy footwear. Carry water when hiking. Altitude range: 914-1 247 metres above sea level.

AVAILABLE LITERATURE: Brochure planned; located on Government Printer's 1:50 000 topographic map '2328 DA Skrikfontein'.
CLIMATE: Summer is very hot. April to November, best months for hiking.

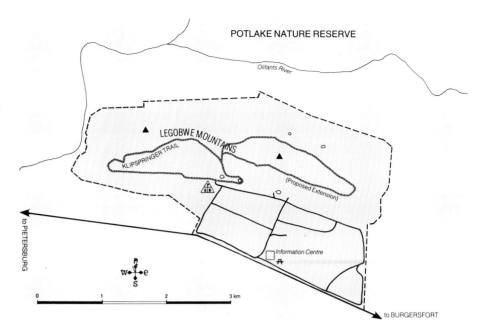

320. Moletsi Nature Reserve

PIETERSBURG

AUTHORITY-IN-CHARGE: Department of Agriculture and Environmental Conservation, Lebowa.
SIZE: Approximately 200 hectares.
DURATION: Approximately 2 hours.
MAIN ATTRACTIONS: Bird sanctuary (bald ibis, Cape vulture, black eagle and lanner falcon breed in the reserve); granite rock boulders; rich variety of animal and plant life for such a small reserve.
FACILITIES/AMENITIES: Two self-guided nature trails; information centre; braai/picnic sites; office; ablution block.
PERTINENT INFORMATION: This reserve provides environmental education for the local people and is a sanctuary for breeding colonies of birds. Before visiting the reserve, contact the head of the Nature Conservation branch of the Department of Agriculture and Environmental Conservation for

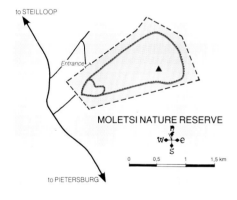

Opposite page, top: The mixed bushveld with its associated birdlife is sure to delight the naturalist in the Haakdoorndraai Nature Reserve.

Opposite page, bottom left: Artefacts of cave-dwelling peoples are well preserved in the Haakdoorndraai Nature Reserve.

Opposite page, bottom right: Moletsi Nature Reserve provides habitat for many plant and animal species.

Right: Hikers reward themselves with a braai in Potlake Nature Reserve.

permission and details of progress on the development of facilities.
AVAILABLE LITERATURE: Interpretive brochures; bird, tree, grass and insect checklists; located on Government Printer's 1:50 000 map '2329 CB Kalkbank'.
CLIMATE: Winter: warm, sunny days. Summer: hot days with rain.

Rising out of open grassveld, only 40 kilometres north-west of Pietersburg, are two granite koppies which remind me of the lower Spitzkoppe in Namibia. It is comforting to know that these formations and the surrounding small area of flat grassy Pietersburg plateau are under the watchful eye of the Nature Conservation authorities of Lebowa, for here lies the northernmost breeding ground of the bald ibis, endemic to South Africa.

An insect-eater, and not a pest to farmers, the bald ibis can be identified by its iridescent blue-green plumage, red legs, naked white head and bright crimson crown and bill. Black eagles and lanner falcons, both predators of bald ibis nests, also breed here.

Moletsi Nature Reserve's small area is astonishingly rich in all sorts of life. Bushveld birds include the whitebrowed sparrow-weaver, violeteared waxbill, orangebreasted bush shrike, whitethroated robin, barthroated apalis and spotted eagle owl. The nature conservation officer had identified more than 70 species of trees at the time of my visit, and had hopes of finding others. It is remarkable, too, that jackal, baboon, steenbok, duiker, klipspringer, impala and dassie all coexist in the 200-hectare reserve.

Besides conservation, the main objective of Moletsi is education. Two self-guided interpretive trails (one a short walk to the summit of the small koppie, and the other a 1,5-2 hour walk around the larger koppie and past the nests of black eagles, bald ibises and Cape vultures) are laid out.

321. Potlake Nature Reserve

SEKHUKHUNELAND

AUTHORITY-IN-CHARGE: Department of Agriculture and Environmental Conservation, Lebowa.
SIZE: 2 786 hectares.
LENGTH/DURATION: 8 km/2-3 hours (to be extended).
MAIN ATTRACTIONS: Large game species; arid sweet bushveld with attractive tree species; Legobwe Mountain.
FACILITIES/AMENITIES: Nature walks; kiosk; interpretive centre; picnic/braai sites.
PERTINENT INFORMATION: Carry water while hiking and wear sturdy footwear to walk on the mountain; in summer, walk during the cool of the day.
AVAILABLE LITERATURE: *Potlake Nature Reserve*, brochure; located on Government Printer's maps '2429 BB Bewaarkloof' and '2429 BD Ga-Mankopane'.

CLIMATE: Average annual rainfall: 430 millimetres, falling mostly in summer (September to March). Average annual temperature range: 18,4-30 °C.

Easily accessible by road and only 85 kilometres south-east of Pietersburg, Potlake Nature Reserve offers marked nature trails in the wildlife-rich, flat *Acacia* woodland, as well as along Legobwe Mountain (1 183 m) where the dry, sweet bushveld looks particularly attractive in its autumn colours.

Some of the dominant tree species include the acacias: the umbrella thorn, *Acacia tortilis*; the horned thorn, *A. grandicornuta*; and the black thorn, *A. mellifera*. The last named appears stunted and is a very thorny tree. Also common are the flat-crown, *Albizia adianthifolia*, which makes a good shade tree; the puzzle bush, *Ehretia rigida*, a good luck charm; and *Commiphora pyracanthoides*, whose bark flakes in small, papery strips.

Most of the large animals, except for the impala and kudu, have been introduced. These include blue wildebeest, eland, gemsbok, waterbuck, giraffe, Burchell's zebra, red hartebeest and ostrich.

For those naturalists with an affinity for the bushveld, Potlake will be a very popular reserve. A view of the Olifants River Valley emerges from the summit of Legobwe Mountain, and there are many round intrusive rock boulders adding scenic interest to the mountain slopes. At present the Klipspringer Trail is an approximately eight-kilometre circular nature route in the western portion of the park; it will be expanded to a figure-of-eight on the eastern side of the mountain. If there is a demand, the authorities will also build a 'meditation hut' for optional overnighting. The interpretive centre adds educational value to the reserve, which is already popular for its braai/picnic sites and kiosk.

322. Strydom Tunnel Hiking Trail

OHRIGSTAD, see Regional Map page 228

AUTHORITY-IN-CHARGE: Department of Agriculture and Environmental Conservation, Lebowa.
DURATION: Approximately 5-day hiking trail planned.
MAIN ATTRACTIONS: Deep kloofs with indigenous forest and large swimming pools; spectacular cliffs and geological formations; birdlife; historical interest.
FACILITIES/AMENITIES: To be decided.
PERTINENT INFORMATION: Proposed route of hiking trail, which will connect the Blyderivierspoort Hiking Trail (see page 236) to the Wolkberg Wilderness Area (see page 250): Blyde River Canyon,

MAPULANENG NATURE TRAILS

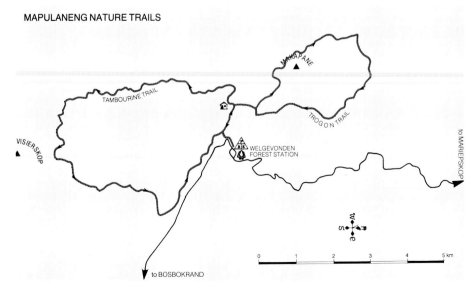

Drakensberg, Strydom Tunnel area, Old Coach Road, Olifants Sekororo, Lekgalameetse Nature Reserve, Thabina Nature Reserve.
AVAILABLE LITERATURE: In process of being compiled.
CLIMATE: Summer rainfall area.

323. *Mapulaneng Nature Trails*

BUSHBUCK RIDGE (BOSBOKRAND)

AUTHORITY-IN-CHARGE: Department of Agriculture and Environmental Conservation, Lebowa.
LENGTH: Tambourine Trail: 17 km. Trogon Trail: 11 km.
MAIN ATTRACTIONS: Tropical wet and dry indigenous forest; waterfalls; streams; forest birds, including the Narina trogon; butterflies; views of the Lowveld.
FACILITIES/AMENITIES: Luxurious three-room log cabin, equipped with 6 beds, hot water, stove, refrigerator, cutlery and crockery; fully serviced.
PERTINENT INFORMATION: Bring your own food. The hut is reached after a 2-km walk from the parking area. Anti-malaria precautions are recommended. Extension of trails to Mariepskop is planned.
AVAILABLE LITERATURE: Brochure planned; the northern part of Mapulaneng is located on the Blyderivierspoort Hiking Trail map by Peter Slingsby, Mapcape (trails are not indicated).
CLIMATE: Average annual rainfall: 1 367 millimetres. December, January and February, wettest and hottest months. June, July and August, driest and coldest months. September to April, mist common. August to April, lightning common.

Many hikers, especially those who use the NHWS, are familiar with the Blyderivierspoort Hiking Trail. However, few are aware that just east of the canyon is an afforested escarpment called Mapulaneng. The Mapulaneng forestry region includes several plantations and also large areas of unspoilt montane forest, the origin of many Lowveld streams. The Lebowa authorities have developed one of these lovely forestry areas, Welgevonden, for nature enthusiasts and day walkers.

Opposite page, top: The Klipspringer Trail meanders to the summit of Legobwe Mountain in the western portion of the park.
Opposite page, centre: Hikers encounter large game species, such as giraffes, on the lower slopes of Legobwe Mountain in the Potlake Nature Reserve.
Top: A luxurious log cabin has been erected for hikers on the Mapulaneng Nature Trails.

Deep in the heart of the jungle-like environment is one secluded, luxury log cabin, situated 1 051 metres above sea level, where up to six people can delight in the intricacies of forest ecology. (You must park your vehicle at the forest station and walk the easy two-kilometre path to the hut.) The cabin is surrounded by tall tropical montane forest species such as yellowwood, Cape wild fig, wild peach, terblans, waterboom, Cape beech, white stinkwood and Cape chestnut.

Radiating from the hut are two circular nature trails. These are cut deep inside the forest, occasionally offering views of the distant Lowveld or the towering quartzitic cliffs that shade the canopy in the late afternoon. The Tambourine Trail runs west from the hut to Visierskop (1 796 m), and the Trogon Trail leads to Makapane (1 554 m). The trails display both the dry forests of the northern slopes and the wetter forests of the southern slopes. A conspicuous feature of these forests is the variety of lianes and ephiphytes, including members of the orchid and streptocarpus families; the forests have strong affinities with those in tropical East Africa and the Chimanimanis of Zimbabwe.

In summer, bird-watchers have a good chance of spotting the elusive Narina trogon, as well as breeding gymnogenes and crowned eagles, orange thrushes, Knysna loeries and many more avian species. Samango monkeys, baboons, bushbuck, duiker and bushpig are common. Lepidopterists will be delighted by the variety of butterflies to be found in Mapulaneng.

324. *Thabina Nature Reserve*

NEAR LENYENYE (MAAKETOWN)

AUTHORITY-IN-CHARGE: Department of Agriculture and Environmental Conservation, Lebowa.
SIZE: 1 153 hectares.
MAIN ATTRACTIONS: Scenically situated Mogoboya Ramodike Dam, fed by mountain streams; high cliffs and waterfalls; subtropical Lowveld trees (marula, lavender tree, mobola plum, pigeonwood, acacia and stamvrug) and pockets of indigenous forest in ravines; rich birdlife, including purplecrested loeries, crowned eagles and gorgeous bush shrikes; wildlife, including bushbuck, duiker, baboon and bushpig.
FACILITIES/AMENITIES: Intensive luxury development planned. Hiking hut near

325. Modjadji Nature Reserve

BOLOBEDU

🚶

AUTHORITY-IN-CHARGE: Department of
Agriculture and Environmental
Conservation, Lebowa.
SIZE: 306 hectares.
MAIN ATTRACTIONS: Modjadji cycad forest;
large game species; tribal history; angling in
dam.
FACILITIES/AMENITIES: Nature walks;
information centre; kiosk; picnic and braai
sites.
PERTINENT INFORMATION: Permits and
entrance fees payable at the gate; open daily
07h00-17h00.
AVAILABLE LITERATURE: *Modjadji Nature
Reserve*, brochure; preliminary bird and tree
checklists; located on Government Printer's
1:50 000 map '2330 CB Ga-Modjadji'.
CLIMATE: Summer rainfall area; mist
common. March to August, best months to
visit.

Emerging from the misty heights above the
Modjadji Valley is the most fascinating
population of plants seen on any nature trail
in southern Africa. Once the main diet of
the dinosaur, the Modjadji cycad, *Encephalartos transvenosus*, forms a unique natural
forest which can be viewed in its prehistoric
state thanks to its strict protection by succeeding generations of 'rain queens', the hereditary rulers in the area. In fact, here the
hiker has the privilege of experiencing the
'Alice in Wonderland' atmosphere of the
largest concentration of a single cycad species in the world. These 200-400 million-
year-old plants not only grow in profusion
but are giants in the genus of 29 species,
with specimens up to 13 metres high, and
bearing cones that may weigh up to 34
kilograms.

Only five kilometres from the reserve, interested people can visit the Modjadji Nursery where little cycads are raised from the
seeds collected in this forest. Young plants
grow about 2,5 centimetres per year, their
growth rate slowing as they get older.

The setting is superb. When mist does not
obscure the view, the hiker gazes over the
cycad forest to the Lowveld and the Kruger
National Park. Approximately 12 kilometres
of well-constructed walks drop from the cycad forest to the acacia and grassveld below
where large game such as blue wildebeest,
waterbuck, nyala, impala and bushbuck,
and over 170 species of birds, dwell in land
once trampled by the cycad-eating dino-

waterfalls planned. Yachting, sailing and
fishing (kurper) allowed on dam; no
motorboats permitted.
PERTINENT INFORMATION: The reserve
borders the eastern edge of the Wolkberg
Wilderness Area (see page 250) and is
situated 45 km from Tzaneen. Altitude
range: 740-1 300 metres above sea level.
Carry water on the trail. Dam is free of
bilharzia.
AVAILABLE LITERATURE: Brochure planned;
located on Government Printer's 1:50 000
topographic map '2430 AA The Downs'.
CLIMATE: Average annual rainfall: 460-
1 600 millimetres. Summer: very hot.
Winter: dry and cool; best season to hike.

saurs. There is an approximately 300-metre change in elevation from the cycad forests to the dam, and this is reflected in the variety of vegetation.

The lands of the Modjadji tribe, a matriarchal society that has produced five rain queens (the present queen speaks only to females), surround the reserve, and the traditional vernacular architecture and culture seen on the reserve's periphery add interest to the trails.

Opposite page, top: Thabina Nature Reserve, bordering the Wolkberg Wilderness Area, is especially rich in subtropical lowveld trees.

Opposite page, centre: The Thabina Nature Reserve surrounds the Mogoboya Ramodike Dam. Fishing, sailing and walks in the area are permitted.

Left: The Modjadji Nature Reserve was created to protect the Modjadji cycad, Encephalartos transvenosus, *once the main diet of the dinosaur.*

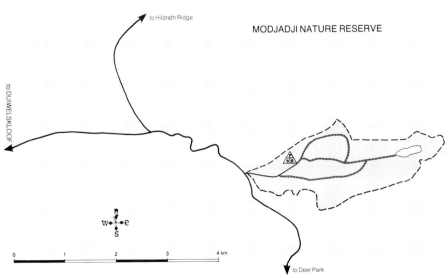

MODJADJI NATURE RESERVE

to Hildreth Ridge

to DUIWELSKLOOF

to Deer Park

0   1   2   3   4 km

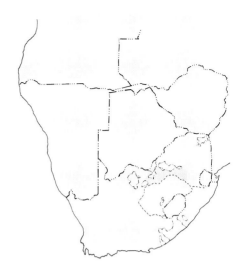

THE HIGHVELD

The Highveld is the flat, grassy plateau comprising the interior of South Africa; most of the central and south-western Transvaal falls into this region. The Transvaal Highveld is South Africa's population hub and its area of greatest urban sprawl. Environmental education and relaxation from the strains of city life are provided by a system of spruits, urban parks, green pockets and wildflower and bird sanctuaries which are linked by semi-urban, self-guided trails. In addition, most mountainous areas around Pretoria and Johannesburg, such as the Witwatersrand and Magaliesberg, are developed with hiking and nature trails and are heavily utilized. Educational centres and guided trails are growing in popularity.

The climate in the Transvaal Highveld is more predictable than in many areas of South Africa. Summers are warm, with thunderstorms common in the late afternoons. Winters are dry and sunny with cool days (perfect for hiking) but very cold nights, and sometimes heavy frosts.

ECOLOGICAL ZONE: HIGHVELD

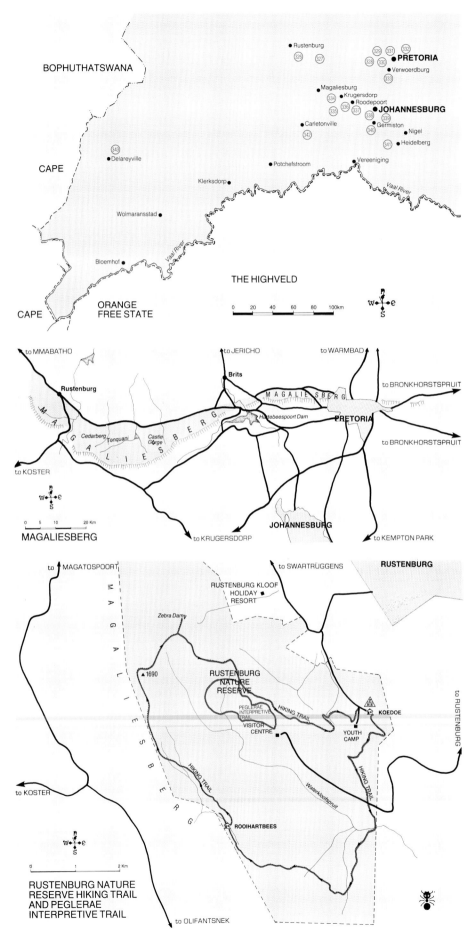

BOPHUTHATSWANA

CAPE

THE HIGHVELD

ORANGE
FREE STATE

CAPE

MAGALIESBERG

RUSTENBURG NATURE
RESERVE HIKING TRAIL
AND PEGLERAE
INTERPRETIVE TRAIL

326. Magaliesberg

SOUTH-CENTRAL TRANSVAAL

AUTHORITIES-IN-CHARGE: Several local governments and private landowners.
LENGTH: 125 km.
MAIN ATTRACTIONS: Deep kloofs; rock climbing; caves and rock paintings; diverse plant and animal life; clean, clear water.
FACILITIES/AMENITIES: Holiday resorts and camp-sites; Hartebeespoort Dam Recreational Complex.
PERTINENT INFORMATION: Seriously threatened by quartzite mining and urban expansion. Very popular during weekends; strict control regulations.
AVAILABLE LITERATURE: *The Preservation of the Magaliesberg*, MCSA report, 1974.
CLIMATE: Summer: hot days with rain. Winter: clear, cool days and cold nights.

For the Highveld mountaineer, the Magaliesberg provides the only suitable environment close to home. Declared a Natural Area in 1977, this range, comprising hard, resistant quartzites, and rising an average of 330 metres above the surrounding plains, remains the last relatively untouched area in the south-central Transvaal since the arrival of white settlers in the 19th century. The pressures being placed on the region, valued both in terms of residential expansion and for its mineral wealth, should therefore be viewed with great concern.

Stretching 125 kilometres from east to west and spanning an elevation between 1 372 and 1 829 metres, the Magaliesberg forms a conspicuous divide between the lower-lying, hotter bushveld to the north and the cooler highveld to the south. Because flora and fauna distinct to both regions merge along the range, the Magaliesberg harbours a considerable diversity of indigenous species. Examples of the many interesting plants are the endemic *Aloe peglerae* and the kloof-dwelling tree fern, *Cyathea dregei*.

More than 150 species of birds have been recorded, including the colourful crimson-breasted shrike, plumcoloured starling, paradise whydah, crested barbet and a large number of raptors. The endangered Cape vulture breeds on the steep southern cliffs. Mammals frequently seen are chacma baboons and vervet monkeys, dassies, grey duiker, reedbuck and klipspringer. Although most of the indigenous big game has been exterminated, predators such as leopard, brown hyaena and aardwolf have managed to survive.

Numerous climbing kloofs such as Castle Gorge, Tonquani and Cedarberg have become so popular over the past several years that access to them is now strictly controlled. In addition, some areas are carefully patrolled by the Mountain Club of South Africa. The hiker is responsible for obtaining

permission or permits for his trip. Take care not to trespass on private land.

The NHWB has proposed the establishment of a hiking trail along the entire length of the Magaliesberg; this may well be the best method of controlling and preserving this valuable mountain range.

327. Rustenburg Nature Reserve Hiking Trail and Peglerae Interpretive Trail

MAGALIESBERG

AUTHORITY-IN-CHARGE: Division of Nature Conservation, Transvaal Provincial Administration.
LENGTH/DURATION: Rustenburg Hiking Trail: 20,5 km/2 days. Peglerae Interpretive Trail: 4,7 km/2-3 hours.
MAIN ATTRACTIONS: Reintroduced large game animals; protected plants; 265 species of birds; massive quartzitic rocks.
FACILITIES/AMENITIES: Two rustic huts with

mattresses, fireplace and firewood, large pots, lanterns and toilets; 10 beds per hut in two separate rooms, between which is a covered sitting and eating area with a table and benches. Youth camp; information centre.
PERTINENT INFORMATION: For bookings: The Officer-in-Charge, Rustenburg Nature Reserve, P.O. Box 511, Rustenburg 0300. Weekends are usually fully booked.
AVAILABLE LITERATURE: *Rustenburg Nature Reserve, Hiking Trail Information*, pamphlet; *Rustenburg Hiking Series 2*, map, no text; *Peglerae Interpretive Trail*, guide; *General Information, Rustenburg Nature Reserve*; animal and plant checklists (all available from the Division of Nature Conservation).
CLIMATE: Very cold winter nights.

On the summit and northern slopes of the western Magaliesberg lies one of the most interesting reserves on the Highveld. The two-day hiking trail through the reserve traverses a variety of habitats: the bush-clad mountain ridge which reaches an altitude of 1 690 metres; a large valley basin with an extensive reed-swamp; and the western open grassland plateau. Although the ascents and descents are steep, the distances covered each day (9 and 12 kilometres respectively) are short enough to allow leisurely walking

and plenty of time to appreciate wildlife. It is planned to extend the trail into another section of the reserve, to the south-east.

Oribi, reedbuck, impala, springbok, eland, sable antelope, waterbuck, red hartebeest, kudu and zebra are commonly seen by trailists. These species have been reintroduced to the region, but others such as the klipspringer, mountain reedbuck and grey duiker have always been present. Predators – the leopard, endangered brown hyaena, caracal and blackbacked jackal – are largely nocturnal and therefore unlikely to be observed. Bird-watchers will see species typical of the sour bushveld and acacia and protea woodlands, including the black eagle, Scops owl and redchested cuckoo, which are fairly common.

The two huts, constructed from wooden poles, reed and thatch, blend well with the environment. Koedoe Hut, situated at the base of the mountain, is for visitors arriving the evening before starting their hike. It has tap water, while hikers at Rooihartbees Hut on the summit can take advantage of the nearby stream.

In addition to the Rustenburg Hiking Trail, casual visitors can walk the Peglerae Interpretive Trail on the northern crest of the Magaliesberg. Using the trail booklet, which is full of sketches and diagrams, ramblers are directed to the best viewpoints and also learn about important geological features, trees and aloes, as well as common wildlife.

Top left: Looking over the Highveld from the Magaliesberg, near Castle Gorge.
Top right: Tonquani is one of the most popular rambling and climbing kloofs in the Magaliesberg.
Far left: The cooking 'boma' on the Rustenburg Hiking Trail.
Left: One of the Magaliesberg's natural pools.

328. Moreleta Spruit Nature Trail

(AND PROPOSED WALKER SPRUIT AND APIES RIVER TRAIL)
PRETORIA

AUTHORITY-IN-CHARGE: Parks and Recreation Department, Pretoria City Council.
LENGTH: Moreleta Spruit Nature Trail: 27,5 km of main trail plus 17 km of tributary trails.
MAIN ATTRACTIONS: Indigenous trees and shrubs which support a diverse and prolific birdlife.
FACILITIES/AMENITIES: Farm dams surrounded by trees; urban parks, bird sanctuaries, museums and trim parks; municipal bus service (weekdays only, excluding public holidays) operates close to the trail.
AVAILABLE LITERATURE: 'The Moreleta Spruit Nature Trail', information sheets and maps in *Parks and Recreation, Pretoria*, booklet.

Much credit must go to the city fathers of Pretoria for linking the capital's attractive natural assets in a series of pleasant walking trails. The Moreleta Spruit Nature Trail stretches from the source of the Moreleta Spruit on the Highveld, to the Pienaars River Dam (Roodeplaat Dam), north-east of Pretoria.

The spruit flows in a more or less northerly direction through eastern Pretoria suburbs such as Garsfontein, Faerie Glen, Lynnwood Glen, Lynnwood Manor, Murrayfield and Silverton, and then through a gap in the Magaliesberg at Derdepoort until it joins the Hartebeest Spruit *en route* to the Pienaars River Dam. The trail also links many urban amenities such as the Meyerspark Bird Sanctuary, Meyerspark Trimpark, the Pioneer Open Air Museum (the oldest existing dwelling in Pretoria), the Derdepoort Regional Park (Pretoria's newest picnic resort), and the Faerie Glen Regional Park (undeveloped).

About 17 kilometres of subsidiary 'looping' trails along the tributaries of the Moreleta (for example, the Waterkloof Spruit, the Wolwe Spruit and the Garston Spruit) are also being developed as nature rambles.

Along the river valleys, ramblers can study the many fine shrubs and trees such as the bushwillow, white stinkwood and hookthorn. Bird-watching, too, is rewarding, and patient observers are likely to spot an interesting variety of species, including the blackcollared barbet, pintailed whydah and bishop bird.

As a result of the popularity of the Pretoria and Johannesburg trail systems, another trail, the Walker Spruit and Apies

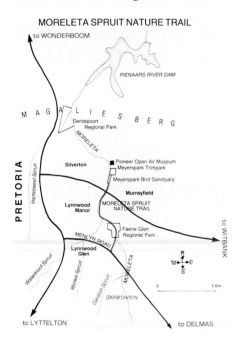

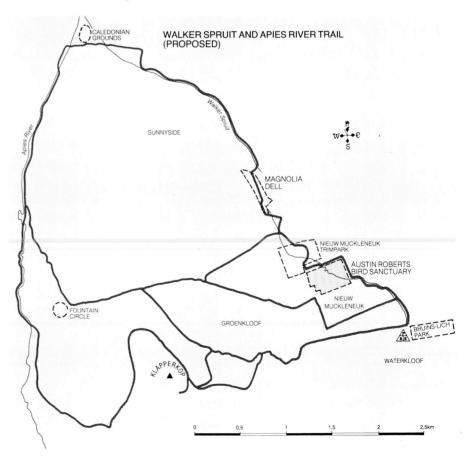

Top: The beautiful terraced gardens of the Union Buildings. The buildings serve as the administrative headquarters of the South African government.

Opposite page, left: The Pretoria National Botanical Garden has the full spectrum of South Africa's flora.

Opposite page, right: Colourful cosmos flowers are a beautiful sight in the Highveld autumn, carpeting fields and growing along roadsides in disturbed soil.

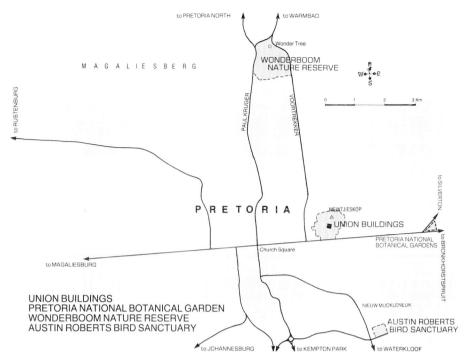

to PRETORIA NORTH   to WARMBAD

Wonder Tree

WONDERBOOM
NATURE RESERVE

MAGALIESBERG

to RUSTENBURG

PAUL KRUGER   VOORTREKKER

P R E T O R I A

MEINTJIESKOP
UNION BUILDINGS

to SILVERTON

PRETORIA NATIONAL
BOTANICAL GARDENS

to BRONKHORSTSPRUIT

Church Square

to MAGALIESBURG

NIEUW MUCKLENEUK

AUSTIN ROBERTS
BIRD SANCTUARY

UNION BUILDINGS
PRETORIA NATIONAL BOTANICAL GARDEN
WONDERBOOM NATURE RESERVE
AUSTIN ROBERTS BIRD SANCTUARY

to JOHANNESBURG   to KEMPTON PARK   to WATERKLOOF

0   1   2   3 Km

River Trail, is being planned. This route starts north of Bruins-Lich Park in Water-kloof and passes various amenities, including the Austin Roberts Bird Sanctuary, the Nieuw Muckleneuk Trimpark, Magnolia Dell, Fountains Valley Nature Reserve, the National Zoological Gardens and Wonderboom Nature Reserve.

329. *Union Buildings*

PRETORIA

AUTHORITY-IN-CHARGE: Pretoria City Council.
MAIN ATTRACTIONS: Beautiful terraced gardens; Meintjies Kop; jacarandas; bushbabies.
FACILITIES/AMENITIES: Footpaths and benches.
PERTINENT INFORMATION: The buildings serve as the administrative headquarters of the South African government; they were designed by Sir Herbert Baker. Do not walk alone after dark.
AVAILABLE LITERATURE: Included in general brochures on Pretoria.
CLIMATE: Summer rainfall area.

330. *Pretoria National Botanical Garden*

PRETORIA

AUTHORITY-IN-CHARGE: Botanical Research Institute, Plant Exploration Section.
SIZE: 61 hectares.
MAIN ATTRACTIONS: Full spectrum of South Africa's flora.
FACILITIES/AMENITIES: Labelled plants; nature trails; nursery.
PERTINENT INFORMATION: Open daily 08h00-17h00. Walks on the northern slopes display subtropical vegetation (lowveld and coastal forest); walks on the cooler south-

facing slopes display temperate vegetation (high forest and fynbos). Garden is located on Brummeria Road, 10 km from Pretoria.
AVAILABLE LITERATURE: *Botanical Research Institute: Department of Agriculture and Fisheries*, booklet.
CLIMATE: Summer rainfall area. Spring is the best time to visit.

331. *Wonderboom Nature Reserve*

PRETORIA

AUTHORITY-IN-CHARGE: Pretoria City Council, Department of Parks and Recreation.
MAIN ATTRACTIONS: The 'wonder tree', wild fig tree (*Ficus salicifolia*).
FACILITIES/AMENITIES: Nature walks.
PERTINENT INFORMATION: The fig tree is 50 m in diameter and 23 m tall; secondary trees develop from 'layering' (heavy branches touch the ground, take root and produce new trees); carbon dating puts the tree at 1 000 years old. The reserve is open daily from sunrise to sunset. It is located on the old Warmbaths road, north of Pretoria.
AVAILABLE LITERATURE: Included in general brochures on Pretoria.
CLIMATE: Summer rainfall area.

332. *Austin Roberts Bird Sanctuary*

PRETORIA

AUTHORITY-IN-CHARGE: Pretoria City Council, Parks and Recreation Department.
SIZE: 13 hectares.
MAIN ATTRACTIONS: 170 species of birds; large animals.
FACILITIES/AMENITIES: Bird-watching; large hide.
PERTINENT INFORMATION: The sanctuary is a national monument. It is open on

weekends and public holidays, 07h00-17h00. Birds and buck are visible from pavements surrounding the perimeter fence. The Walker Spruit and Apies River Trail passes the sanctuary.
AVAILABLE LITERATURE: Included in general brochures on Pretoria.
CLIMATE: Summer rainfall area.

333. Verwoerdburg Trail

VERWOERDBURG, see Regional Map page 270

AUTHORITY-IN-CHARGE: Municipality of Verwoerdburg, P.O. Box 14013, Verwoerdburg 0140.
LENGTH: 17 km.
MAIN ATTRACTIONS: Rivers; the Sesmylspruit; nature reserves.
FACILITIES/AMENITIES: Cricket stadium; lake with sports facilities; trim park; waterpark; indoor sports centre.
PERTINENT INFORMATION: The trail starts near the Verwoerdburg Sports Complex (opposite the Verwoerdburgstad shopping centre) and ends at Zwartkops Nature Reserve; it is planned to extend the trail to join the Pretoria municipal trails and Rietvlei Dam. Open all year; no permits necessary. Trail is flooded after heavy rains.
AVAILABLE LITERATURE: Planned.
CLIMATE: Summer rainfall area.

334. Sterkfontein Caves

KRUGERSDORP

AUTHORITY-IN-CHARGE: Deputy Registrar (Research), University of the Witwatersrand; tel. (011) 716-3556/70.
SIZE: I. E. Stegmann Nature Reserve: 20 hectares.
DURATION: 45-60 minutes.
MAIN ATTRACTIONS: Caves consist of an extensive network of underground caverns and passageways; underground lake; museum with important fossils.
FACILITIES/AMENITIES: Small museum; trained guides; tape-recorded explanations; restaurant and shop; parking and toilet facilities.
PERTINENT INFORMATION: Visitors are not permitted to enter any parts of the caves other than on the clearly demarcated main trail. The caves can be very dangerous. A nominal entrance fee is charged. The caves are closed from the second week in January to the first week in February. Guided tours

STERKFONTEIN CAVES
NOT TO SCALE
PRETORIA
HEKPOORT
Sterkfontein Caves
MAGALIESBURG
KRUGERSDORP
JOHANNESBURG
N1

are available Thursday to Sunday. Open 10h00-17h00 in summer, 10h00-16h30 in winter.
AVAILABLE LITERATURE: Enquire at the restaurant/shop.
CLIMATE: Typical Highveld. Warm to hot in summer, rain possible. Mild to bracing or very cold in winter, usually very dry with danger of grass fires.

In 1936, in the low, grassy hills and wild olive groves of the Sterkfontein Valley, Dr Robert Broom made one of the world's most important archaeological discoveries – the fossilized female skull and jawbone of the man-ape, *Plesianthropus transvaalensis* (now known as *Australopithecus africanus*). This difficult name was shortened by newspaper reporters to the nickname by which the famous skull, one of the most complete 'ape-man' skulls ever discovered, is now widely known: 'Mrs Ples'. She lived more than two million years ago. The small museum explaining the scientific importance of the Sterkfontein Caves is attached to the restaurant, not far from the cave entrance.

This find made famous the Sterkfontein Caves, a series of six large interconnecting chambers containing stalactites, stalagmites and flowstone 'curtains'. A crystal-clear underground lake, 46 metres below the surface, hosts a rare, tiny, sightless freshwater shrimp.

A part of the dolomitic cave system has been developed as a tourist trail. Trained guides conduct visitors through the series of chambers and passages, including the Hall of Elephants which, at 91 metres long and 23 metres high, is the largest chamber. Tape-recorded explanations of important scientific aspects of Sterkfontein are given at a number of points along the route. I found the reflections of the dripstone formations in the underground lake particularly beautiful.

The caves are set in the I. E. Stegmann Nature Reserve, which covers approximately 20 hectares of open grassveld with scattered clumps of bushes; the bushes usually indicate the presence of sinkholes in the underlying dolomitic rock. Only 10 kilometres from Krugersdorp on the Krugersdorp-Hekpoort Road, it takes about 40 minutes from Johannesburg to reach the caves.

335. Krugersdorp Game Reserve

KRUGERSDORP

AUTHORITY-IN-CHARGE: Trails are controlled by the Krugersdorp Centre of the Wildlife Society of Southern Africa.
SIZE: 1 400 hectares.
LENGTH/DURATION: Variable; about 4 km/4 hours.
MAIN ATTRACTIONS: Large diversity of highveld animals; undulating grassland, forest, bushveld and riverine vegetation.
FACILITIES/AMENITIES: Guided trails by the Wildlife Society. Accommodation in reserve: 12 rondavels, each with three beds;

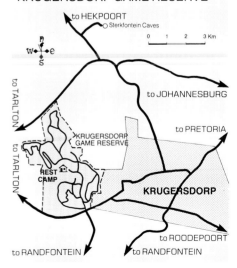
KRUGERSDORP GAME RESERVE
to HEKPOORT
Sterkfontein Caves
0   1   2   3 Km
to TARLTON
to JOHANNESBURG
to TARLTON
KRUGERSDORP GAME RESERVE
to PRETORIA
REST CAMP
KRUGERSDORP
to RANDFONTEIN
to ROODEPOORT
to RANDFONTEIN

six family units, each with six beds. 12 caravan sites; playground, swimming pool, children's pool, fireplaces and picnic sites; kiosk serving light meals; take-away food but no groceries.

PERTINENT INFORMATION: Trails are conducted on Saturday and Sunday mornings throughout the year; they start between 06h30 and 07h30, depending on the season. Maximum of 8 people per trail party (minimum age 10 years); maximum of 2 parties per day. Trails can be arranged to suit special interests.

AVAILABLE LITERATURE: Trailists are supplied with leaflets (when available) discussing the reserve and spoor identification, as well as checklists of birds and other animals; a comprehensive handbook is being compiled by the Wildlife Society.

Once offering only a drive through a zoo-like game park, the Krugersdorp Game Reserve now serves as a valuable educational trail venue on the fringes of the Witwatersrand urban and industrial sprawl. Experienced volunteer officers of the Krugersdorp Centre of the Wildlife Society lead half-day educational trails within a demarcated zone, away from public game-viewing roads.

Although the park is only 1 400 hectares in extent, its diversity of habitats (grassland, forest, bushveld and riverine vegetation) supports reintroduced blesbok, kudu, eland, giraffe, hartebeest, roan and sable antelope, wildebeest, nyala and waterbuck; the smaller antelope, such as duiker, steenbok, impala and springbok; vervet monkey; and 143 species of birds. Lion, white rhino and buffalo can be seen in separate enclosures.

The guided trails are free, but donations to nature conservation are welcomed. In existence since 1980, the Krugersdorp trails are popular with local residents, schoolchildren and foreign tourists.

336. *Witwatersrand National Botanic Garden*

ROODEPOORT

AUTHORITY-IN-CHARGE: National Botanic Gardens.
SIZE: 296 hectares.
MAIN ATTRACTIONS: Developed gardens with plants from the Witwatersrand; Witpoortjie Falls.
FACILITIES/AMENITIES: Conducted and self-guided walks and trails; interpretive centre; labelled plants; nursery (closed to general public); toilets.
PERTINENT INFORMATION: This recently opened reserve is undergoing intensive

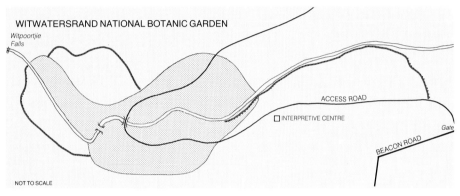

WITWATERSRAND NATIONAL BOTANIC GARDEN

Witpoortjie Falls

ACCESS ROAD

INTERPRETIVE CENTRE

Gate

BEACON ROAD

NOT TO SCALE

development. In 1988, the garden will probably be open every day to the public; until then, open 14h00-17h00 on Sundays. Conducted walks leave from the interpretive centre at 14h30 and 15h30.
AVAILABLE LITERATURE: Pamphlet with map.
CLIMATE: Summer rainfall area.

337. *Kloofendal Nature Reserve*

ROODEPOORT

AUTHORITY-IN-CHARGE: Roodepoort City Council, Parks and Recreation Division, Roodepoort 1725.
SIZE: 150 hectares.
MAIN ATTRACTIONS: Typical Highveld scenery; birdlife, indigenous trees and other plants; dam; national monument (Confidence Reef mine shaft).
FACILITIES/AMENITIES: Self-guided nature trail; amphitheatre; picnic area.
PERTINENT INFORMATION: Entrance is free;

open daily from sunrise to sunset, September to April. For information: The Chief Nature Conservation Officer, Roodepoort City Council.
AVAILABLE LITERATURE: *Kloofendal Highveld Park and Nature Trails, Roodepoort*, brochure and sketch map, issued by the Wildlife Society of Southern Africa; official brochure for the reserve, produced by the City Council, in process of being compiled.
CLIMATE: Summer rainfall area.

The tranquil Kloofendal Nature Reserve with its attractive kloofs, krantzes and dam is situated among the koppies of the Witwatersrand Ridge System in the middle of the city of Roodepoort, only a short drive from the centre of Johannesburg.

The rocks of this region are more than 3 000 million years old and form part of the

Opposite page: A lion club in the Krugersdorp Game Reserve bares its teeth.

Above: Although attractive, the prickly pear cactus is an exotic pest plant, found in many reserves in South Africa.

Lower Witwatersrand System. These ancient quartzites and shales form the basis of the rich soils which support the abundant indigenous plant life. The rich vegetation, in turn, provides an ideal habitat for many birds and small mammals.

From the reserve's picnic site, a number of easy walks lead into the koppies. In addition, the Parks and Recreation Division of the Roodepoort City Council has demarcated circular self-guided nature trails of two and six kilometres, which meander in the nature conservation area of the reserve. Facets of the region's geology and gold-mining history, as well as its flora and wildlife, are highlighted *en route*.

A visit to the Confidence Reef mine shaft (a national monument), where the first payable gold on the Witwatersrand was discovered by Fred and Harry Struben, can be arranged by appointment with the curator of the Roodepoort City Museum, tel. (011) 672-6641, ext. 229/225.

338. Central Witwatersrand Metropolitan Open Space Trails System

JOHANNESBURG

AUTHORITY-IN-CHARGE: City of Johannesburg, Urban Planning Branch, P.O. Box 30733, Braamfontein 2017; tel. (011) 777-1111.

LENGTH/DURATION: A complex of urban nature walks of varying lengths; each can be completed in one day.

MAIN ATTRACTIONS: Birdlife, small mammals and reptiles; historic buildings; old mansions; archaeological and geological sites; granite outcrops, waterfalls and natural areas.

FACILITIES/AMENITIES: Picnic and braai sites; benches; caravan park (in Bezuidenhout Park); trail sections marked by signboards with appropriate logos and maps; bird sanctuaries, zoos, botanic gardens and boating areas; trails for walkers, cyclists and horse-riders.

PERTINENT INFORMATION: Useful information and guide books available from the Johannesburg Publicity Association, P.O. Box 4580, Johannesburg 2000, and the Braamfontein Spruit Trust, Sandton Civic Centre, Sandton 2146.

AVAILABLE LITERATURE: Note that the following booklets and maps, with their detailed natural and historical descriptions, diagrams and photographs, are essential for prospective trailists: *Braamfontein Spruit Trail*, guide booklet with map; *Braamfontein Trail*, map by Map Studio; *The Parktown*

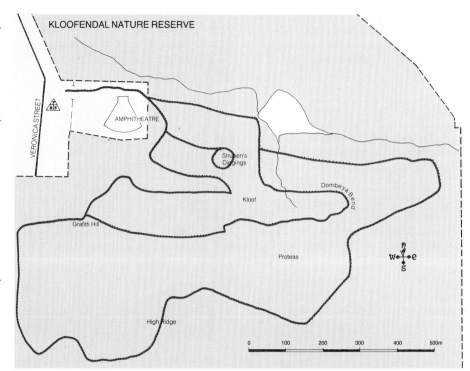

and *Westcliff Urban Walk*, guide booklet with map; *Bloubos*, brochure with map; *Sandspruit Nature Trail*, guide booklet with map; *The Mervyn King Ridge Trail*, guide booklet with map; *The Jukskei Trail and Randlords Heritage Walk*, brochure with map; other brochures with maps for planned sections; *The Sandton Field Book*, V.C. Carruthers, The Sandton Nature Conservation Society, Rivonia, 1982.

CLIMATE: Summer rainfall area; thunderstorms are common in summer. Cold winter nights; cool, sunny winter days.

The development of urban 'green areas' for informal educational and recreational use by the general public is gaining momentum in

southern Africa and, on the Witwatersrand, a prime mover of this laudable trend is Coccos (Co-ordinating Committee for Community Open Space). This joint planning and management team of professionals and officials from the local authorities of Johannesburg, Randburg and Sandton is devising and developing an extensive, metropolitan-wide trail system within the 9 500-hectare Braamfontein Spruit water catchment area.

The Braamfontein Spruit, defined by its floodplain and all contiguous open spaces, is a 25-kilometre river course with four main tributaries – the Montgomery, Westdene, Richmond and Zoo Lake spruits. From its source on the Hillbrow Ridge, the Braamfontein Spruit drains northwards through the suburbs of Johannesburg, Randburg and Sandton, eventually joining the Jukskei River which terminates in the Limpopo River System.

The Central Witwatersrand Metropolitan Open Space Trails System, following urban rivers and ridges and criss-crossing the large Johannesburg metropolitan area, is open to ramblers, hikers, dog-walkers, joggers, horse-riders and, during high water periods, canoeists. Although the pressures imposed by enclosing urban development are great, the trails environment retains much of natural value, and plants and wildlife are remarkably diverse. About 225 bird species frequent the river system, in addition to mammals such as the blackbacked jackal, caracal, dassie, spotted genet, meerkat and water mongoose, 16 frog species, and reptiles including tortoises, turtles and eight snake species.

The Witwatersrand with its typical rocky outcrops adds to the interest of the route, as do the many noteworthy archaeological sites. Discoveries include Stone Age overhangs, earlier Stone Age tools from 250 000 years ago, rock paintings, and Late Stone

CENTRAL WITWATERSRAND METROPOLITAN OPEN SPACE TRAILS SYSTEM (BRAAMFONTEIN/WESTDENE SPRUIT, OUTSPAN SPRUIT, SANDSPRUIT, MERVYN KING RIDGE TRAIL)

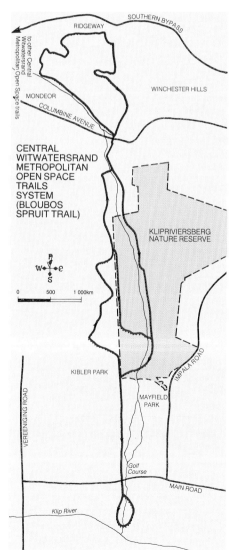

Age grindstones. Also of cultural interest along the route are the many fine homes built during the early boom years of Johannesburg. Some have been declared national monuments and others, especially in Parktown, are worthy of such designation.

The major sections of the trails system are:
1. The Parktown/Westcliff Urban Walk, an urban route with historical interest, which forms the first part of the trail. This area is chock-full of magnificent mansions such as 'Hohenheim', 'Pallinghurst' and 'Emoyeni', built by the 'randlords' (the 19th century mining magnates), and is considered one of the prime historic areas of Johannesburg. The actual Parktown/Westcliff walk is the most direct route from Pieter Roos Park to Dale Lace Park. However, five adjoining, self-guided circular trails, each one hour or less in duration, enable the Parktown/Westcliff Urban Walk to function as an historical outing in its own right. These trails are the Jubilee Road Walk, the Office Park Walk, the Baker Walk, the Parktown West Walk and the Westcliff Walk.
2. Dale Lace Park to Delta Park, including two alternative sections: the Parkview Link, which follows the main course of the Braamfontein Spruit; and the Melville Koppies/Westdene Spruit Trail, following a ridge and tributary of the Braamfontein Spruit.

The latter section includes the Melville Koppies Nature Reserve, a 66-hectare reserve which is both a national monument and a sanctuary for birds and other wildlife. Here, among the rocky outcrops of the main Witwatersrand ridge, indigenous highveld plants flourish undisturbed. Also preserved in this haven from the noise and confusion of the city, is an ancient iron-smelting furnace. Open only on the fourth Sunday of each month, the reserve offers guided tours by the Johannesburg Council for Natural History. If prior arrangements are made, however, the Johannesburg City Council will admit groups at other times.

A guide book, obtainable from the Johannesburg Parks and Recreation Department

or the Johannesburg Council for Natural History, P.O. Box 6428, Johannesburg 2000, describes indigenous flora and fauna, geology and the archaeological sites within the Melville Koppies Nature Reserve.

This section also includes the Johannesburg Botanic Gardens, situated in Jan van Riebeeck Park, on the western shore of Emmarentia Dam, to the north-west of the city centre. The oldest part of the Johannesburg Botanic Gardens, the Rose Garden, displays a fascinating collection of 4 500 roses and their hybrids from all over the world. The attractive booklet, *Rosarium: The Johannesburg Botanic Gardens*, published by the Parks and Recreation Department, gives fascinating historical and ecological details of the roses growing in the seven terraced and informal gardens. Other features of unusual interest within the gardens include the plantings of culinary as well as indigenous and exotic medicinal herbs, and a groundcover and hedge demonstration garden.

Open every day from sunrise to sunset, the Botanic Gardens provide a valuable educational centre for Johannesburg residents and visitors.
3. Delta Park to the Sandton Field and Study Centre, a suburban route along the principal course of the spruit. Delta Park (108 hectares), in the suburb of Victory Park, is the largest open space along the Braamfontein Spruit Trail. It is a relaxing place to ramble and observe birds. The 10-hectare enclosed Florence Bloom Bird Sanctuary has viewing and photography hides situated around a dam. Here you can see approximately 180 species of birds such as paradise flycatchers, Egyptian geese, spotted eagle owls, hamerkops, bishop birds, kingfishers and woodpeckers; it is not uncommon to spot 40 species during an afternoon. The Delta Park trail guide describes the exotic vegetation such as the palm, maple, eucalyptus, plane and poplar

Opposite page: A sacred ibis, seen in the Florence Bloom Bird Sanctuary.

trees and fields of flowering cosmos, in addition to the indigenous birds, other fauna and geology of the area. Guided tours are arranged by the Parks and Recreation Department.

Delta Park also serves as the South African Nature Conservation Centre which promotes all aspects of environmental awareness, as well as providing facilities for 18 conservation and allied societies, one of which is the Transvaal Branch of the Wildlife Society of Southern Africa.

Delta Park is open from sunrise to sunset. Braai facilities with water, but no wood, are available.

4. Sandton Field and Study Centre to the Sandton boundary, a countryside ramble.

5. Montgomery Spruit Trail, which follows the Montgomery Spruit until it joins the Westdene Spruit.

6. Sandspruit Trail, a 12-kilometre continuous strip along the Sandspruit from Sandton's southern boundary at Bramley to the confluence with the Braamfontein Spruit. The main course of the Sandspruit rises in The Wilds, a 20-hectare park of lawns with attractive flora, in the suburb of Houghton Estate. The spruit then flows adjacent to the Killarney Golf Course and into James and Ethel Gray Park in Melrose, where the Melrose Bird Sanctuary is located. This 10-hectare reserve fascinates me for its ability to support over 120 highveld species, including water-birds on its lake and reed-lined banks, within one of Africa's largest cities. The Sandspruit Trail also includes architectural and historical features such as 15 Pine Road in Orchards, the house formerly occupied by Gandhi during his South African visit in

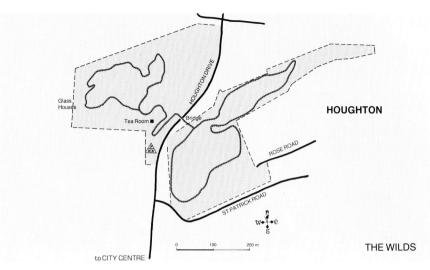

Above: The beautiful blood-red flower of the common coral tree, Erythrina lysistemon.

Opposite page: A chameleon, member of the family Chamaeleontidae, attempts to camouflage itself in the Suikerbosrand Nature Reserve.

the first quarter of this century, and the Johannesburg Melrose Siva Subramaniar Temple, and 80-year-old stronghold of the Hindu religion in South Africa.

7. Outspan Spruit Trail, a 2,8-kilometre walk along the Outspan Spruit to where it joins the Braamfontein Spruit at St. James Street.

8. Bloubos Spruit Trail, a 19-kilometre, circular walk which will eventually link with the Braamfontein Spruit Trail, and the Witwatersrand and Klipriviersberg ridges. This trail is named after the commonly seen Transvaal bluebush, *Diospyros lyciodes*, var. 'guerkii'. The Bloubos Spruit Trail is unusual in that it is an urban trail with natural features. Part of the trail goes through the 550-hectare Klipriviersberg Nature Reserve. Although the trail can be walked at any time of the year, the section through the Klipriviersberg Nature Reserve is guided, and is open only at 09h00 on the second Sunday of each month.

9. The Mervyn King Ridge Trail, an eight-kilometre link between historic 'old Johannesburg' at the little Ockerse Street Park and rural Johannesburg at Gillooly's Farm. This route extends east along the Highlands and Observatory ridges and then drops into the broad Jukskei River Valley. It connects with the Braamfontein Spruit and Sandspruit trails and the Parktown/Westcliff Urban Walk, in Hillbrow. The Mervyn King Ridge Trail extends entirely through the original 4 000-hectare Doornfontein Farm. Today it features grand old houses, parks and open spaces, the Nugget Hill pedestrian bridge, geological sites of interest, a remnant sample of protea savanna with malachite and whitebellied sunbirds, memorials, and the Jukskei River. The Jukskei is Johannesburg's largest north-flowing river, and is regarded to be the source of the Limpopo.

10. The Jukskei Trail and the Randlords Heritage Walk, beginning in eastern Johannesburg where the Mervyn King Ridge Trail ends. The Jukskei Trail extends beyond Sandton and west from the Links-

field Ridge, along the Witwatersrand escarpment as far as Krugersdorp. The first part of the Jukskei Trail is the Randlords Heritage Walk. The Jukskei catchment area boasts archaeological sites, buildings as old as the original gold-rush days, pre-1886 farmhouses, national monuments and historical places. The first gold found in South Africa was in the Jukskei in 1853.

Two further trails are planned:

11. Northcliff Ridge and the Klein Jukskei River, which connects the Braamfontein Spruit across Northcliff to Roodepoort and Randburg. This three-town (Roodepoort, Randburg and Sandton) trail is distinguished by the enormous amount of water along it, mostly in the form of dams and weirs.

12. The Klipriviersberg Trail, which will connect the Bloubos Spruit across the southern ridges to the Natal Spruit in Moffat Park.

339. *The Wilds*

JOHANNESBURG

AUTHORITY-IN-CHARGE: Johannesburg City Council, Parks and Recreation Department.
SIZE: 20 hectares.
MAIN ATTRACTIONS: Indigenous and introduced flora on rocky ridges overlooking Johannesburg's northern suburbs; waterfalls, streams and ponds; four greenhouses.
FACILITIES/AMENITIES: Guided tours for schoolchildren; cut-flower display house; nursery; tea kiosk run by the Rotary Club, open 10h00-17h00.
PERTINENT INFORMATION: The Wilds is a national monument. It is within walking distance of the Yeoville-Berea-Hillbrow complex, situated on Houghton Drive in Houghton Estate.
AVAILABLE LITERATURE: *The Wilds*, trail guide with sketch map, obtainable from the

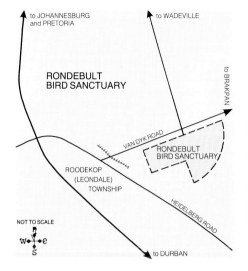

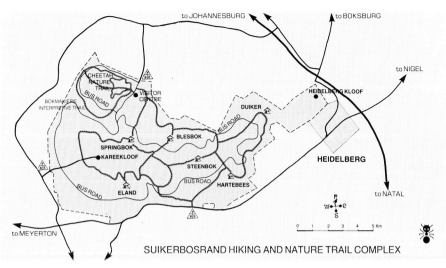

SUIKERBOSRAND HIKING AND NATURE TRAIL COMPLEX

Johannesburg Parks and Recreation Department.
CLIMATE: Average annual rainfall: 635-760 millimetres, falling mostly in summer. September and October are the best times to visit.

The Wilds, proclaimed a national monument in 1978/9, is a well-loved venue for rambling and relaxing, and provides a pleasant contrast to Johannesburg's city centre, only 2,5 kilometres to the south. Here, weary urbanites can refresh themselves on two colour-coded nature walks as well as the several other paths that meander around a large variety of indigenous plants, rocky ridges, shady lawns, waterfalls and streams.

By obtaining the trail guide from the Parks and Recreation Department of Johannesburg's City Council, the rambler can learn much about the ecology of the more than 65 plant species, including the original climax vegetation of the Witwatersrand, the proteas and ericas of the Cape fynbos, and also endangered species such as cycads, yel-

lowwoods and widdringtonias. This large diversity of plants attracts a rich birdlife.

On request, the horticulturist of The Wilds will provide guided walks for schoolchildren and their teachers. For travellers and mountaineers from coastal areas, The Wilds, located at an altitude of between 1 695 and 1 750 metres, serves as an excellent park to become acclimatized for the more demanding Highveld trails.

340. Rondebult Bird Sanctuary

GERMISTON

AUTHORITY-IN-CHARGE: Department of Parks, Sports and Recreation, Municipality of Germiston, P.O. Box 374, Germiston 1400.
SIZE: 95 hectares.
MAIN ATTRACTIONS: Rich wetland habitat, famous for its ducks; rare breeding records (avocet, blackwinged stilt and Hottentot teal); open water, marsh and wetlands in fenced grassland.
FACILITIES/AMENITIES: Seven bird hides; guides will be provided by arrangement with the Witwatersrand Bird Club and the Wildlife Society of Southern Africa.
PERTINENT INFORMATION: Open daily 06h00-18h00; prior arrangements for earlier arrivals or later stays can be made. Entrance is free.
AVAILABLE LITERATURE: *Rondebult Bird Sanctuary, Germiston*, brochure; checklists.
CLIMATE: Spring and summer are the best times to visit, although numbers and species of birds vary throughout the year.

Only a 10-minute drive from the centre of Johannesburg, Rondebult Bird Sanctuary is one of South Africa's prime bird habitats situated near an urban complex. In fact, it boasts observations of every waterfowl spe-

cies breeding in southern Africa, with the exception of the African pygmy goose.

Although walking within the sanctuary is relaxing and pleasant, the serious birdwatcher will find sitting quietly in one of the comfortable hides most rewarding. From these shelters, the great variety of wetland birds and their diverse behaviour can be enjoyed – the remarkable nest-weaving abilities of bishop birds and masked weavers, the many duck species going about their business in closely knit family groups, and the highly specialized feeding habits of the greater flamingo being but a few examples. Don't forget your binoculars and your *Roberts'* bird book.

341. Suikerbosrand Hiking and Nature Trail Complex

SUIKERBOSRAND NATURE RESERVE, HEIDELBERG

AUTHORITY-IN-CHARGE: Division of Nature Conservation, Transvaal Provincial Administration.
SIZE: 13 337 hectares.
LENGTH/DURATION: Hiking trail: 66 km/ 1-6 nights (variable). Cheetah Nature Trail: 4 km. Bokmakierie Interpretive Trail: 10 km or 17 km.
MAIN ATTRACTIONS: Natural area amidst developed Vaal triangle; reintroduced wildlife; 200 species of birds; archaeological relics and ruins; diverse topography.
FACILITIES/AMENITIES: Six huts along the route, with outdoor cooking area, utensils, gas lamps, water, firewood, bunks and mattresses; maximum of 10 people per hut per night (see text); 'meditation' hut for one person only; three group camps accommodating 50, 50 and 100 people respectively; environmental education

programmes; visitor centre with displays, lectures and films; picnic site; guided bus tour; Kareekloof Public Resort (administered by the Board for Public Resorts, Transvaal Provincial Administration) with caravan, camping and picnic sites, tennis courts and swimming pool; public pay phone; kiosk planned.

PERTINENT INFORMATION: Day visits, 07h00-18h00, for a nominal fee, with parking limited to the first 200 cars. Private vehicles, motorbikes and bicycles are not allowed in the reserve except *en route* to the visitor centre and Kareekloof Public Resort, from which bus tours originate. For information: Suikerbosrand Nature Reserve, Private Bag H616, Heidelberg 2400.

AVAILABLE LITERATURE: *Suikerbosrand Nature Reserve*, general information; *Suikerbosrand Nature Reserve – Trail User's Guide*, with sketch map; *Suikerbosrand Hiking Map Series 1*, map, no text; *The Cheetah Nature Trail*, trail booklet; *Bokmakierie Interpretive Trail*, map; *A Guide to the Frogs of the Suikerbosrand Nature Reserve*, Vincent and Jane Carruthers, Transvaal Nature Conservation Division, 1979; numerous interpretive materials.

CLIMATE: Warm temperate climate with summer rainfall. November to January, wettest months. June to August, driest months. Summer maximum temperature: 36 °C. Winter minimum temperature: 2 °C.

Gone are the days when you could ramble about the 13 337 hectares of the Suikerbosrand Nature Reserve with only zebra and eland for company. Situated approximately 50 kilometres south of Johannesburg, this reserve has been developed for resource con-

Top left: Suikerbosrand Nature Reserve before the construction of the hiking and nature trails.

Top right: A brilliant display of Haemanthus *sp. in the Abe Bailey Nature Reserve.*

Opposite page: Bird-watching from a canoe on Barberspan can be very rewarding.

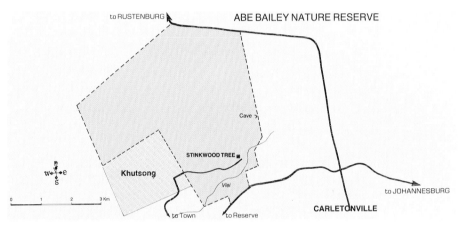

servation, environmental education, outdoor recreation and research.

The 66 kilometres of hiking trail covering high hills, plateaux, kloofs, valleys and ridges are managed as a complex of walks rather than as one continuous trail. Each of the six overnight huts is booked individually so, with the aid of the hiking series map, the trailist must decide beforehand on his route. Many permutations are possible: some routes are gentle, while others are longer and require a greater degree of endurance. In several places the trail intersects the road built for guided bus tours. To provide hikers with privacy, each hiking hut is restricted to one party, irrespective of its size.

Plant communities such as aloe and acacia forest, acacia bushveld, protea savannah, vlei reedbeds and grasslands are all included in the Bankenveld vegetation covering the reserve, and these provide ideal habitats for a very diverse wildlife. Animals that have always populated the region include the grey duiker, steenbok, grey rhebok, mountain reedbuck and baboon. But it is also exciting to hike through an environment rich in large game such as blesbok, springbok, red hartebeest, black wildebeest, zebra, oribi, eland, steenbok, kudu, cheetah and brown hyaena, all of which have been reintroduced. Birds abound in the reserve: some 200 species

have been recorded and here many of the bushveld birds reach the southernmost limit of their distribution. Also inhabiting the reserve are 13 species of frog.

Forefathers of the Tswana once hunted in this region; ruins and relics, some dating back to the Iron Age, remain as proof.

An unusual facility offered at Suikerbosrand is the small 'meditation' hut in the magnificent protea veld. Single accommodation is provided and visitors are transported to and from the hut by reserve staff.

For day visitors who cannot hike the extensive overall route, the Cheetah and Bokmakierie trails are ideal alternatives. The Cheetah Nature Trail is a four-kilometre, undemanding walk beginning at the visitor centre. Interpretation, provided by the guide booklet, stresses human history and its effects on ecology, descriptions of the most interesting plant species and vegetation types, and the consequences of erosion and pollution.

The Bokmakierie Interpretive Trail is also a circular route starting at the visitor centre, but is divided into 10- and 17-kilometre walks. Wildlife and birdlife are unusually abundant in the typical Bankenveld vegetation. A maximum of 100 people are allowed on this trail per day, so it is important to start early to ensure access.

342. Abe Bailey Nature Reserve

CARLETONVILLE

AUTHORITIES-IN-CHARGE: Transvaal Branch of the Wildlife Society of Southern Africa (education centre); Division of Nature Conservation, Transvaal Provincial Administration (nature reserve).
SIZE: Approximately 5 000 hectares.
MAIN ATTRACTIONS: Valuable wetland habitat; limestone caves; large mammals.
FACILITIES/AMENITIES: Guided tours and educational programmes; hide. 100-hectare inner camp is being developed by the Wildlife Society as an education centre, with dormitories.
PERTINENT INFORMATION: Visits to the reserve are by prior arrangement only, with either the Wildlife Society or the Transvaal Provincial Administration. Snakes are abundant in the hotter months.
AVAILABLE LITERATURE: In process of being compiled.
CLIMATE: Average annual rainfall: 500-600 millimetres, falling mostly in summer in the form of thunderstorms. Cold winter days.

First impressions of the Abe Bailey Nature Reserve are deceptive: the reserve appears flat and monotonous, traversed by power-lines and edged by gold mine dumps and the tracks of South Africa's luxurious Blue Train. However, Abe Bailey, one of South Africa's mining magnates, knew the ecological value of this land, and established a hunting lodge here. Today, the Wildlife Society is in the process of renovating Mr Bailey's farm for environmental education, complete with an interpretive centre, dormitories and staff housing. Programmes run by the Wildlife Society and general interest visits to the reserve must be arranged prior to arrival. Phone the Wildlife Society officer on (01491) 3015 or the Transvaal Provincial Administration officer on (01491) 2908.

The valuable wetlands form the focal point of the Abe Bailey Nature Reserve, and a hide has been constructed on their edge.

BARBERSPAN NATURE RESERVE

Of the 185 species of birds identified, a large number are wetland species. The sight of a goliath heron landing among a flock of hundreds of circling queleas and bishop birds is a magnificent treat. The wetlands are abundant in crakes, gallinules, herons and waders, and even a painted snipe has been observed. The more conspicuous land birds are the black korhaan and anteating chat, the latter often seen standing on termite mounds.

The Cape vulture flies from the Magaliesberg to dine on crushed cattle bones, provided by the Division of Nature Conservation for this purpose. Do not be dismayed at the powerlines; they serve to double the vultures' range, providing vantage food-searching points. (Escom refers to the lines as 'dancing ballerinas'.)

Other large birds include the raptors: kestrels, fish eagles, martial eagles, marsh harriers and hawk eagles; and the owls: the spotted, barn and marsh owls. During my investigation of one of the several caves in this dolomitic system, I saw a spotted eagle owl, in broad daylight, guarding the entrance to the cave.

Mammal life on the Bankenveld grassland (a type of sourveld), acacia and wild olive parkland is also abundant. Twenty-one species, including zebra, red hartebeest, black wildebeest, springbok, duiker, blesbok, steenbok, ground squirrel (look for their holes), jackal, porcupine, spring hare, meerkat and hedgehog, are present.

The main problems faced by this reserve, because of its location in South Africa's largest urban area, are feral dogs and microlight planes (the latter buzz the waterfowl).

343. Barberspan Nature Reserve

BARBERSPAN

AUTHORITY-IN-CHARGE: Division of Nature Conservation, Transvaal Provincial Administration.
SIZE: 3 068 hectares.
LENGTH: 14 km.
MAIN ATTRACTIONS: 351 species of birds; large mammals, including blesbok, red hartebeest, zebra and black wildebeest; small mammals, including steenbok, jackal, porcupine, yellow mongoose and ground squirrel; fishing for smallmouth yellowfish and carp.
FACILITIES/AMENITIES: Bird-watcher's walk around 1 800-hectare pan, and hide. Caravan and camping site with braai area and toilets.
PERTINENT INFORMATION: The reserve is world-famous for its research on the migratory habits of water-birds; it also researches general ecology and bird behaviour. Bird-watching from canoe (bring your own) is rewarding. The reserve is flat and grassy. Open daily 06h00-18h00. For information: The Officer-in-Charge, Barberspan Nature Reserve, P.O. Barberspan 2765.
AVAILABLE LITERATURE: Included in annual reports of the Division of Nature Conservation.
CLIMATE: Summer rainfall area. Summer is the best time to visit.

BOPHUTHATSWANA

The Republic of Bophuthatswana, independent since December 1977, is larger than Switzerland. However, it is divided into seven separate geographical units. Six units are situated between the populated gold-mining and industrial heart of South Africa and the Kalahari Desert, while the seventh area is to the south-east in wheat-growing country.

Ranging in altitude between 1 000 and 2 000 metres above sea level, Bophuthatswana is flat to gently undulating, supporting highveld mountain grassveld to tropical bush, and savannah and Kalahari thornveld. Internationally acclaimed game reserves developed on these lands have reintroduced indigenous large game species and offer guided and self-guided trails. A subscription to *Tshomarelo News*, the booklet of the National Parks and Wildlife Management Board, will keep you updated on all trailing and conservation developments.

When entering from South Africa, Bophuthatswana's border formalities are minimal and only visitors who arrive by air into Mmabatho, the capital, are asked to show a passport or Book of Life. Visits exceeding 14 days require prior permission from the magistrate or embassy.

In general, the climate is similar to a dry steppe. Bophuthatswana's average annual rainfall is 300-700 millimetres, falling mostly during the summer months (November to early April). During this time the days are warm to hot; midsummer average temperatures range between 22,5 and 25 °C. Although winters are cool (10-12,5 °C) and frost is common, the days are sunny and pleasant for walking.

ECOLOGICAL ZONES: ACACIA
SAVANNAH OR KALAHARI,
HIGHVELD, DRY WOODLANDS

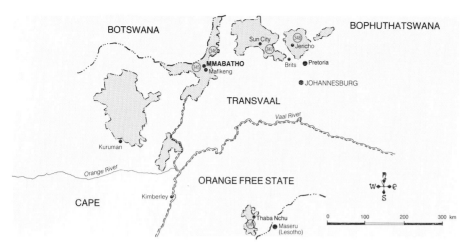

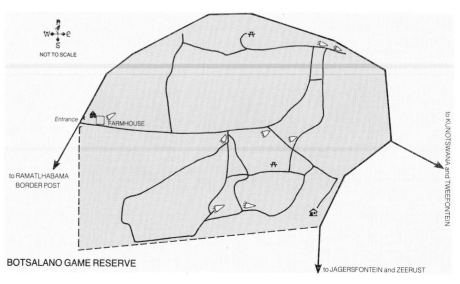

344. Maria Moroka National Park

THABA NCHU

AUTHORITY-IN-CHARGE: National Parks Board, Bophuthatswana.
SIZE: 3 400 hectares.
DURATION: Eland Trail: 4-4,5 hours. Ostrich Trail: 1,5 hours. Thaba Nchu guided trail: 6-10 hours.
MAIN ATTRACTIONS: Scenic landscapes; open plains and Thaba Nchu (Black Mountain); Groothoek Dam (240 hectares); 1 500 head of game, including springbok, blesbok, zebra, red hartebeest and eland; 150 recorded species of birds, including waterfowl.
FACILITIES/AMENITIES: Nature trails and guided walks; conducted game drives; fishing. Accommodation at the Thaba Nchu Sun Hotel.
PERTINENT INFORMATION: All hiking trails begin at the hotel entrance. No tourist vehicles are admitted, except for conducted game drives; all other visitors enter on foot. For information: The Game Ranger's

Console, Thaba Nchu Sun Hotel, tel. (05265) 2161; or The Manager, Maria Moroka National Park, P.O. Box 246, Thaba Nchu 9780, Bophuthatswana.
AVAILABLE LITERATURE: *Maria Moroka National Park*, brochure with map; *Ostrich Trail* and *Eland Trail*, maps.
CLIMATE: Semi-arid area. Average annual rainfall: 570 millimetres (higher in the mountains).

Maria Moroka National Park, situated on farms which once belonged to members of the Barolong Chieftainship, is located south of the bulk of Bophuthatswana, 60 kilometres east of Bloemfontein in the Orange Free State.

On the open plains of sweet grassveld thrive the large mammals that in days gone by inhabited this land – springbok, blesbok, zebra, red hartebeest and eland. The Groothoek Dam and Kgabanyane River attract waterfowl and the Cymbopogon-Themeda veld swarms with grassland birds, while raptors are also common. The blue korhaan is a speciality due to its restricted distribution in the Orange Free State/southern Bophuthatswana region. The Cymbopogon-Themeda veld type is a sweet grassveld, low shrub savannah. Its grasses are palatable, but the dominant shrubs, *Euclea crispa* and *Rhus erosa*, are unpalatable to browsing animals.

Guided walks up Thaba Nchu mountain are flexible, to suit the preferences of the hiker. In addition, two self-guided nature trails, the Ostrich and Eland trails, offer superb views of the game-rich plains and birdlife. For both self-guided walks, participants are ferried to the northern shore of the dam by motorboat and returned to the hotel after they have completed the walk.

Above: Termites building a chimney-like nest in Pilanesberg National Park, a venue for various guided nature trails.

Opposite page: The water pump is a gathering place for residents of 'the stadt', the old section of Mmabatho, capital of Bophuthatswana. Interesting walks through this city are available.

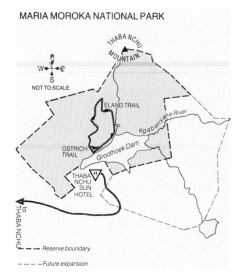

MARIA MOROKA NATIONAL PARK

BOTSALANO GAME RESERVE

345. Botsalano Game Reserve

MMABATHO

AUTHORITY-IN-CHARGE: National Parks Board, Bophuthatswana.
SIZE: 5 800 hectares.
MAIN ATTRACTIONS: Large game, including white rhinoceros, hartebeest, impala, eland, zebra, blesbok, wildebeest, reedbuck, ostrich, kudu, tsessebe, giraffe, gemsbok, sable antelope and waterbuck; abundant bushveld birdlife, including vultures.
FACILITIES/AMENITIES: Conducted day walks, by arrangement; picnic sites and braai places. Botlhaba Camp, an A-frame chalet with six beds; Mogobe Camp, four safari tents on concrete aprons, each tent accommodating 2 or 3 people, rustic dining area with a view of the Mogobe Dam, kitchen with gas stove, refrigerator, deep freeze, crockery, cutlery and cooking equipment, paved lapa; camping area with hot and cold water, shower and toilet.
PERTINENT INFORMATION: For bookings: The Manager, Botsalano Game Reserve, Private Bag X2078, Mafikeng 8670, Bophuthatswana. Botsalano is a developing reserve; consult the manager for the latest details.
AVAILABLE LITERATURE: *Botsalano Game Reserve*, brochure; news of reserve developments in *Tshomarelo News*.
CLIMATE: Summer rainfall area. Very arid.

Botsalano Game Reserve is one of the more recently established national parks in Bophuthatswana. Situated about 40 kilometres from Mmabatho and Mafikeng, this reserve is popular with the residents of these towns, as well as with wildlife fans from afar.

Botsalano's low hills with their gentle slopes and depressions are ideal habitats for game such as white rhinoceros, tsessebe, hartebeest, giraffe, impala, eland, gemsbok, zebra, blesbok, sable antelope, waterbuck, wildebeest, reedbuck and ostrich. Kudu, steenbok, duiker, warthog, jackal, aardwolf, porcupine and antbears, as well as bushveld birds and vultures, are also common in the area. The vegetation which supports this

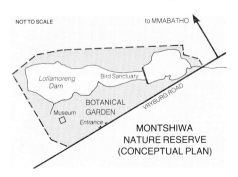

varied fauna comprises grassland, wooded grassland and woodland. Interesting outcrops of quartzite, ironstone and lavas of the Dominion Reef, Black Reef and Ventersdorp systems dot the landscape.

346. Montshiwa Nature Reserve

MMABATHO

AUTHORITY-IN-CHARGE: National Parks Board, Bophuthatswana.
MAIN ATTRACTIONS: Lotlamoreng Dam, with flamingos and abundant waterfowl; Boer cemetery; fishing.
FACILITIES/AMENITIES: The following are planned: environmental education classroom; duck trap; traditional cultural village; picnic sites, pool and recreational games; botanical garden; yachting, canoeing

and rowing; predator zoo; museum; restaurant and curio shop.
PERTINENT INFORMATION: This reserve is in the planning stages.
AVAILABLE LITERATURE: News of developments in *Tshomarelo News*.
CLIMATE: Summer rainfall area.

347. Pilanesberg National Park

SUN CITY

AUTHORITY-IN-CHARGE: National Parks Board, Bophuthatswana.
SIZE: 50 000 hectares.
DURATION: Tshukudu Trail: 3,5 days. Wilderness Leadership School Trail: 2 days (sometimes 3- and 5-day trails are available).
MAIN ATTRACTIONS: 8 000 head of game, including black and white rhino, elephant,

cheetah, giraffe and hippo; 300 species of birds; located in a faunal transition zone (arid western Kalahari/moist eastern Lowveld); unique volcanic alkaline ring complex; diverse landscape; historically interesting sites such as the old Pilanesberg magistrate's court, now renovated and known as the Pilanesberg Centre.
FACILITIES/AMENITIES: Tshukudu Trail: 'luxurious' guided trail, where trailists return to tented camps each night; camps provide all equipment except sleeping bags and food. Wilderness Leadership School trails: 'rustic' guided trails providing all gear except sleeping bags. Approximately 100 km of tourist roads. Conservation education and information centres. Accommodation: trails camp, tented camps, full-service chalets, dormitory-type camp for schoolchildren, caravan park; Kwa Maritane timesharing and hotel resort; Pilanesberg Centre, with restaurant, shop and interpretive centre; Manyane Complex, with caravan park, shopping centre, Bosele group facility for scholars and other large groups of visitors, licensed restaurant and swimming pools; Sun City hotel complex, nearby. Picnic sites, game-viewing hides and braai places.
PERTINENT INFORMATION: Trails are operated on rugged terrain, so hiking boots are recommended. Maximum of 6 and minimum of 4 people permitted on all trails. For information and bookings: Pilanesberg National Park, P.O. Box 1201, Mogwase 0302, Bophuthatswana.
AVAILABLE LITERATURE: Brochures such as *Pilanesberg Trails*, *Pilanesberg National Park, Visitor's Guide* and *Where to Stay*; bird lists.
CLIMATE: Summer rainfall area.

Approximately 42 kilometres north-west of Rustenburg lies a roughly circular mass of lava and syenite, 27 kilometres in diameter.

Below left: Mankwe tented camp on the Tshukudu Trail in Pilanesberg National Park.
Below right: Well-situated hides in Pilanesberg.
Opposite page, top: Pilanesberg National Park.
Opposite page, bottom: Paradise flycatcher.

Rising 600 metres above the surrounding bushveld plains, this mass, named Pilanesberg, is obvious evidence of ancient volcanic intrusion into the Bushveld Igneous Complex.

The rugged north-western section of the 50 000-hectare reserve is the venue for the Tshukudu (rhino) Trail. Although big game – white and black rhino and elephant, among others – has been introduced into this area, educational trails in the Pilanesberg stress the understanding of the entire ecological spectrum and present the opportunity to observe the development of a wildlife sanctuary. At present, casual visitors who wish to walk in the park may do so if they notify the officer-in-charge well in advance so that he can arrange for a game scout to accompany them.

The Pilanesberg National Park is also used as a venue for the Wilderness Leadership School's two-day 'weekend' trails. These trails, departing from Johannesburg, are limited to six participants over 15 years old. All gear, except sleeping bags and daypacks, is provided.

348. Borakalalo National Park

JERICHO

AUTHORITY-IN-CHARGE: National Parks Board, Bophuthatswana.
SIZE: 13 000 hectares.
MAIN ATTRACTIONS: Varied sand bushveld and riverine vegetation; 300 species of birds, including abundant waterfowl; 30 species of large mammals; the park surrounds the 1 000-hectare Klipvoor Dam in which there is excellent fishing (curper, carp and catfish).
FACILITIES/AMENITIES: Self-guided day walks; guided trails for hikers and horse-riders; game-viewing drives. An entrance fee to the park is charged. Camping allowed for organized groups; simple, rustic campsite planned; picnic and braai places with

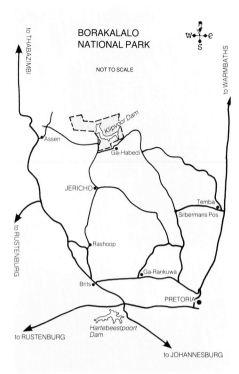

ablution blocks; shop for basic supplies and curios.
PERTINENT INFORMATION: This is a developing park; contact the manager for details. Borakalalo serves as a venue for Wilderness Leadership School trails, as well as for other approved clubs and organizations. No boating or swimming permitted on dam; fishermen must possess a valid licence and permit, obtainable at the gate; fishing is permitted only at allocated sites. Open 05h00-20h00 October to March, 06h00-19h00 April to September. Overnight accommodation and other facilities planned. For bookings: The Reservations Office, Borakalalo National Park, P.O. Box 240, Jericho 0264, Bophuthatswana.
AVAILABLE LITERATURE: *Borakalalo National Park*, brochure with map; news of developments in *Tshomarelo News*; trail guides available at the gate.
CLIMATE: Summer rainfall area.

Under the authority of the National Parks Board of Bophuthatswana since 1983, Borakalalo has been developed from an overused and abused recreational area, ripe with poaching, to a tranquil, beautiful reserve deserving of its Setswana name, which means 'the place where the people relax'.

As the second-largest park in Bophuthatswana, Borakalalo offers a diversity of landscapes and vegetation types such as riverine bush along the Moretele (Pienaars) River, kloofs, vleis, koppies and rolling sandveld. These diverse habitats support many large mammals such as sable, tsessebe, waterbuck, giraffe and zebra, as well as an astonishing 300 or more bird species, including abundant waterfowl on the eight kilometre-

long Klipvoor Dam. In addition to excellent fishing, controlled canoe trails are permitted on the dam.

Borakalalo National Park also owes its popularity to its close proximity (only a two-hour drive) to the Pretoria-Witwatersrand-Vereeniging area.

The Bophuthatswana National Parks Board is keen to provide quality environmental education experiences for its citizens and visitors. A diversity of self-guided day walks and wilderness trails is offered here. Clearly marked, easy walks from one to four hours in duration radiate in wooded terrain from the central braai area near the Klipvoor Dam. They encompass a variety of terrains, from the riverside to a gentle climb up Pit-jane Koppie with its excellent views. Maps are provided at the gate. Although game-viewing by motorcar is permitted, the greater portion of the park (approximately 6 000 hectares) is zoned as wilderness where both horse and walking trails for recognized organizations and clubs, led by an approved guide from the club, are permitted.

One such organization is the Wilderness Leadership School, which runs weekend (two-day) guided trails for groups of six, either youngsters over 12 years old or adults. The school provides transport, food and camping equipment but not sleeping bags or daypacks. The Johannesburg Hiking Club is also an approved club which leads trails. Other organizations are welcome to apply, including horse trail groups, on a 'bring-your-own-horse' basis.

For small groups or single visitors wishing to walk on their own and off marked trails, a guide must be booked in advance by phoning the park on 0020 Jericho 1430 or (01401) 3-2582. Eventually the park staff will operate their own guided trails.

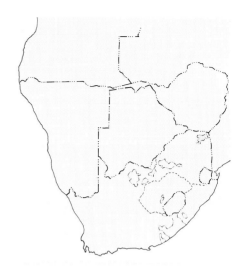

VENDA

Venda, an independent republic since 1979, is a relatively small (6 500 km^2), mountainous country. Completely surrounded by the Transvaal, its eastern border is the Kruger National Park. Gazankulu adjoins it in the south and a narrow strip of land separates it from Zimbabwe in the north.

Straddling the subtropical Soutpansberg range, Venda boasts an atmosphere of unadulterated Africa. Traditional settlements dot mountain slopes; Lake Fundudzi and Lwamondo Kop not only are set in beautiful surroundings but are also riddled with spiritual mystery; here are rock art sites and sacred indigenous forests; the Sagole tribal warmwater baths, a spectacular gorge on the Mutale River; and giant cycads. Big game trails are planned for the Levubu River Valley area.

Border formalities do not exist in Venda but people visiting the country for a period exceeding 14 days should apply for permission from the Director-General, Department of Internal Affairs, Private Bag X2249, Thohoyandou 0970, Venda. Visitors should always be in possession of a passport or other identity document.

Venda's pleasant subtropical climate is shared with the northern Transvaal: high temperatures, humidity and rain in summer, and temperate, dry, frost-free winters.

ECOLOGICAL ZONE: DRY
WOODLANDS

349. Mabuda-Shango Hiking Trail

TATE VONDO PLANTATION, SOUTPANSBERG

AUTHORITY-IN-CHARGE: Department of Agriculture and Forestry, Private Bag X2247, Sibasa 0970, Venda.
LENGTH/DURATION: 55 km/4 days (3rd day optional).
MAIN ATTRACTIONS: Beautiful viewpoints; sacred lake; mountain and forest; traditional Venda rural life; Tshivhase tea production valley.
FACILITIES/AMENITIES: Two overnight sites with thatched shelters, firewood, water and toilets. Hut at start of trail with two beds, kitchen, toilet, shower and braai.
AVAILABLE LITERATURE: Black and white sketch map and notes on trail; tree list.
CLIMATE: Subtropical. Occasional heavy rains and lightning storms. High summer temperatures.

I spent my first week in Africa on the Soutpansberg Hiking Trail, where distant views of Venda villages in clearing mist made an unforgettable impression on me. A decade later I hiked the Mabuda-Shango trail, planned to link up with the Soutpansberg trail. However, because circular trails reduce transportation problems, they have proved to be more popular than linear trails, and the linking of trails is now a low priority. The Mabuda-Shango Hiking Trail starts and ends at the Tate Vondo Plantation, where vehicles can be safely parked and a converted forester's house serves as a convenient base hut for hikers before or after the trail.

Distances each day are relatively short, allowing hikers to walk at their leisure, enjoying the many views and absorbing the sacred significance of the trail's highlights. The first night is spent at the lovely Fundudzi rest camp on the banks of the Mutale River. Here, longtailed wagtails, hopping and flitting from boulder to boulder, amuse the weary hiker. I arrived early, so I dropped my heavy pack and bird-watched in the veld around the Fundudzi Sacred Lake, referred to as the 'real heart of Venda'. Its setting among a ring of mountains is magnificent; the lake itself was created by a landslide across the Mutale River. Of the many legends told about the lake, one of my favourites concerns a poacher who snared not a duiker, but a supernatural being, injuring his only leg. The poacher promised to keep the incident a secret; however, he confided his story to a beer-drinking audience and was struck dumb for life.

Lwamondo Kop, seen on the first day's hike, is well-known for its sacred baboons

Distances each day on the Mabuda-Shango Hiking Trail are short, so hikers can enjoy the many views. Although thatched shelters (opposite page, centre) do exist, hikers would be well advised to take tents.

which cry out to warn of approaching enemies. Legend dictates that killing these baboons will result in an attack by the enemy.

The magic of the sacred forest, the burial place of the chiefs, also permeates into the hiker's experience. Remember your *National List of Trees* as some of the impressive specimens of yellowwood, fig, lemonwood, forest iron-plum and wild gardenia are identified. Sounds of samango monkeys and Knysna loeries echo in the canopy.

The most rewarding moment for me on the trail occurred in the broadleafed woodlands on the first day, when I surprised a flock of crested guineafowl with their distinctive head plumes, a species I seldom see in South Africa.

Another vivid memory of my hike should serve as a warning to others: the two over-

night camps each supply an open thatched shelter; however, after getting drenched at night in a torrential downpour, I strongly recommend that hikers carry tents in the rainy summer season.

The Mabuda-Shango Hiking Trail was originally routed on forestry roads, marked with x's. Later it was re-routed on foot-paths, marked with white footprints. At times these markings were indistinct and I lost my way. However, the marking of the trail is a maintenance task which should be remedied in time.

On the third day of the trail, an optional 12,2-kilometre round-trip from an impressive waterfall to the Tshatshingo potholes is unfortunately marred by the construction of a dam; the access roads and quarries detract from the beauty of the trail.

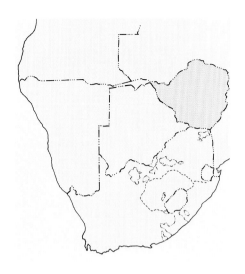

ZIMBABWE

Zimbabwe, with its huge land mass of 390 245 km² (the equivalent area of the American state of California and three times the size of England) is today, after many years of civil war, regaining its former reputation as one of Africa's most lovely, diverse and exceptional outdoor attractions. Zimbabwe is landlocked between Zambia and Mozambique in the north and east, and Botswana and South Africa in the west and south. Twelve per cent of the land is pre-served for parks and game sanctuaries, a heritage providing endless opportunities for rambling, wilderness backpacking and game-viewing on foot.

Here you will find the exquisite Victoria Falls; the Hwange National Park, an elephant haven; wildlife-rich Lake Kariba and its surrounding bushveld reserves; the Great Zimbabwe national monument (Zimbabwe Ruins); highveld semi-urban parks; and the Eastern Highlands, the backpacker's mecca where mountain wonderlands such as the Chimanimanis beckon the energetic. Canoe-ing and rafting trips have also been introduced on the mighty Zambezi River.

Visitors staying less than six months enter Zimbabwe with few formalities: a valid passport, return ticket or enough money to purchase one, and visas for certain nationals.

Zimbabwe's climate is subtropical. The coldest months are between May and August, when the temperature averages 13 °C, dropping in the highlands. The hot season is from September to December; October and November are the hottest months, with temperatures often reaching more than 32 °C. The rains begin in December and end in mid-March. Average annual rainfall varies between 300 and 1 500 millimetres.

Trailists off the beaten track should be aware than dissidents could still be hiding in bush camps within forested hills. Obtain the latest information from the authorities. Also be aware that bilharzia is possible in all rivers and dams and therefore swimming in and drinking these waters should be avoided.

ECOLOGICAL ZONE: DRY
WOODLANDS

350. Matobo National Park

NEAR BULAWAYO

AUTHORITY-IN-CHARGE: Department of National Parks and Wildlife Management, Zimbabwe.

SIZE: 44 200 hectares.

MAIN ATTRACTIONS: High granite outcrops weathered into scenic formations; caves with Bushman paintings; rock lizards and dassies; 300 species of birds (half the known number in Zimbabwe), including the world's greatest concentration of black eagles, plus crowned and martial eagles; sable antelope, white rhinoceros and African python; adjoining 2 600-hectare Whovi Wild Area game park (no walking permitted).

FACILITIES/AMENITIES: Drives; marked trails; lodges, camping and caravan sites; fishing, with licence, in dams; boating, with permission.

PERTINENT INFORMATION: Park is situated 54 km south of Bulawayo. Bilharzia present in all waters of park (dam and rivers).

AVAILABLE LITERATURE: Located on Government Printer's 1:50 000 topographic map 'Silozwi 2028 dl-Matopos', which covers the Toghwana Dam region (trails area); 'Rebuilding a Wilderness: The Matopos National Park', by Nick Greaves, *African Wildlife*, Vol. 41, No. 1.

CLIMATE: Subtropical. Winter (May to August): mild, sunny days and cool nights; frost possible. Summer (September/mid-October to December): thunderstorms possible; October and November, very hot. December to mid-March, rainy season.

A corruption of an Ndebele term, Matobo means 'the bald heads', an appropriate description of the ancient boulder-strewn granite hills of the park. The powerful feel-

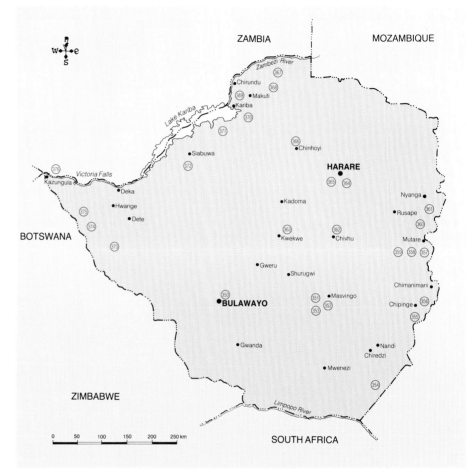

ing of primeval wilderness is reinforced by the world-famous balancing rock formations, worn into their weird shapes by more than 2 000 million years of erosion.

The geology of the region is fascinating, and the Matobo National Park is also a naturalist's delight, with a myriad intriguing discoveries awaiting the enthusiastic rambler. Black eagles abound, and not surprisingly, for the rocky terrain provides an ideal habitat for the dassie, the almost exclusive prey of this raptor. Also prolific are klipspringer

and *Platysaurus capensis*, the teasingly tame, rainbow-coloured rock lizard.

Acacia-mopane woodland lies thickly in the valleys, while aloes, cycads and numerous wildflowers flourish in the rocky terrain.

The Matobos also contain huge caves, well decorated with fine examples of Bushman art, while World's View, the summit of the great granite dome, is the site of Cecil John Rhodes' grave.

Marked day walks to the cave paintings and a trail system in the Togwe Wilderness area within the park are being restored.

351. Mushandike Sanctuary

MUSHANDIKE DAM, MASVINGO, see map page 296

AUTHORITY-IN-CHARGE: Department of National Parks and Wildlife Management, Zimbabwe.

SIZE: 12 900 hectares.

MAIN ATTRACTIONS: Antelope and birdlife; irrigation dam; Bushman rock shelters; ecological training centre and wild herbivore domestication project.

FACILITIES/AMENITIES: Camping and

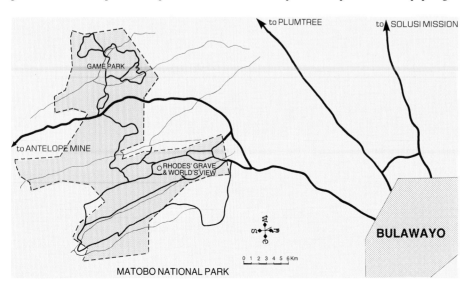

caravan sites; good gravel roads; fishing, with licence, in dam for black bass, bream and catfish.
PERTINENT INFORMATION: Masvingo was formerly known as Fort Victoria, and is the oldest town in Zimbabwe.
AVAILABLE LITERATURE: Included in general tourist brochures produced by the Zimbabwe Tourist Development Corporation.
CLIMATE: Subtropical. Winter (May to August): mild, sunny days and cool nights; frost possible. Summer (September/mid-October to December): thunderstorms possible; October and November, very hot. December to mid-March, rainy season.

Rambling in the well-developed Mushandike Sanctuary is rather 'tame' compared with many of Zimbabwe's more remote parks. However, for the family or inexperienced trailist, walks through the *Brachystegia* woodlands, koppies and *Hyparrhenia* grasslands are enjoyable, and encounters with browsing animals such as sable, kudu, waterbuck, klipspringer, grysbok and

Above: Two hikers rest on one of the ancient granite hills in the Matobo National Park. Matobo means 'the bald heads', an appropriate description of these ancient, boulder-strewn hills with their world-famous balancing rock formations.

duiker are likely, as are sightings of the large flocks of flamingos.

Mushandike houses the Natural Resources College run by the Department of National Parks and Wildlife Management. It is also the site of a project to domesticate wild herbivores such as eland; this is the reason for the large paddocks in the sanctuary.

352. *Great Zimbabwe Park and National Monument*

MASVINGO, see map page 296

AUTHORITY-IN-CHARGE: Department of National Parks and Wildlife Management, Zimbabwe.
SIZE: 723 hectares.
MAIN ATTRACTIONS: Zimbabwe Ruins: the most impressive single complex of ruins south of the Sahara Desert, with an intricate and large array of dry-stone walls and enclosures, and sacred places (1200-1450 AD); Zimbabwe birds (soapstone). Park: botanically valuable, flowering aloes.
FACILITIES/AMENITIES: Nature and history rambles; Site Museum (displays of

prehistory and history of Zimbabwe, local artefacts and Zimbabwe birds); accommodation and camp-sites nearby.
PERTINENT INFORMATION: The ruins are open daily 08h00-17h00; the museum closes at 16h30.
AVAILABLE LITERATURE: *Around Zimbabwe, No. 3: Great Zimbabwe, Lake Kyle*, brochure available from the Zimbabwe Tourist Development Corporation.
CLIMATE: Moderate relative to the rest of the country.

353. *Lake Kyle Recreation Area*

LAKE KYLE, MASVINGO

AUTHORITY-IN-CHARGE: Department of National Parks and Wildlife Management, Zimbabwe.
SIZE: 16 900 hectares.
MAIN ATTRACTIONS: Recreation area, including game enclosure with pony trails; prolific birdlife around the lake and its islands.
FACILITIES/AMENITIES: Game-viewing on foot is permitted in certain areas; pony trails accompanied by guide; lake fishing, with

licence, for black bass; wide range of camp-sites, fully equipped lodges and commercial resorts.

PERTINENT INFORMATION: 'Lake' Kyle is man-made.

AVAILABLE LITERATURE: *Around Zimbabwe, No. 3: Great Zimbabwe, Lake Kyle*, brochure available from the Zimbabwe Tourist Development Corporation.

CLIMATE: Subtropical. Winter (May to August): mild, sunny days and cool nights; frost possible. Summer (September/mid-October to December): thunderstorms possible. October and November, hottest months. December to mid-March, rainy season.

The attractions of this park to the trailist are the pony trails operated within the game area, and those specific areas where game-viewing on foot is allowed.

Lake Kyle, Zimbabwe's second-largest man-made lake, is bordered in the north by an 8 900-hectare game park. The rolling hills, covered with *Brachystegia* woodlands, koppie vegetation and grassland, enhance the park's pleasant setting. Although kudu and reedbuck occur naturally, most ante-lope, buffalo, giraffe and other large species were introduced; the white rhinos, for instance, were brought all the way from the Umfolozi Game Reserve in Natal (see page 211). Birdlife in the bays and inlets along the secluded wooded shores is abundant.

Rambling in the other game parks listed in this section is fairly strenuous, so I recommend the Lake Kyle Recreation Area for the family and the not-so-fit, as well as less experienced, naturalist.

354. *Gonarezhou National Park*

SOUTH-EAST ZIMBABWE

AUTHORITY-IN-CHARGE: Department of National Parks and Wildlife Management, Zimbabwe.

SIZE: 496 400 hectares.

MAIN ATTRACTIONS: Large concentration of big game, including black rhino and nyala; river landscapes; Chilojho Cliffs.

FACILITIES/AMENITIES: Game-viewing on foot; chalets; camping sites (cleared areas only); fishing for bream and tigerfish in the Lundi River; Chilojho Trails (private walking safaris).

PERTINENT INFORMATION: Only four-wheel drive vehicles permitted on certain roads. Open 1 May to 31 October. Anti-malaria precautions necessary. Bilharzia is possible. Permission to enter necessary, obtainable in writing from The Warden, Chipinda Pools, Private Bag 7003, Chiredzi, Zimbabwe (Chipinda Pools area), or The Warden,

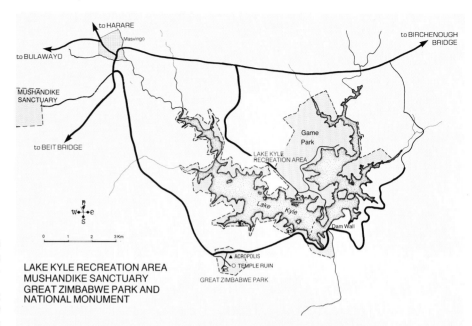

LAKE KYLE RECREATION AREA
MUSHANDIKE SANCTUARY
GREAT ZIMBABWE PARK AND
NATIONAL MONUMENT

Mabalauta Camp, Private Bag 7017, Chiredzi, Zimbabwe (Mabalauta area).

AVAILABLE LITERATURE: Contact the Zimbabwe Tourist Development Corporation; *Chilojho Trails: Gonarezhou*, brochure available from Safari Interlink (Pvt) Ltd, P.O. Box MP 192, Mount Pleasant, Harare, Zimbabwe.

CLIMATE: Extremely hot in summer.

This vast, remote park, whose name means 'the horn (tusk) of the elephant' can be a wonderful experience. Large tuskers, re-introduced black rhino, nyala, suni, hippo, hartebeest and giraffe are just a few of the game species which can be seen in this south-eastern lowveld reserve.

Much of the dense riverine vegetation has been damaged by elephants; other vegetation includes large tracts of rugged mopane tree savannah and acacia woodlands. Bao-babs grow on the lower slopes of the magnificent sandstone Chilojho Cliffs which rise above and range alongside the Lundi River

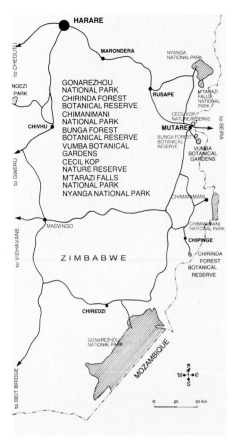

for 32 kilometres. The cliffs glow a vibrant red when touched by the rays of the setting sun.

Mike Fynn, previously a warden of the park, now operates a luxury safari camp and the guided Chilojho Trails through the heart of this wilderness. Ten people can be accommodated in thatched, two-bed chalets with showers and toilets. For information and bookings for these trails, contact Safari Interlink (Pvt) Ltd.

355. *Chirinda Forest Botanical Reserve*

CHIPINGE, EASTERN ZIMBABWE

AUTHORITY-IN-CHARGE: Department of National Parks and Wildlife Management, Zimbabwe.
SIZE: 949 hectares.
MAIN ATTRACTIONS: Evergreen montane forest, noted for ironwoods, wild figs and red mahogany trees, and including a number of tropical plants; also noted for butterflies and moths which feed on rotting vegetation.
FACILITIES/AMENITIES: Situated near Mount Selinda Mission; picnic site.
PERTINENT INFORMATION: 'Chirinda' comes from the Shangane word *tshirinda*, which means 'a refuge'. The red mahogany (*Khaya*

nyasica) is Zimbabwe's tallest indigenous tree. Chirinda borders on Mozambique; there is a border gate, and a road leading to Espungabera in Mozambique.
AVAILABLE LITERATURE: Contact the Zimbabwe Tourist Development Corporation.
CLIMATE: Subtropical. Winter (May to August): mild, sunny days and cool nights; frost possible. Summer (September/mid-October to December): thunderstorms possible. October and November, hottest months. December to mid-March, rainy season.

Zimbabwe's tallest indigenous tree, the 66 metre-tall, 400-year-old red mahogany, along with a diverse selection of evergreen montane plants, is preserved at Chirinda, on the east-facing escarpment edge. More than 100 tree species, as well as a mass of mosses, ferns, creepers and tree orchids, grow here in dense profusion. Also found is the rare blue orchid, *Callianthus natalensis*.

Many rare birds and mammals are present, including the trumpeter hornbill, Livingstone's loerie, the rarely seen crested guineafowl, Swynnerton's robin, Swynnerton's red squirrel, sun squirrel, samango monkey, tree civet and blue duiker. Tropical plants occurring as far afield as Madagascar and Nigeria are present in Chirinda, the 'place of refuge', thus contributing to the theory that in long bygone times much of the continent of Africa was blanketed by continuous rainforest vegetation.

Spring is the best time to visit the reserve, for then the ironwoods are in bloom – a mass of white, pea-like blossoms. Butterflies, especially abundant during and after the rains, can be seen, together with moths, feeding on rotting vegetation.

356. *Chimanimani National Park*

EASTERN HIGHLANDS

AUTHORITY-IN-CHARGE: Department of National Parks and Wildlife Management, Zimbabwe.
SIZE: 17 110 hectares.
MAIN ATTRACTIONS: Rugged grandeur of Zimbabwe's mountain wilderness; endemic plants and animals; streams.
FACILITIES/AMENITIES: Small mountain chalet with minimal furnishings, limited cooking utensils, cold showers and toilet; Mutekeswane camp-site at the foot of the mountains (no advance booking possible); camping is permitted anywhere in the wilderness area; footpaths; trout fishing permitted in Bundi River, with licence, between 1 October and 21 April.
PERTINENT INFORMATION: Access on foot

only; camping at camper's own risk; trailists are advised to check political safety conditions and precautions with the local office of Chimanimani National Park, Private Bag 2063, Chimanimani, Zimbabwe. Permits necessary, obtainable from the local office. The border with Mozambique is unfenced, therefore it is possible to wander across it – don't!
AVAILABLE LITERATURE: *Around Zimbabwe, No. 4: The Eastern Highlands*, available from the Zimbabwe Tourist Development Corporation; maps available from the Department of National Parks and Wildlife Management; 1932-D4, Surveyor-General's map of the park.
CLIMATE: Winter (May to August), best hiking season. Drizzle can be expected at any time of the year. Region subject to sudden storms and/or mist.

The 2 400-metre rugged quartzite and sandstone Chimanimanis derive their name from that of the pass through which the Musapa River flows. This pass is known to the Ndawu tribe as *Tschimanimani*, meaning 'to be squeezed together'. Certainly one of southern Africa's most beautiful wilderness regions, this is an area frequented only by the most enthusiastic mountaineers, as access is only on foot.

Numerous paths radiate from the Mutekeswane base camping site, but the way into the range follows the ancient slave trade and traditional gold pedlars' route from Chimanimani Village over the western slopes, across the inner valley, down via Skeleton Pass into Mozambique and on to the coastal ports. The first three hours of strenuous walking along this path bring you to Chimanimani's only mountain chalet. This simple structure comprises two dormitories, bunk-beds, a fireplace in a communal room, limited cooking utensils and a cold shower. Although the hut cannot be booked in advance, it is crowded only on weekends and during school holidays.

The central range, one of the three parallel north-south ranges within the national park, is the climbing area. It contains numerous caves for overnighting, well-trodden paths, plenty of water, natural swimming holes and waterfalls. The landscape is dominated by Point 71 (2 440 m), Turret Towers (2 399 m) and Uncontoured Peak (2 213 m). The base of Turret Towers is reached in less than a day's hike from the mountain chalet and it is a scramble to the summit. Fraser's Falls, a very high, impressive waterfall, can also be reached within a day from the chalet.

The Chimanimanis are also popular because of the lovely camp-sites amidst the diverse plant communities which flank fast-flowing perennial streams.

Although the vegetation of Chimanimani is basically dry sub-montane forest and

Opposite page: Steenbok, Gonarezhou National Park.

grassy flats, many hikers compare the rock formations and plant life to those of the Western Cape. The mountain ranges support proteas and pincushions, everlastings and ericas, and cedars and yellowwoods on sedimentary rock. Chimanimani has its own endemic *Podocarpus* trees, in addition to endemic amphibians and reptiles. Interspersed with its temperate flora are tropical ferns and orchids.

In the secluded kloofs and slopes of these grand mountains live sable, eland, bushbuck, klipspringer and the rare blue duiker, along with the baboon and its arch enemy, the leopard. Spectacular birdlife, including the purplecrested loerie, trumpeter hornbill, malachite sunbird and eagle, is also present.

357. *Bunga Forest Botanical Reserve*

MUTARE, EASTERN HIGHLANDS, see map page 297

AUTHORITY-IN-CHARGE: Department of National Parks and Wildlife Management, Zimbabwe.
SIZE: 39 hectares.
MAIN ATTRACTIONS: Dense indigenous forest; monkeys and forest buck.
FACILITIES/AMENITIES: Nature trails on a network of footpaths; hotels, caravan- and camp-sites in the vicinity.
PERTINENT INFORMATION: The reserve is sometimes temporarily closed during bad weather.
AVAILABLE LITERATURE: *Around Zimbabwe, No. 4: The Eastern Highlands*, brochure available from the Zimbabwe Tourist Development Corporation.
CLIMATE: Subtropical. Winter (May to August): mild, sunny days and cool nights; frost possible. Summer (September/mid-October to December): thunderstorms possible. October and November, hottest months. December to mid-March, rainy season.

358. *Vumba Botanical Gardens*

MUTARE, EASTERN HIGHLANDS, see map page 297

AUTHORITY-IN-CHARGE: Department of National Parks and Wildlife Management, Zimbabwe.
SIZE: 200 hectares (indigenous woodland); 76 hectares (landscaped botanical garden).
LENGTH: 24 km of nature trails.
MAIN ATTRACTIONS: Landscaped garden;

flowering plants from around the world; natural woodland; views over the plains of Mozambique, 1 000 metres below; ornamental lake.
FACILITIES/AMENITIES: Footpaths; camping and caravan site; holiday resorts in vicinity.
PERTINENT INFORMATION: *Vumba* means 'mountains of drizzle'. Open sunrise to sunset, year-round. For booking of camping and caravan sites: The National Parks Central Booking Office, P.O. Box 8151, Causeway, Harare, Zimbabwe. The lake in the gardens is located at 1 524 metres above sea level.
AVAILABLE LITERATURE: *Around Zimbabwe, No. 4: The Eastern Highlands*, brochure available from the Zimbabwe Tourist Development Corporation.
CLIMATE: Average annual rainfall: 1 676 millimetres.

359. *Cecil Kop Nature Reserve*

MUTARE, see map page 297

AUTHORITY-IN-CHARGE: Manicaland Branch of the Wildlife Society of Zimbabwe, P.O. Box 820, Mutare, Zimbabwe.
SIZE: 1 700 hectares.
MAIN ATTRACTIONS: Mountain grassland, forest, open woodland and vlei; large game and birdlife.
FACILITIES/AMENITIES: Viewing platform, hides and roads; rambling and pony riding; trees labelled with their national tree list numbers; educational programmes, Rupert Fothergill open-air classroom.
PERTINENT INFORMATION: Open sunrise to sunset.
AVAILABLE LITERATURE: Contact the Manicaland Branch of the Wildlife Society.
CLIMATE: Subtropical. Winter (May to August): mild, sunny days and cool nights; frost possible. Summer (September/mid-October to December): thunderstorms possible. October and November, hottest months. December to mid-March, rainy season.

Under the auspices of the Manicaland Branch of the Wildlife Society of Zimbabwe, 1 700 hectares of public commonage on the northern perimeter of the city of Mutare have been preserved as the Cecil Kop Nature Reserve. Rising from 1 036 metres to 1 707 metres, the Cecil Kop range comprises a variety of plant communities, including montane grassland, evergreen forest, open msasa woodland and grassy vleis. These habitats are rich in species peculiar to Zimbabwe's eastern districts, for example, blue duiker, sun squirrels, samango monkeys, Gurney's sugarbirds, Nyasa crimsonwings, grey waxbills and crowned eagles.

Whitefaced whistling ducks and redbilled teals are common around the dams.

The reserve is divided into two areas: the primary game and wild areas (stocked with elephant, white rhinoceros, eland, buck, giraffe and tsessebe), which offer viewing platforms, hides and a road system; and the wilderness area (481 hectares), where rambling and pony riding on cleared trails among 'non-dangerous' game are permitted. Interesting trees are numbered.

The reserve's major asset has been its overwhelming popularity as the venue for educational programmes serving schoolchildren throughout Zimbabwe. A museum education officer leads trails and uses the Rupert Fothergill open-air classroom for informal lectures.

360. *M'Tarazi Falls National Park*

SOUTHERN BOUNDARY OF NYANGA NATIONAL PARK, see map page 297

AUTHORITY-IN-CHARGE: Department of National Parks and Wildlife Management, Zimbabwe.
SIZE: 2 495 hectares.
MAIN ATTRACTIONS: Wilderness comprising montane moorland and mist forest; M'Tarazi Falls (762 m, Zimbabwe's highest); samango monkeys, blue duikers and crowned eagles.
FACILITIES/AMENITIES: Nature rambles; carpark and picnic/braai site near the falls.
PERTINENT INFORMATION: Administered as a unit with Nyanga National Park.
AVAILABLE LITERATURE: *Around Zimbabwe, No. 4: The Eastern Highlands*, brochure available from the Zimbabwe Tourist Development Corporation.
CLIMATE: High rainfall area.

361. *Nyanga National Park*

EASTERN HIGHLANDS, see map page 297

AUTHORITY-IN-CHARGE: Department of National Parks and Wildlife Management, Zimbabwe.
SIZE: 28 900 hectares.
MAIN ATTRACTIONS: Mountain landscapes (modified by pine plantations); stone ruin terraces; Zimbabwe's highest mountain and waterfall.
FACILITIES/AMENITIES: Footpaths and scenic drives; trout fishing; recreation facilities, including tennis, boating and pony

trails; hotels, fully equipped lodges, camp-sites and caravan parks.
PERTINENT INFORMATION: Camping is permitted only in the tourist camping grounds, not in the park itself.
AVAILABLE LITERATURE: Tourist maps, issued by the Troutbeck Inn, P.O. Troutbeck via Mutare, tel. Nyanga 305; *Around Zimbabwe, No 4: The Eastern Highlands*, brochure available from the Zimbabwe Tourist Development Corporation.
CLIMATE: High rainfall area, reaching approximately 2 200 millimetres in December.

Although not as popular for mountaineering as the Chimanimani range, Nyanga, lying at the northern end of a long mountain chain, has its own particular character and boasts superb views stretching all the way to Mulanje in Malawi. The park, with its pine plantations, fruit orchards and holiday resorts, is much more developed than the highlands to the south, but nevertheless has many refreshing walks through moist and sub-montane forest, grassland and heath-like scrub similar to the fynbos of the Western Cape.

Within Nyanga, the famous Pungwe Falls (243 metres) and M'Tarazi Falls (at 762 metres, Zimbabwe's highest), as well as many others, can be reached via a short, signposted walk from the hotels, or by driving. Zimbabwe's highest peak, Inyangani (2 593 m), is reached via a clear, beaconed path from the carpark, which is located

Above: Precautions against mosquitoes are necessary in some parts of the country.

about a quarter of the way up the mountain. The walk, which takes approximately 1-1,5 hours, is closed during periods of heavy rains, usually in the summer, between December and February. Thick mist during this time creates dangerous hiking conditions and inexperienced trailists could lose their way and fall over Inyangani's steep cliffs.

Wildlife is fairly prolific and treats in store for nature ramblers include possible sightings of the samango monkey, blue duiker and crowned eagle.

362. *Ngezi Recreation Park*

CHIVHU

AUTHORITY-IN-CHARGE: Department of National Parks and Wildlife Management, Zimbabwe.
SIZE: 6 326 hectares.
MAIN ATTRACTIONS: Game-viewing (reedbuck, sable antelope, hippo and crocodile).
FACILITIES/AMENITIES: Nature rambles; four fully equipped lodges; camping and caravan sites; fishing in dam.
PERTINENT INFORMATION: Open sunrise to sunset, year-round. For bookings: The National Parks Central Booking Office, P.O. Box 8151, Causeway, Harare, Zimbabwe.
AVAILABLE LITERATURE: General brochures; contact the Zimbabwe Tourist Development Corporation.
CLIMATE: Subtropical. Winter (May to August): mild, sunny days and cool nights; frost possible. Summer (September/mid-October to December): thunderstorms possible. October and November, very hot. December to mid-March, rainy season.

363. *Sabakwe Recreation Park*

KWEKWE

AUTHORITY-IN-CHARGE: Department of National Parks and Wildlife Management, Zimbabwe.
SIZE: 2 510 hectares.
MAIN ATTRACTIONS: Game-viewing; fishing; cliff scenery.
FACILITIES/AMENITIES: Nature rambles; fishing in dam.
PERTINENT INFORMATION: Open sunrise to sunset, year-round. For information: The Senior Ranger, Sabakwe Recreation Park, P.O. Box 636, Kwekwe, Zimbabwe.
AVAILABLE LITERATURE: General brochures; contact the Zimbabwe Tourist Development Corporation.
CLIMATE: Subtropical. Winter (May to August): mild, sunny days and cool nights; frost possible. Summer (September/mid-October to December): thunderstorms possible. October and November, hottest months. December to mid-March, rainy season.

364. *Lake McIlwaine Recreation Park*

HARARE

AUTHORITY-IN-CHARGE: The Warden, Lake McIlwaine, Private Bag 962, Norton, Zimbabwe.
SIZE: 55 000 hectares (1 600-hectare game park).
MAIN ATTRACTIONS: Recreation park with resort facilities; bush trails through game

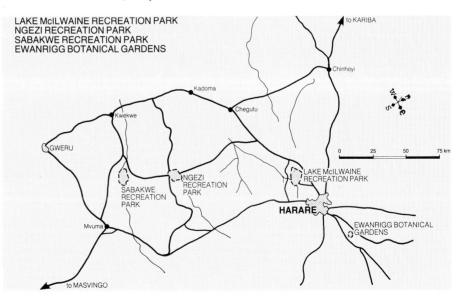

LAKE McILWAINE RECREATION PARK
NGEZI RECREATION PARK
SABAKWE RECREATION PARK
EWANRIGG BOTANICAL GARDENS

area with large mammals; rock paintings in granite hills; plentiful birdlife.

FACILITIES/AMENITIES: Signposted bush trails; camping and caravan sites; hotel and tea garden; sailing and angling (tigerfish, bream and catfish); resort facilities; picnic sites.

PERTINENT INFORMATION: Open sunrise to sunset, year-round.

AVAILABLE LITERATURE: *Around Zimbabwe, No 5: Harare, Chinhoyi, Midlands*, brochure available from the Zimbabwe Tourist Development Corporation.

CLIMATE: Subtropical. Winter (May to August): mild, sunny days and cool nights; frost possible. Summer (September/mid-October to December): thunderstorms possible. October and November, very hot. December to mid-March, rainy season.

365. *Ewanrigg Botanical Gardens*

NEAR HARARE, see map page 299

AUTHORITY-IN-CHARGE: Department of National Parks and Wildlife Management, Zimbabwe.

SIZE: 283 hectares.

MAIN ATTRACTIONS: Indigenous woodland; exotic aloes and cycads; water garden.

FACILITIES/AMENITIES: Nature rambles on a network of footpaths; picnic site.

PERTINENT INFORMATION: Located 40 km from Harare on the road to Shamva. Best time is during peak flowering season (late June to early August, or September to

October). Gardens open sunrise to sunset.

AVAILABLE LITERATURE: General brochures; contact the Zimbabwe Tourist Development Corporation.

CLIMATE: Subtropical. Winter (May to August): mild, sunny days and cool nights; frost possible. Summer (September/mid-October to December): thunderstorms possible. October and November, very hot. December to mid-March, rainy season.

366. *Chinhoyi Caves National Park*

CHINHOYI, see map page 306

AUTHORITY-IN-CHARGE: Department of National Parks and Wildlife Management, Zimbabwe.

SIZE: 148 hectares.

MAIN ATTRACTIONS: Deep, flooded calcite caves formed by erosive action of water on soft limestone; 100 metre-deep, blue sinkhole pool lit by the sun, in which fish and rock formations are visible several metres below the surface; evidence of Stone Age people.

FACILITIES/AMENITIES: Cave walk; caravan and camping site; picnic site; restaurant.

PERTINENT INFORMATION: Located in *Brachystegia* woodlands at the foot of the Hunyani Hills.

AVAILABLE LITERATURE: *Around Zimbabwe, No. 5: Harare, Chinhoyi, Midlands*, brochure available from the Zimbabwe Tourist Development Corporation.

CLIMATE: Subtropical. Winter (May to

August): mild, sunny days and cool nights; frost possible. Summer (September/mid-October to December): thunderstorms possible. October and November, hottest months. December to mid-March, rainy season.

367. *Canoeing and Rafting Trails*

ZAMBEZI RIVER, ZIMBABWE AND ZAMBIA, see map page 306

AUTHORITIES-IN-CHARGE: Various private companies run trails; two of the most active are Canoeing Safaris, P.O. Box 2997, Harare, Zimbabwe (flat and white-water canoeing, and white-water rafting), and Sobek Expeditions, P.O. Box 60957, Lusaka, Zambia (white-water rafting only).

LENGTH: Varies from 3 days, 2 nights to 9 days, 8 nights.

MAIN ATTRACTIONS: Navigating thrilling rapids; birdlife (bee-eater colonies); wildlife; fishing.

FACILITIES/AMENITIES: All equipment and food provided; trail led by experienced person; camping along the river.

PERTINENT INFORMATION: Check with the company as to the equipment provided, age restrictions, arrival and departure points, etc. Anti-malaria precautions are necessary. Bilharzia is possible in water near human habitations. Beware of crocodiles, especially when swimming near sand banks. Portaging is done around waterfalls. Although most companies encourage clients by insisting that no experience is necessary, I suggest participants be familiar with canoeing or river rafting and, if pertinent, white-water techniques.

AVAILABLE LITERATURE: Brochures obtainable from private companies and travel agents.

CLIMATE: Subtropical. Winter (May to August): mild, sunny days and cool nights; frost possible. Summer (September/mid-October to December): thunderstorms possible. October and November, hottest months. December to mid-March, rainy season.

The Zambezi River, with its unparalleled game-viewing and bird-watching opportunities and remote wilderness atmosphere, has finally been discovered by private canoe and river-rafting operators. They class the Zambezi as one of the world's most exciting river corridors. The adventure-seeker can choose from a variety of trips along flat or white-water sections of the mighty Zambezi, and travel in Canadian-style canoes, modified kayaks or rubber rafts.

The most frequented stretch of water for long-distance canoeing safaris is the lower

Zambezi, the area of river stretching from below the Kariba Dam wall to Kanyemba on the Mozambique border, a distance of over 256 kilometres. Canoeing Safaris runs a nine-day, eight-night trip through this area, which includes Kariba Gorge, Mana Pools National Park, Mupata Gorge and other spectacular areas. (Shorter trips are also available.) When travelling by canoe, all supplies are transported within the canoes.

The upper Zambezi River (from Kazangula on the Botswana/Zimbabwe border to the A'Zambezi River Lodge at Victoria Falls, a distance of approximately 80 kilometres) is also canoeing territory. As this section of the river contains strong, medium-sized rapids, trailists ride in modified two-person Klepper kayaks. A Land Rover back-up carries camping equipment and food. In this section it is best not to attempt any rapids which you do not have the confidence or experience to handle. Rather portage the kayak around these rapids.

Sobek Expeditions, a company that runs river-rafting trips all over the world, offers a seven-day white-water rafting stretch from the base of Victoria Falls to Lake Kariba.

This trip, in addition to the crocodiles and hippos in the river and the antelope grazing on the shore, boasts two spectacular water-falls, where the river drops over seven-metre basalt cliffs. (Sobek dictates that these falls necessitate portages!)

A very popular one-day trip is operated from August to mid-December. Starting at the Boiling Pot Trail at Victoria Falls, rafters run 14 sensational rapids in 22 kilometres, ending at Batoka Gorge. Rafts are oar-powered by experienced guides. Each raft holds seven people and a maximum of three rafts float down the river together.

Although the safety record of canoeing and rafting trips is excellent, accidents can happen. In 1986, a crocodile attacked a schoolboy while he was swimming off a sand bank. His father, who jumped in the water to save his son, had his arm severed in the ensuing struggle. Remember that these river trips take you into the raw heart of Africa. Be on the alert, use your common sense and co-operate with the guides and your fellow canoeists, and you will be assured of the unique fascination of one of the few true wilderness areas left on this continent.

368. Mana Pools National Park

ZAMBEZI RIVER, see map page 306

AUTHORITY-IN-CHARGE: Department of National Parks and Wildlife Management, Zimbabwe.
SIZE: 219 600 hectares.
MAIN ATTRACTIONS: Prolific bush and river birdlife; varied and abundant mammal life; attractive floodplains.
FACILITIES/AMENITIES: Good fishing for tigerfish, bream and giant vundu; Nyamepi Camp (camping and caravan sites with full ablution facilities); lodges; Mana Tree Lodge; primitive fishermen's camps; private

Opposite page: Elephant are abundant in Mana Pools National Park.

Above: Breathtaking guided canoeing and rafting trails on the Zambezi River start below the Kariba Dam wall.

safari camps, offering walking tours, situated along the river banks.

PERTINENT INFORMATION: Fishermen and trailists must be wary of crocodiles. Anti-malaria precautions are necessary. Park is open 1 May to 31 October, depending on the rains; advance bookings are necessary.

AVAILABLE LITERATURE: *Around Zimbabwe, No 2: Lake Kariba, Mana Pools*, brochure available from the Zimbabwe Tourist Development Corporation.

CLIMATE: Subtropical. Winter (May to August): sunny, mild days and cool nights; frost possible. Summer (September/mid-October to December): thunderstorms possible. October and November, hottest months. December to mid-March, rainy season.

Mana Pools National Park, in the extreme north of Zimbabwe, stretches southward from the Zambezi River to its escarpment. The park's isolated location contributes greatly to its wilderness atmosphere, thus enhancing its appeal to true lovers of nature. Wandering on foot through the riverine and mopane acacia woodland is very rewarding, for you are likely to encounter, among a wide range of animals, elephant, hippo, buffalo, black rhino, eland, impala, lion, leop-

ard, wild dog and crocodiles, as well as a great many birds.

Mana means 'four', a reference to the park's most outstanding feature – the group of small lakes and pools within the fertile river terraces. Any exploration of these crocodile-infested pools is at the trailist's own risk and can be further hampered by mosquitoes, tsetse flies and the year-round heat. However, if you are willing to bear these inconveniences, the bird-watching and game-viewing are superb – especially when the large herds and lion prides come down from the hills of the escarpment to drink.

369. Ruckomechi Camp Safaris

MANA POOLS NATIONAL PARK

AUTHORITY-IN-CHARGE: Ruckomechi Camp, P.O. Box 2997, Harare, Zimbabwe.
LENGTH/DURATION: Canoeing safari: 40 km/4 days, 3 nights. Walking safari: 45 km/4 days, 3 nights. Sketching safari: variable/3 days, 2 nights. Photographic

safari (on foot, boat or Land Rover): variable.
MAIN ATTRACTIONS: Zambezi River wilderness; Mana Pools National Park; abundant wildlife and prolific birdlife.
FACILITIES/AMENITIES: Safaris are fully inclusive of food and accommodation; canoeing safaris include canoes and canoeing equipment.
PERTINENT INFORMATION: May to October, camp can be reached by road (four-wheel drive vehicle not necessary) or by air from Kariba; November to April, access is by motorboat from Chirundu. Camp accommodates a maximum of 16 people in seven chalets; camp is closed from 30 November to 15 March each year. Permits necessary, issued free of charge at the National Parks Office at Marongora between 07h00 and 15h30. Anti-malaria precautions are necessary. Fishermen must bring their own equipment and bait.

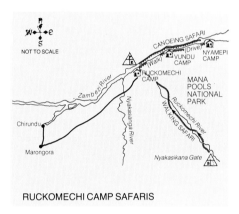

RUCKOMECHI CAMP SAFARIS

Minimum age for canoeing safari, 14 years, unless accompanied by an adult; minimum age for walking, sketching and photographic safaris, 12 years.
AVAILABLE LITERATURE: *Mana Pools Wildlife Safaris: Ruckomechi Camp*, brochure with maps.
CLIMATE: Summer rainfall area. Winter (May to August): evenings are chilly.

Most of Zimbabwe's safari lodges are located in exquisite bush country and offer guided walking trails on request. Ruckomechi Camp specializes in canoe and walking trails, and also combinations of the two. In addition, sketching and photographic safaris are offered for people with an interest in these arts. In fact, if sufficient numbers are available, special interest safaris in ornithology, entomology, botany and lepidoptery can also be arranged.

The canoeing safaris operate from May to October, on the Zambezi River, and are limited to eight clients. I consider these to be fairly luxurious trips as a vehicle serves as a back-up and camp is prepared for the canoeists each night. Should the walking urge strike, short excursions can be made into the wildlife-rich Mana Pools National Park. There is plenty of time to investigate and ex-

plore, fish and photograph, as the safari covers only 40 kilometres in four days.

The walking safari operates in a different area. Departing from the Nyakasikana Gate at the Ruckomechi River bridge, trailists follow in the footsteps of the great hunter and naturalist, Frederick Courteney Selous. This is a leisurely walk, covering only 15 kilometres a day, and porters carry everything but your daypack. To avoid the hot, rainy season, these safaris are run only in April, May, June and July.

The combination walking and canoeing safaris are usually operated on the lower Zambezi and cover a distance of approximately 70 kilometres.

370. Charara Safari Area

LAKE KARIBA, see map page 306

AUTHORITY-IN-CHARGE: Department of National Parks and Wildlife Management, Zimbabwe.
SIZE: 170 000 hectares.
MAIN ATTRACTIONS: Diverse wildlife, especially large game; Lake Kariba scenery.
FACILITIES/AMENITIES: Game-viewing on foot; network of gravel roads suitable for four-wheel drive vehicles only; angling for tigerfish and tilapia; launching slipway for boats; Nyanyana camp for caravanning and camping.
PERTINENT INFORMATION: For information: Charara Safari Area, Private Bag 2002, Kariba, Zimbabwe.
AVAILABLE LITERATURE: Contact the Zimbabwe Tourist Development Corporation.
CLIMATE: Subtropical. Winter (May to August): mild, sunny days and cool nights;

frost possible. Summer (September/mid-October to December): thunderstorms possible. October and November, hottest months. December to mid-March, rainy season.

Bordering the north-east shore of Lake Kariba, Charara Safari Area provides trailists with the opportunity of watching many animals (including black rhino) as they come down to the water to drink. The safari area overlies rich deposits of coal, copper, mica, chrome and tin and although the inevitable mining scars are present, the *Brachystegia-Colophosperum* woodland is relatively untouched by man.

Opposite page: Abundant wildlife makes each of Zimbabwe's national parks a nature lover's paradise: from prehistoric-looking crocodiles (top left) to steenbok (top right) and kudu (bottom), through to the large carnivores such as lion and leopard.

Top: Elephant, a typical sight in Zimbabwe, can be viewed from the many safari camps which border Matusadona National Park.

Above: Walking, canoeing and sailing safaris on Lake Kariba begin at the large, thatched social meeting shelter on Fothergill Island. A number of private lodges organize safaris to Matusadona.

371. Matusadona National Park

SOUTHERN SHORES OF LAKE KARIBA, see map page 306

AUTHORITY-IN-CHARGE: Department of National Parks and Wildlife Management, Zimbabwe.
SIZE: 137 000 hectares.
MAIN ATTRACTIONS: Large mammals, including black rhino, hippo, elephant and buffalo; scenic lake shore with winding, tree-lined creeks and waterfalls; Zambezi escarpment; Sanyati Gorge (fjord-like finger of Lake Kariba).
FACILITIES/AMENITIES: Backpacking trails conducted by private companies; game scouts provided for private walking trips; three exclusive camps, each accommodating 12 people; camp-sites on the shore at Sanyati West and Tashingya (on the Ume River); bush roads, suitable for four-wheel drive vehicles only; fishing for tigerfish, bream and vundu (no licence required).
PERTINENT INFORMATION: Beware of crocodiles (there are approximately 400 adult crocodiles living in the waters around the park). Tsetse fly is present. Exclusive camps are self-contained; bring only your own food. Entry by boat is allowed throughout the year; entry by road only between 1 May and 31 October; float planes are common vehicles of access. The upland mountainous area (south of the lake) is a wilderness area; permits are required here.
AVAILABLE LITERATURE: *Around Zimbabwe, No. 2: Lake Kariba, Mana Pools*, brochure available from the Zimbabwe Tourist Development Corporation.
CLIMATE: Subtropical. Winter (May to August): mild, sunny days and cool nights; frost possible. Summer (September/mid-October to December): thunderstorms possible. October and November, hottest months. December to mid-March, rainy season.

A beautiful way to incorporate Matusadona National Park into a trailing experience is to canoe along the shoreline, watching for elephant, buffalo, impala, kudu and waterbuck and, of course, the thriving aquatic birds. Then ramble through the *Commiphora-Combretum* thickets along the lower plains and the *Brachystegia* woodland on the escarpment, where rhino, eland, sable, roan and lion are frequently seen.

Many of these animals are 'refugees' saved from drowning during 'Operation Noah', one of the most successful wildlife rescue projects of all time, when the Zambezi Valley, which swarmed with wildlife, began to flood with the filling of Lake Kariba.

Fothergill Island (Private Bag 2081, Kariba, Zimbabwe) and Tiger Bay (P.O. Box

102, Kariba, Zimbabwe) are two of a number of private lodges which organize walking safaris and sailing or canoe trips to Matusadona. For example, Fothergill offers a guided, 3-5 day wilderness backpacking trip into the rugged Matusadona Mountains. Tiger Bay, on the Ume River, offers short walks, a four-day hike and also environmental education courses for youngsters. Each lodge concentrates on different areas of the park.

372. Chizarira National Park

NORTH-WEST ZIMBABWE, SOUTH OF LAKE KARIBA, see map page 306

AUTHORITY-IN-CHARGE: Department of National Parks and Wildlife Management, Zimbabwe.
SIZE: 191 000 hectares.
MAIN ATTRACTIONS: Large variety of big game, including elephant, buffalo, tsessebe, sable, roan, black rhino, crocodile, leopard and lion; spectacular and varied mountain scenery; streams, gorges and views over the Zambezi Valley.
FACILITIES/AMENITIES: Game-viewing on foot, with permit; two wilderness campsites.
PERTINENT INFORMATION: Chizarira is a Batlonka word meaning 'barrier'. Access is difficult, and possible by four-wheel drive vehicle only. Permission to enter necessary, obtainable in writing from The Provincial Warden (Matabeleland North), Private Bag DT 5925, Victoria Falls, Zimbabwe.
AVAILABLE LITERATURE: Contact the Zimbabwe Tourist Development Board.
CLIMATE: Cool uplands on escarpment; hot lowveld on Busi River (in the south).

For outdoor enthusiasts seeking a 'real' wilderness experience, Chizarira's relatively undeveloped, magnificently diverse and rugged terrain is an unforgettable experience. Backpackers can retreat to the wilds with a game scout and backpack for at least 10 days, following their own chosen route.

Chizarira lies in the remote north-west of Zimbabwe where *Brachystegia-Colophosperum* woodlands, scrub savannah and *Hyparrhenia* grassland clothe the slopes bordering the steep Zambezi escarpment. Wildlife, too, is diverse and includes many 'refugees' displaced from the Zambezi Valley when the river was dammed to create Lake Kariba. The most notable inhabitants are tsessebe, waterbuck, roan, buffalo, black rhino, elephant, lion and leopard.

Note: Two other safari areas which are equally remote and allow backpacking with scouts are the Chirisa Safari Area (for information: The Provincial Warden, Private Bag DT 5779, Dete, Zimbabwe) and the Chewore Safari Area (for information: The Provincial Warden, Department of National Parks and Wildlife Management, P.O. Box 193, Chinhoyi, Zimbabwe).

Above: The blue wildebeest favours open, grassy plains dotted with thorny bushes in relatively dry areas. The diverse wildlife seen in Zimbabwe's national parks includes 'refugees' displaced from the Zambezi Valley during 'Operation Noah', when the river was dammed to create Lake Kariba.

Opposite page: Numerous foot, vehicle and night safaris start from the luxurious Hwange Safari Lodge.

373. *Hwange National Park*

NORTH-WESTERN ZIMBABWE, see map page 306

AUTHORITY-IN-CHARGE: Department of National Parks and Wildlife Management, Zimbabwe.

SIZE: 1 465 100 hectares.

MAIN ATTRACTIONS: Large concentrations of big game which are attracted to the natural pans; prolific birdlife (401 species).

FACILITIES/AMENITIES: Foot safaris; waterhole platforms; four camps offering hut accommodation and/or caravan and camping sites; three 'exclusive' camps (Deka, Bamboosi and Lukosi); Hwange Safari Lodge offering vehicle, foot and night safaris, bunkee and tree hides; network of game-viewing drives.

PERTINENT INFORMATION: Trailists must provide their own food on the Department's trails. Anti-malaria precautions are necessary.

AVAILABLE LITERATURE: *Around Zimbabwe, No 1: Victoria Falls, Hwange*, brochure available from the Zimbabwe Tourist Development Corporation.

CLIMATE: May to November, the dry season, is the best time for game-viewing.

For the trailist, Hwange's principal attractions are the 'exclusive' camps and guided trails. Exclusive camps are fully equipped, permanent accommodation units for groups of not more than 12 people who, for the period of their stay, have sole use of the area within a five-kilometre radius of their accommodation, for game-viewing. Guided trails or foot safaris are operated within the park. A maximum of six trailists is taken on a three-day walking safari accompanied by both a ranger and a game scout. The cost of the trail includes tents and camp equipment, which is carried by pack donkeys, but does not include food.

Walking in Hwange, the largest of Zimbabwe's national parks and one of the great elephant sanctuaries of Africa, is a very rewarding experience, as it is reputed to have the greatest variety as well as one of the densest populations of wild animals in the world.

The largest area of the park is covered by Kalahari sand, supporting bushveld savannah and grassy plains, the natural habitat of many herding animals. But it is probably the region's large natural pans, rich in salts, sodium, lime and other minerals, that play the greater part in attracting many of the animals. The pans are continuously enlarged by animals wallowing in the mud and drinking at their edges. North of the main watershed, a hilly area of granite outcrops with mopane woodland, is the popular haunt of the elephants; consequently, this area suffers extensive damage from large herds.

In addition to elephants, trailists may see many of the 70 species of large animals such as buffalo, giraffe, lion, reintroduced black and white rhino, wildebeest, ostrich, warthog, spotted and brown hyaena, jackal, hippo and crocodile. The diversified antelope population includes hartebeest, eland, sable, roan, impala, kudu, waterbuck, tsessebe and gemsbok. Present but not readily seen are Hwange's seven centimetre-long pygmy mouse and the South African hedgehog. The birdlife, especially migrants, is prolific.

374. *Matetsi Safari Area*

MATETSI, NEAR HWANGE NATIONAL PARK, see map page 306

AUTHORITY-IN-CHARGE: Matetsi Wildlife Leisure Resort, P.O. Box 160, Victoria Falls, Zimbabwe.

SIZE: 6-hectare wildlife resort within wilderness area.

MAIN ATTRACTIONS: Game animals similar to those found in Hwange National Park, particularly sable, waterbuck and reedbuck.

FACILITIES/AMENITIES: Game-viewing on foot or from a vehicle; chalets; facilities for school groups; conferences; airstrip; hunting.

PERTINENT INFORMATION: Anti-malaria precautions are necessary.

AVAILABLE LITERATURE: *Around Zimbabwe, No. 1: Victoria Falls, Hwange*, brochure available from the Zimbabwe Tourist Development Corporation.

CLIMATE: Subtropical. Winter (May to August): mild, sunny days and cool nights; frost possible. Summer (September/mid-October to December): thunderstorms possible. October and November, hottest months. December to mid-March, rainy season.

375. *Kazuma Pan National Park*

WESTERN SECTION OF MATETSI SAFARI AREA, see map page 306

AUTHORITY-IN-CHARGE: Department of National Parks and Wildlife Management, Zimbabwe.

SIZE: 31 290 hectares.

MAIN ATTRACTIONS: Open grassland savannah with seasonally flooded natural pans; excellent birdlife; gemsbok, giraffe, cheetah and other game species.

FACILITIES/AMENITIES: Nature rambles; game-viewing on foot.

PERTINENT INFORMATION: Permission to enter the park necessary, obtainable from The Provincial Warden, Private Bag DT 5776, Dete, Zimbabwe.

AVAILABLE LITERATURE: Contact the Zimbabwe Tourist Development Corporation.

CLIMATE: Subtropical. Winter (May to

August): mild, sunny days and cool nights; frost possible. Summer (September/mid-October to December): thunderstorms possible. October and November, hottest months. December to mid-March, rainy season.

376. The Victoria Falls and Zambezi National Parks

ZAMBEZI RIVER, WESTERN ZIMBABWE

AUTHORITY-IN-CHARGE: Department of National Parks and Wildlife Management, Zimbabwe.
SIZE: 56 000 hectares, including 2 340-hectare Victoria Falls National Park.
MAIN ATTRACTIONS: One of the world's largest and most sensational waterfalls.
FACILITIES/AMENITIES: Hotels, chalets, lodges, camping and caravan sites; Kandahar and Sansimba fishing camps in Zambezi National Park.
PERTINENT INFORMATION: Raincoat, umbrella and waterproof camera are useful. The Victoria Falls National Park is the area surrounding the falls and the river's edge.
AVAILABLE LITERATURE: *Amazing Zimbabwe: A Very Special Country*, map; *Around Zimbabwe, No. 1: Victoria Falls, Hwange*, brochure (both available from the Zimbabwe Tourist Development Corporation).
CLIMATE: Summer (November to March): rainy and very hot. Winter (June and July): cool and dry; night frosts possible. August to November, best months for photography.

Rising in the north-west Zambian highlands, the Zambezi, the fourth-longest river in Africa, flows eastwards through the flat Barotse plains, gaining momentum in rocky gorges, until it takes its magnificent leap over a chasm eroded in basalt rock. It is difficult to describe the sheer size and grandeur of the Victoria Falls. The Kololo name *Mosi o Thunya* ('the smoke that thunders') captures their evocative spirit and power; when David Livingstone first saw them in 1855 he exclaimed that 'scenes so lovely must have been gazed upon by angels in their flight', and named the spectacle in honour of his queen.

Today, while following what is surely Africa's most awe-inspiring nature walk, the Victoria Falls are seen from the very safe network of paths leading through the Rain Forest, along the opposite bank of the gorge into which the river plunges.

The dense and luxuriant riparian forest which flourishes in the moisture from the falls' spray is also worthy of attention. The

THE VICTORIA FALLS AND ZAMBEZI NATIONAL PARKS, CHINHOYI CAVES NATIONAL PARK, CANOEING AND RAFTING TRAILS, MANA POOLS NATIONAL PARK, CHARARA SAFARI AREA, MATUSADONA NATIONAL PARK, CHIZARIRA NATIONAL PARK, HWANGE NATIONAL PARK, MATETSI SAFARI AREA, KAZUMA PAN NATIONAL PARK

attractive herbaceous plants towered over by figs, ebonies, waterberry and olive trees are of great botanical interest. Trumpeter hornbills and Knysna loeries are often seen in the tall trees and thick undergrowth.

For people planning their first visit to Victoria Falls, I recommend the first half of summer (November or December) as the best time; although these are very hot months, the waters are at their lowest level, comparatively little spray is produced and consequently the geological formation of the region can be better appreciated. At peak flood times (March and April) water volumes increase thirty-fold, making the spray so dense that the bottom of the 103 metre-deep chasm or the full 1 708-metre width of the falls are difficult to see. If possible, try to experience the majestic atmosphere of the falls under full moon or in the late afternoon when rainbows arc through the sprays.

The Zambezi National Park starts at the Victoria Falls and includes 46 kilometres of the Zambezi River upstream of the falls, as well as a large area south of the river. The park is noted for fishing, large mammals and crocodiles. Visitors wishing to explore this park on foot should contact the Department of National Parks and Wildlife Management in Harare for permission and details.

Opposite page: Walk the Victoria Falls nature trail at different times of the day to experience its many moods. In the late afternoon, rainbows arc through the spray.

Above: A cheetah, photographed at the crocodile farm at Victoria Falls.

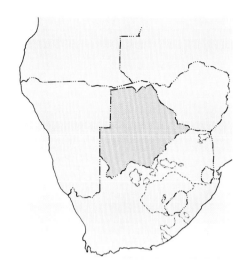

BOTSWANA

Botswana is synonymous with wilderness. Its 580 000 km²-area (more than twice the size of West Germany) is bordered by Namibia in the west, Zimbabwe in the east and South Africa in the south. This vast area is inhabited by less than one million people; a commendable 17 per cent of the country is under the control of the Department of Wildlife and National Parks. Here roam the greatest wildlife herds in southern Africa, together with a most spectacular and varied birdlife.

Although landlocked, Botswana boasts the world's largest inland delta. The Okavango, drowning 16 000 km² of potential desert, receives floodwaters from the Angolan highlands, 1 000 kilometres away. These waters transform the delta into a canoeing paradise of animals and tropical plants, with ecosystems as varied as dry savannah and riparian woodland, mopane forest, floodplain, reedbeds and permanent swamp. The waterless Kalahari, covering two-thirds of the country, contains grassed and bare pans, dry

riverbeds, fossil dunes and rolling grasslands, all rich in wildlife.

Entry to Botswana requires a valid passport or travel document and a visa for some non-South African and non-Commonwealth nationals. Visas must be obtained before entering the country, as they are not available at the border. Visitors are required to pass through a border post or an airport gazetted as a port of entry.

The rains fall as short thunderstorms from November to March or April, and the temperature ranges from 38 °C in the day to 19 °C at night. In the dry winter (May to September) when skies are clear, temperatures may reach 28 °C, but sometimes fall to below freezing at night.

Although you can travel farthest in the delta in late June and July when the water is at its highest, the other months have their advantages: birdlife excels in May, trees flower in September and tigerfish bite in October; October and November are probably the best months for game-viewing. Avoid visiting the area between December and April when the Okavango starts to rise in Angola but has not yet reached Botswana; at this time it is often unpleasantly hot, and although rains occur in torrential downpours, there is little standing water.

ECOLOGICAL ZONE: ACACIA
SAVANNAH OR KALAHARI

Safaris in Botswana
There are no self-guided, constructed hiking trails or walks in Botswana, but there is limitless opportunity for walking and canoeing. Most of the country is a vast wilderness, alive with game, birds and smaller forms of

life. The aim of the trailist in Botswana should be intimate encounters with nature.

It is possible to canoe 600 kilometres from Shakwe village in the north to Maun at the southern end of the Okavango Delta. Camping is popular on the sandy banks of reed-choked channels or on small uninhabited islands. You can either paddle and navigate on your own or hire a guide who is familiar with the ways of the wild.

In Moremi Wildlife Reserve, the area of big game, you are allowed to walk where you wish, as is the case in many of the country's reserves. However, judging from the many safari companies operating in Botswana, there is a vast demand for guided walks, canoe trips and organized camping or more luxurious accommodation.

Most safari companies boast the 'ultimate safari programme and services of professional game rangers and camp staff'. Activities during safaris usually include walking, boating, fishing, game-viewing drives and bird-watching. Most safaris supply all your needs, except cameras, binoculars and clothing, the latter limited to a modest baggage allowance. A few of the companies which include walks as part of their safaris in Botswana are listed below. This list is neither comprehensive nor purports to be a recommendation for any company. It is best to consult your travel agent or wildlife club for the latest information.

Call of the Wild, P.O. Box 51812, Randburg 2125, South Africa.
Gametrackers Botswana (Pty) Ltd, Private Bag 0077, Gabarone, Botswana.
Okavango Tours and Safaris, P.O. Box 784782, Sandton 2146, South Africa.
Okavango Wilderness Safaris (Pty) Ltd, Private Bag 14, Maun, Botswana.
Penduka Safaris, P.O. Box 55413, Northlands 2116, South Africa.
Sitatunga Safaris, Private Bag 47, Maun, Botswana.

377. Mashatu Game Reserve

TULI ENCLAVE

AUTHORITY-IN-CHARGE: Privately owned; member of the Safmarine/Rennies Group.
SIZE: 30 000 hectares.
MAIN ATTRACTIONS: Bushveld wilderness famous for its large population of elephants; 44 mammal species; 375 bird species; archaeological sites.
FACILITIES/AMENITIES: Guided trails by arrangement; open Land Rover drives; walking trails; nocturnal spotlighting drives. Majale luxury lodge with swimming pool; tented bush camp.
PERTINENT INFORMATION: For bookings: Safren House, P.O. Box 32501, Braamfontein 2017, South Africa. The Mashatu elephants constitute the largest

single population of elephants in Africa surviving on privately owned land. Accommodation in lodges and camps is kept to a minimum to ensure an intimate and personal experience. No set itineraries are followed. The Mashatu Ivory Trail runs through the reserve.
AVAILABLE LITERATURE: *Mashatu Game Reserve*, detailed information and ecological package; *Mashatu News*, official newsletter of the Mashatu Wildlife Foundation.
CLIMATE: Summer (October to April): hot and rainy. Winter (May to September): cool to cold and dry.

Below: The acacia-mopane veld provides ideal habitat for a rich variety of large animal life and birdlife, seen on the guided tours offered by the many safari companies operating in Botswana.

Opposite page: One of the three habitat types – water channels and lagoons – explored in the Okavango Swamps, a canoeing paradise of animals and tropical plants.

378. Mashatu Ivory Trail

MASHATU GAME RESERVE, NORTH-EASTERN TULI ENCLAVE

AUTHORITY-IN-CHARGE: Educational Wildlife Expeditions.
DURATION: 5 days.
MAIN ATTRACTIONS: Elephants and other large animals; birdlife (375 species); ruins and artefacts of archaeological interest.
FACILITIES/AMENITIES: Permanent, fully equipped tented camps on banks of Limpopo River; fresh foods are provided. Canoeing.
PERTINENT INFORMATION: Trails leave at 06h00 every Thursday from the Sunnyside Park Hotel in Parktown, Johannesburg, and return on Monday. Maximum of 8 people per group. Book well in advance.
AVAILABLE LITERATURE: Contact Educational Wildlife Expeditions for their latest brochures.
CLIMATE: Summer (October to April): hot and rainy. Winter (May to September): cool to cold and dry.

Situated in a rugged wilderness well known for its large elephant herds, the Mashatu Ivory Trail is a favourite among nature enthusiasts. Its venue is the Mashatu Game Reserve in the north-eastern Tuli Enclave which lies between the Shasti and Limpopo rivers in south-eastern Botswana, 600 kilometres north of Johannesburg via Pietersburg to Pont Drift. (The adjacent conservation area in Zimbabwe is called the Tuli Conservation Area.)

The acacia-mopane veld and riverine bush of the area provide ideal habitats for eland, impala, zebra, wildebeest, waterbuck, buffalo, sable, cheetah, lion, leopard, bateared fox, jackal, hyaena and abundant birdlife. Because hippopotamus are not plentiful, canoeing on the Limpopo is relatively safe and one of the highlights of the trail.

The Tuli Block is an area steeped in history. Inhabited by the Maphungubwe tribe during the Iron Age, a hunting ground of the great Selous, and having close associations with ancient Zimbabwean cultures, the Tuli area possesses many artefacts left by hunters, prospectors and missionaries which add archaeological interest to this area.

The Mashatu Ivory Trail is flexible, to suit the interests of the group. The trained field staff will take the trailist on long or short walks, concentrate on big-game tracking, wildlife photography, bird-watching or ecological discussions of interesting natural phenomena. If possible, book as a group with similar interests.

379. Fish Eagle Trail

OKAVANGO SWAMPS AND SAVUTI CHANNEL

AUTHORITY-IN-CHARGE: Educational Wildlife Expeditions.
DURATION: 5 days.
MAIN ATTRACTIONS: Savuti Channel in Chobe National Park; Okavango wilderness; wildlife and birdlife – one of the richest areas left in Africa.
FACILITIES/AMENITIES: Food and utensils,

best way to enjoy the Okavango Swamps, especially if your time is limited. The venue is reached by air from Johannesburg, and from the bushveld airstrip in the swamps you travel by mokoro dug-out to a secluded tract of land near Chief's Island, your sleeping base for your stay.

Three habitat types – water channels and lagoons; bands of large forest trees and bushy swathes along waterways; and dry woodlands – provide myriad niches for the diversified and specialized fauna. The lechwe, one of the most typical representatives of the Okavango, provides a good example of such adaptation. This swamp-dwelling buck has well-developed lateral hooves which, by providing wider and more stable 'platforms', facilitate the animal's passage over marshy terrain.

The Fish Eagle Trail also includes one and a half days in the Savuti Channel in Chobe National Park. The Savuti is best known for its predatory and marsh birds, especially the painted and Ethiopian snipes, openbill stork, glossy ibis, night heron and hamerkop.

380. Okavango Discovery Trail

OKAVANGO DELTA

AUTHORITY-IN-CHARGE: Educational Wildlife Expeditions.
DURATION: 8 days.
MAIN ATTRACTIONS: Okavango wilderness; 400 species of birds; reedbuck, lechwe, sitatunga, hippo, crocodile and other large animals; dug-out canoe rides; semi-permanent and permanent swamps; Chief's Island; leisurely pace of activities.
FACILITIES/AMENITIES: Transport, food and camping equipment provided; mokoro hire; trained field officers.
PERTINENT INFORMATION: Trails leave every Saturday from the Sunnyside Park Hotel in Johannesburg; fly to Maun and then Xaxaba Camp in the Okavango Delta.
AVAILABLE LITERATURE: Contact Educational Wildlife Expeditions for their latest brochures.
CLIMATE: October/November to March/April: short thunderstorms; temperatures range from 19 °C at night to 38 °C during the day. May to September: dry; temperatures range from 0 °C at night to 28 °C during the day.

The Okavango Discovery Trail differs from the Fish Eagle Trail, also run by Educational Wildlife Expeditions, in that it is longer, more leisurely, follows a circular route, and is located only in the delta itself. Three major ecozones are visited: semi-permanent or seasonally inundated areas; permanent

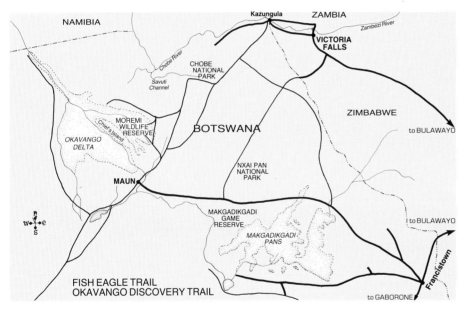

FISH EAGLE TRAIL
OKAVANGO DISCOVERY TRAIL

camping equipment, mosquito nets, sleeping bags, linen, stretchers, mattresses and tents provided; shower and toilets.
PERTINENT INFORMATION: Maximum of 8 people per trail. Trails depart at 06h00 on Fridays from Johannesburg, April to October, on scheduled dates. Trail price includes the charter flight from Johannesburg to Maun and return. Anti-malaria precautions are necessary; binoculars, insect repellent, sunscreen lotion and Elastoplast are recommended. Maximum baggage allowance, 7 kg (backpacks with frames are too bulky). Valid passport and entry visa to Botswana necessary. Non-South Africans must also obtain a re-entry visa to South Africa.
AVAILABLE LITERATURE: Contact

Educational Wildlife Expeditions for their latest brochures.
CLIMATE: October/November to March/April: short thunderstorms; temperatures range from 19 °C at night to 38 °C during the day. May to September: dry; temperatures range from 0 °C at night to 28 °C during the day.

Rising in the Bié Plateau of Angola and flowing 1 000 kilometres south towards the Kalahari, the Okavango River, in its lower reaches, forms a 16 000-km² inland delta, the site of the Fish Eagle Trail. These immense swamplands house a wealth of fauna unsurpassed elsewhere in southern Africa.

A 'wilderness trail' such as this, led by an experienced trails officer and tracker, is the

swamp with perennial surface water (Xoa Flats); and Chief's Island, a high, dry land mass with sandveld and mopane woodland extending into permanent swamp.

Time is spent gliding on mokoros (dug-out canoes) while fishing, bird-watching and game-viewing, or walking to various points of interest. Depending on the advice of the guides, and based on their personal knowledge of the area and recent game movements, a base camp is established and from here daily excursions inland are made. The itinerary is flexible to suit the interests of the group, and the simple camp is easily moved. The northern and southern areas of Chief's Island are visited. Characteristic of Educational Wildlife Expeditions' trails, the guides discuss not only the ecology but also man's place in the area, its geography, history, archaeology and anthropology.

Opposite page: Three habitat types – water channels and lagoons, bands of large forest trees (pictured here), and dry woodlands – provide myriad niches for the fauna found in the Okavango delta.

Above: The Makgadikgadi salt pan is a huge, barren depression located south-east of the Okavango. Most safari companies pay it a visit en route *to the lusher regions of Botswana.*

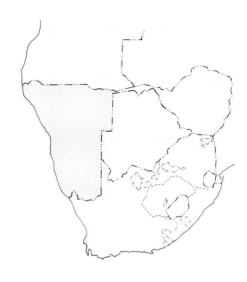

NAMIBIA

Namibia is situated north of the Orange River, and is bordered by Angola in the north, Botswana in the east, South Africa in the south and the Atlantic Ocean in the west. The Hottentots named this huge territory (823 144 km² – over three times the size of West Germany) 'Namibia', which means 'plain'. Despite its vast and harsh desert to semi-desert waterless environment and the long distances between population centres, Namibia continues to draw outdoor enthusiasts. Endless rocky plains, desert dunes, desolate coastlines, dry riverbeds, beautiful birdlife and unusual plants offer the trailist a sense of tranquillity, beauty and silence.

A unique combination of natural colours and angles combines with wide horizons and pollution-free skies to produce magnificently aesthetic lighting: crimson glowing dunes, silver shining pans, pastel mountains at dawn and dusk, and brilliant wildflowers blooming after the rains. Photography here is a dream.

There are no border formalities for people entering Namibia from South Africa; visitors arriving from other countries must have a passport, possibly a visa, and be able to furnish proof of their intention and financial ability to leave the country.

Hikers must be prepared to tolerate extremes of temperature. The summer hiker experiences hot days (in midsummer the temperatures may rise to above 40 °C) and cool nights; winter is a more agreeable time to visit Namibia, when the days are comfortably warm, although at night the temperature can fall to below freezing.

The interior of Namibia has two rainy seasons: the short one, between October and December, when rain falls sporadically, and the main rainfall period, accompanied by thunderstorms, between mid-January and April. During this time, wise campers should be aware of the potential for flash-flooding.

ECOLOGICAL ZONES: COASTAL DESERT, SEMI-DESERT, KALAHARI

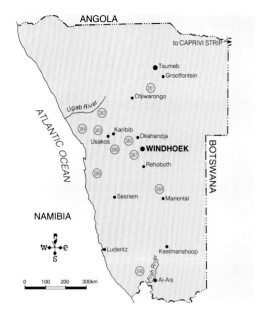

ANGOLA
to CAPRIVI STRIP

Tsumeb
Grootfontein

Otjiwarongo

Ugab River

Karibib
Okahandja
Usakos
WINDHOEK
Rehoboth

BOTSWANA

ATLANTIC OCEAN

NAMIBIA

Sesriem
Mariental

Luderitz
Keetmanshoop

Fish River

Ai-Ais

0 100 200 300km

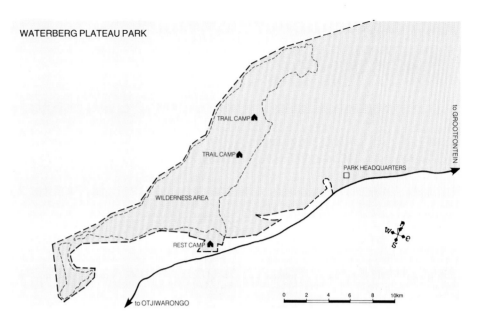

WATERBERG PLATEAU PARK

TRAIL CAMP

TRAIL CAMP

PARK HEADQUARTERS

to GROOTFONTEIN

WILDERNESS AREA

REST CAMP

to OTJIWARONGO

0 2 4 6 8 10km

381. Waterberg Plateau Park

NEAR OTJIWARONGO

AUTHORITY-IN-CHARGE: Directorate of Nature Conservation and Recreation Resorts, Department of Agriculture and Nature Conservation, Namibia.
LENGTH/DURATION: Approximately 15 km (maximum) per day/4 days.
MAIN ATTRACTIONS: Interesting rock sculptures; rock paintings and engravings; rich and varied vegetation, animal and birdlife in a wilderness atmosphere.
FACILITIES/AMENITIES: Guided hiking trail; base camp with tents and stretchers, ablution block, water and firewood.
PERTINENT INFORMATION: The trail runs from Thursday to Sunday afternoon every second, third and fourth weekend from 1 April to 30 November. Only one group (minimum of 6 and maximum of 8 people) permitted on the trail each weekend. Bookings in advance to the Directorate's booking office, Private Bag 13267, Windhoek 9000, Namibia.
AVAILABLE LITERATURE: *Waterberg Wilderness Trail*, brochure.

CLIMATE: Summer rainfall area (October to April). June, July and August are the driest months.

Namibia is a land of scenic surprises, and the table mountain formation of the Waterberg Plateau, abruptly rising hundreds of metres above the surrounding plains, is one such striking contrast. The plateau, a remnant of the original crust which existed before the surrounding land eroded away, hosts an interesting gradient of vegetation from the summit plateau, down through the sandstone cliffs and slopes of the mountain to its base. Some plants growing at Waterberg Plateau Park are found nowhere else in Namibia.

Large trees such as *Ficus* grow around the free-flowing springs which are a special feature of this park; in fact, a whole series of frog species has evolved within the numerous springs.

Animals relocated to the huge, undisturbed mountain plateau include the endangered sable and roan antelope, buffalo and white rhino.

382. The Brandberg

NORTHERN NAMIBIA

AUTHORITY-IN-CHARGE: Chief Damara Affairs Commissioner, Namibia.
SIZE: 500-km² oval base.
MAIN ATTRACTIONS: The White Lady and other rock paintings and engravings; rugged rock scenery; spectacular sunrises and sunsets; unusual plants; birdlife.
FACILITIES/AMENITIES: Picnic spots; no firewood or water.
PERTINENT INFORMATION: Water is severely limited. Permits are not necessary.
AVAILABLE LITERATURE: Included in

general tourist promotion brochures.
CLIMATE: Extreme temperature variations with very hot days and cool to cold nights.

Considering the Brandberg's other names – Desolate or Forsaken Mountain and Fire Mountain – one can understand why only the toughest mountaineers climb Königstein Peak (2 579 m), the highest point in Namibia. Towering 2 000 metres above the surrounding plains, this impressive granite massif lies on the border of the Namib and the semi-desert steppe of grass and bush. Toughness, however, is but one aspect, as experience is equally important, and only mountaineers of long standing should attempt the Brandberg – its excessive daytime temperatures, bitterly cold nights, the lack of water (except in hidden springs and waterholes) and its jumble of rock, ravine and natural rubble combine to create a formidable goal.

For those other than experienced climbers, there is an alternative to a full-scale attack on the mountain, as a well-marked, approximately one-hour nature ramble exists along the main ravine. This leads to the White Lady, one of the most famous rock paintings in Namibia, and one which has over the years evoked a myriad hypotheses as to its origin and meaning.

Rambles at the base of the Brandberg reveal rare and unusual plants such as cobas, a thickset succulent tree which bears a red, grape-like fruit containing poisonous oxalic acid, and the African moringo, another conspicuous, thickset tree with edible bark,

Left: Namaqua chameleon, Chamelio namaquensis.
Opposite page, top: One of the tall, pinnacled termite mounds, typical of this region.
Opposite page, bottom left: The Brandberg.
Opposite page, right: The White Lady, one of Namibia's most famous rock paintings.

stem and roots. Birdlife is plentiful in the protected, vegetation-rich ravines at the base of the massif.

Whether climbing, camping or rambling, always carry plenty of water.

383. *Spitzkoppe*

NEAR USAKOS

AUTHORITY-IN-CHARGE: Chief Damara Affairs Commissioner, Namibia.
HEIGHT: 1 829 metres.
MAIN ATTRACTIONS: Unusual Matterhorn-like shape; rock climber's challenge; rock art and artefacts; semi-precious stones.
FACILITIES/AMENITIES: None.
PERTINENT INFORMATION: Permits are not necessary.
AVAILABLE LITERATURE: Included in general tourist promotion brochures.

Rising as abruptly as it does from the surrounding plains, it is easy to understand why the Spitzkoppe – a volcanic granite 'Matterhorn', capped with 700 metre-high sheer, naked stone – draws expert rock climbers, gapers, photographers, artists and nature-lovers.

I include the Spitzkoppe in this collection of trails principally to relate my own experience, an episode which, I hope, will teach you the same lessons it taught me.

Don, a friend, and I reached the base of the mountain on a perfect late winter's afternoon. After setting up camp, Don was

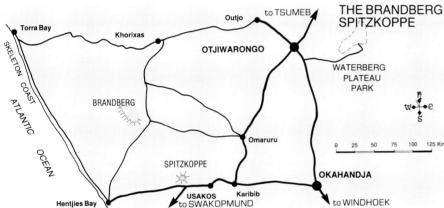

keen to scramble up the coarse and rough granite on the lower slopes, but I preferred to ramble through the vegetation in search of the rosyfaced lovebird. We separated, agreeing to return by dark to cook dinner. My idea to go bird-watching was a good one: there were so many new and exciting species to observe that I became completely engrossed, scrambling over the granite boulders of all shapes and sizes to follow small flocks of birds flitting from thorn tree to shrub. By dusk, not realizing it, I was completely disorientated. Unwittingly compli-

dark – until I realized that the loud cracks were rocks contracting from the sudden, sharp drop in temperature.

Totally exhausted, I found an overhang and lay down with only my binoculars as a pillow and *Roberts'* bird book to cover my body. By this stage I was miserable, confused and shivering uncontrollably – the crisp, cold desert air had finally penetrated my adrenaline-heated arteries and my sweat-soaked T-shirt.

I had in the past few hours done everything that went against good sense and my training – not only had I set out alone to explore the mountain slopes, I had also not taken any warm clothes, food, water or other emergency equipment. I had in fact

placed my life, and those of my companions who would come looking for me, in danger. I did not deserve immediate relief from my self-induced plight, but I have no quarrel with what happened next. Over the Spitzkoppe's needle-like spire rose the most brilliant full moon I could ever wish to see. Fear and confusion overcome, I sat revelling in the sheer beauty of the scene around me.

The rest of the episode was rather an anticlimax. The route was now obvious – I descended a long valley, guided by both moonlight and memory, into the headlights of the Land Rovers of a search party. Still clad in only a damp T-shirt and shorts, with binoculars and the remains of my bird book cover hanging around my neck, I probably

cating my predicament, I continued climbing higher to photograph the varied pink and purple hues blanketing the late afternoon desert landscape.

I then caught sight of a series of rock beacons some distance above, which I assumed had been placed by the local mountain club. I was inexplicably mesmerized by them and, foolishly but instinctively, I set out to investigate, climbing higher and higher until the beacons faded with the rays of the setting sun.

A moonless desert night sharply contrasts with a cloudless, harshly lit desert day and I was rudely faced with my folly. My only thought was to return to camp as rapidly as possible. The route I had taken now seemed excessively complex to retrace, so I opted for climbing higher over a nek and down the other side to where Don would (I hoped) be tending the fire and boiling the water for coffee.

After an hour and a half of frantic crawling, scrambling and feeling my way, I realized that the higher I climbed, the wider grew the cracks, the longer grew the overhangs, and the larger grew the boulders. To make the mountain appear even more formidable, the scanty vegetation was either prickly or poisonous.

It suddenly struck me that I wasn't alone. A herd of 'who-knows-whatsits' galloped past at great speed. I was then frightened by another noise which sounded like a barrage of bullets blasting at my head. I could only guess it was poachers shooting wildly in the

Top: An impressive collection of whitebrowed sparrow-weavers' nests in a tree near the lower slopes of the Spitzkoppe.

Above right: A kokerboom or quiver tree, Aloe dichotoma, *in the area of the Spitzkoppe. At one time, Bushmen made quivers for their arrows from the soft branches of the tree, which gave rise to its common name.*

Right: A sociable weaver's nest, a common sight in Namibia. The nest is in fact a communally built nest mass which accommodates many pairs of birds, including other species such as pygmy falcons.

Oppposite page: The endemic Welwitschia mirabilis.

appeared strange to Don and his warmly clad rescue team, all snug within their down jackets. And at last I could enjoy that cup of steaming coffee . . .

I had been very fortunate not to have come off worse, and I hope that in recounting this experience, other trailists, irrespective of their skills and training, will be careful not to fall into similar traps.

384. The Ugab River Hiking Trail

SKELETON COAST PARK

AUTHORITY-IN-CHARGE: Directorate of Nature Conservation and Recreation Resorts, Department of Agriculture and Nature Conservation, Namibia.
SIZE: 1 690 000 hectares.

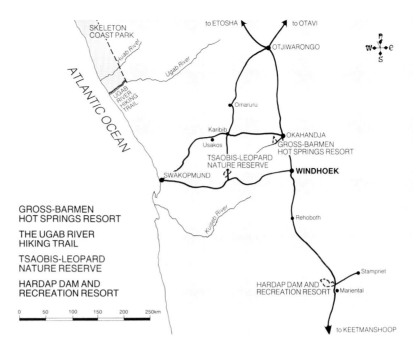

GROSS-BARMEN HOT SPRINGS RESORT

THE UGAB RIVER HIKING TRAIL

TSAOBIS-LEOPARD NATURE RESERVE

HARDAP DAM AND RECREATION RESORT

LENGTH/DURATION: 50 km (variable)/ 3 days.
MAIN ATTRACTIONS: Rugged wilderness-like environment; fascinating geology; canyonlands; sand dunes; unique desert flora; large game, and smaller animals uniquely adapted to desert life; interesting birdlife.
FACILITIES/AMENITIES: Hikers are provided with drinking water *en route*, firewood, and transport from endpoint to beginning of trail; Mile 108 camp-site can accommodate hikers before they start the trail.
PERTINENT INFORMATION: Hikers must form their own groups (minimum of 6 and maximum of 8 people); hikers meet at 09h00 at the Ugab River Gate (43 km north of Mile 108 camp-site). Trails run every second and fourth Tuesday of the month. Medical certificate issued 40 days prior to commencement of hike is required, and is checked at the Ugab River mouth at the start of the trail.
AVAILABLE LITERATURE: Trail information sheet available from the Directorate; brochure and map in process of being

compiled; 'The Ugab River Trail' by Horst Windisch, *Great Outdoors*, No. 54, November/December 1985.
CLIMATE: Days: hot with cooling sea breezes and overcast mornings. Nights: clear to foggy and cold. Freak rainy weather possible. Mid-May to July (after rainy season), best months to hike.

Although the Ugab River guided trail can extend 50 kilometres inland from the mouth of the river, it is tailored to suit group stamina, interests, enthusiasm and prevailing weather conditions. Located in the dry river course of the Ugab River Valley, the trail actually runs along the southern boundary of the Skeleton Coast Park, an immense area of more than a million and a half hectares, composed of sand dunes, gravel plains and desolate, wild coastline. Inland the park boasts a rare, silent beauty of jagged mountains, canyons and abundant wildlife.

Trailists experience a good slice of this unique corner of Africa. As they follow the river course upstream from the mouth, an ever-changing landscape emerges. The open, granitic gravel plains are followed by folded rocky outcrops composed of biotite schists (a metamorphic rock of dark brown to black mica) interlayered with marble bands. These mountains are sliced by 125 million-year-old dolerite dykes and are edged on the southern river banks by sand dunes. Overnight camps in this impressive canyon landscape are chosen at random, often in a rocky side canyon under a large ana (*Acacia albida*) tree.

Desert flora and fauna compete with landform for the hiker's attention. Camel thorn and ebony trees provide shade and shelter while shrubs such as brack-bush, Bushman's candle and euphorbias, and smaller plants such as the vygies, are common. Along the marshy areas of the riverbed, vari-

ous sedge-like plants and reeds form evergreen oases.

Trailists have a good chance of spotting gemsbok, springbok, Hartmann's zebra, baboons and even leopards, although the latter are common only after the river has flooded. Cheetah, lion, rhinoceros, brown hyaena, blackbacked jackal, warthog, Cape hare, striped polecat and honey badger, as well as a healthy snake population (including the horned adder), lizards, chameleons and insects especially adapted to desert conditions are present.

Bird-watchers will be delighted by ostrich, Rüppel's korhaan and Ludwig's bustard, resident raptors such as augur buzzards, chanting goshawks and rock kestrels, lappetfaced vultures and, of course, all the smaller birds of bush and river valley.

385. Gross-Barmen Hot Springs Resort

NEAR OKAHANDJA

AUTHORITY-IN-CHARGE: Directorate of Nature Conservation and Recreation Resorts, Department of Agriculture and Nature Conservation, Namibia.
MAIN ATTRACTIONS: Ruins of old mission station; riverine walks; game; water-birds.
FACILITIES/AMENITIES: Nature rambles; large indoor thermal bath; open-air swimming pool (tepid water); air-conditioned luxury units; small bungalows; restaurant; shop and filling station; tenniquoit and tennis courts.
PERTINENT INFORMATION: Site of old Rhenish mission station, originally known as Otjikango. The station was renamed

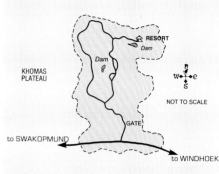

temperatures falling to below freezing. Rain possible October to December (short rains) and mid-January to April (frequent thunderstorms). Dry and cloudless at other times.

387. Daan Viljoen Game Park

NEAR WINDHOEK

AUTHORITY-IN-CHARGE: Directorate of Nature Conservation and Recreation Resorts, Department of Agriculture and Nature Conservation, Namibia.
SIZE: 4 951 hectares.
MAIN ATTRACTIONS: Abundant wildlife and birdlife, especially when the dam is full; rambling anywhere in the reserve is permitted; game-viewing drives; fishing, when there is water in the dam; sensitive application of landscape architecture techniques.
FACILITIES/AMENITIES: Marked trails; bungalows; caravan and camping sites; picnic sites; restaurant and shop; swimming pool.
AVAILABLE LITERATURE: *Daan Viljoen*, brochure with sketch map; bird and tree guide, available on site.

Situated 24 kilometres west of Windhoek at an altitude of 2 000 metres, the Daan Viljoen Game Park is an excellent stopover *en route* to other hiking and scenic areas in Namibia.

Essentially an area for rambling, bird-watching and game-viewing, the reserve is bounded on the west by the rolling hills of the Khomas plateau and in the east by the Windhoek Valley. The skills of landscape architects and planners in creating this man-made oasis in such stark surroundings are impressive, for they have transformed the land into a tiny wildlife paradise.

Trails are laid out, and the rambler is also free to explore the hills, ravines and precipices at will, where he is quite likely to see a number of the mammals that typify the

---

Barmen after the German town where the missionaries studied theology. (The second European house in Hereroland can still be seen in Otjikango.) The mission station closed in 1890 after exhaustive attacks by the Hottentots on the Hereros. Ramblers can walk anywhere along the riverbed and rocky outcrops.
AVAILABLE LITERATURE: Included in general tourist promotion brochures.
CLIMATE: Summer: hot days, cool nights. Winter: warm days, possibility of pre-dawn temperatures falling to below freezing. Rain possible October to December (short rains) and mid-January to April (frequent thunderstorms). Dry and cloudless at other times.

Above: The dam at Daan Viljoen Game Park has created an oasis in otherwise stark surroundings. It attracts abundant wildlife and birdlife during times of high water.

Opposite page, left: The Namib is full of surprises, and only the sensitive hiker can fully appreciate its intricate nature in a seemingly barren landscape.

Opposite page, right: Rambling in the impressive gorges of the Sesriem Canyon.

386. Tsaobis-Leopard Nature Reserve

NEAR KARIBIB, see map page 319

AUTHORITY-IN-CHARGE: Tsaobis-Leopard Nature Reserve, P.O. Box 143, Karibib 9000, Namibia.
SIZE: 35 000 hectares.
MAIN ATTRACTIONS: Chuos Mountains; leopards and other game, including giraffe, kudu, blue wildebeest, red hartebeest and springbok.
FACILITIES/AMENITIES: Horse-riding; rest camp with air-conditioned bungalows; swimming pool; four-wheel drive vehicle tours; nocturnal drives.
PERTINENT INFORMATION: The reserve was established in 1969 by Dr August Juchli, a Swiss conservationist, to breed and study leopards. The leopards are not readily observed on trails or tours.
AVAILABLE LITERATURE: Available from the reserve.
CLIMATE: Summer: hot days, cool nights. Winter: warm days, possibility of pre-dawn

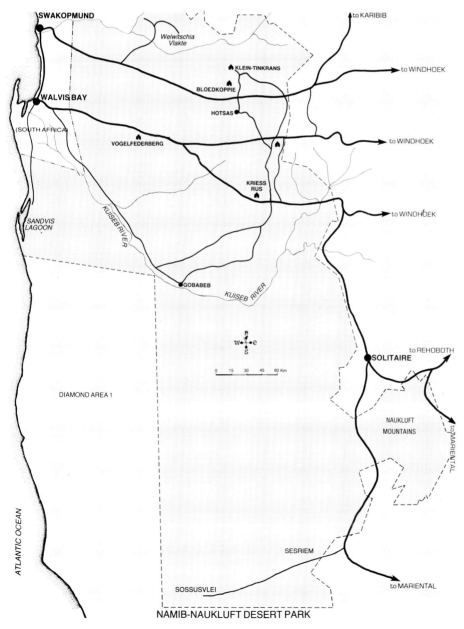

NAMIB-NAUKLUFT DESERT PARK

Namibian highlands – mountain zebra, gemsbok, kudu, wildebeest, red hartebeest, eland, springbok, impala and baboon. Bush-dwelling birds and waterfowl (when the dam is full) are also attractions. Trees are labelled with their national tree list numbers. The rock art, once a highlight of the region, has been vandalized beyond recognition.

388. Namib-Naukluft Desert Park

WEST-CENTRAL NAMIBIA

AUTHORITY-IN-CHARGE: Directorate of Nature Conservation and Recreation Resorts, Department of Agriculture and Nature Conservation, Namibia.
SIZE: 2 340 150 hectares.
MAIN ATTRACTIONS: Coastal desert and escarpment, including Sandvis Lagoon, Sossusvlei (reputedly the highest dunes in the world), the Kuiseb and Sesriem canyons with their abundant wildlife, and the Naukluft Mountain massif; Welwitchias (ancient and unique plants).
FACILITIES/AMENITIES: Naukluft camp-site with cold water, cold showers, toilets, cooking places, firewood and dishwashing facilities; camp-sites in Namib section of the park do not supply firewood or water.
PERTINENT INFORMATION: Permits necessary to sleep in or drive through the park, obtainable from the Directorate; permits required when travelling on sign-posted roads for the Namib section of the park, obtainable from the tourist office in Swakopmund. Restrictions applicable to the Naukluft section: one group of 8 people per camping site per night; four sites available, maximum of 3 nights per visit. Sossusvlei permits day visitors only. Camping at

Sesriem Canyon is allowed but no facilities are provided.

AVAILABLE LITERATURE: *Namib*, brochure; printed materials available from the Directorate; see *SWA Accommodation Guide for Tourists* for permit information.

CLIMATE: Average annual rainfall: 75 millimetres.

In 1978 the borders of the Namib Park and the highland plateau of the Naukluft Mountain Zebra Park were 'merged' to form one huge reserve.

Camping and rambling are allowed in most places in the Namib section, providing that you have obtained the necessary permit. Particularly interesting are the Sandvis Lagoon, Sossusvlei, the Sesriem Canyon and the Kuiseb Canyon, which are richly endowed with unusual wildlife such as the barking gecko (heard at night), the desert gerbil, and the Namib chameleon, which preys on desert toktokkies (a species of wingless tenebrionid beetle).

A three-day hiking trail of approximately 52 kilometres is planned in the Naukluft section of the park, originally founded for the conservation of the mountain zebra. The trail includes gorges, caves and springs deep in the dolomite formations. Contact the Directorate for details.

389. Hardap Dam and Recreation Resort

NEAR MARIENTAL, see map page 319

AUTHORITY-IN-CHARGE: Directorate of Nature Conservation and Recreation Resorts, Department of Agriculture and Nature Conservation, Namibia.
SIZE: 25 000 hectares.
MAIN ATTRACTIONS: Rich birdlife on dam; scenic setting of stone koppies and thorn trees.
FACILITIES/AMENITIES: Nature rambles; fishing; game-viewing drives; game paths for hiking; modern rest camp with

bungalows, restaurant, and caravan and camping sites; watersports.
PERTINENT INFORMATION: Motorists in the game reserve on the dam's southern shore may leave their vehicles and ramble wherever they like.
AVAILABLE LITERATURE: Included in general tourist promotion brochures.
CLIMATE: Summer: hot days, cool nights. Winter: warm days; possibility of pre-dawn temperatures falling to below freezing. Rain possible October to December (short rains) and mid-January to April (frequent thunderstorms); dry and cloudless at other times.

390. Fish River Canyon

SOUTHERN NAMIBIA

AUTHORITY-IN-CHARGE: Directorate of Nature Conservation and Recreation Resorts, Department of Agriculture and Nature Conservation, Namibia.
LENGTH/DURATION: Approximately 86 km/ 4 days; can vary from 2 to 5 days.
MAIN ATTRACTIONS: Spectacular and unique canyon scenery; hot springs; wilderness atmosphere.
FACILITIES/AMENITIES: In canyon, none. Main look-out provides picnic hut, two sunshades, covered braai facilities, toilets and sleeping shelters, each accommodating 10 people. Ai-Ais Hot Springs, at the end of the hike, provides a wide range of

accommodation and amenities, including camping and caravan sites, shop, restaurant, postal agency, swimming pool, tennis court, playground and a petrol station.
PERTINENT INFORMATION: For long hikes into the canyon permits are necessary, obtainable from the Directorate (applications must be accompanied by a medical certificate, and should be made not more than one year and not less than one month before the starting date). The hiking season runs from May to the end of August. Group size is limited to between 3 and 40 people (minimum age 10 years); no-one may hike alone. Water supply varies with rainfall; mosquitoes can be a problem at times. Fishing by permit only, obtainable at Ai-Ais. It is best to leave your car at Ai-Ais and get a lift to the look-out point the day before the descent.
AVAILABLE LITERATURE: *Fish River Canyon Hiker's Guide*, information sheet with map, and *Ai-Ais*, brochure, both issued by the Directorate; *Fish River Canyon*, map by Mapcape, published by Camp and Climb (Pty) Ltd; *Fish River Canyon and Ai-Ais Hot Springs*, AA Bulletin TBE-52; 'Hike the Canyon, Fish River Canyon, S-W Africa' by T. Payne, *Great Outdoors*, No. 24, March 1982, pp. 6-9.
CLIMATE: Hot days with warm to cool nights. Freak rainy weather possible during the hiking season.

Descending into geological history, experiencing magnificent sunrises and sunsets, being totally surrounded by the Fish River's sensational wind- and water-hewn sculptures: this is what hiking the Fish River Canyon is all about, an endeavour which will

FISH RIVER CANYON

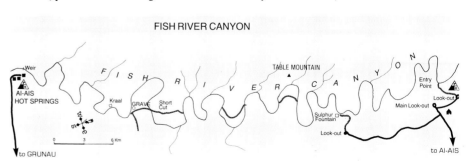

remain one of the 'specials' in your mountaineering accomplishments.

The Fish River rises in the Naukluft Mountains, south-east of Swakopmund, and travels 800 kilometres before flowing into the Orange River. For approximately 65 kilometres along its route, the river has sliced an impressive gash through the surrounding plateau. The canyon is actually a combination of two geological processes: the upper section, a huge trough with a flattish floor, is the result of faulting, while the lower is attributed to water erosion as the Fish River has cut back into the upper canyon's floor. Many other natural eroding forces, such as sand-blasting winds, have worked on the canyon's sides, carving out crags, buttresses and turrets in the ancient rock strata. These eroding forces reveal, in the deepest parts, the Archaean granite and gneisses of the Basement Complex – of rock more than 2 600 million years old. (The Grand Canyon in the United States, to which the Fish River Canyon is often compared, has its oldest rocks dating back only 2 000 million years.)

Traditionally, the hike through the canyon begins at the main viewing point, where you scramble down an eroded track for approximately 45 minutes to the canyon's floor. Once you arrive at the Fish River, simply follow its meandering course, zigzagging across the stream to be on whichever bank offers the easiest walking. The hike is slightly downhill all the way; the only factors presenting physical difficulties are the stretches of small round rock or soft sandy banks. The amount of water in the riverbed often determines the mood of the hike, the difficulty of the river crossings and the quantities of water hikers must carry.

Although there are no obligatory overnight places, the best areas are obvious. The most-used is an area of hot sulphur springs among some isolated palm trees. These palms are believed to have been planted during the First World War by escaping German prisoners.

There are plenty of birds in the canyon, especially water-associated species such as the fish eagle and pied kingfisher. Mammals are not frequently seen but it is possible to spot klipspringer, dassie, baboon and mountain zebra. Fishermen may try their luck for yellowfish, catfish, carp or blue kurper, while trailists more interested in plants can identify the scattered vegetation which varies from the unusual kokerboom and wild fig to the many species of thorn tree.

Most hikers terminate their hike when the river reaches Ai-Ais, a thermal spring rich in mineral waters, around which a spa and resort complex have been built.

Opposite page, left: A kokerboom forest.
Opposite page, right: Hiking in the wilderness of the Fish River Canyon.
Left: The stark landscape of Namibia.

MALAWI

Malawi is a small country: 901 kilometres long and varying from 81 to 161 kilometres wide, little more than twice the size of the Kruger National Park. Bordered by Tanzania in the north, Mozambique in the east and Zambia in the west, this country embraces a diversity of natural environments. Lake Malawi with its shores of long sweeping beaches, rocky headlands and sheltered coves, the highland plateau of Nyika, and the often mist-shrouded mountain massifs of Zomba and Mulanje, are just a few of the natural features in this country of limitless hiking and mountaineering potential.

Although Malawi is one of the most densely populated countries in Africa, this does not in the least detract from its value as an outdoors haven. The people are among the most helpful and courteous I have met and their natural charm is likely to remain an outstanding impression of your visit. There is no doubt in my mind why Malawi is affectionately known as 'the warm heart of Africa'.

All visitors require valid passports; some nationals (including South Africans) do not need visas. In general, immigration formalities are minimal for visitors intending to stay less than three months.

Malawi lies not far south of the equator and there are times of the year, especially along the shores of the lake and in the Shire River Valley in the summer months, when the sticky heat is unpleasant. However, because of the country's diverse topography, you can always escape into the high mountains with their cool glades and streams which provide a beautiful retreat from the oppressive humidity of the lowlands. Most rain falls from December to March, and the frequent thunderstorms take the edge off the heat; from time to time the 'Chiperone', a cool misty cloud, blows up from the Mozambique plains. From June to October the weather is generally cool and dry and, in many ways, this is the finest time of the year for hiking.

Malawi has two social codes which are surprisingly well enforced and apply equally to visitors and residents. In public places, women must wear skirts which cover their knees; although this is unnecessary in out-of-the-way places such as Zomba, Mulanje, Dedza, Viphya and Nyika, as well as the lake shore resorts, it is always wise to carry a skirt with you, especially if you are likely to walk through villages. A simple cotton skirt that can double as a pillow case when camping overnight on mountaineering trips is ·fine. The other restriction applies to men's hairstyles: long hair (covering the neck and ears) is illegal.

ECOLOGICAL ZONE: RIFT VALLEY

391. Lengwe National Park

SOUTHERN MALAWI

AUTHORITY-IN-CHARGE: Department of National Parks and Wildlife, Malawi.
SIZE: 12 950 hectares.
LENGTH: 2,5 km.
MAIN ATTRACTIONS: Diverse wildlife, including buffalo and Livingstone's suni; nyala are plentiful and easily seen; prolific birdlife.
FACILITIES/AMENITIES: Self-guided nature trail; observation hides; picnic shelter; limited chalet accommodation; network of game-viewing drives.
PERTINENT INFORMATION: Entrance is free. Permission to walk the trail is necessary, obtainable from the warden when at the park.
AVAILABLE LITERATURE: Booklet for the nature trail, available from the National Faunal Preservation Society of Malawi.
CLIMATE: May to October, dry season. November/December to March/April, rainy season.

Lengwe National Park, a flat, lowland alluvial plain covered by thicket and riparian forest, is a fantastic little game reserve situated 74 kilometres south of Blantyre. Its wildlife is abundant and diverse, but of special interest is the nyala. This large, beautifully marked antelope is found in great numbers in the park and here reaches the northernmost limit of its distribution.

Livingstone's suni and the crested guineafowl are other species with limited distributions which can be readily seen. Sharp eyes will spot them drinking at forested water-holes. Buffalo, lion, bushbuck, kudu, hartebeest, impala, duiker, samango monkey and banded mongoose are some of the common species.

The National Faunal Preservation Society of Malawi has produced a guide booklet, designed for use by school parties, to accompany their 2,5-kilometre nature trail. Otherwise, walking is restricted to the short tracks leading from the carpark to the hides, and around the chalets. Ask the warden for permission to ramble elsewhere.

392. Elephant Marsh

CHIKWAWA

AUTHORITY-IN-CHARGE: Department of National Parks and Wildlife, Malawi.
SIZE: 18 km at widest point, 65 km long.
MAIN ATTRACTIONS: Huge semi-permanent marsh: channels, lagoons and pools; waterbirds and small animal life; hippos and crocodiles; 300 species of birds.
FACILITIES/AMENITIES: Walking is possible on a railway track which is built on raised ground running through the area, giving bird-watchers a dry, high vantage point.
PERTINENT INFORMATION: Watch out for trains. Mosquitoes can be irritating.
AVAILABLE LITERATURE: Contact the Malawi Department of Tourism.
CLIMATE: May to October, dry season. November/December to March/April, rainy season.

Above: The beautifully marked nyala is plentiful in Lengwe National Park.

Opposite page: Water lilies float on Elephant Marsh, a good place for bird-watchers.

393. *Thyolo Mountain*

SOUTH OF BLANTYRE

AUTHORITY-IN-CHARGE: Ministry of Forestry and Natural Resources, Malawi.
MAIN ATTRACTIONS: Prolific birdlife, including greenheaded oriole; significant area of sub-montane evergreen forest.
FACILITIES/AMENITIES: Nature walks on clear paths running the length of the forest.
PERTINENT INFORMATION: Thyolo Mountain rises to 1 462 metres. It is located 50 km south of Blantyre. Permission to enter necessary, obtainable from Satemwa Tea Estate on arrival.
AVAILABLE LITERATURE: None.
CLIMATE: May to October, dry season. November/December to March/April, rainy season.

394. *Mulanje Mountain*

SOUTHERN REGION

AUTHORITY-IN-CHARGE: Ministry of Forestry and Natural Resources, Malawi.
SIZE: Mulanje Massif, including Michese Mountain, covers 64 000 hectares.
DURATION: Hiking trips lasting 7-9 days recommended.
MAIN ATTRACTIONS: Beautiful mountain area; montane evergreen forest, including the endemic Mulanje cedar; wildflowers and birdlife; trout fishing.
FACILITIES/AMENITIES: Numerous footpaths and firebreaks. Local porters available. Six huts (on Lichenya and Thuchila plateaux, and in Chambe, Ruo (Chinzama Hut), Sombani and Madzeka basins) with tables, chairs, cooking places, firewood, water, emergency first-aid kit and latrines; huts accommodate 8-20 people (depending on hut); forestry cottage at Chambe accommodates 6 people (see Pertinent Information); Red Route shelter (at base of Sapitwa Peak), made of corrugated steel with an earthern floor, accommodates 8 people, no amenities provided.
PERTINENT INFORMATION: Huts have watchmen who will perform minor chores and who should be tipped. The Malawi Mountain Club maintains its own equipment (beds, mattresses, lamps, utensils and porters' blankets) under lock and key at each hut; club members or reciprocal members can obtain keys. Porters are paid according to prescribed rates. The forestry cottage at Chambe was destroyed by fire, so confirm its replacement before booking. A new shelter, the Minunu Shelter, is proposed, and will be a basic

LENGWE NATIONAL PARK, ELEPHANT MARSH, THYOLO MOUNTAIN, CHIRADZULU MOUNTAIN, SOCHE MOUNTAIN, NDIRANDE MOUNTAIN, DEDZA MOUNTAIN, DZALANYAMA RANGE, NYIKA NATIONAL PARK

structure of wood (contact the authorities for details). Huts should be booked well in advance by writing to The Chief Forester, P.O. Box 50, Mulanje, Malawi; confirmation letters should be carried and must be produced on request. Payments should be made in cash at the Likhubula forestry office before setting out. Michese Mountain is situated to the north-east of Mulanje's highest peak, Sapitwa. It is separated from Mulanje by a broad, high valley known as the Fort Lister Gap.

AVAILABLE LITERATURE: *Guide to the Mulanje Massif*, Frank Eastwood, 1979, fully comprehensive book covering ecology, general visitor information, routes, maps and photographs; *Mulanje – Advice for Climbers*, Malawi Mountain Club; *Mulanje Mountain*, 1:30 000 topographic map with some written information.

CLIMATE: Mid-April to end of July is the best climbing season, although wet, misty conditions and night frosts can occur. August to November is hot and dry, with views hazy from bush fire smoke. November to April, thunderstorms can cause flash floods. Mid-April to end of September, 'Chiperone' possible (*Chiperone* is the local name for the thick, wet, cold mist that reduces visibility and may cover the mountain for three to five days).

'a mist-shrouded cedarclad granite mass
emerged from the depths of the earth
as a crystallized fountain of living rock
conceived and nurtured in a primeval fiery
    womb
and given birth at its appointed
    Cosmic time . . .'

Deon Krige

So begins Deon's account of our expedition to Mount Mulanje, the highest massif in south-central Africa. One of the best aspects of Mulanje is that any reasonably fit person can hike and climb on the mountain, as the steep footpaths to the plateau, requiring a 1 000-1 500-metre ascent, can be negotiated with the aid of porters. Once on the 1 830-2 133-metre plateau, the numerous footpaths and firebreaks allow for relatively easy

going. Huts are approximately a half day's walk apart, allowing time to climb Mulanje's high peaks, 20 of which reach 2 500 metres or more. The highest point, Sapitwa (3 002 m), is a reasonable day's round-trip from the Red Route shelter, and involves considerable rock scrambling. The route is marked with painted arrows.

Mulanje is blessed with such topographic and ecological diversity that everyone, from the nature explorer to the rock climber, is well catered for. Divided by the Ruo River's deep valley, the 26- by 22-kilometre massif consists of rolling, grassy uplands; deep, forested kloofs and gullies; rocky, boulder-

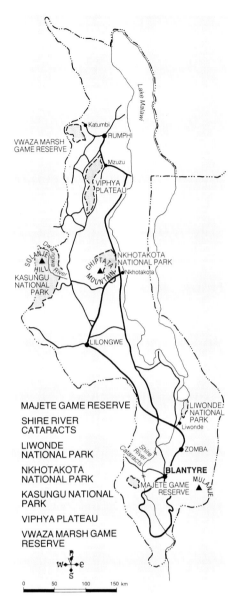

MAJETE GAME RESERVE

SHIRE RIVER
CATARACTS

LIWONDE
NATIONAL PARK

NKHOTAKOTA
NATIONAL PARK

KASUNGU NATIONAL
PARK

VIPHYA PLATEAU

VWAZA MARSH GAME
RESERVE

of indiscriminate hunting, the latter because of the altitude. Bird-watching is both exciting and frustrating when you try to spy on forest species. The hiker who sits quietly near a path in the rainforest may be fortunate enough to spot the Rameron pigeon, Knysna loerie, whitetailed flycatcher and other elusive species. The augur buzzard, lanner falcon and rock kestrel are frequently seen on the wing.

F. Eastwood's *Guide to the Mulanje Massif* (1979) provides a list by habitat of commonly seen bird species. Lizards and butterflies, many endemic to Mulanje, are often observed.

Also in his guide, Eastwood comprehensively describes routes to the huts from the plains, climbs to the peaks from the plateau, and rock climbs. I recommend a 7-9 day circular route of Mulanje, sleeping in each of the forestry huts, with mornings or afternoons left to climb the peaks and explore the forests and ravines.

395. *Majete Game Reserve*

CHIKWAWA

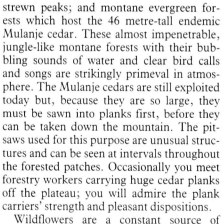

AUTHORITY-IN-CHARGE: Department of National Parks and Wildlife, Malawi.
MAIN ATTRACTIONS: Kapichira Falls; elephant, leopard, kudu, waterbuck and sable antelope; water-birds; hilly area of miombo and riverine woodland.
FACILITIES/AMENITIES: Guided walks with game guards to prime game-viewing areas; minimal camping facilities (wood-burning stove); shallow bathing pools in the river.
PERTINENT INFORMATION: The reserve is

situated at the confluence of the Shire and Wankurumadzi rivers. Four-wheel drive vehicles needed for access during the wet season. Permission to enter necessary, obtainable from The Chief Game Warden, Department of National Parks and Wildlife, P.O. Box 30131, Lilongwe 3, Malawi.
AVAILABLE LITERATURE: Contact the Malawi Department of Tourism.
CLIMATE: May to October, dry season. November/December to March/April, rainy season.

396. *Shire River Cataracts*

CHIKWAWA

AUTHORITY-IN-CHARGE: For information: Malawi Department of Tourism.
LENGTH: Cataracts extend for 64 km.
MAIN ATTRACTIONS: Cataracts; fishing for tigerfish and vundu; grave of Richard Thornton (Livingstone's geologist, 1863), national monument.
FACILITIES/AMENITIES: Nature walks on footpaths; signposted roads.
PERTINENT INFORMATION: Some roads are not recommended for use after heavy rains. The most accessible of the falls are

Opposite page, top: Enormous tree ferns line the footpaths in the evergreen forests of Mulanje.

Opposite page, centre: Young boys waiting in the Mulanje foothills, hoping for employment as porters.

Opposite page, bottom: Elephant in Majete Game Reserve.

Below: Livingstone's cataracts on the Shire River, a formidable barrier to water travel.

strewn peaks; and montane evergreen forests which host the 46 metre-tall endemic Mulanje cedar. These almost impenetrable, jungle-like montane forests with their bubbling sounds of water and clear bird calls and songs are strikingly primeval in atmosphere. The Mulanje cedars are still exploited today but, because they are so large, they must be sawn into planks first, before they can be taken down the mountain. The pit-saws used for this purpose are unusual structures and can be seen at intervals throughout the forested patches. Occasionally you meet forestry workers carrying huge cedar planks off the plateau; you will admire the plank carriers' strength and pleasant dispositions.

Wildflowers are a constant source of beauty. As a result of the varying altitudes, aspects and moisture regimes, the species are highly diversified; some flowers are endemic, while many resemble those found in Cape fynbos.

Mammals and snakes are not numerous on the Mulanje plateau, the former because

Kapachira Falls (southern end) and
Mfumba Falls (northernmost major falls).
AVAILABLE LITERATURE: Contact the
Malawi Department of Tourism; included
in *Malawi: A Guide for the Visitor*, brochure
available from the Malawi Department of
Tourism.
CLIMATE: May to October, dry season.
November/December to March/April, rainy
season.

397. *Chiradzulu Mountain*

NEAR BLANTYRE, see map page 327

AUTHORITY-IN-CHARGE: Ministry of
Forestry and Natural Resources, Malawi.
MAIN ATTRACTIONS: *Brachystegia* woodland;
sub-montane evergreen forest; montane
grassland.
FACILITIES/AMENITIES: None.
PERTINENT INFORMATION: Chiradzulu
Mountain rises to 1 772 metres in the Shire
highlands; footpaths are indistinct.
AVAILABLE LITERATURE: Contact the
Malawi Department of Tourism.
CLIMATE: May to October, dry season.
November/December to March/April, rainy
season.

398. *Soche Mountain*

BLANTYRE, see map page 327

AUTHORITY-IN-CHARGE: Ministry of
Forestry and Natural Resources, Malawi.
MAIN ATTRACTIONS: *Brachystegia* woodland;
sub-montane evergreen forest; riparian
woodland.
FACILITIES/AMENITIES: Nature walks on two
paths to the summit (1 533 m); the red route
is approximately 1 km, the yellow route is
longer and more obscure.

PERTINENT INFORMATION: The forests are
under threat from exploiters of wood for
fire.
AVAILABLE LITERATURE: None.
CLIMATE: May to October, dry season.
November/December to March/April, rainy
season.

399. *Zomba Plateau*

SOUTHERN REGION

AUTHORITY-IN-CHARGE: Forestry
Department, Malawi.
SIZE: 13 300 hectares.
MAIN ATTRACTIONS: Panoramic views;
waterfalls and kloofs; indigenous forest
patches; abundant birdlife; fishing for
rainbow trout.
FACILITIES/AMENITIES: Two self-guided
nature walks; 24 km of circular drives with
look-out at KuChawe Inn; camp-site with
water and toilets, within walking distance of
the hotel.
PERTINENT INFORMATION: The entire

Zomba Plateau is a forest reserve.
AVAILABLE LITERATURE: *Welcome to the
Zomba Plateau and KuChawe Inn*,
information pamphlet with sketch map;
Zomba Mountain – A Walker's Guide, H. M.
Cundy; nature trail booklets available from
KuChawe Inn, P.O. Box 71, Zomba,
Malawi, or the National Faunal Preservation
Society of Malawi.
CLIMATE: Similar to Mulanje Mountain (see
page 328).

From the town of Zomba, a narrow tarred
road winds steeply upwards through thick
forest to the top of Zomba Plateau, a syenitic
rock massif rising 1 000 metres above the
surrounding plains. All along the nature
trails, roads and climbing routes that criss-
cross the plateau, the hiker is rewarded with
magnificent views. Overnight accommodation is available at the hotel and camp-site.

The plateau is a forest reserve with
streams, pools, pine and cedar stands, indigenous montane evergreen forest and grassland. Various peaks rise from the 1 830-
metre table, notably Chiradzulu or Zomba
Peak (2 088 metres), Norimbe and Chagwa.
Rock climbing is possible on Zomba's steep

ZOMBA PLATEAU

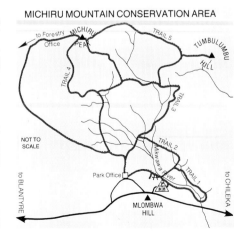

MICHIRU MOUNTAIN CONSERVATION AREA

cliffs. To the east and south, the plateau is bounded by a sheer 762-metre scarp, while to the west it is bounded by one of the main Rift Valley faults – a spectacular 1 220-metre drop to the Shire River Valley floor.

The Chingwe's Hole Nature Trail, with its informative guide to the natural history of the plateau (especially emphasizing orchids, succulents, fungi and birds), is one of my favourite short walks. It begins at Chingwe's Hole on the western side of Zomba Plateau. This and other nature trails are projects of the National Faunal Preservation Society of Malawi, which has done a fine job promoting ecological awareness of natural areas remaining on the plateau.

Zomba Plateau is easily reached from Blantyre, Malawi's principal commercial, industrial and communications centre.

400. Ndirande Mountain

BLANTYRE, see map page 327

AUTHORITY-IN-CHARGE: Ministry of Forestry and Natural Resources, Malawi.
MAIN ATTRACTIONS: Rock climbing; pine plantations; riparian forest; sub-montane evergreen forest.
FACILITIES/AMENITIES: Nature walks; short, dry, steep 1-km gully ascent to the summit.
PERTINENT INFORMATION: *Ndirande* means 'the sleeping man mountain'; it rises to 1 164 metres. For information: Department of Forestry, Malawi.
AVAILABLE LITERATURE: None.
CLIMATE: May to October, dry season. November/December to April, rainy season.

401. Michiru Mountain Conservation Area

BLANTYRE

AUTHORITY-IN-CHARGE: Ministry of Forestry and Natural Resources, Malawi.
SIZE: 5 000 hectares.
DURATION: Five trails varying from 30 minutes to 5 hours.
MAIN ATTRACTIONS: Largest natural woodlands near Blantyre (*Brachystegia* forest, riparian forest and sub-montane forest); splendid views from ridge walks; 200 species of birds; mammal life.
FACILITIES/AMENITIES: Environmental education project; marked footpaths; picnic and braai site; overnight camp-sites in cleared areas; curio shop at office.
PERTINENT INFORMATION: Bookings are not necessary, but large groups are asked to give advance notice of their arrival. For information: Michiru Mountain Park, P.O. Box 619, Blantyre, Malawi.
AVAILABLE LITERATURE: Information sheet and map, available from Michiru Co-ordinator, Michiru Mountain Park, P.O. Box 619, Blantyre, Malawi.
CLIMATE: May to October, dry season. November/December to March/April, rainy season.

The Michiru Mountain Conservation Area, adjacent to Blantyre and on the edge of the Rift Valley, is an exciting environmental education and recreation centre. This scientifically managed, diverse area comprises the largest natural woodlands near Blantyre: steep slopes of *Brachystegia* forest, riparian forest in stream valleys, and patches of sub-montane forest near the 1 473-metre summit. *Eucalyptus* and pine plantations are also present. Ridge walking yields superb views over the plains to the Kirk Range, the mountains around Ncheu and Dedza, as well as to Mulanje and Zomba.

As an environmental education project, three areas receive emphasis: forestry, farming and wildlife. The forestry reserve portrays a good example of successful wood plantations. The farming area covers about 400 hectares devoted to raising dairy cattle for milk, butter and cream. In addition to maize and bananas grown for silage, several freshwater ponds provide good waterfowl habitats.

The wildlife section has five main trails. Trail 1, along the lower part of the Mikwawa River, points out the park's indigenous trees. Trails 2 and 3 wind about the base of Michiru Mountain and into the Mikwawa River Valley, passing hyaena caves, and crossing the river and its streams many times. The fourth trail ascends the peak, while the fifth trail runs along the mountain's summit to Tumbulumbu Hill. Night hiking to see nocturnal animals such as hyaena, leopard, serval, wildcat, civet, genet, jackal, porcupine, bushpig and galago, is permitted.

402. Liwonde National Park

LIWONDE, see map page 329

AUTHORITY-IN-CHARGE: Department of National Parks and Wildlife, Malawi.
MAIN ATTRACTIONS: Shire River scenery; swamp, floodplain, palm savannah, woodland and thicket; elephant, hippo, crocodile, lion, leopard, warthog and sable antelope; rich and varied birdlife, including Lilian's lovebird.
FACILITIES/AMENITIES: Guided nature walks with game scout on untarred network of

roads; boats permitted on river; rondavel camp on Shire River with basic facilities only, so guests must bring their own food, bedding and cooking and eating utensils.
PERTINENT INFORMATION: The park is situated south of Lake Malawi.
AVAILABLE LITERATURE: *Wildlife in Malawi*, brochure available from the Malawi Department of Tourism.
CLIMATE: April to November, dry season. Best time to spot game is second half of dry season, when it is concentrated along the river.

Opposite page: The wide expanse of Malawi, seen from the Zomba Plateau.

Top: The yellow baboon has lighter coloration than its southern relative, the chacma.

Above: A spotted eagle owl, seen along the trails in the Michiru Mountain Conservation Area.

LAKE MALAWI NATIONAL PARK

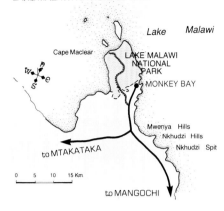

403. *Lake Malawi National Park*

CAPE MACLEAR

AUTHORITY-IN-CHARGE: Department of National Parks and Wildlife, Malawi.
SIZE: 8 800 hectares.
MAIN ATTRACTIONS: Nankumba Peninsula and offshore islands; over 450 species of tropical freshwater fish (largest number of species of fish in any freshwater lake in the world); dramatic lake scenery, beaches, dunes and reed marshes; prolific birdlife and mammal life; missionary graves at Cape Maclear (historical monument).
FACILITIES/AMENITIES: Camp-site, with a bar but no food, at Cape Maclear; other facilities are planned; hotels nearby.
PERTINENT INFORMATION: Lake Malawi National Park is the first park in the world to give protection to a tropical deep-water rift valley lake.
AVAILABLE LITERATURE: Contact the Malawi Department of Tourism.
CLIMATE: Lake Malawi receives less rain than the rest of the country, approximately 80-300 millimetres monthly. The surface water temperature varies from 24 °C to 28 °C. Average temperatures vary from 21 °C to 27 °C.

Created in December 1980, Lake Malawi National Park is the first park in the world to give protection to a tropical deep-water rift valley lake. The park incorporates the Nankumba Peninsula and its offshore islands, the Mwenya and Nkhudzi Hills and Nkhudzi Spit, the latter a low-lying marshland and sandy bar. Although no formal trails have yet been established, this area is wonderful rambling country, and the lake's crystal-clear waters and dazzling tropical fish make snorkelling a unique experience.

A three- to four-hour ramble traverses the headland from Monkey Bay to Cape Maclear. Although this is a hot, dry walk, following inland valleys and wooded rocky hills instead of the shoreline, once you reach Cape Maclear you can refresh yourself in Lake Malawi.

The lake contains the largest number of fish species of any lake in the world – over 450, of which about 350 are endemic. The brightly coloured 'mbuna' fish of the Cichlid family is the one most obvious to snorkellers, as it feeds off algae found on rocks close to the shore.

In addition to rambling around the hills of Cape Maclear and snorkelling in the lake, you can ask the local fishermen to take you out in their dug-out canoes to catch fish – the succulent, delicate flesh of the lake bream, chambo, makes excellent eating for your evening braai. I was fascinated by the fishermen's skill in filleting and roasting my dinner on the hot coals.

The little cemetery at Cape Maclear contains the graves of Dr Black (a medical missionary), the South African missionary Shadrack Ngunana, and other victims of fever, and remembers those individuals of the 'Old Livingstonia' mission (1875-1881). This Mission of the Free Church of Scotland failed because of disease, death and the difficulties involved in converting people who were culturally linked to the Swahili coast.

404. *Dedza Mountain*

DEDZA, see map page 327

AUTHORITY-IN-CHARGE: Ministry of Forestry and Natural Resources, Malawi.
MAIN ATTRACTIONS: Rocky cliffs; indigenous flora; pine plantations.
FACILITIES/AMENITIES: Nature walks on forestry roads and footpaths; Dedza rest house, accommodating 6 people, can be used as a base.
PERTINENT INFORMATION: Dedza Mountain rises to 2 189 metres. The town of Dedza is situated 275 km from Blantyre on the main road.
AVAILABLE LITERATURE: Contact the Malawi Department of Tourism.
CLIMATE: May to October, dry season. November/December to March/April, wet season.

405. *Chongoni Mountain*

NORTH OF DEDZA, see map page 327

AUTHORITY-IN-CHARGE: Ministry of Forestry and Natural Resources, Malawi.
MAIN ATTRACTIONS: Six painted rock shelters dating from the Stone Age to the early 20th century; *Brachystegia* woodland; montane grassland; sub-montane evergreen forest.
FACILITIES/AMENITIES: None.
PERTINENT INFORMATION: Do not deface the rock paintings.
AVAILABLE LITERATURE: Contact the Malawi Department of Tourism.
CLIMATE: May to October, dry season. November/December to March/April, rainy season.

406. *Lilongwe Nature Sanctuary*

LILONGWE

AUTHORITY-IN-CHARGE: Department of National Parks and Wildlife, Malawi.
SIZE: 119 hectares.
LENGTH: More than 5 km of trails.
MAIN ATTRACTIONS: Abundant and varied

Opposite page: Sunset at Cape Maclear in the Lake Malawi National Park.

Top left: On the shores of Lake Malawi, which contains the largest number of fish species of any lake in the world.

Top right: Along the nature walk in the woodlands of the Lilongwe Nature Sanctuary.

Centre: Cycling in Malawi gives the trailist the opportunity to visit the warm-hearted people of the country. This family lives on the lakeside near Chilumba.

birdlife; Lingadzi River; acacia and *Combretum* woodland.

FACILITIES/AMENITIES: Education centre; bird hides; two self-guided nature trails.

PERTINENT INFORMATION: From time to time there are wildlife displays at the centre.

AVAILABLE LITERATURE: *A Nature Walk in the Heart of Lilongwe – Lilongwe Nature Sanctuary*; *South Trail Guide* and *North Trail Guide*, brochures (all available at the education centre).

CLIMATE: May to October, dry season. November/December to March/April, rainy season.

The Malawian authorities are to be commended for setting aside this 119-hectare site, between the old town and the new capital of Lilongwe, as a nature centre and wildlife sanctuary. It functions as a venue for environmental education as well as relaxation. Wildlife in this small woodland reserve is amazingly diverse, with more than 200 bird species, small mammals such as the lesser galago (nagapie or Senegal bushbaby), greater bushbaby and duiker, and large

mammals such as bushbuck, leopard and hyaena. In addition, the Lingadzi River, home of crocodile, otter and 14 fish species, flows through the sanctuary.

Lilongwe Nature Sanctuary is open year-round for day use only. Two of the footpaths have been developed as self-guided nature trails which wind through acacia and *Combretum* woodland and along the bamboo-sheltered Lingadzi River. The accompanying trail brochures are very informative. Both of these 2-3 kilometre trails are laid out on flat terrain, and each can be completed with ease in approximately one hour.

407. *Malawi Cycle Trail*

LILONGWE, see Regional Map page 326

AUTHORITY-IN-CHARGE: Trailblazers.

DURATION: 18 days.

MAIN ATTRACTIONS: A unique way to tour the mountains and lake of Malawi.

FACILITIES/AMENITIES: Accommodation in rest houses and at camp-sites; tarmac and gravel roads; all equipment, food and transport provided; cost of tour does not include cycle hire, so trailists are welcome to use their own bicycles.

PERTINENT INFORMATION: Maximum of 10 people per group. Fat-tyre (all-terrain) bicycles recommended. A back-up vehicle lifts cycles up main escarpments; most of the riding is downhill, so the trail requires only moderate fitness.

AVAILABLE LITERATURE: Brochures available from Trailblazers.

CLIMATE: May to October, dry season. November/December to March/April, rainy season.

Cycling through Malawi is a unique way to see this compact but diverse country. Many

LILONGWE NATURE SANCTUARY

NOT TO SCALE

HIGHWATER TRAIL

Hide

Hide

LINGADZI RIVER

Rock Outcrop

Firebreak

LINGADZI RIVER

Hide

Paddocks

Pond

EDUCATION CENTRE

to NEW LILONGWE

to OLD LILONGWE

of Malawi's natural assets, in addition to a cross-section of its warm-hearted people, can be viewed from the road.

After flying to Lilongwe from Johannesburg, participants take their first ride on flat to rolling terrain at Dedza, followed by a long downhill to Ntchea. The back-up vehicle transports the group to Liwonde National Park. Trailists visit Blantyre, the Mulanie Massif, Zomba, Cape Maclear on Lake Malawi, Chipoka, the Viphya plateau, Mzuzu and the lake shore at Chilumba and Nkhata Bay. Optional hikes are offered on the Mulanje Massif and in historic Livingstonia, and cyclists are ferried on Lake Malawi from Monkey Bay to Chipoka.

408. Dzalanyama Range

MOZAMBIQUE BORDER, see map page 327.

AUTHORITY-IN-CHARGE: Ministry of Forestry and Natural Resources, Malawi.
MAIN ATTRACTIONS: Wild region of rolling hills covered by *Brachystegia* woodland; patches of evergreen forest.
FACILITIES/AMENITIES: None.
PERTINENT INFORMATION: Dzalanyama Range rises to 1 713 metres. Footpaths are indistinct.
AVAILABLE LITERATURE: Contact the Malawi Department of Tourism.
CLIMATE: May to October, dry season. November/December to March/April, rainy season.

409. Nkhotakota National Park

NKHOTAKOTA, see map page 329

AUTHORITY-IN-CHARGE: Department of National Parks and Wildlife, Malawi.
MAIN ATTRACTIONS: Scenery and vegetation, *Brachystegia* to dense rainforest on Chipata Mountain; excellent fishing in Bua River; elephant, buffalo, zebra, crocodile, leopard, lion and antelope; rich birdlife.
FACILITIES/AMENITIES: Guided walks with game scout. Camp-sites: Tongoli (unfurnished rondavel), Bua (on the river) and Chipata (under the mountain).

Right: A great white egret and an openbill stork sharing the same perch.
Opposite page, left: In Nyika National Park.
Opposite page, right: The Manchewe Falls.

PERTINENT INFORMATION: Animals are scarce but the scenery is excellent. Permission to enter necessary, obtainable from the Chief Game Warden, P.O. Box 30131, Lilongwe 3, Malawi.
AVAILABLE LITERATURE: Contact the Malawi Department of Tourism.
CLIMATE: May to October, dry season. November/December to April, rainy season.

410. Kasungu National Park

CENTRAL REGION, see map page 329

AUTHORITY-IN-CHARGE: Department of National Parks and Wildlife, Malawi.
SIZE: 207 000 hectares.
LENGTH: 10-km nature trail.
MAIN ATTRACTIONS: Elephant, hippo, buffalo, rhino, kudu, lion, spotted hyaena, warthog, eland, oribi, common duiker, zebra, hartebeest, sable and reedbuck; 200 species of birds; geometric rock painting near Solanje Hill; iron smelting kiln on Dwangwa River.
FACILITIES/AMENITIES: Game-viewing drives on untarred roads; game scout guides; Lifupa Lodge with rondavels, restaurant and bar overlooking Lifupa Waterhole; fully equipped tents; swimming pool; petrol; passenger vehicle for hire.
PERTINENT INFORMATION: The park is located 112 km north-west of Lilongwe. Although walking is not an emphasized activity, ask the game warden for scouts to point out game and places of interest, such as rock paintings.
AVAILABLE LITERATURE: Contact the Malawi Department of Tourism.
CLIMATE: December to March, rainy season. September to May, warmest season. June to August, coolest season. Game-viewing is best in the dry season.

411. Viphya Plateau

MZUZU, see map page 329

AUTHORITIES-IN-CHARGE: Various landowners.
MAIN ATTRACTIONS: Enormous vistas; heavily forested slopes.
FACILITIES/AMENITIES: Nature walks; Mzuzu luxury hotel, nearby.
PERTINENT INFORMATION: Kamuzu's View looks out over a 17 000 km²-area of pine forests and indigenous woodland.
AVAILABLE LITERATURE: Contact the Malawi Department of Tourism.
CLIMATE: May to October, dry season. November/December to April, rainy season.

412. Vwaza Marsh Game Reserve

KATUMBI, see map page 329

AUTHORITY-IN-CHARGE: Department of National Parks and Wildlife, Malawi.
MAIN ATTRACTIONS: Elephant and hippo; one of the highest densities of animals in Malawi marshland, mixed mopane *Brachystegia* woodland and rocky hills; Lake Kazuni; rich birdlife.
FACILITIES/AMENITIES: Game-viewing and bird-watching on foot, accompanied by a game guard; three tents on raised concrete slabs with thatched canopies, each with two beds; toilets and showers; camping with minimal facilities.
PERTINENT INFORMATION: This is a developing reserve, so check details before planning your trip. Four-wheel drive vehicle necessary. Permission to enter necessary, obtainable from The Chief Game Warden, P.O. Box 30131, Lilongwe 3, Malawi.
AVAILABLE LITERATURE: Included in general tourist brochures.
CLIMATE: May to October, dry season. November/December to March/April, rainy season.

413. Nyika National Park

RUMPHI, see map page 327

AUTHORITY-IN-CHARGE: Department of National Parks and Wildlife, Malawi.
SIZE: 93 240 hectares.
MAIN ATTRACTIONS: Herds of game animals; birdlife; undulating montane grassland and evergreen forest.
FACILITIES/AMENITIES: Seven trails; guided

walks on request; dams with bird hides; fishing for rainbow trout; Chelinda Game Camp with chalets or rooms, a shop and petrol; cabin in Juniper Forest; 224 km of game-viewing tracks for vehicles or pedestrians.

PERTINENT INFORMATION: For information: Nyika National Park, Private Bag 6, Rumphi, Malawi.
AVAILABLE LITERATURE: Contact the Malawi Department of Tourism; map with walking tracks, available from the park on arrival.
CLIMATE: In general, bracing and invigorating with mild and sunny days. Frost common in June and July, when nights are cold. December to April, rainy season.

I was fortunate to arrive at Nyika to find that there was no petrol available. Fortunate? Yes, for I was left with no alternative but to walk the dirt roads, taking short-cuts on the myriad game paths which cross the highest (2 135 metres on average, and in places rising to 2 400 metres) and most extensive plateau in central Africa.

Nyika is bounded on all sides by steep scarps, and to the north-east forms the main wall of the Rift Valley. The plateau is also a major watershed and here Malawi's northern rivers have their source in the wide, flat dambos, reminiscent of the peat bogs of the temperate northern hemisphere.

Rivers, shallow valleys with evergreen forest and undulating montane grassland provide an excellent environment for viewing wildlife. Hikers will easily identify southern reedbuck and herds of eland, zebra and roan antelope, and the more observant will see bushbuck, warthog, klipspringer, hartebeest and vervet monkey. Predators are not seen as readily. The large birds such as the wattled crane and Stanley's bustard are particularly impressive.

Seven wilderness trails combine hiking and game-viewing in this superb setting.

414. *Manchewe Falls and Livingstonia*

NEAR RUMPHI

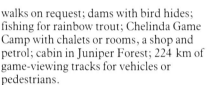

AUTHORITY-IN-CHARGE: The Principal, Overtoun Institution, P.O. Livingstonia, Malawi.
LENGTH: 1-km road walk beginning at the picnic sites; 19-km dirt road from Lake Malawi to Livingstonia.
MAIN ATTRACTIONS: Manchewe Falls; Gorodi escarpment; Livingstonia, with its old buildings and museums, and handcrafts; views of Lake Malawi and Tanzania.
FACILITIES/AMENITIES: Picnic site; camping permitted; rest house in Livingstonia; small museum and shop.
PERTINENT INFORMATION: The museum is closed on Sundays. There is an alternative, less rugged road to Livingstonia, starting at Rumphi.
AVAILABLE LITERATURE: *Shell Guide to Livingstonia*, brochure available from the Overtoun Institution; included in general tourist brochures, available from the Malawi Department of Tourism.
CLIMATE: May to October, dry season. November/December to April, rainy season.

If you have a car, it is well worth driving the 19 kilometres of hairpin bends from the lake to Livingstonia up the Gorodi escarpment. The dirt road (built by missionaries) with its

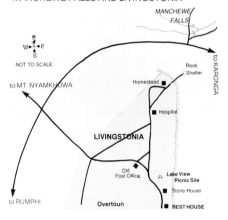

MANCHEWE FALLS AND LIVINGSTONIA

magnificent views can be walked, but take into consideration that it is a steady 1 000-metre incline. Camp at the picnic site, five kilometres outside Livingstonia. The path to Manchewe Falls is very short; the sight of the Chitimba River's twin cascades plunging 70 metres is breathtaking. Escarpment and lake views are also impressive. Access to the caves behind the falls is difficult, requiring agility and rock scrambling. (Phoka tribesmen used to hide from marauding Ngoni warriors in the caves.) I suggest you ask a local resident to guide you there.

Some 750 metres above Lake Malawi, on the 6-km² Khondowe plateau jutting out from the Nyika Mountains, lies the town of Livingstonia and the Mission of the Free Church of Scotland, established in 1894. A walk around the early buildings, now protected under the Monuments Act – the post office and its clock tower (1905), the Stone House (1903), formerly the home of Dr Laws, the founder of the missions, the church (1916), homestead and hospital (1910) – is very interesting.

FURTHER INFORMATION

Trailing checklist

KEY

N	Necessary	UP	Usually provided (check information sheet from company operating the trail, or trail brochure)
S	Suggested		
D	Dependent on season		
A	Dependent on ecotype	I	Inquire when and if needed (necessary when crossing political boundaries)
O	Optional		
–	Not needed		

	NATURE (Day Trips)	WILDERNESS (Guided)	HIKING (with Hut System)	MOUNTAINEERING
CAMPING/SLEEPING				
Overnight backpack	–	–	N	N
Daypack	N	S	S	S
Tent, poles, pegs	–	UP	–	N
Spare cord	O	–	O	S
Sleeping bag and stuffsack	–	UP	N	N
Foam pad or air mattress	–	UP	UP	N
Ground sheet or space blanket	S	S	S	N
Pillow	–	O	O	O
EATING				
Camp-stove	O,D	UP	S	N
Pots (if not included with camp-stove)	O,D	UP	N	N
Pot gripper (if not included with camp-stove)	O,D	UP	S	N
Dishes (if not included with camp-stove)	O	UP	N	N
Fuel container	O,D	UP	N	N
Fuel	O,D	UP	N	N
Water bottle (1 litre capacity)	N	UP	N	N
Mug/cup	S	UP	N	N
Can opener	O	UP	O	O
Matches (waterproofed)	S	UP	N	N
Plastic rubbish bags	N	UP	N	N
Biodegradable washing-up powder	O	UP	N	N
Scouring pad	–	UP	N	N
Knife, fork, spoon set	O	UP	N	N
Water purification tablets	S,A	UP	S,A	S,A
Fresh foods	S	UP	O	O
Dried foods	O	UP	S	S
Dehydrated/freeze-dried foods	O	UP	S	S
Spare foods (emergency high-energy rations)	N	UP	N	N
Tea	N	UP	N	N
Coffee	O	UP	O	O
Isotonic powders	O	UP	S	S
TOILETRIES				
Toilet paper	N	N	N	N
Toilet trowel	S	UP	N	N
Toothbrush/toothpaste	–	N	N	N
Biodegradable body soap	–	N	N	N
Towel	O	N	N	N
Moisturizing cream	S	S	S	S
Insect repellent	D,A	S,A	D,A	D,A
Sun-screen cream	N	N	N	N
Lip salve	N	N	N	N

	NATURE (Day Trips)	WILDERNESS (Guided)	HIKING (with Hut System)	MOUNTAINEERING
Shaving kit	–	O	O	O
Mirror (also useful for emergency signalling)	N	O	N	N
Foot powder	O	N	N	N
Hair brush/comb	O	S	S	S
FIRST AID/EMERGENCY				
Bandages	N	N	N	N
Gauze bandages	N	N	N	N
Adhesive first-aid tape	N	N	N	N
Moleskin/plaster	N	UP	N	N
Scissors/knife	N	S	N	N
Personal medication (prescription pills)	N	N	N	N
Malaria pills	A	A	A	A
Mosquito nets	–	A,UP	A	A
Pain killer (e.g. aspirin)	N	N	N	N
Antiseptic ointment	N	N	N	N
Antihistamines	N	N	N	N
Eye bandage	N	N	N	N
Thermometer	O	UP	S	S
First-aid manual	S	UP	S	S
Snake-bite kit	O	UP	O	O
Tweezers	N	N	N	N
Emergency fire starter	O	UP	N	N
Whistle	N	N	N	N
Compass	N	O	N	N
Candle	O	UP	N	N
Safety pins	O,S	O	N	N
Rubber bands	O,S	O	N	N
Small change (5c, 10c, 20c pieces)	N	O	N	N
Spare spectacles	O	N	N	N
Sunglasses	N	N	N	N
Needle and thread	O	UP,S	S	S
Spare bootlaces	N	N	N	N
Pen/pencil/paper	N	S	N	N
Wristwatch	N	S	N	N
Torch with spare batteries and bulb	N	N	N	N
CLOTHING				
Socks	N	N	N	N
Wool	N	N	N	N
Cotton/silk	N	N	N	N
Spare socks	O,S	N	N	N
Underwear	N	N	N	N
Thermal underwear	O,D	D	D	D
Tracksuit	–	S	O	O

	NATURE (Day Trips)	WILDERNESS (Guided)	HIKING (with Hut System)	MOUNTAINEERING
Sunhat with chin strap	N	N	N	N
Wool hat/balaclava	D	D	N	N
Waterproof rain jacket or poncho	N	N	N	N
Waterproof rain pants	D	D	N	N
Boots	N	N	N	N
Spare footwear	O	N	N	N
Gloves/mittens	D	D	N	N
Long pants	N	N	N	N
Shorts	S	S, avoid bright colours	N	N
Bathing costume	S	S	S	S
T-shirt	S	O, avoid bright colours	S	S
Long-sleeved shirt	N	N, avoid bright colours	N	N
Wool sweater	N	N, avoid bright colours	N	N
Windjacket	S	S	S	S
Down jacket/vest	D	D	D	D

	NATURE (Day Trips)	WILDERNESS (Guided)	HIKING (with Hut System)	MOUNTAINEERING
Gaiters for snow (long)	D	D	D	D
for vegetation (short)	S	S	S	S
Down booties/mukluks	–	O	D,O	D,O
Handkerchief	S	S	S	S
MISCELLANEOUS				
Maps	N	S	N	N
Personal identification	N	N	N	N
Passport/visas	I	I	I	I
Vaccination certificate	I	I	I	I
Permit	N	UP	N	N
Brochure/trail guide	N	S	N	N
Camera/film	O	O	O	O
Binoculars	S	N	S	S
Walking stick	O	O	O	O
Field guides	S	S	S	S
Life jacket	A	UP	–	–
Fishing equipment	O	O	O	O
Waterproof bags	N	UP	N	N
Goggles, sun	D	–	D	D
Ice axe	–	–	–	D
Crampons	–	–	D,O	D
Altimeter	O	–	S	S
Rope/karabiners	–	–	–	A

Further reading list

* indicates field guides or first-aid booklets suitable for backpacks. Some of the publications listed below may be out of print, but if they can be obtained make worthwhile reading.

GENERAL – Mountaineering, outdoor skills, backpacking and camping

Books

Bradt, H. and Bradt, G., 1977. *Backpacker's Africa: 17 Walks off the Cape to Cairo Route*. Bradt Enterprises, Bucks., England.

Bristow, D., 1985. *Mountains of Southern Africa*. C. Struik, Cape Town.

Bundu Book of Geology, Gemmology and Archaeology. Standing Conference of National Voluntary Youth Organizations, Longman Rhodesia, Salisbury, Rhodesia, 1968.*

Bundu Book of Meteorology, Wayfinding and Rock Climbing. Standing Conference of National Voluntary Youth Organizations, Longman Rhodesia, Salisbury, Rhodesia, 1971.*

Clarke, J. and Coulson, D., 1983 *Mountain Odyssey in Southern Africa*. MacMillan South Africa, Johannesburg.

Cleare, J., 1979. *Collins' Guide to Mountains and Mountaineering*. Collins, London.

Corfield, T., 1984. *The Wilderness Guardian: A Practical Guide to Fieldwork Related to Wildlife Conservation*. David Sheldrick Wildlife Appeal, Kenya.

Cornell, J.B., 1979. *Sharing Nature With Children*. Wilderness Press, Berkeley, CA.

Dodwell, C., 1984. *An Explorer's Handbook: Travel, Survival and Bush Cookery*. Hodder and Stoughton, London.

Duggan, A. (ed.), 1983. *Reader's Digest Illustrated Guide to the Game Parks and Nature Reserves of Southern Africa*. Reader's Digest Association of South Africa, Cape Town.

Grainger, Col. D. H., 1982. *Don't die in the Bundu* (12th edition). Howard Timmins, Cape Town.*

Hennig, H., 1978. *The South African Backpacker*. Purnell and Sons, Cape Town.

Kjellstrom, B., 1972. *Be an Expert with Map and Compass*. Scribner, New York.*

Langmuir, E., 1984. *Mountain Craft and Leadership*. The Scottish Sports Council, Edinburgh and the Mountain Walking Leader Training Board, Manchester. (Although emphasis is on Great Britain, this book contains material relevant to all countries.)

Levy, J., 1984. *Practical Trail Design*. Ciskei Holiday and Tourist Trust, Bisho, Ciskei. (For technicians and trail planners.)

Milner, D., 1977. *Photoguide to Mountains for the Backpacker and Climber*. Focal Press Ltd, London.*

Pyatt, E., 1980. *Guinness Book of Mountains and Mountaineering: Facts and Feats*. Guinness Superlatives, Ltd, Great Britain.

Silverman, G., 1986. *Backpacking with Babies and Small Children* (2nd edition). Wilderness Press, Berkeley, CA.

Steyn, A., 1982. *Backpack for Pleasure*. Intergrafix, Pretoria.

Thomas, L., 1980. *The Backpacking Woman*. Doubleday and Company, Inc., New York.

Periodicals

Backpacker. Backpacker Inc., P.O. Box 2784, Boulder, Colorado 80321, USA. (Very good for latest equipment news, and international trail coverage.)

Climber and Rambler: The Journal of the British Mountaineering Council. Holmes McDougall Ltd, 12 York Street, Glasgow G28JL, Scotland.

Great Outdoors. P.O. Box 84436, Greenside 2034, South Africa.

International Backpackers. Association Bulletins, P.O. Box 85, Lincoln Centre, Maine 04458, USA.

Natal Parks Board's Game and Nature Reserves, Resorts and Parks in Natal. Natal Parks Board, P.O. Box 662, Pietermaritzburg 3200. (For latest information on trails, bookings and addresses.)

Nature Conservation in the Cape. Annual Reports of the Cape Department of Nature Conservation and Museum Services.

FIRST-AID
Books
Manual of First Aid. South African Red Cross Society, Cape Town, 1974.★

Mitchell, D., 1972. *Mountaineering First Aid: A Guide to Accident Response and First Aid Care*. The Mountaineers, Seattle, Washington, USA.★

Renouf, J. and Hulse, S., 1978. *First Aid for Hill Walkers and Climbers*. Penguin Books, England.

Wilkerson, J.A., 1975. *Medicine for Mountaineering*. The Mountaineers, Seattle, Washington, USA.★

Periodicals
Sandell, Dr R. *Mountaineering Medicine: Some Experiences on Aconcagua (7 000 m)*. MCSA Journal, Cape Town Section of the Mountain Club of South Africa, 1978.

PHYSICAL FITNESS
Books
Complete South African Kilojoule, Calorie and Carbohydrate Counter (3rd edition). C. Struik, Cape Town, 1986.

Gover, B. and Shepherd, J., 1978. *Runner's Handbook: A Complete Fitness Guide for Men and Women on the Run*. Penguin Books, New York, USA.

Higdon, H., 1974. *Fitness After Forty*. World Publications, California, USA.

Morehouse, L.E. and Gross Hart-David, L., 1975. *Total Fitness in 30 Minutes a Week*. MacGibbon, London.

Physical Fitness. Royal Canadian Air Force, Penguin, London, 1981. (5BX 11 minutes-a-day plan for men; XBX 12 minutes-a-day plan for women.)

GENERAL ECOLOGY
Books
Atlas of Southern Africa. Reader's Digest Association of Southern Africa, Cape Town, 1984.

Greyling, T. and Huntley, B.J. (eds.), 1984. *Directory of Southern African Conservation Areas*. South African National Scientific Programmes Report Number 98, CSIR, Pretoria.

Gordon, R., 1984. *The National Parks of Southern Africa*. C. Struik, Cape Town.

Guinness, A. (ed.), 1977. *Joy of Nature: How to Observe and Appreciate the Great Outdoors*. The Reader's Digest Association, Inc., New York. (Suitable for children.)

Kench, J., 1984. *The Coast of Southern Africa*. C. Struik, Cape Town.

Odum, E.P., 1971. *Fundamentals of Ecology*. W.B. Saunders and Company, Philadelphia and London.

Potgieter, D.J., Du Plessis, P.C. and Skaife, S.H., 1971. *Animal Life in Southern Africa*. Nasou Ltd, Cape Town.

Richards, D. and Walker, C., 1975. *Walk through the Wilderness*. Purnell and Sons, Cape Town. (Suitable for children.)

Sharpe, G.W., 1976. *Interpreting the Environment*. John Wiley and Sons, Inc., New York. (For rangers, conservation and forestry officers and technicians.)

Wannenburgh, A., 1984. *The Natural Wonder of Southern Africa*. C. Struik, Cape Town.

Woodhouse, B. *When Animals Were People: A-Z of Animals of Southern Africa as the Bushmen Saw and Thought Them and as the Camera Sees them Today*. Chris van Rensburg Publications, Melville.

Periodicals
Environment RSA. Department of Environment Affairs, Private Bag X213, Pretoria 0001. (Often reviews trails and/or new reserves.)

The Lammergeyer. Journal of the Natal Parks, Game and Fish Preservation Board, P.O. Box 662, Pietermaritzburg 3200.

GEOLOGY
Books
Du Toit, A.T., 1926. *Geology of South Africa*. Oliver and Boyd, Edinburgh and London.

King, L.C., 1963. *South African Scenery: A Textbook of Geomorphology*. Oliver and Boyd, Edinburgh and London.

Rogers, P.W. and Du Toit, A.L., 1909. *An Introduction to the Geology of the Cape Colony*. Longman, Green and Co., London.

Wellington, J.H., 1955. *South Africa: A Geographical Study, Volume 1 – Physical Geography*. Cambridge University Press, Cambridge.

MARINE LIFE
Books
Branch, G., 1981. *Living Shores of Southern Africa*. C. Struik, Cape Town.

Day, J.H., 1974. *A Guide to Marine Life on South African Shores*. A.A. Balkema, Cape Town.★

Richards, D., 1981. *South African Shells – A Collector's Guide*. C. Struik, Cape Town.★

FLORA
Books
Acocks, J.P.H., 1975. 'Veld Types of South Africa'. *Memoirs of the Botanical Survey of South Africa*, No. 40, BRI and DATS, Pretoria.

Baker, H.A. and Oliver, E.G.H., 1967. *Ericas in Southern Africa*. Purnell and Sons, Cape Town.

Batten, A., 1986. *Flowers of Southern Africa*. Frandsen Publishers, Fourways, South Africa.

Bottomley, A.M. and Talbot, P.H.B., 1954. *Common, Edible and Poisonous Mushrooms in South Africa*. Bulletin No. 324 of the Union Department of Agriculture, Pretoria.★

Chippindall, L.K.A. and Crook, A.O., 1976. *Grasses of Southern Africa*. M.O. Collins (Pty) Ltd, London.

De Winter, B., De Winter, M. and Killick, D.J.B., 1966. *Sixty-six Transvaal Trees*. Transvaal Provincial Administration, Pretoria.

De Winter, B. and Vahrmeijer, J., 1972. *National List of Trees*. Van Schaik, Pretoria.★

Eliovson, S., 1965. *Proteas for Pleasure*. Macmillan South Africa, Johannesburg.

Eliovson, S., 1962. *Discovering Wildflowers of Southern Africa*. Howard Timmins, Cape Town.

Fox, F.W. and Young, M.E.N., 1982. *Food from the Veld: Edible Wild Plants of Southern Africa*. Delta Books, Johannesburg.

Harrison, E.R., 1981. *Epiphytic Orchids of Southern Africa*. Natal Branch of the Wildlife Society of Southern Africa, Durban.★

Hobson, N.K. and Jessop, J.P., 1975. *Veld Plants of Southern Africa*. Macmillan South Africa, Johannesburg.

Levin, H., Branch, M., Rappoport, S. and Mitchell, D., 1985. *A Field Guide to the Mushrooms of South Africa*. C. Struik, Cape Town.

Moll, E., 1981. *A Comprehensive Field Guide to Over Seven Hundred Indigenous and Naturalized Species*. University of Cape Town, Eco-Lab Trust Fund, Cape Town.★

Palgrave, K.C., 1977. *Trees of Southern Africa*. C. Struik, Cape Town.

Palmer, E., 1986. *A Field Guide to the Trees of Southern Africa*. Collins, Johannesburg.

Rourke, J.P., 1980. *Proteas of Southern Africa*. Purnell and Sons, Cape Town.

Stirton, C.H. (ed.), 1978. *Plant Invaders: Beautiful, But Dangerous*. Department of Nature and Environmental Conservation, Cape Provincial Administration, Cape Town.★

Von Breitenbach, F., 1984. *National List of Introduced Trees*. Dendrological Foundation, Pretoria.

Watt, J.M. and Breyer-Brandwijk, M.G., 1962. *Medicinal and Poisonous Plants of Southern and Eastern Africa* (2nd edition). E. and S. Livingstone Ltd, Edinburgh.

MAMMALS
Books
Bosman, P. and Hall-Martin, A., 1986. *Elephants of Africa*. C. Struik, Cape Town.

Cillie, B., 1987. *A Field Guide to the Mammals of Southern Africa*. Frandsen Publishers, Fourways, South Africa.

Dorst, J. and Dandelot, P., 1970. *A Field Guide to the Larger Mammals of Africa*. Collins, London.★

Eltringham, S.K., 1979. *Ecology and Conservation of Large African Mammals*. Macmillan, London.

Kenmuir, D. and Williams, R., 1975. *Wild Mammals*. Longman Rhodesia, Salisbury, Rhodesia.★ (A Bundu Series guide.)

Nicol, M. *A Young Naturalist Book: Mammals of Southern Africa*. C. Struik, Cape Town.

The Mammals of the Southern African Subregion. Mammal Research Institute, University of Pretoria, Pretoria, 1982. (English and Afrikaans).

Rose, P., 1967. *What Antelope Is That?* Purnell and Sons, Cape Town.★

Smithers, R.H.N., 1966. *Mammals of Rhodesia, Zambia and Malawi*. Collins, London.★

Walker, C., 1985. *Signs of the Wild* (2nd edition). C. Struik, Cape Town.★ (A field guide to the spoor and signs of the mammals of southern Africa.)

Zaloumis, E.A. and Cross, R., 1974. *Field Guide to the Antelope of South Africa*. Natal Branch of the Wildlife Society of Southern Africa, Durban.★

BIRDS
Books

Broekhuysen, C.J., 1969. *Field Guide to the Birds of the South African Sea-shore*. Howard Timmins, Cape Town.

Brown, L., 1970. *African Birds of Prey*. Collins, London.

Ginn, P., 1973. *Birds Afield: A Beginner's Guide to Bird Watching in Southern Africa*. Longman Rhodesia, Salisbury, Rhodesia.★ (A Bundu Series guide.)

Kemp, Dr A. and Finch-Davies, C.G., 1986. *Gamebirds and Waterfowl of Southern Africa*. Winchester Press, Johannesburg.

Maclean, G., 1981. *Aids to Bird Identification in Southern Africa*. University of Natal Press, Pietermaritzburg.★

McLachlan, G.R. and Liversidge, R., 1978. *Roberts' Birds of South Africa* (revised edition). The Trustees of the John Voelcker Bird Book Fund, Cape Town.★ (The most comprehensive reference on the subject; essential for all serious bird-watchers.)

Newman, K., 1983. *Birds of Southern Africa*. Macmillan South Africa, Johannesburg.

Newman, K., 1979. *Bird Life in Southern Africa* (2nd edition). Macmillan South Africa, Johannesburg.

Prozesky, O.P.M., 1970. *A Field Guide to the Birds of Southern Africa*. Collins, London.★

Sinclair, I. and Goode, D., 1986. *Birds of Prey*. C. Struik, Cape Town.★

Sinclair, I., 1984. *Field Guide to the Birds of Southern Africa*. C. Struik, Cape Town.

Skead, C.J., 1967. *Sunbirds of Southern Africa: also Sugarbirds, White-eyes and the Spotted Creeper*. A.A. Balkema, Cape Town.

Tuck, G., 1979. *Field Guide to the Seabirds of Southern Africa and the World*. Collins, London.★

Williams, J.G., 1980. *A Field Guide to the Birds of East Africa*. Collins, London.★

REPTILES AND AMPHIBIANS
Books

Broadley, D. and Cock, E., 1975. *Snakes of Rhodesia*. Longman Rhodesia, Salisbury, Rhodesia.★ (A Bundu Series guide.)

FitzSimons, V.F.M., 1970. *A Field Guide to the Snakes of Southern Africa*. Collins, London.★

Marais, J. *Snake Versus Man: A Guide to the Dangerous and Common Harmless Snakes of Southern Africa*. Macmillan South Africa, Johannesburg.

Passmore, N. and Carruthers, V.C. *South African Frogs*. Witwatersrand University Press, Johannesburg.

Patterson, R. and Meakin, P., 1986. *Snakes*. C. Struik, Cape Town.★

Reitz, C.J., 1978. *Poisonous South African Snakes and Snakebite*. Department of Health, National Health Education Programme, Government Printer, Pretoria.★

Visser, J. (undated). *Dangerous Snakes: Species Identification and Treatment of Bites*. Booklet produced by Dettol in co-operation with the South African Retail Chemists and Druggists Association.★

Visser, J., 1966. *Poisonous Snakes of Southern Africa and the Treatment of Snakebite*. Howard Timmins, Cape Town.

Visser, J., 1972. *What Snake Is That?* Purnell and Sons, Cape Town.

Visser, J., 1979. *Common Snakes of South Africa*. Purnell and Sons, Cape Town.★

Visser, J. and Chapman, D., 1978. *Snakes and Snakebite*. Purnell and Sons, Cape Town.

Wager, V.A., 1965. *A Guide to the South African Frogs*. Natal Branch of the Wildlife Society of Southern Africa, Durban.★

INVERTEBRATES
Books

Henning, S. and Abbott, C., 1984. *Southern Africa: Butterflies*. Macmillan South Africa, Johannesburg.

Holm, E. and De Meillon, E., 1986. *Insects*. C. Struik, Cape Town.★

Newlands, G. and De Meillon, E., 1986. *Spiders*. C. Struik, Cape Town.★

Skaife, S.H., 1979. *African Insect Life*. C. Struik, Cape Town.

Williams, J., 1969. *A Field Guide to the Butterflies of Africa*. Collins, London.★

Yates, J.H., 1968. *Spiders of Southern Africa*. Books of Africa, Cape Town.

RECORDINGS

Reucassel, D and Pooley, T. (cassette); Adendorff, D. and Reucassel, D. (record); and Rouse, H. (script and narration). *Calls of the Bushveld*. Contact Dick Reucassel, P.O. Box 11327, Johannesburg 2000.

TRIBAL LIFE
Books

Levitas, B. and Morris, J. *Tribal Life Today*. College Press, Cape Town.

CENTRAL SOURCE OF GOVERNMENT PRINTER'S MAPS OF SOUTH AFRICA
Government Printer, Private Bag X85, Pretoria 0001.

WESTERN CAPE
Books

Anderson, T., 1984. *52 Day-Walks in and around Cape Town*. C. Struik, Cape Town★.

Berrisford, A.B., 1980. *55-60 Years of Mountaineering in South Africa*. Mills Litho Printers, Cape Town.

Brossy, S., 1985. *A Walking Guide for the Hout Bay Mountains and Silvermine Nature Reserve (north)*. Shirley Brossy, Cape Town.

Brossy, S., 1984/5. *A Walking Guide for Table Mountain* (2nd edition). Shirley Brossy, Cape Town.

Brossy, S., 1984. *A Walking Guide for the Kalk Bay Mountains and Silvermine Nature Reserve (south)*. Shirley Brossy, Cape Town.

Burman, J. *Where to Walk from the Cableway*. Human and Rousseau, Cape Town.

Burman, J., 1984. *Day Walks in the South-Western Cape*. Human and Rousseau, Cape Town.

Burman, J., 1979. *Latest Walks in the Cape Peninsula*. Human and Rousseau, Cape Town.★

Burman, L. and Bean, A., 1985. *Hottentot Holland to Hermanus: S.A. Wild Flower Guide No. 5*. Botanical Society of S.A., Cape Town.★

Claassens, A.J.M. and Dickson, C.G.C., 1980. *Butterflies of the Table Mountain Range with the Inter-relationship of their Flora*. C. Struik, Cape Town.

Jackson, W.P.U., 1977. *Wild Flowers on Table Mountain*. Howard Timmins, Cape Town.

Jackson, W.P.U., 1980. *Wild Flowers of the Fairest Cape*. Howard Timmins, Cape Town.

Le Roux, A and Schelpe, E.A.C.L.E., 1981. *Namaqualand and Clanwilliam – South African Wild Flower Guide I*. Botanical Society of South Africa, Cape Town.★

Lotz, E. (undated). *Jonkershoek en sy Berge, 'n Gids vir Klimmers en Stappers*. Cabo, Stellenbosch.★

Lundy, M., 1985. *Twenty Walks around Hout Bay*. Mican Investments, Hout Bay.

Mason, H., 1972. *Western Cape Sandveld Flowers*. C. Struik, Cape Town.

Moll, E.J. and Campbell, B.M., 1976. *Ecological Status of Table Mountain*. Department of Botany, University of Cape Town, Cape Town. (Also referred to as *Table Mountain, A Conservation and Management Report*.)

Moll, E.J. and Scott, L., 1981. *Trees of the Cape Peninsula: A Field Guide*. University of Cape Town, Eco-Lab Trust Fund, Cape Town.★

Quail, B.M. (ed.), 1983. *Table Mountain Guide: Walks and Easy Climbs on Table Mountain, Devil's Peak and Lion's Head* (5th edition). Cape Town Section of the Mountain Club of South Africa, Cape Town.

Rycroft, B., 1980. *Kirstenbosch*. Howard Timmins, Cape Town.★

Stokes, H., 1985. *Flora of Table Mountain*. Murray Coombes, Cape Town.★

Trout in the Kloofs. Cape Piscatorial Society, Cape Town, 1962.

Van Huyssteen, T., 1979. *Foot-loose in Stellenbosch: A Guide for Walkers*. Tafelberg, Cape Town.★

Wilson, P.A.S., 1981. *Leaf Key to 45 Common Trees of Table Mountain*. Directorate of Forestry and Environmental Conservation, Pamphlet 257, Pretoria.★

Periodicals

Rourke, J.P. 'Fernkloof Nature Reserve – A Sanctuary for Montane Fynbos'. *Veld and Flora*, September 1976, Botanical Society of South Africa, Cape Town.

Taylor, H.C. 'Fynbos'. *Veld and Flora*, Vol. 2, No. 4, December 1972. Botanical Society of South Africa, Cape Town.

Woods, D.H. 'From the Koue Bokveld to Porterville'. *MCSA Journal*, Cape Town Section of the MCSA, 1953. (An interesting account of the Groot-Winterhoek Catchment Area when it was still farmland.)

SOUTHERN CAPE
Books

Burman, J., 1980. *Trails and Walks in the Southern Cape*. Human and Rousseau, Cape Town.★

Carter, N., 1977. *Elephants of Knysna*. Purnell and Sons, Cape Town.

MacKay, M., 1983. *The Knysna Elephants and their Forest Home*. Knysna Centre of the Eastern Province Branch of the Wildlife Society of Southern Africa, Knysna.

Seagrief, S.C., 1967. *Seaweeds of the Tsitsikama Coastal National Park*. National Parks Board, Pretoria.★

Tietz, R.M. and Robinson, G.A., 1974. *Tsitsikama Shore*. National Parks Board, Pretoria.★

Von Breitenbach, F., 1974. *Southern Cape Forests and Trees*. The Government Printer, Pretoria.

Von Breitenbach, F., 1985. *Southern Cape Tree Guide, with a Leaf-key to 116 Indigenous Tree and Tall Shrub Species of Outeniqualand and the Tsitsikamma*. Forestry Branch, Pamphlet 360, Department of Environment Affairs, Pretoria.

Periodicals

Trees of the Tsitsikama National Parks. National Parks Board, Pretoria, 1980.★

EASTERN CAPE
Books

Glendhill, E., 1981. *Eastern Cape Veld Flowers*. Department of Nature and Environmental Conservation, Cape Provincial Administration, Cape Town.★

Von Gadow, K., 1977. *100 Indigenous Trees of the Eastern Cape Border Region: A Leaf Key*. Department of Forestry, Pamphlet 195, Pretoria.★

KAROO AND NORTHERN CAPE
Books

De Graaff, G., Robinson, G.A., Van der Walt, P.T., Bryden, B.R. and Van der Hoven, E.A., 1979. *Karoo National Park: Beaufort West*. National Parks Board of Trustees, Pretoria.★

Green, L.G. 1973. *Karoo*. Howard Timmins, Cape Town.

Hobson, N.K., Jessop, J.P., Ginn, M.C. van der R., 1970. *Karoo Plant Wealth*. Pearston Publications, Pearston.

Owens, M. and Owens, D., 1985. *Cry of the Kalahari*. Collins, Johannesburg.

Palmer, E., 1966. *The Plains of Camdeboo*. Collins, London.

TRANSKEI
Books

Republic of Transkei. Chris van Rensburg Publications, Johannesburg, 1976.

LESOTHO
Books

The Guide to Botswana, Lesotho and Swaziland: A Comprehensive Companion for Visitors and Investors. Winchester Press, Saxonwold, 1983.

Schmitz, M., 1982. *Wild Flowers of Lesotho*. Essa (Pty) Ltd, Roma, Lesotho.

NATAL
Books

Ackhurst, J., Irwin, D. Irwin, P., 1980. *Field Guide to the Natal Drakensberg*. Natal Branch of the Wildlife Society of Southern Africa, Durban.★

Berjak, P., Campbell, G.K., Huckett, B. and Pammenter, N.W., 1977. *In the Mangroves of Southern Africa*. Natal Branch of the Wildlife Society of Southern Africa, Durban.★

Bruton, M.N. and Cooper, K.H. (eds.), 1980. *Studies on the Ecology of Maputoland*. Rhodes University, Grahamstown, and the Natal Branch of the Wildlife Society of Southern Africa, Durban.

Bulpin, T.V., 1966. *Natal and the Zulu Country*. Books of Africa, Cape Town.

Dodds, D.A., 1975. *Cradle of Rivers: The Natal Drakensberg*. Purnell and Sons, Cape Town.

Gibson, J.M., 1975. *Wild Flowers of the Natal Coastal Region*. The Trustees of the Natal Publishing Trust Fund, Durban.

Liebenberg, D.P., 1972. *The Drakensberg of Natal*. Bulpin, Cape Town.

The Natal Bushveld: Land Forms and Vegetation. Shuter and Shooter, Pietermaritzburg, in conjunction with the Natal Parks Board, Pietermaritzburg, 1981.★

Pearse, M.L., 1980. *A Camera in Quathlamba: Photographing the Drakensberg*. Howard Timmins, Cape Town.

Pearse, R.O., 1973. *Barrier of Spears: Drama of the Drakensberg*. Howard Timmins, Cape Town.

Pearse, R.O., 1978. *Mountain Splendour: The Wild Flowers of the Drakensberg*. Howard Timmins, Cape Town.

Player, I., 1972. *The White Rhino Saga*. Collins, London.

Reardon, M. and Reardon, M., 1984. *Zululand: A Wildlife Heritage*. C. Struik, Cape Town.

Steele, D. and Cubitt, G., 1981. *Natal: Province of Contrasts*. Don Nelson, Cape Town.

Tainton, N.M., Bransby, D.I. and Booysen, P. de V., 1976. *Common Veld and Pasture Grasses of Natal*. Shuter and Shooter, Pietermaritzburg.

Travseld, W.R., 1969. *Wild Flowers of the Natal Drakensberg*. Purnell and Sons, Cape Town.

Wager, V.A. (undated). *The Frogs that Inhabit the Wildlife Sanctuaries of Natal*. Wildlife Protection and Conservation Society of South Africa, Durban.

Wager, V.A., 1976. *Dwindling Forests of the Natal Coast*. Umhlanga Centre of the Natal Branch of the Wildlife Society of Southern Africa, Durban.★

Periodicals

Bourquin, O. and Channing, A. 'Herpetofauna of the Natal Drakensberg: An Annotated Checklist.' *Lammergeyer*, 30, October 1980. Natal Parks Board, Pietermaritzburg.

De Jesus, Sister M. 'First Trans-Lesotho Trip, October 29-November 4, 1867.' *MCSA Journal*, Mountain Club of South Africa, Cape Town, 1977.

ORANGE FREE STATE, SWAZILAND AND TRANSVAAL
Books

Braack, L., 1983. *The Kruger National Park*. C. Struik, Cape Town.

The Guide to Botswana, Lesotho and Swaziland: A Comprehensive Companion for Visitors and Investors. Winchester Press, Saxonwold, 1983.

Trees and Shrubs of the Witwatersrand. Tree Society of Southern Africa, Witwatersrand University Press, Johannesburg, 1964.★

Carruthers, V. (ed.), 1982. *The Sandton Field Book: A Guide to the Natural History of the Northern Witwatersrand*. Sandton Nature Conservation Society, Sandton.

Newman, K., 1980. *Birds of Southern Africa 1: Kruger National Park*. Macmillan South Africa, Johannesburg.★

Onderstall, J. *Transvaal Lowveld and Escarpment including the Kruger National Park: South African Flower Guide 4*. C. Struik, Cape Town.

Ryan, B., 1987. *52 Day-Walks in and around Johannesburg and Pretoria* (2nd edition). C. Struik, Cape Town.★

Van Wyk, P., 1985. *Field Guide to the Trees of the Kruger National Park*. C. Struik, Cape Town.

Yenter, H.J.T., 1976. *Trees and Shrubs of the Orange Free State*. P.J. de Villiers Publishers, Bloemfontein.

Periodicals

Napper, D.G. (ed.). *Transvaal Weekender and Holiday Guide*, including Orange Free State and Swaziland. Dagmar Publications, Johannesburg. (Published sporadically.)

Pienaar, U. de V., Rautenbach, I.L. and De Graaff, G. 'Small Mammals of the Kruger National Park.' *Koedoe*, 7, 1964. National Parks Board, Pretoria.

CISKEI
Books

Levy, J.R., 1986. *Ciskei Hiking Trails*. Ciskei Tourist Board, Bisho, and John Gibbs Associates, Durban.

ZIMBABWE
Books

Phillipson, D.W. (ed.), 1975. *Mosi-oa-Tunya: A Handbook to the Victoria Falls Region*. Longman Rhodesia, Salisbury, Rhodesia.

BOTSWANA
Books

Cambell, A., 1980. *The Guide to Botswana*. Craighall, Johannesburg.

Ginn, P., 1979. *Birds of Botswana*. Chris van Rensburg Publications, Johannesburg.★

The Guide to Botswana, Lesotho and Swaziland: A Comprehensive Companion for Visitors and Investors. Winchester Press, Saxonwold, 1983.

Johnson, P. and Bannister, A., 1986. *Okavango: Sea of Land, Land of Water*. C. Struik, Cape Town.

Symposium on the Okavango Delta and its Future Utilization. Botswana Society, Gaborone, Botswana, 1976.

Tinley, K.L., 1966. *An Ecological Reconnaissance of the Moremi Wildlife Reserve, Botswana.* Okavango Wildlife Society, Gaborone.

Periodicals
Berl, L. '3rd Bridge' and Sandenbergh, P. 'Okavango'. *Great Outdoors*, Vol. 60, 1987.

NAMIBIA
Books
Clinning, C.F. and Jensen, R.A.C., 1973. *Birds of Daan Viljoen Game Park.* Nature Conservation and Tourism Division of the SWA Administration, Windhoek.
Lambrechts, H., 1985. *Namibia: A Thirstland Wilderness.* C. Struik, Cape Town.

Martin, H., 1974. *The Sheltering Desert.* SWA Scientific Society, Windhoek.
Reardon, M., 1986. *The Besieged Desert.* C. Struik, Cape Town.
Schoeman, A., 1984. *Skeleton Coast.* Macmillan, Johannesburg.

MALAWI
Books
Checklist of the Birds of Malawi. Benson and Benson, Society of Malawi, Blantyre, 1978.★
Eastwood, F., 1979. *Guide to the Mulanje Massif.* Lorton Publications, Johannesburg.★
Pike, J.G. and Rimmington, G.T., 1965. *Malawi: A Geographical Study.* Oxford University Press, London.

Van der Post, L., 1952. *Venture to the Interior.* Hogarth Press, London.
Williamson, J., 1975. *Useful Plants of Malawi.* University of Malawi, Zomba.★

Periodicals
The JTPE Hiking and Camping Guide to Malawi. (Joint Tourism Promotional Effort.)
Orchids of Malawi, SARTOC, P.O. Box 564, Blantyre, Malawi.
Wildlife in Malawi, Malawi Department of National Parks and Wildlife, P.O. Box 30131, Lilongwe 3, Malawi.

Evolution of Southern Africa

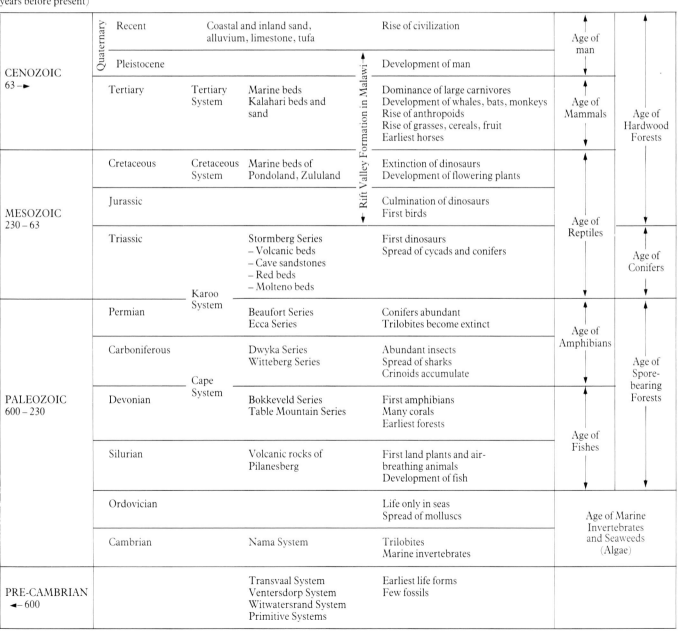

ERA (millions of years before present)	PERIOD		FORMATION		CORRELATION WITH ANIMAL AND PLANT EVOLUTION		
CENOZOIC 63 →	Quaternary	Recent		Coastal and inland sand, alluvium, limestone, tufa	Rise of civilization	Age of man	Age of Hardwood Forests
		Pleistocene			Development of man		
		Tertiary	Tertiary System	Marine beds Kalahari beds and sand	Dominance of large carnivores / Development of whales, bats, monkeys / Rise of anthropoids / Rise of grasses, cereals, fruit / Earliest horses	Age of Mammals	
MESOZOIC 230 – 63		Cretaceous	Cretaceous System	Marine beds of Pondoland, Zululand	Extinction of dinosaurs / Development of flowering plants	Age of Reptiles	
		Jurassic			Culmination of dinosaurs / First birds		Age of Conifers
		Triassic	Karoo System	Stormberg Series – Volcanic beds – Cave sandstones – Red beds – Molteno beds	First dinosaurs / Spread of cycads and conifers		
PALEOZOIC 600 – 230		Permian		Beaufort Series Ecca Series	Conifers abundant / Trilobites become extinct	Age of Amphibians	Age of Spore-bearing Forests
		Carboniferous	Cape System	Dwyka Series Witteberg Series	Abundant insects / Spread of sharks / Crinoids accumulate		
		Devonian		Bokkeveld Series Table Mountain Series	First amphibians / Many corals / Earliest forests	Age of Fishes	
		Silurian		Volcanic rocks of Pilanesberg	First land plants and air-breathing animals / Development of fish		
		Ordovician			Life only in seas / Spread of molluscs	Age of Marine Invertebrates and Seaweeds (Algae)	
		Cambrian		Nama System	Trilobites / Marine invertebrates		
PRE-CAMBRIAN ◄– 600				Transvaal System Ventersdorp System Witwatersrand System Primitive Systems	Earliest life forms / Few fossils		

Rift Valley Formation in Malawi

Useful addresses

'Authorities-in-Charge' of Trails – where not stated under trail entry in text.

* Where an asterisk appears following the name of the Authority-in-Charge in the trails directory, this address may change. This includes those trails falling within the mountain catchment areas of the Forestry Branch, Department of Environment Affairs, which are now run by their respective provincial conservation authorities.

CISKEI
Ciskei Department of Tourism and Aviation, Private Bag 0026, Bisho.
Department of Forestry, Private Bag X501, Zwelitsha 5608.
Division of Wildlife Resources and Parks, ULMICOR, P.O. Box 59, Bisho.

BOPHUTHATSWANA
National Parks Board, Private Bag X2078, Mafikeng.

LEBOWA
Department of Agriculture and Environmental Conservation, Private Bag X01, Chuniespoort 0745.

MALAWI
National Faunal Preservation Society of Malawi, P.O. Box 1429, Blantyre.
Department of Tourism, P.O. Box 402, Blantyre.
For Mulanje:
Ministry of Forestry and Natural Resources, Mulanje Mountain, P.O. Box 50, Mulanje.
For Ndirande:
Department of Forestry, P.O. Box 5493, Limbe.
Michiru Mountain Park, P.O. Box 619, Blantyre.
Department of National Parks and Wildlife, P.O. Box 30131, Lilongwe 3.

NAMIBIA
Chief Damara Affairs Commissioner, Private Bag 2005, Khorixas 9221.
Directorate of Nature Conservation and Recreation Resorts, Department of Agriculture and Nature Conservation, Private Bag 13306, Windhoek 9000.

SOUTH AFRICA
Ananda Hotel, P.O. Box 15, Rustenburg 0300.
Barberton Publicity Association, P.O. Box 221, Barberton 1300.
Botanical Research Institute, Private Bag X101, Pretoria 0001.
Caledon Divisional Council, P.O. Box 5, Caledon 7230.
Cape Divisional Council, P.O. Box 1073, Cape Town 8000.
Cape Town Municipality, P.O. Box 1694, Cape Town 8000.
Cape Town Visitors' Information Bureau (Captour), P.O. Box 1403, Cape Town 8000.
Cathedral Peak Forest Station, Gewaagd, P.O. Winterton 3340.
Cathedral Peak Hotel, P.O. Winterton 3340.
Cathkin Park Lake Hotel, P.O. Loskop 3330.
Champagne Castle Hotel, Private Bag X8, Winterton 3340.
Department of Nature and Environmental Conservation, Cape Provincial Administration, Private Bag 9086, Cape Town 8000.

Regional Offices:
Eastern Cape Regional Office, DNEC, Private Bag 1006, Grahamstown 6140.
Northern Cape Regional Office, DNEC, Private Bag, Hartswater 8750.
Southern Cape Regional Office, DNEC, Private Bag X6546, George 6530.
Western Cape Regional Office, DNEC, Private Bag 5014, Stellenbosch 7600.
Dias Divisional Council, P.O. Box 318, Port Elizabeth 6000.
Forestry Branch, Private Bag X313, Pretoria 0001.
Regional Offices:
The Principal, College for Foresters, Saasveld, Private Bag 531, George 6530.
The Regional Director, Eastern Cape Forest Region, P.O. Box 119, King William's Town 5600.
The Regional Director, Eastern Transvaal Forest Region, Private Bag X503, Sabie 1260.
The Regional Director, Natal Forest Region, Private Bag 9029, Pietermaritzburg 3200.
The Regional Director, Northern Transvaal Forest Region, Private Bag 2413, Louis Trichardt 0920.
The Regional Director, Southern Cape Forest Region, Private Bag 12, Knysna 6570.
The Regional Director, Southern Transvaal Forest Region, Private Bag 11201, Nelspruit 1200.
The Regional Director, Tsitsikamma Forest Region, Private Bag X37, Humansdorp 6300.
The Regional Director, Western Cape Forest Region, Private Bag 9005, Cape Town 8000.
The Regional Director, Zululand Forest Region, Private Bag 506, Eshowe 3815.
Division of Nature Conservation, Transvaal Provincial Administration, Private Bag X209, Pretoria 0001.
Dragon Peaks Caravan Park, P.O. Loskop 3330.
Drum Rock Hotel, P.O. Box 622, Nelspruit 1200.
Eagle Ridge Forest Resort, P.O. Box 127, Stutterheim 4930.
Educational Wildlife Expeditions, P.O. Box 645, Bedfordview 2008.
Eiland Mineral Baths, Private Bag, Letsitele 0885.
El Mirador, P.O. Winterton 3340.
Enviro-Venture, c/o Albany Museum, Somerset Street, Grahamstown 6140.
Evans, A.L., Mount Sheba Nature Reserve, P.O. Box 4, Pilgrim's Rest 1290.
False Bay Park, P.O. Hluhluwe 3960.
Germiston Publicity Association, 115 Rutland Place, Germiston 1400.
Giant's Castle Game Reserve, Private Bag 755, Estcourt 3310.
For Hillside Camp-site:
Officer-in-Charge, Hillside, P.O. Box 288, Estcourt 3310.
Halse, Robin (Black Eagle Wilderness Trail), Carnarvon Estates, P.O. Halseton, Cape Province.
Hans Merensky Nature Reserve, Private Bag X502, Letsitele 0885.
Hermanus Publicity Association, P.O. Box 117, Hermanus 7200.
Hluhluwe Game Reserve, P.O. Box 25, Mtubatuba 3935.

Isidenge State Forest, Private Bag X32, Stutterheim 4930.
Johannesburg City Council, Parks and Recreation Department, P.O. Box 2824, Johannesburg 2000.
Kamberg Nature Reserve, P.O. Rosetta 3301.
KwaZulu Government: The Secretary, Bureau of Natural Resources, Private Bag X23, Ulindi, Zululand 3838.
Loteni Nature Reserve, P.O. Box 14, Himeville 4585.
Mdedelo Wilderness Area (Monk's Cowl Forest Station), P.O. Winterton 3340.
Mkuzi Game Reserve, P.O. Mkuze 3965.
Natal Parks Board, P.O. Box 662, Pietermaritzburg 3200.
National Botanic Gardens of S.A., Kirstenbosch, Private Bag X7, Claremont 7735.
National Hiking Way Board, Private Bag X447, Pretoria 0001.
National Monuments Council, P.O. Box 4637, Cape Town 8000.
National Parks Board, P.O. Box 787, Pretoria 0001.
Nest Hotel, Private Bag X14, Winterton 3340.
New Agatha State Forest, Private Bag 4009, Tzaneen 0850.
Overvaal Resorts, Private Bag X182, Pretoria 0001.
Port Elizabeth Historical Society, P.O. Box 12070, Port Elizabeth 6006.
Port Elizabeth Municipality, P.O. Box 116, Port Elizabeth 6000.
Pretoria City Council, Parks and Recreation Department, P.O. Box 1454, Pretoria 0001.
Public Resorts Board, Transvaal Provincial Administration, P.O. Box 3046, Pretoria 0001.
Queenstown Municipality, P.O. Box 22, Queenstown 5320.
Rivermen and Funbikers, P.O. Box 17229, Congella 4013.
Rustenburg Kloof Holiday Resort, P.O. Box 16, Rustenburg 0300.
Rustenburg Nature Reserve, P.O. Box 511, Rustenburg 0300.
School in the Wilds (South African Exploration Society, S.O.S.), P.O. Box 153, Villiersdorp 7170.
Shlaralumi Reserve, P.O. Box 121, Hoedspruit 1380.
Silverstrand Camp-site, P.O. Box 52, Robertson 6705.
Solitude Mountain Resort, P.O. Box 9, Cramond 3420.
St. Lucia Estuary, Trails Officer, Natal Parks Board, Private Bag, St. Lucia Estuary 3936.
Stellenbosch Divisional Council, P.O. Box 80, Stellenbosch 7600.
Stellenbosch Publicity Office, Visitors' Bureau, 46 Alexander Street, Stellenbosch 7600.
Trailblazers, P.O. Box 18692, Hillbrow 2038.
Umfolozi Game Reserve, P.O. Box 99, Mtubatuba 3935.
Umgeni Valley, P.O. Box 394, Howick 3290.
Vergelegen Nature Reserve, P.O. Himeville 4585.
Vredenburg-Saldanha Municipality, Private Bag X12, Vredenburg 7380.
White Mountain Resort, P.O. Box 609, Estcourt 3310.
Wilderness Leadership School, P.O. Box 53058, Yellowwood Park 4011.

Wildlife Society of Southern Africa, P.O. Box
44189, Linden 2104.
Branches:
Cape Town Branch, WLS, P.O. Box 1313,
Cape Town 8000.
Natal Branch, WLS, P.O. Box 2985, Durban
4000.
Transvaal Branch, WLS, P.O. Box 44344,
Linden 2104.
Krugersdorp Centre, P.O. Box 1064,
Krugersdorp 1740.
Witwatersrand University, P.O. Box 1176,
Johannesburg 2000.
Woodbush State Forest, Private Bag 4013,
Tzaneen 0850.

ZIMBABWE
Department of National Parks and Wildlife
Management, P.O. Box 8365, Causeway,
Harare.
Zimbabwe Tourist Board, P.O. Box 8052,
Causeway, Harare.

MOUNTAIN, CLIMBING AND RAMBLING
CLUBS – hiking clubs are multiplying at a
tremendous rate; this list is not comprehensive.

Algoa Ramblers, 18 Mowbray Street, Newton
Park, Port Elizabeth 6045.
Bellville Hiking Club, P.O. Box 1089, Oakdale
7534.
Bloemfontein Hiking Club, c/o Deon Basson,
P.O. Box 7779, Bloemfontein 9300.
Border Outdoor Adventure Association (Hiking
Club of East London), P.O. Box 13200,
Vincent, East London 5217.
Breede Valley Hiking Club, P.O. Box 271,
Worcester 6850.
Club International, P.O. Box 160, Wingatepark
0153.
CSIR Hiking Club, 263 Marais Street, Brooklyn
0181.
Cycad Hiking Club, P.O. Box 93, Middelburg
1050.
Durban Rambling and Hiking Club, P.O. Box
1623, Durban 4000.
East Rand Hiking Club, 44 Dean Crescent,
Northmead Ext. 7, Benoni 1500.
Eshowe Ramblers Club, P.O. Box 5, Eshowe
3815.
Exploratio, University of Pretoria, SRC Office,
Tindall Road, Pretoria 0002.
Gantouw Hiking Club, P.O. Box 316, Strand
7140.
Hamba Gahle Stapklub, P.O. Box 1775, Alberton
1450.
Harmonie-pakstapklub, P.O. Box 8859,
Minnebron 1549.
Helderberg Hiking Club, P.O. Box 857, Somerset
West 7130.
Highland Mountain Club, P.O. Box 1035,
Bethlehem 9700.
Hiking Federation of South Africa, P.O. Box
17247, Groenkloof, Pretoria 0027. (National
body, recognized by the Government as
representing the interests of rambling, hiking
and backpacking clubs in South Africa;
publishes a very informative newsletter.)
Hottentots Holland Hiking Club, P.O. Box 5325,
Helderberg 7135.
IBM Hiking Club, P.O. Box 70243, Bryanston
2021.
Iscor Hiking Club, P.O. Box 34048, Erasmia
0023.
Johannesburg Hiking Club, P.O. Box 2254,
Johannesburg 2000.

Kalender Hiking Club, P.O. Box 28591,
Sunnyside 0132.
Kimberley Hiking Club, 24 Jan van Zyl Street,
Monumenthoogte, Kimberley 8301.
Klipspringer Hiking Club, Private Bag X381,
Pretoria 0001.
Kruinstadstappersklub, Private Bag X30,
Roodepoort 1725.
Lowveld Rambling Club, P.O. Box 1929,
Nelspruit 1200.
Momentum Stap-en-Bergklimklub, University of
OFS, P.O. Box 569, Bloemfontein 9300.
Mountain Club of Malawi, P.O. Box 240,
Blantyre, Malawi.
Mountain Club of South Africa (MCSA; 11
sections throughout South Africa). Head
Office: 97 Hatfield Street, Cape Town 8001.
Mountain Club of Zimbabwe, P.O. Box 1945,
Harare, Zimbabwe.

Ndaba Hiking Club, 368 Christoffel Street,
Pretoria West 0183.
Nomade-Bergklimklub, P.O. Box 2383, Pretoria
0001.
Norkem Park High School Hiking Club, Private
Bag X04, Birchleigh 1621.
Ore Hiking Club, P.O. Box 16041, Atlasville
1465.
Overtuur, 101 Disbashof, Kraai Street,
Kwaggasrand 0183.
Paarl Hiking Club, P.O. Box 478, Paarl 7620.
Pakstappers, 31 Botanica, 2 Malana Avenue,
Brumeria 0184.
Panorama-stapklub, Department of External
Affairs, Private Bag X152, Pretoria 0001.
Peninsula Ramblers, P.O. Box 982, Cape Town
8000.
Pietermaritzburg Ramblers Club, P.O. Box
10073, Scottsville 3209.
Pietersburg Staptoerklub, P.O. Box 598,
Pietersburg 0700.
Pretoria Wandelaars, 711 Ben Swart Street,
Rietfontein 0084.
Roodepoort Hiking Club, P.O. Box 21007,
Helderkruin 1732.
Rugsak-en-Stewelsstapklub, P.O. Box 28560,
Sunnyside, Pretoria 0132.
Sanlam Staptoerklub, P.O. Box 1, Sanlamhof
7532.
SAP Hiking Club, P.O. Box 391, Durban 4000.
SAS Immortelle, Private Bag X104, Pretoria
0001.
Sasolburg Bergklimklub, P.O. Box 725,
Sasolburg 9570.

South African Climbers Club, P.O. Box 64,
Newlands 7700.
Stellenbosch Hiking Club, 17 Het Heerenhof,
6 Oudebaan, Stellenbosch 7600.
Swartland Hiking Club, P.O. Box 283,
Malmesbury 7300.
Unisa Hiking Club, (University of South Africa),
P.O. Box 392, Pretoria 0001.
University of Cape Town Mountain and Ski Club,
Sports Union, University of Cape Town,
Rondebosch 7700.
University of Natal Mountain Club, SRC,
University of Natal, Pietermaritzburg 3200,
and Durban 4000.
Vereeniging Hikers, 70 Myrtle Street, Three
Rivers, Vereeniging 1930.
Vlugvoet-voetslaanklub, 39 Rhodes Street,
Geduld Extension, Springs 1650.
Western Province Mountain Club, P.O. Box 54,
Crawford 7770.

SKI CLUBS
Ben Mac Ski Club, c/o Bonnyvale, Barkly East
5580.
Letseng Ski Club, P.O. Box MU 126, Maputsoe,
Lesotho.
Maluti Ski Club, P.O. Box 31163, Braamfontein
2017.
Ski Club of South Africa, 'Lalapanzi', Cecil Road,
Hout Bay 7800.
Springbok Ski Club, 6th Floor, Hunts Corner,
Cnr. Eloff Street and New Street South,
Johannesburg 2001.
University of Cape Town Mountain and Ski Club,
University of Cape Town, Rondebosch 7700.
Wits Ski Club, c/o Wits University, 1 Jan Smuts
Avenue, Johannesburg 2001.

SELECTED CONSERVATION-
ORIENTATED SOCIETIES FOR AMATEUR
NATURALISTS
Botanical Society of South Africa, Private Bag
X7, Claremont 7735.
Cape Bird Club, P.O. Box 5022, Cape Town
8000.
Dendrological Society, P.O. Box 104, Pretoria
0001.
Eastern Cape Wild Bird Society, P.O. Box 1305,
Port Elizabeth 6000.
Entomological Society of South Africa, P.O. Box
103, Pretoria 0001.
'Enviroe', University of Natal, Pietermaritzburg
3200.
Faunal Preservation Society of Malawi, P.O. Box
5135, Limbe, Malawi.
Friends of the Earth, P.O. Box 11435, Brooklyn,
Pretoria 0001.
Geological Society of South Africa, P.O. Box
1017, Johannesburg 2000.
Limnological Society of South Africa, P.O. Box
662, Pietermaritzburg 3200.
Natal Bird Club, P.O. Box 1, Snell Parade,
Durban 4074.
National Veld Trust, P.O. Box 26192, Arcadia
0007.
South African Aloe and Succulent Society, P.O.
Box 1193, Pretoria 0001.
South African Archaeological Society, P.O. Box
1038, Johannesburg 2000.
South African Camping Club, 2 Ivy Road,
Norwood 2192.
South African Hunters and Game Conservation
Society, P.O. Box 1703, Pretoria 0001.
South African National Council for Conservation
of Coastal Birds, P.O. Box 17, Rondebosch
7700.

Southern African Ornithological Society, P.O. Box 87234, Houghton 2041.
Transvaal Horticultural Society, P.O. Box 7616, Johannesburg 2000.
Tree Society of Southern Africa, P.O. Box 4116, Johannesburg 2000.
Vulture Study Group, P.O. Box 4190, Johannesburg 2000.
Wildlife Protection and Conservation Society of South Africa, P.O. Box 489, Pinetown 3600.
Wildlife Society of Southern Africa, P.O. Box 44189, Linden 2104.
Witwatersrand Bird Club, P.O. Box 7048, Johannesburg 2000.

PRIVATE OPERATORS SPECIALIZING IN HIKING, CYCLING AND RIVER TRAILS –
the listing of a company here is not in itself a recommendation; this list does not purport to be fully comprehensive.

Adventure Organizers, P.O. Box 300, Constantia 7848.
Basotho Adventures, P.O. Box 1071, Maseru 100, Lesotho.
Budget Travel and Safaris, P.O. Box 2839, Blantyre, Malawi.
Canoeing Safaris, P.O. Box 2997, Harare, Zimbabwe.
Drifters, P.O. Box 48434, Roosevelt Park 2129.
Educational Wildlife Expeditions, P.O. Box 645, Bedfordview 2008.
Funbikers, P.O. Box 17229, Congella 4013.
Inkosana Lodge and Trekking, P.O. Box 60, Winterton 3340.
Namib Wilderness Safaris, P.O. Box 6850, Windhoek, Namibia. (Correspondence to Wilderness Safaris, P.O. Box 651171, Benmore 2010.)
Okavango Wilderness Safaris (Pty) Ltd, Private Bag 14, Maun, Botswana. (Correspondence to Wilderness Safaris, P.O. Box 651171, Benmore 2010.)
The Rivermen, P.O. Box 17229, Congella 4013.
The River Rafters, P.O. Box 14, Diep River 7800.
Roaming Tours, P.O. Box 295, Constantia 7848.

Trailblazers, P.O. Box 18692, Hillbrow 2038.
Veld and Vlei Adventure Trust, Head Office, P.O. Box 396, Port Elizabeth 6000. (Offices at Elgin in the Western Cape, Sedgefield in the Southern Cape and Estcourt in Natal.)
Wanderlust, Ersula Stevens, P.O. Box 154, Rondebosch 7700.
Wilderness Leadership School, P.O. Box 53058, Yellowwood Park 4011.

BACKPACKING AND CAMPING EQUIPMENT
Retailers
Adventure Centre, Rondebosch (Cape Town).
Army Surplus Store, Pinetown (Durban).
Berhuis, Cape Town.
Boland Canvas and Rope Company, Cape Town.
Cambrian Electrical, Scottburgh (Natal).
Camp and Climb, Claremont (Cape Town), Cape Town, Braamfontein (Johannesburg), Port Elizabeth and Sunnyside (Pretoria).
Campcraft, Durban
Campcraft Camping Equipment, Florida (Transvaal).
Camping and Outdoor Living, Sunnyside (Pretoria).
Campus Sports, Port Elizabeth.
Camp-Trails, Port Elizabeth.
Capital, Maseru (Lesotho).
Cymot, Windhoek, Swakopmund and Tsumeb (Namibia).
Dudley's, Witbank (Transvaal).
Farrer's, King William's Town (Cape).
Fereday and Sons, Harare (Zimbabwe).
Harkin Enterprises, Harare (Zimbabwe).
Henry's Canvas, Johannesburg.
Kimberley Sprite, Kimberley.
King's Sports, Pietermaritzburg.
Leisure World Agencies, La Rochelle (Johannesburg).
Lemkus, Cape Town and suburban branches, and Johannesburg.
M.E. Stores, Germiston, Randburg (Johannesburg), Pretoria and other branches.
Midco Kamp and Gas, Nelspruit.
The Nest Outdoor Living Centre, Carletonville (Transvaal).

Orange Free State Canvas, Bloemfontein.
Outdoor Centre, Pietermaritzburg.
Outdoor Inn, Durban.
Outdoor Living, Ferndale (Transvaal).
Outdoor Living and Canvas Centre, East London.
Outdoor Pursuits, Cape Town and Port Elizabeth.
PMB Gas Company, Pietermaritzburg.
Reo's Safari, Benoni (Transvaal).
Saffier Uit en Tuis, Pietersburg.
Safrics, Johannesburg.
Seaking Camping Equipment, Roodepoort (Transvaal).
Simpsons of Pretoria, Gezina.
South African Canvas, Port Elizabeth and East London.
Sparks and Ellis (Cape Union Mart), Cape Town.
Sports and Boat Boutique, Humansdorp (Cape).
Sport and Camping Paradise, Louis Trichardt (Transvaal).
Sunshine Camping Centre, Klerksdorp (Transvaal).
Taylors Canvas, Harare (Zimbabwe).
Tent and Tarpaulin, Bellville and Salt River (Cape Town).
Tents and Tarpaulins, Gabarone (Botswana).
Uitenhage Outdoor Life, Port Elizabeth.
Upington Caravan Sales, Upington.
Varsity Sports, Johannesburg, Pretoria, Germiston, Bloemfontein and Cape Town.
Voortrekkerwinkels Co-op., Bethal.
Vrystaad Sprite Caravans, Bloemfontein.
Welkom Gas Centre, Welkom.
Zulu Gypsey, Empangeni (Natal).

Wholesalers
Backpacker Products, Claremont.
Campcraft, Pretoria
Karrimor International, Kenwyn, Cape.
Mountain Safety Research, Seattle, Washington, USA.
Olympic, Cape Town.
Optimus, Upplands Väsby, Sweden.
Preddy Brothers, Germiston.
Survival Equipment Company, Auckland Park.
Three Spears, Lansdowne, Cape.

Glossary of ecological, geological and mountaineering terms

This section provides definitions and explanations of ecological, geological and mountaineering terms, in addition to translations of relevant Afrikaans words which occur in the text.

BASALT – a hard, dark-coloured rock of volcanic origin.
BASEMENT COMPLEX – deposits of chiefly metamorphic and igneous rocks under the stratified rocks of a region. Basement or Primitive formations date back to the beginnings of geological history.
BATHOLITH – a great mass of granite or other igneous rock intruded below the surface, commonly along the axis of a mountain range, sometimes exposed by erosion.
BENZINE – white or unleaded petrol, used in camp-stoves.
CATARACT – a large, steep waterfall.
CLIMBING GRADES –
  'A', a walk
  'B', a rock scramble
  'C', a rock-climb with good hand-holds

'D', 'E', etc., rock-climbs requiring ropes and sometimes, in higher grades, artificial aids.
CRETACEOUS – the last geological period of the Mesozoic era, characterized by the formation of chalk deposits, dinosaurs becoming extinct and the development of flowering plants.
DIURNAL – active only during the day (biological); a complete 24-hour period or a recurring daily phenomenon (meteorological).
DOLERITE – a coarse-grained basalt.
ENDEMIC – indigenous to a certain locality, and not occurring elsewhere.
FAMILY – a group of related animals or plants ranking below an order and above a genus.
FAULT LINE – a line which marks the intersection of a fault plane with the earth's surface.
FOLDED MOUNTAINS – mountains with bends and flexures formed by tremendous pressures after their stratification.
FOOD CHAIN – a series of organisms interrelated by the fact that each member of the group forms food for the next higher organism in the series.
FOOD WEB – a group of interrelated food chains.

GENUS – a group of related plants or animals, generally consisting of two or more species, but sometimes of a single species, possessing certain common structural characteristics distinct from any other group. A genus ranks below a family and above a species.
GEOPHYTE – a plant which survives the winter by storing its foods in deep subterranean buds.
GNEISS – a coarse-grained, metamorphic rock composed of quartz, feldspar and mica or hornblende. It is distinguished from granite by its foliated or laminated structure.
GRABEN – a rift valley, q.v.
GRANITE – a hard, igneous rock comprising grains of other rocks, chiefly quartz and feldspar, and usually with one or more minerals, such as mica or hornblende.
IGNEOUS – produced by intense heat or volcanic action.
INSELBERG – a residual stump or core of a mountain left rising above a surrounding plain, primarily the result of wind erosion.
KAROO SYSTEM – gently inclined beds of rock,

dating from late Carboniferous to Triassic times, which cover the greater surface of the interior of South Africa. The Karoo System is composed of stratified formations of shale and sandstones and volcanic rock intrusions.

KLOOF – a ravine, steeper than a valley but less steep than a gorge.

KRANTZ – a rock precipice.

LIANA – common name for a climbing or twining plant.

METHYLATED SPIRITS – alcohol used in camp-stoves.

NEK – a narrow pass.

NOCTURNAL – active during the night.

PENEPLAIN – a formerly mountainous or hilly area so reduced by erosion as to be almost a plain.

PLEISTOCENE – the geological epoch commonly called the Ice Age, followed by the Recent (Holocene) and characterized by vast glaciation of the earth's surface.

PRE-CAMBRIAN – the earliest geological division of time in the earth's history.

POORT – a narrow pass through a mountain.

QUARTZITE – a metamorphic, granular rock formed from siliceous sandstone.

QUATERNARY – the geological period marked by the onset of glaciation and including the Pleistocene and Recent (Holocene) epochs.

RESOURCE CONSERVATION – to preserve from impairment or to use wisely all significant objects and features of nature.

RIFT BLOCK – a mass of displaced rock between two faults, lifted above or sunk below the general level.

RIFT VALLEY – a valley formed by the lowering of an area of land between two nearly parallel faults.

SANDSTONE – a sedimentary rock formed by the consolidation of sand, the grains being held together by a cement of silica or the like.

SCHIST – a crystalline metamorphic rock composed mainly of mica. It splits easily into layers.

SHALE BAND – a layer of shale sandwiched between sandstone or other rocks, prominent in the Cape folded mountains. Because shale has better water retention, a higher nutrient content and is less porous than sandstone, the shale band supports different vegetation than its neighbouring sandstone layers.

SLATE – a fine-grained, bluish-grey metamorphic rock formed from shale. It flakes easily into thin, smooth layers.

SPOOR – footprints, tracks, scents or droppings of animals, including man.

TEMPERATURE INVERSION – an atmospheric condition in which a layer of warm air develops above a layer of cool air.

TOPOCADASTRAL MAP – a map which indicates both the surface features of a region, and the extent and ownership of land.

UPWELLING – the movement of nutrient-rich, cold oceanic waters upwards to replace warmer surface waters blown away by off-shore winds. Upwelling of the Benguela Current, which originates in sub-Antarctic water and which is rich in nutrients, diatoms and phytoplankton, is responsible for the productivity of the Atlantic coast of South Africa and Namibia.

VLAKTE – (Afrik.) flat land, usually grassed or, if in fynbos, covered mainly with restios.

VOETSLAANPAD – (Afrik.) hiking trail.

WAG-'N-BIETJIE – (Afrik.) literally meaning 'wait a bit', referring to trees with thorns that entangle your clothes and tear at your skin; for example, *Ziziphus mucronata*.

WANDELPAD – (Afrik.) nature walk.

XEROPHYTE – a plant that loses very little water and can grow in deserts or very dry ground.

Common and scientific names referred to in the text

AMPHIBIANS

frog, dainty *Cacosternum* spp.
frog, East African puddle *Phrynobatrachus acridoides*
frog, ghost *Heleophryne purcelli*
frog, golden reed *Afrixalus brachycnemis brachycnemis*
frog, grey tree *Chiromantis xerampelina*
frog, Hogsback *Anhydrophryne rattrayi*
frog, rain *Breviceps* spp.
toad, Amatola *Bufo amatolica*

REPTILES

adder, berg (mountain adder) *Bitis atropos atropos*
adder, gaboon *Bitis gabonica*
adder, horned *Bitis caudalis*
adder, mountain *Bitis atropos atropos*
adder, Peringuey's desert or side-winding adder *Bitis peringueyi*
adder, rhombic night *Causus rhombeatus*
agama (koggelmander) *Agama* spp.
agama, mountain (rock agama) *Agama atra*
boomslang *Dispholidus typus*
chameleon, Namib *Meroles cuneirostris*
cobra *Naja* spp.
cobra, Cape *Naja nivea*
crocodile *Crocodylus niloticus*
crocodile, Nile *Crocodylus niloticus*
gecko Gekkonidae (family)
gecko, barking *Ptenopus garrulus garrulus*
gecko, Peringuey's leaf-toed *Phyllodactylus peringueyi*
koggelmander (agama) *Agama* spp.
leguan, rock *Varanus exanthematicus*
leguan, water (Nile monitor) *Varanus niloticus*
lizard, red sand *Eremias undata rubens*
lizard, rough-scaled, dark girdled *Cordylus warreni depressus*
mamba *Dendroaspis* spp.
puff adder *Bitis arietans*
python, African *Python sebae*
skaapsteker *Psammophylax* spp.
skink, bluetailed rock *Mabuya quinquetaeniatus margitifer*
snake, grass *Psammophis* spp.

snake, northern green *Philothamnus irregularis irregularis*
snake, tree (boomslang) *Dispholidus typus*
tortoise, angulate *Chersine angulata*
tortoise, mountain *Geochelone pardalis*

BIRDS – this list has been compiled in accordance with the Southern African Ornithological Society's Checklist but, for convenience, Roberts' *Birds* (5th edition) numbers have been included.

albatross Diomedeidae (family)
apalis, Rudd's, 649 *Apalis ruddi*
apalis, yellowbreasted, 648 *Apalis flavida*
babbler, pied, 563 *Turdoides bicolor*
barbet, blackcollared, 464 *Lybius torquatus*
barbet, crested, 473 *Trachyphonus vaillantii*
barbet, pied, 465 *Lybius leucomelas*
barbet, white-eared, 466 *Stactolaema leucotis*
bateleur, 146 *Terathopius ecaudatus*
batis, Cape, 700 *Batis capensis*
batis, Woodwards', 704 *Batis fratrum*
bee-eater, carmine, 441 *Merops nubicoides*
bee-eater, whitefronted, 443 *Merops bullockoides*
bishop bird *Euplectes* spp.
bishop, golden, 826 *Euplectes afer*
bishop, red, 824 *Euplectes orix*
bokmakierie, 746 *Telophorus zeylonus*
broadbill, African, 490 *Smithornis capensis*
bulbul, Cape, 566 *Pycnonotus capensis*
bulbul, sombre, 572 *Andropadus importunus*
bunting, Cape, 885 *Emberiza capensis*
bustard Otididae (family)
bustard, kori, 230 *Ardeotis kori*
bustard, Ludwig's, 232 *Neotis ludwigii*
bustard, Stanley's, 231 *Neotis denhami*
buzzard, augur, 153 *Buteo augur*
buzzard, forest, 150 *Buteo oreophilus*
buzzard, jackal, 152 *Buteo rufofuscus*
canary, forest, 873 *Serinus scotops*
chat, buffstreaked, 588 *Oenanthe bifasciata*
chat, familiar, 589 *Cercomela familiaris*
chat, tractrac, 590 *Cercomela tractrac*
cisticola *Cisticola* spp.

coot, redknobbed, 228 *Fulica cristata*
cormorant *Phalacrocorax* spp.
cormorant, reed, 58 *Phalacrocorax africanus*
cormorant, whitebreasted, 55 *Phalacrocorax carbo*
coucal, Burchell's, 391 *Centropus superciliosus*
courser Glareolidae (family)
crake, black, 213 *Amaurornis flavirostris*
crane, blue, 208 *Anthropoides paradisea*
crane, crowned, 209 *Balearica regulorum*
crane, wattled, 207 *Grus carunculatus*
crimsonwing, redfaced, 836 *Cryptospiza reichenovii*
cuckoo, black, 378 *Cuculus clamosus*
cuckoo, redchested, 377 *Cuculus solitarius*
cuckooshrike, black, 538 *Campephaga flava*
curlew, 289 *Numenius arquata*
dabchick, 8 *Tachybaptus ruficollis*
dikkop *Burhinus* spp.
dikkop, Cape or spotted, 297 *Burhinus capensis*
dove, Cape turtle, 354 *Streptopelia capicola*
dove, greenspotted, 358 *Turtur chalcospilos*
dove, Namaqua, 356 *Oena capensis*
duck, African black, 105 *Anas sparsa*
duck, maccoa, 117 *Oxyura maccoa*
duck, whitefaced, 99 *Dendrocygna viduata*
duck, yellowbilled, 104 *Anas undulata*
eagle, Ayre's, 138 *Hieraaetus ayresii*
eagle, black, 131 *Aquila verreauxii*
eagle, crowned, 141 *Stephanoaetus coronatus*
eagle, fish, 148 *Haliaeetus vocifer*
eagle, longcrested, 139 *Lophaetus occipitalis*
eagle, martial, 140 *Polemaetus bellicosus*
eagle, Wahlberg's, 135 *Aquila wahlbergi*
egret, cattle, 71 *Bubulcus ibis*
eremomela, Karoo, 654 *Eremomela gregalis*
falcon, pygmy, 186 *Polihierax semitorquatus*
falcon, peregrine, 171 *Falco peregrinus*
finch, redheaded, 856 *Amadina erythrocephala*
finch, scalyfeathered, 806 *Sporopipes squamifrons*
firefinch, bluebilled, 840 *Lagonosticta rubricata*
flamingo *Phoenicopterus* spp.
flycatcher, bluemantled, 708 *Trochocerus cyanomelas*
flycatcher, chat, 697 *Melaenornis infuscatus*
flycatcher, paradise, 710 *Terpsiphone viridis*

345

INSECTS/INVERTEBRATES

giant earthworm, *Microchaetus* spp.
malaria mosquito Anophelinae (subfamily)
mopane worm *Gonimbrasia belina*
peripatus Peripatopsidae (family)
solifuge (sun-spider) Solifugae (order)
trap-door spider Ctenizidae (family)
tsetse fly *Glossina* spp.

MARINE AND FRESHWATER LIFE

barbel Tachysuridae (family)
bass, black *Micropterus* spp.
carp *Cyprinus* spp.
catfish (rock barbel) *Gephyroglanis sclateri*
dolphin *Delphinus delphis*
eel, freshwater *Anguilla* spp.

grunter *Pomadasys* spp.
humpback (whale) *Megaptera novae-angliae*
kob (kabeljou) *Argyrosomus hololepidotus*
kurper, blue *Tilapia mossambica*
leatherback *Dermochelys coriacea*
mudskipper *Periophthalmus kolreuferi*
mullet *Mugil* spp.
mussel *Pelecypoda* spp.
oyster *Crassostrea margaritacea*
perch *Perca* spp.
perlemoen *Haliotis midae*
prawn, sand and mud *Macrura* group of Crustacea
rock bait (red bait) *Pyura stolonifera*
scaly fish *Barbus natalensis*
shark, Zambezi *Carcharhinus leucas*
springer *Elops machnata*
stumpnose, white *Rhabdosargus globiceps*
tigerfish *Hydrocynus vittatus*
trout, brown *Salmo trutta*
trout, rainbow *Salmo gairdneri*
vundu *Heterobranchus longifilis*
whale, southern right *Eubalaena australis*
yellowfish, smallmouth *Barbus holubi*

MAMMALS

aardwolf *Proteles cristatus*
anteater, scaly *Manis temmincki*
antelope, roan *Hippotragus equinus*
antelope, sable *Hippotragus niger*
ape, blue (blue monkey) *Cercopithecus mitis*
baboon, chacma *Papio ursinus*
blesbok *Damaliscus dorcas phillipsi*
bontebok *Damaliscus dorcas dorcas*
buffalo, Cape *Syncerus caffer*
bushbaby, lesser (night ape) *Galago senegalensis*
bushbaby, greater *Galago crassicaudatus*
bushbuck *Tragelaphus scriptus*
bushpig *Potamochoerus porcus*
caracal *Felis caracal*
cheetah *Acinonyx jubatus*
civet *Viverra civetta*
dassie Procaviidae (family)
dassie, yellowspotted *Heterohyrax brucei*
duiker Cephalophinae (subfamily)
duiker, blue *Cephalophus monticola*
duiker common (Grimm's duiker or grey duiker)
    Sylvicapra grimmia
duiker, red *Cephalophus natalensis*
eland *Taurotragus oryx*
elephant *Loxodonta africana*
fallow deer (exotic) *Cervus dama*
fox, bateared *Otocyon megalotis*
fox, Cape *Vulpes chama*
gemsbok (oryx) *Oryx gazella*
genet cat *Genetta* spp.
gerbil Gerbillinae (subfamily)
gerbil, hairy-footed *Gerbillurus paeba*
giraffe *Giraffa camelopardalis*
grysbok *Raphicerus melanotis*
hare Leporidae (family)
hare, Cape *Lepus capensis*
hare, Natal red or red rock *Pronolagus
    crassicaudatus*
hare, scrub *Lepus saxatilis*
hartebeest, red or Cape *Alcelaphus caama*
hedgehog, South African *Erinaceus frontalis*
Himalayan tahr (exotic) *Hemitragus jemlahicus*
hippopotamus *Hippopotamus amphibius*
honey badger *Mellivora capensis*
hunting dog *Lycaon pictus*
hyaena Hyaenidae (family)
hyaena, brown *Hyaena brunnea*
hyaena, spotted *Crocuta crocuta*
hyrax (dassie) *Procavia* spp.
hyrax, Cape rock *Procavia capensis*
hyrax, tree *Dendrohyrax arboreus*

impala *Aepyceros melampus*
jackal *Canis* spp.
jackal, blackbacked *Canis mesomelas*
jackal, sidestriped *Canis adustus*
klipspringer *Oreotragus oreotragus*
kudu *Tragelaphus strepsiceros*
lechwe *Kobus leche*
lemur Lemuridae (family)
leopard *Panthera pardus*
lion *Panthera leo*
lynx (caracal) *Felis caracal*
meerkat Herpestinae (subfamily)
mole, golden Chrysochloridae (family)
mole, giant golden *Chrysospalax trevelyani*
mole-rat Bathyergidae (family)
mongoose, banded *Mungus mungo*
mongoose, Cape grey *Herpestes pulverulentus*
mongoose, Egyptian *Herpestes ichneumon*
mongoose, water *Atilax paludinosus*
mongoose, yellow *Herpestes (Galerella) ochracea*
monkey, samango *Cercopithecus albogularis*
monkey, vervet *Cercopithecus pygerythrus*
mouse, field or grass *Rhabdomys pumilio*
mouse, pygmy *Mus minutoides*
nyala *Tragelaphus angasi*
oribi *Ourebia ourebi*
oryx *Oryx gazella*
otter Lutrinae (subfamily)
otter, Cape clawless *Aonyx capensis*
polecat, striped *Ictonyx striata*
porcupine *Hystrix* spp.
puku *Kobus vardoni*
quagga *Equus quagga*
reedbuck, common (southern) *Redunca
    arundinum*
reedbuck, mountain *Redunca fulvorufula*
rhebok, grey or vaal *Pelea capreolus*
rhinoceros Rhinocerotidae (family)
rhinoceros, black *Diceros bicornis*
rhinoceros, white *Ceratotherium simum*
rooikat (caracal, African lynx) *Felis caracal*
serval *Felis (Leptailurus) serval*
sheep, barbary (exotic) *Ammotragus lervia*
sheep, mouflon (exotic) *Ovis musimon*
sitatunga *Tragelaphus spekei*
skunk (striped polecat) *Ictonyx striatus*
spring hare *Pedetes capensis*
springbok *Antidorcas marsupialis*
squirrel, ground *Xerus inauris*
squirrel, sun *Heliosciurus* spp.
squirrel, Swynnerton's red *Paraxerus palliatus
    swynnertoni*
squirrel, Tonga orange (red) *Paraxerus palliatus
    tongensis*
steenbok *Raphicerus campestris*
suni *Nesotragus moschatus*
tsessebe *Damaliscus lunatus*
warthog *Phacochoerus aethiopicus*
waterbuck, common *Kobus ellipsiprymnus*
waterbuck, Defassa *Kobus defassa*

white-naped weasel *Poecilogale albinucha*
wild cat *Felis libyca*
wild dog *Lycaon pictus*
wild pig (bushpig) *Potamochoerus porcus*
wildebeest, black *Connochaetes gnou*
wildebeest, blue (brindled gnu) *Connochaetes
    taurinus*
wildebeest, Cookson's *Connochaetes taurinus
    cooksoni*
zebra, Hartmann's mountain *Equus (Hippotigris)
    zebra hartmannae*
zebra, mountain *Equus (Hippotigris) zebra zebra*
zorilla *Ictonyx striatus*

PLANTS – with national tree list numbers where
relevant

African holly, 397 *Ilex mitis*
aloe, spiral *Aloe polyphylla*
aloe, Wylliespoort, 28,4 *Aloe angelica*
aloe, Zimbabwe 28,8 *Aloe excelsa*
ana tree, 159 *Acacia albida*
arum lily *Zantedeschia aethiopica*
assegai, 570 *Curtisia dentata*
banana, wild (Cape), 32 *Strelitzia alba*
banana, wild (Natal), 34 *Strelitzia nicolai*
baobab, 467 *Adansonia digitata*
Barberton daisy *Gerbera jamesonii*
bastard lightning bush, 305 *Andrachne ovalis*
bastard saffron, 414 *Cassine peragua*
beech, Cape, 578 *Rapanea melanophloeos*
beech, red, 364 *Protorhus longifolia*
beech, Transvaal, 75 *Faurea saligna*
beechwood, 75 *Faurea saligna*
bitterbos *Chrysocoma tenuifolia*
bitter karoo *Chrysocoma tenuifolia*
black-thorn, 176 *Acacia mellifera*
blackberry *Rubus allegheniensis*
blackwood *Acacia melanoxylon*
bluebush, 605 *Diospyros lycioides*
berg hard pear, 514 *Olinia emarginata*
boer-bean, Karoo, 201 *Schotia afra*
botterboom, 137,1 *Cotyledon paniculata*
box, Cape, 358 *Buxus macowanii*
brack-bush *Suaeda plumosa*
broad-leaved protea, 88,3 *Protea eximia*
buchu, round-leaved *Agathosma betulina*
buffalo-thorn, 447 *Ziziphus mucronata*
bulrush, Cape *Typha capensis*
bush-tick berry, 736,2 *Chrysanthemoides
    monilifera*
Bushman's candle *Sarcocaulon mossamedense*
Bushman grass, short *Aristida ciliata*
Bushman grass, tall *Aristida uniplumis*
buttercup *Ranunculus raeae*
cabbage tree, 564 *Cussonia spicata*
cabbage tree, forest, 561,1 *Cussonia
    sphaerocephala*
cabbage tree, lowveld, 564 *Cussonia spicata*
cactus, jointed *Opuntia aurantiaca*
camel thorn, 168 *Acacia erioloba*, sometimes
    incorrectly referred to as *Acacia giraffae*
camphor bush, 733 *Tarchonanthus camphoratus*
candelabra tree, 28 *Aloe bainesii*
candlewood, 212 *Cassia abbreviata*
Cape Beech, white, 618,1 *Olea capensis capensis*
Cape holly, 397 *Ilex mitis*
Cape honeysuckle, 673,1 *Tecomaria capensis*
Cape plane, 479, 482 *Octina arborea*
cassia, long-tail, 212 *Cassia abbreviata*
cat-thorn, 451 *Scutia myrtina*
cedar, Clanwilliam, 19 *Widdringtonia juniperoides*
cedar, mountain, 20 *Widdringtonia cupressoides*
cedar, Mulanje, 20 *Widdringtonia cupressoides*
cedar, Willowmore, 21 *Widdringtonia schwarzii*
cheesewood, 139 *Pittosporum viridiflorum*

INDEX

Captions to photographs appearing on opening pages of each chapter

p. 36: A view over Western Cape farmlands, with Table Mountain in the distance.
p. 73: On the Kranshoek Coastal Nature Walk in the Southern Cape.
pp.94-5 (left): A wheatfield crowned by rainbow in the Eastern Cape; (right): The 39 Steps Waterfall in the Hogsback area of the Eastern Cape.
pp. 118-19 (left and right): On the Orange Gorge Kayak Trail in the Northern Cape.
pp.132-3 (left): A horseman, a common sight in the Qwa-Qwa Conservation Area; (right): On

the Brandwater Hiking Trail in the Orange Free State.
pp. 146-7 (left): The rolling vistas awaiting hikers in Ciskei; (right): A game guard in Tsolwana Game Park in Ciskei.
pp.158-9 (left): One of many stunning rock formations to be seen on the Transkei Hiking Trail; (right): Watsonia sp.
pp. 164-5 (left): Trailists discovering the inner mountain kingdom of Lesotho the relaxed way, on one of Lesotho's Horse Trails; (right): A spiral aloe, Aloe polyphylla.

pp. 170-1 (left): The Amphitheatre, a landmark in the Drakensberg; (right): Snow in the Leslie's Pass area of the 'Berg.
pp. 184-5 (left): Ndumu Pan, a haven for waterbirds, in northern Natal; (right): Oribi Gorge, a spectacular landscape feature near the lower south coast of Natal.
pp. 218-9 (left): Nkomati picnic site in Swaziland; (right): A blue crane, Anthropoides paradisea.
pp. 226-7 (left): A kudu, spotted in the Kruger National

Park; (right): In the beautiful Wolkberg Wilderness Area of the Northern Transvaal.
pp. 268-9 (left): Barberspan, the summer home for thousands of birds, on the Highveld; (right): An excursion into Tonquani Gorge in the Magaliesberg, a 'getaway' for Highveld mountaineers.
pp.282-3 (left): The Pilanesberg in Bophuthatswana; (right): A white rhino and her calf in Pilanesberg National Park.
pp. 288-9 (left): On the Mabuda-Shango Hiking Trail

in Venda; (right): A strangler fig, Ficus sp.
pp. 292-3 (left): A grey heron, Ardea cinerea; (right): Elephant, a common sight in Zimbabwe's nature reserves.
pp. 308-9 (left): Lake Ngami, located in the south-west corner of the Okavango Swamps; (right): Safaris in Botswana.
pp. 314-15 (left): The kokerboom, Aloe dichotoma; (right): In the Namib-Naukluft Desert Park in Namibia.
p. 324: Lake Chilwa, located to the east of the Shire Highlands in Malawi.